Cloud Computing for Machine Learning and Cognitive Applications

Cloud Computing for Machine Learning and Cognitive Applications

Kai Hwang

The MIT Press
Cambridge, Massachusetts
London, England

This book was set in Syntax LT Std and Times LT Std by Westchester Publishing Services. Printed and bound in the United States of America.

Library of Congress Cataloging-in-Publication Data

Names: Hwang, Kai.
Title: Cloud computing for machine learning and cognitive applications / Kai Hwang.
Description: Cambridge, MA : The MIT Press, [2017] | Includes bibliographical references and index.
Identifiers: LCCN 2016057874 | ISBN 9780262036412 (hardcover : alk. paper)
Subjects: LCSH: Cloud computing. | Machine learning. | Data mining. | Big data.
Classification: LCC QA76.585 .H95 2017 | DDC 004.67/82—dc23
LC record available at https://lccn.loc.gov/2016057874

10   9   8   7   6   5   4   3   2   1

Contents

PART IV: CLOUD PROGRAMMING AND PERFORMANCE BOOSTERS   401

Preface

Ever since the turn of the millennium, the world of computing and information technology has gone through some major changes in scales, machines, and platforms. Thousands of data centers around the globe are being converted into clouds to benefit a hundred million individual, business, and government users. Three billion smartphones are in use, interacting with social-network clouds. All of these have changed human activities and interactions greatly. The *Internet of things* (IoT) and machine intelligence are reshaping our lifestyles. All of these advances in information technology are transforming our society into an economy of scale supported by many *artificial intelligence* (AI) and automated cognitive solutions. In fact, we are entering an era of having cloud data analysis, smart robots, and machine cognitive services.

To realize the new computing and communication paradigms, we must upgrade the cloud computing ecosystem with new capabilities for machine learning, IoT sensing, data analytics, and cognitive power that can mimic or augment human intelligence. The ultimate goal is to build up a big data industry to provide cognitive services to offset human shortcomings in handling labor-intensive tasks with higher efficiency. Successful cloud systems, web services, and data centers must be designed to store, process, learn, and analyze big data to discover new knowledge or make critical decisions. These goals can be achieved through hardware virtualization, machine learning, deep learning with training, neuromorphic computer architecture, and cognitive services. For example, new cloud services may include learning as a service (LaaS), analytics as a service (AaaS), or security as a service (SaaS).

Today, IT companies, large enterprises, universities, and governments are gradually converting their data centers into cloud facilities to support mobile and networked applications. Supercomputers having a cluster architecture similar to clouds are also under transformation to deal with the large data sets or data streams. Smart clouds are greatly in demand to support social, media, mobile, business and government operations. Companies like Google, Amazon, Microsoft, Facebook, Apple, Baidu, Alibaba, Tencent QQ, and IBM are competing in developing IoT devices, smart robots, self-driving cars, flying vehicles, and cognitive systems. The high technology industry is entering a new world of challenges and opportunities.

A Quick Glance at the Book

This textbook is designed to train college seniors or graduate students to master modern cloud system architectures, machine learning algorithms, parallel and distributed programming, software tools for big data mining, predictive analytics, and cognitive service applications. It can also act as a major reference for professionals, scientists, or engineers. This book is a result of the author's research, teaching, and lecturing experiences of the past two decades. Readers can leverage the cloud and machine learning skills learned here to push for career advancement and business transformation in the era of big data and machine intelligence.

The book is divided as follows:

- Part I has two introductory chapters on fundamental principles of cloud computing, data science, and adaptive computing in big data applications. These two chapters lay the necessary theoretical foundation and technological bases for the subsequent eight chapters in the remaining parts.
- Part II has three chapters covering cloud architecture, virtual machines, Docker containers, mobile clouds, IoT, and multi-cloud mashup services. Case studies include Amazon AWS, Google Cloud, Microsoft Azure, IBM SmartCloud, Salesforce clouds, SGI Cyclone, Apple iCloud, NASA Nebula, and CERN Cloud.
- Part III features two chapters on principles of machine learning, deep learning, AI machines, smart robots, neuromorphic processors, brain-like computers, augmented reality (AR), and virtual reality (VR). In particular, Google's Brain Project, DeepMind, X-Lab programs, IBM SyNapse, Bluemix and Cognitive initiatives, and China's Cambricon neural chips are covered.
- Part IV presents three chapters on cloud programming paradigms and software tools and application development based on MapReduce, Hadoop, Spark, TensorFlow, and GraphX. The final Chapter is devoted to cloud performance, privacy, and security issues. All cloud systems, programming paradigms, machine learning methods, and software tools are illustrated with concrete application examples throughout the book.

Empowering Clouds and IoT Platforms with AI Capabilities

This book blends big data theories with emerging technologies in smart clouds and explores distributed data centers with new applications. Today, *cyber-physical systems* (CPSs) appear in smart cities, autonomous car driving, emotion-detection robotics, delivery drones, virtual reality, augmented reality, and cognitive services.

To promote effective big data computing on smart clouds or data centers, the author takes a technological fusion approach by integrating big data theories with cloud design principles and supercomputing standards. IoT sensing enables large-scale data collection and filtering.

Machine learning and data analytics help intelligent decision making on clouds or IoT platforms, automatically and without human interference. Augmenting clouds and super-computers with AI features is our fundamental goal. These AI and machine learning tasks are supported by Hadoop, Spark, and TensorFlow programming libraries in real-life applications.

Data analysts, cognitive scientists, and computer professionals must work together to solve practical problems. This collaborative learning must involve clouds, mobile devices, data centers, and IoT resources. The ultimate goal is to discover new knowledge or make impor-tant decisions, intelligently. For many years, we have sought to build brain-like computers that can mimic or augment human functions in sensing, memory, recognition, and com-prehension. Today, Google, IBM, Microsoft, Facebook, the Chinese Academy of Sciences, and Baidu are all exploring AI in cloud, machine learning, and IoT applications.

This book covers some new neuromorphic chips and software platforms that were built by leading research centers to enable cognitive computing. It examines these advances in hardware, software, and ecosystems. It emphasizes not only machine learning in pattern recognition, speech/image understanding, and language translation and comprehension with low cost and low power requirements, but also emerging new approaches to building a future cyberspace of mobile phones, robots, IoT platforms, data centers, and computing clouds.

Intended Audience and Reader/Instructor Guide

This book is written to meet the growing demand for an updated curriculum in computer science and electrical engineering education. By teaching various subsets of the ten chap-ters, instructors can use it at both the senior and graduate level. It will also benefit com-puter professionals who wish to transform their skills to meet new IT challenges.

Instructors can choose to teach different chapters that match their own expertise and best serve the interests of students at various levels. To teach a cloud computing course, at least eight chapters should be covered; Chapters 2 and 7 could be skipped if the teaching time is limited. For a machine learning course, Chapters 3 or 10 could be skipped. For a senior course, seven chapters (1, 2, 3, 4, 5, 6, 8) are sufficient. All ten chapters should be taught in any course covering both topics of cloud computing and machine learning. The book is also suit-able for use as a reference in courses on big data science, IoT, and distributed computing.

High-tech, computer, Internet and professional engineers, scientists, and managers should also find this book a useful reference. For example, Intel engineers may find the book use-ful to push the concept of IoT; software engineers and big data analysts at Amazon, Google, Microsoft, Apache, Databricks, and Cloudera may find it useful in their daily work; and Google Brain, X Lab, and DeepMind developers may use the book in deep learning services on speech, text, and image understanding, healthcare, and autonomic ve-hicle driving.

In the emerging cognitive industry, IBM has identified IoT and cognitive services to broaden their business in societal and government sectors. Facebook, Apple, and Baidu may want to explore new AI features, social services, and personalized entertainment based on augmented and virtual realities (AV/VR) technology. Finally, buyers and sellers on Amazon and Alibaba clouds may want to expand their online shopping and transaction business beyond e-commerce and P2P social services.

Acknowledgments

The author is grateful to his academic peers and collaborators: Gorden Bell, Lotfi Zadeh, Michael Flynn, John Hennessy, Bill Dally, David Patterson, Ian Foster, Jack Dongarra, Geoffrey Fox, Jeffrey Dean, David Silver, Dennis Gannon, H. J. Siegel, Raj Buyya, Albert Zomaya, Deyi Li, Keqin Li, and Hai Jin for sharing their vast knowledge, insightful visions, and professional innovations. In particular, he wishes to thank Min Chen and Fan Zhang for stimulating discussions that lead to some collaborative joint work on machine learning, IoT sensing, cloud mashups, and healthcare systems.

In addition, the author appreciates his colleagues at the University of Southern California (USC) for joint research efforts and technical support: Michael Arbib, George Bekey, Ellis Horowitz, Viktor Prasanna, Sandeep Gupta, and Clifford Neumann. He is also grateful to Choli Wang, Richy Kwok and Paul Cheung at Hong Kong University; Weiming Zheng, Yongwei Wu, Xiaoying Bai, Junwei Cao, Wenquang Chen, and Wen He at Tsinghua University. He wants to thank Guojie Li, Zhiwei Xu, Gaogang Xie, and Dan Meng at the Chinese Academy of Sciences for joint scientific work in the past decade.

The author is indebted to two of his current Ph.D. students at USC, Wenhao Zhang and Yue Shi, for their help in material collection, artwork, homework solutions, and proofreading of several versions of this manuscript. He want to acknowledge the academic undertakings that he had completed with his former Ph.D. students at Purdue and USC, in particular with Lionel Ni, D. K. Panda, Joydeep Ghosh, Zhiwei Xu, Ahmed Lourie, Jiyuan Chin, Jian Xu, Shanshan Song, Yu Chen, Min Cai, Xiaosong Lou, and Runfang Zhou over the years.

Finally, the author would like to dedicate this book to his children, Tony, Andrew, Katherine, and Annie, and his wife Jennifer, for their love and understanding during the long process of writing and producing this book over the past three years.

Kai Hwang
January 12, 2017

PART I

CLOUD, BIG DATA, AND COGNITIVE COMPUTING

Part I contains two introductory chapters on the fundamental principles of cloud computing, data science, and cognitive computing in the context of big data applications. Chapter 1 introduces cloud computing principles. Chapter 2 presents necessary background on big data science and technological support. We attempt to integrate three mutually supportive fields: cloud computing, cognitive services, and big data science.

These two chapters lay the necessary theoretical foundation and technological bases for reading the eight chapters in the subsequent three parts of this book. Part II presents virtualization, cloud architecture, mobile clouds, social media, and mashup services. Part III deals with machine learning and data analytics principles and algorithms. Finally, big data programming support and cloud performance boosters are treated in Part IV.

Chapter 1: Principles of Cloud Computing Systems

Summary: This opening chapter is devoted to establishing the necessary foundations of smart and efficient clouds that are user-friendly in terms of programmability and productivity. Basic cloud models and generic architecture are introduced. In particular, we address the scalability, availability, mobility, and performance issues in using elastic clouds. Basic cloud service models are specified. Chapter 1 presents special architectural supports for big data computing on clouds. Subsequent chapters follow up with more details about these hardware, software, and networking technologies.

Chapter 2: Data Science, Internet of Things, Analytics, and Cognitive Computing

Summary: Data science and cloud analytics are introduced in this chapter. We also cover related issues on the Internet of things (IoT) and cognitive computing. We first review big data characteristics and then proceed with basic knowledge on data mining and machine learning techniques. We then introduce the basic architectural support for cloud data analytics. Finally, we present the key concept of cognitive computing and neuro-informatics. Neuromorphic processors, brain-like computers, and cognitive research projects at IBM, Google, and the Chinese Academy of Sciences are reviewed as examples.

Chapter 1

Principles of Cloud Computing Systems

1.1 Elastic Cloud Systems for Scalable Computing

Over the years, traditional computer systems have emphasized *high-performance computing* (HPC) applications in terms of raw speed in batch processing. Now that the Internet is used by billions of people each day, the new demand for network-based computing requires *high-throughput computing* (HTC) systems, which are built with parallel and distributed computing technologies. This demand has triggered the upgrading of many data centers into Internet clouds that can serve millions of users simultaneously. This chapter focuses on building HTC clouds using low-cost servers, distributed storage systems, and high-bandwidth networks in order to advance big data computing in web, cloud, and *Internet of things* (IoT) services. It describes cloud system design principles, hardware and software infrastructure, and virtualized resources management.

1.1.1 Enabling Technologies for Cloud Computing

The key driving forces behind cloud computing are the ubiquity of broadband and wireless networking, falling storage costs, and progressive improvements in Internet computing software. Cloud users are able to demand more capacity at peak hours, reduce costs, experiment with new services, and remove unneeded capacity, whereas service providers can increase the system utilization via multiplexing, virtualization, and dynamic resource provisioning.

The concept of cloud computing has evolved from cluster, grid, and utility computing. Cluster and grid computing leverage the use of many computers in parallel. Utility and *software as a service* (SaaS) provide the computing resources. Cloud computing leverages dynamic resources to deliver a large number of services to end users. It frees up users to focus on user applications development by outsourcing the job execution to cloud providers.

Enabling Technologies

Clouds are enabled by the progress in developing new hardware, software, and networking technologies (see Table 1.1). These technologies play instrumental roles in making cloud computing a reality. Most of these technologies are mature enough today to meet the increasing demand. In the hardware area, the rapid progress in multicore CPUs, memory chips, and disk arrays has made it possible to build faster data centers with huge storage spaces. Resource virtualization enables rapid cloud deployment with HTC and disaster recovery capabilities.

The progress of providing SaaS, Web 2.0 standards, and Internet performance have all contributed to the emergence of cloud services. Today's clouds are designed to serve a large number of tenants over massive volumes of data. The availability of large-scale, distributed storage systems is the underlying foundation of today's data centers. Of course, cloud computing is greatly benefitted by the progress made in license management and automatic billing techniques.

Private clouds within an organization are easier to secure and are more trustworthy than public clouds. Once the private clouds become mature and more secure, they could be opened or converted to public clouds. Therefore, the boundary between public and private clouds might blur in the future. Most future clouds will likely be hybrid in nature.

Convergence of Technologies

Cloud computing is enabled by the convergence of four technologies, as illustrated in Figure 1.1: (1) hardware virtualization and multicore chips make it possible to have

Table 1.1
Cloud-enabling technologies in hardware, software, and networking.

Technology	Requirements and Benefits
Fast Platform Deployment	Fast, efficient, and flexible deployment of cloud resources to provide dynamic computing environment to users.
Virtual Clusters on Demand	Virtualized cluster of VMs provisioned to satisfy user demand and virtual cluster reconfigured as workload changes.
Multitenant Techniques	SaaS distributes software to a large number of users for their simultaneous uses and resource sharing if so desired.
Massive Data Processing	Internet search and web services often require massive data processing, especially to support personalized services.
Web-Scale Communication	Support e-commerce, distance education, telemedicine, social networking, digital government, digital entertainment, etc.
Distributed Storage	Large-scale storage of personal records and public archive information demand distributed storage over the clouds.
Licensing and Billing Services	License management and billing services greatly benefit all types of cloud services in utility computing.

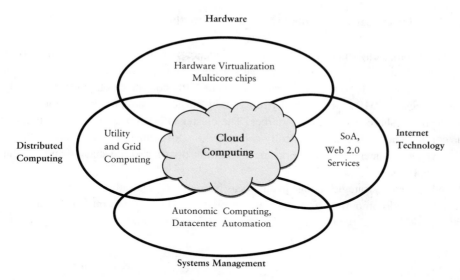

Figure 1.1
Technological convergence enabling cloud computing over the Internet.

dynamic configurations in clouds; (2) utility and grid computing technologies lay the necessary foundation for cloud computing; (3) recent advances in *service oriented architecture* (SoA), Web 2.0, and mashups of platforms are pushing the cloud another step forward; and (4) autonomic computing and automated data center operations have enabled cloud computing.

Cloud computing explores multicore and parallel computing technologies. To realize the vision of data-intensive systems, one needs to integrate hardware, Internet, and data centers. Today's Internet technology emphasizes SoA and Web 2.0 services. Utility and grid computing lay the distributed computing foundation needed for cloud computing. Finally, one cannot ignore the widespread use of data centers with virtualization techniques applied to automate the resources provisioning process in clouds.

Utility computing is based on a business model by which customers receive computing resources from cloud or IoT service providers. This presents some technological challenges in almost all aspects of computer science and engineering. For example, users may demand new network-efficient processors, scalable memory and storage schemes, distributed *operating systems* (OS), middleware for machine virtualization, new programming models, effective resource management, and application program development. These hardware and software advances are necessary to facilitate mobile cloud computing in various IoT application domains.

1.1.2 Evolution of Scalable Distributed/Parallel Computing

The general computing trend is toward increased leveraging on shared web resources over the Internet. As illustrated in Figure 1.2, we see the evolution from two tracks of system development: HPC systems and HTC systems. On the HPC side, supercomputers (massively parallel processors, MPP) are gradually replaced by clusters of cooperative computers out of the desire to share computing resources. The cluster is often a collection of homogeneous compute nodes that are physically connected in close range to one another. On the HTC side, peer-to-peer (P2P) networks are formed for distributed file sharing and content delivery applications.

There has been a strategic change in emphasis from the HPC paradigm to the HTC paradigm. P2P, cloud computing, and web service platforms focus more on HTC than HPC applications. The HTC paradigm pays more attention to high-flux multicomputing, where

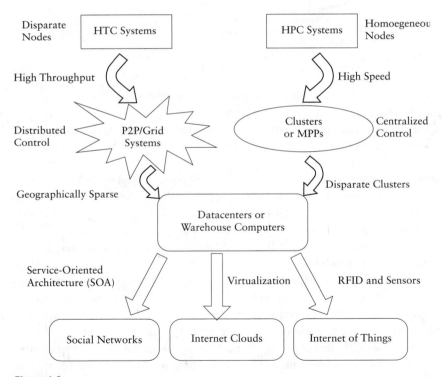

Figure 1.2
Evolutionary trend of parallel, distributed, and cloud computing using clusters, MPPs, P2P networks, computing grids, Internet clouds, web services, and the IoT. HPC: high-performance computing; HTC: high-throughput computing; P2P: peer-to-peer; MPP: massively parallel processors; RFID: radio-frequency identification.

Internet searches and web services are requested by millions of users simultaneously. Thus, the new performance goal has shifted from speed to measuring the *high throughput* or the number of tasks completed per unit of time. Furthermore, cost, energy efficiency, security, and reliability in clouds are also of vital importance.

In this era of big data, we are facing a data deluge problem. Data comes from IoT sensors, lab experiments, simulations, society archives, and the web in all scales and formats. Preservation, movement, and access of massive data sets require generic tools supporting high-performance, scalable file systems, databases, algorithms, workflow, and visualization. A new data-centric paradigm of scientific discovery is based on data-intensive technologies. New tools for data capture, data creation, and data analysis are needed. The cloud and IoT technologies are driven by the surge of interest in the data deluge situation.

The Internet and World Wide Web are used by billions of people every day. As a result, large data centers or clouds must be designed to provide not only big storage but also distributed computing power to satisfy the requests from a large number of users simultaneously. The emergence of public or hybrid clouds requires upgrading many data centers using larger server clusters, distributed file systems, and high-bandwidth networks. With massive smartphone and tablet usage requesting services, the cloud engines, distributed storage, and mobile networks must interact closely with the Internet to deliver mashup services in web-scale mobile computing over the social and media networks.

Advances in virtualization make it possible to use Internet clouds to process a huge number of user service requests. In fact, the differences among clusters, P2P systems, and clouds may become blurred. Some view the clouds as computing clusters with modest changes in virtualization. Others anticipate the effective processing of huge data sets generated by web services, social networks, and the IoT. In this sense, many users consider cloud platforms a form of utility computing or service computing.

The basic architecture and design considerations of data centers are presented in the following sections. A cloud architecture is built with commodity hardware and network devices. Almost all cloud platforms choose the popular x86 processors. Low-cost terabyte disks and gigabit Ethernet are used to build data centers. Data center design focuses more on the performance/price ratio than speed performance alone. Storage and energy efficiency are more important than sheer speed performance.

Data Center Growth and Cost Breakdown

A large data center may be built with thousands of servers, while smaller ones are built with only hundreds of servers. As of 2010, there were approximately 43 million servers worldwide. The cost to build and maintain data center servers has increased over the years and the cost of utilities exceeds the cost of hardware after just three years. According to a 2009 International Data Corporation Report (Figure 1.3), typically, 30% of data center costs

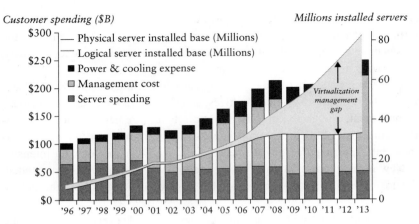

Customer spending ($B)   *Millions installed servers*

Figure 1.3
Growth and cost breakdown of data centers over the years. Source: IDC Report 2009.

are attributed to the purchasing of *information technology* (IT) equipment (such as servers, disks, etc.), 33% to cooling, 18% to *uninterruptible power supply* (UPS), 9% to computer room air conditioning, and the remaining 7% to power distribution, lighting, and transformer costs. Thus, the cost to run a data center is dominated by about 60% in management and maintenance costs. The server purchase cost did not increase much with time, yet the cost of electricity and cooling did increase from 5% to 14% in 15 years.

Low-Cost Design Philosophy
High-end switches or routers may be too cost-prohibitive in building data centers. Thus, using high-bandwidth networks may not fit the economics of cloud computing. Given a fixed budget, commodity switches and networks are preferred in data centers. Similarly, using commodity x86 servers is more desirable over the use of expensive mainframes. The software layer handles the network traffic balancing, fault tolerance, and expandability. Currently, nearly all the cloud computing data centers use the Ethernet as the fundamental network technology.

Science and our society are facing a data deluge problem. Data comes from sensors, lab experiments, simulations, individual archives, and the web in all different scales and formats. Preservation, movement, and access to massive data sets require generic tools supporting high-performance scalable file systems, databases, algorithms, workflow, and visualization. With science becoming data-centric, a new paradigm of scientific discovery is based on data-intensive technologies.

There exists a cycle of interactions among four technical areas: The cloud technology is driven by the surge of interest on data deluge. Cloud computing impacts the eScience greatly, which explores the multicore and parallel computing technologies, which in turn enable a data deluge. To realize the vision of data-intensive systems and building of generic tools, one needs to address workflows, databases, algorithms, and virtualization.

By linking computer science and technologies with scientists, spectrum of eScience or eResearch applications in biology, chemistry, physics, social science, and humanities has generated new insights into interdisciplinary activities. Cloud computing is a transformative approach as it promises much more than the data center model as well as fundamentally changing how we interact with information. The cloud provides services on demand, such as infrastructure, platform, or software. At the platform level, MapReduce offers a new programming model that transparently handles data parallelism with natural fault tolerance capability.

1.1.3 Virtualized Resources in Cloud Systems

According to Gordon Bell, Jim Gray, and Alex Szalay [3]: "Computational science is changing to be data-intensive. Supercomputers must be balanced systems, not just CPU farms but also petascale I/O and networking arrays." In the future, working with large data sets will typically mean sending the computations (programs) to the data, rather than copying the data to the workstations. This reflects the trend in IT that moves computing and data from desktops to large data centers, where on-demand provision of software, hardware, and data as a service are available. Data explosion promoted the idea of cloud computing.

Cloud computing has been defined differently by many users and designers. IBM [5] has defined cloud computing as: "A cloud is a pool of virtualized computer resources. A cloud can host a variety of different workloads, including batch-style backend jobs and interactive, user-facing applications." By this definition, a cloud allows workloads to be deployed and scaled out quickly through the rapid provisioning of *virtual machines* (VMs) or *physical machines* (PMs). The cloud supports redundant, self-recovering, highly scalable, programming models that allow workloads to recover from many unavoidable hardware or software failures. Finally, the cloud system should be able to monitor resource use in real time to enable rebalancing of allocations when needed.

Internet Clouds

Cloud computing applies a virtualized platform with elastic resources on demand by dynamically provisioning hardware, software, and data sets (see Figure 1.4). The idea is to move desktop computing to a service-oriented platform using server clusters and huge databases at data centers. Cloud computing leverages its low cost and simplicity that benefit both users and providers. Machine virtualization has enabled such cost-effectiveness. Cloud computing is intended to satisfy many user applications simultaneously, therefore the cloud ecosystem must be designed to be secure, trustworthy, and dependable. Some computer users think of a cloud as a centralized resource pool. Others consider a cloud as a server cluster which practices distributed computing over all utilized servers.

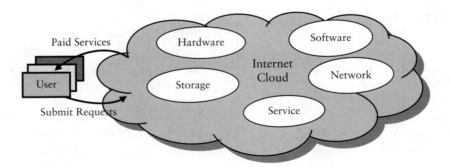

Figure 1.4
Virtualized resources from data centers form an Internet cloud, provisioned with hardware, software, storage, network, and services for paid users to run their applications.

Foster et al. [13] defined cloud computing as: "A large-scale distributed computing paradigm that is driven by economics of scale, in which a pool of abstracted virtualized, dynamically-scalable, managed computing power, storage, platforms, and services are delivered on demand to external customers over the Internet." Six common characteristics of the Internet clouds are identified as follows:

1. The cloud platform offers a scalable computing paradigm built around the data centers.
2. Cloud resources are dynamically provisioned by data centers upon user demand.
3. The cloud system provides compute, storage, and flexible platforms for upgraded web services.
4. Cloud computing relies heavily on the virtualization of all kinds of resources.
5. Cloud computing defines a new paradigm for collective computing, data consumption, and delivery of information services over the Internet.
6. Clouds stress the cost of ownership reduction in mega data centers.

Traditionally, a distributed computing system tends to be owned and operated by an autonomous administrative domain (e.g., a research laboratory or company) for on-premises computing needs. However, these traditional systems have encountered several performance bottlenecks: constant system maintenance, poor utilization, and increasing costs associated with hardware/software upgrades. Cloud computing as an on-demand computing paradigm resolves or provides relief from these difficulties.

1.1.4 Cloud Computing versus On-Premise Computing

Conventional computing systems involve buying the hardware equipment, acquiring the necessary system software, installing the system, testing the configuration, and executing the application codes and management of resources, etc. In the case of clouds, all hardware and software resources are leased from the provider without much capital investment on the part of the user. Only the execution phase requires some service charge. One can easily save 80–95% of the cost to execute small jobs by using the cloud, something very appealing to small businesses as it eliminates the need to invest in permanent and expensive computers or servers.

Traditional computing applications are primarily executed on local hosts that are on the premise, such as desktops, desk-side workstations, notebooks, tablets, etc. On-premise computing differs from cloud computing primarily in resource control and infrastructure management. In Table 1.2, we compare three basic cloud service models with the on-premise computing paradigm. We consider five types of hardware and software resources: storage, servers, VMs, networking, and application software (see Table 1.2).

Basic cloud service models are *infrastructure as a service* (IaaS) or infrastructure cloud, *platform as a service* (PaaS) or platform cloud, and *software as a service* (SaaS) or application cloud. In the case of on-premise computing at local hosts, all resources must be acquired by the users except networking, which is shared between users and the provider. This creates a heavy burden and operating expense on the part of the users. In cloud computing, users entrust their program execution to a remote cloud through the Internet thereby eliminating such an expense.

Cloud computing differs from conventional network computing or outsourced computing in that users leave most or all infrastructure management and program execution to the cloud platform, which acts as a compute/storage rental company. Users lease the computing power from the cloud providers. A cloud platform provides many VM opportunities that execute dedicated services to a large number of users, both separately and simultaneously. Therefore, clouds can benefit individuals, families, communities, and organizations, concurrently.

In IaaS clouds such as AWS EC2, the user only needs to worry about application software deployment. The VMs are jointly deployed by the user and provider. The vendors are responsible for providing the remaining hardware and networks. In PaaS clouds, such as Google App Engine, both application codes and VMs are jointly deployed by the user and

Table 1.2
Comparing three cloud service models with the on-premise computing in terms of resources management responsibilities.

Resource Types	On-Premise Computing	IaaS Model	PaaS Model	SaaS Model
App Software	User	User	Shared	*Vendor*
Virtual Machines	User	Shared	Shared	*Vendor*
Servers	User	*Vendor*	*Vendor*	*Vendor*
Storage	User	*Vendor*	*Vendor*	*Vendor*
Networking	Shared	*Vendor*	*Vendor*	*Vendor*

vendor and the remaining resources are provided by the vendors. Finally, in the SaaS model, used in the Salesforce cloud, everything is provided by the vendor including the application software. In conclusion, we see that cloud computing reduces a user's infrastructure management burden from two resources to none, as one moves from IaaS to PaaS and SaaS services. This clearly shows the advantages to users of separating the application from resources investment and management.

Cloud Design Objectives

Despite the controversy surrounding the replacement of desktop or desk-side computing by centralized computing and storage services at the data centers or big IT companies, the cloud computing community has reached some consensus on what has to be done to make cloud computing universally acceptable. Six design objectives for cloud computing are outlined as follows.

1. ***Shifting computing from desktops to data centers:*** The shift of computer processing, storage, and software delivery away from the desktop and local servers to data centers over the Internet.

2. ***Service provisioning and cloud economics:*** Providers supply cloud services by signing SLAs with consumers and end users. The services must be economically feasible with efficiency in computing, storage, power consumption, etc. Pricing models are based on a *pay-as-you-go* policy.

3. ***Scalability in performance:*** The cloud platforms and software and infrastructure services must be able to increase in performance as the number of users increase.

4. ***Data privacy protection:*** The concern regarding users' data and record privacy must be addressed to make clouds a successful and trusted service.

5. ***High-quality of cloud services:*** The QoS of cloud computing must be standardized to make clouds interoperable among multiple providers.

6. ***New standards and interfaces:*** This refers to solving the data lock-in problem associated with data centers or cloud providers. Universally accepted *application programming interfaces* (APIs) and access protocols are needed to provide high portability and flexibility of virtualized applications.

Many executable application codes are much smaller than the web-scale data sets they process. Cloud computing avoids large data movement during execution. This will result in less traffic on the Internet and better network utilization. We will model the performance of cloud computing in Chapter 10 along with data protection, security measures, service availability, fault-tolerance, and operating cost. The core of a cloud is the server cluster (or VM cluster). The cluster nodes are used as compute nodes and a few control nodes are used to manage and monitor of the cloud activities.

The scheduling of user jobs on a cloud requires assigning the work to virtual clusters created for users. The gateway nodes provide the access points of the service from the outside world. These gateway nodes also can be used for security control of the entire cloud platform. In physical clusters, users expect a static demand of resources. Clouds are designed to face fluctuating workloads and thus dynamically demand varying amounts of resources. Data centers and supercomputers have some significant similarities and distinctions. In the case of data centers, the scaling is a fundamental requirement. The data center server clusters are built with low-cost servers. For example, Microsoft has a data center in the Chicago area that has 100,000 8-core servers housed in 50 containers. In a supercomputer, a separate storage disk array is used, while a data center uses local disks attached to the server nodes.

1.2 Cloud Architectures Compared with Distributed Systems

This section studies the generic architecture of contemporary clouds. We present a cloud taxonomy based on service models, applications, ownership, etc. Clouds can be treated as centralized systems due to the fact that most clouds are converted from big data centers and warehouse computer systems. On the other hand, clouds can be also considered distributed systems because (1) many clouds are used in co-locations or mashup configurations and (2) cloud applications are often distributed to distance clouds from where the big data is located. We will compare clouds with other parallel and distributed systems.

1.2.1 Basic Cloud Platform Architectures

Generic cloud architecture and the hierarchical development of cloud platforms are introduced below.

Generic Cloud Architecture

A generic cloud architecture is shown in Figure 1.5. The Internet cloud is envisioned as a massive cluster of servers. These servers are provisioned on demand to perform collective web services or distributed applications using data center resources. The cloud platform is formed dynamically by the provisioning, or de-provisioning, of servers, software, and database resources. Servers in the cloud can be PMs or VMs. User interfaces are applied to request services. The provisioning tool carves out the cloud system to deliver the requested service. In addition to building the server cluster, the cloud platform demands distributed storage and accompanying services. The cloud computing resources are built in data centers, typically owned and operated by a third-party provider, and consumers do not need to know the underlying technologies.

In a cloud, software becomes a service. The cloud demands a high level of trust of massive data retrieved from large data centers. A framework must be built to process large-scale data stored in the storage system which demands a distributed file system over the database system. Other cloud resources are added into a cloud platform including the storage area networks, database systems, firewalls, and security devices. Web service providers offer

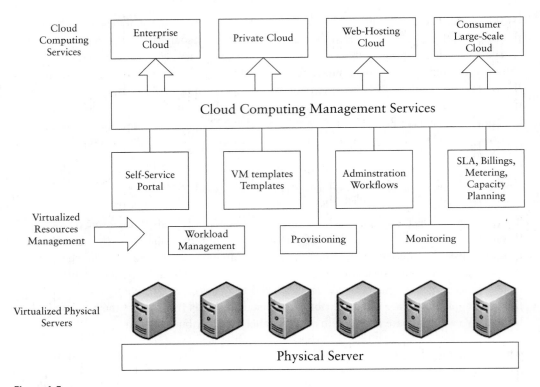

Figure 1.5
A generic architecture of cloud computing system, where physical servers are virtualized as VM instances under the control of a resource management system.

special APIs that enable developers to exploit Internet clouds. Monitoring and metering units are used to track the usage and performance of provisioned resources.

Virtual Machines

Multiple VMs can be started and stopped on demand on a single PM to meet accepted service requests, hence providing maximum flexibility to configure various partitions of resources on the same PM to different specific requirements of service requests. In addition, multiple VMs can concurrently run applications based on different operating system environments on a single PM since each VM is isolated from one another on the same PM. Details of VM and containers will be addressed in Chapter 3.

The software infrastructure of a cloud platform must handle all resource management and do most of the maintenance, automatically. Software must detect the status of each node, server joining and leaving, and perform the tasks accordingly. Cloud computing providers, such as Google and Microsoft, have built a large number of data centers all over the world.

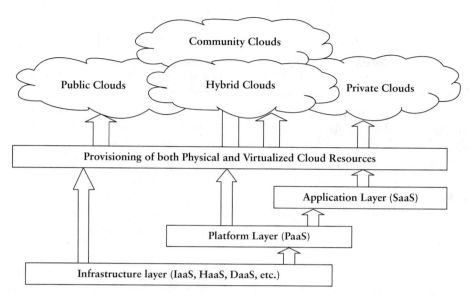

Figure 1.6
Layered architectural development of the cloud platform for IaaS, PaaS, and SaaS applications over the Internet.

Each data center may have thousands of servers and its location is chosen in order to reduce power and cooling costs. Thus, the data centers are often built around a hydroelectricity power stop. The cloud's physical platform builder is more concerned with the performance/price ratio and reliability issues than shear speed performance.

Layered Development of Service Clouds

The architecture of a cloud is developed in three layers: infrastructure, platform, and application, as demonstrated in Figure 1.6. These three development layers are implemented with virtualization and standardization of hardware and software resources provisioned in the cloud. The services to public, private, and hybrid clouds are conveyed to users through the networking support over the Internet and Intranets involved. It is clear that the infrastructure layer is deployed first to support IaaS types of services. This infrastructure layer serves as the foundation upon which the platform layer of the cloud for supporting PaaS services is built. In turn, the platform layer is a foundation for the implementation of the application layer for SaaS applications.

1. The *infrastructure layer* is built with virtualized compute, storage, and network resources. The abstraction of these hardware resources is meant to provide the flexibility demanded by users. Internally, the virtualization realizes the automated provisioning of resources and optimizes the infrastructure management process. It should be noted that

not all cloud services are restricted to a single layer. In fact, many applications may apply resources at mixed layers. After all, the three layers are built from the bottom up with a dependence relationship.

2. The *platform layer* is for general purposes and repeated usage of the collection of software resources. This layer provides users with an environment in which to develop their applications, test the operation flows, and monitor the execution results and performance. The platform should be able to assure the users of scalability, dependability, and security protection. In a way, the virtualized cloud platform serves as a "system middleware" between the infrastructure and application layers of the cloud.

3. The *application layer* is formed from a collection of all necessary software modules for SaaS applications. Service applications in this layer include daily office management work, such as information retrieval, document processing, calendar managment, and authentication services. This layer is also heavily used by enterprises in business marketing and sales, as it enhances the consumer relationship.

From the provider's perspective, the services at various layers demand different amounts of function support and resource management by the providers. In general, the SaaS demands the most work from the provider, the PaaS the middle amount, and IaaS the least. For example, Amazon EC2 provides not only virtualized CPU resources to users but also the management of these provisioned resources. Services at the application layer demand more work from the providers. The best example is the Salesforce CRM service in which the provider supplies not only the hardware at the bottom layer and the software at the top layer, but also provides the platform and software tools for user application development and monitoring.

It should be noted that the IaaS clouds can be utilized directly by users. IaaS clouds often share the resources with large websites such as Amazon.com or search engines such as Google and they can be also used as the foundation for the PaaS clouds or SaaS clouds. Many companies like Salesforce started without an IaaS platform. They simply rented the facilities from Amazon clouds. Now, these companies can afford to build their own infrastructure clouds to support PaaS or SaaS applications. As a matter of fact, the three cloud types are often built on the same hardware. With cloud operating system support, one can easily convert an IaaS cloud into a PaaS cloud. Then, with a cloud platform established, one can easily provide SaaS application software to users.

1.2.2 Public, Private, Community, and Hybrid Clouds

The cloud offers significant benefits to IT companies by freeing them from the menial task of setting up the hardware (servers) and managing the system software tools. Cloud computing applies a virtual platform with elastic resources put together by on-demand provisioning of hardware, software, and data sets, dynamically. The main idea is to move desktop computing to a service-oriented platform using server clusters and huge databases at data

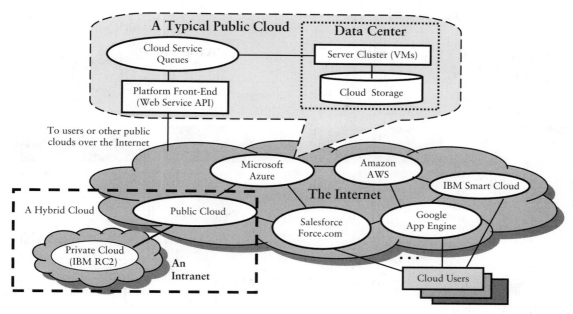

Figure 1.7
Public, private, and hybrid clouds. The callout box shows the architecture of a typical public cloud. A private cloud is built within an Intranet. A hybrid cloud involves both types in its operation range. Users access the clouds from a web browser or through a special API tool.

centers. Cloud computing leverages its low cost and simplicity to both providers and users. Four families of cloud platforms are introduced in the sections that follow.

Centralized versus Distributed Computing

Some people argue that cloud computing is centralized computing at data centers. Others claim that cloud computing is indeed practicing distributed parallel computing over data center resources. These represent the two opposing views of cloud computing. All computations in cloud applications are distributed to the servers in a data center. These are mainly VMs in virtual clusters created out of data center resources. In this sense, cloud platforms are indeed distributed systems through virtualization. As shown in Figure 1.7, both public clouds and private clouds are developed over the Internet. These clouds are characterized separately below, although they may complement each other in their functionalities.

As many clouds are generated by commercial providers or by enterprises in a distributed manner, they can be interconnected over the Internet to achieve scalable and efficient computing services. Commercial cloud providers like Amazon, Google, and Microsoft created their platforms and distributed them geographically. The distribution is partially attributed to fault tolerance, response latency reduction, and even legal reasons. The Intranet-based

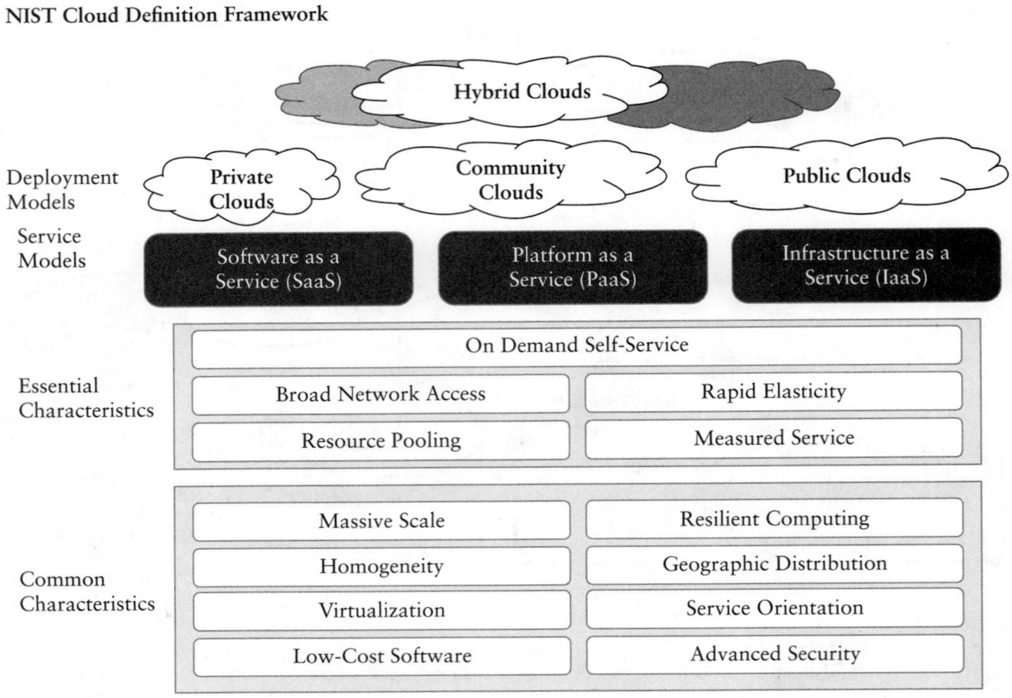

NIST Cloud Definition Framework

Figure 1.8
Public, private, community, and hybrid clouds. Courtesy of National Institute of Standards and Technology, 2013.

private clouds are linked to the public clouds in order to get additional resources. Nevertheless, European users may not feel comfortable computing their applications in U.S. clouds,
and vice versa, until extensive *service level agreements* (SLAs) are developed between the
two user communities. These cloud families are illustrated in Figure 1.8 based on the
National Institute of Standard and Technology's (NIST) definition of cloud computing.

Public Clouds
A public cloud is built over the Internet, which can be accessed by any user who has paid
for the service. Public clouds are owned by service providers and are accessed by subscrip-
tion. Well-known public clouds include the Google App Engine (GAE), Amazon Web Service (AWS), Microsoft Azure, IBM Smart Cloud, Salesforce Sales Cloud, etc. These providers
offer a publicly accessible remote interface for creating and managing VM instances within
the system.

Community Clouds

This is a growing subclass of public clouds. These clouds appear as a collaborative infrastructure shared by multiple organizations with some common social or business interest, scientific discovery, high availability, etc. Community clouds are often built over multiple data centers. In recent years, community clouds have grown rapidly in education, business, enterprises, and government sectors to meet the growth of big data applications.

Private Clouds

The private cloud is built within the domain of an Intranet owned by a single organization. Therefore, they are client owned and managed. A private cloud is supposed to deliver more efficient and convenient cloud services while giving users a flexible and agile private infrastructure to run service workloads within their administrative domains. Private clouds may wish to retain greater customization and organizational control.

Hybrid Clouds

A hybrid cloud is built with all cloud families. Private clouds support a hybrid cloud model by supplementing local infrastructure with computing capacity from an external public cloud. For example, the *research compute cloud* (RC2) is a private cloud owned by IBM. The RC2 interconnects the computing resources at eight IBM Research Centers scattered in the United States, Europe, and Asia. A hybrid cloud provides access to the client, partner network, and a third party.

In summary, public clouds promote standardization, preserve capital investigation, and offer application flexibility. The private clouds attempt to achieve customization and offer higher efficiency, resiliency, security, and privacy. The hybrid clouds operate in the middle with many compromises in resources sharing. In general, the private clouds are easier to manage while public clouds are easier to access. The trend of cloud development is that more and more clouds are becoming hybrid. We will cover all these requirements in subsequent chapters. Overall, cloud systems require both HPC and HTC power. Furthermore, one should emphasize on-demand and self-service in any cloud system.

1.2.3   Physical Clusters versus Virtual Clusters

A physical cluster is a collection of servers (PMs) interconnected by a physical network like a LAN. The physical clusters are identified by its controller at the top boxes and servers are shown by small boxes at the bottom. Here, we introduce virtual clusters, study their properties, and explore potential applications. The differences between physical clusters and virtual clusters are illustrated in Figure 1.9. Virtual clusters are built with multiple VMs installed at servers belonging to one or more physical clusters. The VMs in a virtual cluster are interconnected logically by a virtual network across several physical networks. Each virtual

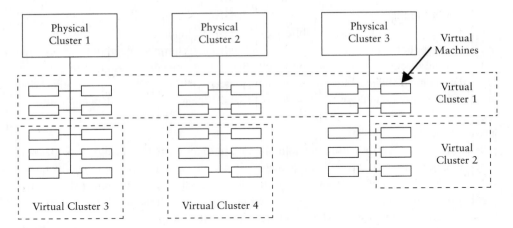

Figure 1.9
A cloud platform built with four virtual clusters over three physical clusters. Each virtual cluster is formed with
VMs hosted in multiple physical clusters.

cluster is formed with PMs or VMs hosted by multiple physical clusters. The virtual clusters'
boundaries are shown with distinct boundaries. The provisioning of VMs to a virtual cluster is dynamically done. Virtual clusters have the following interesting properties:

1. The virtual cluster nodes can be either PMs or VMs. Multiple VMs running with different OSs can be deployed on the same physical node.

2. A VM runs with a guest OS, which is often different than the host OS that manages the
   resources in the PM, where the VM is implemented.

3. The purpose of using VMs is to consolidate multiple functionalities on the same server.
   This will greatly enhance the server utilization and application flexibility.

4. VMs can be colonized (replicated) in multiple servers for the purpose of promoting distributed parallelism, fault tolerance, and disaster recovery.

5. The size (number of nodes) of a virtual cluster can grow or shrink dynamically, similar
   to the way an overlay network varies in size in a P2P network.

6. The failure of any physical nodes may disable some VMs installed on the failing nodes
   but the failure of VMs will not pull down the host system.

Example 1.1 Formation of Virtual Clusters out of Physical Clusters

Consider three physical clusters on the top of Figure 1.9. Four virtual clusters are created on the right and bottom over the physical clusters. The PMs are known as host systems. In contrast, the VMs are guest systems. The host and guest systems may run with
different operating systems. Each VM is installed on a given server or replicated on

multiple severs belonging to the same or different physical clusters. The boundary of a virtual cluster can change as VM nodes are added, removed, or migrated dynamically over the time.

Important design issues of a virtual cluster include deployment, monitoring, and management over a large-scale physical cluster. The designer must consider VM instance creation, job scheduling, load balancing, server consolidation, fault tolerance, and other techniques. The different shadings in boxes represent the nodes in different virtual clusters. In a virtual cluster system, it is important to store the large number of VM machine images efficiently. ∎

Data Center Networking Structure

The core of a cloud is the server cluster (or VM cluster). The cluster nodes are used as compute nodes and a few control nodes are used to manage and monitor cloud activities. The scheduling of user jobs requires assigning the work to virtual clusters created for users. The gateway nodes provide the access points of the service from the outside world. These gateway nodes also can be used for security control of the entire cloud platform. In physical clusters and traditional grids, users expect static demand of resources. Clouds are designed to face fluctuating workload and thus demand varying amounts of resource, dynamically. It is anticipated that private clouds will satisfy this demand more efficiently.

Data centers and supercomputers do have some similarities as well as fundamental distinctions. In the case of data centers, the scaling is a fundamental requirement. The data center server clusters are built with thousands to even a million servers (nodes). For example, Microsoft has a data center in the Chicago area that has one hundred thousand 8-core servers that are housed in 50 containers. In supercomputers, a separate data farm is used, while a data center uses disks on server nodes plus memory cache and databases.

Supercomputers and data centers also differ in networking requirements, as illustrated in Figure 1.10. Supercomputers use custom-designed high bandwidth networks like fat trees or 3D torus networks. Networks in data centers are primarily IP-based commodity networks such as 10 Gbps Ethernet, which is optimized for Internet access. Figure 1.10 shows a multilayer structure to access the Internet. The server racks are at the bottom layer (L) and are connected through fast switches (S) at layer 2 (the hardware core). The data center is really connected at layer 3, then a large number of switches are connected to L3 access routers at layer 3. Then L3 boarder routers are used to access the Internet.

For example, NASA (National Aeronautics and Space Administration) is building a private cloud to enable researchers to run climate models on remote systems provided by NASA. This can save the users from capital expenses in HPC at local sites. Furthermore, NASA can build the complex weather models around their data centers, which is more cost effective. Another good example is the cloud built by CERN (European Organization for Nuclear Research). This is a very big private cloud to distribute data, applications, and computing resources to thousands of scientists around the world.

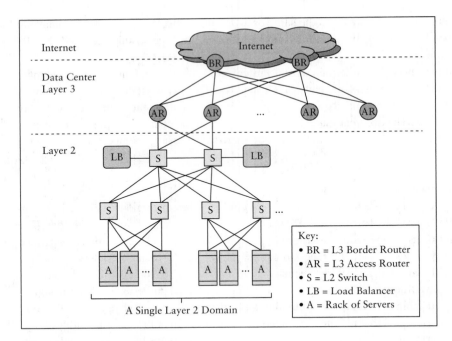

Figure 1.10
Standard data center networking for the cloud to access the Internet. Courtesy of Dennis Gannon, keynote address at IEEE Cloudcom, 2010.

1.2.4 Comparison with Other Parallel/Distributed Systems

Major computing paradigms and their system distinctions are revealed below. The high-technology communities have argued for many years over the precise definitions of these computing terminologies. In general, distributed computing is defined in contrast with centralized computing. The field of parallel computing does overlap with distributed computing to a large extent. Cloud computing overlaps with all three paradigms. We assess below their overlapping areas and identify the subtle differences. These architectural and operational differences will become more transparent after reading the subsequent chapters.

1. *Centralized computing:* A computing paradigm by which all computer resources are centralized at one physical system. All resources (processors, memory, and storage) are fully shared and tightly coupled under one integrated OS. Many data centers and supercomputers are centralized systems but are used in parallel, distributed, and cloud computing applications.

2. *Parallel computing:* All processors are either tightly coupled with centralized shared memory or loosely coupled distributed memories. Some authors refer to this discipline

as parallel processing. Interprocessor communication is done through shared memory or by message passing. The computer system capable of parallel computing is a parallel computer. A program running in a parallel computer is called a parallel program. The process of writing parallel programs is often called parallel programming.

3. **Distributed computing:** This is a field of computer science/engineering that studies distributed systems. A distributed system consists of multiple autonomous computers, each with its own private memory, that communicate through a computer network. Information exchange in a distributed system is done through *message passing*. The computer program that runs in a distributed system is known as a *distributed program*. The process of writing distributed programs is known as *distributed programming*.

4. **Cloud computing:** An Internet cloud of resources can be either a centralized or a distributed computing system. The cloud applies parallel or distributed computing or both. Clouds could be built with physical or virtualized resources over large data centers that are centralized or distributed. Some authors consider cloud computing to be a form of utility computing or service computing.

Other authors may prefer the terms as *concurrent computing or concurrent programming*, which often refer to the union of parallel computing or distributing computing. Biased practitioners may interpret them differently. *Ubiquitous computing* refers to computing with pervasive devices at any place and time using wired or wireless communications. The IoT, connecting any objects (including computers, sensors, human, objects, etc.) on the Earth, is supported by Internet clouds to practice ubiquitous computing. Finally, *Internet computing* is an even broader term that covers all computing paradigms over the Internet. This book covers all of the above-mentioned computing paradigms with more emphasis on distributed and cloud computing and their working systems including clusters, grids, P2P, and cloud systems.

Ever since the mid-1990s, technologies for building P2P networks and networks of clusters have been consolidated into many national projects to establish wide-area computing infrastructures known as computational grids or data grids. More recently, there has been a surge of interest in exploring Internet cloud resources for data-intensive applications. Internet clouds result from moving desktop computing to a service-oriented computing using server clusters and huge databases at data centers. This chapter introduces the basics of various parallel and distributed families. Grids and clouds are disparity systems with great emphasis on resource sharing in hardware, software, and data sets.

Both HPC and HTC demand multicore processors that can handle hundreds or thousands of computing threads, tens of kilo-thread node prototypes, and mobile cloud services platform prototypes. Both types of systems emphasize parallelism and distributed computing. Future HPC and HTC systems must satisfy the huge demand of computing power in terms of throughput, efficiency, scalability, reliability, etc. The term "efficiency" is decided by both speed performance and work efficiency, including the programming and energy efficiency in terms of throughput per watt of energy consumed. To meet these goals, four key design goals must be achieved.

1. *Efficiency* measures utilization rate of resources in an execution model by exploiting massive parallelism in HPC. For HTC, efficiency is related more to job throughput, data access, storage, and power efficiency.

2. *Dependability* in terms of reliability and self-management from the chip to system and application levels. The purpose is to provide high-throughput service with QoS assurance even under failure conditions.

3. *Adaptation* in the programming model which can support billions of job requests over massive data sets and virtualized cloud resources under various workload and service models.

4. *Flexibility* in application deployment. Distributed systems should be designed to run well in both HPC in science and engineering and business HTC applications.

A massively parallel and distributed computing system, or in short a massive system, is built over a large number of autonomous computer nodes. These node machines are interconnected by *system-area networks* (SAN), *local-area networks* (LAN), or *wide-area networks* (WAN) in a hierarchical manner. By today's networking technology, a few LAN switches can easily connect hundreds of machines as a working cluster. A WAN can connect many local clusters to form a very large cluster of clusters. In this sense, one can build a massive system to have millions of computers connected to edge networks in various Internet domains.

Massive systems are considered highly scalable to reach a web-scale connectivity, either physically or logically. In Table 1.3, massive systems are classified into four groups: clusters,

Table 1.3
Classification of parallel and distributed computing systems.

Functionality, Applications	Computer Clusters	Peer-to-Peer Networks	Computational Grids	Cloud Platforms
Architecture, Network Connectivity, and Size	Network of compute nodes interconnected by SAN, LAN, or WAN, hierarchically	Flexible network of client machines logically connected by an overlay network	Heterogeneous clusters interconnected by high-speed network links over selected resource sites	Virtualized cluster of servers over data centers via service-level agreement
Control and Resources Management	Homogeneous nodes with distributed control, running Unix or Linux	Autonomous client nodes, free in and out, with self-organization	Centralized control, server oriented with authenticated security	Dynamic resource provisioning of servers, storage, and networks
Applications and Network-Centric Services	High-performance computing, search engines, web services, etc.	Most appealing to business file sharing, content delivery, and social networking	Distributed super-computing, global problem solving, and data center services	Upgraded web search, utility computing, and outsourced computing services
Representative Operational Systems	Google search engine, Sun Blade, IBM Road-Runner, Cray XT4, etc.	Gnutella, eMule, BitTorrent, Napster, KaZaA, Skype, JXTA	TeraGrid, GriPhyN, UK EGEE, D-Grid, ChinaGrid, etc.	Google App Engine, IBM Smart Cloud, AWS, and Microsoft Azure

P2P networks, computing grids, and Internet clouds over huge data centers. In terms of node number, these four system classes may involve hundreds, thousands, or even millions of computers as participating nodes. These machines work collectively, cooperatively, or collaboratively at various levels. The table entries characterize these four system classes in various technical and application aspects.

From an application perspective, clusters are most popular in supercomputing applications. In 2009, 417 out of the top 500 supercomputers were built with a cluster architecture. It is fair to say that clusters have laid the necessary foundation for building large-scale grids and clouds. P2P networks appeal most to business applications, however the content industry was reluctant to accept P2P technology due to lack of copyright protection in ad hoc networks. Many national grids built in the past decade were underutilized for lack of reliable middleware or well-coded applications.

1.3 Service Models, Ecosystems, and Scalability Analysis

This section specifies various cloud models and the ecosystem that was built over a decade. Then we study three fundamental issues: mobility, scalability, and availability surrounding cloud deployment.

1.3.1 Cloud Service Models: IaaS, PaaS, and SaaS

Cloud computing benefits the service industry and advances business computing with a new paradigm. It has been forecasted that global revenue in cloud computing may exceed $300 billion by 2017. Basic advantages of cloud computing lie in providing ubiquitous services, resource sharing efficiency, and application flexibility. Users are able to access and deploy applications from anywhere in the world at very competitive costs.

- *Infrastructure as a Service (IaaS):* This model puts together infrastructures demanded by users, namely servers, storage, networks, and data center fabric. The user can deploy and run on multiple VMs running guest OS on specific applications. The user does not manage or control the underlying cloud infrastructure, but can specify when to request and release the needed VMs and data. The best IaaS examples are the AWS, GoGrid, Rackspace, Eucalyptus, FlexiScale, RightScale, etc.

- *Platform as a Service (PaaS):* This model allows the user to deploy user-built applications onto a virtualized cloud platform. PaaS includes middleware, database, development tools, and some runtime supports like Web 2.0 and Java. The platform includes both hardware and software integrated with specific programming interfaces. The provider supplies the API and software tools (e.g., Java, Python, Web 2.0, .NET) and the user is freed from managing the cloud infrastructure. PaaS provides a programming environment to build and manage cloud applications. The best examples of PaaS platforms are Google App Engine, Microsoft Azure, Salesforce, etc.

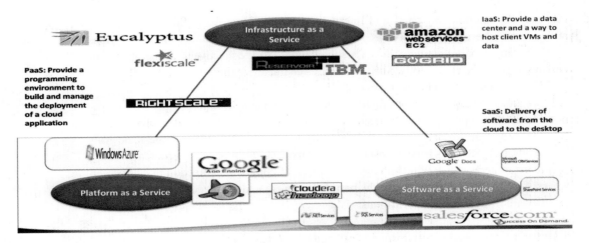

Figure 1.11
Three cloud service models deployed by major providers. Courtesy of Dennis Gannon, keynote address at IEEE Cloudcom, 2010.

- *Software as a Service (SaaS):* This refers to browser-initiated application software delivered to thousands of paid cloud customers. The SaaS model applies to business processes, industry applications, consumer relationship management (CRM), enterprise resources planning (ERP), human resources (HR), and collaborative applications. On the customer side, there is no upfront investment in servers or software licensing. On the provider side, costs are rather low compared with conventional hosting of user applications. The best SaaS examples are Cloudera, Hadoop, Salesforce, .NETService, Google Docs, Microsoft Dynamics CRM Service, SharePoint service, etc.

Figure 1.11 shows the cloud landscape with major cloud providers. All three cloud service models are applied. Internet clouds offer four deployment modes: private, public, community, and hybrid. These modes demand different levels of security implications. The different SLAs imply the security to be a shared responsibility of all the cloud providers, the cloud resource consumers, and the third-party cloud-enabled software providers. Advantages of cloud computing have been advocated by many IT experts, industry leaders, and computer science researchers.

The idea is to move desktop computing to a service-oriented platform using server clusters and huge databases at data centers. Cloud computing leverages its low cost and simplicity that benefit both users and providers. Machine virtualization has enabled such cost-effectiveness. Cloud computing intends to satisfy many user applications simultaneously and the cloud ecosystem must be designed to be secure, trustworthy, and dependable. Otherwise, it may deter the users from accepting the outsourced services. Cloud computing applies a virtualized platform with elastic resources on demand by provisioning hardware.

It should be noted that most clouds have started to provide infrastructure services to host client VMs, good examples of which are the AWS EC2, Rackspace, Eucalyptus, GoGrid, and IBM Reservoir. Some other clouds provide both IaaS and PaaS services such as the AWS and App Engine. In fact, today's AWS offers all three type of services.

Example 1.2   Amazon Web Services Virtual Private Clouds (VPC)

Amazon Web Services (AWS) is by far the most popular IaaS public cloud serving an enormous number of users, simultaneously. A user could build a private server cluster on AWS for use in computations, exclusively. AWS offers the Elastic Compute Cloud (EC2), Simple Storage Service (S3), and Virtual Private Cloud (VPC) to its users. These services operate at 11 geographical regions across the world. Figure 1.12 shows the concept of VPC resources provisioning. The Amazon VPC addresses users' privacy concerns to protect their sensitive data and software. As of December 2014, AWS clouds operated with an estimated 1.4 million servers across 28 availability time zones.

AWS was reported to be profitable, with annual sales of $8 billion in 2015. The VPC allows the user to isolate the provisioned AWS processors, memory, and storage from interference from other users. Both auto scaling and elastic load balancing services are available to support VPC. Auto scaling enables the user to increase or decrease his VM instances, automatically. This can uphold the desired performance level when the workload varies. Lately, a new Amazon EC2 Container Service (ECS) became available at AWS. We will study the details of EC2, S3, and ECS in Chapter 4.

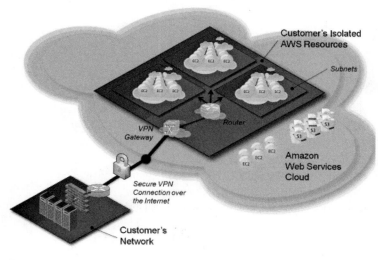

Figure 1.12
Amazon virtual private cloud (VPC). http://aws.amazon.com/vpc/.

Cloud Service Distribution Trends in Recent Years

Figure 1.13 plots the market share projected by Gartner Research for global distribution of the cloud service models from 2014–2020. Ever since the introduction of clouds in 2008, growth has increased at a rate higher than 20%, reaching its peak in 2014. The left Y-axis shows the total sales in dollars and the right Y-axis plots the growth rate plotted by the black curve. The sectioned bars show the market shares of IaaS, PaaS, and SaaS models. The general trend is that both IaaS and SaaS grow rapidly and SaaS growth is faster than IaaS. The PaaS model has a much smaller sale with almost no growth.

By 2016, the worldwide market of cloud services reached $65 billion with a growth rate of 25.36%. By 2020, Gartner projects that the total sales will reach $143 billion with a growth rate of 118.65%. The average growth rate in this six-year period is 22%. In 2015, North America dominated the cloud market with a 56% share. Amazon AWS alone had an annual income of almost $8 billion in 2015. The remaining market shares are spread over Europe, Asia, Latin America, and Australia. The growth rate is expected to continue with an average annual rate of at least 20% worldwide. Based on these trends, the SaaS market will be $72 billion, IaaS $61.5 billion, and the PaaS $10 billion by 2020. Based on these numbers alone, it is obvious that SaaS and IaaS will dominate future cloud services.

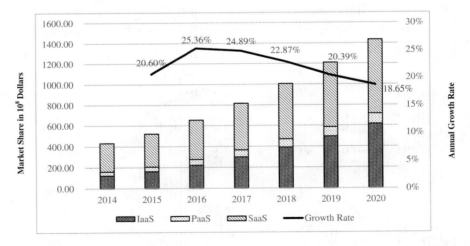

Figure 1.13
Worldwide distribution of cloud service models and the growth rate based on projections by Gartner Research from 2014–2020.

1.3.2 Scalability Laws in Evaluating Cloud Performance

There are predictable trends in technology that drive computing applications. Designers and programmers want to predict the technological capabilities of the future systems. Moore's Law indicates that the processor speed doubles every 18 months. This was indeed true for the past 30 years, however it is hard to say if Moore's Law can continue to hold in the future.

Gilder's Law indicates that the network bandwidth doubled yearly in the past. Can that continue in the future? The tremendous price/performance ratio of commodity hardware was driven by the desktop, notebook, and tablet computing market. This has also driven the adoption and use of commodity technologies in large-scale computing. The answers to these computing trends are given in subsequent chapters. Distributed systems emphasize both resource distribution and concurrency or high degree of parallelism (DoP). We will first review various types of parallelism before proceeding further with the special requirements for cloud computing.

When hardware was bulky and expensive 50 years ago, most computers were designed in a bit-serial fashion. Bit-level parallelism (BLP) converts bit-serial processing to word-level processing gradually. Over the years, users moved from 4-bit microprocessors to 8-, 16-, 32- and 64-bit CPUs. The next wave of improvement is the *instruction-level parallelism* (ILP). By shifting from using processors to execute single instructions to executing multiple instructions simultaneously, we have practiced ILP through pipelining, superscalar, *very-long instruction word* (VLIW), and multithreading. ILP demands branch prediction, dynamic scheduling, speculation, and compiler support.

Data-level parallelism (DLP) was made popular through SIMD (single-instruction and multiple-data) and vector machines using vector or array types of instructions. DLP demands both even more hardware support and compiler assistance to work properly. Ever since the introduction of multicore processors and *chip multiprocessors* (CMP), we explore the *task-level parallelism* (TLP). A modern processor explores all of the above parallelism types.

The BLP, ILP, and DLP are all well supported by advances in hardware and compilers. However, the TLP is far from being very successful due to the difficulty in programming and compilation of codes for efficient execution on multicores and CMPs. As we move from parallel processing to distributed processing, we will see the increase of computing granularity to *job-level parallelism* (JLP). It is fair to say that the coarse-grain parallelism is built on top of the fine-grain parallelism.

In what follows, we study two fundamental issues on cloud performance: the scalability and availability of cloud clusters. To achieve high scalability, we apply Amdhal's and Gustafson's Laws. To support high availability, we present the basic formula that relates availability to *mean time to failure* (MTTF) and *mean time to repair* (MTTR). These basic laws lay the foundation for studying cloud or any other computer architecture.

The total execution time of the program is calculated by $\alpha T + (1-\alpha)T/n$, where the first term is the sequential execution time on a single server and the second term is the parallel execution time on n servers. For simplicity, all system and communication overheads among the n servers are ignored here. The input/output (I/O) time or exception handling time are also excluded in the following analysis of CPU (or server) performance. Amdahl's Law states that the *speedup factor* of using the n-server cluster over the use of a single server is expressed by:

$$Speedup = S = T / [\alpha T + (1 - \alpha) T / n] = 1 / [\alpha + (1 - \alpha) / n]. \tag{1.1}$$

The maximum speedup of n is achieved only if the *sequential bottleneck* α is reduced to 0 or the code is fully parallelizable with $\alpha = 0$. As the cluster becomes sufficiently large, i.e., $n \to \infty$, S approaches $1/\alpha$, which is the upper bound on the speedup S. Surprisingly, this upper bound is independent of the cluster size n.

Sequential bottleneck is the portion of the code that cannot be parallelized. For example, the maximum speedup achievable is 4, if $\alpha = 0.25$ or $1 - \alpha = 0.75$, even if one uses hundreds of processors. Amdahl's Law implies that one should make the sequential bottleneck of all programs as small as possible. Increasing the cluster size alone may not give a good speedup as the program structure is essentially sequential in nature.

Amdahl's Law assumes the workload (or problem size) is fixed regardless how large a cluster is used. Hwang [18] refer to this as *fixed-workload speedup*. To execute a fixed workload on n servers, parallel processing may lead to a *cluster efficiency* defined by:

$$E = S / n = 1 / [\alpha n + 1 - \alpha]. \tag{1.2}$$

This cluster efficiency decreases rapidly with the increase of the cluster size n. For example, to execute the above program with a sequential bottleneck $\alpha = 0.25$ on a cluster with $n = 256$ servers, we expect a very low efficiency $E = 1 / [0.25 \times 256 + 0.75] = 1.5\%$. To increase the efficiency to 60%, the sequential bottleneck must be reduced to 0.13%, which is impossible in most user programs. This is due to the fact that large sequential bottlenecks lead to many idle servers in the cluster.

$$S' = W' / W = [\alpha W + (1 - \alpha) n W] / W = \alpha + (1 - \alpha) n. \tag{1.3}$$

This speedup is known as Gustafson's Law. By fixing the parallel execution time at level W, the following efficiency expression is obtained:

$$E' = S' / n = \alpha / n + (1 - \alpha). \tag{1.4}$$

For the above program with a scaled workload, we can improve the efficiency of using a 256-server cluster to $E' = 0.25/256 + 0.75 = 0.751$. One should apply Amdahl's Law and Gustafson's Law under different workload conditions. For a fixed workload, apply Amdahl's Law; for scaled problems, Gustafson's Law should be applied with a proportional increase of workload as the cluster size increases.

Scalability versus OS Image Count

In Figure 1.14, scalable performance is estimated against the multiplicity of OS images in distributed systems deployed up to 2010. Scalable performance implies that the system can achieve higher speed performance by adding more processors or servers, enlarging the physical node memory size, extending the disk capacity, or adding more I/O channels. The OS image is counted by the number of independent OS images observed in a cluster, grid, P2P network, or the cloud. The SMP and NUMA are included in the comparison. A *symmetric multiprocessor* (SMP) server has a single system image which could be a single node in a large cluster. By the 2010 standard, the largest shared-memory SMP node was limited to a few hundred processors. The scalability of an SMP system is limited primarily by packaging as a shared-memory system.

Nonuniform memory access (NUMA) machines are often made out of SMP nodes with distributed shared memories. A NUMA machine appears often as a multicomputer distributed system that runs with multiple operating systems. It can scale to a few thousand processors communicating with a *message passing interface* (MPI) library. For example, an NUMA machine may have 2,048 processors running by 32 SMP operating systems. Thus, there are 32 OS images in such a 2,048-processor NUMA system. The cluster nodes can be

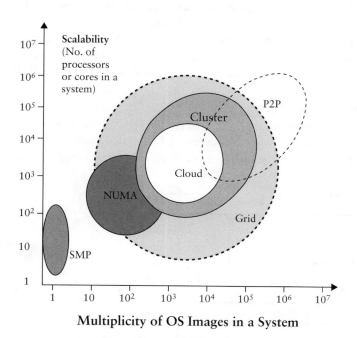

Figure 1.14
System scalability versus multiplicity of OS images based on 2010 technology.

either SMP servers or high-end servers that are loosely coupled together. Therefore, computing clusters have much higher scalability than NUMA machines. The number of OS images in a cluster is counted by the cluster nodes concurrently in use. By the end of 2016, the largest cloud will have installed millions of virtual cores or VMs.

Reviewing the fact that many cluster nodes are SMP (multiprocessor) or multicore servers, the total number of processors or cores in a cluster system is one or two orders of magnitude greater than the number of OS images running in the cluster. The grid node could be a server cluster, or a mainframe, or a supercomputer, or a MPP. Therefore, OS image count in a large grid structure could be hundreds or thousands of times smaller than the total number of processors in the grid. A P2P network can easily scale to millions of independent peer nodes, essentially desktop machines. The P2P performance depends on the QoS in a public network. The low-speed P2P networks, Internet clouds, and computer clusters should be evaluated at the same networking level.

1.3.3 Cloud Ecosystem and User Environments

With the emergence of various Internet clouds, an ecosystem for providers, users, and technologies has surfaced (see Figure 1.15). This ecosystem has evolved around public clouds. Strong interest is growing in open source cloud computing tools that let organizations build their own IaaS clouds using their internal infrastructures. Private and hybrid clouds are not exclusive, since public clouds are involved in both. A private/hybrid cloud allows remote access to its resources over the Internet using remote web services interfaces like that used in Amazon EC2.

An ecosystem was suggested to build private clouds with levels of ecosystem development. At the user-end level, consumers demand a flexible platform. At the cloud management level, cloud managers provide virtualized resources over an IaaS platform. At the virtual infrastructure management level, the manager allocates VMs over multiple server

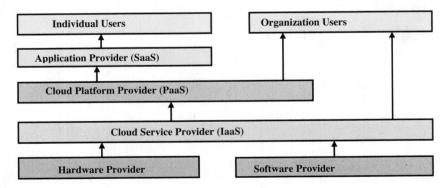

Figure 1.15
Individual versus organization users of cloud computing and their services, hardware, and software providers.

clusters. Finally, at the VM management level, the VM managers handle VMs installed on individual host machines. An ecosystem of cloud tools must cover cloud management. Integrating these two layers is complicated due to the lack of open and standard interfaces between them. An increasing number of startup companies are using cloud resources, spending very little or no capital to manage their own IT infrastructures. We require a flexible and open architecture to enable organizations to build private/hybrid clouds.

Computing and IT administrators, software vendors, and end users demand cloud services. Figure 1.15 introduces five levels of cloud players. At the top level, individual users and organizational users demand very different services. The application providers at the SaaS level primarily serve individual users. Most business organizations are serviced by IaaS and PaaS providers. The infrastructure services (IaaS) provide compute, storage, and communication resources to both applications and organizational users. The cloud environment is defined by the PaaS or platform providers. Note that the platform providers support both infrastructure services and organization users directly.

Mashup of Cloud Services
Presently, public clouds are in use by a growing number of users. Due to the concern over the leaking of sensitive data in the business world, more and more enterprises, organizations, and communities are developing private clouds that demand deeper customization. An enterprise cloud is used by multiple users within the organization. Each user may build some strategic applications on the cloud. The user demands customized partition of the data, logic, and database in the metadata representation.

Table 1.4 shows cloud users', providers', and vendors' perspectives. Popular APIs include Google Maps, Twitter, YouTube, Amazon eCommerce, and Salesforce. Various cloud players have different perspectives toward using cloud platforms. The providers are primarily concerned with the compliance of the SLAs. Software developers (vendors) prefer the least effort in SaaS mode. End users prefer to develop or test web software, while business users prefer to use business software provided by SaaS vendors.

Using Clouds for Utility Computing
The cloud industry leverages the growing demand by many enterprises and business users to outsource their computing and storage jobs to clouds. The provider service charges are

Table 1.4
Cloud perspectives from providers, vendors, and users.

Cloud Players	IaaS	PaaS	SaaS
IT Administrators/ Cloud Providers	Monitor SLAs	Monitor SLAs and enable service platforms	Monitor SLAs and deploy software
Software Developers (Vendors)	Deploy and store data	Enable platforms via configurator and APIs	Develop and deploy software

often much less than it would cost the user to replace obsolete servers. Based on a 2010 Google search survey, cloud mashup resulted from the need to use multiple clouds simultaneously or in a sequence. For example, an industrial supply chain may involve the use of different cloud resources or services at different stages of the chain. Another example is the ProgrammableWeb, which provides a public repository of thousands of service APIs and mashups for web commerce services.

In Table 1.5, we enlist a number of cloud service examples. These services differ from conventional web services, P2P, and grid computing tasks in many ways. Web 2.0 uses a network as its platform across many computing facilities and a cloud is indeed based on a centralized data center platform, however clouds and Web 2.0 are not mutually exclusive. In fact, they can be mashed up together to provide composite services. A cloud can behave in different ways: (1) it could be user-centric even it has a high degree of resource sharing; (2) it could be mission-centric using predefined services; (3) it is scalable from small to very large in capacity; (4) it is easy to access with low cost based on the pay-as-you-go model; and (5) it is programmable and automated in many ways.

Both HPC and HTC systems desire transparency in many aspects of application. For example, data access, resource allocation, process location, concurrency in execution, job replication, and failure recovery should be made transparent to both users and system management. In Table 1.5, we identify a few key applications that have driven the development of parallel and distributed systems over the years. These applications spread across many important domains in science, engineering, business, education, healthcare, traffic control, Internet and web services, military, and government applications.

Table 1.5
Cloud application trends beyond web services and Internet computing.

Categories	Some Cloud Service Examples
Document and Databases	Collaborative word processing using docs.google.com, joint co-authorship using Dropbox for synchronization
Community/ Communications	Group exchanges, community services, security watch, social welfare, alert, and alarming systems
Storage and Data Sharing	Backup storage on Dropbox, records on iCloud, photo sharing on Facebook, and professional profiling and job hunting on LinkedIn
Activity/Event Management	Calendar, contacts, event planning, family budgeting, school events, exercise team, and scheduling
Project/Mission Management	Joint design, collaborative project, virtual organizations, mission coordination, strategic defense, battlefield management, crisis handling, etc.
e-Commerce and Business Analytics	Online shopping on Amazon, Taobao, Jingdong, eBay, Salesforce CRM, and sales clouds
Healthcare and Environment	Big data for healthcare through hospitals and public clinics, pollution control, environmental protection, emotion control, caring for the elderly
Social Media and Entertainment	Centralized e-mail services like the Outlook Web App (OWA) through MS Office 365, Facebook, Twitter, Gmail, QQ, LinkedIn, cloud gaming, etc.

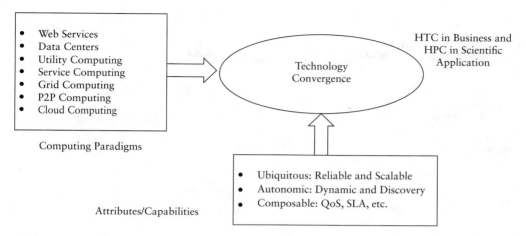

Figure 1.16
The vision of using clouds for HPC in science and HTC in business applications by merging various distributed computing paradigms.

In Figure 1.16, major computing paradigms are identified to facilitate the study of distributed systems and their applications. These paradigms are attributed to some common characteristics. First, they all ubiquitously appear in our daily lives. Reliability and scalability are two major design objectives in these computing models. Second, they are aimed at autonomic operations that can be self-organized to support dynamic discovery. Finally, these paradigms are composable with *quality of service* (QoS), *service level agreement* (SLA), etc.

All grid/cloud platforms are regarded as utility service providers. However, cloud computing offers a broader concept than utility computing. Distributed cloud applications run on any available server in some edge networks. Major technological challenges include all aspects of computer science and engineering. For example, users demand new network-efficient processors, scalable memory and storage schemes, distributed OS, middleware for machine virtualization, new programming models, effective resource management, and application program development. These hardware and software supports are necessary to build distributed systems that explore massive parallelism at all processing levels.

1.3.4 Gartner Hype Cycle for Cloud Computing

Gartner's Hype Cycles are released annually by Gartner Research for all emerging new technologies. They vary from year to year depending on the growth rate and degree of maturity. Gartner also assesses progress of new technologies in specific areas. Figure 1.17 shows the Hype Cycle for cloud computing in 2015. The cycle shows the growth of technology in

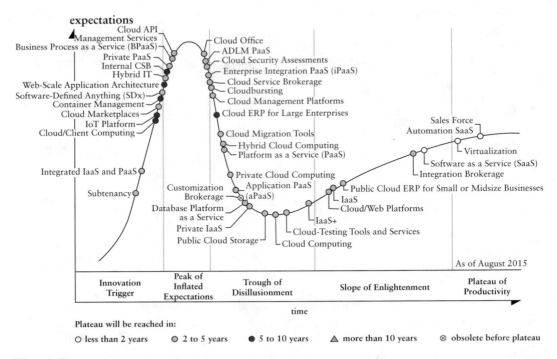

Figure 1.17
Gartner's Hype Cycle for cloud computing in August 2015. Reprinted with permission from Gartner Research, Inc.

five stages as it rises sharply from the trigger stage to a peak of inflated expectations. Through disillusionment, the cycle drops sharply to a valley and then increases steadily along a slope of enlightenment, before reaching the plateau of industrial productivity. This Hype Cycle assesses more than 2,000 technologies on their market excellence, maturity, benefit, etc. The number of years for an emerging technology to become mature and reach the plateau of productivity can be anywhere from two to ten years.

The entries on the Hype Cycle change yearly. It is interesting to compare the Hype Cycles of the past three years to reveal the trendy development of new technologies. Clouds were first introduced in 2008 and reached the peak of their development by 2014. Therefore, by 2015, most cloud technologies were relatively more mature than in previous years. Many of the cloud technologies that may reach productivity in two to five years include integrated IaaS, PaaS, and SaaS service brokerage, cloud migration tools, private cloud computing, private clouds, and public cloud storage cloud/web platforms.

Only three cloud technologies were shown to be mature enough to reach the industrial plateau of productivity in less than two years (hollow circles): SaaS, virtualization, and Salesforce automation SaaS. Some clouds, such as IoT platform, cloud/client computing, internal CSB, web-scale application architecture, and cloud ERP for large enterprises, may

Table 1.6
Top 10 strategic technology trends for cloud computing in 2015.

Merging the Real World and the Virtual World	1	Computing everywhere
	2	The Internet of things
	3	3D printing
Intelligence Everywhere	4	Advanced, pervasive, and invisible analytics
	5	Context-rich systems
	6	Smart machines
The New IT Reality Emerges	7	Cloud/client computing
	8	Software-defined application and infrastructure
	9	Web-scale IT
	10	Risk-based security and self-protection

take a longer time (five to ten years) to become mature, as represented by dark circles in Figure 1.17. By 2015, the hottest cloud computing technologies appeared near the peak of expectation hills. They were cloud API, *business process as a service* (PaaS), cloud office, ADLM cloud, cloud security assessment, private clouds, etc. There is only one technology, customization brokerage, identified as having become obsolete before the plateau. See Table 1.6 for the top ten strategic technology trends in cloud computing for 2015.

In a 2005 Hype Cycle report, hot technologies were identified as 3D printing, smart robots, IoT, biochips, machine learning, software-defined networks, etc. However, quite a few technologies are on the trailing slope of disillusionment. Hot technologies such as wearable computers, social networks, crypto-occurrences, consumer 3D printing, nature-language question answering, social networks, *near-field communication* (NFC), 3D scanners, consumer telematics, and speech recognition now are becoming much more mature or heavy in industrial production. They therefore will not appear in Hype Cycles released in the future.

The top three technologies (computing everywhere, IoT, 3D printing) attempt to merge the real world with the virtual world. The analytics, context-rich systems, and smart machines are designed to establish machine intelligence everywhere. New IT realities are emerging in cloud/client computing, software—defined apps and infrastructure, web-scale IT and risk-based security, and self-protection. Interested readers may want to follow up with those future development trends. In Chapter 2 (Figure 2.2), we show another Hype Cycle that covers all technologies in all IT fields and Figure 7.1 in Chapter 7 shows a third Hype Cycle for smart machines.

1.3.5 Interaction among SMACT Technologies

Almost all applications demand computing economics, web-scale data collection, system reliability, and scalable performance. For example, distributed transaction processing is often practiced in the banking and finance industry. Transactions represent 90% of the existing market for reliable banking systems. Users must deal with multiple database servers in distributed transactions. How to maintain the consistency of replicated transaction records

Table 1.7
SMACT technologies characterized by basic theories, typical hardware, software tooling, networking, and service providers needed.

SMACT Technology	Theoretical Foundations	Hardware Advances	Software Tools and Libraries	Networking Enablers	Representative Service Providers
Mobile Systems	Telecommunication, radio access theory, mobile computing	Smart devices, wireless, mobility infrastructures	Android, iOS, Uber, WeChat, NFC, iCloud, Google Play	4G LTE, WiFi, Bluetooth, radio access networks	AT&T Wireless, T-Mobile, Verizon, Apple, Samsung
Social Networks	Social science, graph theory, statistics, social computing	Data centers, search engines, and www. infrastructure	Browsers, APIs, Web 2.0, YouTube, WhatsApp, WeChat	Broadband Internet, sofware-defined networks	Facebook, Twitter, QQ, LinkedIn, Baidu, Amazon, Taobao
Big Data Analytics	Data mining, machine learning, artificial intelligence	Data centers, clouds, search engines, big data lakes, data storage	Spark, Hama, BitTorrent, MLlib, Impala, GraphX, KFS, Hive, HBase	Co-location clouds, mashups, P2P networks, etc.	AMPLab, Apache, Cloudera, FICO, Databricks, eBay, Oracle
Cloud Computing	Virtualization, parallel/distributed computing	Server clusters, clouds, VMs, interconnection networks	OpenStack, GFS, HDFS, MapReduce, Hadoop, Spark, Storm, Cassandra	Virtual networks, OpenFlow networks, software-defined networks	AWS, GAE, IBM, Salesforce, GoGrid Apache, Azure, Rackspace, DropBox
Internet of Things (IoT)	Sensing theory, cyber physics, pervasive computing	Sensors, RFID, GPS, robotics, satellites, ZigBee, gyroscope	TyneOS, WAP, WTCP,IPv6, Mobile IP, Android, iOS, WPKI, UPnP, JVM	Wireless LAN, PAN, MANET, WMN Mesh, VANET, Bluetooth	IoT Council, IBM, social media, Smart Earth, Google, Samsung

is crucial in real-time banking services. Other complications include short of software support, network saturation, and security threats in these applications. In recent years, five cutting-edge information technologies, namely Social, Mobile, Analytics, Cloud, and IoT (known as SMACT technologies) have become very hot and demanding. Table 1.7 summarizes the underlying theories, hardware, software and networking advances, and representative service providers.

Interactions among Technologies

Large amounts of sensor data or digital signals are generated by mobile systems, social networks, and various IoT domains. Sensing of RFID, sensor network, and GPS-generated data is needed to capture the data in a timely manner and selectively, as unstructured data can be disrupted by noises or air loss. Sensing demands high-quality data so filtering is often used to enhance the data quality. Figure 1.18 shows the interactions among SMACT technologies. Three observations are given below to show the close relationship between big data and other supportive information technologies.

1. Data mining involves the discovery, collection, aggregation, transformation, matching, and processing of large data sets. Data mining is a fundamental operation incurred with big data information systems. The ultimate purpose is knowledge discovery from data.

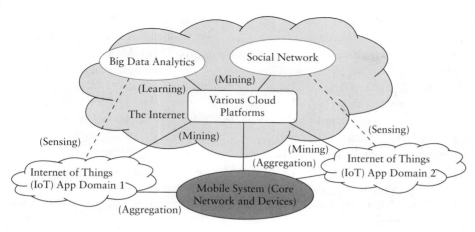

Figure 1.18
Interactions among social networks, mobile systems, big data analytics, and cloud platforms over various Internet of things (IoT) domains.

Numerical, textual, object pattern, image, and video data can be mined. Chapter 2 will cover the essence of big data mining in particular.

2. Data aggregation and integration refers to data preprocessing to improve data quality. Important operations include data cleaning, removing redundancy, checking relevance, data reduction, transformation, discretization, etc.

3. Machine learning and big data analytics is the foundation for using a cloud's computing power to analyze large data sets scientifically or statistically. Special computer programs are written to automatically learn to recognize complex patterns and make intelligent decisions based on data. Chapters 5–10 cover machine learning, big data analytics, and their programming applications.

Technology Fusion to Meet the Future Demand

The IoT extends the Internet of computers to any object. The joint use of clouds, IoT, mobile devices, and social networks is crucial for capturing big data taken from all sources. This integrated system is envisioned by IBM researchers as a "smart earth" which enables fast, efficient, and intelligent interactions among humans, machines, and any objects surrounding us. A smart earth must have intelligent cities, clean waters, efficient powers, convenient transportation, safe food supplies, responsible banks, fast telecommunications, green IT, better schools, healthcare, and abundant resources to share. This sounds like a dream, but it will gradually become a reality in the years to come.

In general, mature technology is supposed to be adopted quickly. The combined use of two or more technologies may demand additional effort to integrate them for the common purpose. Thus, integration may demand some transformational changes. In order to enable innovative new applications, core technology transformation posts a challenge. Disruptive technology is even more difficult to integrate due to higher risk as it may demand more research and experimentation or prototyping efforts. This leads us to consider technology fusion by blending different technologies together to complement one another.

All five SMACT technologies are deployed within the mobile Internet (otherwise known as wireless Internet). The IoT networks may appear in many different forms at different application domains. For example, we may build in IoT domains for national defense, healthcare, green energy, social media, smart cities, etc. Social networks and big data analysis subsystems are built in the Internet with fast database search and mobile access facilities. Large storage and processing power are provided by domain-specific cloud services on dedicated platforms. In spite of all these advances, we still have a long way to go before we see widespread use of domain-specific cloud platforms for big data or IoT applications in the mobile Internet environment.

1.4   Availability, Mobility, and Cluster Optimization

Cloud hardware is essentially built around a large cluster of servers. Clusters are inherently highly available due to redundancy brought by independent servers used in the cluster. In case of a single server failure, the jobs running on VMs hosted in the failing server can be migrated to surviving server hosts under software control. In this section, we first study the availability of server clusters on clouds. Then we study mobile clouds and their access methods. Fault tolerance in virtual clusters is also studied, and, finally, we present life migration techniques on VMs.

1.4.1   Availability Analysis of Cloud Server Clusters

High availability (HA) is desired in all server clusters. Since a cloud system is essentially built on server clusters, HA also becomes a crucial requirement in cloud systems. A cluster system is highly available if it has long MTTF and short MTTR. The MTTF is the average system uptime between two adjacent failures. The MTTR accounts the average downtime after a failure or maintenance shutdown. The cluster availability is formally defined as follows:

$$Cluster\ Availability = MTTF\ /\ (MTTF + MTTR). \tag{1.5}$$

The larger the MTTF, the higher the availability. On the other hand, the lower the MTTR, the higher the availability. The values of these two parameters are attributed to many factors. All hardware, software, and network components may fail. Any failure that will pull down the operation of the entire system is called a *single point of failure*. The rule of thumb is to design a HA cluster system with no single point of failure. Adding hardware redundancy,

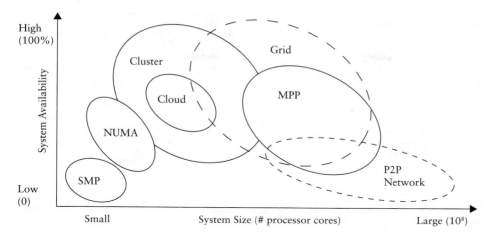

Figure 1.19
Estimated system availability by system size of common configurations.

increasing component reliability, and allowing VM migration all help enhance the cluster availability. In Figure 1.19, the effects on system availability are estimated by scaling the system size in terms of the number of processor cores in a system.

In general, as a distributed system increases in size, the availability decreases due to a higher chance of failure and difficulty to isolate the failure. Both SMP and MPP are very vulnerable with centralized resources under one OS. The NUMA machine has improved in availability due to use of multiple OSs. Most clusters are designed to have HA with failover capability. Private clouds are created out of virtualized data centers. Hence, a cloud has an estimated availability similar to that of the hosting cluster. A grid is visualized as a hierarchical cluster of clusters. They have higher availability due to the isolation of faults. Therefore, clusters, clouds, and grids have a decreasing availability as the system gets larger. A P2P file-sharing network has the highest aggregation of client machines. However, because they operate independently with low availability even many peer nodes depart or fail simultaneously.

Example 1.3 High Availability of a Dual-Server Cluster System

Consider the following two server-client cluster configurations in Figure 1.20. Part (a) is built with a single server and a single disk, which may become a single point of failure pulling the entire cluster down when either the server or the disk fails. Part (b) adds an extra server and another disk. The purpose is to use double redundancy to eliminate all possible single points of failure. Here we assume that all client hosts, Ethernet, and small computer system interface (SCSI) bus are fail-free. The two servers share the disks via

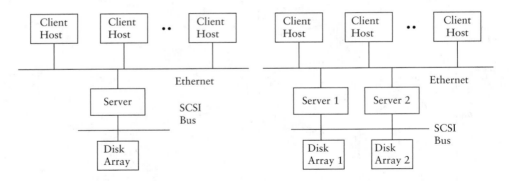

Figure 1.20
A high-availability cluster of two servers sharing two disks to eliminate all single points of failure. The availability in part (b) is 99.31% improved from 96.2% in part (a).

a SCSI bus. When a server fails, its workload is switched to the surviving server in a negligible time. Similarly, the two disks are images of one another to provide the double-redundancy protection.

Assume that each server has a MTTF of 200 days and a MTTR of 5 days. The shared disk has a MTTF every 800 days and a MTTR every 10 days. In part (a), the cluster is considered down if the server fails, or the disk fails, or both fail at the same time. Note that the server and the disk may fail independently. The MTTR may be attributed to either natural failure or scheduled maintenance. We simple lump the two times together in a statistical sense. The availability of each server is $200/(200+5)=97.5\%$. The availability of the disk is $800/(800+10)=98.7\%$. The availability of the system is when both server and disk are up and thus calculated by the joint events $97.5\% \times 98.7\% = 96.2\%$.

Now consider the availability of the double-redundancy cluster in part (b). This cluster is down when both servers are down, when both disks are down, or when all four components are down. The failure rate of both servers is $(1-97.5\%)^2=0.625\%$. The failure rate of both disks is $(1-98.7\%)^2=0.169\%$. The failure rate of the four components at the same time is $(0.625\%) \times (0.169\%) = 0.105\%$. Thus, the total cluster availability in part (b) becomes $1-[0.625\%+0.169\%-0.105\%]=1-(0.689\%)=99.31\%$. This availability is improved from the case of part (a). If one considers the downtime per year (365 days), part (a) cluster is down 13.87 days per year, while part (b) cluster is only down 2.52 days per year. ∎

Consider the use of a cluster of n homogeneous servers in a cloud system. Let p be the *availability* of a single server in the cluster. Therefore, $1-p$ is the *failure rate* of a single server. The cluster system is considered *available* or *acceptable* in normal operation if at least k out of n servers are operating normally without failure. Formally, we define the *system availability* of the cluster by the following probabilistic expression:

(1.6)

$$A = \sum_{i=k}^{n} \binom{n}{i} p^i (1-p)^{n-i}$$

$$= \binom{n}{k} p^k (1-p)^{n-k} + \binom{n}{k+1} p^{k+1} (1-p)^{n-k-1}$$

$$+ \cdots + \binom{n}{n-1} p^{n-1} (1-p)^1 + \binom{n}{n} p^n (1-p)^0,$$

where $1 \le k \le n$ and the $n - (k-1) = n - k + 1$ terms correspond to the probabilities of having $k, k+1, \ldots, n-1$ and n servers working properly in the cluster. For example, given that $n = 8$, $p = 0.99$, and $k = 7$, we obtain the system availability $A = 51.36\%$ by substituting the parameter values in Equation 1.6. It is observed that A is monotonic, increasing the function of k. It approaches 100% system availability, when k approaches n.

1.4.2   Fault Tolerance in Virtual Cluster Operations

Fault tolerance refers to the fact that program execution on a server cluster will not be interrupted or suspended with server failure in the cluster. This can be achieved through two redundancy approaches. The first method is to use redundant servers that can be hot switched to replace the failing servers. In general, double redundancy can tolerate a single failure by failing from one server to another, while triple redundancy can enable double error detection and single error correction. The second method is to use a software approach in a virtual cluster. Figure 1.21 shows the reconfiguration overhead experienced with physical cluster and virtual clusters.

VM technology requires advanced disaster recovery schemes. One scheme is to recover a PM by another PM. The second scheme is to recover a VM by another VM. As shown in the top timeline of Figure 1.21, the traditional disaster recovery from PM to PM is rather slow, complex, and expensive. The total recovery time is attributed to the hardware

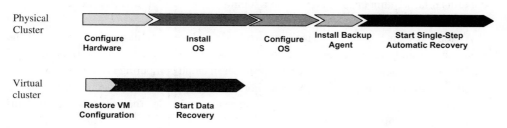

Figure 1.21
Recovery overhead on a physical cluster compared with that of a virtual cluster.

configuration, installing and configuring the OS, installing the backup agents, and the long time it takes to restart the PM. To recover a VM platform, the installing and configuration times for OS and backup agents are eliminated. Therefore, we end up with a much shorter disaster recovery time, about 40% of that to recover from failing PMs. VMs and virtual clusters will be studied in Chapter 3.

1.4.3   Queuing Model of Multiserver Clusters in Clouds

In the last decade, cloud computing has become a mature technology and cost-effective way to consolidate computing resources with massive user services. By centralized management of resources and services, cloud computing delivers hosted services over the Internet, such that access to shared hardware, software, databases, information, and all resources are provided to consumers on demand. Cloud computing is able to provide a cost-effective and energy-efficient way of computing resources management. Cloud computing has proven that it has really become an information appliance or utility commodity using the pay-as-you-go pricing model.

Today's Cloud Computing Paradigm

Cloud computing can be cost-effective, but it will never be free. Understanding the economics of cloud computing is critically important. One attractive cloud computing environment is a three-tier structure, which consists of infrastructure vendors, service providers, and consumers. An infrastructure vendor maintains basic hardware and software facilities. A service provider rents resources from the infrastructure vendors, builds appropriate multiserver systems, and provides various services to users. Such a paradigm is known as *multitenant technology* to globally face the general public.

A consumer or simply a cloud user submits a service request to a service provider, receives the desired result from the service provider subject to certain SLA, and pays for the service based on the amount of the service and the QoS. A service provider can build different multiserver systems for different application domains, such that service requests of different natures are sent to different multiserver systems. Each cloud cluster system contains a large number of servers. The system can be devoted to serve various types of service requests and applications.

A cloud system S is characterized by two basic features: the number of servers in the cloud cluster and the execution speed (or throughput) of the servers, collectively. Like all businesses, the pricing model of a service provider in cloud computing is based on two components, namely the income and the cost. For a service provider, the income or revenue is the service charge to users, and the cost is the renting cost plus the utility cost paid to infrastructure vendors.

Queuing Modeling of Cloud Services

The cloud service time is a random variable, which is determined by the task waiting time once a cloud system is established. There are many different service performance metrics in a SLA such as the task response time (or turnaround time), which includes task waiting time and task execution time. The SLA is the promised time to complete a service, which is a constant times the expected length of a service. If the actual length of a service is (or, a service request is completed) within the SLA, the service will be fully charged. However, if the actual length of a service exceeds the SLA, the service charge will be reduced. In other words, there is penalty for a service provider to break a SLA.

The approach is to treat a multiserver cloud system as an M/M/m queuing model, such that the optimization problem can be formulated and solved analytically. In queuing theory, the M/M/c queue is a multiserver queuing model. This is a system where arrivals form a single queue and are governed by a Poisson process, in which c servers and job service times are exponentially distributed. The model can be described as a continuous time Markov chain as illustrated in Figure 1.22, where λ is the requested arrive rate and μ is the service rate. There are an infinite number of states $\{0, 1, 2, 3, \ldots\}$ in this transition diagram, corresponding to the number of service requests in the queuing system.

One can apply two different server speed and power consumption models, namely, the idle-speed model and the constant-speed model. We must derive the *probability density function* (PDF) of the waiting time of a newly arrived service request. Then we calculate the expected service charge to a service request. Based on these results, we get the expected net business gain per unit of time, and obtain the optimal server size and the optimal server speed, accordingly.

Understanding the economics of cloud computing becomes important not only to cloud providers but also to cloud users. To maximize the profit, a service provider should understand both service charges and business costs. They need to determine the optimal configuration of a multiserver system to satisfy the demand from a large number of users concurrently. In what follows, we briefly present the main results from solving the M/M/m queuing model. We outline the ideas of cloud cluster optimization, based on the work of Cao et al. [9].

Consider a multiserver cloud system S has m identical servers. The cloud cluster is treated as an M/M/m queuing system specified as follows. There is a Poisson stream of service requests with *arrival rate* λ, i.e., the interarrival times are random variables with mean $1/\lambda$. The system maintains a queue with infinite capacity for waiting tasks when all m servers are busy.

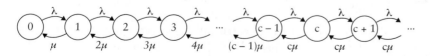

Figure 1.22
Markov chain model of an M/M/c queue for c servers.

The *first-come-first-serve* (FCFS) queuing discipline is adopted. The task execution requirements are random variables r. The m servers have identical execution speed s. Hence, the task execution times on the servers of S are random variables $x = r/s$ with mean $\bar{x} = \bar{r}/s$.

Let $\mu = 1/\bar{x} = s/\bar{r}$ be the average service rate, or the average number of service requests that can be done per unit time by m servers in the cluster S. The *server utilization* is the average percentage of time that system S is busy, which is computed by $\rho = \lambda/m\mu = \lambda\bar{x}/m = \lambda/m \cdot \bar{r}/s$. Let p_k be the probability that there are k service requests in the M/M/m queuing system for S. Then, we have:

$$p_k = \begin{cases} p_0 \dfrac{(m\rho)^k}{k!}, & k \le m; \\ p_0 \dfrac{m^m \rho^k}{m!}, & k \ge m, \end{cases} \quad \text{and} \quad p_0 = \left(\sum_{k=0}^{m-1} \frac{(m\rho)^k}{k!} + \frac{(m\rho)^m}{m!} \cdot \frac{1}{1-\rho} \right)^{-1}. \tag{1.7}$$

We calculate below the wait probability of a newly submitted service request that must wait in the queue, because all servers are busy.

$$P_q = \sum_{k=m}^{\infty} p_k = \frac{p_m}{1-\rho} = p_0 \frac{(m\rho)^m}{m!} \cdot \frac{1}{1-\rho}. \tag{1.8}$$

The average number of service requests in waiting or under execution in S is thus computed by:

$$\bar{N} = \sum_{k=0}^{\infty} k p_k = m\rho + \frac{\rho}{1-\rho} P_q. \tag{1.9}$$

Applying Little's Law, we get the average task response time as follows:

$$\bar{T} = \frac{\bar{N}}{\lambda} = \bar{x} \left(1 + \frac{P_q}{m(1-\rho)} \right) = \bar{x} \left(1 + \frac{P_m}{m(1-\rho)^2} \right). \tag{1.10}$$

The average waiting time of a service request is thus computed by:

$$\bar{W} = \bar{T} - \bar{x} = \frac{P_m}{m(1-\rho)^2} \bar{x}. \tag{1.11}$$

1.4.4 Multiserver Cluster Optimization for Cloud Computing

The waiting time is the source of customer dissatisfaction. A service provider should keep the waiting time to a minimum by providing enough servers and/or increasing server speed, and be willing to compensate a customer in case the waiting time exceeds a certain limit. In what follows, we seek an optimal solution to this queuing problem in normal cloud service operations. The goal is to achieve optimization of cloud services to have a win-win situation for both cloud users and cloud providers

Factors or Policies Affecting Cloud Pricing of Services

The pricing model used by a cloud provider includes many considerations, such as the amount of a service, the workload of an application environment, the system configuration (the size and the speed), the SLA between users and provider, the satisfaction of a consumer, the QoS guaranteed such as task waiting time and response time, the penalty of a low-quality service, the cost of renting, the cost of energy consumption, and a service provider's margin and profit. The profit or the net business gain is the income minus the cost. To maximize the profit, a service provider should consider both service charges and business costs, and in particular, how they are determined by the characteristics of the applications and the configuration of a multiserver system.

The service charge to a service request is determined by two factors: the expected length of the service and the actual length of the service. The expected length of a service is the execution time of an application on a standard server with a baseline or reference speed. Once the baseline speed is set, the expected length of a service is determined by a service request itself, i.e., the service requirement measured by the number of instructions to be executed. The longer the expected length of a service is, the greater the service charge. The actual length of a service depends on the size of a multiserver system, the speed of the servers, and the workload of the system.

The cost of a service provider includes two components, i.e., the renting cost and the utility cost. The renting cost is proportional to the number of servers used in the system. The utility cost is essentially the cost of energy consumption and is determined by both the size and the speed of a multiserver system. The faster the speed, the greater the utility cost. To calculate the cost of energy consumption, we need to establish certain server speed and power consumption models. To increase the revenue of business, a service provider can construct and configure a multiserver system with many high-speed servers.

Since the actual service time contains task waiting time and task execution time, more servers reduce the waiting time and faster servers reduce both the waiting time and execution time. Hence, a powerful system reduces the penalty of breaking a SLA and increases the revenue. However, more servers increase the cost of facility renting from the infrastructure vendors and the cost of base power consumption. Furthermore, faster servers increase the cost of energy consumption. Such increased cost may counterweight the gain from penalty reduction. Therefore, for an application environment with a specific workload, which includes the task arrival rate and the average task execution requirement, a service provider needs to decide on the optimal size and speed of a multiserver system such that the expected profit is maximized.

Optimization on Waiting Time and Service Charge

A utility function measures the value and importance of tasks as well as the user's tolerance to delay and sensitivity to QoS. We need to support market-based bidding, negotiation, and admission control. By taking an economic approach to providing service-oriented utility computing, a service provider allocates resources and schedules tasks in such a way that the total profit earned is maximized. In a system-centric performance, one needs to minimize the average task response time. On the other hand, we need to achieve computational economy with a user-centric optimization. The approach is to maximize the total utility delivered to users. In what follows, we present the waiting time distribution and cloud service charges.

Let W be the waiting time of a new service request that arrives to a multiserver system. We find the pdf of $f_W(t)$ of W. To this end, we consider W in different situations, depending on the number of tasks in the queuing system when a new service request arrives. Let W_k be the waiting time of a new task that arrives to an M/M/m queuing system under the state of having k tasks in the system. The pdf of the waiting time W of a newly arrived service request is computed by:

$$f_W(t) = (1 - P_q)u(t) + m\mu p_m e^{-(1-\rho)m\mu t}, \tag{1.12}$$

where $P_q = p_m / (1-\rho)$ and $p_m = p_0 (m\rho)^m / m!$. The proof is explained in the work of Cao et al. [9].

If all the servers have a fixed speed s, the execution time of a service request with execution requirement r is known as $x = r/s$. The response time to the service request is $T = W + x = W + r/s$. The response time T is related to the service charge to a customer of a service provider in cloud computing. To study the expected service charge to a customer, we need a complete specification of a service charge based on the amount of a service, the SLA, the satisfaction of a consumer, the QoS, the penalty of a low-quality service, and a service provider's margin and profit. Let s_0 be the baseline speed of a server. We define the service charge function for a service request with execution requirement r and response time T to be as follows:

$$C(r,T) = \begin{cases} ar, & \text{if } 0 \le T \le \dfrac{c}{s_0} r; \\[2ex] ar - d\left(T - \dfrac{c}{s_0} r\right), & \\[1ex] & \text{if } \dfrac{c}{s_0} r < T \le \left(\dfrac{a}{d} + \dfrac{c}{s_0}\right) r; \\[2ex] 0, & \text{if } T > \left(\dfrac{a}{d} + \dfrac{c}{s_0}\right) r. \end{cases} \tag{1.13}$$

Now, we are ready to compute the expected charge to a service request as follows:

$$C = a\bar{r}\left(1 - \frac{P_q}{((ms - \lambda\bar{r})(c/s_0 - 1/s) + 1)} \frac{1}{((ms - \lambda\bar{r})(a/d + c/s_0 - 1/s) + 1)}\right), \quad (1.14)$$

where $P_q = p_m/(1-\rho)$ and $p_m = p_0(m\rho)^m/m!$

Optimal Cluster Size and Speed to Satisfy Business Demand

Net business gains and profit maximization are addressed in this section. We choose the optimal cluster size and multiserver speed to achieve the goal. The theoretical findings from the queuing model offer the solutions nicely. Since the number of service requests processed per unit time is in a stable M/M/m queuing system, the expected service charge per unit time is λC, which is actually the expected revenue of a service provider. Let β be the rental cost of one server per unit time. Also, assume that the cost of energy is γ per Watt. The cost of a service provider is the sum of the cost of infrastructure renting and the cost of energy consumption, i.e., $\beta m + \gamma P^*$ .. _Then, the expected net business gain (i.e., the net profit) of a service provider in one unit of time is $G = \lambda C - (\beta m + \gamma(\lambda\bar{r}\xi s^{\alpha-1} + mP))$ for the idle-speed model and $G = \lambda C - (\beta m + \gamma m(\xi s^\alpha + P^*))$ for the constant-speed model. Now, we are ready to estimate the expected to a service request as follows:

$$C \approx a\bar{r}\left(1 - \frac{1}{\left(\sqrt{2\pi m}(1-\rho)(e^\rho/e\rho)^m + 1\right)\left((ms - \lambda\bar{r})(c/s_0 - 1/s) + 1\right)}\right.$$
$$\left. \times \frac{1}{\left((ms - \lambda\bar{r})(a/d + c/s_0 - 1/s) + 1\right)}\right). \quad (1.15)$$

Our ultimate goal is to determine the optimal size m of the server cluster to be used. We optimize the cluster size m by making the derivative of the business gain G zero.

$$\frac{\partial G}{\partial m} = \lambda\frac{\partial C}{\partial m} - (\beta + \lambda P^*) = 0. \quad (1.16)$$

Furthermore, we need to find the *optimal server* speed that can maximize the business gain.

$$\frac{\partial G}{\partial s} = \lambda\frac{\partial C}{\partial s} - \gamma\lambda\bar{r}\xi(\alpha-1)s^{\alpha-2} = 0. \quad (1.17)$$

We have presented a pricing model for cloud computing which takes many factors into consideration, such as the requirement r of a service, the workload λ of an application environment, the configuration (m and s) of a multiserver system, the SLA c, the satisfaction (r and s_0) of a consumer, the quality (W and T) of a service, the penalty d of a low-quality service, the cost (β and m) of renting, the cost (α, γ, P^*, and P) of energy consumption, and a service provider's margin and profit a. By using an M/M/m queuing model, we formulated and solved the problem of optimal multiserver configuration for profit maximization in a cloud computing environment. This queuing model is very useful as it could allow providers to make critical platform design decisions that would make the cloud service successful and profitable.

1.5   Conclusions

Cloud platforms and service principles were covered in this introductory Chapter. The best way to master cloud computing is to use the clouds. You can use cloud services provided by public clouds such as Amazon AWS, Apple's iCloud, Google App Engine, Salesforce, Microsoft Azure, IBM SmartCloud, etc. You can gain concrete hands-on experience by practice. Machine virtualization techniques will be introduced with hypervisors and Docker containers in Chapter 3. More on cloud infrastructure design and various services applications is provided in Chapters 4 and 5. In the remaining Chapters 5 through 10, readers will learn the principles of machine learning, AI machines, cloud programming, data privacy, and security issues.

This book is significantly extended and updated from the author's earlier book *Distributed and Cloud Computing* published in 2012 [20]. This book offers more theoretical foundations, updated cloud architecture designs, Spark and TensorFlow programming, machine learning, and AI machines, which were not treated in the earlier book. Hwang and Chen have written *Big Data Analytics* (Wiley 2017) [19], which can serve as a companion book to this one. That book introduces clouds briefly, but offers a comprehensive coverage of machine and deep learning algorithms, IoT sensing, and cloud-assisted healthcare applications. These two books complement one another in learning contents and different application domains.

Homework Problems

1.1: Briefly characterize the differences in the following computing paradigms and explore computer architecture, parallel processing, distributed computing, Internet technology, and web services.

(a) PMs versus VMs

(b) public clouds versus private clouds

(c) mashups in web and cloud services

1.2: Briefly characterize the following basic terminologies, techniques, and technologies that are related to recent advances in computer architecture, parallel processing, distributed computing, and web services.

(a) high-performance computing (HPC) systems

(b) high-throughput computing (HTC) systems

(c) peer-to-peer (P2P) networks

(d) computer clusters vs. computational grids

(e) VM vs. virtual cluster

(f) public clouds vs. private clouds

1.3: Circle only one correct answer in each of the following questions.

(1) In 2010's Top 500 list of the fastest computer systems, which architecture dominates?

    a. Symmetric shared-memory multiprocessor systems

    b. Centralized massively parallel processor (MPP) systems

    c. Clusters of cooperative computers

(2) Which global network system was designed to best eliminate isolated resource islands?

    a. The Internet for computer-to-computer interaction using Telnet command

    b. The web service for page-to-page visits using http:// command

    c. The grid service using middleware to establish interactions between applications running on a federation of cooperative machines

(3) In a cloud formed by a cluster of servers, all servers must be selected as follows:

    a. All cloud machines must be built on physical servers.

    b. All cloud machines must be built with virtual servers.

    c. The cloud machines can be either physical or virtual servers.

1.4: Consider a program to multiply two large-scale $N \times N$ matrices, where N is the matrix size. The sequential multiply time on a single server is $T_1 = c\,N^3$ minutes, where c is a constant decided by the server used. A MPI-code parallel program requires $T_n = cN^3/n + dN^2/n^{0.5}$ minutes to complete execution on an n-server cluster system, where d is a constant determined by the MPI version used. You can assume the program has a zero-sequential bottleneck ($\alpha = 0$). The second term in T_n accounts for the total message passing overhead experienced by n servers.

Answer the following questions for a given cluster configuration with $n = 64$ servers and $c = 0.8$ and $d = 0.1$. Parts (a, b) have a fixed workload corresponding to the matrix size $N = 15{,}000$. Parts (c, d) have a scaled workload associated with an enlarged matrix size $N' = n^{1/3} N = 64^{1/3} \times 15{,}000 = 4 \times 15{,}000 = 60{,}000$. Assume the same cluster configuration to process both workloads. Thus, the system parameters n, c, and d stay unchanged. Running the scaled workload, the overhead also increases with the enlarged matrix size N'.

(a) Using Amdahl's Law, calculate the speedup of the n-server cluster over a single server.

(b) What is the efficiency of the cluster system used in part (a)?

(c) Calculate the speedup in executing the scaled workload for an enlarged $N' \times N'$ matrix on the same cluster configuration using Gustafson's Law.

(d) Calculate the efficiency of running the scaled workload in part (c) on the 64-processor cluster.

(e) Compare the above speedup and efficiency results and comment on their implications.

1.5: Answer the following questions on personal computing (PC) and high-performance computing (HPC).

(a) Explain why the PC and HPC were evolutionary rather revolutionary for the past 30 years.

(b) Discuss the drawbacks in disruptive changes in processor architecture. Why is memory wall a major problem in achieving scalable changes in performance?

(c) Explain why x86 processors are still dominating the PC and HPC markets.

1.6: Multicore and many-core processors have experienced widespread use in both desktop computers and HPC systems. Answer the following questions in using advanced processors, memory devices, and system interconnects.

(a) What are the differences between multicore CPU and GPU in architecture and usages?

(b) Explain why parallel programming cannot match with the progress of processor technology.

(c) Suggest ideas and defend your argument by some plausible solutions to this mismatch problem between core scaling and effective programming and use of multicores.

(d) Explain why flash memory SSD can deliver better speedups in some HPC or HTC applications.

(e) Justify the prediction that InfiniBand and Ethernet will continue to dominate the HPC market.

1.7: Discuss the major advantages and disadvantages in the following challenging areas.

(a) Why are VMs and virtual clusters suggested in cloud computing systems?

(b) What are the breakthrough areas needed to build virtualized cloud systems cost effectively?

(c) What are the impacts of cloud platforms on the future of HPC and HTC industry?

1.8: Characterize the following three cloud computing models.

(a) What is an IaaS cloud? Give one example system.

(b) What is a PaaS cloud? Give one example system.

(c) What is a SaaS cloud? Give one example system.

1.9: Consider a multicore processor with four heterogeneous cores labeled as A, B, C, and D. Assume cores A and D have the same speed. Core B runs twice faster as core A. Core C runs three times faster than core A. Assume that all four cores start the execution of the following application at the same time and no cache misses are encountered in all core operations. Suppose an application needs to compute the square of each element of an array of 256 elements. Assume 1 unit time for cores A or D to compute the square of an element. Thus, core B takes 1/2 unit time and core C takes 1/3 unit time to compute the square of an element.

(a) Compute the *total execution time* (in time units) for using the 4-core processor to compute the squares of 256 elements in parallel. The four cores have different speeds. Some faster cores finish the job and may become idle, while others are still busy computing until all squares are computed.

(b) Calculate the *processor utilization rate*, which is the amount of the total time the cores are busy (not idle) divided by the total execution time in using all cores in the processor to execute the above application.

1.10: Solve the following cluster performance problems using Amdahl's Law and Gustafson's Law, separately. Answer the questions posted.

(a) Consider a user application program with a sequential bottleneck α. Let T be the sequential execution time on a single server and $T(n, \alpha)$ be the parallel execution time on n servers. Derive an expression for the achievable speedup S based on Amdahl's Law.

(b) Determine and prove the upper bound on the above speedup S. What is the implication of this upper bound?

(c) Explain Gustafson's Law and its improvement over the Amdahl's Law. You need to derive formula here.

1.11: Compare on-premise (desktop) computing with three cloud service models. The resources and user application software are divided into five categories: network, storage, servers, VMs, and application software. Each resource category could be controlled by user, vendor, or shared between user and vendor. Draw a table to illustrate the modes of resource control responsibilities.

1.12: Consider the System Availability (A) of a server cluster in terms of three parameters: namely the mean time to failure (MTTF), the mean time to repair (MTTR), and a regular maintenance time (RMT). The MTTF reflects the average uptime between two adjacent natural failures. The MTTR is the downtime due to natural failure. The RMT refers to scheduled down time for hardware/software maintenance or updates.

(a) Given a cloud system with a demanded availability $A = 98\%$. If the MTTF is known to be two years (or $365 \times 24 \times 2 = 17{,}520$ hours) and the MTTR is known 24 hours, what is the value of RMT in hours per month that you can schedule for this cloud system?

(b) Consider a cloud cluster of three servers. The cluster is considered available (or acceptable with a satisfactory performance level), if at least k servers are operating normally where $k \leq 3$. Assume that each server has an availability rate of p (or a failure rate of $1 - p$). Derive a formula to calculate the total cluster availability A (i.e., the probability that the cluster is available satisfactorily). Note that A is a function of k and p.

(c) Given that each server has an availability $p = 0.98$, what is the largest minimum number of servers that must be available to achieve a total cluster availability A, which is higher than 96%? You have to check the effect of all possible values of k in part (b) in order to answer this question correctly.

1.13: Study the paper on cluster optimization to reduce the service waiting time and energy consumption [9]. You have learned the basic concept in Section 1.4.4. After an in-depth study, you are asked to extend the performance model to cover many other factors that affect the QoS in providing cloud services. You will find more coverage on cloud performance in Chapter 10.

References

[1] Baker, M., and R. Buyya. "Cluster Computing at a Glance." In *High-Performance Cluster Computing, Architecture and Systems*, edited by R. Buyya, vol. 1, chap. 1. Prentice-Hall, 1999.

[2] Barroso, L., and U. Holzle. "The Data Center as a Computer: An Introduction to the Design of Warehouse-Scale Machines." In *Synthesis Lectures on Computer Architecture*, edited by M. Hill. Morgan & Claypool Publishers, 2009.

[3] Bell, G., J. Gray, and A. Szalay. "Petascale Computational Systems: Balanced Cyberstructure in a Data-Centric World." *IEEE Computer Magazine*, 2006.

[4] Birman, K. *Reliable Distributed Systems: Technologies, Web Services, and Applications.* Springer Verlag, 2005.

[5] Boss, G., et al. "Cloud Computing—The BlueCloud Project." www.ibm.com/developerworks/websphere/zones /hipods/, October 2007.

[6] Buyya, R., D. Abramson, J. Giddy, and H. Stockinger. "Economic Models for Resource Management and Scheduling in Grid Computing." *Concurrency and Computation: Practice and Experience* 14 (2007): 1507–1542.

[7] Buyya, R., J. Broberg, and A. Goscinski, eds. *Cloud Computing: Principles and Paradigms.* Wiley Press, 2011.

[8] Buyya, R., C. S. Yeo, S. Venugopal, J. Broberg, and I. Brandic. "Cloud Computing and Emerging IT Platforms: Vision, Hype, and Reality for Delivering Computing as the Fifth Utility." *Future Generation Computer Systems* 25 no. 6 (2009): 599–616.

[9] Cao, J., K. Hwang, K. Li, and A. Zomaya. "Optimal Multiserver Configuration for Profit Maximization in Cloud Computing." *IEEE Transactions on Parallel and Distributed Systems* (2013).

[10] Chou, T. *Introduction to Cloud Computing: Business and Technology.* Lecture Notes at Stanford University and at Tsinghua University. Active Book Press, 2010.

[11] Clark, C., et al. "Live Migration of VMs." Proc. of Second Symposium of Networked System Design and Implementation (NSDI), 2005.

[12] Dongarra, J., et al., eds. *Source Book of Parallel Computing.* Morgan Kaufmann, 2003.

[13] Foster, I., Y. Zhao, J. Raicu, and S. Lu. "Cloud Computing and Grid Computing 360-Degree Compared." Grid Computing Environments Workshop, November 12–16, 2008.

[14] Gannon, D. "The Client+Cloud: Changing the Paradigm for Scientific Research." Keynote Address, Cloud-Com2010, Indianapolis, IN, November 2, 2010.

[15] Google, Inc. "Google and the Wisdom of Clouds." http://www.businessweek.com/magazine/content/ 0752 / b4064048925836.htm.

[16] Hey, T., S. Tansley, and K. Tolle, eds. *The Fourth Paradigm: Data-Intensive Scientific Discovery.* Microsoft Research, 2009.

[17] Hill, M. D., ed. *Synthesis Lectures on Computer Architecture.* Morgan & Claypool Publishers, 2009.

[18] Hwang, K. *Advanced Computer Architecture.* McGraw-Hill, 2010.

[19] Hwang, K., and M. Chen. *Big Data Analytics for Cloud, IoT and Cognitive Learning.* Wiley, 2017 (in press).

[20] Hwang, K., G. Fox, and J. Dongarra. *Distributed and Cloud Computing.* Morgan Kaufmann, 2012.

[21] Hwang, K., and D. Li. "Trusted Cloud Computing with Secure Resources and Data Coloring." *IEEE Internet Computing,* Special Issue on Trust and Reputation Management (September 2010): 14–22.

[22] Hwang, K., and Z. Xu. *Scalable Parallel Computing.* McGraw-Hill, 1998.

[23] Pfister, G. F. *In Search of Clusters*, 2nd ed. Prentice-Hall, 2001.

Chapter 2

Data Analytics, Internet of Things, and Cognitive Computing

2.1 Big Data Science and Application Challenges

This section introduces the basic concepts of data science, supporting technologies, and their innovative applications.

2.1.1 Data Science and Big Data Characteristics

Formally, *data science* can be defined as the process of extracting useful knowledge directly from data through data discovery and hypothesis formation and analysis. A data scientist is a practitioner with sufficient business expertise, domain knowledge, analytical skills, and programming expertise to manage the end-to-end scientific process through each stage in the big data lifecycle.

Data science requires the discovery, aggregation, matching, and sorting of huge amounts of data elements. As depicted in Figure 2.1, it is at the intersection of three interdisciplinary areas—computer programming, application domains, and statistics/data mining—and it calls on cross-disciplinary expertise in algorithm creation, analytic systems, and the research field of modeling or problem formation. Data science has a wide range of applications, for instance, in government use, military operations, business transactions, scientific discovery, environmental protection, green energy, clinical trials, biological science, agriculture, medical care, and social networks. The value chain of big data divides into four phases: data generation, data acquisition, data storage, and data analysis. Data generation and data acquisition exploit raw data in a process known as data preprocessing. Then data storage and data analysis form a production process to extract or add value to the raw data.

Cloud architecture, algorithms, and programming systems are studied throughout the book. Major big data application domains are identified in the discussion on machine learning methods in Part III. Big data problem modeling must be worked out jointly between data scientists and domain experts. Because so many cross-disciplinary skills are needed, cloud programmers, data scientists, analytics experts, and *artificial intelligence* (AI) professionals are very much in demand today.

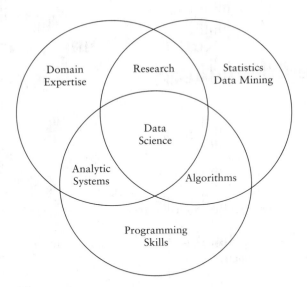

Figure 2.1
Data science encompasses three interdisciplinary areas: computer programming, application domains, and statistics/data mining, with cross-disciplinary skills in algorithm creation, analytic systems, and the research field of modeling or problem formation.

The concept of data science has a long history but only recently has attracted widespread interest with the increasing use of clouds and the IoT for building a smart world. As shown in Table 2.1, today's big data possesses five important attributes: data in large *volume,* demanding high *velocity* to process it, and appearing in a *variety* of data types. The *veracity* attribute refers to the fact that most data is difficult to trace or to verify with proof of its integrity. Finally, the *value* of data varies with the data types and the way they are used in different applications. These attributes are known as the five V's of big data. Their characteristics and the challenges they present to data centers and cloud users are shown in the table.

By current standards, 1 TB or greater of data is considered big data. The International Data Corporation (IDC), a market research firm, has estimated that 40 ZB of data was processed worldwide in 2013. With 7 billion people existing today, that means each person may need to deal with 5.2 TB of data directly or regularly. This large volume demands large storage capacity and analytical capabilities to handle a massive amount of data.

All the V's make it difficult to capture, manage, and process data using existing hardware/software infrastructure. The pervasive use of data centers, large search engines, super-cluster systems, and cloud platforms have provided new sensing, storage, and compute facilities to handle big data effectively. In fact, these new information resources generate new opportunities for big data applications. In subsequent chapters, we will learn how to

Table 2.1

Five attributes (5 V's) that characterize the modern world of big data.

Attributes	Data Characteristics and Contents	Challenges
Volume	Terabytes, records/archive, transactions, tables, files	Storage and processing
Velocity	Batch processing, real-/near-time, processes, streaming	Need HPC/HTC system
Variety	Structured, unstructured, multifactor, probabilistic	Too many varieties to handle
Veracity	Trust, reputation, authenticity, tracing, accountability	Not traceable, lack of trust
Value	Statistical, snowball effects, aggregation, hypothetical	Varies with big data domains

use smart clouds, social, and IoT sensing networks to support big data operations efficiently with reduced costs and limited energy demands, often referred to as green computing for the future.

Forbes, Wikipedia, and the National Institute of Standards and Technology (NIST) provide some historical reviews of data science. To illustrate its evolution to a big data era, we divide the timeline into four stages. In the 1970s, data science was equivalent to *datalogy*, as noted by Peter Naur: "The science of dealing with data, once they have been established, while the relation of the data to what they represent is delegated to other fields and sciences" [19]. At one time, data science was regarded as part of statistics in a wide range of applications. Since the 2000s, the scope of data science has enlarged significantly. It has become a continuation of the field of data mining and predictive analytics, also known as the field of *knowledge discovery and data* mining (KDD).

In this context, programming is viewed as part of data science. Over the past two decades, data has increased in escalating scale in various fields. The data science evolution enables the extraction of knowledge from massive volumes of data that are structured or unstructured. Unstructured data include e-mails, videos, photos, social media, and other user-generated contents. The management of big data requires scalability across large amounts of storage, computing, and communication resources.

2.1.2 Gartner Hype Cycle for the Internet of Things

Figure 2.2 examines Gartner's Hype Cycle for the IoT in 2016. It may take two to ten years for an emerging technology to become mature and reach the plateau of productivity. By 2016, the most expected technologies are identified at the peak of the hype cycle. The top ten hot technologies for IoT development are identified as IoT architecture, wide-area IoT networks, embedded software and systems security, event stream processing, the IoT, machine learning, predictive analytics, IR/OT integration, and low-cost development boards.

As identified by the dark solid circles, several IoT technologies are still at the innovation trigger stage, which may take five to ten years to mature. These include the licensing and

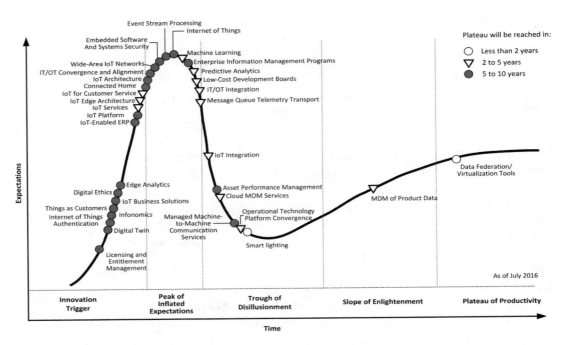

Figure 2.2
Hype Cycle for the Internet of Things in 2016. Source: Gartner Research, Hype Cycle, July 2016.

entitlement management, IoT authentication, Infonomics, digital twins, things as customers, IoT business solutions, digital ethics, edge analytics, and managed M2M communication services. The IoT for customer service, IoT edge architecture, IoT services, IT/OT integration, message queue telemetry transport, IoT integration, cloud MOM services, and MDM of product data may become mature in two to five years. The smart lighting, data federation, and virtualization tools are reaching the plateau of productivity within two years. Asset performance management, cloud MOM services, operational technology, and platform convergence are at trough of disillusionment at the low valley of the hype cycle.

It has been well accepted that new technology will become more human-centric. This implies that transparency is expected between people, businesses, and things. This relationship will surface more as the evolution of technology becomes more adaptive, contextual, and fluid within the workplace, at home, and interacting with the businesses world. As hinted above, we see the emergence of IoT technologies applied at all works of life. In Chapter 7, we will identify smart machine technologies with another Hype cycle (Fig.7.1).

There are predictable trends in technology that drive computing applications. Designers and programmers want to predict the technological capabilities of future systems. Jim Gray's *"Rules of Thumb in Data Engineering"* paper is an excellent example of how technology affects applications and vice versa. Moore's Law indicates that the processor speed doubles every eighteen months. This was indeed true over the past thirty years. However, it is hard to say that Moore's Law will be viable in the future. Gilder's law indicates that the network bandwidth has doubled annually. The tremendous price/performance ratio of commodity hardware was driven by smartphone, tablets, and the notebook market. This has also enriched commodity technologies in large-scale computing.

It is interesting to see the high expectation of IoT in recent years. The cloud computing in mashup or other applications demand computing economics, web-scale data collection, system reliability, and scalable performance. For example, distributed transaction processing is often practiced in the banking and finance industries. Transactions represent ninety percent of the existing market for reliable banking systems. Users must deal with multiple database servers in distributed transactions. How to maintain the consistency of replicated transaction records is crucial in real-time banking services. Other complications in these business applications include a shortage of software support, network saturation, and security threats.

2.1.3 Towards a Big Data Industry

In the big data era, we are facing a data deluge problem. Data comes from IoT sensors, lab experiments, simulations, society archives, and the web in all scales and formats. Preservation, movement, and access of massive data sets require generic tools supporting high-performance scalable file systems, database, algorithms, workflow, and visualization. With science becoming data-centric, a new paradigm of scientific discovery is based on data-intensive technologies. We need to foster tools for data capture, data creation, and data analysis. The cloud and IoT technologies are driven by the surge of interest in the data deluge situation.

As shown in Table 2.2, we had a database industry in the 1960 to 1990s. At that time, most data blocks were measured as MB, GB, and TB. Data centers became widely in use from 1980 to 2010 with data sets that easily ranged from TB to PB or even EB. After 2010, we saw the gradual formation of a new industry called *big data*. To process big data in the future, we expect EB to ZB or even YB. The market size of the big data industry reached $34 billion in 2013. Exceeding $100 billion in big data applications is within reach by 2020.

The Internet and WWW are used by billions of people every day. As a result, large data centers or clouds must be designed to provide not only big storage but also distributed computing power to satisfy the requests from a large number of users simultaneously. The emergence of public or hybrid clouds demands the upgrade of many data centers using larger server clusters, distributed file systems, and high-bandwidth networks. With massive

Table 2.2
Evolution of the big data industry in three development stages.

Stage	Databases	Data Centers	Big Data Industry
Time Frame	1960–1990	1980–2010	2010 and beyond
Data Sizes	MB, GB, TB	TB, PB, EB	EB, ZB, YB
Market Size and Growth Rate	Database market, data/knowledge engineering	$22.6 billion market by IDC 2012; 21.5% growth	$34 billion in IT spending (2013), predicted to exceed $100 billion by 2020; 4.4 million new big data jobs (2015)

amounts of smartphones and tablets requesting services, the cloud engines, distributed storage, and mobile networks must interact closely with the Internet to deliver mashup services in web-scale mobile computing over the social and media networks. To thrive in the digital economy, enterprise or business leaders must proactively discover the emerging new technologies. Success demands transformational business models for competitive advantage. The developers must maximize value through reduction of operating costs, and overcome legal and regulatory hurdles.

Table 2.3 identifies the software tools and libraries developed in the IT and cloud computing industry or from open sources. These tools are identified with specific skill areas at various subspaces, divided into three intersected tool spaces. For example, for data analytics, one may find the UCI machine learning repository, the RapidMiner for data mining, the Baidu Institute of Deep Learning (IDL) for deep learning with neural networks, and the Stanford Network Analysis Platform (SNAP) for social network and graph analysis. The OpenNLP provides a modeling tool in natural language processing. The table entries are by no means exhaustive; these are only a small number of representative software packages.

MATLAB is a well-known tool for solving linear algebra and mathematical programming. The IDL tool is a domain expertise tool for data visualization. IMES is used for medical engineering and science applications. For programming skills, we find Hadoop for MapReduce computations, BOINC for distributed computing, and Spark for scalable computing at streaming and GraphX modes. We will study some of these programming tools in Chapters 8 and 9. In particular, we will introduce the Google TensorFlow software platform in Chapter 9, which is used for deep learning or cognitive computing with artificial neural networks.

Most data scientists started as domain experts who mastered mathematical modeling, data mining techniques, and data analytics. Combining domain knowledge with mathematical skills, specific models are developed and new algorithms designed. Data science runs across the entire data lifecycle. It incorporates principles, techniques, and methods from many disciplines and domains, including data mining and analytics, especially when machine learning and pattern recognition are applied. Statistics, operations research,

Table 2.3
Software libraries for cloud and cognitive computing over big data sets.

Category	Software	Brief Description	Web Link
Big Data Analytics	Apache Mahout	Scalable machine learning for data analytics, clustering, and classification	Mahout.apache.org
	RapidMiner	Data mining and predictive analytics	Rapidminer.com
	PaddlePaddle	Baidu deep learning for intelligence	Paddlepaddle.org
	SNAP	Stanford network analysis platform with graph mining library	Snap.stanford.edu
Mathematic/ Statistical Modeling	OpenNLP	Java machine learning toolkit for natural language processing	Opennlp.org/projects
	SAS	SAS software—statistics for mining, analytics, and data management	sas.com
	Bayesian Classifier	Statistical decision theory for data classification and prediction	En.wikipedia.org/wiki/ Naïve_Bayes_classifier
Algorithms	MATLAB	Linear algebra and matrix manipulation	mathworks.com/produsts/matlab
	Graphstream	Open-source dynamic graph analysis	graphstream-project.org
Programming Tools	Hadoop	Java-implemented MapReduce library	Hadoop.apache.org
	Spark	Scalable computing with DAG model	Spark.apache.org
	HDFS	Hadoop distributed file system	Hadoop.apache.org
	BOINC	Berkeley open infrastructure for network computing	Github.com/BOINC/boinc
	TensorFlow	Deep learning with neural networks	tensorflow.org
App Domain Expertise	X Lab	Google research for disruptive technology and smart machines	solveforx.com
	IMES	MIT Institute for Medical Engineering and Science	Imes.mit.edu

visualization, and domain knowledge are also indispensable. Data science teams solve very complex data problems. Some open challenges in big data research, development, and applications are as follows:

- structured vs. unstructured data with effective indexing;
- identification, de-identification, and re-identification;
- ontologies and semantics of big data;
- data introspection and reduction techniques;
- design, construction, operation, and description;
- data integration and software interoperability;
- immutability and immortality;
- data measurement methods; and
- data range, denominators, trending, and estimation.

2.1.4 Big Data Applications: An Overview

A large number of big data applications have been reported in the open literature. We will treat big data and cloud applications later in Parts III and IV. Here in Table 2.4, we give a global overview of various big data applications. The U.S. National Institute of Standards and Technology (NIST) has identified 51 application cases of big data application. These tasks are grouped into nine categories. As a matter of fact, many data-driven applications have emerged in the past two decades. For example, business intelligence has become a prevailing technology in business applications. Network search engines are based on a massive data mining process. We briefly introduce a few of these applications as follows.

Commercial Applications

The earliest business data was generally structured data, collected by companies from old systems and then stored in relational database management systems (RDBMSs). Analytical technologies used in such systems were dominant in the 1990s and were intuitive and simple, e.g., reports, instrument panels, special queries, search-based business intelligence,

Table 2.4
Application categories of big data: From TBs to PBs (NIST, 2013).

Category	Brief Description	Example Applications
Government	National Archives and Records, federal/ state administration, Census Bureau, etc.	CIA, FBI, police forces, etc.
Business and Commercial	Finance in cloud, cloud backup, Mendeley (citations), web search, digital materials, etc.	Netflix, cargo shipping, online shopping, P2P
Defense and Military	Sensors, image surveillance, situation assessment, crisis control, battle management, etc.	Pentagon, Home Security Agency
Healthcare and Life Science	Medical records, graph and probabilistic analysis, pathology, bioimaging, genomics, epidemiology, etc.	Body-area sensors, genomics, emotion control
Deep Learning, Social Media	Self-driving cars, geolocate images/cameras, crowdsourcing, network science, NIST benchmark data sets	Machine learning, pattern recognition, perception, etc.
Scientific Discovery	Sky surveys, astronomy and physics, polar science, radar scattering in atmosphere, metadata, collaboration, etc.	Large Hadron Collider at CERN and Belle Accelerator in Japan
Earth and Environment	Earthquake, ocean, Earth observation, ice sheet radar scattering, climate simulation data sets, atmospheric turbulence identification, biogeochemistry	AmeriFlux and FLUXNET gas sensors, IoT for smart earth
Energy Research	New energy resources, wind power, solar systems, green computing, etc.	Smart Grid Project

online transaction processing, interactive visualization, score cards, predictive modeling, and data mining. Since the beginning of the 21st century, networks and websites have provided a unique opportunity for organizations to have an online presence and directly interact with customers.

Abundant products and customer information, including clickstream data logs and user behavior, can be acquired from the websites. Product layout optimization, customer trade analysis, product suggestions, and market structure analysis can be conducted by text analysis and website mining technologies. The quantity of mobile phones and tablet PCs first surpassed that of laptops and PCs in 2011. Mobile phones and IoT based on sensors are opening a new generation of innovation applications, and searching for a larger capacity of supporting location-sensing, people-oriented, and context operations.

Network Applications

The early Internet mainly provided e-mail and webpage services. Text analysis, data mining, and webpage analysis technologies have been applied to the mining of e-mail content and the building of search engines. Nowadays, most applications are web-based, regardless of their application field and design goals. Network data accounts for a major percentage of the global data volume. The web has become the common platform for interconnected pages, full of various kinds of data, such as text, images, videos, pictures, and interactive contents.

Advanced technologies are in great demand in semistructured or unstructured data. For example, image analysis technology can extract useful information from pictures, e.g., face recognition. Multimedia analysis technologies are applied to automated video surveillance systems for business, law enforcement, and military applications. Online social media applications, such as Internet forums, online communities, blogs, social networking services, and social multimedia websites, provide users with great opportunities to create, upload, and share content. Different user groups may search for daily news and publish their opinions with timely feedback.

Scientific Applications

Scientific research in many fields is acquiring massive data with high-throughput sensors and instruments such as astrophysics, oceanology, genomics, and environmental research. The U.S. National Science Foundation (NSF) has recently announced a big data initiative to promote research efforts to extract knowledge and insight from large and complex collections of digital data. Some scientific research disciplines have developed massive data platforms and obtained useful outcomes.

For example, in biology, the iPlant project applies network infrastructure, physical computing resources, coordination environment, virtual machine resources, and interoperative analysis software and data service to assist researches, educators, and students in enriching all plant sciences. iPlant data sets have high varieties in form, including specification or reference data, experimental data, analog or model data, observation data, and other derived data. Big data has been applied in the analysis of structured data, textual data, website data, multimedia data, network data, and mobile data.

Enterprise Applications

At present, big data primarily comes from, and is mainly used in, enterprises, while *business intelligence* (BI) and *online analytical processing* (OLAP) can be regarded as the predecessors of big data applications. The application of big data in enterprises can enhance their production efficiency and competitiveness in many aspects. In particular, in marketing, with correlation analysis of big data, enterprises can accurately predict consumer behavior.

In sales planning, after comparison of massive data, enterprises can optimize their commodity prices. In operations, enterprises can improve their operation efficiency and operation satisfaction, optimize the input of labor force, accurately forecast personnel allocation requirements, avoid excess production capacity, and reduce labor costs. In supply chains, using big data, enterprises may conduct inventory optimization, logistic optimization, supplier coordination, etc., to mitigate the gap between supply and demand, control budgets, and improve services.

Example 2.1   Big Data in Financial and e-Commerce Applications

The use of big data in financial and commercial applications has grown rapidly in recent years. For example, the Industrial and Commercial Bank of China (ICBC) applies data analysis to recognize that such activities as multiple-times score accumulation and score exchange in shops are effective for attracting good-quality customers. By building a customer loss early warning model, the bank can sell high-yield financial products to the top 20% of customers in a loss ratio so as to retain them. As a result, the loss ratios of customers with luxury or average credit cards have been reduced by 15% and 7%, respectively. By analyzing customers' transaction records, potential small corporate customers can be effectively identified. Utilizing remote banking, cloud referral platforms can help implement cross-selling; considerable performance gains have occurred in recent years.

Clearly, the classic application of big data is in e-commerce. Tens of thousands of transactions are conducted daily on Taobao—an online shopping website in China—with transaction times, commodity prices, and purchase quantities recorded. In addition, such information matches age, gender, address, and even hobbies and interests of buyers and sellers. Data Cube is a big data application on the Taobao platform through which merchants can be aware of the market conditions of their brands, and consumers' characteristics and behaviors, and make production and inventory decisions accordingly. Meanwhile, more consumers can purchase their favorite commodities at preferred prices.

The e-commerce company Alibaba automatically analyzes and judges whether to extend loans to enterprises through enterprise transaction data acquired by virtue of big data technologies (there is no manual intervention in the entire process). So far, Alibaba has lent more than $5 billion with a bad loan rate of only 0.3%, which is much lower than that of commercial banks. ■

Healthcare and Medical Applications

Medical data is continuously and rapidly growing, containing abundant and various information values. Big data has unlimited potential for effectively storing, processing, querying, and analyzing medical data. The application of medical big data will profoundly influence human health. The IoT is revolutionizing the healthcare industry. Sensors collect patient data, and microcontrollers process, analyze, and communicate the data over wireless Internet. Microprocessors enable rich graphical user interfaces. Healthcare clouds and gateways help analyze the data with statistical accuracy. The healthcare industry's use of big data is growing rapidly.

Example 2.2   Big Data Applications in the Healthcare Industry

Aetna Life Insurance Company selected 102 patients from a pool of 1,000 patients to complete an experiment in order to help predict the recovery of patients with metabolic syndrome. In an independent experiment, it scanned 600,000 laboratory test results and 180,000 claims through a series of detection test results of metabolic syndrome in patients over three consecutive years. In addition, it summarized the final result into a personalized treatment plan to assess the danger factors and create the main treatment plans of patients.

This way, doctors may reduce morbidity by 50% over the next ten years by prescribing statins and helping patients to lose weight or suggesting that patients reduce the total triglycerides in their bodies if the sugar content in their bodies is over 20%. The Mount Sinai Medical Center in New York utilizes the technologies of Ayasdi, a big data company, to analyze all genetic sequences of *Escherichia coli*, including over 1 million DNA variants, to discover why bacterial strains resist antibiotics. Ayasdi's technology uses topological data analysis to understand data characteristics.

HealthVault of Microsoft launched an excellent application of medical big data in 2007. The goal was to manage individual health information in individual and family medical equipment. Presently, health information can be entered and uploaded with mobile smart devices and imported into individual medical records by a third-party agency. In addition, it can be integrated with a third-party application with the *software development kit* (SDK) and open interface. ■

IoT Sensing and Crowdsourcing

With the rapid development of wireless communication and sensor technologies, mobile phones and tablet computers have integrated more and more sensors, with increasingly stronger computing and sensing capacities. As a result, crowdsensing is coming to the center stage of mobile computing. In crowdsensing, a large number of general users utilize mobile devices as basic sensing units to conduct coordination with mobile networks for distribution of sensed tasks and collection and utilization of sensed data. The goal is to complete large-scale and complex social sensing tasks. In crowdsensing, participants who complete complex sensing tasks do not need to have professional skills.

Crowdsensing modes represented by crowdsourcing have been successfully applied to geotagged photography, positioning and navigation, urban road traffic sensing, market forecast, opinion mining, and other labor-intensive applications. Crowdsourcing, a new approach for problem-solving, takes a large number of general users as the foundation and distributes tasks in a free and voluntary way. Crowdsourcing can be useful for labor-intensive applications, such as picture marking, language translation, and speech recognition.

The main idea of crowdsourcing is to distribute tasks to general users and to complete tasks that users could not individually complete or do not anticipate completing. With no need for intentionally deploying sensing modules and employing professionals, crowdsourcing can broaden the sensing scope of a sensing system to reach the city scale and even larger scales. As a matter of fact, crowdsourcing has been applied by many companies before the emergence of big data. For example, P&G, BMW, and Audi improve their R&D and design capacities by virtue of crowdsourcing.

In the big data era, spatial crowdsourcing has become a hot topic. Three operational characteristics of spatial crowdsourcing are observed below.

1. Users may request the service and resources related to a specified location.

2. The mobile users who are willing to participate in the task will move to the specified location to acquire related data (such as video, audio, or pictures).

3. The acquired data will be sent to the service requester. With the rapid growth of usage of mobile devices and the increasingly complex functions provided by mobile devices, it can be forecasted that spatial crowdsourcing will be more prevalent than traditional crowdsourcing, e.g., Amazon Turk and Crowdflower.

2.2 The Internet of Things and Cloud Interactions

Integrating cyberspace into the physical world web is the ultimate goal of the IoT. This could be regarded as the third evolution of the information industry. First, the network scale that can interconnect an enormous number of things in the physical world becomes very large. Second, network mobility increases rapidly due to pervasive use of mobile and vehicular devices. Third, the fusion of heterogeneous networks becomes deeper with various types of devices connected to the Internet. Furthermore, mobile Internet, cloud computing, big data, software-defined networking, and 5G cellular systems have all accelerated IoT development.

Figure 2.3 shows a three-dimensional web space where objects can be instrumented, interconnected, and interacted intelligently. The communications are done between people and things or among the things themselves. The H2H, H2T, and T2T communications are identified for human to human, human to things, and things to things, respectively. The importance is to connect any things at any time and any place with low costs. The dynamic connections will grow exponentially into the IoT, a new universal network of networks. The IoT is strongly tied to specific application domains. Different application domains are embraced by different community cycles or groups in our society. We simply call them the IoT domains or IoT networks.

The traditional Internet connects machines to machines or web pages to web pages. The IoT refers to the networked interconnection of everyday objects, tools, devices, or computers. The things (objects) of our daily lives can be large or small. The idea is to tag every object using *radio-frequency identification* (RFID) or related sensor or electronic technologies like *global positioning systems* (GPS). With the introduction of IPv6 protocol, there are 2^{128} IP addresses available to distinguish all objects on the earth, including all mobile, embedded devices, computers, and even some biological objects. It is estimated that an average person is surrounded by 1,000 to 5,000 objects on a daily basis. The IoT needs to be designed to track 100 trillion static or moving objects simultaneously. For this reason, the IoT demands unique addressability of all objects.

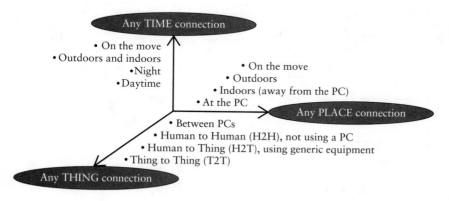

Figure 2.3
Physical layout of the IoT by interconnecting any things (objects) on earth at any time in any place. Source: http://en.wikipedia.org/wiki/InternetofThings, 2016.

2.2.1 IoT Sensing and Platform Architecture

With the rapid advances in electronics, electromechanics, and nanotechnologies, ubiquitous devices are getting larger in number and smaller and smaller in size. In the context of IoT, such objects are also called *things*, such as computers, sensors, people, actuators, refrigerators, TVs, vehicles, mobile phones, clothes, food, medicines, books, passports, and luggage. They are expected to become active participants in business, information, and social processes. These participants can react autonomously to "real/physical world" events and influence them by triggering actions and creating services either with or without direct human intervention. Lots of sensor devices are deployed for object sensing and information gathering. The senor node is a combination of sensing, communications, and local information processing. The architecture of a typical IoT platform is depicted in Figure 2.4.

RFID Technology

The first step to enabling smart services is to collect contextual information about the environment, things, and objects of interest. For example, sensors can be used to continuously monitor a person's physiological activities and actions, such as health status and motion patterns, and RFID techniques can be utilized for collecting crucial personal information and storing it in a low-cost chip that is attached to an individual at all times.

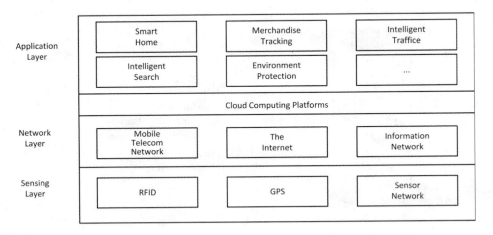

Figure 2.4
The architecture of an IoT and its underlying technologies. Source: K. Hwang, et al., *Distributed and Cloud Computing*, Morgan Kaufmann, 2012.

RFID is a *radio-frequency* (RF) electronic technology that allows automatic identification or locating of objects, people, and animals in a wide variety of deployment settings. In the past decade, RFID systems have been incorporated into a wide range of industrial and commercial systems, including manufacturing and logistics, retail, item tracking and tracing, inventory monitoring, asset management, antitheft, electronic payment, antitampering, transport ticketing, and supply-chain management.

A typical RFID application consists of an RFID tag, an RFID reader, and a backend system. With a simple RF chip and an antenna, an RFID tag can store information that identifies the object to which it is attached. There are three types of RFID tags: passive tags, active tags, and semiactive tags. A passive tag obtains energy through RF signals from the reader, while an active tag is powered by an embedded battery, which enables larger memory or more functionality. Although a semiactive tag communicates with RFID readers like a passive tag, additional modules can be supported through an internal battery. When it comes within the proximity of an RFID reader, the information stored in the tag is transferred to the reader, and onto a backend system, which can be employed on a computer for processing this information and controlling the operation of other subsystem(s).

Sensors and Sensor Networks

In the last decade, we witnessed a growing interest in deploying a sheer number of microsensors that collaborate on data gathering and processing in a distributed manner. Sensor nodes are expected to be inexpensive and can be deployed in various environments. A *wireless sensor network* (WSN) consists of spatially distributed autonomous sensors to monitor physical or environmental conditions, such as temperature, sound, or pressure, and to cooperatively pass their data through the network to a main location. The sensor nodes form a multihop ad hoc wireless network.

A WSN is a group of specialized transducers with a communications infrastructure intended to monitor and record conditions at diverse locations. Commonly monitored parameters are temperature, humidity, pressure, wind direction and speed, illumination intensity, vibration intensity, sound intensity, power-line voltage, chemical concentrations, pollutant levels, and vital body functions. A sensor network consists of multiple detection stations called sensor nodes, each of which is small, lightweight, and portable. Every sensor node is equipped with a transducer, microcomputer, transceiver, and power source. The transducer generates electrical signals based on sensed data.

One of the most widely used sensor technologies is ZigBee, an IEEE 802.15.4-based device. The radio frequency applied in ZigBee results in low data rate, long battery life, and secure networking. They are used mainly in monitory and remote control IoT or mobile applications. Many supermarkets, department stores, and hospitals are installed with ZigBee networks. The data rate ranges from 20 to 250 Kbps and they can operate up to 100 m.

However, ZigBee devices can be networked together to cover a much large area. ZigBee networks are highly scalable and are used in wireless home-area networks (WHAN). The ZigBee technology is simpler to use and less expensive than Bluetooth or WiFi.

Basic IoT architecture is introduced below in three layers, namely the sensing, networking, and application layers. The IoT system is likely to have an event-driven architecture. In Figure 2.4, IoT development is shown with a three-layer architecture. The top layer is formed by the driven applications. The bottom layer consists of various types of sensing and automatic information generation devices: namely sensors, ZigBee devices, RFID tags, road-mapping GPS navigators, etc. The sensing devices are locally or wide-area connected in the form of sensor networks, RFID networks, and GPS systems, etc. Signals or information collected at these sensing devices are linked to the applications through the cloud computing platforms at the middle layer.

The signal-processing clouds are built over the mobile networks, the Internet backbone, and various information networks at the middle layer. In the IoT, the meaning of a sensing event does not follow a deterministic or syntactic model. In fact, the *service-oriented architecture* (SoA) model is adoptable here. Large numbers of sensors and filters are used to collect the raw data. Various compute and storage clouds and grids are used to process the data and transform them into information and knowledge formats. The sensory data is used to put together a decision-making system for intelligence applications. The middle layer is a semantic web or grid. Some actors (services, components, avatars) are self-referenced.

2.2.2 IoT Value Chains and Development Road Map

Gartner estimated that 6.4 billion connected "things" were in use in 2016, up 30% from 2015. This implies a huge market value in IoT products and applications. The IoT really resulted from the fast rise of wireless communication, smart mobile devices, sensors, GPS services, and big data applications in the past decade. The sensors are based on the principles of optics, touch/pressure, chemistry, and electromagnetics. In the networking area, we have benefited from the widespread coverage of WiFI, Bluetooth, and *long-term evolution* (LTE) technologies in our living environment. In addition, the appearance of clouds also helped solve the problems associated with discovery, storage, and processing of huge IoT-generated big data.

According to the analysis by IoT PaaS platform Xively, there will be 80 billion pieces of equipment connected to various forms of IoT platforms by 2020. It is estimated that 12 billion IoT platforms will be set up at major enterprises by then. These may bring a 30% increase in company revenue. The manufacturing industry has also increased 35% in using various forms of smart sensors to automate their production processes. A similar increase in IoT adoption appears in petroleum, gas energy, mining, insurance, smart homes/cities, banking, healthcare, government, and military applications. Overall, the annual increase by 30% is observed on all IoT products, equipment, and platforms.

Table 2.5
IoT value chain among major players and estimated value share.

Objects or Users	Sample Objects, Users, Operators, Providers, Distributors, or Customers	Estimated Share
Building Components	Embedded chips, modules, wireless modems, sensors, cameras, routers, gateways, antennas, and cables	5–10%
Smart Objects	Smart bins, solar cells, temp sensor, fire extinguisher, meters, ATM, cameras	
Network Operators	Spectrum allocation, network infrastructure, connectivity, availability, billing, customer services	15–20%
Service Enablers	Software, infrastructure, technology selection, consulting, solution design	30–40%
System Integrators	Interfaces, enterprise system integration, app development, security, data management, hardware and installation	15–20%
Service Providers	Analysis, app managers, access control, data managers, QoS, service provision	15–20%
Distributors/Resellers	Product distribution, road services, forward supply chains	Unknown
Clients or Customers	Buyer service and user services	Unknown

Table 2.5 lists an IoT value chain among all IoT suppliers and clients. The IoT value shares among seven user categories are given at the right column with a total share of 100%. The IoT value chain is formed from device provider to network provider, platform provider, and application in a sequence, with the largest value share coming from service enablers. The next contributors are from network operators, system integrators, and software providers. It is low in the value chain on contributions by IoT components, sellers, and customers.

As shown in Figure 2.5, the IoT was primarily applied to expedite supply chain management in early 2000. Vertical market and ubiquitous positioning applications began to dominate IoT applications after 2010. Eventually, we will see widespread use of IoT in a physical world web, where teleoperations and telepresence will enable monitoring and controlling of any remote object. Ultimately, the IoT will enable the creation of a physical world web so that everything is connected on earth.

This will make our daily lives more convenient and well informed on events taking place in almost all the world. This will help us make smarter decisions, save human life, avoid disasters, and reduce human burdens during crises. On the other hand, the rise of IoT brings some negative impact. For example, we may lose privacy. Criminals or enemies could use IoT to stage even more destruction. Legal systems must be established to prevent or avoid possible negative impacts from the IoT development.

Many IoT challenges are wide open, yet to be solved. Specific challenges include privacy, participatory sensing, data analytics, geographic information system- (GIS-) based

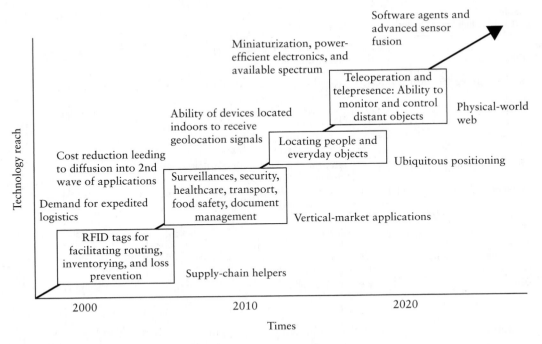

Figure 2.5
Technology road map of IoT applications. Courtesy of SRI: Consulting Business Intelligence, "Disruptive Technologies Global Trends 2025."

visualization, and cloud computing. Other areas are related to IoT architecture standardization, energy efficiency, security, protocols, and QoS. Standardization of frequency bands and protocols plays a pivotal role in accomplishing this goal. A roadmap of key developments in IoT applications is shown in Figure 2.6. This diagram shows the expected growth of five key IoT application domains from 2010 to 2025.

In 2016, the worldwide IoT market was identified with ten huge critical trends. We review a few these trends in this chapter with some updated comments from the perspectives of both IoT developer and user communities. It is expected that the number of IoT acquisitions will grow even faster than before. The IoT field is complex and must involve partnership from different disciplines. Security is still a major barrier. IoT will shine in industrial applications with huge success in the small home market. It seems that the most keen interest in the IoT is outside the United States. However, IBM and Intel are trying hard to enter the IoT competition along with cognitive services. Smart cities and self-driving cars are gaining traction. The IoT is now more about the data it generates than the things it connects. Optimistically, the hype is over and the IoT is becoming a reality.

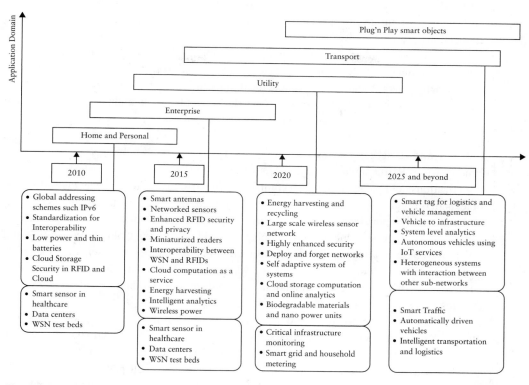

Figure 2.6

Projected upgrades in five IoT application domains from 2010 to 2025. Courtesy of J. Gubbi et al., "Internet of Things (IoT): A Vision, Architectural Elements, and Future Directions," *Future Generation Computer Systems* 29 (2013).

2.2.3 Stand-alone and Cloud-centric IoT Applications

Typically, stand-alone IoT focuses on some stable environments in which new applications would likely improve the quality of our lives: at home, while traveling, when sick, at work, when jogging, at the gym, just to cite a few. These environments are now equipped with objects with only primitive intelligence, most of the time without any communication capabilities. Giving these objects the possibility to communicate with each other and to interact with their surroundings enables a very wide range of IoT applications. These can be grouped into the following domains: transportation and logistics domain; healthcare domain; smart environment (home, office, plant) domain; personal and social domain. We may distinguish between those either directly applicable or closer to our current living habits and those that are futuristic, which we can only fancy of at the moment, since the technologies and/or our societies are not ready for their deployment. In the following subsections we provide a review of the short-medium term applications for each of these categories and a range of futuristic applications.

RFID technology plays an important role in business and the marketplace. Many industrial, government, and community services can benefit from these applications. These include activities or initiatives to promote the development of better and more efficient societies, cities, and governments. The typical RFID IoT applications include retailing and logistics services and supply chain management.

Retailing and Logistics Services

Emergence of RFID applications depends strongly on their adoption by retailers, logistics organizations, and package-delivery companies. In particular, retailers may tag individual objects in order to solve a number of problems at once: accurate inventorying, loss control, and ability to support unattended walk-through point of sale terminals (which promise to speed checkout while reducing both shoplifting and labor costs). Cold-chain auditing and assurance could require tagging food and medicine with temperature-sensitive materials and/or electronics. Assuring or monitoring whether perishable materials are intact and/or need attention may entail communications among things, refrigeration systems, automated data logging systems, and human technicians.

For example, at the grocery store you buy a carton of milk. The milk containers will have an RFID tag that stores the milk's expiration date and price. When you lift the milk from the shelf, the shelf may display the milk's specific expiration date, or the information could be wirelessly sent to your personal digital assistant or cell phone. As you exit the store, you pass through doors with an embedded tag reader. This reader tabulates the cost of all the items in your shopping cart and sends the grocery bill to your bank. Product manufacturers know what you've bought and the store's computers know exactly how many of each product needs to be reordered.

Once you get home, you put your milk in the refrigerator, which is equipped with a tag reader. This smart refrigerator is capable of tracking all of the groceries stored in it. It can track the foods you use, how often you restock your refrigerator, and let you know when that milk and other foods spoil. Products are also tracked when they are thrown into a trash can or recycle bin. Based on the products you buy, your grocery store gets to know your unique preferences. Instead of receiving generic newsletters with weekly grocery specials, you might receive one created just for you.

Supply Chain Management

Supply chain management can be aided by a RFID system. The idea is to manage a whole network of related businesses or partners involved in product manufacturing, delivery, and service as required by the end customers. At any given time, market forces could demand changes from suppliers, logistics providers, locations, and customers, and from any number of specialized participants in a supply chain. This variability has significant effects on the supply chain infrastructure, ranging from the foundational layers of establishing the electronic communication between the trading partners to the more complex configuration of the processes, and the arrangement of work flows that are essential to the fast production process.

A supply line combines the processes, methodologies, tools, and delivery options to guide collaborative partners to work in a sequence to conduct business with high efficiency and delivery speed. The cooperative companies must work in lockstep quickly as the complexity and speed of the supply chain increases due to the effects of global competition, rapid price fluctuations, surging oil prices, short product life cycles, expanded specialization, and talent scarcity. A supply chain is an efficient network of facilities that procures materials, transforms these materials to finished products, and finally distributes the finished products to customers. The following example could explain how supply chains can be aided by the IoT, which is particularly tailored to promote business efficiency and fast growth.

Example 2.3   Supply Chain Management Aided by the Internet of Things

Supply chain management is a process used by companies to ensure that their supply chain is efficient and cost effective. In Figure 2.7 the supply chain for the production and sales of consumer products is illustrated. The supply chain involves material or component suppliers, distribution centers, communication links, cloud data centers, large numbers of retail stores, corporate headquarters (like Wal-Mart), banks, etc. These are business partners that are linked by satellite, Internet, wired and wireless networks, truck, train or shipping companies, and electronic banking, cloud providers, etc.

Sensors, RFID tags, and GPS devices could be placed everywhere along the supply chain. The whole idea is to promote online business, e-commerce, or mobile transactions. Supply chain management is comprised of five major stages of operations.

1. *Planning and coordination:* A plan or strategy must be developed to address how a good or service can satisfy the needs of customers.

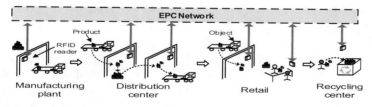

Figure 2.7
Supply chain management in a multipartner business pipeline.

2. *Material and equipment supplies:* This phase involves building a strong relation with the raw material suppliers and also planning methods for shipping, delivery, and payment.

3. *Manufacturing and testing:* The product is tested, manufactured, and scheduled for delivery.

4. *Delivery of products:* Customer orders are taken and delivery of the goods is planned.

5. *After-sale service and returns:* At this stage, customers may return defective products and the company also addresses customers' demands. Supply chain software is used by many companies for efficient supply chain management. ∎

Example 2.4   A Smart Power Grid Supported by the Internet of Things

A smart grid includes an intelligent monitoring system that keeps track of all electricity flowing in the system. Smart meters and sensors, a digital upgrade of current utility meters, tracks energy usage in real time so both the customer and the utility company know how much is being used at any given time. Energy is paid for using "time of day" pricing, meaning electricity will cost more at peak times of use. The smart power grid is supported by IoT in the areas of home, office, store, factory, distributed data collection of environmental changes, green energy generation, consumption reduction, natural disaster recovery, etc. With the development of WSNs, as well as low-power embedded systems and cloud computing, cloud-assisted IoT systems are gradually maturing to support smart and computation-intensive IoT applications involving big amounts of data. The home IoT applications can be upgraded by the emerging cloud computing environment. The scalable and elastic cloud-assisted framework shifts computation and storage into the network to reduce operational and maintenance costs.

For example, when power is least expensive the user can allow the smart grid to turn on selected home appliances such as washing machines or factory processes that can run at arbitrary hours. At peak times it could turn off selected appliances to reduce demand. More involved users will be able to use the smart meter to view energy usage remotely and make real-time decisions about energy consumption. A refrigerator or air conditioning system could be turned down remotely while residents are away. ∎

Cloud-centric IoT Systems Applications

The information delivered from different domains (e.g., smart grid, healthcare) is difficult to understand and handle for the computer in the cloud service. With the support of the semantic model, an ontology-based approach can be used to implement information interaction and sharing in cloud-assisted home IoT. As shown in Figure 2.8, separate cloud systems can interoperate, with an additional root cloud providing different services for health care, energy management, convenience, entertainment, etc.

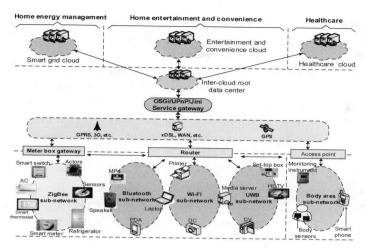

Figure 2.8

Cloud-centric IoT system for smart home development. Reprinted with permission from K. Hwang and M. Chen, *Big Data Analytics for Cloud, IoT and Cognitive Learning*, Wiley, 2017.

The service gateway implements various technologies, protocols, standards, and services to diversify communications capabilities and integrate devices. Currently, most service gateways implement well-defined software modes and systems, such as Jini, UPnP, and OSGi. In addition, the communication of heterogeneous objects in IoT is a major problem because different objects provide different information in different formats for different purposes. Semantic web technologies and models may also be used to help solve this problem. Semantic web technologies can be applied to facilitate communication in home IoT applications.

In recent years, cloud computing has provided novel perspectives in cloud-assisted technologies for distinct purposes. A cloud-assisted communication system may include multiple cloud systems operating with different policies to share resources, so that end-to-end QoS to users can be maintained even in the event of large fluctuations in computing load that cannot be handled by a single cloud system. It is known that the previous architectures for IoT have not taken into account cloud-assisted capabilities. In our view, it is an important factor for the IoT to achieve functional completeness. Therefore, compared to previous survey literature, we propose a cloud-assisted layer for the advancement of IoT architecture, for example, the joint effort between Intel and China Mobile toward the development of 5G mobile core networks.

2.2.4   Smart City and Smart Community Development

In 2016, more than half of the world's population was living in cities. By 2050, more than 70% will live in cities. More than 60% of those cities are still underdeveloped. Cities are traditionally developed with these possible models: economy-driven, energy-driven, and vanity-driven. To build a smart city, the ultimate goal is to build a highly intelligent, human-centric living environment. This can be greatly aided by using big data collected from the use of IoT and cloud platforms. We need big data to be visible, analytical, and highly responsive by leveraging new technologies like IoT and clouds.

Example 2.5   Solutions to Build Safe and Comfortable Communities and Cities
REDtone is a developer company for smart cities. Their solution is to apply crowdsourcing by using smartphones to acquire large amounts of real data from residents or visitors. The city management uses the big data to make meaningful classifications of events and predictions of disasters. The end purpose is to make the city safe, convenient, and comfortable to live, work, or play in. Their crowdsourcing mass includes those using iOS or Android smartphones to run the CityAct applications. The initial goal is to help people recognize high crime zones, avoid road construction areas, and escape from fire, flood, or terror attacks. Table 2.6 lists some desired features in building a smart city.

Smart cities must be able to prevent public facilities or private properties from being destroyed or intruded upon. Environmental protection, and monitoring of traffic and pollution, are just a few example of acheiving this. REDtone designers are also considering integrating Twister, SMS, WhatsApp, Facebook, and WeChat as methods to help protect cities from crime or attack. Extensive use of sensors, meters, and GPS can help and so does visual information on TVs, iPads, or notebooks.

Table 2.6
Use of IoT devices and platforms for smart city/community development

IoT features	Functional Requirements	Sensing Device or Framework
Environmental Monitoring	Temperature, CO, fire hazards, noise control, drought, earthquake, etc.	Sensors, meters, sensor networks, detection stations, etc.
Traffic Intensity Monitoring	Traffic volumes, road occupancy, vehicle speed, queue length, pedestrian crossings, etc.	RFID, sensors at main city entrances, GPS receivers, etc.
River, Ocean, and Weather Monitoring	Water quality, water level, flow sensors, weather and flood warning, hurricanes, tornadoes, tsunamis, etc.	Measuring devices, sensors (such as pH sensor), flow meters, etc.
Outdoor Parking and Management	Parking period, payments, violation, theft, trapped children, guidance to free parking lots, etc.	Parking sensors, meters, guide signs, surveillance cameras, etc.
Smart Citizens with Crowdsensing	Detection and prevention of event accidents, riots, terrorist attacks, etc.	Smartphone applications, Twitter messages, GPS, etc.
Smart Waste Management	City sewage treatment, garbage collection, waste dumping, ground monitoring, etc.	Sensors in waste bins, garbage trucks, sewage outlets, etc.

The building of cloud-centric IoT healthcare systems, or daily care centers or assisted living facilities for the elderly and Alzheimer patients, is also being suggested for intelligent IoT applications. The requirement for building a smart city, smart community, smart classroom, smart hospital, and smart home is to have common or specific goals, such as the importance of passing on timely information to its citizens or residents in case of emergency, like fire, war, earthquake, etc. Figure 2.9 shows a suggested design of an urban IoT network base on mashup web services.

The urban IoT system is built with a web service approach, which requires the deployment of suitable protocol layers in different elements of the network. The protocol stacks are depicted in each IoT node or gateway. Besides the key elements in communication protocols applied, we need to decide on the link layer technologies that can be used to interconnect the different devices attached to the IoT network. For details, readers are referred to Zanella et al. [22]. ∎

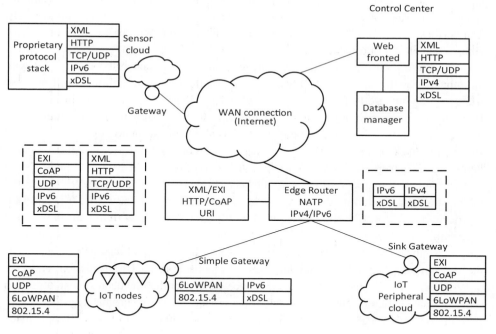

Figure 2.9

Conceptual design of an IoT network for smart cities. Reprinted with permission from A. Zanella et al., "Internet of Things for Smart Cities," *IEEE Internet of Things Journal* 1, no. 1 (2014).

2.3 Data Collection, Mining, and Analytics on Clouds

Big data analytics is the process of examining large amounts of data of a variety of types (big data) to uncover hidden patterns, unknown correlations, and other useful information. Such information can provide competitive advantages over rival organizations and result in higher business intelligence or scientific discovery, such as more effective marketing or increased revenue. The primary goal of big data analytics is to help companies make better business decisions by enabling data scientists and other users to analyze huge volumes of transaction data that may be left untapped by conventional business intelligence (BI) programs.

2.3.1 Data Quality Control and Representations

For many years, *high-performance computing* (HPC) systems emphasized raw speed performance, but now there is a strategic change in focus from HPC to *high-throughput computing* (HTC). The HTC paradigm pays more attention to high-flux multicomputing for Internet searches and web services that are requested by millions of users simultaneously. The performance goal is thus shifted to measure high throughput, or the number of tasks completed per unit of time.

In 2015, the total data stored in all forms on earth is estimated to be 300+ EB with an annual growth rate of 28%. However, the total data transmitted among all possible sources is about 1,900+ EB per year (www.martinhilbert.net/WorldInfoCapacity.html). In the old days, most information items were expressed in analog format. Digital storage devices became popular in 2002 and quickly replaced most analog devices. Table 2.7 shows only 6% (19 EB) in analog and 94% (280 EB) on digital devices in 2007. Analog items are primarily stored on audio/video tapes (94%). Digital information is spread across many different kinds of storage devices. PC/server hard drives have contributed the most (44.5%) including those used in large data centers. The next are DVD and Blu-ray devices (22.8%). Clearly, the secondary storage devices now dominate the storage spectrum.

Data acquisition includes data collection, data transmission, and data preprocessing. At the second phase, data acquisition includes data collection, data transmission, and data preprocessing. During big data acquisition, once we collect the raw data, we can utilize an efficient transmission mechanism to send it to a proper storage management system to support different analytical applications. The collected data sets may sometimes include much redundant or useless data, which unnecessarily increases storage space and affects the subsequent data analysis. Table 2.8 summarizes major data acquisition methods and preprocessing operations.

For example, high redundancy is very common among data sets collected by sensors for environmental monitoring. Data compression technology can be applied to reduce the redundancy. Therefore, data preprocessing operations are indispensable to ensure efficient

Table 2.7
Global information storage capacity in terms of total bytes in 2007.

Technology	Storage Devices	Distribution
Analog, 19 EB, 6% of the total	Paper, film, audio tape, and vinyl	6.0%
	Analog videotapes	94.0%
Digital, 280 EB, 94% of the total capacity	Portable media and flash drives	2.0%
	Portable hard disks	2.4%
	CDs and mini disks	6.8%
	Digital tapes	11.8%
	DVD and Blu-ray	22.8%
	PC/server hard disks	44.5%
	Others (memory cards, floppy disks, mobile phone, PDSs, cameras, video games, etc.)	< 1.0%

Table 2.8
Some big data acquisition sources and major preprocessing operations.

Collection Sources	Logs, sensors, crawlers, packet capture, mobile devices, etc.
Preprocessing Steps	Integration, cleaning, and redundancy elimination
Data Generators	Social media, enterprises, IoT, Internet, biomedical, government, scientific discovery, environments, etc.

data storage and exploitation. Data collection utilizes special data collection techniques to acquire raw data from a specific data generation environment. Many common data collection and generation sources and data generators are introduced below, separately.

Log Files

As one widely used data collection method, log files are record files automatically generated by the data source system, so as to record activities in designated file formats for subsequent analysis. Log files are used in nearly all digital devices. For example, web servers record in log files number of clicks, click rates, visits, and other property records of web users. To capture activities of users at websites, web servers mainly include the following three log file formats: public log file format, expanded log format, and IIS log format.

All three types of log files are in ASCII text format. Databases other than text files may sometimes be used to store log information to improve the query efficiency of the massive log store. There are also some other log files based on data collection, including stock indicators in financial applications and determination of operating states in network monitoring and traffic management.

Methods for Acquiring Network Data

At present, network data acquisition is accomplished using a combination of web crawler, word segmentation system, task system, and index system, etc. Web crawler is a program used by search engines for downloading and storing web pages. Generally speaking, web crawler starts from the uniform resource locator (URL) of an initial web page to access other linked web pages, during which it stores and sequences all the retrieved URLs. Web crawler acquires a URL in the order of precedence through a URL queue and then downloads web pages, identifies all URLs in the downloaded web pages, and extracts new URLs to be put in the queue.

This process is repeated until the web crawler is stopped. Data acquisition through a web crawler is widely applied in applications based on web pages, such as search engines or web caching. Traditional web page extraction technologies feature multiple efficient solutions, and considerable research has been done in this field. As more advanced web page applications are emerging, some extraction strategies are used to cope with rich Internet applications. The current network data acquisition technologies mainly include traditional libpcap-based packet capture technology, zero-copy packet capture technology, as well as some specialized network monitoring software such as Wireshark, SmartSniff, and WinNetCap.

Table 2.9 summarizes interesting properties and attributes that affect data quality. We introduce the methods, architectures, and tools for big data analysis. Our studies are by no means meant to cover all progress made in this field. We identify the key concepts and some representative tools or database models used in this context. Big data sources come from business transactions, textual and multimedia contents, qualitative knowledge data, scientific discovery, social media and sensing data from IoT. The quality of the data is often poor, because of the massive volume, data variety due to unpredictable data types, and data veracity for lack of traceability.

The quality control of big data involves a circular cycle of four stages. One must (1) identify the important data quality attributes; (2) have the ability to measure or assess the data quality level; (3) be able to analyze the data quality and any major problems; and finally, (4) to improve the data quality by suggesting concrete actions to take. Unfortunately, none of these tasks is easy to implement. In Table 2.9, we identify the important attributes involved in data quality control. Among these data quality control dimensions, intrinsic attributes and representational and access control mechanisms are equally important.

Data can be represented in many different ways. Four major representation models suggested for big data are as follows: (1) <key, value> pairs are often used to distribute data in MapReduce operations (to be presented in Chapter 8) Dynamo Voldemort is a good example of using key-value pairs; (2) Table Lookup or relational databases such as Google's BigTable and Apache Cassandra software; (3) graphic tools like GraphX used in Spark for

Table 2.9
Attributes for data quality control, representation, and database operations.

Category	Attributes	Basic Definitions and Questions
Intrinsic and Contextual	Accuracy and trust	Data correctness and credibility; true, fake, or accurate?
	Integrity and reputation	Biased or impartial data? Reputation of data source?
	Relevance and value	Data relevance to task at hand and value added or not?
	Volume and completeness	Data volume tested and any value present?
Representation and Visualization	Easy to comprehend	Data clarity and easy to understand without ambiguity
	Interpretability and visualization	Data well represented in numbers, text, graphs, images, videos, profiles, or metadata, etc.
Accessibility and Security	Access control	Data availability, access control protocols, easy to retrieve
	Security precaution	Restricted access or integrity control from alteration or deletion

social graph analysis; and (4) special database systems such as MongoDB, SimpleDB, and CouchDB that are commonly used by the big data community.

Data science, data mining, data analytics, and knowledge discovery are closely related terms. In many cases, they are used interchangeably. These big data components form a big data value chain built on top of statistics, machine learning, biology, and kernel methods. Statistics covers both linear and logistic regression. Decision trees are typical machine learning tools. Biology refers to artificial neural networks, genetic algorithms, and swarm intelligence. Finally, the kernel method includes the use of support vector machines.

Compared with traditional data sets, big data generally includes masses of unstructured data that need more real-time analysis. In addition, big data brings about new opportunities for discovering new values, helps us to gain an in-depth understanding of hidden values, and incurs new challenges, e.g., on how to effectively organize and manage such data. At present, big data has attracted considerable interest from industry, academia, and government agencies. Recently, the rapid growth of big data mainly comes from people's daily lives, especially that relate to Internet, web, and cloud services.

The rapid growth of cloud computing and IoT also triggers the sharp growth of data. Cloud computing provides safeguarding, access sites, and channels for data assets. In the paradigm of IoT, sensors all over the world are collecting and transmitting data to be stored and processed in the cloud. Such data in both quantity and mutual relations will far surpass the capacities of the IT architectures and infrastructure of existing enterprises, and its real-time requirement will greatly stress available computing capacity. The following example highlights some representative big data values driven by the massive data volume involved.

Big Data Discovery and Aggregation

The data generated far surpasses the capacities of IT architectures and infrastructures of existing enterprises, and the major data types include Internet data, sensory data, etc. This is the first step of big data. Given Internet data as an example, a huge amount of data in terms of searching entries, Internet forum posts, chatting records, and microblog messages are generated. Such Internet data may be valueless individually, but, through the exploitation of accumulated big data, useful information such as habits and hobbies of users can be identified, and it is even possible to forecast users' behaviors and emotional moods.

Moreover, generated through longitudinal and/or distributed data sources, data sets are more large-scale, highly diverse, and complex. Such data sources include sensors, videos, clickstreams, and/or all other available data sources. At present, some main sources of big data are the operation and trading information in enterprises, logistic and sensing information in the IoT, human interaction information and position information in the Internet world, and data generated in scientific research. Not only does the information surpass the capacities of IT infrastructures of existing enterprises, its real-time requirement also pushes existing computing capacity beyond its limit.

Loading is the most complex procedure among the three, which includes operations such as transformation, copy, clearing, standardization, screening, and data organization. A virtual database can be built to query and aggregate data from different data sources, but this database does not contain data. On the contrary, it includes information or metadata related to actual data and its positions. Such "storage-reading" approaches do not satisfy the high-performance requirements of data flows or search programs and applications. Compared with queries, data in these approaches is more dynamic and must be processed during data transmission.

Generally, data integration methods are accompanied with flow-processing engines and search engines.

- *Data selection:* Select a target data set or subset of data samples on which discovery is to be performed.

- *Data transformation:* Simplify the data sets by removing unwanted variables. Then, analyze useful features that can be used to represent the data, depending on the goal or task.

- *Data mining:* Search for patterns of interest in a particular representational form or a set of such representations as classification rules or trees, regression, clustering, and so forth.

- *Evaluation and knowledge representation:* Evaluate knowledge patterns, and utilize visualization techniques to present the knowledge vividly.

Big Data Storage, Cleaning, and Integration

This refers to the storage and management of large-scale data sets while achieving reliability and availability of data accessing. The explosive growth of data has placed more strict requirements on data storage and management. We consider the storage of big data as the third component of big data science. The storage infrastructure needs to provide information storage services with reliable storage space, and it must provide a powerful access interface for querying and analysis of a large amount of data.

Considerable research on big data promotes the development of storage mechanisms for big data. Existing storage mechanisms of big data may be classified into three bottom-up levels: (1) file systems, (2) databases, and (3) programming models. File systems are the foundation of the applications at upper levels. Google's GFS is an expandable distributed file system to support large-scale, distributed, data-intensive applications. GFS uses cheap commodity servers to achieve fault-tolerance and provides customers with high-performance services. Microsoft developed Cosmos to support its search and advertisement business. Facebook utilizes Haystack to store large amounts of small-sized photos.

It is necessary to cleanse and preprocess data by deciding on strategies to handle missing fields and alter the data as per the requirements. Data cleaning is a process to identify inaccurate, incomplete, or unreasonable data, and then modify or delete such data to improve data quality. Generally, data cleaning includes five complementary procedures: defining and determining error types, searching and identifying errors, correcting errors, documenting error examples and error types, and modifying data entry procedures to reduce future errors.

During cleaning, data formats, completeness, rationality, and restriction are inspected. Data cleaning is of vital importance to maintain data consistency, which is widely applied in many fields, such as banking, insurance, the retail industry, telecommunications, and traffic control. In e-commerce, most data is electronically collected, which may have serious data quality problems. Classic data quality problems mainly come from software defects, customized errors, or system misconfigurations. Some perform data cleaning in e-commerce using crawlers and regularly recopying customer and account information.

Data integration is the cornerstone of modern commercial informatics, which involves the combination of data from different sources and provides users with a uniform view of data. This is a mature research field for traditional databases. Historically, two methods have been widely recognized: data warehouse and data federation. Data warehousing includes a process named ETL (*extract, transform, and load*). Extraction involves connecting source systems and selecting, collecting, analyzing, and processing necessary data. Transformation is the execution of a series of rules to transform the extracted data into standard formats. Loading means importing extracted and transformed data into the target storage infrastructure.

2.3.2 Data Mining and Data Analytics

We classify data mining into three categories: association analysis, classification, and cluster analysis. We divide machine learning techniques intro three categories: (1) supervised learning such as regression model, decision tree, etc.; (2) unsupervised learning, which includes clustering, anomaly detection, etc.; and (3) other forms of learning, such as reinforcement learning, transfer learning, active learning, and deep learning (see Figure 2.10).

Data mining and machine learning are closely related. Data mining is the computational process of discovering patterns in large data sets involving methods at the intersection of AI, machine learning, statistics, and database systems. The overall goal of the data mining process is to extract information from a data set and transform it into an understandable structure for further use. Aside from the raw analysis step, it involves database and data management aspects, data preprocessing, model and inference considerations, interestingness metrics, complexity considerations, postprocessing of discovered structures, visualization, and online updating.

Machine learning explores the construction and study of algorithms that can learn from and make predictions on data. Such algorithms operate by building a model from example inputs in order to make data-driven predictions or decisions, rather than following strictly

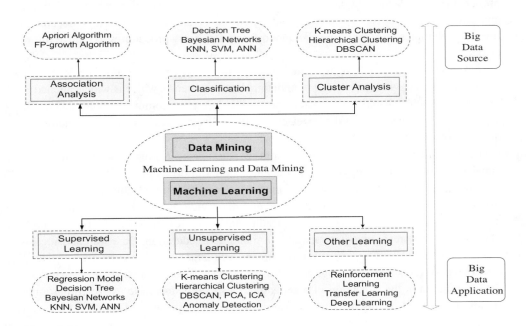

Figure 2.10

The interaction between data mining and machine learning operations. Reprinted with permission from K. Hwang and M. Chen, *Big Data Analytics for Cloud, IoT and Cognitive Learning*, Wiley, 2017.

static program instructions. These two terms are commonly confused, as they often employ the same methods and overlap significantly. Machine learning is closer to applications and the user end. It focuses on prediction, based on known properties learned from the training data.

Data mining is closer to the data source. It focuses on the discovery of unknown properties of the data, which is also considered as the analysis step of knowledge discovery in databases. As shown in Figure 2.10, the typical data mining techniques are classified into three categories: (1) association analysis including the Apriori and FP-growth algorithms; (2) classification, which includes decision trees, support vector machines (SVMs), the K-nearest neighbors (KNN) algorithm, naive Bayesian and Bayesian belief networks, and artificial neural networks (ANNs); and (3) clustering analysis, including K-means, hierarchical clustering, and density-based spatial clustering of applications with noise.

Supervised Machine Learning

Supervised means that the *machine learning* (ML) methods are trained with labeled sample data. This category includes the regression model, decision tree, SVM, Bayesian classifier, hidden Markov model, and deep learning, all to be addressed in Chapter 6.

Unsupervised Machine Learning

The category has no training samples to apply in prediction model development. This category includes dimension reduction, *principal component analysis* (PCA), clustering, etc. In Chapter 6, we will also study these unsupervised models.

Other Machine Learning Techniques

This category includes reinforcement learning and *Markov decision processes* (MDPs), which provide a mathematical framework for modeling decision making in situations, where the outcomes are partly random and partly under the control of a decision maker. Another class is the transfer leaning model. The purpose is to reduce time-consuming and labor-intensive processing costs. After some labeling and validation through transfer learning, the training sets are established.

2.3.3 Upgrading Data Analytics on Clouds

Big data sources must be protected in web server logs and Internet clickstream data, social media activity reports, mobile-phone call records, and information captured by sensors or IoT devices. Big data analytics can be done with the software tools commonly used as part of advanced analytics disciplines such as predictive analytics and data mining. Figure 2.11 shows the goals and requirements of today's cloud analytics compared with those of the basic analysis used for small amounts of data in the past.

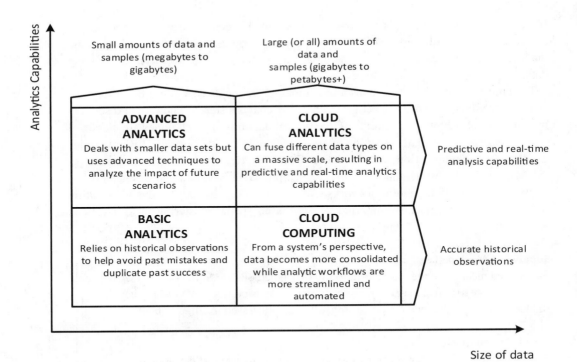

Figure 2.11
The evolution from basic analysis of small data (MB to GB) in the past to sophisticated cloud analytics over big data sets (TB ~ PB) by 2016 standard.

In the old days, we handled "small data" objects in terms of MB to GB. On the X-axis, we evolved from small data to "big data" that ranges from TB to PB based on the 2015 standard. On the Y-axis, we show the analytics capability in two ascending levels: accurate historical observations versus predictive and real-time analysis capabilities. The performance space is divided into four subspaces:

1. The *basic analysis* of small data relies on historical observations to help avoid past mistakes and duplicate the past success story.

2. The *advanced analytics* system on small data is improved from the basic capability by using advanced techniques to analyze the impact on future scenarios.

3. As we move to cloud computing, most existing clouds provide a better coordinated analytics workflow in streamlined and automated fashion, but still lack predictive or real-time capabilities.

4. For an ideal *cloud analytics* system, we expect to handle scalable big data in streaming mode with real-time predictive capabilities.

Table 2.10
Some big data analysis methods and practice tools.

	Traditional Methods	Big Data Methods and Tools
Data Analysis Methods	Clustering, factor, correlation, bucket testing, regression, statistics, data mining, etc.	Bloom filters, hashing, triel, indexing, MapReduce, Hadoop, Spark, Yarn, etc.
Commonly Used Analytics Tools	R, Excel, Rapid-i (RapidMiner), LNMINE, Impala, Spark, MLlib, GraphX, etc.	

Traditional data analysis means to use proper statistical methods to analyze massive first-hand and second-hand data to concentrate, extract, and refine useful data hidden in a batch of chaotic data, and to identify the inherent law of the subject matter, so as to develop functions of data to the greatest extent and maximize the value of data. Data analysis plays a huge guidance role in making development plans for a country, as well as understanding customer demands and predicting market trends by enterprises. Big data analysis can be deemed as the analysis of a special kind of data. Therefore, many traditional data analysis methods may still be utilized for big data analysis. Several representative traditional data analysis methods are examined in the following, many of which are from statistics and computer science.

The data analytic system often performs the following set of machine analysis and learning tasks in the cloud. Table 2.10 summarizes some big data analytics methods and tools commonly used. These data analysis operations are briefly introduced below. More coverage of these topics will be given in Parts III and IV. The raw data may be structured such as relational databases or semi-structured data in the forms of textual graphical, and image or video data, or even heterogeneous data distributed on the network. Methods of discovering knowledge may be mathematical or nonmathematical and deductive or inductive. Discovered knowledge may be used for information management, query optimization, decision support, and process control, as well as data maintenance.

Mining methods are generally divided into machine learning methods, neural network methods, and database methods. Machine learning may next be divided into inductive learning, example-based learning, genetic algorithms, etc. Neural network methods may be divided into feedforward neural networks, self-organizing neural networks, etc. Database methods mainly include multidimensional data analysis or *online analytical processing* (OLAP), as well as attribute-oriented inductive methods.

Various data mining algorithms have been developed, including AI, machine learning, mode identification, statistics, database community, etc. In 2006, the *IEEE International Conference on Data Mining* series identified the ten most influential data mining algorithms through a strict selection procedure, including C4.5, K-means, SVM, Apriori, EM, Naive Bayes, Cart, etc. These ten algorithms cover classification, clustering, regression, statistical learning, association analysis, and linking mining. In addition, other advanced algorithms such as neural networks and genetic algorithms can be applied to data mining in cognitive applications. Some prominent applications are gaming, business, science, engineering, and supervision, etc. Data mining is often referred to as *knowledge discovery in database* (KDD).

Example 2.6   System Context for Data Analytics Applications on Clouds

Figure 2.12 shows the workflow for performing big analytics operations in a modern cloud. The diagram illustrates the flow of data from possible sources like DBMS or a data warehouse to a data management stage involving preprocessing, filtering, aggregation, and other transformation operations. Then the cleaned data aggregation feeds into the analytical modeling stage. Finally, the selected model is analyzed at the last stage. There exist two feedback loops. The analyzed data is feedback at the lower loop to train the modeling process. The upper loop feeds back to the preprocessing stage in order to iterate the process for optimization purposes.

Data analytics will provide the necessary system support to any smart clouds in the future. The system contexts for data analytics applications on various cloud types are shown in Figure 2.12. These include (in the top row) data clouds, PaaS clouds like Azure, and analytics clouds with deep learning capabilities. The middle row of the

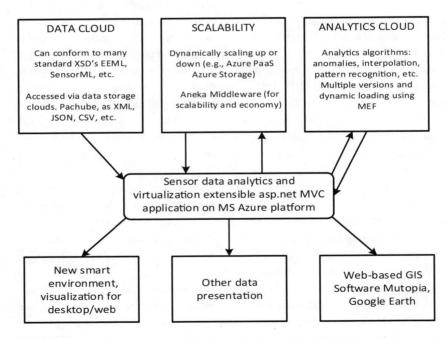

Figure 2.12
System contexts for data analytics applications on various cloud types. Courtesy of J. Gubbi et al., "Internet of Things (IoT): A Vision, Architectural Elements, and Future Directions." *Future Generation Computer System*s 29 (2013).

diagram corresponds to IoT sensing data with analytics and visualization support. Various kinds of applications are shown in the bottom boxes. Among them, Google Earth offers a user-friendly GIS for navigation and positioning applications. The message being conveyed here is that big data must grow in the years to come with intelligent use of clouds and IoT capabilities.

In the United States, the topological data analysis program supported by the Defense Advanced Research Project Agency (DARPA) seeks the fundamental structure of massive data sets. To use big data analytics, most users prefer direct-attached storage like *solid state drive* (SSD) and distributed disks in cloud clusters. The traditional *storage area network* (SAN) and network-attached storage (NAS) are too slow to meet big data analysis demands. Cloud designers must be concerned about system performance, commodity infrastructure, low cost, and real-time responses to inquiries.

The cloud access latency problem is also a major concern in the use of clouds. Another concern is the scalability problem as data sets grow dramatically. Shared storage has the advantage of being faster, but lacks scalability. Big data analytics practitioners prefer distributed storage in large clusters for its scalability and low cost. Big data for manufacturing demands an infrastructure for transparency. Predictive manufacturing demands near-zero downtime, availability, and productivity. ∎

2.3.4   Cloud Resources for Supporting Big Data Analytics

The cloud ecosystem is changing toward big data applications. Cloud computing, IoT sensing, database, and visualization technologies are indispensable for analyzing big data. These technologies play a fundamental role in cognitive services, business intelligence, machine learning, face recognition, natural language processing, etc. Multidimensional data arrays known as *tensors*, which were introduced with the TensorFlow library, will be studied in Chapter 9. Additional technologies crucial to big data management include data mining, distributed file systems, mobile networks, deep learning chips, and cloud-based infrastructure.

Big Data Cloud Platform Architecture

In general, we build a cloud for big data computing with a layered structure, as illustrated in Figure 2.13. At the bottom layer, we have the cloud *infrastructure management* control, which handles resources provisioning, deployment of agreed resources, monitoring the overall system performance, and arranging the workflow in the cloud. All big data elements collected from all sources form the *data lake*. Data can be structured or unstructured or come-and-go in streaming mode. This lake stores not only raw data but also the metadata for data management.

At the middle layer, we need to provide *views and indexes* to visualize and access data smoothly. This may include geographic data, language translation mechanisms, entity relationship, graphs analysis, streaming index, etc. At the next higher level, we have the *cloud processing*

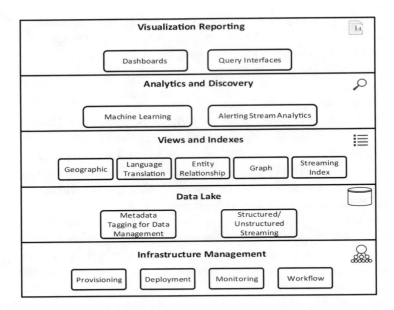

Figure 2.13
Layered development of cloud platform for big data processing and analytics applications.

engine, which includes data mining, discovery, and analytics mechanisms to perform machine learning, alerting, and data stream processing operations. At the top level, we have to report or display the analytics results. This includes *visualization* support for reporting with dashboards and query interfaces. The display may come as histograms, bar graphs, charts, video, etc.

Workflow in a Big Data Processing Engine

Figure 2.14 shows the conceptual workflow in a typical big data analytics cloud. The big data comes as data blocks or data streams from various sources from the top. The cloud platform resources are divided into four infrastructure parts: mainly used to store, retrieve, transform, and process the data flowing through the large cluster of servers forming the cloud core. The resources management and security units control the data flow on the left half. In the middle, the data flow control mechanisms manage and secure data movement through the cloud engine on the left. This engine performs various data transformation functions including collection, aggregation, matching, and mining operations, before feeding the extracted or sorted data to various applications at the bottom box.

Cloud Analytics Requirements

Listed below are critical issues that must be addressed to design smart clouds for big data applications. Figure 2.15 shows the architectural support needed to build up a cloud analytics system. The data infrastructure is needed to control the data flow through the cloud.

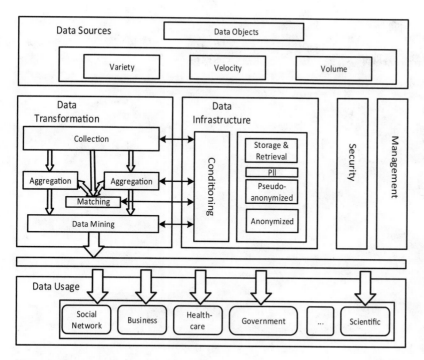

Figure 2.14
Conceptual architecture of a modern cloud system for big data computing applications.

The data transformation part forms the core of data mining and analytics processing. Management and security are needed to protect the cloud storage and processing engine and enforce the data privacy and access control policies.

- **Unstructured data:** Traditional relational databases cannot support unstructured data. Thus, we require NoSQL processing of incomplete data from noisy and dirty sources. These data are often short of veracity or not traceable. Many blogs or social exchanges cannot be easily verified, requiring data filtering and integrity control.

- **Social graphs, API, and visualization tools** are needed to handle unstructured social media data effectively. This demands cost-effective clouds and distributed file systems to aggregate, store, process, and analyze big data. Bottom-up techniques are needed to uncover unknown structures and patterns.

- **Data analytics software tools** are needed in a big data cloud. In subsequent chapters, we will address some open-source or commercial tools for big data analysis. These tools must be integrated to maximize their collaborative effect. Business intelligence must be upgraded to inductive statistics or support predictive analytics for critical decision making.

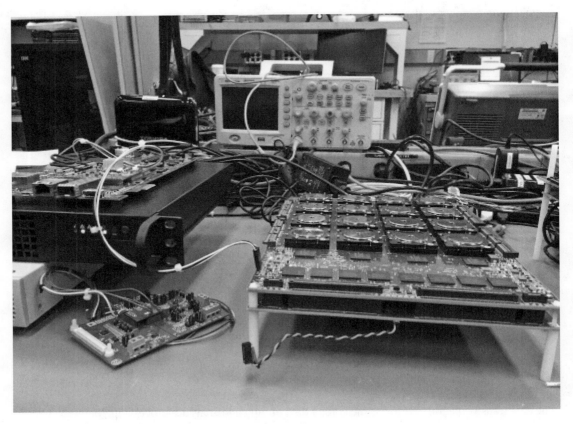

Figure 2.15
The prototype neurocomputing system built at IBM Almaden Research Center. Courtesy of D. Modha's Brain-Inspired Computing website: http://www.modha.org/.

- *Machine learning and cloud analytics algorithms* are greatly in demand for supervised or unsupervised machine or deep learning. These will be studied in Chapter 6. Data scientists must have sufficient domain knowledge, statistical data mining, social science, and programming skills; all demand experts from crossover domains to work cooperatively.

- *Data governance and security* demand data privacy, integrity control, SLA compliance, accountability, trust management, etc. Security control must be deployed on a global scale. Data privacy must be preserved down to a fine-grain access control level.

2.4 Neuromorphic Hardware and Cognitive Computing

Human cognition and intelligence are closely supportive of each other. It is similar to link machine intelligence to cognitive services in computing. In this section, we link machine intelligence to big data applications. Machine intelligence is attributed to smart clouds with applied IoT sensing and data analytics capabilities. We will assess some cognitive computing technologies and prototype systems built in recent years. We study the SyNAPSE program at the IBM Almaden Research Center, and the Google Brain team and DeepMind projects.

2.4.1 Cognitive Computing and Neuromorphic Processors

Cognitive science is interdisciplinary in nature. It covers the areas of psychology, AI, neuroscience, linguistics, etc. It spans many levels of analysis from low-level machine learning and decision mechanisms to high-level neuromorphic circuitry to build brain-like computers. The concept of cognitive science is related to the thinking that can be represented by its structures in the mind and operations performed on those structures.

Neuroinformatics attempts to combine informatics research and brain modeling to benefit both fields of science. Traditional computer-based informatics facilitates brain data processing and handling. Through hardware and software technologies, one can arrange databases, modeling, and communication in brain research. Or, conversely, enhanced discoveries in neuroscience may invoke the development of new models of brain-like computers. The term *cognitive computing* is derived from cognitive science and artificial intelligence.

For years, we have worked to build a computer that can compute as well as learn by training to achieve some human senses or intelligence. Such a brain-like computer is built with special hardware and/or software that can mimic basic human brain functions. Such a machine should be able to handle fuzziness and perform affective or cognition functions. It can handle some ambiguity and uncertainty beyond traditional computers. To this end, we require a cognitive machine that can model the human brain and senses to learn, reason, and respond to external stimulus, autonomously and tirelessly.

Cognitive computing hardware and applications could be more effective and influential by creating design choices that make a new class of problems computable. Such a system offers a synthesis not just of information sources but of influences, contexts, and insights. In other words, cognitive computing systems make some well-defined "context" computable. IBM researchers created neuromorphic systems that learn at scale, reason with purpose, and interact with humans naturally.

What Is Neuromorphic Computing?

Neuromorphic computing is a term that was first introduced by Carver Mead in the late 1980s. The idea was to apply *very-large-scale integration* (VLSI) analog circuits to mimic neurobiological architectures present in the human nervous system. Now the term has been extended to describe analog, digital, mixed-mode analog/digital VLSI, and software systems. These systems implement models of neural systems for possible use in perception, motor control, or multisensory integration applications. To achieve these goals, the first step is to understand the morphology interactions of individual neurons, circuits, systems, and target applications. This involves the application of machine learning or deep learning to design artificial neural systems, such as vision systems, head-eye systems, auditory processors, and autonomous robots.

In the traditional von Neumann architecture, the CPU executes instructions sequentially on data fetched from memory. In contrast, neuromorphic computing applies a connectionist model that computes over a very large number of neurons, each communicating with thousands of other neurons through synapses. Ongoing projects at various research centers explore this architecture and are developing programming environments that take advantage of neural computers. Over a period of 30 years, Mead has long recognized the extraordinary energy stinginess of biological computing. However, the industrial follow-up was still rather limited until the surge of interest in AI and cognitive services in recent years.

System Features of Cognitive Computing and Applications

A neuromorphic system redefines the relationship between humans and their pervasive digital environment. It may play the role of assistant or coach for the user, and it may act virtually autonomously in many situations. In general, three approaches are adopted in cognitive computing applications: (1) apply software library on computers or cloud of servers to perform machine learning operations; (2) use representation and algorithms to relate the inputs and outputs of artificial neural computers; and (3) use neuromorphic chips to implement brain-like computers for machine learning and intelligence. The computing results of a cognitive system could be suggestive, prescriptive, or instructive in nature. Some desired characteristics of a cognitive computing system are as follows:

- *Adaptive in learning:* It may learn as information changes and as goals and requirements evolve. It may resolve ambiguity and tolerate unpredictability. It may be engineered to feed on dynamic data in real time or near real time.

- *Interactive with users:* Users can define their needs as a trainer of the cognitive system. It may also interact with other processors, devices, and cloud services, as well as with people.

- *Iterative and stateful:* It may redefine a problem by asking questions or finding additional source input if a problem statement is ambiguous or incomplete. It may "remember" previous interactions iteratively.

- *Contextual in information discovery:* It may understand, identify, and extract contextual elements such as meaning, syntax, time, location, appropriate domain, regulations, user's profile, process, task, and goal. It may draw on multiple sources of information, including both structured and unstructured digital information, as well as sensory inputs such as visual, gestural, auditory, or sensor-provided.

Cognitive computing platforms have emerged and become commercially available, evidence that real-world applications are starting to surface. Organizations that adopt and use these cognitive computing platforms have purposed them to develop applications to address specific use cases with each application, utilizing some combination of available functionality. Examples of such real-world use cases include: (1) speech understanding; (2) sentiment analysis; (3) face recognition; (4) election insights; (5) autonomous driving; and (6) deep learning applications. Many more examples are available on cognitive computing platform provider blog websites, helping to demystify the possibilities of real-world applications.

Cognitive systems differ from current computing applications in that they move beyond tabulating and calculating based on preconfigured rules and programs. Although they are capable of basic computing, they can also infer and even reason based on broad objectives. In addition, cognitive computing systems can be extended to integrate or leverage existing information systems and add domain or task-specific interfaces and tools. Some current commercial applications partially exhibit some of the above features.

Neuromorphic Processors and Neural Processing Units

For decades, CPUs, GPUs, and DSPs appeared as traditional chips for general-purpose computing, graph, and signal processing applications. Now chip manufacturers are under pressure to upgrade their processors to meet the demands from deep learning and cognitive applications. In the past, most CPU and GPU chips leveraged the multicore or many-core microarchitectures, respectively. However, machine learning algorithms are implemented on these chips with a software approach, which may not be able to yield real-time responses efficiently on traditional CPUs and GPUs.

To amend the problem, many application-specific or neuromorphic processors are appearing gradually as *tensor processing units* (TPUs) or *neural processing units* (NPUs). These new chips are designed to accelerate the massive computations in training, learning, and applications of *artificial neural networks* (ANN) or *deep convolutional neural networks* (DCNN). We will cover ANN and DCNN in Chapter 7. Table 2.11 summarizes several neuromorphic or cognitive processors built by IBM, Nvidia, Google, Intel, Qualcomm, and the Chinese Academy of Sciences (CAS) in recent years.

2.4.2 SyNAPSE and Related Neurocomputer Projects at IBM

This section describes some new processor chips, non–von Neumann architecture, and ecosystem development for cognitive computing at IBM, Nvidia, Intel, and the Institute of Computing Technology at the Chinese Academy of Sciences. These projects are still at the research stage, but they represent the emerging technologies that combine computing with cognition to enhance human capacity and understanding of the environment surrounding us.

Table 2.11
Neuromorphic processors and neural processing units developed up to 2016

Processor and (Relevant Section)	Brief Technical Description and Current Status
Nvidia Tesla GPU P1000	Targeting stream processing, graph processing, and deep learning in AI applications on the supercomputer DGX-1 built by Nvidia for the OpenAI program. The GPU must work with CPU jointly.
Intel Xeon Phi Processor Knights Mill	Intel Knights Hill processor is based on 10 nm many-core technology. It extends from Xeon Phi processor to accelerate deep learning applications. Unlike GPU or TPU, the Intel design is a stand-alone processor, which need not attach to a CPU.
IBM TrueNorth Chip in SyNAPSE (Section 2.4.2)	Deep learning chip consisting of 1.6 million neurons with 4 billion synapses as presented in in Section 2.4.2. Prototype system built at IBM Almaden Research Center.
IBM Neurocomputer built at Zurich (Section 2.4.2)	Phase change neuron chip design with GST technology in nano scale. Prototype system was built with 500 GST neurons as shown in Figure 2.17.
Cambricon NPU (Section 2.4.3)	Cambricon is an NPU built by the Chinese Academy of Sciences with a special instruction set designed for processing deep neural networks.
Google TPU in TensorFlow (Sections 2.4.4, 9.3)	TPU (Example 2.9) is an accelerator module, specifically designed to upgrade CPU/GPU performance in AlphaGo competition (Section 9.3). TensorFlow computations in Chapter 9.
Cadence Tensilica Vision P5 and Synopsys EV DSP	Both processors are upgraded on top of their existing DSP chips. Transforming traditional SIMD DSP chip to neural network processing, not a true NPU.
Qualcomm Zeroth NPU (Section 2.4.1)	An AI-accelerator platform for deep learning on mobile devices such as the Snapdragon 820 processor. Targeted for image/sound processing, speech/face/gesture recognition, and battery life extension. Software operates locally on mobile devices rather than on a cloud.

SyNAPSE Program at IBM Almaden Research Center

IBM has a SyNAPSE research program devoted to the development of new hardware and software for cognitive computing. This project has been supported by DARPA in the United States. In 2014, IBM unveiled a neurosynaptic computer chip design in *Science Magazine*, known as the TrueNorth processor (Figure 2.15). This processor can mimic the human brain's computing abilities and power efficiency. The chip design could enable wide-ranging applications, such as assisting visually impaired people to navigate safely through their environment.

This chip could cram supercomputer-like powers into a microprocessor the size of a post-age stamp. Rather than solving problems through brute-force mathematical calculations, the chip was designed to understand its environment, handle ambiguity, and take action in real time and in context. It is estimated that an average human brain has 100 billion neurons and 100 trillion to 150 trillion synapses. Modeled after the human brain, the TrueNorth chip incorporates 5.4 billion transistors, the most IBM has ever put on a chip. The chip features 1 million programmable neurons and 256 million programmable synapses.

This synaptic chip could be applied to power small rescue robots, automatically distinguish between voices in a meeting, and create accurate transcripts for each speaker.

Other potential uses include tsunami alerts, oil-spill monitoring, or enforcement of shipping lane rules. What is amazing is that the chip consumes only 70 mW of power to perform the above functions, about the same level consumed by a hearing aid. The chip is still in the prototype stage. It was announced at a conference that IBM may spend $3 billion to push for the future of such computer chips and explore their cognitive service potentials. It does not require the heavy computational load needed for complex operations as in biological cognitive systems. For example, if a robot run with today's microprocessors was walking toward a pillar, it would depend on image processing and huge computing resources and power to avoid a collision. By comparison, a robot using a synaptic chip would steer clear of the danger by sensing the pillar, much as a person would do, with little power consumption.

Experts believe an innovation like SyNAPSE's TrueNorth could help overcome the performance limits of the von Neumann architecture, the mathematics-based system at the core of almost every computer built since 1948. IBM expects the chip to help transform science, technology, business, government, and society by enabling vision, audition, and multisensory applications. This could be the first step in designing future computers based on the human brain model.

Neuromorphic Hardware Design at IBM Zurich Research Center

Another neuron-like computer is under development at IBM Zurich Research Center. In 2016, they announced the construction of the world's first artificial neuron with nanotechnology that allows stochastic phase changes. This makes the system programmable in computing or learning operations. The team built a prototype neurocomputer system with an array of 500 such man-made neurons. The neural array simulates human brain functions in signal-processing applications.

Such a phase-change neuron is built with GST nanotechnology. GST stands for *germanium-antimony-tellurium*, which can change its phase in nano-time. The cell design is extremely small in size and thus has the potential to switch states much faster and consume very little energy compared with a conventional computer built with silicon chips. The stochastic feature of the IBM design implies that the phase-change neuron may produce slightly different signals with the same input signals at different times. This is similar in operational characteristics of biological neurons in human brains. Figure 2.16 shows the concept of the IBM neuromorphic processor array design.

The neuron soma at the top is built with a neuronal membrane that receives the summed input from the dendrites and generates spike events as output to other neurons through axon terminals. The input end is formed with plastic synapses that receive input spike trains as well as back propagation spike events. These synapses generate postsynaptic potential signals as output to the neuron soma. The neuronal membrane is the nucleus of the neuron. At the bottom of Figure 2.16, the biological neuron and artificial neuron are compared

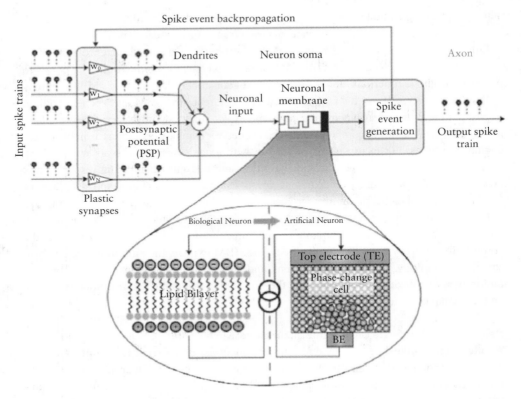

Figure 2.16
Comparison between biological neuron and neuromorphic hardware design. Courtesy of IBM Zurich Research Center, 2016.

graphically. The biological neuron is built with neuronal membrane in lipid bilayer. The artificial neuron is built with phase-change cells connected to top and bottom electrodes as shown in the lower right box.

In either case, the neuronal membrane or the phase-change cells act like resistance and capacitance that control neural signal current flow-through and absorb energy at the same time. When energy is absorbed to a sufficient level, it generates its own signal to excite nearby neurons. This process is repeated constantly. In the IBM neuron design, the phase-exchange cells are made of composite pieces of GST material. This GST cell performs the stochastic phase-change operations. Through extremely low laser or current energy, the cell can change between two binary phases: *crystal* state versus *inactive* state. The crystal state conducts current and the inactive state impedes current and thus generates no excitation signals.

Due to so many noises in the human body that affect the neurons, biological neurons acts stochastically. IBM researchers produced similar stochastic behavior in the man-made neuron. Thus, no one can predict the signals generated in each cycle. The importance is that the artificial neuron cells are made from mature GST material, are small in size (reported as 90 nm), consume very low energy, and have a long usage life in billions of times without failure. This is considered a milestone breakthrough in recent years of work on building artificial brains.

When a very large number of the neuron cells are used concurrently, the system has the potential to compete with the human brain in decision making or performing cognitive functions. According to IBM researchers, they are building an array of 10×10 cells as building blocks. With five blocks, they can construct a larger array of 500 neurons. The work is continuing to simulate human brain functions. This prototype may be programmable as the human brain is. With N artificial neurons, the system may have 2^N bit information, if N is sufficiently large. One single GST chip may host tens of thousands of artificial neurons. This hints that the future of cognitive computing is getting closer to reality.

2.4.3 Cambricon NPU at the Chinese Academy of Sciences

This project started as a joint research program between Dr. Tianshi Chen of the Institute of Computing Technology (ICT) at the Chinese Academy of Sciences and Professor Oliver Tenam of French INRIA. The joint research team developed a series of hardware accelerators, known as Cambricon, for neural network and deep learning applications. The chip was built as a synaptic processor to power artificial neural computing in machine learning operations. Cambricon stays away from the classic von Neumann architecture in order to match with the special kind of operations performed in artificial neural network computations.

Machine learning tasks are becoming pervasive in a broad range of systems from embedded systems to data centers. For example, deep learning algorithms using convolutional and deep neural networks (CNNs and DNNs to be treated in Chapter 7), take a long learning cycle to be trained to be useful on a conventional computer. The Cambricon accelerator was designed to focus on large-scale CNNs and DNNs solutions. The joint ICT-INRIA team proved that it is possible to build accelerators with high throughput capable of performing 452 GOP/s (key neural network operations in synaptic weight multiplications).

The chip was fabricated on a small footprint of 3.02 mm^2 and 485 mW silicon technology. The team has also worked out a new instruction set architecture (ISA) for efficient use of such a brain-like processor. This new ISA is specially tailored for neural networks or cognitive computing. Comparing with a 128-bit 2 GHz SIMD GPU accelerator, the accelerator chip achieved a speedup of 117 times faster with 21 times reduction in power consumption. With an extended 64-chip machine-learning architecture, the team has shown a speedup of 450 times over an array of GPU chips with a power reduction of 150 times.

Through multinational efforts, human-oriented cognitive computing is coming closer to a reality. It is interesting to watch the development of special-purpose neuron-based synaptic processors in multicore or many-core multiprocessor chips and the use of massive numbers of such chips to build future cognitive supercomputers. We will study machine learning and deep learning algorithms in Chapters 6 and 7. These ML/DL algorithms could be applied in the design of future cognitive computing systems.

2.4.4 Google's TPU and Related AI Programs

In research and industry, speech recognition is always in great demand. It would be nice to have an intelligent recording machine that can listen to human speech and produce documented textual reports. Similarly, the United Nations needs to have automatic language translation systems, not only translation between text documents but also between speech and documented reports in different languages. In this section, we introduce Google's AI program briefly. More details will follow in Chapter 9 when we study TensorFlow programming tools.

Example 2.7 Google's Brain Team Developing New AI Products

Google's Brain project started in 2011 as a joint effort between Jeff Dean, Greg Corrado, and Andrew Ng. They built a large-scale, deep-learning software system called *DistBelief* on top of Google's cloud computing infrastructure. In 2012, the *New York Times* reported that a cluster of 16,000 computers used to mimic some aspects of human brain activity had successfully trained itself to recognize a cat based on 10 million digital images from YouTube videos. Figure 2.17 lists some active cognition projects installed by various Google Brain teams.

In 2013, Geoffrey Hinton, a leading researcher in the deep learning field, joined Google. Subsequently, Google acquired DeepMind Technologies and released TensorFlow. Notable Google products developed out of the Brain team, including the Android speech recognition system, Google photo search, and video recommendations in YouTube. The team also worked on developing mobile and embedded machine intelligence applications, starting with Android and then moving on to iOS services. In addition, the Brain team worked with Google X and the Quantum Artificial Intelligence Lab at NASA in joint space.

In May 2016, Google announced a custom *application-specific integrated circuit* (ASIC) chip they built specifically for machine learning tailored for TensorFlow programming. They installed the TPUs inside their data centers for more than a year, and have found them to deliver an order of magnitude performance gain per watt in machine learning operations.

The TPU is a pretrained chip to support TensorFlow computing with a high volume of low-precision (e.g., 8-bit) arithmetic. The TPU is indeed programmable as the TensorFlow program changes. The TPU is likely fabricated at the two largest chip foundry companies: Taiwan Semiconductor Manufacturing and GlobalFoundries. TensorFlow

The Promise (or Wishful Dream) of Deep Learning

Figure 2.17
The promise of deep learning at Google's Brain Project. Courtesy of slide presentation by Jeff Dean, Google Brain Team, 2016.

offers a software platform for deep learning applications that will be covered in Chapter 9. The TPU accelerates TensorFlow computations. Android support of TensorFlow is available for mobile execution. Intel has also optimized their high-end server processor for neural computing. ∎

Google's DeepMind AI Programs

In 2010, a British artificial intelligence company started DeepMind Technologies, which received the 2010 "Company of the Year" award by Cambridge Computer laboratory in the United Kingdom. Subsequently, in 2014 DeepMind was acquired by Google at a cost of $500 million. This project applies convolutional deep networks that learn to play video games in a fashion that mimics the short-term memory of the human brain. Multiple TPUs were used in AlphaGo match. Go is a very complex game for both human players and computers due to the huge search space involved.

In 1997, IBM's computer Deep Blue beat world chess champion Garry Kasparov in an open match. Ever since then, the strongest AI program to play Go only reached approximately amateur 5-dan level, which still could not beat a professional Go player without handicaps. For example, the software program Zen, running on a four-PC cluster, beat Masaki Takemiya (9p) two times at five- and four-stone handicap. The program Crazy Stone beat Yoshio Ishida (9p) at four-stone handicap.

The Go game is played with black and white stones on a 19×19 mesh board. The game has a search tree complexity equal to b^d, where b is the game's breadth (number of the illegal moves at each state) and d is the depth (number of moves before the game is over). This means that brute force search is impossible for computers to evaluate who is winning. In the past, no computers had ever beaten human Go players until March 2016. In fact, Go is much more complex than any other game such as chess. This is attributed to the much larger number of possibilities on the Go game board. The complexity involves deep steps that even professional players cannot keep tracking beyond certain steps with possible rewards accurately evaluated.

The AlphaGo research project was formed around 2014 to test how well a neural network using deep learning could win over Go professional players. It represents a significant improvement over previous Go programs. AlphaGo running on multiple computers won 500 games played against other Go programs. The distributed system used in an October 2015 match used 1,202 CPUs and 176 GPUs. In January 2016, the team published a paper in the journal *Nature* that describes the algorithms used in AlphaGo. In March 2016, this computer program beat Lee Sedol, a 9-dan Go player, 4 to 1 in a five-game match.

AlphaGo was not specifically trained to face Lee and it won the game out of entirely machine intelligence without handicap. Although it lost to Lee Sedol in the fourth game, Lee resigned in the final game. In recognition of beating Lee Sedol, AlphaGo was awarded an honorary 9-dan by the Korea Baduk Association. The Google DeepMind program is aimed to solve very difficult intelligence problems that leverage machine learning and neuroscience systems.

The AlphaGo and Lee match proves that computers can be trained to formalize the human intelligence process. In addition to the Go match, seven Atari video games (Pong, Breakout, Space Invaders, Seaquest, Beamrider, Enduro, and Q*bert) were also tested using similar computer programs. All of these games involve strategic thinking out of imperfect or uncertainty information contents. DeepMind claims that their AI program is not preprogrammed. Each move is limited to 2 s. The program learns from experience using only raw pixels as data input. Technically, the program uses deep learning on a convolutional neural network.

The DeepMind team proposed a novel scheme Q-learning based on reinforcement learning. The Google DeepMind team has developed a reinforcement learning system named Gorila. This system was implemented on large clusters of servers at Google. With 64 search threads, a distributed cluster of 1,930 CPUs and 280 GPUs was used in the AlphaGo and Lee competition. Parallel acting generates new interactions with distributed replay memory to save iterations. Parallel learning computes gradients from replayed iterations. The distributed CNN updates the network with gradients. Google also has other AI-related programs in its X Lab such as self-driving cars, merchandise delivery drones, and smart machines, all of which will be covered in Chapter 7.

2.5 Conclusions

This chapter introduced the basic definitions and key concepts of big data science and cognitive computing. The purpose is to prepare our readers to study the in-depth material of the subject matter found in subsequent chapters. Smart clouds were sketched for IoT sensing support and hardware/software of a big data analytics system. In-depth coverage of virtualization techniques, various cloud architectures, security, and performance issues will follow in Chapters 3 to 5 in Part II. Chapters 6 and 7 cover machine learning and deep learning algorithms. Cloud programming systems are covered in Chapters 8 and 9 to train readers to use the clouds with hands-on experience.

We emphasized the interactions or fusion of various technologies for big data processing. Social media networking and mobile access of cloud services will be treated in Chapter 5 on mobile cloud computing. The cloud architectural support given in Section 2.3.3 will be expanded in subsequent chapters for deep data analytics applications. We introduced the fundamentals of data mining, machine learning, data analytics, and cognitive computing in Sections 2.3 and 2.4. In Parts III and IV of this book, these topics will be studied in much deeper coverage. This chapter introduced only a few industrial initiatives on designing brain-inspired computers or clouds for AI-related applications including the projects at IBM, Google, and the Chinese Academy of Sciences.

Homework Problems

2.1: This homework requires you to do some research. Write an updated assessment report of the SMACT technologies. Discuss the strengths and weaknesses and pros/cons of each technology. You need to dig out a few relevant technical reports or white papers from relevant industries, especially from major industrial players like Facebook, AT&T, Google, Amazon, IBM, etc. Reading some published papers in leading *ACM/IEEE* magazines or conferences would be useful for you to make insightful assessments with concrete evidence.

2.2: Briefly explain the problems (challenges) associated with four "V's" of big data characteristics: (1) volume, (2) velocity, (3) variety, and (4) veracity. Discuss the resource demands and associated processing requirements and limitations to meet the challenges.

2.3: In data science, what is the intersection of application domain expertise and the field of mathematics or statistics? Also, explain the intersection of programming skills and the required mathematics or statistics background.

2.4: Figure 2.2 shows the Gartner Hype Cycle up to July 2016. Check the Internet to find a more recent release of the Hype Cycle and discuss it with technology assessment and potential acceptance by the industry.

2.5: Consider the following two cloud/IoT service applications, dig out more examples from open literature about smart cities in Example 1.5 and healthcare cloud services in Example 1.6. You need to report your findings on how machine leaning and big data analytics can help out in their success stories.

2.6: Explain why big data can be more cost-effectively handled by clouds than using a super-computer. Why do big data scientists require domain expertise? Also, explain the difference between supervised and unsupervised machine learning techniques.

2.7: Table 2.3 identified a number of software tools provided by companies or research centers. Consider the following three software packages: the MATLAB library for computing algorithms, the Apache Mahout for scalable machine learning, and the OpenNLP for natural language processing. Consult their websites or other online sources about their functionalities and their usage requirements for big data computing.

2.8: Design a healthcare system which consists of body sensors and wearable devices to collect human physiological signals. This system should possess the following functions: real-time monitoring, disease prediction, and early detection of chronic diseases. Also design a monitoring and management system that can optimize the distribution of medical resources and facilitate the data sharing for such resources.

2.9: Design a video analytics system for security checks through video surveillance. Such a system demands real-time response and accurate verification. With increasing use of high-definition cameras, your system should be able to transmit video surveillance data and track theft or criminals in real time. Describe how to use artificial intelligence and machine learning technology to analyze massive video files and automatically locate the suspects in a moving path based on target features.

2.10: Based on the introduction of the IBM GST-based neuron chip design for building brain-like computers in the future, visit the IBM Zurich Research Center website or contact the design team members about the technical details of the project. Write a technical report about your findings.

2.11: Repeat Problem 2.10 on the SyNAPSEs program conducted at the IBM Almaden Center. Their project has released more technical information recently. Your technical report should be easier to write.

2.12: Based on the introduction of the Google Brain team work in Example 2.7 or the Deep-Mind programs introduced in Section 2.4.4, write a technical report about your follow-up research findings. More details of the Google AI programs can be found in Section 7.1 of Chapter 7.

2.13: Having studied the material on IoT sensing and applications in Section 2.2, you are asked to make an assessment of the road map of IoT development in Figure 2.5. Discuss two milestone IoT achievements reported in the literature. To narrow the scope of your assessment, focus on specific commercial products or academic reports on experimental IoT systems. Report only technical progress in hardware, software, and networking (do not include sales pitches).

2.14: Based on the introduction of China's Cambricon project in Section 2.4.3, study three published papers on Cambricon from the IEEE ISCA, Micro, and ASPOS conferences. Write a survey report to assess their progress on building brain-like computers, compared with the use of traditional x86 CPU or GPU for the same purpose in machine learning or deep learning applications.

2.15: Visit the iCloud website (https://www.icloud.com) or check on Wikipedia to find out the functionality and application services provided by Apple iCloud. In particular, answer the following questions.

(1) Briefly, specify the main services provided by iCloud. How many users reported up until now?

(2) What are the data types or information items that are handled by iCloud?

(3) Explain the procedure to find an old friend using the Find My Friend service on the iCloud?

(4) Explain the iCloud features of Find My iPhone to locate your lost or stolen iPhone.

References

[1] Baesens, B. *Analytics in a Big Data World: The Essential Guide to Data Science and Its Applications.* Wiley, 2015.

[2] Chaouchi, H. *The Internet of Things.* Wiley, 2010.

[3] Chen, M. *Big Data Related Technologies.* Springer Computer Science Series. Springer, 2014.

[4] Ellis, B. *Real-Time Analytics: Techniques to Analyze and Visualize Streaming Data.* Wiley, 2014.

[5] Farnham, S. *The Facebook Association Ecosystem.* O'Reilly Radar Report, 2008.

[6] Gardner, D., and G. M. Shepherd. "A Gateway to the Future of Neuroinformatics." *Neuroinformatics* 2 no. 3 (2004): 271–274.

[7] Gubbi, J., R. Buyya, S. Marusic, and M. Palaniswarni. "Internet of Things (IoT): A Vision, Architectural Elements, and Future Directions." *Future Generation Computer Systems* 29 (2013): 1645–1660.

[8] Han, J., M. Kamber, and J. Pei. *Data Mining: Concepts and Techniques*, 3rd ed. Morgan Kaufmann, 2012.

[9] Hansmann, U., et al. *Pervasive Computing: The Mobile World*, 2nd ed. Springer, 2003.

[10] Hilber, M., and P. Lopez. "The World's Technological Capacity to Store, Communicate and Compute Information." *Science*, 332 no. 6025 (2011).

[11] Hough, A. "Nate Silver: Politics 'Geek' Hailed for Barack Obama Wins US Election Forecast." *The Telegraph* (London), November 7, 2012.

[12] Hwang, K., and M. Chen. *Big Data Analytics for Cloud, IoT and Cognitive Learning.* Wiley, 2017.

[13] Hwang, K., G. Fox, and J. Dongarra. *Distributed and Cloud Computing.* Morgan Kaufmann, 2012.

[14] Hype Cycle, http://www.gartner.com/newsroom/id/2819918, August 2014.

[15] Karau, H., et al. *Learning Spark: Lightning Fast Data Analysis.* O'Reilly, 2015.

[16] Kelley, J., III. "Computing, Cognition and the Future of Knowing." http://www.research.ibm.com/software/IBMResearch/multipmedia/Computing_Cognition_WhitePaper, October 2015.

[17] Liu, R. H. *Introduction to Internet of Things.* Science Press, 2011.

[18] Miller, G. A. "The Cognitive Revolution: A Historical Perspective." *Trends in Cognitive Sciences* 7 (2003): 141–144.

[19] Naur, P. *Concise Survey of Computer Methods.* Student Litteratur, 1975.

[20] Silver, D., A. Huang, C. Maddison, A. Guez, L. Sifre, G. Driessche, J. Schrittwieser, I. Antonoglou, and V. Panneershelvam. "Mastering the Game of Go with Deep Neural Networks and Tree Search." *Nature* 529 no. 7587 (2016): 484–489.

[21] Weiser, M. "The Computer for the 21st Century." *Scientific American* (1991).

[22] Zanella, A., N. Bui, A. Castellani, L. Vangelista, and M. Zorzi. "Internet of Things for Smart Cities." *IEEE Internet of Things Journal* 1 no. 1 (2014).

[23] Zaslavsky, A., C. Perera, and D. Georgakopoulos. "Sensing as a Service and Big Data." Proc. Int. Conf. Advanced. Cloud Computing (ACC), Bangalore, India, July 2012, pp. 21–29.

PART II

CLOUD ARCHITECTURE AND SERVICE PLATFORM DESIGN

Part II contains three chapters covering cloud architecture, virtual machines, Docker containers, mobile clouds, IoT, social media, and mashup services. Case studies include the Amazon AWS, Google Cloud, Microsoft Azure, IBM SmartCloud, Salesforce clouds, SGI Cyclone, Apple iCloud, NASA Nebula, and CERN Cloud. Chapter 3 lays the foundation of virtualization for converting data centers into clouds. Chapter 4 deals with cloud architecture and service platforms. Finally, Chapter 5 relates cloud services to mobile networks, IoT, social media processing, and multi-cloud mashup services. Thirty-seven cloud systems and services are presented as illustrative examples in this part.

Chapter 3: Virtual Machines, Docker Containers, and Server Clusters

Summary: This chapter presents virtualization of computer hardware by software means. First, we present various abstraction levels to create virtual machines (VM). We learn how to convert data centers into clouds through dynamic deployment of virtual clusters. We study both VM and Docker container architectures and their management issues to match with the workload demands. Finally, we study VM migration techniques to recover from failures. We also cover virtualization supports in cloud software systems: Eucalyptus, OpenStack, and vSphere.

Chapter 4: Cloud Architectures and Service Platform Designs

Summary: This chapter is devoted to cloud systems architecture, design principles, and infrastructure management. We review the multitenant market-oriented cloud architecture and its design objectives. Major cloud service models (IaaS, PaaS, and SaaS) are characterized, along with services provided and business uses. The goal of service platform design is to satisfy a large number of cloud users simultaneously. Practical cloud systems and their platform management issues are presented with 18 illustrative cloud examples and case studies.

Chapter 5: Mobile, IoT, Social Media and Mashup Clouds

Summary: The *Internet of things* (IoT) is made possible by rapid progress in wireless and sensor technologies, smartphones and mobile devices, and networks. We study cloud-centric IoT architecture and wireless access of clouds known as *mobile clouds*. We examine the interactions among IoT sensing, artificial intelligence, and mobile clouds. Cloudlets for wireless access of remote clouds are introduced. Social media clouds in mashup services are presented. We emphasize cloud mashups for agility and scalability in real-life cloud and cognitive applications.

Chapter 3

Virtual Machines, Docker Containers, and Server Clusters

3.1 Virtualization in Cloud Computing Systems

The reincarnation of VMs presents a great opportunity for parallel, cluster, grid, cloud, and distributed computing. Virtualization technology primarily benefits the computer and IT industry as it allows for the sharing of expensive hardware resources by multiplexing VM on the same set of hardware hosts.

3.1.1 Basic Concept of Machine Virtualization

The conventional computer has a simple architecture, as seen in Figure 3.1(a), where the operating system (OS) manages all hardware resources at the privileged system space and all applications run at the user space under the control of the OS. After virtualization, different user applications managed by their own operating systems (*guest OS*) can run on the same hardware, independent of the *host OS*. This is often done by adding additional software, known as a *virtualization layer*. In Figure 3.1(b), the VMs are shown in the upper boxes, where applications run with their own guest OS over the virtualized CPU, memory, and I/O resources.

A VM is essentially built as a software package that can be loaded into a host computer to execute certain user applications. Once the jobs are done, the VM package can be removed from the host computer. The host acts like a "hotel" to accommodate different "guests" at different timeframes. In this sense, VMs offer a high degree of resources shared within a computer. Multiple VMs could co-exist in the same host, as long as the host has enough memory to handle the guest VMs. Two guest VMs are being hosted by the computer shown in Figure 3.1(b). Note that the two VMs could run with different guest OS. The virtual resources allocated to each VM are known as virtual processors, virtual memory, virtual disks, or virtual I/O devices.

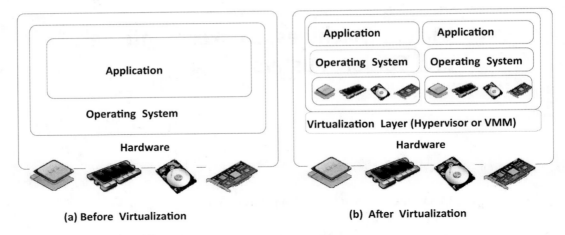

(a) Before Virtualization

(b) After Virtualization

Figure 3.1
The architecture of a computer system before and after virtualization.

Virtualization Operations

The virtual machine monitor (VMM) provides the VM abstraction to the guest OS. With full virtualization, the VMM exports a VM abstraction identical to the physical machine (PM) so that a standard OS, such as Windows 2000 or Linux, can run just as it would on the physical hardware. Mendel Rosenblum [16] classified basic VMM operations into four categories, as illustrated in Figure 3.2:

1. The VMs can be *multiplexed* between hardware machines, as shown in Figure 3.2(a).

2. A VM can be *suspended* and *stored* in a stable storage, as shown in Figure 3.2(b).

3. A suspended VM can be *resumed* or *provisioned* to a new hardware platform in Figure 3.2(c).

4. A VM can be *migrated* from one hardware platform to another, as shown in Figure 3.2(d).

These primitive VM operations enable a VM to cater to any available hardware platform. They make it flexible to carry out distributed application executions. Furthermore, the VM approach significantly enhances the utilization of server resources. Multiple server functions can be consolidated on the same hardware platform to achieve higher system efficiency, thereby eliminating server sprawl via deployment of systems such as VMs. These VMs move transparency to the shared hardware. VMware, a leading virtualization software provider, has claimed that the server utilization could increase from a low rate of 5–15% to 60–80% after virtualization.

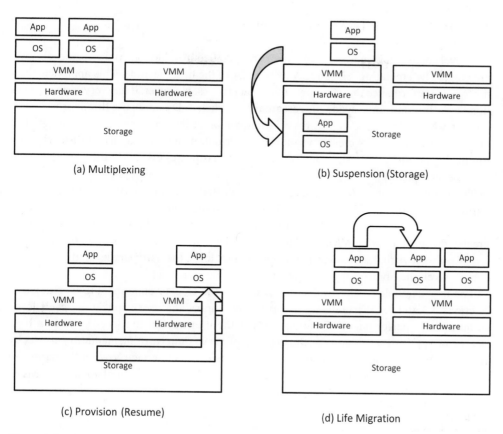

Figure 3.2
VM multiplexing, suspension, provision, and migration in a distributed computing environment. Courtesy of Mendel Rosenblum, "The Reincarnation of Virtual Machines," *ACM QUEUE,* July/August 2004.

Virtual Infrastructures

Physical resources for computing, storage, and networking at the bottom are mapped to the needy applications embedded in various VMs at the top. Hardware and software are then separated. Virtual infrastructure is what connects resources to distributed applications. It is a dynamic mapping of the system resources to specific applications. The result is decreased costs and increased efficiencies and responsiveness, of which virtualization for server consolidation and containment is a good example.

3.1.2 Implementation Levels of Virtualization

Five levels of abstraction for virtualization are specified in Table 3.1. At the ISA level, VMs are created by emulating a given ISA by the ISA of the host machine. This approach gives the lowest performance due the slow emulation process. However, it has very high application flexibility, and some academic research VMs, such as Dynamo, use this approach. The highest VM performance comes from virtualization at the bare-metal or OS levels. The famous hypervisor XEN creates virtual CPU, virtual, memory, and virtual disks right on top of the bare-metal physical devices. However, hardware-level virtualization results in the most complexity.

The main function of the software layer for virtualization is to virtualize the physical hardware of a host machine into virtual resources to be used by VMs. This can be implemented at various operational levels to be introduced below. The virtualization software creates the abstraction of VMs by interposing a layer at various levels of a computer system. Common virtualization layers include the ISA level, the hardware level, the operating system level, the library support level, and the application level.

The best example of OS-level virtualization is the Docker containers to be studied in Sections 3.3 and 3.4. Virtualization at run-time library and user application levels leads to an average performance. Creating VMs at the user application level leads to a high degree of application isolation at the expense of very complex implementation efforts by the users. In this book, we will consider using hypervisors to create VMs at the hardware level and the use of Docker containers at the Linux kernel level. Implementing VMs at

Table 3.1
Relative merits of virtualization at five abstraction levels

Level of Virtualization	Functional Description	Example Packages	Merits, App Flexibility/ Isolation, Implementation Complexity
Instruction Set Architecture	Emulation of a guest ISA by host	Dynamo, Bird, Bochs, Crusoe	Low performance, high app flexibility, median complexity and isolation
Hardware-Level Virtualization	Virtualization on top of bare-metal hardware	XEN, VMWare, Virtual PC	High performance and complexity, median app flexibility, and good app isolation
Operating System Level	Isolated containers of user app with isolated resources	Docker Engine, Jail, FVM	Highest performance, low app flexibility and best isolation, and average complexity
Run-Time Library Level	Creating VM via run-time library through API hooks	Wine, vCUDA, WABI, LxRun	Average performance, low app flexibility and isolation, and low complexity
User Application Level	Deploy HLL VMs at user app level	JVM, .NET CLR, Panot	Low performance and app flexibility, very high complexity and app isolation

the ISA, user, or run-time library levels is most often done in academia, but rarely practiced in industry due to their low performance and the fact that they are very difficult to implement.

Instruction Set Architecture Level

As previously mentioned, at the ISA level virtualization is done by emulating a given ISA by the ISA of the host machine. For example, MIPS binary code can run on an x86-based host machine with the help of ISA emulation. With this approach, it is possible to run a large amount of legacy binary codes written for various processors on any given new hardware host machine. Instruction set emulation leads to virtual ISA created on any hardware machine.

The basic emulation method is through *code interpretation*. An interpreter program interprets the source instructions to target instructions one by one. One source instruction may require tens or hundreds of native target instructions to perform its function. Obviously, this process is relatively slow. For better performance, *dynamic binary translation* is desired. This approach translates dynamic basic blocks of source instructions to target instructions. The basic blocks can be further extended to program traces or super blocks to increase translation efficiency. Instruction set emulation requires binary translation and optimization. A *virtual instruction set architecture* (V-ISA) thus requires adding a processor-specific software translation layer in the compiler.

A conventional computer has a single OS image. This offers a rigid architecture that tightly couples application software to a specific hardware platform. Some software running well on one hardware machine may not be executable on another platform with a different instruction set under a fixed OS management. VMs offer novel solutions to boost underutilized resources, application inflexibility, software manageability, and security concerns in existing PMs. The concept of VMs is illustrated in Figure 3.4. Today, to build large clusters, grids, and clouds, we need to access large amounts of computing, storage, and networking resources in a virtualized manner. We need to aggregate those resources and offer a single system image. In particular, a cloud of provisioned resources must rely on virtualization of processors, memory, and I/O facilities, dynamically.

Most virtualization uses a software or firmware approach to generate the VMs. However, one can also use a hardware-assisted approach to help virtualization. Intel has produced VT-x for this purpose. The purpose is to improve the efficiency of its processors in the VM environment. This requires modifying the CPU to provide hardware support for virtualization. Other types of virtualization also appear in desktop virtualization, memory and storage virtualization, and various levels of virtualization, as introduced in Table 3.2. One can even consider data and network virtualization. For example, the *virtual private network* (VPN) allows a virtual network to be created over the Internet. Virtualization enables the concept of cloud computing. The major difference between traditional grid computing and today's clouds lies in the use of virtualized resources.

Table 3.2
Relative merits of virtualization at various levels

Level of Implementation	Higher Performance	Application Flexibility	Implementation Complexity	Application Isolation
Instruction Set Architecture (ISA)	X	XXXXX	XXX	XXX
Hardware-Level Virtualization	XXXXX	XXX	XXXXX	XXXX
Operating System Level	XXXXX	XX	XXX	XX
Run-Time Library Support	XXX	XX	XX	XX
User Application Level	XX	XX	XXXXX	XXXXX

Hardware Abstraction Level

Hardware-level virtualization is performed right on top of the hardware. On the one hand, this approach generates virtual hardware environments for VMs. On the other hand, the process manages the underlying hardware through virtualization. The idea is to virtualize a computer's resources like processors, memory, and I/O devices with the intention to upgrade the hardware utilization rate by multiple users concurrently. This idea was implemented in the IBM VM/370 in the 1960s. More recently, the XEN attempted to virtualize x86-based machines to run Linux or other guest OS applications.

Operating System Level

The OS level refers to an abstraction layer between traditional OS and user applications. OS-level virtualization creates isolated containers on a single physical server and the OS instances to utilize the hardware and software in data centers. The containers behave like real servers. The OS-level virtualization is commonly used in creating virtual hosting environments to allocate hardware resources among a large number of mutually distrusting users. It is also used, to a lesser extent, in consolidating server hardware by moving services on separate hosts into containers or VMs on one server.

Library Support Level

Most applications use *application programming interfaces* (APIs) exported by user-level libraries rather than using lengthy system calls by the OS. Since most systems provide well-documented APIs, such an interface becomes another candidate for virtualization. Virtualization with library interfaces is possible by controlling the communication link between applications and the rest of a system through API hooks. The software tool Wine has implemented this approach to support Windows applications on top of UNIX hosts. Another example is the vCUDA, which allows applications executing within VMs to leverage GPU hardware acceleration.

User Application Level

Virtualization at the application level virtualizes an application as a VM. On a traditional OS, an application often runs as a process. Therefore, *application-level virtualization* is also known as *process-level virtualization*. The most popular approach is to deploy *high-level language* (HLL) VMs. The virtualization layer sits as an application program on top of an OS. The layer exports an abstraction of a VM that can run programs written and compiled to a particular abstract machine definition. Any program written in the HLL and compiled for this VM will be able to run on it. The Microsoft .NET CLR (*common language runtime*) and JVM (Java VM) are two good examples of this class of VMs.

Another form of application-level virtualization is known as application isolation, application sandboxing, or application streaming. The process involves wrapping the application in a layer that isolates it from the host OS and therefore other applications. The result is an application that is much easier to distribute and remove from user workstations. A typical example is LANDesk, which is an application virtualization platform. It enables the deployment of software applications as self-contained, executable files in an isolated environment without requiring installation, system modifications, or elevated security privileges.

Relative Merits of Different VM Approaches

In Table 3.2, the relative merits of implementing virtualization at various levels are compared. The column headings correspond to four technical merits. Higher performance and application flexibility are self-explanatory. The implementation complexity implies a higher cost of implementation. The application isolation refers to the effort to isolate resources committed to different VMs. Each row corresponds to a particular level of virtualization.

The number of "X's" in the table entries reflects the advantage points of each implementation level. Five "X's" are the best case and one "X" has the lowest rating. Overall, hardware and OS support will yield the highest performance. However, the hardware and application levels are also the most expensive to implement. User isolation is the most difficult to achieve, while ISA implementation offers the best application flexibility.

3.1.3 Resources Virtualization in Cluster or Cloud Systems

Traditional data centers are built with large-scale clusters of servers. Those big clusters are used not only for storing large databases but also for building fast search engines. Ever since the introduction of virtualization, more and more data center clusters are being converted into clouds. Google, Amazon, and Microsoft are all building their cloud platforms this way.

In this section, we cover the resource virtualization techniques. Both hypervisors and Docker engines are introduced. Virtualization can be done at the software process level, the host system level, or at various extended levels. Table 3.3 summarizes five resource

Table 3.3
Resources virtualization and representative software products

Virtualization	Brief Description	Representative Products
Servers	Multiple VMs installed in servers to enhance the utilization rate of shred servers	XenServer, PowerVM, Hyper-V, VMware EXS Server, etc.
Desktops	Upgrade applications flexibility on PCs and workstations	VMware Workstation, *VMware ACE,* XenDesktop, Virtual PC, etc.
Networks	Virtual private networks (VPNs), virtual local area networks, virtual clusters in clouds	Intranet virtualization, OpenStack, Eucalyptus, etc.
Storage	Network storage and NAS virtualization for shared cluster or cloud applications	Dropbox, Apple iCloud, AWS S3, MS One Drive, IBM Datastore, etc.
Application	Software process-level virtualization, such as containers	Docker containers, XenApp, MS CRM, various Salesforce SaaS clouds, etc.

virtualization levels. Among these, server virtualization is indispensable in converting a data center to an operating cloud in order to serve a large number of users simultaneously. Some representative products are also listed in the table.

The main purpose of server virtualization is to upgrade the cluster elasticity and enhance the utilization of shared servers. Desktop virtualization attempts to provide application flexibility by individual users, so that applications able to be run on different OS platforms can be executed on the same hardware host. Virtual storage and virtual networking make clouds more even more powerful on colocation operations. Application virtualization refers to software process-level virtualization. Application software libraries for processing big data are summarized at the end of Table 3.3.

The concept of computer virtualization started in the 1960s. It is a technique to abstract the machine resources logically at different architectural levels. Virtual memory is a typical example of expanding the physical memory beyond its physical capacity by allowing page swapping between physical disks and virtual address space. In this section, we introduce the key concepts of hardware virtualization and other types of virtualization. It is fair to observe that no elastic clouds can be built to satisfy multitenancy operations without resource virtualization.

Hardware Virtualization

This refers to the use of special software to create a VM on a host hardware machine. The VM acts like a real computer with a guest OS. The host machine is the actual machine where the VM is executed. The VM and host machine may run with different OSs. The software that creates VM on the host hardware is called a *hypervisor* or VMM. Three types of hardware virtualization are specified below:

- *Full virtualization:* This refers to a complete simulation or translation of the host hardware to some sort of virtual CPU, virtual memory, or virtual disks for use by the VM using its own unmodified OS.

- *Partial virtualization:* This refers to the fact that some selected resources are virtualized and some are not. Therefore, some guest programs must be modified to run in such an environment.

- *Paravirtualization:* In this case, the hardware environment of the VM is not virtualized. The guest applications are executed in an isolated domain or are sometimes called *software containers.* The guest OS is no longer used. Instead, a VMM is installed at the user space to guide the execution of user programs.

3.2 Hypervisors for Creating Native Virtual Machines

Traditional computers are PMs. Each physical host runs with its own OS. In contrast, a VM is a software-defined abstract machine created by the virtualization process. A physical computer running an OS X executes application programs only specially tailored to the X platform. Other programs written for a different OS Y may not be executable on the X-platform. In using a VM, the guest OS could differ from the host OS. For example, the X-platform is an Apple OS and the Y-platform could be a Windows-based computer. VMs offer a solution to bypass the software portability barrier.

3.2.1 Virtual Machine Architecture Types

The host machine is equipped with the physical hardware (as shown at the bottom of Figure 3.3), for example a desktop with x-86 architecture running its installed Windows OS. The VM can be provisioned to any hardware system. The VM is built with virtual resources managed by a guest OS to run a specific application. Between the VMs and the host platform, one needs to deploy a middleware layer known as VMM. A native VM is installed with the use of a VMM at the privileged mode.

The guest OS could be a Linux system and the hypervisor the XEN system developed at Cambridge University. This hypervisor approach is also called bare-metal VM, because the hypervisor handles the bare hardware (CPU, memory, and I/O) directly. Another architecture is the hosted VM shown in Figure 3.3(b). Here, the VMM runs with a nonprivileged mode. The host OS does not need to be modified. The VM can be also implemented with a dual mode. Part of VMM runs at the user level and another portion runs at the hypervisor level. In this mixed mode, the host OS may have to be modified to some extent. Multiple VMs can be ported to one given hardware system in order to support the virtualization process. The VM approach offers hardware independence of the OS and applications. The user application running on its dedicated OS could be bundled together as a *virtual*

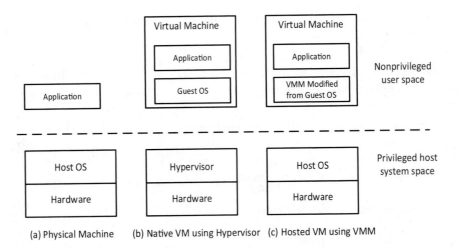

Figure 3.3
Two VM architectures compared with conventional physical machines.

appliance that is ported on any hardware platform. The VM could run on a different OS from that of the host computer.

The conventional computer has a simple architecture shown in Figure 3.3(a), where the OS manages all hardware resources at the privileged system space and all applications run at the user space under the control of the OS. On a *native VM,* the VM consists of the user application control by a guest OS. This VM is created by the *hypervisor* installed at the privileged system space. This hypervisor sits right on top of the bare metal, as shown in Figure 3.3(b). Here, multiple VMs can be ported to one physical computer. The VM approach extends the software portability beyond the platform boundaries. Bare-metal hypervisors run directly on the machine hardware.

Another VM architecture, known as *hosted VM* created by a VMM or a hosted hypervisor implemented on top of the host OS, is shown in Figure 3.3(c). The VMM is a middleware between the host OS and the user application. It replaces the guest OS used in a native VM. Thus, the VMM abstracts the guest OS from the host OS. VMware Workstation, VM player, and VirtualBox are examples of hosted VMs known as *paravirtualization.* In this case, the host OS is left unchanged and the VMM monitors the execution of the user application directly. Unless otherwise specified, we will consider only the native VMs produced by the bare-metal hypervisors.

Hypervisor supports a hardware-level virtualization (Figure 3.4). The hypervisor software sits directly between the physical hardware and its OS. This virtualization layer is called either a VM monitor or hypervisor. The hypervisor provides hypercalls for the guest OSs and applications. Depending on the functionality, a hypervisor can assume micro-kernel

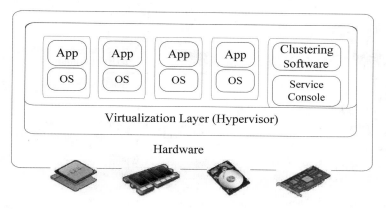

Figure 3.4

A hypervisor is the software layer for virtualization on the bare-metal hardware. This layer converts physical devices into virtual resources to execute user applications.

architecture like the Microsoft Hyper-V or monolithic hypervisor architecture like the VMware ESX for server virtualization.

A micro-kernel hypervisor includes only the basic and unchanging functions (such as physical memory management and processor scheduling). The device drivers and other changeable components are outside of the hypervisor. On the contrary, a monolithic hypervisor implements all of the above functions including device drivers. Therefore, the size of hypervisor code of a micro-kernel hypervisor is smaller than that of a monolithic hypervisor.

Generally speaking, VMware VMM packages (players or VirtualBox) are not responsible for allocation resources for all user programs. They are used to allocate only restricted resources to selected applications. The VMM controls resources explicitly allocated to these selected special applications. In other words, the VMM is tied to selected processor resources. Not all processors meet the VMM requirements. Specific limitations include the inability to trap some privileged instructions.

Hypervisors or VMMs are summarized in Table 3.4. The XEN is the most popular one used in almost all x86-based PCs, servers, or workstations. Hypervisor-created VMs are often heavily weighted because they consist of the user application code (which could be only KB) plus a guest OS which may demand GB of memory. The guest OS supervises the execution of the user applications on the VM. The KVM is a Linux kernel-based VM. The Microsoft Hyper-V is used for Windows server virtualization. In other words, KVM is mostly used in Linux hosts while Hyper-V must be used in Windows hosts. This hypervisor involves OS integration at the lowest level. Malware and rootkits could post potential threats to hypervisor security so researchers from Microsoft and academia have developed some anti-rootkit HookSafe software to protect hypervisors from malware and rootkit attacks.

Table 3.4
Hypervisors or VM monitors for generating VMs

Hypervisor	Host CPU	Host OS	Guest OS	Architecture, Applications, and User Community
XEN	x86, x86–64, IA-64	NetBSD, Linux	Linux, Windows, BSD, Solaris	Native hypervisor (Example 3.1) developed at Cambridge University
KVM	x86, x86–64, IA-64, S-390, PowerPC	Linux	Linux, Windows, FreeBSD, Solaris	Hosted hypervisor based on paravirtualization at the user space
Hyper V	x86 based	Server 2003	Windows servers	Windows-based native hypervisor, marketed by Microsoft
VMWare Workstation, VirtualBox	x86, x86–64	Any host OS	Windows, Linux, Darwin Solaris, OS/2, FreeBSD	Hosted hypervisor with a paravirtualization architecture

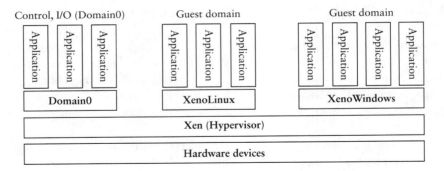

Figure 3.5
The XEN Architecture: Domain0 for resources control and I/O and several guest domains (VMs) are created for executing user applications.

Example 3.1   The Xen Hypervisor Architecture and Resources Control

The Xen is an open-source, micro-kernel hypervisor developed at Cambridge University. The Xen hypervisor implements all mechanisms, leaving the policy to be handled by a Domain0, as shown in Figure 3.5. The Xen does not include any device drivers natively. The core components of a Xen system are the hypervisor, kernel, and applications. The guest OS, which has the control ability, is called Domain0 and the others are called DomainU. Domain0 is a privileged guest OS of Xen. It is initially loaded when Xen boots without any file system drivers.

The Domain0 is designed to access hardware directly and manage devices. Therefore, one function of Domain0 is to allocate and map hardware resources to the guest domains (DomainUs). For example, the Xen is based on Linux and its security level is higher. Its management VM is named Domain0, which has the privilege of managing other VMs implemented on the same host. If the Domain0 is compromised, the hacker can control the entire system. Special security policy is applied to secure Domain0. The Domain0, behaving like a hypervisor, allows users to create, copy, save, read, modify, share, migrate, and rollback VMs as easily as manipulating a file. ∎

3.2.2   Full Virtualization and Hosted Virtualization

Depending on implementation technologies, hardware virtualization can be classified into two categories: *full virtualization* and *host-based virtualization*. Full virtualization does not need to modify the host OS. It relies on *binary translation* to trap and virtualize the execution of certain sensitive, nonvirtualizable instructions. The guest OSs and their applications consist of noncritical and critical instructions. In a host-based system, both a host OS and a guest OS are used. A virtualization software layer is built between the host OS and guest OS. These two classes of VM architecture are introduced below.

Full Virtualization

With full virtualization (Figure 3.6), noncritical instructions run on the hardware directly while critical instructions are discovered and replaced with traps into the VMM to be emulated by software. Both the hypervisor and VMM approaches are considered full virtualization. Why

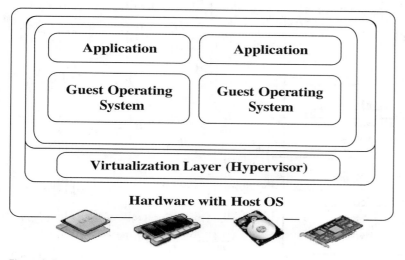

Figure 3.6
The concept of full virtualization using a hypervisor sitting on top of the bare-metal hardware in the host machine.

are only critical instructions trapped in the VMM? This is because binary translation can incur a large performance overhead. Noncritical instructions do not control hardware and threaten the security of the system but critical instructions do. Therefore, running noncritical instructions on hardware cannot only promote efficiency but also ensure system security.

Binary Translation of Guest OS Requests Using a VMM

This approach was implemented by VMware and many other software companies. As shown in Figure 3.7, VMware puts the VMM at Ring 0 and the guest OS at Ring 1. The VMM scans the instruction stream and identifies the privileged, control, and behavior-sensitive instructions. When these instructions are identified, they are trapped in the VMM. The VMM emulates the behavior of these instructions. The method used in emulation is called *binary translation*. Therefore, full virtualization combines binary translation and direct execution. The guest OS is completely decoupled from the underlying hardware. Consequently, the guest OS is not modified.

The performance of full virtualization may not be ideal because it involves binary translation, which is rather time consuming. In particular, the full virtualization of I/O-intensive applications is a big challenge. Binary translation employs code cache to store translated hot instructions to improve the performance, but it increases the cost of memory usage. Currently, the performance of full virtualization on x86 architecture is typically 80–97% that of the host machine.

The user can install this VM architecture without modifying the host OS. The virtualizing software can rely on the host OS to provide device drivers and other low-level

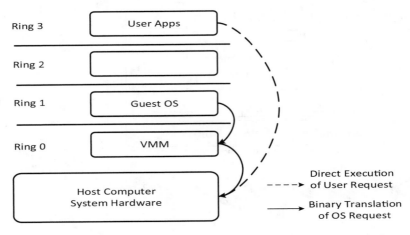

Figure 3.7
Indirect execution of complex instructions via binary translation of guest OS requests using the VMM layer along with direct execution of simple user instructions on host machine. (Ring 2 function is not used here.)

services. This will ease the VM design and its deployment. Second, the host-based approach appeals to many host machine configurations. Compared to the hypervisor/VMM architecture, the performance of host-based architecture may be also low. When an application requests hardware access, it involves four layers of mapping which downgrade the performance significantly. When the ISA of a guest OS is different from the ISA of the underlying hardware, binary translation must be adapted. Although the host-based architecture has flexibility, the performance is too low to be useful in practice.

Host-Based Virtualization

An alternative VM architecture is to install a virtualization layer on top of the host OS. This host OS is still responsible for managing the hardware, but the guest OSs are installed and run on top of the virtualization layer. Dedicated applications may run on the VMs, and certainly some other applications can also run with the host OS directly, as shown by the left box in Figure 3.8. This host-based architecture has some distinct advantages as discussed below.

3.2.3 Paravirtualization with Guest OS Modification

Paravirtualization needs to modify the guest operating systems. A paravirtualized VM provides special APIs requiring substantial OS modifications in user applications. The performance degradation is a critical issue of a virtualized system. No one prefers to use a VM if it is much slower than using a PM. The virtualization layer can be inserted at different

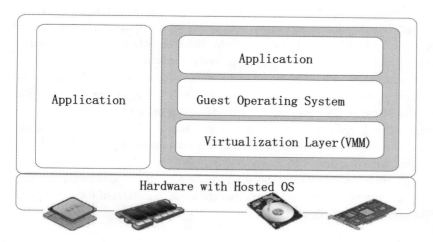

Figure 3.8
A hosted VM installed with a VMM (virtualization layer) at the user space linking the guest OS with the host OS. This differs from the full virtualization architecture shown in Figure 3.6.

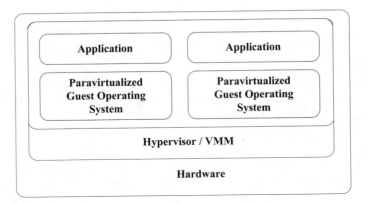

Figure 3.9
Paravirtualization involves modifying the guest OS kernel to replace nonvirtualizable instructions with hypercalls for the hypervisor or the VMM to carry out the virtualization process (see Figure 3.12 for more details).

positions in a machine software stack. However, paravirtualization attempts to reduce the virtualization overhead and thus improve the performance by modifying only the guest OS kernel. The concept of paravirtualized VM architecture is illustrated in Figure 3.9.

Paravirtualization Architecture
When the x86 processor is virtualized, a virtualization layer is inserted between the hardware and the OS. By the x86 ring definition, the virtualization layer should also be installed at ring 0. Different instructions at the same ring 0 may cause some problems. In Figure 3.10, we show that paravirtualization replaces nonvirtualizable instructions with hypercalls that communicate directly with the hypervisor or VMM. However, when the guest OS kernel is modified for virtualization, it can no longer run on the hardware directly.

Although paravirtualization reduces the overhead, it incurs other problems. First, its compatibility and portability may be in doubt, because it must support the unmodified OS as well. Second, the cost of maintaining paravirtualized OSs is high, because it may require deep OS kernel modifications. Finally, the performance advantage of paravirtualization varies greatly due to workload variations. Compared to full virtualization, paravirtualization is relatively easy and more practical. The main problem in full virtualization is its low performance by binary translation. Speeding up binary translation is difficult to achieve, therefore, many virtualization products employ the paravirtualization architecture, of which the popular Xen, KVM, and VMware ESX are good examples.

Kernel-Based Virtual Machine
Kernel-based virtual machine (KVM) is a Linux paravirtualization system—a part of the Linux version 2.6.20 kernel. Memory management and scheduling activities are carried out by the existing Linux kernel. The KVM does the rest, which makes it simpler than

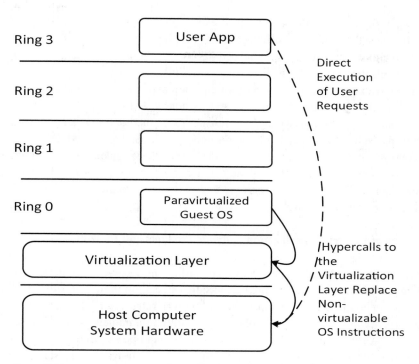

Ring 3

Ring 2

Ring 1

Ring 0

Figure 3.10
The use of a paravirtualized guest OS assisted by an intelligent compiler to replace non-virtualizable OS instructions by hypercalls. (Rings 1 and 2 are not used here).

hypervisor, which controls the entire machine. KVM is a hardware-assisted paravirtualization tool, which improves performance and supports unmodified guest OSs like Windows, Linux, Solaris, and other UNIX.

Paravirtualization with Compiler Support
Unlike the full virtualization architecture, which intercepts and emulates privileged and sensitive instructions at runtime, paravirtualization handles these instructions at compile time. The guest OS kernel is modified to replace privileged and sensitive instructions with hypercalls to the hypervisor or VMM. The Xen assumes such a paravirtualization architecture. The guest OS running in a guest domain may run at ring 1 instead of at ring 0. This implies that the guest OS may not be able to execute some privileged and sensitive instructions.

The privileged instructions are implemented by hypercalls to the hypervisor. After replacing the instructions with hypercalls, the modified guest OS emulates the behavior of the original guest OS. On an UNIX system, a system call involves an interrupt or service routine. The hypercalls apply a dedicated service routine in Xen. As shown in Figure 3.10, the traditional x86 processor offers four instruction execution rings: ring 0, 1, 2, and 3. The lower the ring number, the higher the privilege of instruction being executed. The OS is responsible for managing the hardware and the privileged instructions to execute at ring 0, while user level applications run at ring 3.

The VMM layer virtualizes the physical hardware resources such as CPU, memory, network and disk controllers, and human interface devices. Every VM has its own set of virtual hardware resources. The resource manager allocates CPU, memory disk, and network bandwidth and maps them to the virtual hardware resource set of each VM created. Hardware interface components are device drivers and the VMware ESX Server File System. The service console is responsible for booting the system, initiating the execution of the VMM layer and resource manager, and relinquishing control to those layers. It also provides some functions to facilitate the system administrators.

3.2.4 Comparison of Platform Virtualization Software Products and Toolkits

VMware offers the world's largest selection of virtualization software products, toolkits, and systems. Here we review their products as announced on their website (http://vmware.com/products/vsphere/), with information that was retrieved on July 20, 2016. Table 3.5 lists all VMware software for hardware virtualization, namely the hypervisor products. Some software is supplied from a third party or via open sources. Four software categories are given. "Native" refers to a hypervisor in the traditional sense for bare-metal virtualization. The "hosted" category refers to paravirtualization, which is further subdivided into "specialized" tools vs. "independent" tools. The last group refers to "other tools" with a similar purpose. Additional details can be found from the VMware website provided.

Table 3.5
Summary of hardware virtualization (hypervisors) and hosted software for virtualization

Category	VMware Software Products or Third-Party Software
Native (Hypervisor)	Adeos, CP/CMS, Hyper-V, KVM (Red Hat Enterprise Virtualization), LDoms/Oracle VM Server for SPARC, LynxSecure, SIMMON, VMware ESXi (VMware vSphere, vCloud), VMware Infrastructure, Xen (XenClient), z/VM
Hosted (Specialized)	Basilisk II, bhyve, Bochs, Cooperative Linux, DOSBox, DOSEMU, Linux, Mac-on-Linux, Mac-on-Mac, SheepShaver, SIMH, Windows on Windows, Virtual DOS machine, Win4Lin
Hosted (Independent)	Microsoft Virtual Server, Parallels Workstation, Parallels Desktop for Mac, Parallels Server for Mac, PearPC, QEMU, VirtualBox, Virtual Iron, VMware Fusion, VMware Player, VMware Server, VMware Workstation, Windows Virtual PC
Other Tools	Ganeti, oVirt, VM Manager

Source: http://vmware.com/products/vsphere/, retrieved July 20, 2016.

Table 3.6
Summary of software toolkit for virtualization at OS-level, desktop, application, and network levels

Virtualization Levels	VMware Products or Tool Names from Third Party
OS-Level Virtualization (Containers)	cgroups-based: CoreOS, lmctfy, Linux-V Server, LXC, Docker, OpenVZ, Parallels Virtuozzo, FreeBSD Jail, iCore Virtual Accounts, Kubernetes, Linux namespaces, Solaris Containers, Workload Partitions
Desktop Virtualization	Citrix XenApp, Citrix XenDesktop, Remote Desktop Services, VMware Horizon View
Application Virtualization	Ceedo, Citrix XenApp, Dalvik, InstallFree, Microsoft App-V, Remote Desktop Services, Spoon Symantec Workspace Virtualization, VMware ThinApp, ZeroVM
Network Virtualization	Distributed Overlay Virtual Ethernet (DOVE), NVGRE, Open vSwitch, Virtual security switch, Virtual Extensible LAN (VXLAN)

Source: http://vmware.com/products/vsphere/.

Table 3.6 lists the software toolkits for virtualization at the OS-level, desktop, application, and network levels. The Docker containers are considered as OS-level tools. Again, interested readers are referred to VMware's website for details. Specialization refers to native VM machine at specific guest OS levels such as the cooperative Linux, DOSBox, Mac-on-Linux, etc. The independent hosted VMs refer to hypervisors or VMMs built with guest OS that are independent of the host OS.

The virtualization at the OS level must involve system calls or modification of the host OS. Quite a few of them are related to the *cgroups* in Linux OS including the Docker containers, Google Kubernetes, Solaris containers, etc. The desktop virtualization applies to desktop computers like the Microsoft App-V for Windows PC or servers, etc. The application level virtualization is entirely done at the user application level. Finally, the network virtualization is used to establish virtual networks like Distributed Overlay Virtual Ethernet (DOVE), Virtual Extensible LAN, etc. We will study some of the hypervisors like XEN, KVM, Hyper-V, and many VMware software packages in subsequent sections.

Example 3.2   VMware ESX Server for Paravirtualization

VMware pioneered the software market for virtualization. The company has developed virtualization tools from desktops and servers to virtual infrastructure for large data centers. The ESX is VMM or a hypervisor for bare-metal x-86 SMP servers. It accesses hardware resources such as I/O directly and has complete resource management control. An ESX-enabled server consists of four components: virtualization layer, resource manager, hardware interface components, and service console as shown in Figure 3.11. To improve the performance, the ESX server employs the paravirtualization architecture by which the VM kernel interacts directly with the hardware without involving the host OS. ■

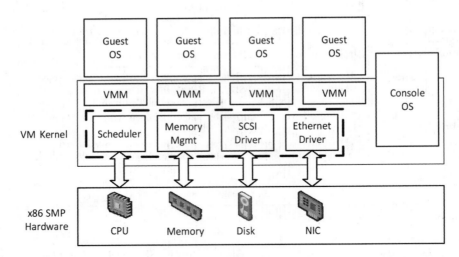

Figure 3.11
The VMware ESX server architecture using paravirtualization. Courtesy of VMware, 2011, http://www.vmware
.com/products.

3.3   Docker Engine and Application Containers

Docker provides an OS-level virtualization on host machines running Linux, Mac OS, and
Windows. In this section, we introduce the Docker engine and Docker containers. Then
we compare the implementation differences and discuss the relative strength and weakness
between the bare-metal hypervisor-created VMs and Docker containers. Most data centers
are built with low-cost x86 servers in a large scale. It is easy to see the growing interest of
cloud builders and providers to switch to Docker containers for scalable user applications.
However, the VMs are still useful in different types of applications. They may coexist for
an extended period of time.

3.3.1   Virtualization at Linux Kernel Level

With the help of VM technology, a new computing mode named cloud computing is emerging. Cloud computing is transforming the computing landscape by shifting the hardware
and staffing costs of managing a computational center to third parties, just like banks. However, there are at least two challenges of cloud computing. The first is the ability to use a
variable number of PMs and VM instances depending on the needs of a problem. For example, a task may need only a single CPU during some phases of execution but may need
hundreds of CPUs at other times. The second one is the slow operation of initializing new
VMs. Currently, the new VMs originate either as fresh boots or replicates of a template

VM, unaware of the current application state. Therefore, to better support cloud computing, a large amount of research and development should be done.

Why OS Level of Virtualization?

As mentioned above, it is slow to initialize a hardware-level VM because each VM creates its own image from scratch. In a cloud computing environment, perhaps thousands of VMs need to be initialized simultaneously. Besides the slow operation, the storage of the VM images also becomes an issue. As a matter of fact, there is considerable repeated content among the VM images. Moreover, full virtualization at the hardware level also has disadvantages of low performance and low density, and paravirtualization needs to modify guest OS. To reduce the performance overhead of hardware-level virtualization, hardware modification is needed. Operating system-level virtualization provides a feasible solution for the above issues of hardware-level virtualization.

Operating system virtualization inserts a virtualization layer inside an operating system to partition the physical resources of a machine. It enables multiple isolated VMs within a single operating system kernel. These kinds of VMs are often called *virtual execution environments* (VEs), *virtual private servers* (VPSs), or simply containers. From the point of view of their users, VEs look like real servers. This means a VE has its own set of processes, file systems, user accounts, network interfaces with IP addresses, routing tables, firewall rules, and other personal settings. Although the VEs can be customized for different people, they share the same operating system kernel. Therefore, operating system-level virtualization is also called *single OS image virtualization*. Figure 3.3 illustrates the operating system virtualization from the point of view of a machine stack.

Benefits of OS Extensions

The benefits of OS-level virtualization versus hardware-level virtualization are twofold: (1) VMs at the operating system level have minimal startup/shutdown costs, low resource requirements, and high scalability; and (2) for an operating system level VM, it is possible for a VM and its host environment to synchronize state changes when necessary. These benefits can be achieved by two mechanisms of OS-level virtualization: (1) all OS-level VMs on the same PM share a single operating system kernel; and (2) the virtualization layer can be designed in a way that allows processes in VMs to access as many resources of the host machine as possible, but never to modify them. In cloud computing, the first and second benefits can be used to overcome the defects of slow initialization of VMs at the hardware level and awareness of the current application state, respectively.

Disadvantages of OS Extensions

The main disadvantage of OS extensions is that all VMs at the operating system level on a single container must have the same kind of guest operating systems. Although different OS-level VMs may have different operating system distributions, they must pertain to the

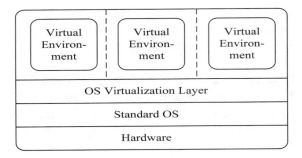

Figure 3.12
The virtualization layer is inserted inside an OS to partition the hardware resources for multiple VMs to run their applications in virtual environments.

same operating system family. For example, a Windows distribution such as Windows XP cannot run on a Linux-based container. However, users of cloud computing are various. Some prefer Windows and others prefer Linux or other operating systems. Therefore, there is a challenge for operating system-level virtualization in such cases. The concept of OS-level virtualization is illustrated in Figure 3.12.

The virtualization layer is inserted inside the OS to partition the hardware resources for multiple VMs to run their applications in multiple virtual environments. To implement OS-level virtualization, isolated execution environments (VMs) should be created based on a single OS kernel. Furthermore, the access requests from a VM need to be redirected to its local resource partition on the PM; the *chroot* command in a UNIX system can create several virtual root directories within a host OS. These virtual root directories are the root directories of all VMs created. There are two ways to implement virtual root directories: (1) duplicating common resources to each VM partition and (2) sharing most resources with the host environment and only creating private resource copies upon VM on demand. The first way incurs significant resource costs and overhead on a PM. This issue neutralizes the benefits of OS-level virtualization, compared with hardware-assisted virtualization. Therefore, OS-level virtualization is often a second choice.

Virtualization on Linux or Windows Platforms
By far, most reported OS-level virtualization systems are Linux based. Virtualization support of Windows-based platforms is less frequent and still at the research stage. The Linux kernel offers an abstraction layer to allow software processes to work with, and operate on, resources without knowing the hardware details. New hardware may need new Linux kernels to support it. Therefore, different Linux platforms use patched kernels to provide special support for extended functionality, as demonstrated in Table 3.7.

However, most Linux platforms are not tied to a special kernel. In such a case, a host can run several VMs simultaneously on the same hardware. Several examples of OS-level

Table 3.7
Virtualization support for Linux and Windows NT platforms

Virtualization Support and Source of Information	Brief Introduction on Functionality and Application Platforms
Linux vServer for Linux platforms (http://linux-vserver.org/)	Extending the Linux kernels to implement a security mechanism to help building VMs by setting resource limits and file attributes and changing the root environment for VM isolation, etc.
OpenVZ for Linux platforms (http://ftp.openvz.org/doc/OpenVZ-Users-Guide.pdf) (Example 3.3)	Creating virtual private servers (VPS), where the VPS has its own files, users, process tree, and virtual devices. These can be isolated from other VPSs with support of checkpointing and live migration.
FVM for virtualizing the Windows NT platforms	FVM (Feather-weight VM) uses system call interfaces to create VMs at NT kernel spaces. Multiple VMs are supported by virtualized namespaces and copy-on-write.

virtualization tools that have developed in recent years are summarized. Two OS tools (Linux VServer and OpenVZ) support Linux platforms to run other platform-based applications through virtualization. These two OS-level tools are illustrated in Example 3.3. The third one, Feather-weight VM (FVM), is an attempt for virtualization on the Windows NT platform.

Example 3.3   Virtualization Support for Linux Platform

The following OpenVZ is an OS-level tool (the OS virtualization layer in Figure 3.3), designed to support Linux platforms to create virtual environments for running VMs under different guest OS. OpenVZ is an open source container-based virtualization solution built on Linux. To support virtualization and isolation of various subsystems, limited resource management, and check-pointing, OpenVZ modifies the Linux kernel. The overall picture of the OpenVZ system is illustrated in Figure 3.13. Several Virtual Private Servers can run simultaneously on a PM. These VPSs look like normal Linux servers. Each VPS has its own files, users and groups, process tree, virtual network, virtual devices, and IPC through semaphores and messages.

The resource management subsystem of OpenVZ consists of three components: (1) two-level disk allocation; (2) two-level CPU scheduler; and (3) resource controller. The size of disk space a VM can use is set by the OpenVZ server administrator. This is the first level of disk allocation. Each VM acts as a standard Linux system. Hence, the VM administrator is responsible for allocating disk spaces for each user and group. This is the second level disk quota. The first level CPU scheduler of OpenVZ decides which VM gets the time slice, taking into account virtual CPU priority and limit settings.

The second-level CPU scheduler is the same as that of Linux. OpenVZ has a set of about 20 parameters, which are carefully chosen to cover all aspects of VM operation.

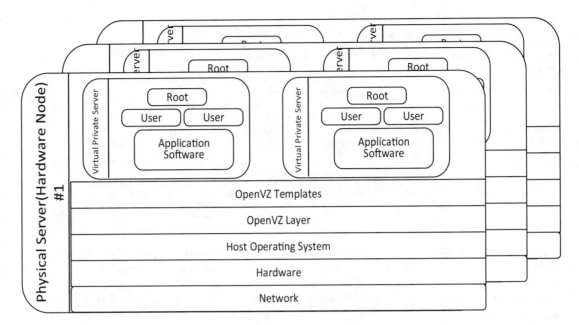

Figure 3.13
OpenVZ inserts a virtualization layer called OpenVZ inside the host OS. This layer provides some OS images to create VMs quickly at the user space. Source: http://ftp.openvz.org/doc/OpenVZ-Users-Guide.pdf.

Therefore, the resource a VM can use is well controlled. OpenVZ also supports check-pointing and live migration. At a moment, the complete state of a VM is saved to a disk file. This file can then be transferred to another PM and the VM can be restored there. It only takes a few seconds to complete the whole process. However, there is still a delay in processing because the established network connections are also migrated. ∎

3.4 Docker Containers and Deployment Requirements

In this section, we introduce the key concept of application *containers* as simplified VMs. The purpose is to reduce the implementation costs and enhance the scalability and orchestration capability. We will also discuss the application opportunities of VMs and containers to satisfy different workload and application demands. Another new approach will be introduced by using unikernels to further simplify the complexity and improve efficiency and performance.

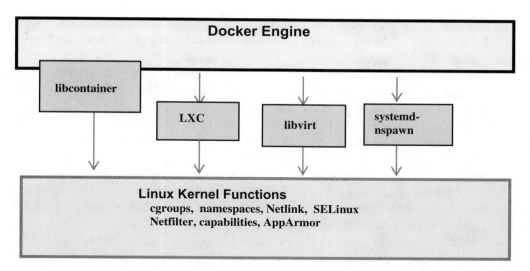

Figure 3.14
The Docker engine applies Linux kernel features for isolated virtualization of different application containers.

3.4.1 Docker Containers Created with Linux Kernel Functions

This is a virtualization software that runs within a container of user application codes and their binaries and libraries over Linux kernel functions. The Docker engine implements a high-level API to provide lightweight containers that run software processes in isolation. The Docker virtualization concept is illustrated in Figure 3.14. The Docker engine uses resources isolation features of the Linux kernel. The cgroups and kernel namespaces allow independent containers to run within separate Linux instances. These isolated containers avoid the overhead of creating VMs.

There is no guest OS needed to run the user applications. The containers apply the kernel functionalities. The resource isolation, including CPU, memory and block I/O, and network, is done using separate namespaces for different applications. Docker applies the kernel's virtualization features directly using the libcontainer library. This interface became available with Docker 0.9. The Docker engine can also access Linux kernel indirectly, through the use of interfaces: LXC (Linux containers), libvirt, or systemd-nspawn. The source code is entrusted to the GitHub website and in alliance with the Apache 2.0 agreement.

Docker Containers

Docker is an open-source project that automates the development of user applications as software containers. The Docker engine provides an additional layer of abstraction and automation of OS-level virtualization in Linux-based host platforms. Docker engine is written in

Go language, running on the Linux platform. Docker differs from the traditional VMs in that it consists of the application plus its needed binaries and library. Each application container takes 10 MB of memory.

Docker engine packages a user application and its dependencies in a virtual container that runs on any Linux server without the use of a guest OS. This helps enable flexibility and portability regarding where the application can run, whether on the premises, public cloud, private cloud, bare metal, etc. Docker implements a high-level API to provide lightweight containers that run processes in isolation. The idea of building a Docker container on top of facilities provided by the Linux kernel (primarily cgroups and namespaces) differs from conventional VMs primarily because it is not using a guest OS. Another advantage in using containers lies in the fact that resources can be isolated, services restricted, and processes provisioned to have a private view of the OS with their own process ID space, file system structure, and network interfaces.

Multiple containers may share the same kernel, but each container can be constrained to use only a predefined amount of resources such as CPU, memory, and I/O. Using Docker to create and manage containers may simplify the creation of highly distributed systems. This will enable multiple user applications, worker tasks, and other processes to run autonomously on a single PM or across multiple VMs. This container approach scales well with systems like Apache Cassandra, MongoDB, or Riak.

Example 3.4 Docker Process to Create Application Containers in an Isolated Execution Environment

Figure 3.15 shows a schematic block diagram for the container creation process using the Docker engine. The client submits the request at the user end using the software *Docker*. The daemon is a backend unit built with a Docker server and engine. Daemon accepts and processes client requests and manages all Docker containers. The server handles http requests, routing, and interfaces with the Docker engine. A Docker engine is the core of all Docker operations, which handles multiple job requests concurrently. The registry is used to store container images.

The daemon interacts with three drivers in a Docker engine. Drivers control the creation of the container execution environment. The *graphdriver* is a container image manager. It communicates with the layered *rootfs* files associated with the containers created at the lower box. The *networkdriver* completes the Docker container deployment. The *execudriver* is responsible for driving the container execution by working with the namespaces and cgroups in the libcontainer, which is written in Go language and used as a base to control all the containers created.

Finally, the containers are created at the lower box. The Docker uses daemon as a manager and libcontainer as an executioner in generating the containers. The containers are similar in function to the VM under an isolated execution environment. In

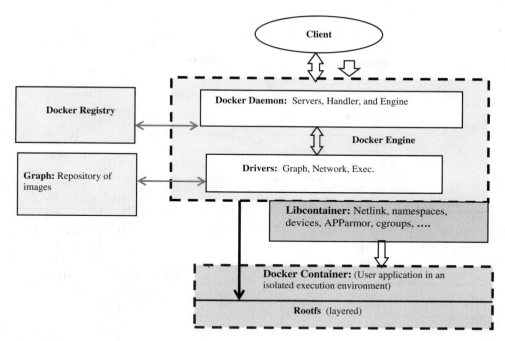

Figure 3.15
Docker engine block diagram for creating and management of Docker containers in isolated execution.

this process, the Docker container is created with low overhead, demands minimum memory, and is well protected with kernel isolation. ∎

3.4.2 Docker Containers versus Virtual Machines

As shown in Figure 3.16(a), a hypervisor-generated VM may demand tens of GB for hosting the guest OS in addition to the application codes. Docker containers are isolated to use their own binaries and libraries, as shown in Figure 3.16(b). There is no guest OS needed in a Docker container. The containers may share binaries and libraries, as shown in Figure 3.16(c). The obvious advantage of the lightweight containers over the heavy-duty VMs is that each must have its own guest OS and binaries /libraries. The contrast is demonstrated by the height disparity between the VMs and the containers in Figure 3.16(b, c). It may cost less to build and use containers than create and use VMs. For this reason, Docker containers are gradually replacing traditional VMs in cloud applications that emphasize orchestrated massive parallelism, especially in scale-out workloads.

The Docker engine generates lightweight virtualized containers on the Linux platform. The system is essentially a container generation and management engine. The Docker

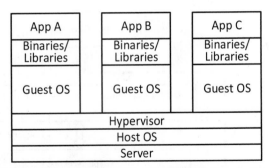

(a) Three hypervisor-created virtual machines (VMs) on the same hardware hosts; each VM is heavily loaded with its own guest OS and specific binaries and libraries

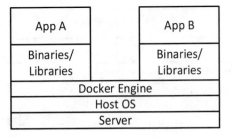

(b) Each container is loaded with its own binaries/libraries which are not shared

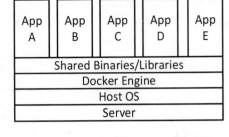

(c) The Docker engine creates many lightweight app containers, which are isolated, but share OS

Figure 3.16
Hypervisor versus Docker engine for creating VMs and application containers, respectively.

source code is too small to fit most computers; it is implemented with Go language. For the clients, Docker assumes a client/server architecture.

For example, a container can be booted and ready for application in 500 ms, while a hypervisor may boot in 20 s according to the OS used. In general, one can conclude that the lightweight containers are suitable for scalable use with multiple copies for cloud orchestration. This implies that containers are in favor of clustering and multiples. For example, containers act in favor of running multiple copies of a single application, say MySQL. The hypervisors are often more suitable for heavy-duty applications that have limited cloud orchestration demand. If you want flexibility of running multiple applications, you use VMs.

These hypervisor-created VMs are compared with Docker containers in Table 3.8. As stated earlier, it may cost less to build and use containers than create and use the VMs. For example, Amazon Web Service Elastic Container 2 (AWS EC2) has already offered the Elastic Container Service (ECS). This offers users containers to implement their applications with significantly lowered memory demand and complexity. Using containers, resources are isolated, service is restricted, and processes are provisioned to have a completely

Table 3.8
Comparison between hypervisor-created VMs and Docker containers

VM Type	Strength and Weakness	Suitable Applications
Hypervisor-Created Virtual Machines	Higher app flexibility in launching different OS apps, but demands more memory and overhead to create and launch the VMs.	More suitable for use in multiple apps without orchestration. VMs appear to run on a wide variety of operating systems.
Docker Containers	Lightweight application containers with low overhead to create and run with better protection in an isolated execution environment in the kernel space.	More suitable for scalable use of the same app in multiple copies under orchestration. Works better with a particular OS version. It may save the operation costs on clouds.

private view of the OS inside their own process ID space, file systems, and network interfaces. For building highly distributed systems, the use of application containers can simplify the creation, security, and management issues significantly, compared with the use of hypervisor-created VMs.

3.4.3 Architectural Evolution from VMs to Containers and Unikernel

Most commercial clouds, public or private, are built on x86 hosts for low-cost considerations. Thus, traditional VMs are mostly created with hypervisors on x86 hosts. The Docker containers are generated at the Linux kernel level. The Docker containers rely on using Linux kernel tools to establish the isolated execution environment for different containers. We assess below the architectural changes in recent Docker containers and introduce the new approach of using unikernels.

Containers Becoming the Mainstream in Cloud Computing

In 2014, OpenStack decided to support containers and third-party developers. It named a new container editing engine for supporting multienvironment container construction. VMware also announced the support of containers. They claimed that it would enhance the security of containers by using VM as the interface in the deployment process. Red Hat also integrated Docker to its RHEL OS using KVM to load Docker. They pushed out the RHEL 7 Atomic HOST virtualization system for containers.

In 2015, Docker version 1.9 included the new product, Swarm, to support multihost interconnections. Docker modified the Compose function to support multiple environments. Recently, Docker also released the YubiKey to enable signature on hardware. This security feature supports Docker Hub with image security scanning and supports user namespace. Amazon also announced the EC2 container service. The ECS is used to support container migration at a reduced cost.

The automation of container operation control depends on how the operation environment is defined. Docker helps developers make sure that the development and execution environments are consistent. This implies total consistency between catalogs, routes, documentation, encrypted names of storage users, access rights, and domain names in both environments. Docker tools must be designed to standardize the environments on different hosts.

Introduction of an Efficient Unikernel Approach

In building VM containers on x86 nodes, the user applications require handling the hardware access and operation at the kernel space of the Linux OS. This results in a frequent switch of user application between user mode and kernel mode and thus lowers the performance to some extent. Recently, a new unikernel technique was developed based on the LibOS. The evolutional changes are illustrated in Figure 3.17. Unikernels are specialized, single-address space machine images constructed by using library operating systems.

In a library operating system, protection boundaries are pushed to the lowest hardware layers, resulting in a set of libraries that implement mechanisms to drive hardware or network protocols. The library contains a set of policies that enforces access control and isolation in the application layer. The first of such systems were Exokernel and Nemesis in the late 1990s. The library OS has the advantage of using only a single address space; there is no need for repeated privilege transitions to move data between user space and kernel space. Therefore, a library OS can provide improved performance by allowing direct access to hardware without context switches. However, unikernel has a drawback in that it lacks

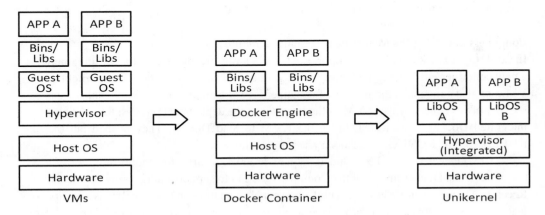

Figure 3.17
Architectural evolution from VMs to Docker containers and unikernels.

separation among running multiple applications side by side as in a library OS. This makes it harder to enforce resource isolation.

OS virtualization can overcome the above drawbacks on commodity hardware. A modern hypervisor creates VMs with CPU time and strongly isolated virtual devices. A library OS running as a VM can depend on the hypervisor to drive the physical hardware. However, protocol libraries are still needed to replace the services of a traditional OS. In the unikernel approach, a developer selects a minimal set of libraries from a modular stack which correspond to the OS constructs required for their application to run. These libraries are then compiled with the application and configuration code to build sealed, fixed-purpose images (unikernels).

The libraries run directly on an integrated hypervisor or hardware without an intervening OS such as Linux or Windows. The hypervisor creates the VMs in the system space as shown by the left stack in Figure 3.17. The containers are created by the Docker engine at the system space at the middle stack. The right stack corresponds to the unikernel approach, which has the application and its execution environment entirely handled by an integrated hypervisor in the kernel space.

The unikernel approach implies complete Ring 0 privileged execution in the x86 CPU. The hardware access is entirely controlled by the hypervisor. Three distinct advantages of this approach are described as: (1) enhanced security with less chance to be attacked at the kernel space; (2) smaller in memory demand by the unikernel hypervisor, which is only 4% of that required to be supported by a complete host OS; and (3) much shorter startup time is expected due to the loading of the entire OS. The shortcoming of this unikernel approach lies in the custom order by the upper application. The host may be less powerful in general-purpose applications. By late 2016, the unikernel model is still at the research and testing stage by ClickOS, Clive, and MirageOS users.

Switching from x86 to ARM, Power, and Sparc as Building Nodes

Currently, the x86 processors are used in almost all server clusters deployed in cloud platforms. The situation may change in the next few years. This is due to the rise of using ARM, Power, and Sparc processors in virtualized cloud computing. In 2013, IBM announced a $1 billion investment in upgrading its power series for Linux applications. For example, the Power 8 architecture is now open to create its own ecosystem. IBM has provided support plans for commercial clouds to switch to Linux-based power hosts. In 2015, Oracle started to shift toward cloud computing. They encouraged the world to use Sparc servers in building future clouds. (Remember, Sun Microsystem Sparc is now part of Oracle.)

ARM processors used in many smartphones have demonstrated their strength in low power consumption and low cost to deliver high performance. Now, Dell, HP, Microsoft, and Amazon are all investing in ARM server development for cloud constructions. The intention is obviously to replace x86 processors in future clusters used in clouds. It is predictable that future clouds may enter an era of keen competition among x86, ARM, Power, and Sparc manufacturers.

Marriage Between Clouds and IoT Platforms

The impact of IoT on cloud computing cannot be ignored. In fact, their marriage is not stoppable due to the sensing and big data requirements in future clouds. With the introduction of Industry 4.0, an industrial Internet will appear soon with the rise of the IoT and cognitive services. All manufacturing sites are fully supported by sensors, robots, machine learning, big data collectors, real-time monitory, intelligent maintenance, online or offline data analytics, etc. Cloud-centric IoT systems will upgrade all economic sectors, including healthcare, smart cities, intelligent transportations, and energy conservation.

Since 2015, IBM, Microsoft, and Amazon have all promoted the cloud–IoT marriage. IBM is pushing its cognitive services to be fully supported by IoT facilities. Microsoft announced its "Azure IoT" services by linking Windows 10 hosts. The goal is to achieve on-site data forwarding to Azure for real-time processing. General Electric pushes the "Predix Cloud" platform for its clients to process the big data at manufacturing sites. Amazon also announced its AWS IoT initiative to serve their cloud clients at smart homes, smart plants, and smart cities (http://aws.amazon.com).

3.5 Virtual Machine Management and Container Orchestration

Cloud infrastructure management involves several issues. First, we consider the VM management from independent service jobs. Then we consider how to put together a large number of lightweight containers as an orchestra of players.

3.5.1 VM Management Solutions

In a cluster built with mixed nodes of host and guest systems, the normal way of operation is to run everything on the PM. When a VM fails, its role could be replaced by another VM on a different node, as long as they both run with the same guest OS. In other words, a physical node can fail over to a VM on another host. This is different from physical-to-physical failover in a traditional physical cluster. The advantage is to enhance failover flexibility. The potential drawback is that a VM must stop playing its role if its residing host node fails. However, this problem can be dealt with by VM live migration. Figure 3.18 shows the process of live migration of a VM from a host A to host B. The migration is done by copying the VM state file from the storage area to the host machine.

There are four ways to manage a virtual cluster. First, we may use *guest-based manager*, by which the cluster manager resides on a guest system. In this case, multiple VMs form a virtual cluster. For example, openMosix is an open-source Linux cluster running

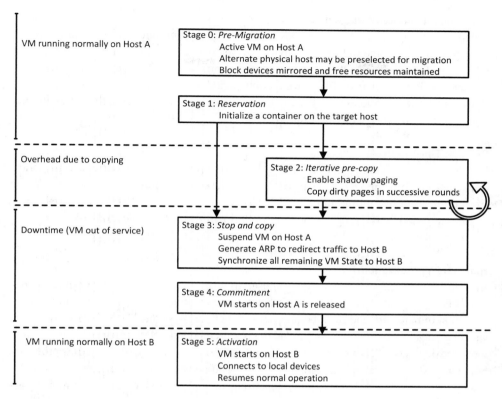

Stage 0: *Pre-Migration*
Active VM on Host A
Alternate physical host may be preselected for migration
Block devices mirrored and free resources maintained

Stage 1: *Reservation*
Initialize a container on the target host

Stage 2: *Iterative pre-copy*
Enable shadow paging
Copy dirty pages in successive rounds

Stage 3: *Stop and copy*
Suspend VM on Host A
Generate ARP to redirect traffic to Host B
Synchronize all remaining VM State to Host B

Stage 4: *Commitment*
VM starts on Host A is released

Stage 5: *Activation*
VM starts on Host B
Connects to local devices
Resumes normal operation

VM running normally on Host A

Overhead due to copying

Downtime (VM out of service)

VM running normally on Host B

Figure 3.18
Steps for live migration of VMs from host computer A to another host B. Reprinted with permission from C. Clark et al., "Live Migration of Virtual Machines," *Proc. of the Second Symposium on Networked Systems Design and Implementation* (NSDI'05), 2005.

different guest systems on top of the Xen hypervisor. Another example is Sun Cluster Oasis: an experimental Solaris cluster of VMs supported by a VMware VMM. Second, one can build a cluster manager on host systems. The *host-based manager* supervises the guest systems and can restart the guest system on another PM. A good example is the VMware HA system that can restart a guest system after failure.

The above two cluster management systems are either guest-only or host-only, but they do not mix. Third, one can use an *independent cluster manager* on both host and guest systems. This will add complexity on the infrastructure management. Finally, one can use an *integrated cluster* on guest and host systems. This means the manager must be designed to distinguish between virtualized resources and physical resources. Various cluster management schemes can be greatly enhanced when VM live migration is enabled with minimum overhead.

Independent Service Management

Independent services request facilities to execute many unrelated tasks. Commonly, the APIs provided are some web services that the developer can use conveniently. In AWS EC2, the Simple Queue Service (SQS) is constructed to provide reliable communication service between different providers. Even an endpoint device does not run while another entity has posted a message in the SQS. By using independent service providers, the cloud applications can run different services at the same time.

Running Third-Party Applications

Cloud platform is often used to execute third-party applications. As current web applications are often provided by using Web 2.0 form, the programming interfaces are different from those used in runtime libraries. The APIs act as services. Web service application engines are used by the programmers for building third-party applications. Web browsers are the user interface for end users.

Hardware Virtualization

In a cloud system, hypervisors are often used to virtualize the hardware resources to create VMs. System-level virtualization demands a special kind of software that simulates the execution of hardware and runs the unmodified operating systems. Virtualized servers, storage, and networks are put together to yield a cloud computing platform. The cloud development and deployment environments should be consistent to eliminate some runtime problems. Some virtualized resources in compute, storage, and network clouds are listed in Table 3.9. The VMs installed on a cloud computing platform are mainly used for hosting third-party applications. VMs provide the flexible runtime services to free users from worrying about the system environment.

Table 3.9
Virtualized resources in compute, storage, and network clouds

Provider	Amazon Web Services (AWS)	Microsoft Azure	Google Compute Engine (GCE)
Compute Cloud with Virtual Clusters	x86 servers, Xen VMs, resource elasticity extends scalability through virtual clustering	VMs provisioned by declarative descriptions	Handlers written in Python, automatic scaling up and down, server fail-over capability
Storage Cloud with Virtual Storage	Elastic block store (EBS) for volume storage, automatic scaling varies from EBS to S3	SQL Data Services, Azure storage service	MegaStore, and BigTable for distributed file management
Network Cloud Services	Declarative topology, security groups, availability zones isolate network failures	User's declarative descriptions or roles of app components	Fixed topology to accommodate a 3-tier web app structure, scaling up and down is automatic

By using VMs, high application flexibility is often a primary advantage over traditional computer systems. As the VM resources are shared by many users, we need a method to maximize the user's privilege and keep the provisioned VMs in an isolated execution environment. Traditional sharing of cluster resources is often set up statically before runtime. Such sharing is not flexible at all. Users cannot customize the system for interactive applications and OS is often the barrier on software portability. Docker containers are better isolated than using hypervisor-created VMs. In general, virtualization can benefit a cloud system by achieving higher availability, disaster recovery, dynamic load balancing, flexible resources provisioning, and most importantly a scalable computing environment.

3.5.2 VM Migration for Disaster Recovery

VM technology requires an advanced disaster recovery scheme. One scheme is to recover a PM by another PM. The second scheme is to recover a VM by another VM. As shown in the top timeline of Figure 3.18, the traditional disaster recovery from PM to PM is rather slow, complex, and expensive. The total recovery time is attributed to the hardware configuration, installing and configuring the OS, installing the backup agents, and the long time to restart the PM. To recover a VM platform, the installing and configuration times for OS and backup agents are eliminated. Therefore, we end up with a much shorter disaster recovery time, about 40% of that to recover the PMs.

The cloning of VMs offers an effective solution. The idea is to make a clone VM on a remote server for every running VM on a local server. Among all clone VMs, only one needs to be active. The remote VM should be in a suspended mode. A cloud control center should be able to activate this clone VM in case of failure of the original VM, taking a snapshot of the VM to enable live migration with minimum time. The migrated VM runs on a shared Internet connection. Only updated data and modified states are sent to the suspended VM to update its state. Security of the VMs should be enforced during the live migration of VMs.

Live VM Migration Steps
VMs can be migrated live from one PM to another. In case of failure, a VM can be replaced by another VM through live migration. Virtual clusters can be applied in computational grids, cloud platforms, and in HPC systems. The major attraction is due to the fact that virtual clustering provides dynamic resources that can be quickly put together upon user demand or after some node failure. In particular, virtual clustering plays a key role in making cloud computing possible today.

An active state refers to a VM that has been activated at the virtualization platform to perform a real task. A paused state corresponds to a VM that has been activated but disabled to process a task or paused in a waiting state. A VM enters the suspended state if its machine file and virtual resources are stored back to the disk.

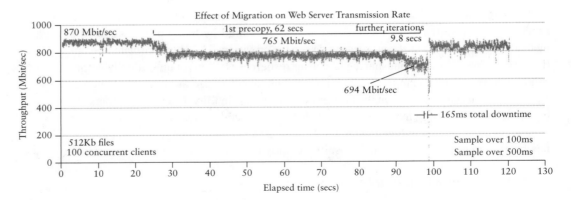

Figure 3.19
Effect on data transmission rate of a VM migrated from one failing web server to another. The downtime of 165 ms was observed. Reprinted with permission from C. Clark et al., "Live Migration of Virtual Machines," *Proc. of the Second Symposium on Networked Systems Design and Implementation* (NSDI'05), 2005.

Figure 3.19 shows the effect on the data transmission rate (Mbit/s) by live migration of a VM from one host to another. Before the copying of the VM with 512 Kb files for 100 clients, the data throughput was 870 Mb/s. The first precopy takes 63 s during which the rate is reduced to 765 Mb/s. Then the data rate reduces to 694 Mb/s in 9.8 s for more iterations of the copying process. The system experiences only 165 ms of downtime before the VM is restored at the destination host. This experimental result shows a very small migration overhead in a live transfer of a VM between host nodes. This is critical to achieve dynamic cluster reconfiguration and disaster recovery as needed in cloud computing.

An *inactive state* is defined by the virtualization platform. With the emergence of widespread cluster computing over a decade ago, many cluster configuration and management systems have been developed to achieve a range of goals. These goals naturally influence individual approaches on cluster management. VM technology has become a popular method for simplifying management and sharing of physical computing resources. Platforms such as VMware and Xen allow multiple VMs with different operating systems and configurations to coexist on the same physical host in mutual isolation. Clustering inexpensive computers is an effective way to obtain reliable, scalable computing power for network services and compute-intensive applications.

Example 3.5   Live Migration of VMs between Two Xen-Enabled Hosts
Xen supports live migration. It is a useful feature and natural extension to virtualization platforms that allow for the transfer of a VM from one PM to another with little downtime of the services hosted by the VM. Live migration transfers the working state and memory of a VM across a network when it is running. Xen also supports VM

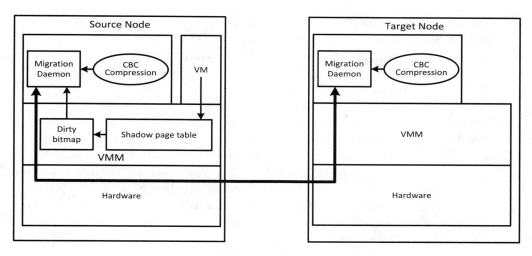

Figure 3.20
Live migration of VM from the Domain0 to that of an Xen-enabled target host.

migration by using a mechanism: *remote direct memory access* (RDMA). The idea is illustrated in Figure 3.20.

It speeds up the VM migration by avoiding TCP/IP stack processing overhead. RDMA implements a different transfer protocol of which origin and destination VMs must be registered before any transfer operations reduce it to a "one-sided" interface. Data communication over RDMA does not need to involve CPU, caches, or context switches. This allows migration with minimum impact on guest operating systems and hosted applications.

Migration daemons are responsible for performing migration. Shadow page tables in the VMM layer trace modifications to the memory page in migrated VMs during the pre-copy phase. Corresponding flags are set in a dirty bitmap. At the start of each pre-copying round, the bitmap is sent to the migration daemon. Then, the bitmap is cleared and the shadow page tables are destroyed and recreated in the next round. The system resides in the management VM of Xen. Memory pages denoted by bitmap are extracted and compressed before being sent to the destination. The compressed data are then decompressed on the target. ∎

3.5.3 Docker Container Scheduling and Orchestration

Docker users would like to scale a large number of containers across many hosts. Clustered hosts present some management challenges. This demands the use Docker schedulers and orchestration tools. First, we identify the challenges and then examine the OpenStack

Magum, one of the container tools that can help managing Docker containers to yield scalable performance. Orchestration is a broad concept that involves container scheduling, cluster management, and even the provisioning of additional hosts.

Container Scheduling

Docker containers need to be loaded into the hosts in a timely fashion to meet the service demand. Scheduling is the ability of a Docker administrator to load a service file onto a host that establishes how to run a specific container. Cluster management is needed to control a group of hosts. This includes the adding or subtracting of hosts from a cluster. The cluster manager must first get the loading information about the current state of the hosts and their loaded containers. The container scheduler must have access to each host in the cluster. Host selection is a big problem for the container scheduler. This selection process should be as automatic as possible. The container and host workload need to be matched with load balancing in a cluster.

Container Orchestration Tools

Cluster management software like OpenStack is meant to support container scheduling, advanced scheduling demand container grouping, and optimization. The administrator must manage the group containers as a single application. Grouping containers may demand the synchronization of the start and stop time. Another issue is host provisioning, which refers to the timely and smooth joining of a new host into an existing cluster. Six popular tools for container scheduling and cluster management are summarized in Table 3.10. Swarm and Compose were developed by Docker teams. Kubernetes was developed by Google to label, group, and set container groups.

OpenStack Orchestration (Magnum)

This is an OpenStack API service developed by the OpenStack container team. The purpose is to make container orchestration engines such as Docker and Kubernetes available as first-class resources on the OpenStack. Example 3.6 illustrates the use of Magnum in

Table 3.10
Host provisioning and container scheduling tools

Tool Name	Brief Description of Tool Functionality
Fleet	Scheduling and cluster management component of the CoreOS
Marathon	Scheduling and service management component in a Mesosphere installation
Swarm	Docker's robust scheduler to spin up containers on provisioned hosts
Mesos	Apache Mesos abstracts and manages the resources of all hosts in a cluster
Kubernetes	Google's scheduler over the containers running on your cloud infrastructure
Compose	Docker's tool that allows group management of containers, declaratively

container orchestration. Magnum applies the Docker Heat to orchestrate an OS image which contains Docker and Kubernetes. Magnum runs the image either in VMs or bare metal in a cluster configuration.

Example 3.6   OpenStack Magnum for Container Scheduling and Orchestration

Magnum is an OpenStack project still under development. The architecture of Magnum is shown in Figure 3.21. Technical details are not available until the system gets stabilized. Magnum allows API to manage application containers, which may differ greatly from Nova machine instances. The Magnum API is an asynchronous tool that is compatible with the Keystone software for multitenant implementation. It relies on OpenStack Orchestration and uses both Kubernetes and Docker as components.

Magnum is designed for OpenStack cloud operators to use. The purpose is to enable self-service solutions to provide containers to cloud users as managed hosted services. Magnum attempts to create application containers to run with existing Nova instances, Cinder volumes, and Trove databases. The major innovations are the ability to scale an application to a specific number of instances to cause the application to re-spawn an instance in the event of a failure automatically, and to pack applications together more effectively than using heavy-duty VMs.

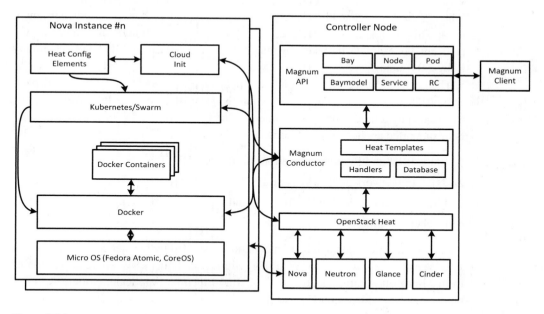

Figure 3.21
Docker container orchestration illustrated by using OpenStack Magnum to deploy container clusters in multiple Nova instances. Courtesy of https://wiki.openstack.org/wiki/Magnum, retrieved August 2015.

Multiple Nova instances are used. Docker Heat, Kubernetes/Swarm, OpenStack Heat and Micro OS (Fedora Atomic, CoreOS) are used as components. The Docker Heat does not provide a resource scheduler: it is specific to Docker and uses Glance to store container images. Layered images are supported by Heat. The major components in the Magnum controller node are the Magnum API and Conductor and OpenStack Heat, which control the Cloud-Init, Kunernetes/Swarm, and Docker in Nova instances to function cooperatively in a coordinated manner.

Finally, it is worth mentioning that the Magnum team at OpenStack is trying to secure multitenancy operations. Resources such as containers, services, pods, and bays started by Magnum can only be viewed and accessed by the owning users. This is a key security feature that containers belonging to the same tenant can pack tightly within the same pods and bays, but run separate kernels in separate Nova instances used by different tenants. Using Magnum provides the same level of security isolation as Nova running VMs. ∎

Example 3.7 AWS Elastic Beanstalk: An Orchestration Service of VMs and Containers

AWS offers an Elastic Beanstalk service for deploying infrastructure that orchestrates various AWS services, including EC2, S3, Simple Notification Service (SNS), Cloud-Watch, Auto Scaling, and Elastic Load Balancers, all of which will be studied in Chapter 4. This is an additional layer of abstraction over prebuilt combination of OS and platform. For example, the user may see a "64-bit Amazon Linux 2014.03 v1.1.0 running Ruby 2.0 (Puma)."

The deployment requires defining an "application" as a logical container. A deployable platform needs to use a "configuration template" that contains information for the Beanstalk environment. An "environment" combines a "version" with a "configuration." Four supported applications and software stacks are:

1. Ruby, PHP, and Python applications on Apache HTTP Server;

2. .NET Framework applications on IIS 7.5;

3. Java applications on Apache Tomcat; and

4. Docker containers.

The deployment of such application containers is aided by Docker containers, Git, or Java Web application Archive (WAR file). Similar container services are also available from Microsoft Azure, Cloud Foundry, IBM Bluemix, AppScale, Google App Engine, etc. The architecture of these clouds will be studied in Chapter 4. ∎

3.6 Eucalyptus, OpenStack, and VMware for Cloud Construction

Seven software packages are listed in Table 3.11. The top six are all open-source codes. The vSphere 4 is developed by VMWare, which is commercially available for converting data centers to clouds. To convert server clusters or data centers into private clouds, Eucalyptus is an open-source software for building clouds on large-scale cluster of servers. The stable version was released in 2010 and is available to the general public. OpenStack is extended from Eucalyptus with much more software support. Let us examine the functionality of Eucalyptus. Then we present the progress made with the OpenStack and vSphere systems.

3.6.1 Eucalyptus for Virtual Clustering in Private Clouds

Eucalyptus is an open-source computer software for building AWS-compatible private and hybrid cloud computing. The software is marketed by the company Eucalyptus Systems. Eucalyptus is the acronym for Elastic Utility Computing Architecture for Linking Your Programs. It enables pooling compute, storage, and network resources that can be dynamically scaled up or down as application workloads change. In March 2012, Eucalyptus Systems announced a formal agreement with AWS to maintain compatibility. This is a free open-source software system (Figure 3.22) for building IaaS clouds.

The system mainly supports virtual networking and management of VMs. Virtual storage is not supported. It was used widely in building private clouds that can interact with end users through the Ethernet or Internet. The system also supports interactions with other private cloud or public clouds over the Internet. It is short of security and features for

Table 3.11
Open-source software for cloud computing (except the vSphere 6)

Software	Cloud Type, License	Language Used	Linux/ Windows	EC2/S3 Compatibility	XEN/KVM/ VMWare
Eucalyptus	IaaS, Rackspace	Java, C	Yes/Yes	Yes/Yes	Yes/Yes/Yes
Nimbus	IaaS, Apache	Java, Python	Unknown	Yes/No	Yes/Yes/ Unknown
Cloud Foundry	PaaS, Apache	Ruby, C	Yes/No	Yes/No	Yes/Yes/Yes
OpenStack	IaaS, Apache	Python	Yes/Unknown	Yes/Yes	Yes/Yes/ Unknown
OpenNebula	IaaS, Apache	C, C++, Ruby, Java, Lex, YaaS, Shell Script	Yes/Unknown	Yes/Unknown	Yes/Yes/ Unknown
ApplScale			Unknown	Yes/Yes	Yes/Yes/Yes
vSphere 4			Yes/Yes	Yes/Yes	Yes/Yes/Yes

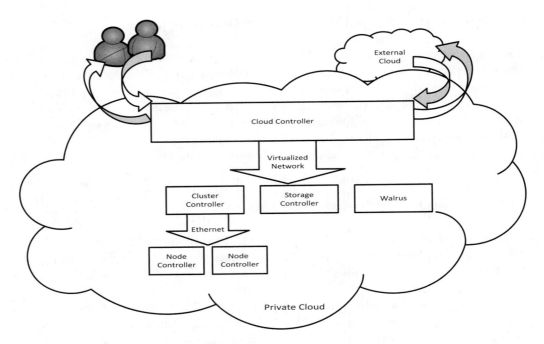

Figure 3.22
The Eucalyptus for building private cloud by establishing virtual network over the VMs linking through Ethernet and the Internet.

general-purpose grid or cloud applications. In terms of functionality, the Eucalyptus serves like AWS APIs. Therefore, it can interact with EC2 and provide a storage API to emulate the Amazon S3 API for storing user data and VM images. Eucalyptus is installed on Linux-based platforms. It is compatible with EC2 and S3 in SOAP, REST, and Query services. The CLI and web portal services can be applied with Eucalyptus.

Example 3.8   Eucalyptus Software Specified in HP Helion Cloud System
In September 2014, Hewlett-Packard acquired Eucalyptus to strengthen HP cloud computing initiatives. The HP Helion Eucalyptus system is shown in Figure 3.23. This system can manage either Amazon or Eucalyptus instances. Users can also move instances between a Eucalyptus private cloud and the Amazon EC2 cloud to create a hybrid cloud. Like all other clouds, hardware virtualization isolates applications from computer hardware details. Again, the system is built on top of data centers that provide the physical hardware infrastructure. Virtualization brings the compute, storage, and network support for building machine instances. Like AWS, Auto Scaling, Elastic Load Balancing, and CloudWatch are services for users. The importance is the AWS compatibility to widen its application scope.

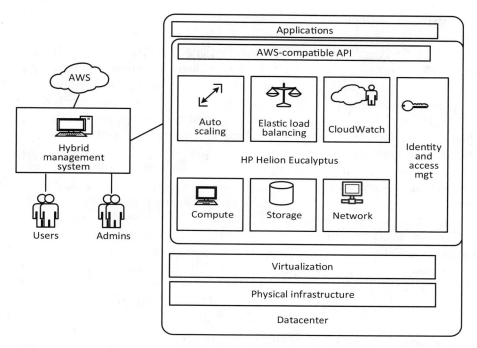

Figure 3.23
The HP Helion Eucalyptus cloud system connected to the AWS cloud for joint applications. Courtesy of Eucalyptus Software: www.eucalyptus.com, 2016.

The Helion Eucalyptus system has six components, defined as follows:

1. The *Cloud Controller* (CLC) is a Java program that offers EC2-compatible interfaces, as well as a web interface to the outside world.

2. *Walrus*, also written in Java, is the Eucalyptus equivalent to AWS Simple Storage Service (S3).

3. The *Cluster Controller* (CC) is the front-end for a cluster within a Eucalyptus cloud and communicates with the Storage Controller and Node Controller.

4. The *Storage Controller* (SC) is the Eucalyptus equivalent to AWS EBS.

5. The *VMware Broker* is an optional component that provides an AWS-compatible interface for VMware environments and physically runs on the Cluster Controller.

6. The *Node Controller* (NC) hosts the VM instances and manages the virtual network endpoints. ∎

3.6.2 OpenStack Software for Building Private or Public Clouds

OpenStack was introduced by Rackspace and NASA in July 2010. The ultimate goal is to create a massively scalable and secure cloud software library for building private and public clouds. Currently, over 200 companies have joined the OpenStack project. The project offers free open-source software under the Apache license. OpenStack cloud software is written in Python. The system is updated every six months. Eight major components of OpenStack are introduced in Figure 3.24 and more details can be found in http://openstack.org/.

OpenStack software controls large pools of compute, storage, and networking resources throughout a data center, managed through a dashboard or via the OpenStack API. OpenStack works with popular enterprises and open-source technologies making it ideal for heterogeneous infrastructures. Many of the world's largest brands rely on OpenStack to run their everyday business, while reducing costs and helping them move faster. OpenStack has a strong ecosystem, and users seeking commercial support can choose from different OpenStack-powered products and services. The software was built by a thriving community of developers, in collaboration with users.

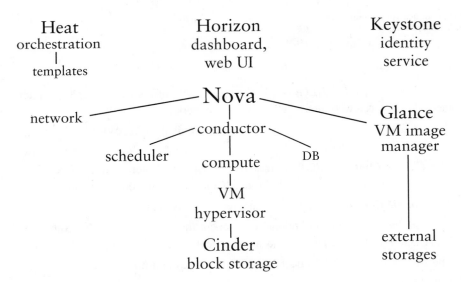

Figure 3.24
OpenStack for constructing private or public clouds in IaaS services. Courtesy of OpenStack, http://openstack .org, Apache License 2.0.

Functional Modules in OpenStack Library

The main services and components of OpenStack are shown in Figure 3.24. Block Storage (Cinder) provides persistent block-level storage devices for use with OpenStack compute instances managed by the dashboard. Networking (Neutron) offers a system for managing networks and IP addresses in a cloud deployment, and gives users self-service ability over network configuration. Dashboard (Horizon) provides administrators and users a graphical interface to access, provision, and automate cloud-based resources. Identity Service (Keystone) provides a central directory of users mapped to OpenStack services. It acts as a common authentication system across the cloud OS and can integrate with existing backend directory like LDAP.

OpenStack Compute (Nova)

This is the OpenStack Compute module. Nova is a controller to set up the internal fabric of any IaaS cloud by creating and managing a large cluster of virtual servers. The system applies KVM, VMware, Xen, Hyper-V, Linux container LXC, and bare-metal HPC configurations. The structure of a typical Nova instance is illustrated in Figure 3.25. The architecture for Nova is based on the concepts of shared-nothing and messaging-based information exchange. Hence, most communication in Nova is facilitated by message queues. To prevent blocking some components waiting for a response from others, deferred objects are introduced to enable callback when a response is received. The AMQP protocol offers such an advanced messaging queuing protocol. The cloud controller uses HTTP and AMQP protocols to interact with other Nova nodes or the AWS S3.

Nova was implemented in Python while utilizing a number of externally supported libraries and components. This includes Boto, an Amazon API provided in Python, and

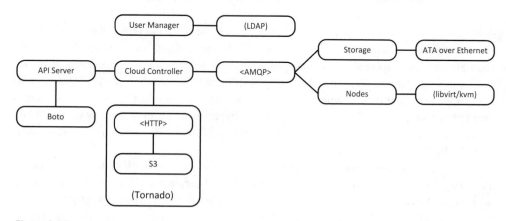

Figure 3.25
OpenStack Nova system architecture, where the resource controller uses HTTP and AMQP protocols to interact with the AWS S3 and other Nova nodes.

Tornado, a fast HTTP server used to implement the S3 capabilities in OpenStack. The API server receives http requests from Boto, converts the commands to and from the API format, and forwards requests to the cloud controller. The cloud controller maintains the global state of the system and assures authorization while interacting with the User Manager via the lightweight direct access protocol (LDAP). The Nova system interacts with the S3 service and manages participating nodes and storage workers. In addition, Nova integrates networking components to manage private networks, public IP addressing, VPN connectivity, and firewall rules.

OpenStack Storage (Swift)

This is a scalable and redundant storage system over multiple disks spread over large data center servers. The Swift solution is to build a number of interacting components, including a proxy server, a ring, object server, a container server, an account server, replication, updaters, and auditors. The proxy server enables inquiries to the location of the accounts, containers, or objects in Swift storage rings and routes the request. Thus, any object is streamed to or from an object server through the proxy server.

A ring represents a mapping between the names of entities stored on disk and their physical location. Separate rings are created for different accounts, containers, and objects. Data objects are stored as binary files with metadata stored in the file's extended attributes. This requires choosing the underlying file system for object server support, which is often not the case for standard Linux installations. To list objects, a container server is utilized. Listing of containers is handled by the account server. Redundancy (thus fault tolerance) is achieved through data replications over distributed disks.

3.6.3   VMware Virtualization Support for Building Hybrid Clouds

VMware provides cloud and virtualization software and services. This is the first company devoted to the virtualization of x-86 servers. VMware products are used to support more than 80% of the market share of enterprise clouds or hybrid clouds. Since 1998, VMware has developed a range of products starting with their hypervisors. VMware became well known for their first type 2 hypervisor known as GSX. This product has since evolved into two hypervisor product lines, VMware's type 1 hypervisors running directly on hardware, along with their hosted type 2 hypervisors. Figure 3.26 shows the VMware software packages for building hybrid clouds.

VMware software supports full virtualization of hardware to work with guest operating systems in a VM. Their software virtualizes the hardware for a video adapter, a network adapter, and hard disk adapters. The host provides pass-through drivers for guest USB, serial, and parallel devices. By doing so, VMware VMs become highly portable between computers. In practice, a system administrator can pause operations on a VM guest, move or

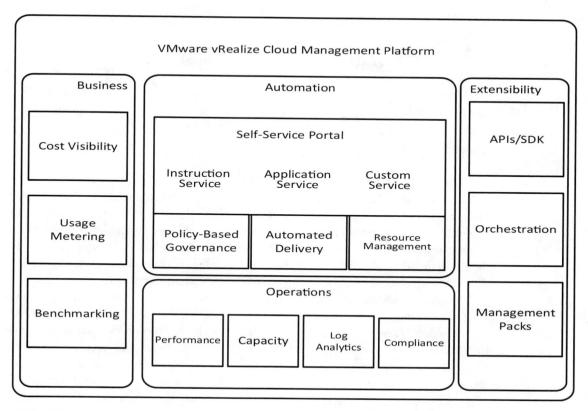

Figure 3.26
VMware software packages for building hybrid clouds: vSphere, NSX, and vSAN work in private clouds, SDN, and distributed storage operations that work jointly with public clouds.

copy that guest to another physical computer, and once there resume execution exactly at the point of suspension. VMware also developed a feature called vMotion, which allows the migration of operational guest VM machines between similar hardware hosts sharing the same disk storage.

VMware Workstation, Server, and ESX take an optimized approach to running target OSs on the host. Their software does not emulate an instruction set for different hardware not physically present. This significantly boosts performance, but can cause problems when moving VM guests between hardware hosts using different instruction sets. It also does not work between hardware hosts with a differing number of CPUs. Software that is CPU agnostic can usually survive such a transition, unless the CPU is agnostic, by forking at startup to stop the guest OS before moving it, then restarting after the move.

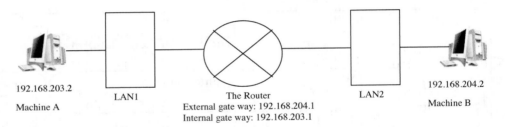

Figure 3.27
The topological of the virtual LAN in Problem 3.10.

VMware predated the virtualization extensions to the x86 instruction set. Their hypervisors are now designed to take advantage of the extensions. When direct execution cannot operate, such as with kernel-level and real-mode code, VMware products use binary translation to rewrite the code dynamically. The translated code gets stored in spare memory at the end of the address space. Thus, VMware operates faster than emulators, running at more than 80% of the speed than the virtual guest OS would run directly on the same hardware. VMs may deal with offending instructions by replacing them, or by simply running kernel-code in user mode.

Although VMware VMs run in user mode, the VMware Workstation itself requires the installation of various drivers in the host OS. Their cloud OS products appear as vSphere kernels and vCenter interfaces. Figure 3.27 shows the VMWare vRealize management platform for supporting hybrid construction. The virtual environments supported include the vSphere for compute purpose, NSX for SDN (server domain name), and vSAN for distributed storage applications. These virtual environments are managed in four subsystems: business, automation, operations, and extensibility of the hybrid cloud. Large numbers of service modules are built inside these subsystems. The main purpose is to build vSphere- or vCenter-based private clouds that can work with external public clouds jointly as a hybrid cloud.

3.7 Conclusions

In this chapter, we covered software technology for virtualization of large server clusters. We demonstrated the know-how in converting data center clusters into clouds at various abstraction levels. Both native VMs and hosted VMs were specified with examples. VM migration techniques for achieving fast disaster recovery were studied. Virtualization is made possible by using hypervisors and Docker engines. They are used to create VMs and application containers, respectively. Traditional VMs must be supported with their own guest OS and thus cost more memory to build. On the other hand, Docker engine creates containers directly with Linux kernel function calls.

Docker containers avoid the use of guest OS, which offers a major simplification from the VMs. Containers are more suitable for use in large-scale clusters with orchestrated containers. The concept of using a unikernel approach to further simplify the containers was introduced at its early stage of development. VMs, containers, and unikernels lay the necessary foundation of cloud construction and elastic resource management in Chapter 4. In particular, we will study the tradeoffs between using hypervisor-created VMs and Docker application containers. Several software tools for orchestration of a large pool of containers are also reviewed for massively parallel processing in machine learning or AI applications.

Homework Problems

3.1: Answer the following two questions briefly. You do not have to repeat everything in the book, just highlight the key points and identify distinctions in various approaches.

(a) How many levels of virtualization can one consider? Comment on their advantages, shortcomings, and limitations. What are the typical systems that you know of that have been implemented at each level in the past?

(b) What are the differences between full virtualization and paravirtualization? Explain the advantages, shortcomings, and limitations in the implementation and application of either class of VMs on today's host machines.

3.2: Describe the approaches used to exchange data among the domains of Xen and design experiments to compare the performance of data communication between the domains. This is designed to familiarize you with the Xen programming environment. It may require a longer time to port the Xen codes, implement the application codes, perform the experiments, collect the performance data, and interpret the results.

3.3: Install the VMware Workstation on your personal computer or laptop, whose operating system is Windows XP or Vista, and then install Red Hat Linux and Windows XP in the VMware Workstation. Configure the network settings of Red Hat Linux and Windows XP to get on Internet. Please write an installation and configuration guide for the VMware workstation, Red Hat Linux, and Windows XP in the Workstation.

3.4: Pick two hardware/virtualization services (HaaS) from the following cloud list: VMware, Intel, IBM, and XenEnterprise. Conduct in-depth studies beyond what you have read in the textbook. You need to uncover useful technical information by visiting the providers' websites or by searching through Google, Wikipedia, and any open literature. The purpose is to report their latest progresses in cloud technology, service offerings, software applications developed, business models applied, and success/failure lessons learned. Make sure that your study report is technically rich in content and avoids sales pitches.

3.5: Download a new kernel package from http://www.kernel.org/. Compile it in the Red Hat Linux in the VMware Workstation installed in problem 3.3 and in a Red Hat Linux on another physical machine. Compare the time used for the two compilations. Which one takes longer time to compile? What are their major differences?

3.6: Install a VM with guest OS: Red Hat Linux using the Xen installed in problem 3.3. Download the NBench from http://www.tux.org/~mayer/linux/bmark.html. Run the NBench on the VM on a real machine. Compare the performance of the programs on the two platforms.

3.7: Install the QEMU on Windows and then install FreeBSD on the QEMU. The QUME on Windows can be downloaded at http://www.h7.dion.ne.jp/~qemu-win/ and the .iso of FreeBSD (any version is okay) from http://www.freebsd.org/where.html. You may need the bximage of Bochs to create an img of FreeBSD for QEMU. It can be downloaded from: http://bochs.sourceforge.net/cgi-in/topper.pl?name=See+All+Releases&url=http://sourceforge.net/project/showfiles.phpqmrkgroup_ideq12580.

3.8: Set up an environment to test the live migration of Xen. Note: Since Xen does not support the mix of x86–32 and x86–64 well, you need to pay more attention to the OS you installed on your machine.

3.9: Leverage the QEMU to find out all processes of a Linux OS manually. Given the platform configuration: Host OS: Windows XP, virtualization layer: QEMU 0.9.1, QEMU VM: CENT OS 5.3 (Linux 2.6.18), and architecture: X86–32. Note: The version of the platforms could be changed to suit your familiarity with the hardware and software that are available in your cloud computing environment.

3.10: Build your own LAN by using VMware Workstation. The topological structure of the LAN is specified in Figure 3.27. Machine A is required to install Red Hat Linux while machine B is required to install Windows XP.

3.11: Explain the differences in the following two machine recovery schemes. Comment on their implementation requirements, advantages and shortcomings, and application potentials.

(a) Recovery of a PM failure by another PM.

(b) Recovery of a VM failure by another VM.

(c) Suggest a method to recover a VM from a failing PM.

3.12: Hardware and software resource deployment is often complicated and time-consuming. Automatic VM deployment can significantly speed up the time to instantiate new services or reallocate resources depending on the user needs. Go to http://wiki.systemimager.org/index.php/Automating_Xen_VM_deployment_with_SystemImager and get experience of automatic deployment using SystemImager and Xen-tools functionalities.

3.13: Design a large-scale virtual cluster system. This project may need three students to work together cooperatively for a whole semester. The functional requirements are as follows:

(a) Users can create multiple VMs at one time. Users can also manipulate and configure multiple VMs at the same time.

(b) Common software such as operating systems or libraries can be preinstalled as templates. These templates enable users to create a new execution environment rapidly.

(c) Users have their own profiles, which store the identification of data blocks for the corresponding VMs in the virtual cluster. New blocks should be created when users modify the data. The identifications for recently created blocks should be inserted into the profiles of the users.

3.14: Compare strengths, weaknesses, and suitable applications of VMs created by hypervisors over bare metal with the application containers created by Docker engine on a Linux host. You should compare them along the lines of resource demands, creation overhead, execution modes, implementation complexity, and execution environment, application isolation, OS flexibility, and host platforms.

3.15: The Magnum in Example 3.6 is a good software project to realize container orchestration and host clustering on OpenStack Nova machine instances. Check the OpenStack website to follow up with the latest release of the Magnum source codes. Write a short technical report to summarize your research findings.

3.16: The Eucalyptus presented in Example 3.8 has been upgraded by HP to support efficient management of IaaS cloud resources. Check the Eucalyptus website to follow up with their latest reported experiences by their registered user groups. Write a short technical report to summarize your research findings.

3.17: The vSphere 6 is a cloud OS commercially available from VMware. Review the open literature that reports the porting and application experiences and measured performance by its clients or user groups. Write a short technical report to summarize your research findings.

3.18: Conduct a comparative survey of the following five computer platform virtualization software products: VMware ESXi, Microsoft App-V, Google Kubernetes, Docker containers, and Citrix XenDesktop. You need to discover useful technical information by visiting the companies' websites or by visiting Google, Wikipedia, or any other open literature. The purpose is to report the latest progress in virtualization by these companies in terms of virtualization architecture, technology applied, and client application services provided. Make sure that your study report is technically solid and avoids the sales pitches from companies.

3.19: VM or container cluster management by orchestration is a hot topic concerning cloud providers and users. Pick two VM/container scheduling and orchestration software tools from seven candidate tools: CoreOS Fleet, Mesosphere Marathon, Docker Swarm, Apache Mesos, Hadoop Yarn, Google Kubernetes, and Docker Compose. Conduct an in-depth comparative study by visiting each company's website to discover technical information to explain the following issues.

(a) Why cluster management and orchestration tools are essential in cloud service.

(b) Briefly illustrate the architecture of each orchestration tool.

(c) Regarding the two VM/container scheduling and orchestration tools you selected, give a critical review about their strengths and challenges.

3.20: A new AWS service is offered for virtualization using Docker Engine to create application software containers. The service is known as Amazon EC2 Container Service (ECS). Explain how it is done on the AWS cloud. Report the ECS applicability and discuss the differences in using containers and VM instances used in the EC2.

3.21: You have studied the basic concepts of live migration of VMs and disaster recovery in Section 3.5.2. Answer the following questions.

(a) Why is VM live migration important in disaster recovery of data center or cloud operations?

(b) What virtualization support is needed to achieve fast cloning of VMs? Explain how VM cloning can enable faster disaster recovery.

3.22: Conduct a deeper study on VM live migration and disaster recovery in establishing fault tolerance in cloud systems. You may have to search for white papers or new R & D reports released from industry. Or, check with IEEE or ACM or Internet Society publications on published cloud papers. Write a short technical report to summarize your technical findings. Again, skip sales pitches and concentrate on technical innovations and new discoveries.

3.23: Study the unikernel and library OS architecture to justify its advantage and disadvantage in building future application containers, compared with the Docker engine over Linux kernel against the traditional VMs created by hypervisors working with traditional host OS.

References

[1] Adams, K., and O. Agesen. "A Comparison of Software and Hardware Techniques for x86 Virtualization." Proc. of the 12th International Conference on Architectural Support for Programming Languages and Operating Systems, October 21–25, 2006, San Jose, CA.

[2] Andre Lagar-Cavilla, H., J. A. Whitney, A. Scannell, P. Patchin, S. M. Rumble, E. de Lara, M. Brudno, M. Satyanarayanan. "SnowFlock: Rapid Virtual Machine Cloning for Cloud Computing." Proc. of EuroSys, Nuremburg, Germany, April 2009.

[3] Barham, P., B. Dragovic, K. Fraser, S. Hand, T. Harris, A. Ho, R. Neugebauer, I. Pratt, and A. Warfield. "XEN and the Art of Virtualization." *Proceedings of the Nineteenth ACM Symposium on Operating System Principles (SOSP19).* ACM Press, 2003.

[4] Chisnall, D. *The Definitive Guide to the XEN Hypervisor.* Prentice Hall International, 2007.

[5] Clark, C., K. Fraser, S. Hand, J. G. Hansen, E. Jul, C. Limpach, I. Pratt, and A. Warfield. "Live Migration of Virtual Machines." *Proc. of the Second Symposium on Networked Systems Design and Implementation (NSDI'05),* 2005, pp. 273–286.

[6] Grit, L., D. Irwin, A. Yumerefendi, and J. Chase. "Virtual Machine Hosting for Networked Clusters: Building the Foundations for Autonomic Orchestration." First International Workshop on Virtualization Technology in Distributed Computing (VTDC), November 2006.

[7] Hwang, K., and D. Li. "Trusted Cloud Computing with Secure Resources and Data Coloring." *IEEE Internet Computing* (September/October 2010): 30–39.

[8] Intel Open Source Technology Center. *System Virtualization—Principles and Implementation.* Tsinghua University Press, 2009.

[9] Jin, H., L. Deng, S. Wu, X. Shi, and X. Pan. "Live Virtual Machine Migration with Adaptive Memory Compression." *Proc. of IEEE Cluster Computing,* August–September 2009.

[10] Kivity, A., et al. "KVM: The Linux Virtual Machine Monitor." Proc. of the Linux Symposium, Ottowa, Canada, 2007, p. 225.

[11] KVM Project. "Kernel-Based Virtual Machines," http://www.linux-kvm.org.

[12] Nick, J. "Journey to the Private Cloud: Security and Compliance." Technical Presentation by EMC Visiting Team, Tsinghua University, Beijing, May 25, 2010.

[13] Nurmi, D., et al. "The Eucalyptus Open-Source Cloud Computing System." Proc. of the International Symposium on Cluster Computing and the Grid (CCGrid), Shanghai, China, September 2009, pp. 124–131.

[14] OpenStack, http://www.openstack.org. 2013.

[15] Qian, H., E. Miller, et al. "Agility in Virtualized Utility Computing." Proc. of Third International Workshop on Virtualization Technology in Distributed Computing (VTDC 2007), November 12, 2007.

[16] Rosenblum, M. "The Reincarnation of Virtual Machines." *ACM QUEUE* (July/August 2004).

[17] Rosenblum, M., and T. Garfinkel. "Virtual Machine Monitors: Current Technology and Future Trends." *IEEE Computer* 38 no. 5 (2005): 39–47.

[18] Shi, L., H. Chen, and J. Sun. "vCUDA: GPU Accelerated High Performance Computing in Virtual Machines." Proc. of the IEEE International Symposium on Parallel & Distributed Processing, 2009.

[19] Smith, J., and R. Nair. "The Architecture of Virtual Machines." *IEEE Computer* (May 2005).

[20] Sun Microsystems. "Solaris Containers: Server Virtualization and Manageability." Technical white paper (September 2004).

[21] Ublig, R., et al. "Intel Virtualization Technology." *IEEE Computer* (May 2005).

[22] VMware. "Understanding Full Virtualization, Paravirtualization, and Hardware Assist," http://www.vmware.com/files/pdf/VMware_paravirtualization.pdf.

[23] VMware. "The vSphere/6 Operating System for Virtualizing Data Centers." News Release, February 2009, http://www.vmware.com/products/vsphere/ 2016.

[24] Voosluys, W., et al. "Cost of VM Live Migration in Clouds: A Performance Evaluation." *Proc. of First International Conference on Cloud Computing,* pp. 267–295. IOS Press, 2009.

Chapter **4**

Cloud Architectures and Service Platform Design

4.1 Cloud Architecture and Infrastructure Design

This section presents cloud architectures and infrastructure design principles. We start with business models for clouds. We study the market-oriented cloud architecture based on multitenant technology. Then we learn how to convert data centers into clouds using the virtualization technology we learned in Chapter 3. Finally, we study resource provisioning methods in cloud management.

4.1.1 Public Clouds and Service Offerings

As consumers rely on cloud providers to supply more resources to satisfy their computing needs, they will require specific *Quality of Service* (QoS) to be maintained by their providers, in order to meet their objectives and sustain their operations. Cloud providers consider and meet different QoS parameters of each individual consumer as negotiated in specific *service-level agreements* (SLAs). To achieve this, the providers cannot deploy a traditional system-centric resource management architecture. Instead, market-oriented resource management is necessary to regulate the supply and demand of cloud resources to achieve market equilibrium between supply and demand.

The designer needs to provide feedback on economic incentives for both consumers and providers. The purpose is to promote QoS-based resource allocation mechanisms. In addition, clients can benefit from potential cost reductions from providers, which could lead to a more competitive market and thus lower prices. Figure 4.1 shows the high-level architecture for supporting market-oriented resource allocation in a cloud computing environment. This cloud is basically built with many entities: essentially the cloud sets no limit on dynamic negotiation of SLAs with competing requests.

Users, Brokers, and Resource Allocators
Users or brokers acting on their behalf submit service requests from anywhere in the world to the data center and cloud to be processed. The SLA Resource Allocator acts as the interface between the data center/cloud service provider and external users/brokers.

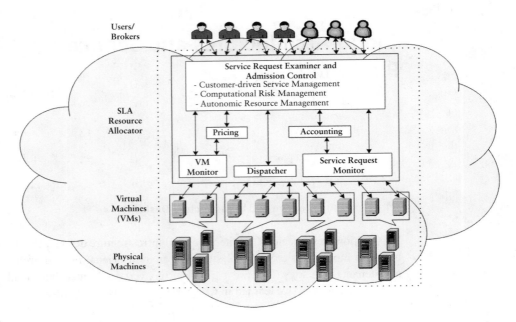

Figure 4.1

Market-oriented cloud architecture to expand or shrink leasing of resources based on QoS/demand from registered users or clients accepted SLA. Courtesy of R. Buyya et al.

The interaction of the following mechanisms are required to support SLA-oriented resource management.

1. **Service request examiner and admission control:** When a service request is first submitted, the Service Request Examiner and Admission Control mechanism interprets the submitted request for QoS requirements before determining whether to accept or reject the request. This ensures that there is no overloading of resources whereby many service requests cannot be fulfilled successfully due to limited resources available. It also needs the latest status information regarding resource availability and workload processing.

2. **Pricing and accounting:** The pricing mechanism decides how service requests are charged. For instance, requests can be charged based on submission time (peak/off-peak), pricing rates (fixed/changing), or availability of resources (supply/demand). Pricing serves as a basis for managing the supply and demand of computing resources within the data center. The accounting mechanism maintains the actual usage of resources by requests so that the final cost can be computed and charged to the users.

3. **VM monitor and dispatcher:** The virtual machine monitor (VMM) mechanism keeps track of the availability of VMs and their resource entitlements. The dispatcher mechanism starts the execution of accepted service requests on allocated VMs. The

service request monitor mechanism keeps track of the execution progress of service requests. Multiple VMs can be started and stopped on demand on a single physical machine to meet accepted service requests, hence providing maximum flexibility to configure various partitions of resources on the same physical machine to different specific requirements of service requests.

Cloud services are demanded by computing and IT administrators, software vendors, and end users. Individual users and organizational users demand very different services. The application providers at the *software as a service* (SaaS) level serve mainly individual users. Most business organizations are serviced by *infrastructure services* (IaaS) and *platform as a service* (PaaS) providers. The IaaS provide compute, storage, and communication resources to both applications and organizational users. The cloud environment is defined by the PaaS or platform providers. Note that the platform providers support both infrastructure services and organization users directly.

An Overview of Major Public Clouds

Cloud services rely on advances in server clustering, machine virtualization, service-oriented architecture, infrastructure management, power efficiency, etc. Consumers purchase cloud services in the form of IaaS, PaaS, or SaaS, as introduced in Chapter 1. There are many public cloud providers selling value-added utility services to all users. The cloud industry leverages the growing demand by many enterprises and business users to outsource their computing and storage jobs to cloud platforms. In Table 4.1, we summarize the profiles of five major clouds using the 2016 standard.

Amazon pioneered the IaaS business in supporting e-commerce and cloud applications used by millions of customers simultaneously. The elasticity in the Amazon cloud comes from the flexibility provided by the hardware and software services. The *Elastic Compute Cloud* (EC2) provides an environment for running virtual servers on demand. The *Simple*

Table 4.1
Five public cloud platforms and their service offerings (2016)

Public Clouds	Platform Model(s)	Typical Service Offerings	Website and Coverage in Book
Amazon Web Service (AWS)	IaaS, PaaS	EC2, S3, SQS, EMR, VPC, EBS, SNS, CloudFront, etc.	http://aws.amazon.com/, Section 4.3
Google App Engine	PaaS, SaaS	Gmail, Docs, GFS, BigTable, Chubby	https://developer.google.com, Section 4.4.1~2
Microsoft Azure	PaaS, SaaS	Live, SQL, Office 365, Dynamic CRM	http://www.windowsazure.com, Section 4.4.3
IBM SmartCloud	PaaS, SaaS, IaaS	Compute, Storage, Backup, Networking, Virtualization	http:/www.ibm.com/cloud-computing, Section 4.5.2
SalesForce Clouds	SaaS, PaaS	CRM, Sales, Marketing, Apex, Visual force	https://salesforce.com, Section 4.5.1

Storage Service (S3) provides unlimited online storage space. Both EC2 and S3 are supported in the *Amazon Web Services* (AWS) platform. Microsoft offers the Windows Azure platform for cloud applications. They have also supported the .NET service, dynamic CRM, Hotmail, and SQL applications. Salesforce offers extensive SaaS applications for online CRM applications using their own Force.com platforms.

All IaaS, PaaS, and SaaS models allow the user to access the services over the Internet, relying entirely on the infrastructures of the cloud service providers. These models are offered based on various SLAs between the providers and users. SLAs are more common in network services as they account for the QoS characteristics of the network services. For cloud computing services, it is difficult to find a reasonable precedent for negotiating an SLA. In a broader sense, the SLAs for cloud computing address service availability, data integrity, privacy, and security protections. More details of these clouds are provided in subsequent sections.

4.1.2 Business Models of Cloud Services

Cloud developers have to consider how to design the system to meet critical requirements such as high throughput, high availability, and fault tolerance. The operating system might need to be modified to meet the special requirements of cloud data processing. Based on the

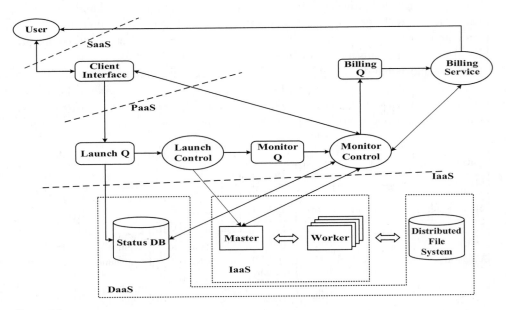

Figure 4.2
SaaS is closest to users to run their chosen applications. PaaS provides a cloud platform for users to develop new applications. The IaaS layer provides virtualized compute, storage, and data resources for users to form their desired working cluster configuration.

observation of some typical cloud computing instances such as Google, Microsoft, Yahoo, etc., the overall software stack structure of cloud computing software can be viewed as layers. Each cloud category has its own purpose and provides the interface for the upper category, such as a traditional software stack.

There exist many service extensions of clouds, as shown in Figure 4.2. The SaaS is closest to users with client interfaces, then PaaS through a sequence of queuing, monitory, and billing services. The player provides virtualized compute, storage, and data services marked as *hardware as a service* (HaaS), *network as a service* (NaaS), etc. The cloud infrastructure layer can be further subdivided as *data as a service* (DaaS) and *communication as a service* (CaaS) in addition to compute and storage in IaaS. *Location as a service* (LaaS) provides a colocation service to house, power, and secure all the physical hardware and network resources. Some authors call this *security as a service* (SaaS).

Table 4.2 classifies various types of clouds into five business models: application clouds, platform clouds, compute/storage clouds, colocation clouds, and network clouds. Their representative cloud service providers are also given in the table. We have already introduced the top three service models as SaaS, PaaS, and IaaS in Chapter 1. The platform cloud provides the PaaS, which sits on top of the IaaS infrastructure. On the top category, the cloud offers software application services (SaaS). The implication is that one cannot launch SaaS applications without a cloud platform. The cloud platform cannot be built if the compute and storage infrastructures are not there. However, the developer can rent the lower level clouds to build the higher level platforms or application portals.

Example 4.1 Colocation Cloud Services by Savvis

A colocation service deals with the management of data centers, where the equipment, space, and bandwidth are available for rental to retail customers. Colocation facilities provide space, power, cooling, and physical security for the server, storage, and

Table 4.2
Five cloud service categories and their representative providers

Cloud Categories	Cloud Service Providers
Application Clouds	OpenTable, Kenexa, NetSuite, RightNow, WebEx, Blackbaud, Concur Cloud, Telco, Omniture, Vocus, Microsoft OWA (Office 365), Google Gmail, Yahoo!, Hotmail
Platform Clouds	Force.com, Google App Engine, Facebook, IBM Blue Cloud, Postini, SQL Server, Twitter, Microsoft Azure, SGI Cyclone, Amazon EMR
Compute and Storage Clouds	Amazon AWS, Rackspace, OpSource, GoGrid, MeePo, FlexiScale, HP Cloud, Banknorth, VMware, XenEnterprise, iCloud
Colocation Clouds	Savvis, Internap, Digital Realty, Trusted Advisor, 365 Main
Network Clouds	AboveNet, AT&T, Qwest, NTT Communications

networking equipment of multiple clouds that interact with others via telecommunications and network service providers. Savvis is such a company, founded in 1996. They provide web hosting and colocation services, including cloud housing and power supply, infrastructure management, networking, and security services to both physical and network resources of many data centers.

Apple was Savvis' first large customer. By leveraging the Apple Computer customer reference and testimonials, Savvis closed additional large contracts with other cloud providers. The company sells managed hosting and colocation services globally, with more than 50 data centers in North America, Europe, and Asia, automated management and provisioning systems, and information technology consulting. By 2015, Savvis had provided colocation services to 2,500 business and government customers, including some large web hosting platforms such as AT&T, Rackspace, Verizon Business, Terremark, and SunGard. In 2006, Savvis' *content delivery network* (CDN) services were booming. They grew rapidly with network assets, customer contracts, and intellectual property used in their CDN business. Several lessons they learned were in spam support allegations and security breaches on IaaS cloud management. One such incidence was the charge of soliciting business from spammers for profit. As a result of the negative media attention, Savvis resumed business using Spamhaus (a worldwide organization of spam fighters) to prevent customer spam attacks. ∎

Business Models for SaaS Applications

Cloud computing enables many small businesses to compete in markets traditionally dominated by multinational corporations. A case study of the game cloud industry is given in Example 4.2. The business model for SaaS applications on commercial clouds is characterized in Table 4.3. The table entries reveal SaaS characteristics, application concerns, and business requirements. The business clouds are a subclass of general-purpose clouds. However,

Table 4.3
Business models for SaaS applications on the clouds

SaaS Characteristics	Application Concerns	Business Requirements
• Server based • Scalable and elastic • Multitenancy • One to many • Usage metering • Internet technology	• Service-level agreement guarantees • Security, including data ownership • Integration with on-premise systems • Transparency of supply chains • Limited customization • Immature technology and standards • Unproven financial and licensing models	• Easy to deploy and deliver • Online purchase and support • Low price, high volume, immediate need • Low competitive advantage • Common business processes • Loose, standard integration • Modest internal IT capacity • Low budgetary expenses

Source: A. Ojala and P. Tyrvainen, "Developing Cloud Business Models: A Case Study on Cloud Gaming," *IEEE Software Magazine*, 2011.

business clouds demand more credit checking, marketing analysis, billing, accounting, advertisement services, etc.

There are many business software applications that can take advantage of the massive storage and timely processing power of public clouds. However, business SaaS demands more SLA compliance, QoS guarantees, security enforcement, metadata governance, and data integrity checking. On-premise IT is safer and easy to control, especially to preserve data privacy. In order to make business clouds successful, we need to establish trust between cloud users and providers. Remote cloud resources must be based on immature technology and standards, limited customization, and unproven financial licensing models. Business requirements include simplicity to deploy and delivery of quality control. These involve online purchase and support, low price, modest internal IT investment, and low budgetary expenses.

Example 4.2   Business Model of a Game Cloud for SaaS Applications

A business model must identify the value a company offers to customers, companies, and network partners. The purpose is to generate profitable and sustainable revenue streams. One of the biggest concerns in online gaming is that of copyright violations. Executing the games on a cloud server makes illegal copying practically impossible. Figure 4.3 shows the business model suggested for online gaming applications on the cloud. The major players involved are the game licensors, the cloud server, network operators, and the endgame players. This diagram shows gaming SaaS content flow from left to right. The revenue flows from the end users to the players on the supplier end. This business model offers package software to SaaS clients, which differs from game play on PC or tablet computers, which involve the purchase of expense playback facilities. Cloud gaming avoids illegal game copying, exploits SaaS advantages, and adapts to infrastructure technology changes. ∎

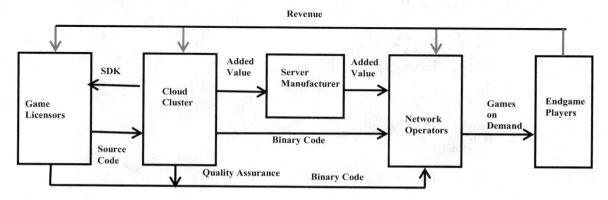

Figure 4.3

The business model of cloud-based game platform for SaaS applications. Source: A. Ojala and P. Tyrvainen, "Developing Cloud Business Models: A Case Study on Cloud Gaming," *IEEE Software Magazine* (2011).

4.1.3 Converting Data Centers to Cloud Platforms

A data center is often built with a large number of servers through a huge interconnection network. In Figure 4.4, we show a very large data center from Microsoft. This data center is as large as a shopping mart (11.5 times the size of a football field) under one roof. Such a megascale data center can house 400,000 to 1 million servers. The data centers are built with economies of scale. A small data center could have 1,000 servers. The larger the size of a data center, the lower the cost. The approximate monthly costs to operate a huge 400-server data center fall into three categories: (1) network-$13/Mbps; (2) storage-$0.4/GB; and (3) administration cost greater than that of a 1,000-server data center. The network cost to operate a small-sized data center is about 7 times greater and the storage cost is 5.7 times greater than those costs to run a very large data center. Microsoft has about 100 data centers distributed globally, and most of them are of very large size with more than tens of thousands of servers. Most data centers are built with commercially available components. An off-the-shelf server consists of a number of processor sockets, each with a multicore CPU and its internal cache hierarchy, local shared, and coherent *dynamic random-access memory (DRAM)*, and a number of directly attached disk drives. The DRAM and disk resources within the rack are accessible through the first-level rack switches and all resources in all racks are accessible via the cluster-level switch. Consider a data center built with 2,000

Figure 4.4
A huge data center that is 11.5 times the size of a football field. This data center houses 400,000 to 1 million servers. Courtesy of D. Gannon, "The Client+Cloud: Changing the Paradigm for Scientific Research." Keynote Address, CloudCom2010, Indianapolis, IN, November 2, 2010.

servers, each with 8 GB of DRAM and four 1-TB disk drives. Each group of 40 servers is connected through a 1-Gbps link to a rack-level switch that has an additional eight 1-Gbps ports used for connecting the rack to the cluster-level switch.

With a scale of tens of thousands of servers, concurrent failure, either hardware failure or software failure, of 1% of nodes is common. There are many failures that can happen in hardware, for example CPU failure, disk IO failure, and network failure. It is even quite possible that the whole data center does not work while facing the situation of a power crash. Moreover, some failures are caused by software. The service and data should not be lost in a failure situation. Reliability can be achieved by redundant hardware. The software must keep multiple copies of data in different locations and keep the data accessible, even when encountering disastrous server failures.

Cooling System of a Data Center Room

Figure 4.5 shows the layout and cooling facility of a warehouse data center. The data center room has a raised floor for hiding cables, power lines, and cooling supplies. The cooling system is somewhat simpler than the power system. The raised floor has a steel grid resting on stanchions about 2–4 ft above the concrete floor. The under-floor area is often used to route power cables to racks, but its primary use is to distribute cool air to the server rack. The *computer room air conditioning* (CRAC) unit pressurizes the raised floor plenum by blowing cold air into the plenum.

This cold air escapes from the plenum through perforated tiles that are placed in front of server racks. Racks are arranged in long aisles that alternate between cold aisles and hot aisles to avoid mixing hot and cold air. The hot air produced by the servers recirculates

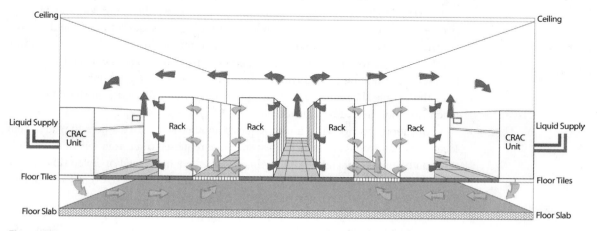

Figure 4.5
The cooling system in a raised-floor data center with hot-cold air circulation supported water heat exchange facilities. Courtesy of DLB Associates, D. Dyer, "Current Trends/Challenges in Data Center Thermal Management—A Facilities Perspective." Presentation at ITHERM, San Diego, CA, June 1, 2006.

back to the intakes of the CRAC units that cool it and then exhaust the cool air into the raised floor plenum again. Typically, the incoming coolant is at 12–14°C and the warm coolant returns to a chiller. Newer data centers often insert a cooling tower to precool the condenser water loop fluid. Water-based free cooling uses cooling towers to dissipate heat. The cooling towers use a separate cooling loop in which water absorbs the coolant's heat in a heat exchanger.

Example 4.3 Apple iCloud for Storage, Backup, and Personal Services

In 2011, Apple Inc. launched the iCloud as a cloud storage and cloud computing service. One of Apple's iCloud data centers is located in Maiden, North Carolina. By 2015, the iCloud service had over 500 million users. iCloud provides its users with means to store documents, photos, and music on remote servers at Apple data centers for download to iOS, Macintosh, or Windows devices. The cloud shares and sends data to other users and manages their Apple devices if lost or stolen.

The iCloud service also provides the means to wirelessly back up iOS devices directly to iCloud, instead of being reliant on manual backups to a host Mac or Windows computer using the iTunes services. The system also allows users to use AirDrop wireless service to share photos, music, and games instantly by linking with their mobile accounts. It also acts as a data syncing center for e-mail, contacts, calendars, bookmarks, notes, reminders (to-do lists), iWork documents, photos, and other data. The backup iOS devices route directly to iCloud, which acts as a data syncing center. These are major improvements from the past using iTunes services directly.

Big data types stored in iCloud include contacts, calendars, bookmarks, mail messages, notes, shared photo albums, iCloud photo library, My Photo Stream, iMessages, text (SMS), MMS messages, etc. Documents saved in iCloud using iOS and Mac applications are on the iCloud.com website. These data types and settings stored on your mobile devices (iPhones, iPads, etc.) are backed up by iCloud daily, even including purchase history for music, movies, TV shows, apps, and books. The iCloud also offers an interesting feature to find friends. Users of Find My Friends share their location with the people they choose. Location is determined using GPS in the iOS device when Location Services is turned on.

Notification appears when a user requests another user to see where they are. Your location is sent from your device when someone requests to see your location. The feature can be turned on and off at any time. To locate a misplaced or stolen iPhone, one can play sound at maximum volume, or cause flashing on screen, even if it is muted. This feature is useful if the device has been mislaid. One can also flag the device in lost mode: the user can lock it with a passcode. People finding the phone can call the owner directly on the lost device. The system can also erase all sensitive iPhone records on a stolen phone. ∎

Data Centers Built in Physical Containers

A modern data center is structured as a shipyard of server clusters housed in truck-towed containers. Figure 4.6 shows the interior details of a truck container of server clusters. Inside the container, hundreds of blade servers are housed in racks surrounding the container walls. An array of fans forces the heated air generated by server racks to go through a heat exchanger, which cools the air for the next rack (detail in callout) on a continuous loop. A single container can house a data center with a capacity to process 7 terabytes of data with 2 petabytes of storage. Modern data centers are becoming a shipyard of container trucks.

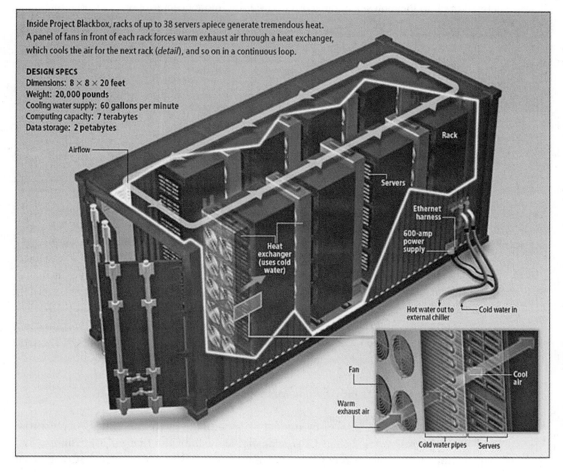

Inside Project Blackbox, racks of up to 38 servers apiece generate tremendous heat. A panel of fans in front of each rack forces warm exhaust air through a heat exchanger, which cools the air for the next rack (*detail*), and so on in a continuous loop.

DESIGN SPECS
Dimensions: 8 × 8 × 20 feet
Weight: 20,000 pounds
Cooling water supply: 60 gallons per minute
Computing capacity: 7 terabytes
Data storage: 2 petabytes

Airflow

Rack

Servers

Ethernet harness

600-amp power supply

Heat exchanger (uses cold water)

Hot water out to external chiller — Cold water in

Fan

Warm exhaust air

Cool air

Cold water pipes   Servers

Figure 4.6
The layout of a data center built inside a truck container cooled by chilled air circulation with cold-water heat exchanges. Courtesy of HP Project Blackbox, 2008.

The modular data center in container trucks was motivated by the demand for lower power consumption, higher computer density, and mobility to relocate data centers to better locations with lower costs in electricity, better cooling water supplies, and cheaper housing for maintenance engineers.

Both chilled air circulation and cold water flow through the heat exchange pipes to keep the server racks cool and easy to repair. Data centers usually are built on the ground where leases and utility for electricity is cheaper and cooling is more efficient. Both warehouse-scale and modular data centers in containers are needed. In fact, the modular truck containers can be used to put together a large-scale data center like a container shipyard. In addition to location selection and power saving in data center operations, one must consider data integrity, server monitory, and security management in data centers. These problems are easier to handle if the data center is centralized in a single large building.

Container Data Center Construction

The data center module is housed in a towable truck container. The modular container design includes the network gear, compute, storage, and cooling systems. One needs to increase the cooling efficiency by varying the water and air flow with better air flow management. Another concern is to meet seasonal load requirements. The construction of the container-based data center may start with one system (server), then move to a rack system design and finally to the container system. The staged development may take different amounts of time and demand an increasing cost.

Building a rack of 40 servers may take a half-day's effort. Extending to a whole container system with multiple racks for 1,000 servers requires proper layout of the floor space with power, networking, and cooling and complete testing. The container must be designed to be weatherproof and easy to transport. Modular data center construction and testing may take a few days to complete if all components are available and power and water supplies are handy. The modular data center approach supports many cloud service applications. For example, the healthcare industry will benefit by installing their data centers at all clinic sites. However, how to exchange information with the central database and maintain periodic consistency becomes a rather challenging design issue in a hierarchically structured data center. The security of colocation cloud services may involve multiple data centers.

4.1.4 Elastic Resources Provisioning Methods

Providers supply cloud services by signing SLAs with the end users. The SLAs must commit sufficient resources such as CPU, memory, and bandwidth that the user can use for a preset time period. Under-provisioning of resources would lead to broken SLAs and penalties. Over-provisioning of resources would lead to resource underutilization and, consequently, a decrease in revenue for the provider. Deploying an autonomous system to efficiently provision resources to users is indeed a very challenging problem.

The difficulty comes from the unpredictability of consumer demand, software and hardware failures, heterogeneity of services, power management, and conflicts in signed SLAs between consumers and service providers. Efficient VM provisioning depends on the cloud architecture and management of cloud infrastructures. The resource provisioning schemes also demand fast discovery of services and data in cloud computing infrastructures. In a virtualized cluster of servers, this demands efficient installation of the VMs, live VM migration, and fast recovery from failures. To deploy VMs, users treat them as physical hosts with customized operating systems for specific applications.

Figure 4.7 shows the resources provisioning effects. The x-axis is the timescale in ms. In the beginning, heavy fluctuations of CPU load are encountered. All three methods demand a few VM instances initially. Gradually, the utilization rate becomes more stabilized with a maximum of 20 VMs (100% utilization) provided for demand-driven provisioning in part (a). However, the event-driven method reaches a stable peak of 17 VMs toward the end of the event and drops quickly in part (b). The popularity provisioning leads to similar fluctuations with a peak VM utilization at the middle of the plot.

Three resource provisioning methods are presented below. The *demand-driven method* provides static resources. The *event-driven method* is based on predicted workload by time. The *popularity-driven method* is based on Internet traffic monitored.

1. ***Demand-driven resource provisioning:*** This method adds or removes computing instances based on current utilization level of the allocated resources. In general, when a resource has surpassed a threshold for some time, the scheme reduces that resource.

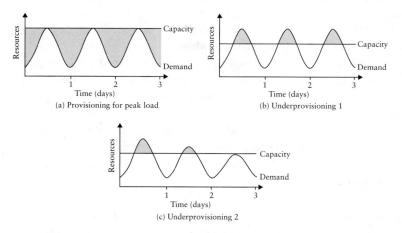

(a) Provisioning for peak load

(b) Underprovisioning 1

(c) Underprovisioning 2

Figure 4.7

Three cloud resource provisioning cases: (a) heavy waste due to over-provisioning of resources, (b) under-resources provisioning, and (c) under-then over-provisioning.

When a resource is below a threshold for a certain amount of time, that resource increases accordingly. Amazon implements such an "Auto Scaling" feature in their EC2 platforms.

2. ***Event-driven resource provisioning:*** This scheme adds or removes machine instances based on a specific time event. The scheme works better for seasonal or predicted events such as Christmas time. In special events, the number of users grows and decreases during the event period. The method results in minimal loss of the QoS, if the event is predicted correctly.

3. ***Popularity-driven resource provisioning:*** In this method, the Internet searches for popularity of certain applications and creates the instances by popularity demand. The scheme anticipates increased traffic with popularity. Again, the scheme has minimal loss of QoS, if predicted popularity is correct. Wasted resources may happen if traffic does not come as expected.

> **Example 4.4   MeePo: A Community Cloud Built at Tsinghua University, China**
>
> In a community cloud, a massive number of data blocks are dynamically shared by many user groups. MeePo presents a new associative data sharing method for effective use of virtual disks in the MeePo cloud shown in Figure 4.8. Innovations in the MeePo cloud design include big-data metering, associative data sharing, data block prefetching, *privileged access control* (PAC), and privacy preservation. These features are improved or extended from competing features implemented in DropBox, CloudViews, and MySpace. The reported benchmark results validate the claimed performance of the MeePo cloud.
>
> Multiple data centers work together in colocations of a community cloud. They must handle the rapid growth of data and tolerate disaster or outage in any single data center. We require a unified access model that applies distributed data sets across multiple data centers transparently. The sharing of big data is motivated by data dependence or common interests among users. Clients can serve as consumers or producers of the shared data blocks. Data could be shared by users registered in the same group or associated with different groups. Data sharing could be better protected by privileged accesses to safeguard the data integrity and preserve privacy. ∎

4.2   Dynamic Deployment of Virtual Clusters

In this section, we study four virtual cluster projects that have been built at academia and research centers. These projects have developed some automatic cluster deployment mechanisms, software tools, or configuration databases. We learn from these projects how best to achieve dynamic deployment of virtual clusters.

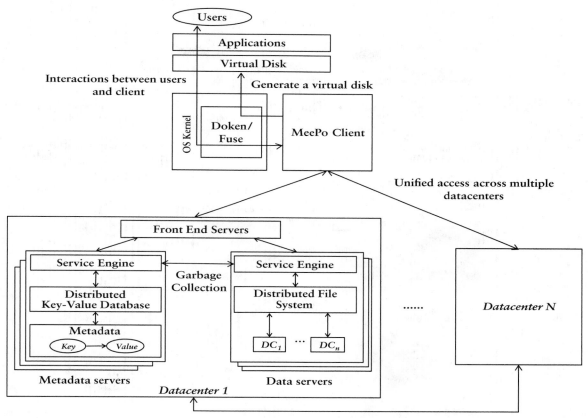

Figure 4.8
MeePo: A community cloud built at Tsinghua University over multiple data centers, where DC stands for data chunks. Courtesy of Wu et al., "Associative Big Data Sharing in Community Clouds—The MeePo Approach," *IEEE Cloud Computing Magazine* (January 2016).

4.2.1 Virtual Cluster Deployment Projects

Three virtual cluster research projects are summarized in Table 4.4. We briefly introduce their design objectives and reported performance results. The Cellular Disco at Stanford is a virtual cluster built in a shared-memory multiprocessor system. The COD and VIOLIN clusters are studied in the examples that follow.

Example 4.5 The Cluster-on-Demand (COD) at Duke University

Researchers at Duke University have reported the *cluster-on-demand* (COD) project. This is a virtual cluster management system for dynamic allocation of servers from a

Table 4.4
Experimental results on three research virtual clusters

Project Name	Design Objectives	Reported Results and References
Cluster-on-Demand (COD) at Duke University [12]	Dynamic resource allocation with a virtual cluster management system	Sharing of VMs by multiple virtual clusters using a Sun Grid Engine scheduler [11]
Cellular Disco at Stanford University	To deploy a virtual cluster on a shared-memory multi-processor	VMs deployed on multiple processors under a VMM called Cellular Disco [7]
VIOLIN at Purdue University [24]	Multiple VM clustering to prove the advantage of dynamic adaptation	Reduce execution time of applications running VIOLIN with the adaptation [32]

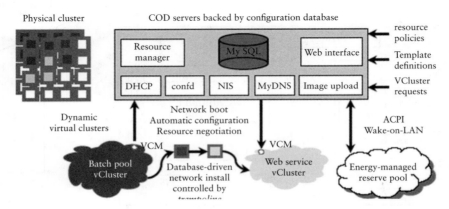

Figure 4.9
Cluster-on-Demand (COD) partitions a physical cluster into multiple virtual clusters. Courtesy of J. Chase, et al., "Dynamic Virtual Clusters in a Grid Site Manager," IEEE 12th Symposium on High-Performance Distributed Computing (HPDC), 2003.

computing pool to multiple virtual clusters. The idea is illustrated by the prototype implementation of the COD in Figure 4.9. The COD partitions a physical cluster into *multiple virtual clusters* (Vclusters). Vcluster owners specify the operating systems and software for their clusters through an XML-RPC interface. The Vclusters run a batch schedule from Sun's Grid Engine (SGE) on a web server cluster. The COD system can respond to load changes in restructuring the virtual clusters dynamically.

Figure 4.10 shows the variation of the number of nodes in each of three virtual clusters during eight days of a live deployment. Three application workloads requested by three user groups are labeled system, architecture, and bioGeometry in the trace plot. The experiments were performed with multiple SGE batch pools on a test bed of 80 rack-mounted IBM xSeries-335 servers within the Duke cluster. This trace plot clearly shows the sharp variation in cluster size (number of nodes) in 8 days. Dynamic provisioning and deprovisioning of virtual clusters are needed in real-life cluster applications.

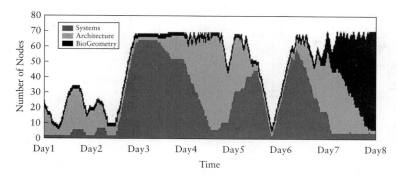

Figure 4.10

The cluster size variation in the COD for eight days at Duke University. Courtesy of J. Chase, et al., "Dynamic Virtual Clusters in a Grid Site Manager," IEEE 12th Symposium on High-Performance Distributed Computing (HPDC), Washington, DC, June 2003.

The Duke researchers use the SGE scheduler to demonstrate that dynamic virtual clusters are an enabling abstraction for advanced resource management in computing utilities like grids. The system supports dynamic, policy-based cluster sharing between local users and hosted grid services. Attractive features include resource reservation, adaptive provisioning, scavenging of idle resources, and dynamic instantiation of grid services. The COD servers are backed by a configuration database. This system provides resource policies and template definition in response to user requests. ∎

4.2.2 Virtual Cluster Configuration Adaptation

Purdue University has developed the VIOLIN Project, which has contributed to a dynamic cluster configuration among several physical clusters. The idea is described in the following cluster design example.

Example 4.6 The Violin Project at Purdue University

The Purdue VIOLIN Project applies live VM migration to reconfigure a virtual cluster environment. The purpose is to achieve better resource utilization in executing multiple cluster jobs on multiple cluster domains. The project leverages the maturity of VM migration and environment adaptation technology. The approach is to enable mutually isolated virtual environments for executing parallel applications on top of a shared physical infrastructure consisting of multiple domains. The idea is illustrated in Figure 4.11 with five concurrent virtual environments, labeled as VIOLIN 1–5, sharing two physical cluster domains.

The squares of various shadings represent the VMs deployed in the physical server nodes. The major contribution by the Purdue group is to achieve autonomic adaptation of the virtual computation environments as active, integrated entities. A virtual execution

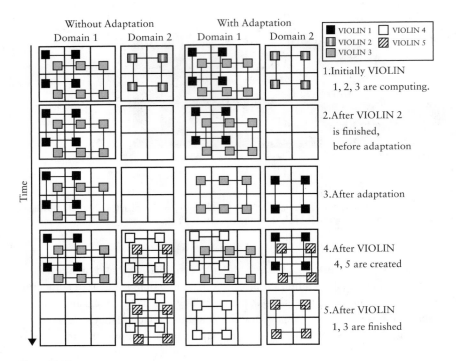

Figure 4.11
VIOLIN adaptation scenario of five virtual clusters on two hosted clusters. There are less idle nodes after the adaptation. Courtesy of P. Ruth et al., "Automatic Live Migration of Virtual Computational Environments in a Multi-Domain Infrastructure," *Technical Report*, Purdue University (2006).

environment is able to relocate itself across the infrastructure. It can scale its share of infrastructural resources. The adaptation is transparent to both users of virtual environments and administrations of infrastructures. The adaptation overhead is maintained at 20 s out of a total time of 1,200 s in solving a large NEMO 3D problem of 1 million particles.

The message being conveyed here is that virtual environment adaptation can enhance resource utilization significantly at the expense of less than 1% of increase of total execution time. The migration of VIOLIN environments does pay off. Of course, the gain in shared resource utilization will benefit many users. The performance gain varies with different adaptation scenarios. We leave the readers to trace the execution of another scenario in problem 4.12 to tell the difference. Virtual networking is a fundamental component of the VIOLIN system. ∎

4.2.3 Virtualization Support for Data Center Clusters

Data centers must be virtualized to serve as a cloud provider. Four *virtual infrastructure* (VI) managers or OS are summarized in Table 4.5. These VI managers and OS are specially

Table 4.5
Open source virtual infrastructure managers and cloud operating systems

Manager/OS, Platforms, License	Resources Being Virtualized, Web Link	Client API, Language	Hypervisors Used	Public Cloud Interface	Special Features
Nimbus, Linux, Apache v2	VM creation, virtual cluster, http://www.nimbusproject.org/	EC2 WS, WSRF, CLI	Xen, KVM	EC2	Virtual networks
Eucalyptus, Linux, BSD	Virtual networking (Example 3.23) http://www.eucalyptus.com/	EC2 WS, CLI	Xen, KVM	EC2	Virtual networks
OpenNebula, Linux, Apache v2	Managing VM, host, virtual network, scheduling tools http://www.opennebula.org/	XML-RPC, CLI, Java	Xen, KVM	EC2, ElasticHosts	Virtual networks, Dynamic provisioning
vSphere/6, Linux, Windows, Proprietary	Virtualizing OS for data centers http://www.vmware.com/products/vsphera/ (Example 4.7)	CLI, GUI, Portal, WS	VMware ESX, ESXi	VMware vCloud partners	Data protection, vStorage, VMFS, high availability

tailored for virtualizing data centers that often own a large number of servers in clusters. Nimbus, Eucalyptus, and OpenNebula are all open-source software, available to the general public. Only the VMWare vSphere 6 is a proprietary OS for cloud resource virtualization and management over the data centers.

These VI managers are used to create VMs and aggregate them into virtual clusters as elastic resources. Nimbus and Eucalyptus support essentially virtual networks. OpenNebula has additional features to provision dynamic resources and make advance reservations. All three public VI managers apply Xen and KVM for virtualization. vSphere 6 uses the hypervisors ESX and ESXi from VMware. Only vSphere 4 supports virtual storage in addition to virtual networking and protecting data. We will study Eucalyptus and vSphere 6 in two examples below.

4.2.4 VMware vSphere 6: A Commercial Cloud Operating System

In what follows, we present the functions of vSphere 6 as a proprietary OS released by VMware. This OS is used to create VMs and aggregate them into virtual clusters as elastic resources. The vSphere 6 uses the hypervisors ESX and ESXi from VMware. Furthermore, vSphere 6 supports virtual storage in addition to virtual networking and protecting data. The proprietary vSphere is compared with the open-source Eucalyptus in Table 4.5. Eucalyptus supports Xen and KVM virtualization and mainly the virtual networking of VMs or containers.

Example 4.7 VMware vSphere 6: A Cloud OS for Hybrid Clouds

The vSphere 6 is a cloud operating system developed by VMware in 2015. vSphere extends from the earlier virtualization software products, namely the Workstation virtualization, ESX for server virtualization, and virtual infrastructure for server clusters. The system interacts with user applications via an interface layer, called vCenter, managed by VMware. The main use of vSphere is to offer virtualization support and resource management of data center resources in building enterprise clouds. VMware claims that the system is the very first cloud OS that supports availability, security, and scalability in general-purpose cloud services. Figure 4.12 shows the key functional modules in VMware vSphere 6.

vSphere 6 was built with two functional software suites: the *infrastructure services* right on top of the hardware and the *application services* toward user applications, shown at the top of Figure 4.12. The infrastructure services are shown at the bottom. This suite has three component packages mainly for virtualization purposes: vCompute is supported by ESX, ESX1, and DRS virtualization libraries from VMWare. vStorage is supported by VMS and thin provisioning libraries. vNetwork offers distributed switching and networking functions. These packages interact with the hardware servers, disks, and networks in the data center. These infrastructure functions also communicate with other external clouds.

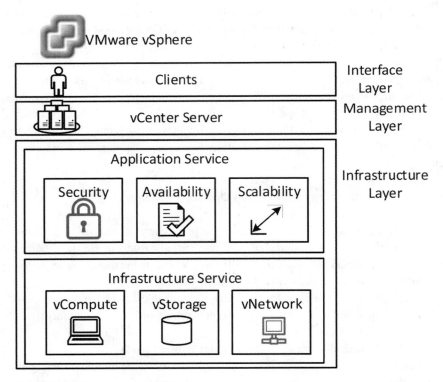

Figure 4.12
Functional modules in VMware vSphere 6 operating system for private/hybrid clouds.

The application services are also divided into three groups: namely availability, security, and scalability. The availability support includes vMotion, storage vMotion, high availability (HA), fault tolerance, and data recovery from VMWare. The security package supports vShield Zones and VMSafe. The scalability package has been built with DRS and Hot Add. The maximum configuration supported by vSphere 6 has the following specifications: 64 hosts per cluster, 8,000 VMs per cluster, 480 CPUs per host, 12 TB of memory, 1,000 VMs per host, 128 vCPUs per VM, and 4 TB RAM per VM.

vSphere Data Protection includes all vSphere Data Protection Advanced functionality such as up to 8 TB of deduped data per VDP appliance, up to 800 VMs per VDP appliance, application level backup and restore of SQL Server, Exchange, SharePoint, replication to other VDP appliances and EMC Avamar, and data domain support. To fully understand the use of vSphere 6, users must also learn how to use the vCenter interfaces to link with existing applications or to develop new applications. ■

Failure Management in vSphere 6

The vSphere fault tolerance is illustrated in Figure 4.13. Continuous availability is achieved by live migration of VMs. Multiple databases are always shared by the primary and secondary VMs. vSphere 6 has built-in three networks for VM management, fault-tolerant logging,

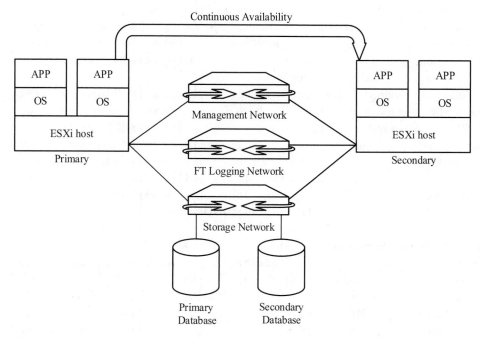

Figure 4.13
Switching over between virtual machines sharing multiple databases in vSphere disaster recovery operations.

and storage accesses. Therefore, all single failures can be fully tolerated through switchover and switchback capabilities.

4.3   Amazon AWS Cloud and Service Offerings

In this section, we first study *service-oriented architecture* (SoA) for building public, private, and hybrid clouds. Then we study the management issues in using the VMs and containers to build virtual clusters for use in cloud services. To this end, we present the three most popular cloud architectures: AWS cloud, OpenStack, and VMware systems.

4.3.1   Three Cloud Architectures and Services Convergence

Cloud computing delivers infrastructure, platform, and software (applications) as services, which are made available as subscription-based services in a pay-as-you-go model to consumers. The IaaS, PaaS, and SaaS models form three pillars on top of cloud computing solutions that are delivered to end users. All three models allow the user to access the services over the Internet, relying entirely on the infrastructures of the cloud service providers.

These models are offered based on various SLAs between the providers and users. In a broad sense, the SLA for cloud computing is addressed in terms of service availability, performance and data protection, and security aspects. The SaaS is applied at the application end using special interfaces by users or clients. At the PaaS layer, the cloud platform must perform billing services and handling of job queuing, launching, and monitoring services. At the bottom layer of IaaS services, databases, compute instances, file systems, and storage must be provisioned to yield user demands.

Most of today's clouds follow the SoA organization. In general, cloud architecture can be described by two layers of resources. The bottom layer is the static infrastructure, system boundary, and user interfaces with the outside world. The upper layer is formed by dynamic resources such as VMs or containers under the management of cloud OS or control centers. In Table 4.6, we compare the three SoAs for building three types of clouds. AWS cloud represents the most popular public cloud. OpenStack is used for private cloud construction in small businesses and protected communities. The commercial VMWare software packages are for building hybrid clouds used by enterprises and large organizations.

Example 4.8   Service-Oriented Architecture of the AWS Public Cloud

SoA architecture differs from the traditional computer architecture in many ways. The components in a traditional computer system are tightly coupled. This has restricted application flexibility and makes it difficult to maintain the system. The concept of SoA started with IBM, HP, and Microsoft in early 2000. The principle of SoA is hinged on loosely coupling the service blocks of a system. Service interfaces are designed to link various service modules. This will free up the binding effects of the system, enabling

Table 4.6
Comparison of three cloud platform architectures

Cloud System Features	Amazon Web Service (AWS): Public Cloud	OpenStack Systems: Private Cloud	VMWare Systems: Hybrid Cloud
Service Model(s)	IaaS, PaaS	IaaS	IaaS, PaaS
Developer/Provider and Design	Amazon (Sec.4.3)	Rackspace/NASA and Apache (Section 2.3.4)	VMWare (Section 2.3.5) Proprietary
Architecture Packages and Scale	Data centers distributed as availability zones in many global regions (Figure 2.14)	Small cloud at owner sites, licensed thru Apache (Figure 2.15)	Private clouds interacting with public clouds (Figure 2.18)
Cloud OS/ Software Support	Supporting both Linux and Windows machine instances with autoscaling and billing	Open source, extending from Eucalyptus and OpenNebula	vSphere and vCenter, supporting x-86 servers with NSX and vSAN
User Spectrum	General public: enterprises and individual users	Research centers or small businesses	Enterprises and large organizations

higher scalability, and modular growth and maintenance. That is exactly what a cloud system should have. Amazon CEO Jeff Bezos has pushed the SoA idea into the development of the AWS cloud, which has been proven successful in getting AWS as the top-choice public cloud.

The AWS cloud is built with a global infrastructure of many data centers located in different regions of the word. For example, the AWS core EC2 has nine regional sites all over the world. Within each region, they group the data centers into *availability zones* (AZ). Each AZ is built with at least three data centers with 50 KM distance between them. The multi-data center approach enhances the performance, reliability, and fault tolerance of the AWS cloud greatly. Amazon global infrastructure distributes resources globally as shown in Figure 4.14. There are a large number of edge data centers that can be added into the AWS cloud operations. AWS cloud started by providing IaaS services in compute and storage functions. Now the services have been extended to the PaaS level as well.

The PaaS services are meant to support big data, database, and data analytics operations. Large numbers of service modules are built into both IaaS and PaaS platforms of AWS. The details of these services will be treated in Section 4.3. Special service interfaces are designed to provide communications among the service modules. The combined IaaS+PasS services are also supported in Microsoft Azure and Google clouds. The cloud management coordinates the entire cloud operation interims of monitory, security, billing, and use of third-party software. ∎

IaaS clouds allow users to use virtualized IT resources for computing, storage, and networking. In short, the service is performed by rented cloud infrastructure. The user can deploy and run his own applications over his chosen OS environment. The user does not

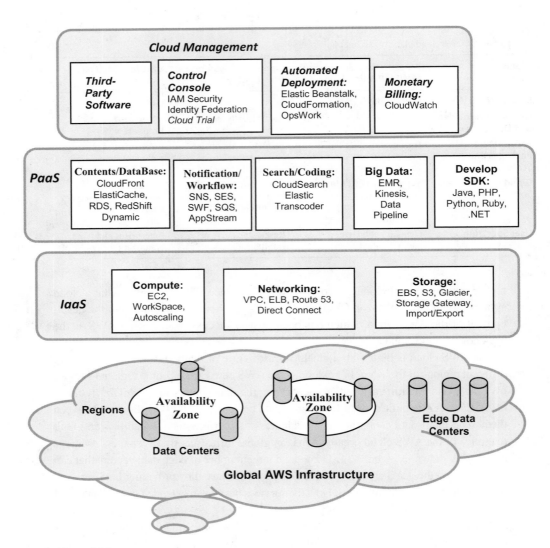

Figure 4.14
The AWS public cloud consisting of the top management layer, PaaS, and IaaS platforms, and the global infrastructure built over data centers in availability zones located in various regions.

Table 4.7
Public IaaS clouds and their VM instance configurations (August 2015)

Cloud Name	Virtual Machine Instance Configurations	API and Access Tools
Amazon EC2	Each instance has 1–20 EC2 processors, 1.7–15 GB memory, and 160 TB storage	CLI or Web Service (WS) portal
GoGrid	Each instance has 1–6 CPUs, 0.5–8 GB memory, and 30–480 GB storage	REST, Java, PHP, Python, Ruby
Rackspace Cloud	Each instance has a 4-core CPU, 0.25–16 GB memory, and 10–620 GB storage	REST, Python, PHP, Java, C#, .NET
FlexiScale in UK	Each instance has 1–4 CPUs, 0.5–16 GB memory, and 20–270 GB storage	Web console

manage or control the underlying cloud infrastructure but has control over the OS, storage, deployed applications, and possibly select networking components. This IaaS model encompasses *storage as a service*, compute *instances as a service*, and CaaS. Some representative IaaS providers are listed in Table 4.7.

The platform cloud is an integrated computer system consisting of both hardware and software infrastructure. The user application can be developed on this virtualized cloud platform using some programming languages and software tools supported by the provider (e.g., Java, Python, .NET). The user does not manage the underlying cloud infrastructure. The cloud provider supports user application development and testing on a well-defined service platform. This PaaS model enables the means to have a collaborated software development platform for users from different parts of the world. This model also encourages third parties to provide software management, integration, and service monitoring solutions.

To develop, deploy, and manage the execution of applications using the provisioned resources demands a cloud platform with some software support. Such a cloud platform includes the operating system and run-time library support. This has triggered the creation of the PaaS model to enable the user to develop and deploy his user applications. PaaS cloud services offered by four providers are shown in Table 4.8. These PaaS service providers include Google App Engine, Microsoft Azure, Salesforce, Amazon Elastic Map-Reduce, and Aneka in Australia.

There is a growing trend that the service models in many public clouds are being upgraded hierarchically. With more platform software support, IaaS clouds are being upgraded to provide PaaS services as well. Many IaaS or PaaS clouds are also being extended to provide SaaS application services. The best example is AWS which started as a pure IaaS cloud. Now it provides PaaS and some SaaS services as well. Both the Google cloud and Azure cloud started as PaaS platforms. Now they both provide some IaaS and SaaS services. Eventually, most public clouds should be able to provide IaaS, PaaS, and SaaS services. Further, many private clouds are being upgraded to become hybrid clouds under new management policies.

Table 4.8
Public clouds offering PaaS services (August 2015)

Cloud Name	Languages and Developer Tools	Programming Models Supported by Provider	Target Applications and Storage Option
Google App Engine	Python, Java, and Eclipse-based IDE	MapReduce, Web programming on demand	Web applications and BigTable storage
Salesforce, Force.com	Apex, Eclipse-based IDE, web-based Wizard	Workflow, Excel-like, Web programming on demand	CRM and add-on app development for business
Microsoft Azure	.NET, Azure tools for MS Visual Studio	Dryad, Twister, .NET Framework	Enterprise and web applications
Amazon Elastic MapReduce	Hive, Pig, Cascading, Java, Ruby, Perl, Python, PHP, R, and C++	MapReduce, Hadoop, Spark	Data processing, e-mail, e-commerce, S3, and WorkDocs

4.3.2 AWS EC2 Compute Engine and S3 Storage Cloud

The global AWS cloud architecture is illustrated in Figure 4.15. In what follows, we give more details of the internal core architecture of the AWS cloud, namely the EC2, as shown in Figure 4.16. The AWS provides extreme flexibility (VMs) for users to execute their own applications. Elastic load balancing automatically distributes incoming application traffic across multiple Amazon EC2 instances and allows user to avoid nonoperating nodes and to equalize load on functioning images.

Both autoscaling and elastic load balancing are enabled by CloudWatch which monitors running instances. CloudWatch is a web service that provides monitoring for AWS cloud resources, starting with Amazon EC2. It provides customers with visibility into resource utilization, operational performance, and overall demand patterns—including metrics such as CPU utilization, disk reads and writes, and network traffic.

Amazon offers a Relational Database Service (RDS) with a messaging interface. The Elastic MapReduce capability is equivalent to Hadoop running on the basic EC2 offering. AWS Import/Export allows one to ship large volumes of data to and from EC2 by shipping physical disks; it is well known that this is often the highest bandwidth connection between geographically distant systems. CloudFront implements a content distribution network. Amazon DevPay is a simple-to-use online billing and account management service.

The Flexible Payments Service (FPS) provides developers of commercial systems on AWS with a convenient way to charge Amazon's customers that use such services built on AWS. Customers can pay using the same login credentials, shipping address, and payment information they already have on file with Amazon. The Fulfillment Web Service allows merchants to access Amazon cloud through simple web services. EC2 and S3 are two core IaaS service modules in the AWS cloud system as shown in Figure 4.15.

The EC2 is mainly used for compute services and S3 is for scalable storage service for users. Worldwide, there are nine regional EC2 facilities distributed on U.S. East and West coasts, Europe, Tokyo, Australia, etc. Users accessing local EC2 should have lower

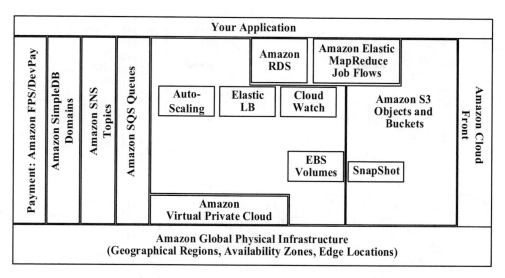

Figure 4.15
The AWS system architecture, services modules, and user-end interfaces.

network delays. The S3 is extremely large in capacity. The following examples give some technical details of these cloud facilities at the AWS cloud.

Example 4.9   AWS Elastic Compute Cloud (EC2) for IaaS

The structure of the EC2 is shown in Figure 4.16. The EC2 supports many cloud services with a cluster of machine instances. Both Linux and Windows instances are available. The Amazon Machine Images (AMI) offers the templates to create machine instances of various types. Public AMIs can be freely used by any user. Private AMIs are created for owners' private use only, while paid AMIs can be shared among users with payment between the users and owners. The AMI launch cycle is shown in the blowout box, where security is enforced with instance-access firewalls.

Automatic scaling and load balancing among the instances are supported in EC2. The machine instances provisioned in an EC2 cluster are selected upon user demand. The cluster configuration should match with the workload anticipated. We will study scale-out and scale-up strategies for EC2 configuration control in Chapter 10. Autoscaling allows you to scale your EC2 size up or down automatically according to some threshold conditions. The number of EC2 instances in a cluster is driven by workload demand. Autoscaling is particularly well suited for applications that experience frequent variability in workload. The scaling technique is automatically triggered by Amazon CloudWatch and available at no additional charge to the users beyond the use of the CloudWatch. ∎

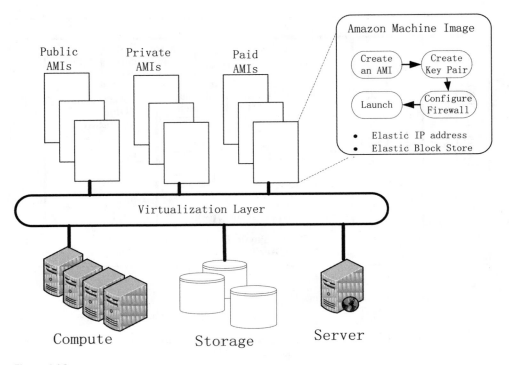

Figure 4.16

The EC2 execution environment where Amazon Machine Image (AMI) can be created from public, private, or paid pools with security protection.

The AWS platform supports many smaller clients and large companies to build their leased clouds to run their businesses and make a profit from a huge number of Internet users. One good example is DropBox, which applied the S3 for a long time to provide their backup data storage operations before they built their own data center storage. The analytics services are newly added. They apply Elastic MapReduce (EMR) using Hadoop or Spark. Real-time streaming and support of the orchestration of containers is also provided.

Example 4.10   AWS S3 Architecture with Block-Oriented Data Buckets

Amazon S3 provides an S3 that can be used to store and retrieve any amount of data, at any time, from anywhere on the web. S3 provides object-oriented storage service for users. Users can access their objects through SOAP protocol with any browser. The S3 execution environment is shown in Figure 4.17. The fundamental operation unit of S3 is an object, which is attributed to value, meta, and access control. Each object is stored in a bucket and retrieved via a unique and developer-assigned key. The bucket is the container of the object.

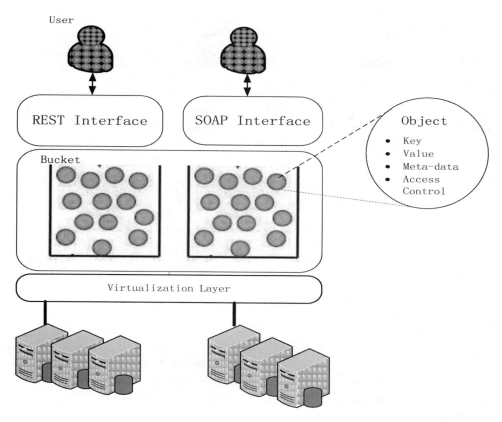

Figure 4.17
The Amazon S3 storage service for holding unlimited data objects.

Authentication mechanisms are provided to ensure that data is kept secure from un-authorized access. Objects can be made private or public, and rights can be granted to specific users. The default download protocol is HTTP. There is no data transfer charge between Amazon EC2 and S3 within the same region. The steps to use S3 are: (1) create a bucket at regions where your bucket and object(s) reside to optimize latency, minimize costs, or address regulatory requirements; (2) upload objects to your bucket, where your data is backed by the Amazon SLA; and (3) the access controls are optional to grant others access to your data from anywhere in the world. ■

4.3.3 Other AWS Cloud Service Offerings

Three tables are given below to summarize the offerings by AWS in three major service areas: Table 4.9 lists 15 compute, storage, database, and networking service offerings by AWS. Many

Table 4.9
Compute, storage, database, and networking services in AWS cloud

Category	Offering	Service Modules or Short Description
Compute	EC2	Virtual servers in the AWS cloud
	Lambda	Run code in response to events
	EC2 Container Service	Run and manage Docker containers
Storage & Content Delivery	S3	Scalable storage in the AWS cloud
	Elastic File System	Fully managed file system for EC2
	Storage Gateway	Integrate on-premises IT facilities with cloud storage
	Glacier	Archive storage in the AWS cloud
	CloudFront	Global content delivery network
Database	RDS	MySQL, PostgreSQL, Oracle, SQL Server
	DynamicDB	Predictable and scalable NoSQL data store
	ElastiCache	In-memory cache
	RedShift	Managed petabyte-scale warehouse service
Networking	VPC	Virtual private cloud as isolated cloud resources
	Direct Connect	Dedicated network connection to AWS
		Scalable DNS and domain name registration

of these are of SaaS type, except users can request their own customized server clusters to run these applications. The application services cover message queuing, real-time streaming, email sending, searching, synchronization, mobile, and analytics workflow orchestration operations. Most of these are newly added features in the AWS cloud in recent years. The mobile services help users synchronize their mobile data with rented S3 storage. Mobile analytics are provided to analyze these data for decision making or responses. The Simple Notification Service (SNS) service handles push notification between mobile phones and the S3 service.

Table 4.10 specifies the application, mobile, and analytics services offered by the AWS cloud. These are indeed SaaS offerings. Table 4.11 summarizes the administration, enterprise, security, and deployment services offered by the AWS cloud. These are related PaaS offerings. In terms of services provided, the AWS is no longer just a pure IaaS cloud. By far, the EC2 and S3 are the most popular IaaS services provided by AWS. Many other IaaS clouds are also trying to make their cloud systems compatible with EC2 and S3. The RDS service supports relational SQL services. DynamicDB supports NoSQL operations over unstructured big data. The networking services support virtual clustering of the network resources.

Example 4.11 Static or Dynamic Web Hosting on AWS S3 and CloudFront Services

Any user can create a personal or company website on the AWS cloud. The idea is to reserve some space in S3 to host the static website content. The Amazon Route 53

Table 4.10
Application, mobile, and analytics services in the AWS cloud

Category	Offering	Service Modules or Short Description
Application Services	SQS	Message queue services
	SWF	Workflow service for coordinating app components
	AppStream	Low-latency application streaming
	Elastic Transcoder	Easy-to-use scalable media transcoding
	SES	E-mail sending and receiving service
	CloudSearch	Managed search service
	API Gateway	Build, deploy, and manage APIs
Mobile Services	Cognito	User identity and app data synchronization
	Device Farm	Test Android, Fire OS, and iOS apps on cloud devices
	Mobile Analytics	Collect, view, and export app analytics
	SNS	Simple push notification service
Analytics Services	EMR	Managed elastic Hadoop (MapReduce) framework
	Kinesis	Real-time processing of streaming data
	Data Pipeline	Orchestration for data-driven workflows
	Machine Learning	Build machine-learning prediction solutions

Table 4.11
Administration, security, enterprise, and deployment services in the AWS cloud

Category	Offering	Service Modules or Short Description
Administration and Security	Directory Service	Managed directory in the AWS cloud
	Identity/Access Manager	Access control and key management
	Trusted Advisor	AWS cloud optimization expert
	CloudTrail	User activity and change tracking
	Configuration	Resource configurations and inventory
	CloudWatch	Resource and application monitoring
	Service Catalog	Personalized catalog of AWS resources
Enterprises and Applications	Workplaces	Desktops in the AWS cloud
	WorkDocs (New)	Secure enterprise storage and sharing service
	WorkMail	Secure email and calendaring service
Deployment and Management	Elastic Beanstalk	AWS application containers
	OpsWorks	DevOps application management service
	CloudFormation	Templated AWS resource creation
	CodeDeploy	Automated code deployments
	CodeCommit	Managed Git repositories
	CodePipeline	Continuous delivery of codes

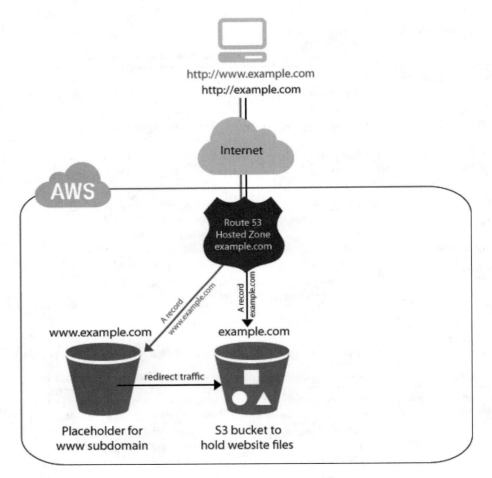

Figure 4.18
Construction of a static website hosted on the AWS S3.

provides custom domain names, and the Amazon CloudFront is applied to reduce latency that customers face while accessing the rented website. Additional services beyond
static web hosting could be applied to make the website dynamically maintained. Figure 4.18 shows the architecture of such a hosted website at AWS S3.

The idea is to use EC2 as a virtual platform to perform server-side processing.
Amazon Elastic Block Store (EBS) provides persistent data storage for the EC2 virtual server. Finally, autoscaling is applied to add or reduce nodes depending on the
workload encountered. Visit the following web link to check out more details on hosting a WordPress blog on the EC2 using Linux Instances: http://docs.aws.amazon.com
/AWSEC2/latest/UserGuide/hosting-wordpress.html. One can also create dynamic

web pages in WordPress by reading the following tutorial: http://www.tutorialized .com/tutorial/How-To-Create-Dynamic-Page- In-WordPress/77386. ∎

Table 4.10 lists most of the application service offerings in AWS cloud. These cover the mobile computing, machine learning (ML), and data analytics applications.

Amazon ML offers a service that allows data scientists to use ML technology. Amazon ML provides visualization tools and wizards that guide user through the process of creating prediction models. This frees up the developers from learning complex ML algorithms and software tools. The Amazon ML makes it easy to obtain predictions using simple APIs. The user does not have to implement custom prediction generation code.

Example 4.12   Three Major Applications of Cloud Services

In general, cloud applications are categorized into three domains. As illustrated in Figure 4.19, business applications cover e-commerce (web store, website, consumer portal, and vendor portal), CRM (consumer relation management), which includes salesforce automation, market campaigns, partner portal, consumer support, and order management. In the accounting and ERP (enterprises resources planning) area, popular services include shipping, financials, purchasing, inventory, and payroll (Figure 4.19a).

In the scientific/technical area, two good examples are automobile design (self-driving cars) and AI big data analytics and ML (Figure 4.19b). In the consumer and social media area, typical applications cover mobile devices, e-mail, games, social networks, documentation, cognitive services, etc., as exemplified in Figure 4.19c. We will study

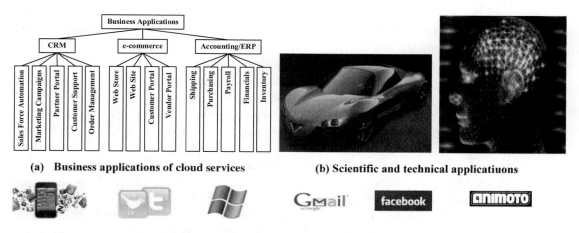

(a)   Business applications of cloud services   (b) Scientific and technical applicatiuons

(c) Consumer, games, e-mail, mobile and social media applications

Figure 4.19
Typical cloud applications in business, science/technical, and social media areas.

many of these examples in more details as we discuss ML in Chapters 6 and 7 and apply Hadoop, Spark and TensorFlow programming in Chapters 8 and 9. ■

In Table 4.11, 16 services for administration, security, deployment, and enterprise operations on the AWS platform are listed. These features are especially attractive to those companies using the AWS platform as a business platform to satisfy their business demands many large and small business companies are renting private virtual clouds for their exclusive use in business transactions, market analysis, event, and accounting managements. Other small or transient users simply rent EC2 instances based on need.

4.4   Google App Engine and Microsoft Azure

In this section, we study two commercial clouds: one is the App Engine cloud built by Google and the other is the Azure cloud by Microsoft. Both are public clouds with a large number of registered uses. You can easily get some trial accounts as a beginner.

4.4.1   Google App Engine and Compute Engine

Google cloud computing platform offers hosting on the same supporting infrastructure that Google uses internally for end-user products like Google Search and YouTube. This platform is part of a suite of enterprise solutions from Google for Work. Google provides a set of modular cloud-based services with a host of development tools. For example, hosting and computing, cloud storage, data storage, translation APIs, and prediction APIs.

Major elements in Google Cloud Platform include Google App Engine (GAE)—a PaaS and IaaS service providing virtual machines similar to Amazon EC2. BigQuery—a PaaS service—provides map reduction services similar to Hadoop. The raw Google infrastructure to support these cloud services is named Google Compute Engine. Other Google cloud platforms include Google Cloud Datastore, Google Cloud Storage, and Google Cloud SQL. More details can be found at https://cloud.google.com.

Google has the world's largest search engine facilities. They have extensive experience in massive data processing that has led to new insights into data center design and novel programming models that scale to incredible size. Google has hundreds of data centers and has installed over millions of servers worldwide. For example, 200 Google data centers were used at one time for some large-scale cloud applications. Data items are stored in text, images, and video and are replicated to avoid faults or failures.

First, we examine design philosophy from the raw infrastructure to build the GAE. The purpose is to reduce user coding effort with an increasing level of agility (Figure 4.20) by increasing the roles of middleware and OS support. The middleware appears as deployment manager and managed VMs. The cloud OS handles the resources management, logging,

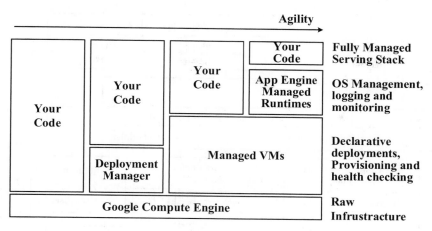

Figure 4.20

Building Google App Engine with increasing agility from raw infrastructure to Compute Engine, using OS support and managed VMs and runtimes to reduce user coding efforts. Courtesy of Google website, http://www.google.com, retrieved October 2016.

and monitoring operations. Declarative deployments are supported by provisioning and health checking middleware.

The GAE is a managed platform with built-in security and autoscaling. Users apply the App Engine APIs in Java, Python, or PHP, etc. The APIs also provide access to advanced functionality such as Memcache, Cloud SQL, etc. The Google Compute Engine architecture is shown Figure 4.21. Compute Engine generates three resource pools: classify pool, trainer pool, and file upload pool. Each pool is essentially an instance group that can autoscale upon user demands. The VM instances are driven by user demands. Users can configure how many vCPUs are desired, as well as RAM and disk storage, and get charged as they go.

Google Cloud Storage is built with disks attached to a large number of servers. Data can be easily replicated to key server locations around the globe, closer to the requesting user. Google's Network Load Balancer allows you to route traffic to the different Compute Engine clusters that you have defined. With Managed VMs, you can run your application in Google Compute Engine while benefiting from the automanagement and services that GAE provides. Moving from an App Engine runtime to a managed VM can be as easy as adding one line to your app.yaml file, such as vm:true. One can design a Google Cloud Deployment Manager to create declarative deployments of cloud platform resources that are constantly health monitored, and autoscaled as needed.

Example 4.13   Google App Engine for PaaS/IaaS Services with Load Balancing

Google has pioneered cloud development by leveraging the large number of data centers they operate. For example, Google pioneered cloud services in Gmail, Google Docs,

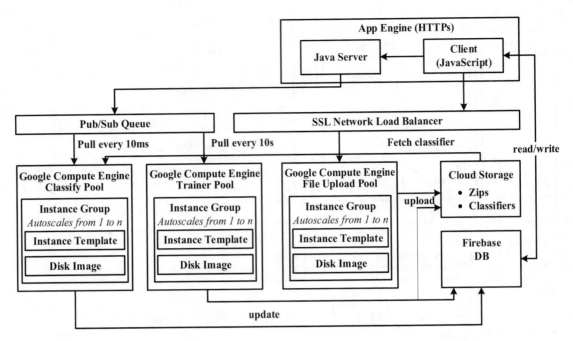

Figure 4.21
The architecture of Google Compute Engine as three functional pools and cloud storage to support Google App Engine applications development and executions.

Google Earth, etc. These applications can support a large number of users simultaneously with high availability. Notable technology achievements include the Google File System (GFS), MapReduce, BigTable, Chubby, etc. In 2008, Google announced the GAE web application platform which is becoming a common platform for many small cloud service providers. This platform specializes in supporting scalable (elastic) web applications. GAE enables users to run their applications on a large number of data centers associated with Google's search engine operations.

Figure 4.22 shows the major building blocks of the Google cloud platform which has been used to deliver the cloud services highlighted above. The GFS is used for storing large amounts of data. MapReduce is used in parallel program execution. Chubby is used for distributed application lock services. BigTable offers major storage for the GAE cloud. A user application can use BigTable by submitting requests to the storage manager. The applications all run in data centers under tight management by Google engineers. Inside each data center, there are thousands of servers forming different clusters.

GAE supports many web applications. One is the storage service to store the application-specific data in Google's infrastructure. The data can be persistently stored in the backend storage server while still providing the facility for queries, sorting, and even transactions similar to traditional database systems. The GAE provides Google's specific

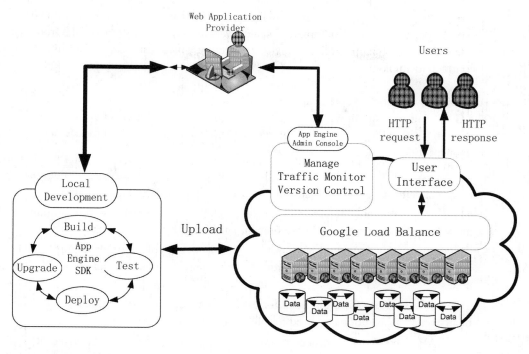

Figure 4.22
Google App Engine platform for PaaS operations with load balancing.

services such as the Gmail account service. In fact, such a service is the login service, where applications can use the Gmail account directly. This can eliminate the tedious work of building the customized user management components in web applications. Thus, web applications built on top of the GAE can use the APIs authenticating users and sending e-mail using Google Accounts.

Users interact with Google applications with the web interface provided by each application. Third-party application providers use the App Engine to build cloud services. The applications are all run in the Google data centers. Inside each data center, there might be thousands of server nodes to form different clusters. Typical configuration of a cluster can run the Google file system, MapReduce jobs, as well as BigTable servers for structure data. Extra services such as Chubby for distributed locks can also run in the clusters. ∎

GAE runs the user program on Google's infrastructure. As a platform running third-party programs, application developers now do not need to worry about the maintenance of servers. The GAE can be understood as the combination of several software components. The front-end is an application framework which is similar to other web application frameworks such as ASP, J2EE, or JSP. Currently, GAE supports Python and Java programming environments. The applications can run just as in the web application containers. The front-end can be used as the dynamic web serving infrastructure which can provide the full support of common technologies.

Functionality of Google App Engine

The GAE platform is built with five major components. The GAE is not an infrastructure platform but rather an application development platform for users. We introduce below the component functionalities, separately (Figure 4.23).

1. The datastore offers object-oriented, distributed, structured data storage services based on BigTable techniques. The datastore secures data management operations.

2. The application runtime environment offers a platform for scalable web programming and execution. It supports two development languages: Python and Java.

3. The software development kit (SDK) is used for local application development. The SDK allows users to execute test runs of local applications and upload application codes.

4. The administration console is used for easy management of user application development cycles, instead of being used for physical resource management.

5. The GAE web service infrastructure provides special interfaces to guarantee flexible use and management of storage and network resources by the GAE.

Google offers essentially free GAE services to all Gmail account owners. Users can register for a GAE account or use their Gmail account name to sign up for the services.

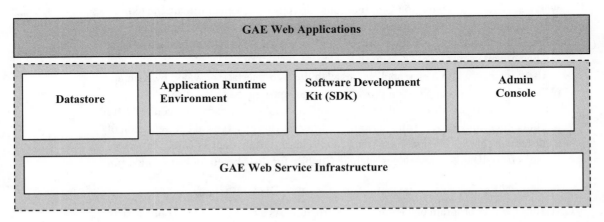

Figure 4.23
Functional components in the Google App Engine (GAE).

The service is free within a quota. If you exceed the quota, the page instructs you how to pay for the services. Then, you download their SDK and read the Python or the Java guide to get started. GAE accepts Python, Ruby, and Java programming languages. This cloud allows the user to deploy user-built applications on top of the cloud infrastructure, which are built using the programming languages and software tools supported by Google (e.g., Java, Python). The user does not manage the underlying cloud infrastructure. The cloud provider supports all application development, testing, and operations.

4.4.2 Google Hardware/Software Support for Machine Learning Services

Google cloud ML platform is built with special hardware and software support. The platform provides pre-trained ML models or allows user-tailored models for machine applications. The neural net-based ML platform achieves high accuracy in large-scale deep learning systems. Major Google applications that use Cloud ML include photos (image search), Google app (voice search), Translate, Inbox (Smart Reply), etc. This cloud platform is now available as a cloud service in many personal or business applications.

The ML platform is portable, fully managed, and integrated with other Google cloud platform products such as Google Cloud Storage, Google Cloud Dataflow, and Google Cloud Datalab. Several representative ML applications that are supported by special hardware and software are introduced as follows:

1. *Google Cloud Vision API* applies a REST-based interface to understand the content of an image by encapsulating powerful ML models. It quickly classifies images into thousands of categories (e.g., "sailboat," "Eiffel Tower"), detects individual objects and faces within images, and finds and reads printed words contained within images.

2. *Google Cloud Speech API* allows users to convert audio to text by applying neural network models. The API recognizes over 80 languages and variants, to support its global user base. It can transcribe the text of users dictating to an application's microphone or enable command-and-control through voice.

3. *Google Natural Language API* is also REST based; it reveals the structure and meaning of text by offering powerful ML models. You can use it to extract information about people, places, events and much more, mentioned in text documents, news articles, or blog posts. You can also use it to understand sentiment about your product on social media or parse intent from customer conversations.

4. *Google Cloud Translate API* provides a simple programmatic interface for translating an arbitrary string into any supported language. Translate API is highly responsive, so websites and applications can integrate with Translate API for fast, dynamic translation of source text from the source language to a target language.

Tensor Processing Units

Most of the above cognitive applications apply various machine learning or deep learning algorithms. These ML cloud apps are supported by the TensorFlow software framework to be introduced in Chapter 9. They are also supported by Google's ML accelerator, known as *tensor processing units* (TPUs). This chip built on a TPU board can achieve 10x efficiency gain over the pure software solution to ML applications. A board with a TPU fits into a hard disk drive slot in Google's data center racks. The TPU is shown in Figure 4.24(a). The data center server racks are shown in Figure 4.24(b).

Tensor analysis is a branch of vector or matric calculus, which forms the basis of Google's open-source TensorFlow framework for machine learning. The TPUs are specifically designed to do only tensor calculations, which means the company can fit more transistors on the chip that do only one thing well—achieving higher efficiency than other types of chips. At Google, more than 100 teams are currently using machine learning in developing new services or to upgrade existing services. TPUs already power many ML applications at Google, including RankBrain, used to improve the relevancy of search results and Street View, to improve the accuracy and quality of our maps and navigation. AlphaGo was powered by TPUs in the matches against Go world champion Lee Sedol, enabling the machine to "think" much faster and look further ahead between moves.

4.4.3 Microsoft Azure and Service Offerings

Microsoft Azure is a cloud computing platform for building, deploying, and managing applications and services through a global network of Microsoft-managed and Microsoft partner-hosted data centers. It provides both PaaS and IaaS services and supports many different programming languages, tools, and frameworks. The platform is divided into three major component platforms. The Windows Azure offers a cloud platform built on Windows OS and based on Microsoft virtualization technology. Applications are installed on VMs deployed on the data center servers. Azure manages all servers, storage, and network resources of the data center.

Microsoft Azure is also the name of the operating system managing Azure resources. This cloud OS runs its cluster hosted at Microsoft's data centers that manage computing and storage resources of the computers. Azure provides the resources to applications running on top of Microsoft Azure. Microsoft Azure has been described as a "cloud layer" on top of a number of Windows server systems, which use Windows Server 2012 and a customized version of Hyper-V, known as the Microsoft Azure Hypervisor, to provide virtualization of services.

Scaling and reliability are controlled by the Microsoft Azure Fabric Controller. The guarantee from Microsoft is that the services and environment do not crash if one of the servers crashes within the Microsoft data center and provides the management of the user's web application like memory resources and load balancing. Azure provides an API built on

Figure 4.24(a)

Figure 4.24(b)
Google tensor processing units installed on server disks in data center racks. Courtesy of Google Cloud Platform .com/, retrieved May 18, 2016.

REST, HTTP, and XML that allows a developer to interact with the services provided by Microsoft Azure. Microsoft also provides a client-side managed class library which encapsulates the functions of interacting with the services. It also integrates with Microsoft Visual Studio, Git, and Eclipse.

Azure service offerings are summarized in Figure 4.25. On top of the infrastructure are the various services for building different cloud applications. They can be considered as the building blocks in the cloud environment. Microsoft has already provided its own cloud applications based on those building blocks. Microsoft's common language runtime (CLR) VM is a common intermediate form executed in a managed environment. Azure storage service is based on declarative descriptions to achieve load balancing among application components.

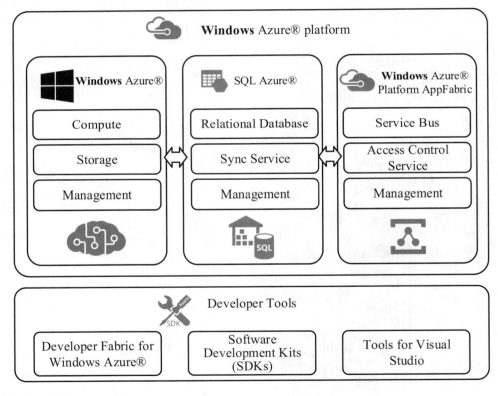

Figure 4.25

Microsoft Windows Azure platform for cloud computing. Courtesy of Microsoft, http://www.microsoft.com /windowsazure, 2016.

The major services offerings by Azure are grouped into three categories under Windows Azure, SQL Azure, and Windows Azure Platform (AppFabric). Windows Azure is mainly responsible for the compute and storage services. SQL Azure manages relational databases and sync services. AppFabric provides the Service Bus and access control services. Development tools are available as developer Fabric for Windows Azure. SDKs are available to clients and developers. There are also rich tools for Visual Studio applications. Listed as follows are major Azure service offerings available up to 2016.

1. *Compute services:* These include the provisional Windows and Linux Virtual Machines, various levels of cloud services such as highly available, infinitely scalable cloud apps, and APIs. The system supports batch processing of large scale parallel and batch compute jobs. It also supports remote applications such as deploy Windows client apps in Azure.

2. *Data and storage services:* These include SQL Database (manage relational SQL database), DocumentDB (manage NoSQL document database), Redis Cache (high throughput, low-latency data access), Azure Storage (durable, highly available cloud storage for blobs, tables, queues, files, and disks), StorSimple (hybrid cloud storage for enterprises), Azure Search (fully managed search as a service), and SQL Data Warehouse (elastic data warehouse).

3. *Web and mobile services:* These include web apps (create and deploy critical web apps that scale your business), mobile apps (build and host backend for any mobile app), logic apps (automate the access engagement and use of data across clouds), API apps (easy build and consume cloud APIs), API management (publish APIs to developers, partners and employees securely), notification hubs (scalable, cross-platform push notification infrastructure), and mobile engagement (data-driven user engagement platform).

4. *Data analytics:* Azure offers HDInsight (managed Hadoop clusters), ML (cloud-based predictive analytics), stream analytics (real-time stream processing), data factory (orchestrate and manage data transformation), event hubs (ingest, persist, and process millions of events per second), SQL Data Warehouse (elastic data warehouse), and data catalog (data source discovery to get more value from existing data sheets)

5. *Internet of Things:* Azure offers Internet of Things (IoT) services in event hubs (receive telemetry from millions of devices), stream analytics (real-time data streaming from IoT devices), machine learning (cloud-based predictive analytic tool), and notification hubs (push notification engine for quickly sending messages).

6. *Networking services:* These include virtual network (provisional private network), ExpressRoute (private network fiber connections to Azure), traffic manager (route incoming traffic for high availability), load balancer (high availability and network performance to apps), DNS (host your DNS domain in Azure), VPN gateway (establish secure, cross-premises connectivity), and application gateway (load balancing and delivery control of scalable websites).

7. *Social media and contents distribution services:* These include media services (encode, store, stream videos, and audios at scale), encoding (studio grade encoding at cloud scale), Azure Media Player (single player for all playback needs), media intelligence (enhance discoverability and accessibility of media), content protection (securely deliver content using AES or PlayReady), live and on-demand streaming (deliver content to all devices with scale), and CDN (deliver content to end user).

8. *Identity, access, and integration services:* These are represented by Azure Active Directory (synchronize on-premises directories and enable single sign on), Azure Active Directory B2C (consumer identity and access management in the cloud), multifactor authentication (safeguard access to data and apps with extra level authentication), BizTalk Server (integrate the enterprise and cloud), Service Bus (connect across private and public cloud environments), Backup (reliable server backup to the cloud), and site recovery (protection and recovery of private clouds).

9. *Developer and management services:* These cover Visual Studio Online (services for teams to share code track work and ship software), Visual Studio Application Insights (diagnose problems and track usage to improve web and mobile apps), Microsoft Azure Preview Portal, Scheduler, Automation (cloud management with process automation), Operational Insights (collect, search, and visualize machine data from on premise and cloud), and Key Vault (safeguard and maintain control keys and other secrets).

All of the above cloud services in Azure platform can interact with traditional Microsoft software applications, such as Windows Life, Office Live, Exchange Online, SharePoint Online, and Dynamics CRM Online. The Azure platform applies the standard web communication protocols SOAP and REST. Azure service applications allow users to integrate the cloud application with other platforms or third-party clouds. You can download the Azure development kit to run a local version of Azure.

The SDK allows Azure applications to be developed and debugged on the users' Windows client. This is done by emulating the Azure cloud environment. Azure provides an API built on REST, HTTP, and XML that allows a developer to interact with the services provided by Microsoft Azure. Microsoft also provides a client-side managed class library that encapsulates the functions of interacting with the services. It also integrates with Microsoft Visual Studio, Git, and Eclipse. Figure 4.26 illustrates the interfaces of Microsoft Azure with the business world including clients and application developers.

Microsoft Azure websites is a web-hosting platform that supports multiple technologies, and programming languages like .NET, Node.js, PHP, and Python. Users with Microsoft Azure accounts can create websites and deploy content and code into the websites. Microsoft Azure websites supports a website creation wizard that allows the user to create a site based on some preconfigured images or create a customized website. Here are some interesting features from the Azure website gallery:

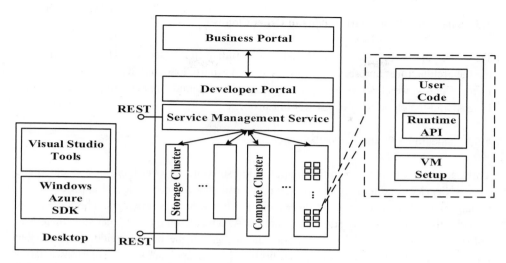

Figure 4.26
Microsoft Azure and its interfaces with business, developer, and client applications.

- User-selected placement in one or multiple data centers across the globe;
- Uptime SLA of 99.95% for standard tier customers [9];
- Continuous monitoring of site metrics such as CPU time, data in, data out, HTTP errors, etc.;
- Setting of monitoring alerts [10];
- Log collection and failed request tracing for tracking and troubleshooting;
- Deployment of a Microsoft SQL or MySQL database to be used with web applications [11];
- Websites are hosted on IIS 8.0 running on a custom version of Windows Server 2012;
- Support for four service tiers: free, shared, basic, and standard (dedicated) [12];
- Basic and standard tiers, support for 3 VM sizes for scaling up [13];
- Pay tiers, support for manual or automatic scaling-out with up to 10 instances of VMs [14];
- Support for integration with Azure Traffic Manager to route traffic manually or automatically between websites in different regions across the globe; and
- Authentication using Microsoft Azure Active Directory.

4.5 Salesforce, IBM SmartCloud, and Other Clouds

The most popular SaaS cloud by Salesforce is studied in this section. Then we will examine the architectures and service offerings at IBM SmartCloud and SGI Cyclone cloud platforms. Finally, we check two very large-scale private clouds, namely the Nebula cloud at NASA, and the cloud built by CERN in Europe.

4.5.1 Salesforce Clouds for SaaS Services

This SaaS refers to browser-initiated application software for over thousands of cloud customers. Services and tools offered by PaaS are utilized in construction of applications and management of their deployment on resources offered by IaaS providers. The SaaS model provides the software applications as a service. As a result, on the customer side, there is no upfront investment in servers or software licensing. On the provider side, costs are kept rather low, compared with conventional hosting of user applications. The customer data is stored in the cloud that is either vendor proprietary or publically hosted. Table 4.12 provides a summary of four SaaS cloud platforms and their service offerings.

The best examples of SaaS services include Google Gmail and Docs, Microsoft SharePoint, and the CRM software from Salesforce. They are all very successful in promoting their own business and are used by thousands of small businesses in their day-to-day operations. Providers like Google and Microsoft offer integrated IaaS and PaaS services, whereas others such as Amazon and GoGrid offer pure IaaS services. Third-party providers such as Manjrasoft offer application development and deployment services on top of commercial clouds. Another well-known SaaS cloud is the Outlook Web Access (OWA) known as Office 365 offered by Microsoft for cloud-hosted e-mail services.

To discover new drugs through DNA sequence analysis, the Eli Lily Company used Amazon's EC2 and S3 platforms with provisioned server and storage clusters. The goal was to conduct high-performance biological sequence analysis without using an expensive supercomputer. The benefit of this IaaS application was a reduced drug deployment time with much lower cost. Another good example is the *New York Times* applying EC2 and S3 services to retrieve useful pictorial information quickly from millions of archival articles and newspapers. The *New York Times* has significantly reduced their time and cost in getting the job done. Many startup cloud companies provide some SaaS service with rented platforms like AWS.

Example 4.14 offers a review of SaaS and PaaS services by Salesforce. This company was established in 1999 to provide online solutions to SaaS, mainly in CRM applications. Initially, they used third-party cloud platforms to run their software services. Gradually, the company launched its own Force.com as a PaaS platform that can execute many SaaS applications or help users to develop add-on applications under PaaS support. Salesforce also offers commercial applications of social networking.

Table 4.12
Four SaaS cloud platforms and their service offerings (August 2015)

Model	Amazon AWS	Google App Engine	Microsoft Azure	Salesforce
Platform Support	AWS EC2, S3, EMR, SNS, etc.	GAE, GFS, BigTable, MapReduce, etc.	Azure, .NET service, Dynamic CRM,	Force.com, Online CRM, Gifttag
SaaS Offerings	Elastic Beanstalk, CodeDeploy, OpsWorks, CodeCommit, Code-Pipeline, Mobile Analytics	Gmail, Docs, YouTube, WhatsApp	Live, SQL, Office 365 (OWA), Hotmail	Sales, service, market, data, collaboration, analytics
Security Features	CloudWatch, Trusted Advisor, Identity/Access Control	Chubby locks for security enforcement	Replicated data, rule-based access control	Admin./record security, use metadata API
APIs and Languages	API Gateway, Latin Pig	Web-based admin. console, Python	Azure portal, .NET Framework	Apex, Visualforce, AppExchange, SOSL, SOQL

Example 4.14   Salesforce Force.com as a Custom PaaS Cloud

In 2008, Salesforce built its Force.com cloud with Dell servers using AMD processors running Linux and some Sun Fire E25K servers with SPARC processors running Solaris. The company uses the Momentum platform from Message Systems to allow its customers to send large amounts of e-mail without encountering deliverability problems. In 2012, Salesforce built a data center in the UK to handle European citizens' personal data. In 2013, Salesforce and Oracle entered a partnership to use Oracle Linux, Exadata, Database, and the Java platform to power its SaaS platform.

The architecture of the Force.com cloud is conceptually shown in Figure 4.27. The platform offers external developers to create add-on applications that integrate into the main Salesforce hosted applications. They aim at enterprise users in business computations. Salesforce pioneered the SaaS model for its customer relationship management (CRM) service. In addition, they provide Apex, a proprietary Java-like programming language, for the Force.com platform. They have an integrated development environment, Visualforce, to simplify the business development cycle. They offer a shared resource pool, AppExchange, for multiple users to interact and perform coordinated work easily. The application services are mainly in CRM database, application development, and customization.

Force.com offers multitenant techniques, metadata, and security services to SaaS users. In the security area, Salesforce provides not only some mechanisms to protect data integrity, but also some access control mechanisms to assure administrative security and record security. They introduced Chatter as a "Facebook for the enterprise" in June 2010. This is a real-time collaboration platform that brings together people and data in a secure environment. The packaging service helps users to release their application innovations.

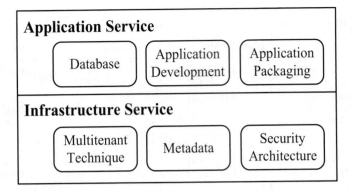

Figure 4.27
Salesforce Force.com cloud platform supporting both PaaS and SaaS applications.

Users can customize their CRM applications in the Force.com platform. The system handles tabs of contacts, reports, and accounts. Each tab contains associated information by adding user-defined custom fields. Users can also add sets of customized /novel tabs for specific features in finance and human resources applications. In addition, the Force.com platform also provides SOAP web service APIs. Mobile support is also provided for subscribers of smartphones. The Salesforce SaaS and PaaS services work in over a dozen international languages. ∎

Example 4.15 SaaS Cloud Services Offered by Salesforce Company
Recently, Salesforce has subdivided its CRM service into seven specific cloud service categories: namely Sales Cloud, Service Cloud, Market Cloud, Data Cloud, Collaboration Cloud, Analytics Cloud and Custom Cloud as illustrated in Figure 4.28. Among these, all provide SaaS applications, except the PaaS Custom Cloud, also known as Force.com. We briefly introduce their functionalities as follows:

1. *Sales Cloud:* For CRM SaaS applications for managing customer profile, track opportunities, optimize campaigns, Salesforce IQ for small business, and Data .com for B2B prospecting and data cleansing.

2. *Service Cloud:* A cloud-based customer service SaaS allowing companies to create, track, and route service cases, including social media networking services, customized support, and help desk.

3. *Market Cloud:* Providing social marketing SaaS applications allowing companies to identify sales leads from social media, discover advocates, offer digital marketing platforms, and Pardot B2B for market automation, etc.

4. *Data Cloud:* For acquiring and managing CRM records.

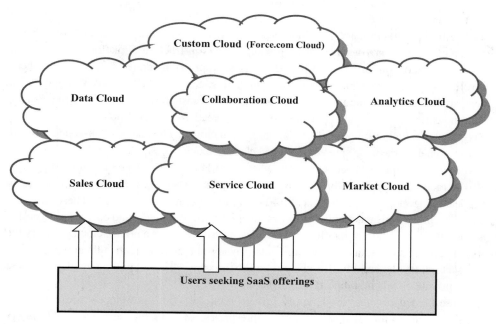

Figure 4.28
Seven Salesforce cloud service offerings: all for SaaS applications except the custom cloud offering PaaS applications.

5. ***Collaboration Cloud:*** For use in business collaborations.

6. ***Analytics Cloud:*** For sales performance analysis based on machine learning, offers Wave Analytics for business analytics and Wave Apps that drive sales insight and customer delight.

7. ***Custom Cloud:*** A PaaS platform for creating add-on apps on top of standard CRM apps offers community services to connect customers, partners, and employees, and chatter for enterprise social networks, Force.com (Lightning apps), Heroku Enterprise for scalable apps for developers. ∎

4.5.2   IBM SmartCloud, IoT, and Cognitive Projects

Several public clouds or commercially available cloud systems are reviewed in this section. These include the IBM SmartCloud, SGI Cyclone cloud, NASA Nebula cloud, and CERN cloud.

IBM Bluemix Initiative

Since 2014 IBM has invested $2 billion to develop a new cloud development platform, known as Bluemix, which applies a "spreading strategy" to construct PaaS platforms in widening cloud applications in all walks of life. Bluemix attempts to integrate IBM OS, WebSphere, Tivoli, and DB2 for flexible hybrid cloud computing. Since 1999, the IBM WebSphere has been applied widely in the financing, stock exchange, transportation, manufacturing, and energy industries. Now the mission of Bluemix is to spread WebSphere applications to all cloud environments including public, private, or hybrid clouds. The use of open-souce DNA in Bluemix enables the wide spreading of IBM cloud ecology.

Bluemix has applied open-source Apache Cloud Foundry PaaS architecture. They have also merged the private cloud Blue Box from OpenStack. Bluemix is open to the public as an application development platform with 140 software tools and cloud services. These cover applications in the big data, mobile, analytics, integration, development and operations, security, and IoT domains. Initially, the Bluemix Local edition operated as a private cloud to satisfy the special demands of security, SLA, and data privacy in the banking, healthcare, and financial sectors. By the end of 2016, the public Bluemix hybrid cloud will be available to host many private clouds in public IDC data centers.

These hosted private clouds apply private APIs to secure the clouds and solve data lock-in problems for clients outside the enterprises. In the Chinese market, a Bluemix Dedicated edition is also supported by IBM's Watson IoT platform and some Chinese cognition services. IBM's cognitive computing is a major thrust to broaden IBM Smart-Cloud applications. The idea is to mix community chaining service with Bluemix middleware, database, and resource management for each specific application domain. This may change the business models in future cloud applications. The IBM cloud operation in Japan is known as the Bluemix Garage, which is being exported to deploy in other countries as well.

IBM SmartCloud Models

IBM has gradually changed from a hardware/software and system company to a computing service company. The IBM cloud platforms are mostly built with IBM server clusters supported by IBM WebSphere and accumulated software assets over the years. Both the z-series and p-series servers at IBM are being upgraded with virtualization capabilities. Since 2007, IBM has launched a number of cloud-related R&D projects. These projects are extended from IBM's work on autonomous computing using the SOA.

IBM Ensemble offers a virtualized cloud system for IaaS services. This system can put together a large resource pool to simplify management complexity. The purpose is to offer application flexibility and efficient resource deployment through dynamic server, storage, and network ensembles. IBM also developed Tivoli Service Automation Manager for rapid design, deployment, and management of service processes. WebSphere CloudBurst offers another platform for managing private clouds. IBM LotusLive offers an SaaS cloud for application service development. The services include online conference service, coordinated office management, and e-mail services.

IBM RC2 Cloud

The computer and IT infrastructures of eight IBM Research Centers are now strongly connected to form a private cloud, called Research Compute Cloud (RC2). RC2 is web-based, allowing more than 3,000 IBM researchers worldwide to share computing resources among themselves. This is indeed IBM's internal test bed for promotion of cloud technology. RC2 provides solutions to establish an autonomous computing environment upon user demand. The system supports machine virtualization, service life-cycle management, and performance monitoring. The whole idea is to reduce computing cost by outsourcing jobs to the best-fit sites for rapid resource deployment and thus optimal execution.

> **Example 4.16   IBM SmartCloud Delivered by Public, Private, and Hybrid Models**
> As illustrated in Figure 4.29, IBM offers three hardware platforms for cloud computing. These platforms support virtualization through IBM WebSphere infrastructure solutions. The management layer of the IBM cloud framework includes IBM Tivoli middleware. Management tools provide capabilities to regulate images with automated provisioning and deprovisioning, monitor operations, and meter usage while tracking costs and allocating billing. The last layer of the framework provides integrated workload tools. Workloads for cloud computing are services or instances of code that can be executed to meet specific business needs. IBM offers tools for cloud-based collaboration, development and testing, application development, analytics, business-to-business integration, and security.
>
> The IBM SmartCloud offers IaaS, SaaS, and PaaS services through public, private, and hybrid cloud delivery models. IBM also builds cloud environments for clients that are not necessarily on the SmartCloud platform. For example, Tivoli management software or IBM Systems Director virtualization can be integrated separately on other cloud platforms. In 2011, IBM SmartCloud integrated Hadoop-based InfoSphere BigInsights for big data, Green Hat for software testing, and Nirvanix for cloud storage. Users may build their own private cloud or purchase services hosted on the IBM cloud. By 2014, the name SmartCloud was replaced with products that have a prefix of "IBM Cloud." The IBM Cloud Manager with OpenStack was offered at that time.
>
> Today, IBM offers five cloud provision models: (1) private cloud, owned and operated by the customer; (2) private cloud, owned by the customer, but operated by IBM; (3) private cloud, owned and operated by IBM; (4) virtual private cloud services based on multitenanted support for individual enterprises; and (5) public cloud services based on the provision of functions to individuals. The majority of cloud users choose a hybrid cloud model, with some workloads being served by internal systems, some from commercial cloud providers, and some from public cloud service providers. ∎

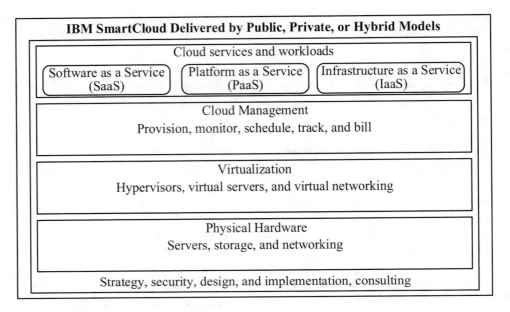

Figure 4.29
Architecture of an IBM SmartCloud offered as public, private, and hybrid platforms based on IBM Tivoli, DB2, WebSphere, and Xen-based virtualization.

4.5.3 Clouds at SGI, NASA, and CERN

Additional commercial and private clouds are presented below. The SGI Cyclone offers high-performance computing services. The NASA and CERN clouds are large-scale private clouds for research use.

Cloud System from SGI

On February 11, 2010, SGI announced the Cyclone as a large-scale on-demand cloud computing service for HPC applications. Both SaaS and IaaS models are offered on the Cyclone. The SaaS model offers users prepackaged technical applications covering a wide range of technical domains. For example, the system applies to *computational fluid dynamics* (CFD) and finite-element analysis, which are used by both the airplane and automobile industries. With the IaaS model, users can access the SGI's fastest Altix servers and ICE clusters, networking and storage systems managed and optimized by SGI experts for specific user applications.

Companies today are dealing with increasingly difficult business problems, with ever-growing amounts of data to manage and process, and pressure to deliver results in record time. Most attack this critical problem by expanding IT infrastructure, which often comes with unforeseen administration and facilities costs and lower than expected throughput due to data bottlenecks. The SGI Altix ICE integrated blade cluster was designed for today's data-intensive problems and avoids these pitfalls. This innovative new platform from SGI raises the efficiency bar, easily scaling to meet virtually any processing requirements without compromising ease of use, manageability, or price/performance. SGI Altix ICE delivers some customer value with efficiency, reliability, and manageability.

Example 4.17   SGI Cyclone Cloud for High-Performance Computing

The architecture of the SGI Cyclone HPC cloud is shown in Figure 4.30. The SGI servers can scale up, scale out, or combine in a hybrid mode to match specific user application requirements. The Cyclone HPC cloud supports many well-known scientific and engineering applications, including OpenFOAM, NUMECA, AcuSolve, etc. These cloud applications benefit many industrial and government sectors including green energy, manufacturing, digital media, entertainment, government finances research, and higher education. Customers can expand their compute and storage capacity with no capital outlay. The advantages are demonstrated by the elimination of lengthy procurement and installation cycles. Users can request infrastructure as they see fit without worry about infrastructure management.

Cyclone is an on-demand cloud computing service specifically dedicated to technical applications. Cyclone supports a number of leading applications partners and five technical domains, including computational fluid dynamics, finite element analysis, computational chemistry and materials, computational biology, and ontology. Cyclone is available in two service models: SaaS and IaaS. With SaaS, Cyclone customers can significantly reduce time to results by accessing leading-edge open-source applications and best-of-breed commercial software platforms from top independent software vendors. The IaaS model enables customers to install and run their own applications. SGI Altix provides scale up, Altix ICE provides scale out, and Altix XE hybrid clusters are used for hybrid management of the cloud servers, all based on Intel Xeon processors. Altix is a line of servers and supercomputers produced by Silicon Graphics, based on Intel processors. ∎

NASA's Nebula Cloud

This is a large-scale cloud that was built at the National Aeronautics and Space Administration (NASA). It is designed for NASA scientists to run climate models on remote systems provided by NASA. This can save thousands of NASA users from the need to acquire supercomputers at their local sites. Furthermore, this enables NASA to build the complex weather models around their data centers, which is more cost effective considering the savings in large data movement.

Nebula is an open-source cloud computing platform that was developed to provide an easily quantifiable and improved alternative to building additional expensive data centers and to provide an easier way for NASA scientists and researchers to share large, complex

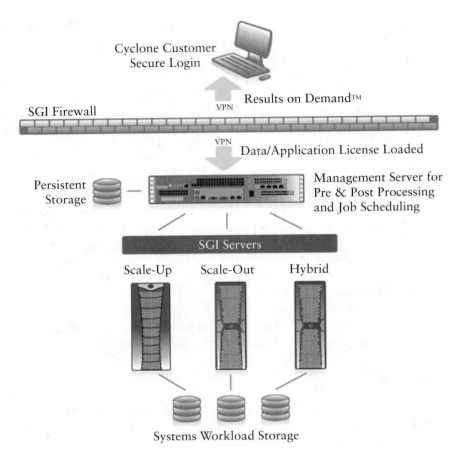

Figure 4.30
SGI Cyclone HPC cloud for enabling SaaS and IaaS applications.

data sets with external partners and the public. Nebula is currently an IaaS implementation that provides scalable compute and storage for science data and web-based applications.

Nebula IaaS allows customers to unilaterally provision, manage, and decommission computing capabilities (virtual machine instances, storage, etc.) on an as-needed basis through a web interface or a set of command-line tools. PaaS scheduled for release in Q4 2010 will provide a consistent set of frameworks, code repositories, and web services to enable NASA developers to deploy secure, policy-compliant web applications that automatically scale to meet variable demand. SaaS and *database as a service* (DBaaS) are planned for 2011.

Nebula's high-density architecture allows for a dramatically reduced data center footprint. Each shipping container data center can hold up to 15,000 CPU cores or 15 petabytes (one petabyte equals 1 million gigabytes), proving 50% more energy efficiency than traditional data centers. In addition, this "green" architecture allows for maximum flexibility and efficiency since these modular shipping container data centers can be modified, upgraded, expanded, and even physically relocated as NASA's computing needs evolve over time.

NASA must comply with a host of data security and privacy policies, which can sometimes create a challenge in finding a collaborative environment in which to share data with its outside partners. By utilizing Nebula, users gain access to powerful IT resources months faster and with far less effort than before. Nebula saves hundreds of staff hours, allowing NASA scientists to focus on mission-critical activities. Nebula's architecture is designed from the ground up for interoperability with commercial cloud service providers such as AWS, offering NASA researchers the ability to easily port data sets and code to run on commercial clouds.

Nicknamed the "Super Cloud," Nebula can effortlessly manage 10,000 or 100,000 times the amount of information as the most powerful commercial cloud computing platforms, accommodating files as large as 8 terabytes and accommodating an individual file system of 100 TB. By contrast, the maximum Amazon EC2 file size and file system size is 1 terabyte. Built upon a converged 10 Gig-E switching fabric, Nebula delivers ten times the networking speed of the fastest available commercial cloud environments, most of which run at 1 GigE, and use only 100 megabits. This combination of high-speed networking, 2.9 GHz CPUs, and hardware RAID configurations allows the Nebula environment to provide massively parallel performance.

CERN Cloud System

This EU cloud is built by the the European Organization for Nuclear Research (CERN) in Geneva. This is a large private cloud to distribute data, applications, and computing resources to thousands of scientists around the world. CERN deals with large data sets and big throughput with a global workforce and finite budget. One can see that most clouds are initially developed with restricted user groups. Figure 4.31 shows a conceptual architecture of the CERN cloud.

Tens of thousands of scientists around the world are feeding off the huge data sets and doing all kinds of research by themselves. CERN believes the cloud project will allow them to deliver increased computing performance and offer better infrastructure services to its 10,000 researchers from 85 countries. At CERN, massive amounts of scientific data are processed and must be distributed to researchers in near real time. As a result, CERN's cloud infrastructure has to provide the capacity necessary to support production and analysis of more than 15 petabytes of data per year, processed by 60,000 CPU cores, allowing scientists to manage workloads themselves as opposed to a centralized IT management department at CERN's laboratory near Geneva.

Because CERN uses Spectrum's LSF grid and workload management solution to enable the extensive scalability to analyze its vast research data, the laboratory chose to

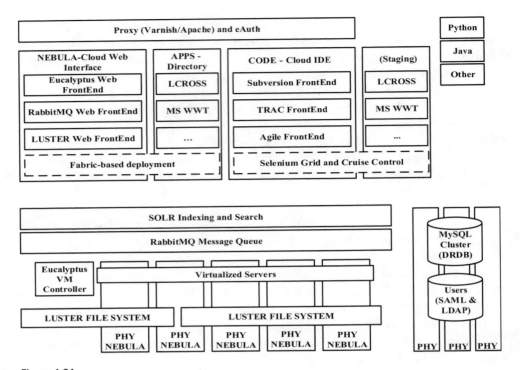

Figure 4.31
The Nebula cloud project at NASA, http://nebula.nasa.gov.

partner again with Spectrum to explore how to more effectively utilize their resources in a virtualized cloud environment. Spectrum LSF and its adaptive cluster provide an open, low-cost common platform for CERN's scientists, allowing the management of both virtual and physical servers in the cloud. In addition, scientists can manage their own application environments and control projects dynamically for maximum flexibility and efficient workload, processing more cost-effectively than with a centralized IT management department.

CERN VM Project

Scientists working on *A Large Ion Collider Experiment*, known as the ALICE collaboration, are conducting heavy ion simulations at CERN. They have been developing and debugging compute jobs on a collection of internationally distributed resources, managed by a scheduler called AliEn to integrate a cloud's dynamically provisioned resources into an existing infrastructure such as the ALICE pool of computers. The purpose is to ensure that the various AliEn services have the same deployment-specific information. CERN VM project has developed a way to provide virtual machines that can be used as a base supporting the production environment for all large experiments at CERN.

4.6 Conclusions

In this chapter, we studied cloud computing architecture and infrastructure design. We established the business models for cloud systems, then we reviewed the experiences of data center conversion into clouds by many enterprises and organizations throughout the world. We evaluated the cloud ecosystems against today's business and public demands of cost effectiveness and data security in using the clouds. Three major cloud types—IaaS, PaaS, and SaaS—were case studied. Specifically, we studied the architectural details of AWS cloud, Google App Engine cloud, and Saleforce clouds. IoT sensing and interactions with clouds were studied to prepare for pervasive use of clouds in social media and mobile networking in the world.

Homework Problems

4.1: We studied many AWS and Salesforce cloud services in class. Visit their websites and report the detailed functionality and service features in six service offerings by AWS, and four service offerings by Salesforce.

(a) AWS services: CloudFront, Mobile Analytics, Data Pipeline, Kinesis, Machine Learning, and Elastic Beanstalk.

(b) Salesforce cloud services: Marketing Cloud, Case Collaborator, Wave Analytics, Custom Cloud.

4.2: Pick two SaaS cloud providers from the following list: Consur, RightNow, Salesforce, Kenexa, WebEx, Blackbaud, NetSuite, Omniture, Kenexa, Vocus, Google App Engine, and Microsoft Azure. Conduct an in-depth study by digging out useful technical information from the providers' websites or by searching through Google, Wikipedia, and any open literature. The purpose is to report their latest progress in cloud technology, service offerings, software applications developed, business models applied, and success/failure lessons learned. Make sure that you report is technically rich in content and avoid sales pitches.

4.3: Visit the iCloud website https://www.icloud.com or Wikipedia to find out the functionality and application services provided by Apple iCloud. In particular, answer the following questions on iCloud.

(a) Briefly, specify the main services provided by iCloud. How many users reported up to now?

(b) What are the data types or information items that are handled by iCloud?

(c) Explain the procedure to find an old friend using the Find My Friend service on the iCloud.

(d) Explain the iCloud features Find My iPhone to locate your lost or stolen iPhone.

4.4: The vSphere 6 is the latest cloud OS released by VMware. Dig out from VMware website, and/or open literature that reports technical details and deployment or application experiences by VMware clients or customers. Write a short technical report to summarize your research findings.

4.5: Pick two colocation cloud services from the following list: Savvis, Internap, NTTCommunications, Digital Realty, Trusted Advisor, and 365 Main. Conduct in-depth studies beyond what you have read in the textbook. You need to dig out useful technical information by visiting the providers' websites or by searching through Google, Wikipedia, and any open literature. The purpose is to report their latest progresses in cloud technology, service offerings, software applications developed, business models applied, and success/failure lessons learned. Make sure that your study report is technically rich in content and avoid sales pitches.

4.6: Compile a table to compare public clouds and private clouds in each of the following four aspects. Also identify their differences, advantages, and shortcomings in terms of design technologies and application flexibility. Give several example platforms that you know of under each cloud class.

(a) Technology leverage and IT resources ownership.

(b) Provisioning methods of resources including data and VMs, and their management.

(c) Workload distribution methods and loading policies.

(d) Security precautions and data privacy enforcement.

4.7: Check the AWS cloud website. Plan a real computing application using the EC2, S3, or the simple queue service (SQS), separately. You must specify the resources requested and figure out the costs charged by Amazon. Carry out the EC2, S3, and SQS experiments on the AWS platform and report and analyze the performance results measured.

4.8: In Examples 4.5 and 4.6, you have learned how the EC2 and S3 services are offered by AWS. Visit the website: https://www.aws.com for an update on the latest services and products from AWS. Dig out the functionality and application of additional services provided by AWS. Your report should be as technical as possible. Do not speculate; everything you report must be substantiated with convincing evidence.

(a) What is the SNS service on the AWS cloud? Explain how it works and the user interfaces for SNS on using the mobile phones to transmit and store photo streams on the S3.

(b) What is EMR on the AWS? How it is implemented? What language is applied to use EMR and how does it works with the Hadoop system?

4.9: Pick two NaaS clouds from the following list: Qwest, AT&T, and AboveNet. Conduct in-depth studies beyond what you have read in the textbook. You need to expose useful technical information by visiting the providers' websites or by searching through Google, Wikipedia, and any open literature. The purpose is to report their latest progresses in cloud technology, service offerings, software applications developed, business models applied, and success/failure lessons learned. Make sure that your study report is technically rich in content and avoid sales pitches.

4.10: Compare strengths, weaknesses, and suitable applications of VMs created by hypervisors over bare metal with the application containers created by Docker engine on a Linux host. You should compare them along the lines of resource demands, creation overhead, execution modes, implementation complexity, execution environment, application isolation, OS flexibility, and host platforms.

4:11: Learn about AWS container service and run an Amazon ECS sample container code. You need to take some screenshots to prove that you have done this correctly. You need to report what you have learned out of this testing run.

Step 1. Learn about Amazon EC2 Container Service (Amazon ECS), watch the video here:

http://aws.amazon.com/ecs/

Look at the developer guide:

http://docs.aws.amazon.com/AmazonECS/latest/developerguide/Welcome.html

Step 2. Before using the service, set up the execution environment with Amazon ECS:

http://docs.aws.amazon.com/AmazonECS/latest/developerguide/get-set-up-for
-amazon-ecs.html

Step 3. Get started with Amazon ECS by running a sample container application:

http://docs.aws.amazon.com/AmazonECS/latest/developerguide/ECS
_GetStarted.html

Step 4. Shut down the container and its host EC2 instance to avoid additional charges.

http://docs.aws.amazon.com/AmazonECS/latest/developerguide/ECS
_CleaningUp.html

4.12: Figure 4.32 shows another VIOLIN adaptation scenario for change in virtual environments. There are four VIOLIN applications running in two cluster domains. Trace the three steps of VIOLIN job execution and discuss the gains in resource utilization after live migration of the virtual execution environment in the two cluster domains. You can check against the cited paper to compare with your observations.

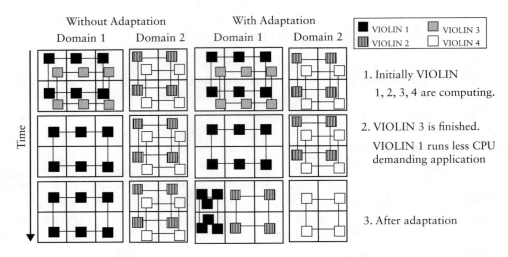

Figure 4.32
The VIOLIN cluster adaptation in Problem 4.13.

References

[1] Amazon EC2 and S3. "Elastic Compute Cloud (EC2) and Simple Scalable Storage (S3)." http://spatten _presentations.s3.amazonaws.com/s3-on-rails.pdf.

[2] Armbrust, M., A. Fox, R. Griffith, A. Joseph, R. Katz, A. Konwinski, G. Lee, D. Patterson, R. Karp, A. Rabkin, I. Stoica, and M. Zaharia. "Above the Clouds: A Berkeley View of Cloud Computing." *Technical Report*, No. UCB/EECS-2009–28, University of California at Berkeley, February 10, 2009.

[3] Bahga, A., and V. Madisetti. *Cloud Computing: A Hands-On Approach*, 1st ed. CreateSpace Independent Publishing Platform, 2014.

[4] Barroso, L., and U. Holzle. *The Data Center as a Computer: An Introduction to the Design of Warehouse-Scale Machines*. Morgan Claypool Publisher, 2009.

[5] Boss, G., P. Malladi, et al. "Cloud Computing—The BlueCloud Project." www.ibm.com/ developerworks /websphere/zones/hipods/, October 2007.

[6] Bugnion, E., S. Devine, and M. Rosenblum. "Disco: Running Commodity Operating System on Scalable Multiprocessor Systems." *ACM Transactions on Computer Systems* 15 no. 4 (November 1997).

[7] Buyya, R., J. Broberg, and A. Goscinski, eds. *Cloud Computing: Principles and Paradigms*. Wiley, 2011.

[8] Buyya, R., C. S. Yeo, and S. Venugopal. "Market-Oriented Cloud Computing: Vision, Hype, and Reality for Delivering IT Services as Computing Utilities." Proc. of the 10th IEEE International Conference on High Performance Computing and Communication, Dalian, China, September 25–27, 2008.

[9] Cao, J., K. Hwang, K. Li, and A. Zomaya. "Optimal Multiserver Configuration for Profit Maximization in Cloud Computing." *IEEE Transactions on Parallel, and Distributed Systems* (Special Issue on Cloud Computing) 24 no. 6 (2013): 1087–1096.

[10] Chase, J. S., et al. "Dynamic Virtual Clusters in a Grid Site Manager." IEEE 12th Symposium on High-Performance Distributed Computing (HPDC), Washington, DC, June 2003.

[11] Chen, M., Y. Hao, D. Wu, Y. Li, and K. Hwang, "Opportunistic Task Scheduling over Co-Located Clouds in Mobile Environment." *IEEE Services Computing* 99 (July 2016).

[12] Chou, T. *Introduction to Cloud Computing: Business and Technology*. Active Book Press, 2010.

[13] Clark, C., K. Fraser, J. Hansen, E. Jul, I. Pratt, and A. Warfield. "Live Migration of Virtual Machines." Proc. of the Symposium on Networked Systems Design and Implementation, Boston, MA, May 2, 2005, pp. 273–286.

[14] Dyer, D. "Current Trends/Challenges in Data Center Thermal Management—A Facilities Perspective." Presentation at ITHERM, San Diego, CA, June 1, 2006.

[15] Foster, I., Y. Zhao, J. Raicu, and S. Lu. "Cloud Computing and Grid Computing 360-Degree Compared." Grid Computing Environments Workshop, Austin, TX, November 12–16, 2008.

[16] Gannon, D. "The Client+Cloud: Changing the Paradigm for Scientific Research." Keynote Address, Cloud-Com2010, Indianapolis, IN, November 2, 2010.

[17] Google App Engine. http://appengine.google.com/, 2012.

[18] Greenberg, A., J. Hamilton, D. Maltz, and P. Patel. "The Cost of a Cloud: Research Problems in Data Center Networks." *ACM SIGCOMM Computer Communication Review* 39 no. 1 (2009).

[19] Hwang, K., X. Bai, Y. Shi, M. Li, W. G. Chen, and Y. Wu. "Cloud Performance Modeling with Benchmark Evaluation of Elastic Scaling Strategies." *IEEE Trans. on Parallel and Distributed Systems* (January 2016).

[20] Hwang, K., and M. Chen. *Big Data Analytics for Cloud, IoT and Cognitive Learning.* Wiley, 2017 (in press).

[21] Jinesh, V. "Cloud Architectures White Paper." http://aws.amazon.com/about-aws/whats-new/2008/07/16/cloud-architectures-white-paper/.

[22] Leavitt, N., et al. "Is Cloud Computing Really Ready for Prime Time?" *IEEE Computer* 42 no. 1 (2009): 15–20.

[23] Linthicum, D. *Cloud Computing and SOA Convergence in Your Enterprise: A Step-by-Step Guide.* Addison Wesley Professional, 2009.

[24] Mell, P., and T. Grance. "The NIST Definition of Cloud Computing." *NIST Special Pub.* No. 800–145 (September 2011).

[25] Norman, W., M. Paton, T. de Aragao, K. Lee, A. Alvaro Fernandes, and R. Sakellarious. "Optimizing Utility in Cloud Computing through Autonomic Workload Execution." *Bulletin of the IEEE Computer Society Technical Committee on Data Engineering* (2009).

[26] Nurmi, D., Rich Wolski, et al. "Eucalyptus: An Elastic Utility Computing Architecture Linking Your Programs to Useful Systems." *UCSB Computer Science Technical Report* No. 2008–10 (August 2008).

[27] Ojala, A., and P. Tyrvainen. "Developing Cloud Business Models: A Case Study on Cloud Gaming." *IEEE Software Magazine* (2011).

[28] Rittinghouse, J., and J. Ransome. *Cloud Computing: Implementation, Management and Security.* CRC Publisher, 2010.

[29] Rochwerger, B., D. Breitgand, E. Levy, et al. "The RESERVOIR Model and Architecture for Open Federated Cloud Computing." *IBM Systems Journal* (2008).

[30] Rosenblum, M., and T. Garfinkel. "Virtual Machine Monitors: Current Technology and Future Trends." *IEEE Computer* (2005): 39–47.

[31] Ruth, P., et al. "Automatic Live Migration of Virtual Computational Environments in a Multi-Domain Infrastructure." *Technical Report*, Purdue University (2006).

[32] Salesforce, Service Oriented Architecture. http://wiki.developerforce.com/SalesforceSOA. Demo, 2013.

[33] Sotomayor, B., R. Montero, and I. Foster. "Virtual Infrastructure Management in Private and Hybrid Clouds." *IEEE Internet Computing* (2009).

[34] VMware, Inc. "vSphere." http://www.vmware.com/products/vsphere/.

[35] Wu, Y., M. Su, W. Zheng, K. Hwang, and A. Zomaya. "Associative Big Data Sharing in Community Clouds—The MeePo Approach." *IEEE Cloud Computing Magazine* (January 2016).

[36] Zhang, F., K. Hwang, S. Khan, and Q. Malluhi. "Skyline Discovery and Composition of Inter-Cloud Mashup Services." *IEEE Transactions on Service Computing* (September 2016).

Chapter 5

Clouds for Mobile, IoT, Social Media, and Mashup Services

5.1 Wireless Internet and Mobile Cloud Computing

In this opening section, we review recent progress in wireless, sensor, and mobile technologies. These advances laid the foundation for wireless Internet and mobile cloud computing. In particular, we will study the issues surrounding the use of cloudlets in a local-area mesh to protect workload offloading from mobile devices to remote clouds.

5.1.1 Mobile Devices and Internet Edge Networks

Mobile devices appear as smartphones, tablet computers, wearable gear, and industrial tools. As shown in Figure 5.1, global users of mobile devices exceeded 3 billion in 2015. In the 1980s, 1G devices were primarily analog phones used for voice communication only. The 2G mobile networks began in the early 1990s. Digital phones appeared accordingly for both voice and data communications. The 2G cellular networks appear as GSM, TDMA, FDMA, and CDMA based on different division schemes to allow multiple callers to access the system simultaneously. The basic 2G network supports 9.6 Kbps of data with circuit switching. The speed was improved to 115 Kbps with packet radio services. As of 2016, 2G networks are only in use in a few developing countries.

Since 2000, 2G mobile devices have been gradually replaced by 3G products. The 3G networks and phones are designed to have 2 Mbps speed to meet the demand of multimedia communications through the cellular system. The 4G LTE (long-term evolution) networks appeared in the 2010s. They were targeted to achieve a download speed of 100 Mbps, an upload speed of 50 Mbps, and a static speed of 1 Gbps. The 3G system is enabled by better radio technology with *multiple-input and multiple-output* (MIMO) smart antennas and *orthogonal frequency-division multiplexing* (OFDM) technology. The 3G systems have received widespread deployment now, but could be replaced gradually by 4G networks. We expect the mixed use of 3G and 4G networks to last for at least another decade. The 5G networks may appear beyond 2020 with a target speed of at least 100 Gbps.

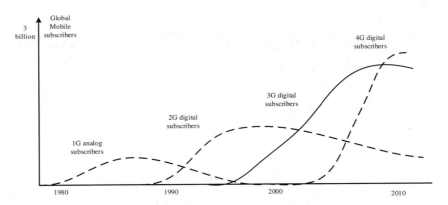

Figure 5.1
Global subscribers of four generations of smartphones and tablet computers exceeded 3 billion by early 2015.

Mobile Core Networks

The *cellular radio access networks* (RANs) are structured hierarchically. Mobile core networks form the backbone of today's telecommunication systems. The core networks have gone through four generations of deployment in the past three decades. As shown in Figure 5.1, the 1G mobile network was used for analog voice communication based on circuit switching technology. The 2G mobile network started in early the 1990s for supporting the use of digital telephones in both voice and data telecommunications exploring packet switching circuits. Famous 2G systems are the Global System for Mobile Communications (GSM) developed in Europe and the Code Division Multiple Access (CDMA) system developed in the United States. Both GSM and CDMA systems were deployed in various countries.

The 3G mobile network was developed for multimedia voice/data communications with global roaming services. The 4G system started in the early 2000s based on the LTE and MIMO radio technologies. The 5G mobile networks are still under heavy development and may appear in 2020. The technology, peak data rate, and driven applications of the five generations of cellular mobile networks are summarized in Table 5.1. Speedwise, the mobile systems improved from 10 Kbps and 2 Mbps to 100 Mbps in four generations. It is projected that the upcoming 5G system may achieve an increase in data rate up to 100 Gbps or higher. The 5G system may be built with *remote radio head* (RRH) and virtual base stations installed in *cloud-based radio access networks* (C-RAN).

Mobile Internet Edge Networks

Most of today's wireless and mobile networks are based on radio signal transmission and reception in various operating ranges—RANs. Figure 5.2 illustrates how various RANs are used to access the mobile core networks, which are connected to the Internet backbone

Table 5.1
Milestone mobile core networks for cellular telecommunication

Generation	1G	2G	3G	4G	5G
Radio and Networks Technology	Analog phones, AMPS, TDMA	Digital phones, GSM, CDMA	CDMA2000, WCDMA, and TD-SCDMA	LTE, OFDM, MIMO, software-steered radio	LTE, Cloud-based RAN
Peak Mobile Data Rate	8 Kbps	9.6 ~ 344 Kbps	2 Mbps	100 Mbps	10 Gbps–1 Tbps
Driving Applications	Voice Communication	Voice/Data Communication	Multimedia Communication	Wideband Communication	Ultra-speed Communication

and many Intranets through mobile Internet edge networks. Such an Internet access infrastructure is also known as *wireless Internet* or *mobile Internet* in the computing community. In what follows, we introduce several classes of RANs known as Wi-Fi, Bluetooth, WiMax, and ZigBee networks. Generally speaking, we consider below several short-range wireless networks, such as *wireless local-area network* (WLAN), *wireless home-area network* (WHAN), *personal-area network* (PAN), *body-area network* (BAN), etc. These wireless networks play a key role in mobile computing and IoT applications.

Bluetooth Devices and Networks

Bluetooth is a short-range radio technology named after a Danish king dating back to the ninth century. A Bluetooth device operates in 2.45 GHz industrial scientific medical band as specified by the IEEE 802.15.1 standard. It transmits omnidirectional (360°) signals with no limit on line of sight, meaning data or voice can penetrate solid nonmetal objects. It supports up to eight devices (one master and seven slaves) in a PAN called *piconet*. Bluetooth devices have low cost and low power requirements. The device offers a data rate of 1 Mbps in ad hoc networking with 10 cm to 10 meters in range. It supports voice or data communication between phones, computers, and other wearable devices. Essentially, Bluetooth wireless connections are replacing most wired cables between computers and their peripherals such as a mouse, keyboard, or printers.

Wi-Fi Networks

Wi-Fi access point, or Wi-Fi networks, are specified in the IEEE 802.11 standard. So far, they have appeared as a series of 11a, b, g, n, and ac networks. The access point broadcasts its signal in a radius of less than 300 ft. The closer it is to the access point, the faster the data rate experienced will be. The maximum speed is only possible within 50–175 ft. The peak data rates of Wi-Fi networks have improved from less than 11 Mbps in 11b to 54 Mbps in 11g and 300 Mbps in 11n networks. The 11n and 11ac networks apply OFDG modulation technology with the use of MIMO radio and antenna to achieve high speed. Wi-Fi

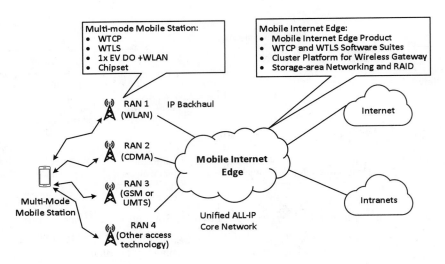

Figure 5.2
The interactions of various radio access networks (RANs) with the unified all-IP-based mobile core networks, Intranets, and the Internet.

enables the fastest WLAN in a mesh of access points or wireless routers. In many places today, they offer almost free access to the Internet within 300 ft.

5.1.2 Wi-Fi, Bluetooth, and Wireless Sensor Networks

With the increasing number of online users in mobile environments, it becomes a critical issue to interconnect mobile devices into the Internet with high speed. The Internet backbone is really built with wire line networks. As shown in Table 5.2, the cellular RANs are applied mainly for wide-area wireless voice or data communications. Some wireless wide-area networks appear as *wireless metropolitan area networks* (WMAN) using broadband WiMax technology. *Wireless local area networks* (WLAN) are primarily supported by WiFi technology with an operating range between 100 and 1,000 ft. *Wireless personal area networks* (WPAN) work short range as body-area networks or room-area networks such as using the Bluetooth, NFC, and ZigBee technologies. The four categorized wireless networks are used in different environments and cooperate with each other to offer convenient network access, so they are important infrastructures to realize IoT.

According to the capabilities of diverse hardware, we classify the measuring techniques into six categories (from fine to coarse grained): location, distance, angle, area, hop count, and neighborhood. Among them, the most powerful physical measurement is directly obtaining the position without any further computation. A *global positioning system* (GPS) is one such kind of infrastructure. We discuss the other five measurements in this chapter, with emphasis on the basic principles of measuring techniques. Basically, distance-related

Table 5.2
Wireless networking used in mobile IoT and cloud computing

Network Types	Cellular WAN	WMAN	WLAN	WPAN	WPAN
Market Name Standard	GSM/GPRS CDMA/1XRTT	WiMaX 802.15.6	Wi-Fi 802.11n	ZigBee 802.15.4	Bluetooth 802.15.1
Application focus	Wide Area Voice and Data	Data, Trans. Bandwidth	Web, E-mail, Video	Monitoring & Control	Cable Replace
Memory (MB)	18+	8+	1+	0.004–0.032	0.25+
Battery (days)	1–7	1–7	0.5–5	100–1000+	1–7
Network Size	1	1	32	2^{64} or more	7
Bandwidth (KBs)	64–128+	75,000	54,000+	20–250	720
Range (KM)	1000+	40 ~ 100	1–100	1–100+	1–10+
Success Metric	Coverage	Speed	Flexibility	Power, Cost	Low cost

information can be obtained by radio signal strength or radio propagation time; angle information by antenna arrays; and area, hop count, and neighborhood information by the fact that radios only exist for nodes in vicinity.

5.1.3 Cloudlet Mesh for Mobile Cloud Computing

Mobile device users may move across a mobile cellular network or another wireless network to access remote clouds. Due to limited resources available on a smartphone or tablet computer, the remote cloud access could be constrained by limited battery life, low CPU power, and small storage capacity. Recently, researchers at Carnegie Mellon University, Microsoft, AT&T, and Lancaster University have proposed a low-cost infrastructure to enable cloud computing using mobile devices. This device is known as a *cloudlet*, which offers a resource-rich portal for upgrading mobile devices with cognitive abilities to access distance clouds. This portal should be designed in a trustworthy fashion, using *virtual machines* (VMs) to explore location-aware cloud applications. Cloudlet makes it possible for mobile devices to offload a heavy database search or machine learning jobs to nearby or remote clouds for processing or analysis and return with short answers or predictions quickly.

Example 5.1: Cloudlet Gateway for Mobile Devices to Access Remote Clouds
As shown in Figure 5.3, the wireless access of remote clouds from mobile devices enables many useful applications in our daily life. In other words, heavy-duty computations initiated by "small" mobile devices could be carried out by "large" clouds. For example, abundant data collected by IoT sensing devices could be passed through a smartphone to a remote cloud for processing or machine learning systems. The cloudlet can help to link the users to remote clouds in performing data mining and machine

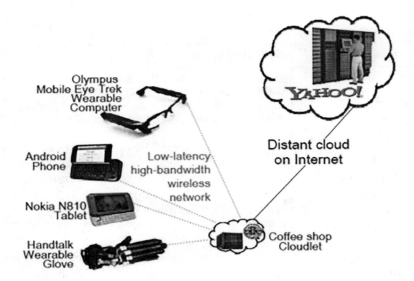

Figure 5.3
Virtual machine-based cloudlet serving as a wireless gateway to access remote clouds. Courtesy of Satyanarayanan, et al., "The Case of VM-Based Cloudlets in Mobile Computing," *IEEE Pervasive Computing* 4 no. 8 (2009).

learning operations. This cloudlet portal is designed to be trustable and uses VMs to explore location-aware cloud applications.

The idea is applied for opportunity discovery, fast information processing, and intelligent decision making on the road, etc. Both mobile devices and centralized clouds or data centers have shortcomings in supporting mobile cloud computing. The mobile handsets face a resource poverty problem with limited CPU power, storage capacity, and network bandwidth on smartphones or tablet computers. Mobile devices cannot be used to handle large data sets. On the other hand, the distant cloud on the Internet faces the wide area network (WAN) latency problem. The clouds have to solve the collision problem with too many (millions) of clients logging into the cloud simultaneously. ∎

Fast VM Synthesis in Cloudlets

A prototype cloudlet called Kimberley was built at Carnegie Mellon University (CMU). This prototype synthesized a VM overlay in the cloudlet host. They reported fast VM synthesis time to be less than 100 s. In other words, they created the VM overlay in transient cloudlets that are customized to bind distant cloud resources to satisfy user needs. Figure 5.4 shows the timeline for dynamic VM synthesis in Kimberley. A small VM overlay is delivered by the mobile device to a cloudlet that already possesses a base VM. The VM overlay

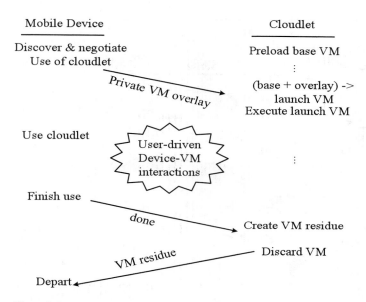

Figure 5.4
Fast VM synthesis in cloudlet built at the CMU Kimberley prototype system. Courtesy of Satyanarayanan et al., "The Case of VM-Based Cloudlets in Mobile Computing," *IEEE Pervasive Computing* 4 no. 8 (2009).

combined with the base VM creates a special execution environment for the mobile device to launch its cloud applications through the cloudlet portal. Trust and security issues are also major factors in cloudlet deployment.

Data protection includes file/log access control, data coloring, and copyright compliance. Disaster recovery is also needed to secure data from being lost due to hardware/software failures. Cloud security can be enforced with establishing the root of trust, securing the VM provisioning process, software watermarking, and the use of firewalls and IDSs at host and network levels. Recently, trust overlay networks and reputation systems were suggested to protect data centers from trusted cloud computing.

The architecture of a *cloudlet mesh* is shown in Figure 5.5. All cloudlets are Wi-Fi-enabled. Each cloudlet server has an embedded Wi-Fi access point. Each cloudlet connects many mobile devices within the Wi-Fi range. The cloudlets are interconnected by wireless links to form the mesh. All cloudlets operate essentially as gateways at the edge network of the Internet. We use multiple cloudlets in the mesh to achieve the following goals. First, we widen the wireless coverage range to serve many more mobile devices. Second, collaborative defense is suggested in using many cloudlets collectively to build a shield to deter intruders and attackers. Finally, caching and load balancing are practiced to upgrade the QoS and throughput during multitask offloading to the remote clouds.

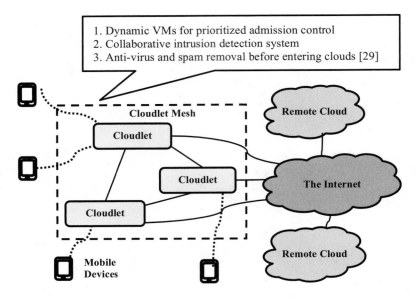

Figure 5.5
Cloudlet mesh architecture for securing mobile cloud computing environment. Courtesy of Shi, Abhilash, and Hwang, "Cloudlet Mesh for Securing Mobile Clouds from Intrusions and Network Attacks," The Third IEEE International Conference on Mobile Cloud Computing (MobileCloud), April 2015.

Deploying cloudlets at convenience stores or coffee shops may take more time to become widely accepted, just like the acceptance of Wi-Fi access points in the past decade. Widely deployed cloudlets enable distributed cloud computing and extended resource handling at convenience stores, classrooms, or by users on the move. The idea is to use the cloudlet as a flexible gateway or portal to access the distant cloud. The cloudlets can be easily implemented on PCs, workstations, or low-cost servers.

Potential threats and defense schemes for protecting mobile cloud computing systems are summarized in Table 5.3. Mobile devices are subject to virus or network worm attacks. Encryption may not be the best solution for mobile devices due to its limited computing power and energy consumption constraints. Some special software tools are available to resist virus or worm attacks on mobile devices. This may involve authentication, URL checking, and spam filtering. With large storage and backup services, mobile users will offload these duties to the clouds.

5.1.4 Mobile Clouds and Colocation Clouds

Mobile devices are rapidly becoming the major service participants. There is a shift of user preferences from traditional cell phones and laptops to smartphones and tablets. Advances

Table 5.3
Threats and defense concerns in protecting mobile cloud computing

Threats/Defense	Mobile Device	Cloudlet Mesh	Remote Clouds
Encryption for Data Protection	Energy cost for encryption is high on mobile devices	Encryption to secure the access of a remote cloud	Encryption fully supported to protect user data lost
Virus, Worms, or Malware Attacks	Privacy and energy cost for detecting malware is high	Protect mobile device by verifying files and content	Perform analytics on the cloud to detect new types of malware
Identity Theft and Authentication	User authentication before offloading to clouds	Need to authenticate all three parties involved	Authentication as a service (AaaS) is needed
Cloud Offloading and File Transfer	Offloading tasks in security-enforced cloudlet mesh	Data caching at cloudlet to improve performance	High latency to offload may create a QoS problem
Data Integrity and Storage Protection	May use secure storage outsourcing protocols	Data stored by the cloudlet is vulnerable to attacks	Clouds may compromise user data through phishing attacks
URL and IP and Spam Filtering	Checking blacklist of IP addresses and URLs	Alert mobile devices with intrusive attacks on clouds	Performs predictive analytics and provides database updates

in the portability and capability of mobile devices, together with widespread 3G/4G LTE networks and Wi-Fi accesses, have brought rich mobile application experiences to end users. Mobile cloud computing is a model for elastic augmentation of mobile device capabilities via ubiquitous wireless access to cloud storage and computing resources. This is further enhanced by context-aware dynamic adaption to the changes in the operating environment. Figure 5.6 shows a typical mobile environment for offloading large jobs to remote clouds from mobile device holders.

With the support of *mobile cloud computing* (MCC), a mobile user basically has a new cloud option to execute the application. The user attempts to offload the computation through Wi-Fi, cellular network, or satellite to the distant clouds. The terminal devices at the user's end have limited resources, i.e., hardware, energy, or bandwidth. The cell phone itself is infeasible to finish some compute-intensive tasks. Instead, the data related to the computation task is offloaded to the remote cloud. Special cloudlets were introduced to serve as wireless gateways between mobile users and the Internet. These cloudlets can be used to offload computations or web services to remote clouds safely.

With the growing popularity of mobile devices, a new type of *peer-to-peer* (P2P) mode for mobile cloud computing has been introduced. By applying short-range wireless networks, one can easily connect to nearby mobile devices using the cloudlets. We introduce below an *opportunistic* task *scheduling scheme* over *colocated clouds* (OSCC). This offers flexible cost-delay tradeoffs between remote cloud services and mobile cloudlets services. In the mobile environment, remote cloud and mobile cloudlets both have advantages and disadvantages for task offloading.

As illustrated in Figure 5.7, mobile users can upload their computing tasks to the cloud. The cloud will then return the result to them after the completion of the computing tasks.

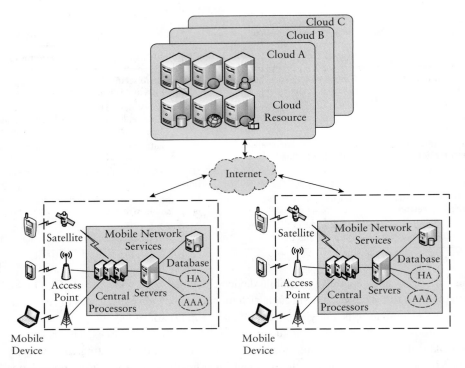

Figure 5.6
The architecture of a mobile cloud computing environment.

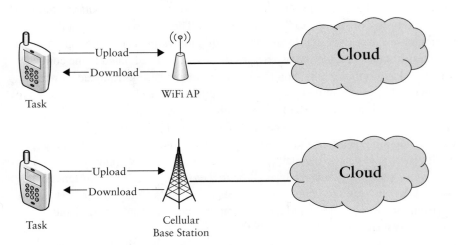

Figure 5.7
Two task offloading methods to access remote clouds (a) via Wi-FI access point and (b) via a cellular network through a base station.

This is traditional task offloading mode. Mobile devices can offload computing-related tasks to the cloud in two ways. One is through Wi-Fi for cost-saving purposes, as shown in Figure 5.7(a), while the other method is through an expensive cellular network (e.g., 3G/4G/5G), as shown in Figure 5.7(b), if Wi-Fi is not available.

We illustrate in Figure 5.8 the OSCC architecture for the use of colocated clouds in a mobile environment. Here, assume that David has a computation-intensive task which cannot be carried out on his mobile phone. Within his mobile range, the phones of his three friends are all idle. So, David divides the computing task into three subtasks and transmits them to his friends' phones to access other available clouds. This task offloading among co-location clouds offers an efficient solution to cope with the growing mobile traffic and the associated computation demand. In the design of the OSCC scheme, a compromise mode is offered between remote cloud and mobile cloudlets. The main advantage is to achieve higher flexibility and better performance in terms of energy saving and latency reduction.

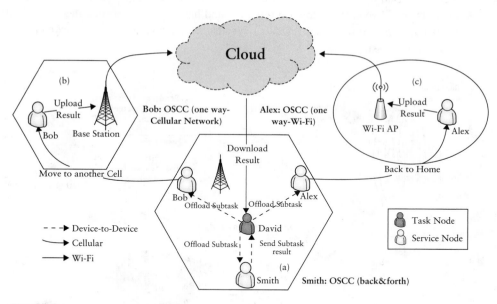

Figure 5.8
Efficient tasks offloading among colocation clouds in a mobile environment. Source: Chen and Hwang, et al., "Body Area Networks: A Survey," *ACM/Springer Mobile Networks and Applications* (MONET) 16 no. 2 (2010): 171–193.

5.2   IoT Sensing and Interaction with Clouds

Integrating the digital and physical worlds is the ultimate goal of IoT. This could be regarded as the third evolution of the information industry. First, network scale becomes very large in order to interconnect an enormous number of things in the physical world. Second, network mobility increases rapidly due to pervasive use of mobile and vehicular devices. Third, the fusion of heterogeneous networks becomes deeper with various types of devices connected to the Internet. Furthermore, mobile Internet, cloud computing, big data, software defined networking, and 5G have all impacted IoT development.

Example 5.2: RFID Technology for Merchandise Tagging or e-Labeling

Electronic labels or RFID tags appear on merchandise or shipping boxes. The e-label is made from polyethylene media, housing small IC chips and printed circuitry driven by a copper coil antenna. The tag itself has no power supply attached to it. The tag is energized by signal waves broadcast from the reader's antenna. Figure 5.9 shows a sequence of six events. Events 1–3 show energization and handshaking between the reader and the tag. Events 4–6 show how an antenna reads the data on the tag to the backend computer for processing.

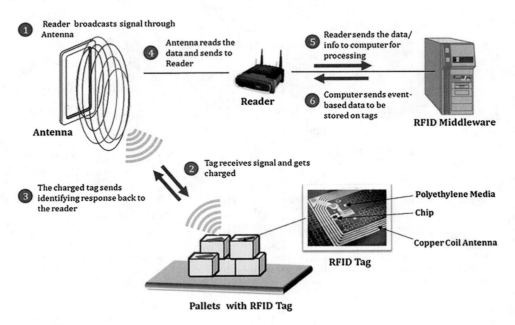

Figure 5.9
Using RFID readers to retrieve product data on e-labels (RFID tags) placed on the package boxes.

The computer sends updated event-based data to be stored on tags for future use. The RFID middleware is executed by the backend computer to complete the reading and updating process. Of course, the idea can be modified to serve other remote identification purposes. For example, RFID labels are also used in department stores, supermarkets, inventory searching, and the shipping industry. ■

5.2.1 Local and Global Positioning Systems

Position techniques are applied to identify location and measure distance, angle, area, hop count, neighborhood, etc. Basically, distance-related information can be obtained by radio signal strength or radio propagation time; angle information by antenna arrays; and area, hop count, and neighborhood information by the fact that radios only exist for nodes in the vicinity.

Local Positioning Technology

One method to determine the location of a device is through manual configuration, which is often infeasible for large-scale deployments or mobile systems. As a popular system, GPS is not suitable for indoor or underground environments and suffers from high hardware cost. Local positioning systems rely on high-density base stations being deployed, an expensive burden for most resource-constrained wireless ad hoc networks.

Localization solutions consist of two basic stages: (1) measuring geographic information from the ground truth of network deployment and (2) computing node locations according to the measured data. Geographic information includes a variety of geometric relationships from coarse-grained neighbor awareness to fine-grained internode ranges (e.g., distance or angle). Based on physical measurements, localization algorithms solve the problem of how the location information from beacon nodes spreads network-wide. Generally, the design of localization algorithms depends on a wide range of factors, including resource availability, accuracy requirements, and deployment restrictions, and no particular algorithm is an absolute favorite across the spectrum.

Satellite Technology for Global Positioning

Global positioning is done with multiple satellites deployed in outer space. Each satellite continually transmits messages that include the transmission time and satellite position. A GPS receiver calculates its position by precisely timing the signals sent by satellites. The receiver uses the messages it receives to determine the transit time and computes the distance to each satellite using light speed. Each of these distances and satellites' locations define a signal sphere. The receiver is located at the intersection of signal spheres from multiple satellites.

Example 5.3: GPS System Developed in the U.S.A.

The U.S. GPS is made up of three segments: (1) the space segment where the satellites are circulating in outer space; (2) the user segment which includes any moving or stationary objects such as an airplane, ships, or moving vehicles on Earth's surface; and (3) the control segment which includes some ground antennas and master and monitor stations on Earth's surface that are scattered globally. The uplink and downlink data types are shown in Figure 5.10. The computed signal travel time is used for displaying the receiver location. A number of applications for GPS make use of this cheap and highly accurate timing, including time transfer, traffic signal timing, and synchronization with cell phone base stations.

In general, four satellites are required to locate a single point on earth's surface. Figure 5.10 shows the equipment deployed in U.S. GPS. The American GPS, monitored continuously by ground stations located worldwide, is built with 24 satellites which orbit at 12,540 miles above the earth. The system was initially developed for military use in 1975, however now the system, under strict regulations, is open for civilian and commercial use, mainly in vehicle tracking and navigation applications. ∎

Four Global Positioning Systems Deployed

Table 5.4 summarizes four global positioning systems used today. In addition to the GPS deployed by the United States, which is now open for global civilian applications by many countries, Russia deployed their Global Navigation Satellite System (GLONASS) for Russian military use exclusively. In the European Union, there is the Galileo positioning system. By 2015, China launched 20 satellites toward a complete system with a goal of establishing 31 satellites by the 2020s.

5.2.2 Cloud-Based RAN for Building Mobile Networks

Based on published projections in Figure 5.11, global mobile traffic increased 66-fold with a compound annual growth rate of 131% between 2008 and 2013. On the other hand, the peak data rate from Universal Mobile Telecommunications Service (UMTS) to LTE-A only increased at a rate of 55%. There exists a large gap between these two rates. To close up the gap, new infrastructure technologies must be developed beyond today's LTE technology. At the same time, mobile operators must hold down their construction and operating costs in order to increase revenue. This implies an alarming pressure on mobile operators to meet user demand. As the demand of higher mobile speed increases rapidly, new technology must satisfy the sharp increase of voice and data volumes as depicted in these curves.

RANs are the foundation of today's mobile cellular networks. Traditional RANs built in 2G to 4G mobile core networks are characterized with the following features:

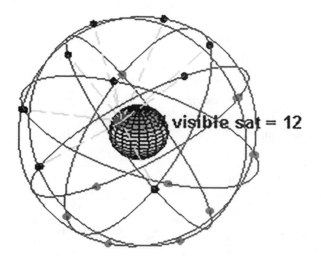

visible sat = 12

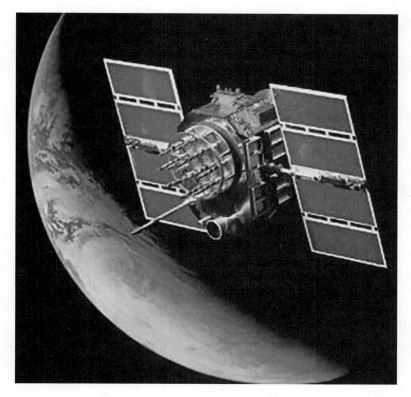

Figure 5.10
The U.S. global positioning system (GPS) deployed with 24 satellites circulating around the Earth with orbital heights 10,180 km in six layers.

Table 5.4
Four global positioning systems in the United States, EU, Russia, and China

Features	GPS	GLONASS	Beidou	Galileo
Owner	United States	Russia	China	European Union
Coding	CDMA	FDMA/CDMA	CDMA	CDMA
Orbital Height	20,180 km (12,540 mi)	19,130 km (11,890 mi)	21,150 km (13,140 mi)	23,220 km (14,430 mi)
Period	11.97 h (11 h 58 min)	11.26 h (11 h 16 min)	12.63 h (12 h 38 min)	14.08 h (14 h 5 min)
Number of Satellites	At least 24	31 (24 operational)	5 GEO, 30 MEO satellites	22 operational satellites supported

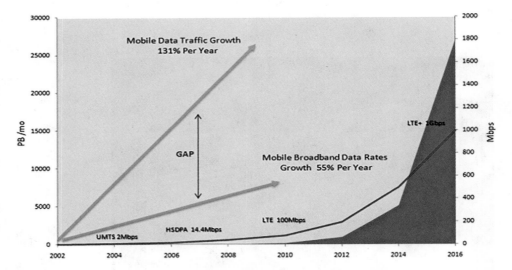

Figure 5.11
Sharp increase of mobile Internet traffic with limited network bandwidth growth (top two curves scaled on the left Y-axis) and mismatch between actual data rate (lower curve) and the desired data rate (shaded curve on the right Y-axis).

1. A large number of base stations (BS) are deployed with fixed sector antennas. Each BS covers a small area and only handles phone signals in its coverage range.

2. The service capacity is limited by interference and handover losses.

3. The BSs are built with high infrastructure costs.

These features have resulted in low spectral efficiency, some air loss, limited QoS (quality of service), high CAPEX (capital expenditure), and OPEX (operational expenditure). To amend these problems, C-RAN was suggested to upgrade or replace GSM, WCDMA/ TD-SCDMA, and LTE in building 5G or future mobile networks.

In other words, existing RANs are becoming far too expensive for mobile operators to remain competitive in the future mobile Internet world. They lack the efficiency to support the sophisticated, centralized, interference management required by future heterogeneous networks, the flexibility to migrate services to network edge for innovative applications, and the ability to generate new revenue from new services. Mobile operators are faced with the challenge of architecting radio networks that enable flexibility. The future RAN should provide mobile broadband Internet access to wireless customers with low bit-cost, high spectral efficiency, and energy efficiency. The C-RAN approach is meant to reduce the cost (CAPEX and OPEX), lower energy consumption, achieve higher spectral efficiency, and support multiple standards and smooth evolution.

Large numbers of base stations are used in current 3G or 4G mobile core networks. They are facing a series of problems, namely, bulky in physical size, slow in data rate, air losses during handover between cells, and they demand appreciable power to keep them running smoothly without interruption. C-RAN is a joint project between Intel and China Mobile toward an efficient solution to these problems. The idea is illustrated in Figure 5.12. The bulky antenna towers used in conventional-based stations are replaced by a large number

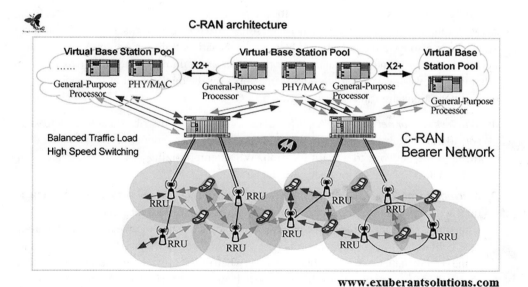

Figure 5.12
Architecture of a cloud-based radio access network (C-RAN) that supports fast, mobile, clean, and energy-efficient 5G telecommunication services. Courtesy of Chen and Ran, China Mobile Research Institute, 2011.

of small *remote radio units* (RRU) that operate with little power (even solar energy can do the job) and get easily distributed with high density in populated user areas. The control and processing in physical based stations are replaced by using *virtual base station* (VBS) pools housed in a hierarchy of cloud-based switching centers.

Balanced traffic load between the RRUs and the VBS pools is enabled by using high-speed optical transport networks and switches with fiber cable and microwave links. The advantages of using C-RAN are summarized as four aspects: (1) centralized processing resource pool can support 10–1,000 cells with high efficiency; (2) collaboration radios are in multicell joint scheduling and processing, which solve the air loss and handover problems; (3) C-RAN offers real-time services by targeting the open IT platform, resources consolidation, and flexible multistandard operation and migration; and (4) a green-energy and clean mobile telecommunication is realized with much less power consumption, lower operating expenses, and fast system rollout. Many other companies have also built similar C-RAN systems including CISCO and Korean Telecommunication.

5.2.3   IoT Interaction Frameworks with Clouds and Devices

Based on the intelligence obtained by data analytics, energy-efficient sensing can be achieved through the interaction between the sensing layer and the analyzing layer; the data analytics also can benefit smart services. As for the network layer, management functions (e.g., network function virtualization together with software defined networks) realized in the analyzing layer also have the potential to help operators satisfy tight service-level agreements, accurately monitor and manipulate network traffic, and minimize operating expenses. In what follows, we specify four wireless frameworks for the deployment of IoT applications. Their interactions are illustrated in Figure 5.13.

1. *Wireless sensor network (WSN):* WSN consists of spatially distributed autonomous sensors to monitor physical or environmental conditions and to cooperatively pass their data through the network to a main location. WSNs emphasizing information perception through all kinds of sensor nodes are the basis of IoT.

2. *Machine to machine (M2M) communication:* Typically, M2M refers to data communications with or without limited human intervention among various terminal devices such as computers, embedded processors, smart sensors/actuators, and mobile devices. The rationale behind M2M communication is based on three observations: (1) a networked machine is more valuable than an isolated one; (2) when multiple machines are interconnected, more autonomous applications can be achieved; and (3) smart and ubiquitous services can be enabled by machine-type devices intelligently communicating with other devices at any time and anywhere.

3. *Body-area network (BAN):* The concept of BAN is shown in Figure 5.14. This sensor network is built with smart clothing using lightweight, small-size, ultra-low-power, and

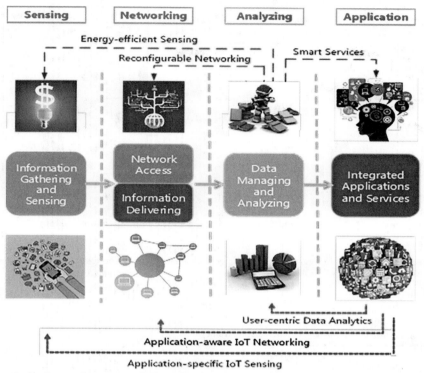

Figure 5.13
Interactions among IoT sensing, mobile monitoring, and cloud analytics. Reprinted with permission from Hwang and Chen, *Big Data Analytics for Cloud, IoT and Cognitive Learning*, Wiley, 2017.

intelligent monitoring wearable sensors. These devices monitor a person's physiological activities such as health status and motion pattern, which can be routed to distant doctors for help in telemedicine applications. Smart cloth with BAN is becoming a growing industry.

4. ***Cyber-physical system (CPS):*** A system of sensor networks, GPS devices, and computer systems that interact with humans or robots in the control loop.

In Table 5.5, we show from one X to four X's (XXXX) to indicate the demand for different IoT frameworks on the relevant features listed in the row headings. More X's refer to a higher demand for that particular feature under the column framework. CPS applications have the potential to benefit from massive wireless networks and smart devices, which would allow CPS applications to provide intelligent services based on knowledge from the surrounding physical world. We observe that WSNs are the very basic scenario of IoT. One

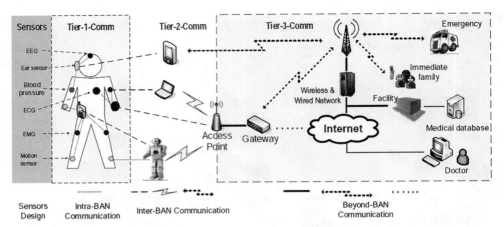

Figure 4.9   A three-tier architecture based on a BAN communications system.

Figure 5.14
Body-Area Network can be built in wearable cloth mounted with smart sensors, Courtesy of M. Chen, et al. "Body Area Networks: A Survey," *ACM/Springer Mobile Networks and Applications* (MONET) 16 no. 2 (2010): 171–193.

Table 5.5
Requirements of four IoT computing and communication frameworks

Framework	WSN	M2M	BAN	CPS
Sensing Requirement	XXXX	XX	XXX	XXX
Networking Demand	XX	XXXX	XX	XXXX
Analyzing Complexity	XX	XX	XXX	XXXX
Application Industrialization	XXXX	XXX	XX	X
Security Demand	X	XX	XXX	XXXX

could consider supplementing M2M to enhance CPS. The CPS is evolved from M2M in terms of machine intelligence.

In practice, the deployment of cognitive services relies on different contexts, such as location information, which is used by services offered over the Internet in order to provide location-aware customization to users. Once mobile devices (phones and tablets) became a popular and integral part of everyday life, context information collected from sensors built into the devices (e.g., accelerometer, gravity, gyroscope, GPS, linear accelerometer, rotation vector, orientation, geomagnetic field, proximity, light, pressure, humidity, temperature) were used to provide context-aware functionality. For example, built-in sensors were used to determine user activities, environmental monitoring, health and well-being, location, and so on.

Today's context information is collected through social networking services (e.g., Facebook, MySpace, Twitter, WeChat) using mobile devices. Some context-aware applications are developed for activity predictions, recommendations, and personal assistance. For example, a mobile application may offer location information retrieved from mobile phones to recommend nearby restaurants that a user might like. Another example is an Internet-connected refrigerator with which a user can check the foods in the refrigerator remotely and decide what to purchase on the way home.

When the user leaves the office, the application autonomously does the shopping and guides the user to a particular shopping market so he can collect the goods it has ordered. To perform such tasks, the application must fuse location data, user preferences, activity prediction, user schedules, information retrieved through the refrigerator (i.e., shopping list), and much more. In light of the above examples, it is evident that the complexity of collecting, processing, and fusing information has increased over time. The amount of information collected to aid decision making has also increased significantly.

IoT Contexts

Context-aware technology provides a methodology to evaluate the performance of an IoT solution. The evaluation is mainly based on three high-level context-aware features, i.e., (a) context-aware selection and presentation, (b) context-aware execution, and (c) context-aware-tagging. However, we have also enriched the evaluation framework by identifying subfeatures under the above-mentioned three features. In Table 5.6 we give examples to evaluate IoT solutions in the smart city application domain.

The primary context data captured by IoT solutions are listed: W denotes web-based; M denotes mobile-based; D denotes desktop-based; and O denotes object-based. We identify touch (T), gesture (G), and voice (V) as three common mechanisms. M means that interactions are carried out through a PC or a smartphone. RT represents an IoT solution that processes data in real time, while A means the IoT solution processes archival data. Other notations in Table 5.6: we have S for IoT sensing, E for energy, UD for user device, R for radio technology, and N for notification. We introduce the name of the IoT project in the leftmost column. The web page links are the most reliable references to a given IoT solution. Such links allow readers to probe further and explore the IoT technology more meaningfully.

In the IoT era, there will be a large number of sensors attached to everyday objects. These objects will produce large volumes of sensory data that have to be collected, analyzed, fused, and interpreted. Sensory data produced by a single sensor will not provide the necessary information that can be used to fully understand the situation. Therefore, data collected through multiple sensors needs to be fused together. In order to accomplish sensor data fusion, contexts need to be tagged together with the sensory data to be processed and understood later. Therefore, context annotation plays a significant role in context-aware computing research.

Table 5.6
Representative IoT contexts in smart city applications

IoT Project, Builder, and (Website)	Primary Context	Secondary Context	Presentation Channel	User Interaction	Real-Time Archival	Notification Mechanism	Learning Ability	Notification Execution
Waste Management Enevo (enevo.com)	Waste fill level	Efficient routes to pick up waste	W	M	RT,A	N,R	ML,UD	E
Indoor Localization, Estimote (estimote.com)	Bluetooth signal strength, Beacon ID	Location, distance	M	M	RT	N,R	UD	T,S,E
Parking Slot Management, ParkSight (streetline.com)	Sound level, road surface temperature	Route for free parking slot	M,W	M	RT,A	N,R	ML,UD	T,S,E
Street Lighting, Tvilight (tvilight.com)	Light, presence, weather, events	Energy usage, patterns, lamps	W	M	RT,A	N,A	ML,UD	T,S,E
Movement Analysis, Scene Tap (scenetap.com)	GPS, video	Crowd profiling by location	M,W,D	M	RT	N,A	ML	T,S
Foot Traffic Monitoring (scanalyticsinc.com)	Floor level	Heat maps tracking movements	W	T,M	RT,A	N	ML,UD	S,E
Crowd Analysis, Livehoods (livehoods.org)	Foursquare check-ins, cloud service	Social dynamics, large cities	W	M	RT,A	-	ML	E

Abbreviations: *M*: mobile, *W*: web services, *D*: desktop-base, *T*: touch technology, *S*: IoT sensing, *RT*: real time, *N*: notification, *A*: archival, *ML*: machine learning, *UD*: user device, *E*: energy.

5.3 Cloud Computing in Social Media Applications

This section gives an overview of social networks, mobile devices, and radio-access networks of all sorts for short-range and wide-range communications and data movement. Social and mobile cloud computing will be assessed. Big data analytics can be applied in building automated healthcare systems with smart clothing, robotics, and clouds. This has provided personalized medicine and prescriptive analytics, clinical risk intervention, and predictive analytics to reduce waste. The system can also automate external and internal reporting of patient data, use standardized medical terms, and provide patient registries and real-time caring solutions. In the education arena, we also see progress in using Audacity to train students on AI and big data applications.

Social media is a major source of big data aggregation in our daily activities. In this section, we assess data analytics technologies applied in the social media industry and its impact in all walks of life. Then we study social networks and graph analysis of social communities. Finally, we present smart cloud resources needed for supporting big-data analytics applications. Online social networks are formed with individuals or organizations over the Internet. These individual or organizational entities are related, connected, or associated with special interests or specific dependencies.

5.3.1 Social Media Big-Data Industrial Applications

We review below typical requirements in big data applications in the social media domain. Marketing profits from microblogs and video streaming, consumer services prefers using forums and mobile systems, sales enjoys products/service reviews, and human resources prefers to leverage business networks. Most organizations apply enterprise social networks. Mobile social media users make use of the location- and/or time-sensitive features of the big data set collected. They aim to manage customer relations, sales promotions, and incentive programs as assessed in the four areas below. The social-economic impact of social-media corporate functions is summarized in Table 5.7. These impact factors range from low to medium, high, and very high. The blank entries refer to almost no impact in those corporate functions. These weighted influence factors are useful in social media information analysis or business decision making.

1. *Marketing research:* In mobile social media applications, the users often collect data from offline consumer movements first, before they move to online companies. Online data collections can escalate rapidly to a large amount. They have to be handled quickly and continuously in a streaming mode. The requirement is to keep all concerned parties or firms well informed with the exact times of transactions and the comments made during the transactions or social network visits.

2. *Communication in social media exchanges:* Mobile social media communication takes the form of: *business to consumer* (B2C), in which a company may establish a

Table 5.7
Social media corporate functions weighted by social-economic impact

Corporate Function	Res. and Develop.	Marketing	Customer Service	Sales	Human Resources	Organization
Blogs	Low	Medium	Low			
Business Networks					Very high	Low
Collaborative Projects	Very high					Very high
Enterprise Networks	High				Medium	
Forums	Medium	Low	Very high		Low	
Microblogs		High				
Photo Sharing		Medium				
Products/Services Review	Low	Medium		Very high		
Social Bookmarking		Medium				
Social Gaming		Medium				
Social Networks	Low	Very high	Medium		Low	Low
Video Sharing		Very high	Low			
Virtual Worlds	Low	High		Low		

connection to a consumer based on its location and provide reviews about user-generated content. For example, McDonald's offered $5 and $10 gift cards to 100 users randomly selected among those checking in at one of its restaurants. This promotion increased sales by 33% and resulted in many blog posts and news feeds through Twitter messages.

3. *Sales promotions and discounts:* Although customers have had to use printed coupons in the past, mobile social media allows companies to tailor promotions to specific users at specific times. For example, when launching its California-Cancun service, Virgin America offered passengers two flights to Mexico for the price of one. Relationship development and loyalty programs could be established to enhance long-term relationships with customers. For example, companies may construct loyalty programs to allow customers who check in regularly at a location to earn discounts or perks.

4. *e-Commerce:* Mobile social media applications such as Amazon.com and Pinterest have started to influence an upward trend in the popularity and accessibility of e-commerce, or online purchases. Such e-commerce events could be conducted as B2B (*business to business*), B2C (*business to customer*), C2B (*customer to business*), or C2C (customer to customer) in a peer-to-peer (P2P) fashion. Recently, O2O transactions are also taking place as *online to offline* or *offline to online* sales or business exchanges.

The building of social networks is based on personal friendship, kinship, professional orientation, common interests, financial exchange, community or racial groups, religious or political beliefs, knowledge or prestige, celebrity fans, etc. In a social network, nodes represent the individuals, and the ties between the nodes represent the relationships such as friendship, kinship, and colleagueship. Online social networking services are built to reflect the social relations among people. These services are introduced as communication tools among people. Traditional online communities are more group-oriented, while modern social websites are mostly built individually. Table 5.8 provides a list of the leading 14

Table 5.8
Top social networks based on global user population in 2016

Social Network	Active Users	Social Network	Active Users
Facebook	1.65 billion	Twitter	320 million
WhatsApp	1.00 billion	Baidu Tieba	300 million
QQ	853 million	Skype	300 million
WeChat	697 million	Viber	249 million
Qzone	640 million	Sina Weibo	222 million
Tumblr	555 million	Line	215 million
Instagram	400 million	Snapchat	200 million

social networks based on the number of active user accounts as of April 2016. These numbers have been growing rapidly in recent years.

Obviously, Facebook and WhatsApp are both very successful in attracting users. In China QQ and WeChat use is booming rapidly and involves almost two-thirds of the population. Social media are built around weak ties. For example, social media's role in democratizing media participation may fall short of ideals. Social media allows anyone with an Internet connection to become a content creator. This may be able to empower the "active" users to inspire the "passive" ones. But international survey data suggests online media audience members are largely passive consumers, while content creation is dominated by a few. The following example assesses the pluses and minuses of the social networks industry in recent years.

Twitter does not copy all offline relationships onto websites. Hence, the attraction to use Twitter is far less than Facebook at present. On the other hand, Facebook is not as open as Twitter. These features make people trust Facebook more than Twitter, because privacy concerns would lead people to choose a more closed system. Facebook is more complex in functionalities than Twitter. Although Twitter has plenty of third-party applications, Twitter is still not convenient for beginning users. Facebook has embedded many common features in the website. If someone does not like to explore third-party applications for some common functions, they would go to Facebook instead of Twitter, based on the current trend.

The social media industry is moving away from flat media such as newspapers, magazines, or television shows. Instead, e-books, mobile payment, Uber cars, online shopping, and social networking are gradually becoming the mainstream. The trick is to catch or target users at optimal times in ideal locations. The ultimate aim is to serve, or convey, a message or content that is in line with the consumer's mindset. For example, e-newspapers and e-books are replacing hardcopy books and newspapers. Targeting of consumers is closely tied to data-capture methods much more than what has been done in the past. This is best seen by finding the correlation of IoT and big data. Various IoT sensing technologies have transformed how the media industry, business companies, and even governments operate. This has affected economic growth and competitiveness.

Example 5.4: Prediction of the 2012 US Presidential Election against Actual Results

Nate Silver is an American statistician and writer who analyzes baseball and elections. He is currently the editor-in-chief of ESPN and a special correspondent for ABC News. In 2012, he successfully predicted the reelection of Barack Obama as the president of the United States. According to the data analytics model he used for prediction, he considered data from many sources. The idea was to use the past to guide the future.

Silver extracted useful statistics from 46 previous presidential elections. He also applied demographic data released in recent decades. He has revealed election data correlations, using Monte Carlo simulations to understand the polls based on probabilities. Figure 5.15 shows the exact match of the predicted 2012 electoral votes in 51 states with the actual voting result of the 312 electoral votes that reelected President Obama. Some of the swing states were even predicted correctly. ∎

The social media industry provides computer-mediated tools that allow people or companies to create, share, or exchange information, career interests, ideas, pictures, and videos in all walks of life. Social media services are presented in the following four areas of daily life activities:

- Social media services are part of Web 2.0 web service applications.
- User-generated content is the lifeblood of the social media organism.
- Users create service-specific profiles for social media organizations and websites.
- Social media facilitates the development of online social networks in societal and business activities.

Social media enables fundamental changes to communication between businesses, organizations, communities, and individuals. These changes demand the social media industry to operate from many sources to many receivers. This differs from traditional media that operates from one source to many receivers. Social media technologies take on many different forms, including blogs, business networks, enterprise social network forums, microblogs, photo sharing, products/services review, social networks, video sharing, and virtual worlds.

Figure 5.15
U.S. 2012 presidential election: Predicted 312 votes for Obama, which matches with the actual count. Source: Michael Cosentino (@Cosentino), Nov. 6, 2012, https://twitter.com/cosentino/status/266042007758200832

5.3.2   Social Networks and API for Social Media Applications

Most social networks provide human services such as friendship connections, personal profiling, professional services, and entertainment. In general, users must register to become a member to access the website. Users can create a user profile, add other users as "friends," exchange messages, post status updates and photos, share videos, and receive notifications when others update their profiles. In addition, users may join common-interest user groups, organized by workplace, school or college, or other characteristics, and categorize their friends into lists such as "People from Work" or "Close Friends." In Table 5.9, we compare several popular social networks and introduce their services briefly.

Facebook is by far the largest social networking service provider with over 1.65 billion users. The Tencent QQ network, based in China, is the second largest social network; the QQ network has over 800 million users. It is really the Facebook of China, with extended services such as e-mail accounts, entertainment, and even some web business operations. Linkedin is a business-oriented social network providing professional services. It is highly used by big enterprises in recruiting and searching for talent. Twitter offers the largest short text message and blogging services today. Other sites are online shopping networks or tied to special interest groups.

Facebook Platform Architecture

With 1.65 billion active users worldwide in 2016, Facebook keeps a huge number of personal profiles, tags, and relationships as social graphs. Most users are in the United States, Brazil, India, and Indonesia. The social graphs are shared by various social groups on Facebook. This website has attracted over 3 million active advertisers with $12.5 billion of revenue reported in 2014. The Facebook platform is built with a collection of huge data centers with a very large storage capacity, intelligent file systems, and searching capabilities. The web must resolve the traffic jams and collisions among all its users.

Table 5.9
Summary of popular social networks and web services provided

Social Network, Year, and Website	Registered Active Users	Major Services Provided
Facebook, *2004,* www.facebook.com	1.65 billion users, 2016	Content sharing, profiling, advertising, events, social comparison, communication, play social games, etc.
Tencent QQ *in China, 1999,* www.tencent.com	853 million users, 2016	An instant messaging service, online games, music, ebQQ, shopping, microblogging, movies, WeChat, QQ Player, etc.
Linkedin, *2002,* www.linkedin.com	364 million users, 2015	Professional services, online recruiting, job listings, group services, skills, publishing, advertising, etc.
Twitter, *2006,* www.twitter.com	320 million users, 2016	Microblogging, news, alerts, short messages, rankings, demographics, revenue sources, photo sharing, etc.

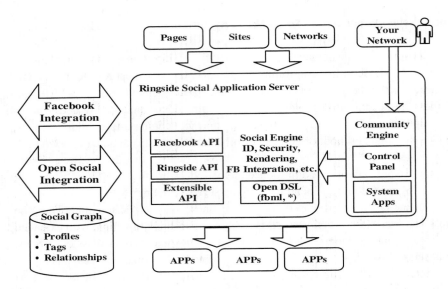

Figure 5.16
Ringside social application server architecture in Facebook cloud (*-fbml is the facebook markup language).

In Figure 5.16, the infrastructure of the Facebook platform is shown. The platform is formed with a huge cluster of servers. The requests are shown as pages, sites, and networks entering the Facebook server from the top. The social engine is the core of the application server. This social engine handles IS, security, rendering, and Facebook integration operations. Large number of APIs are made available to enable users to use more than 2.4 million applications. Facebook has acquired several big applications, including Instagram, WhatsApp, Oculus VR, and PrivateCore.

User requests appear as pages, sites, and networks entering the server cluster from the top. The social engine executes all user applications. Open DSL is used to support application executions. Facebook provides blogging, chat, gifts, marketplace, voice/video calls, etc. There is a community engine that provides networking services to users. Most Facebook applications are helping users achieve their social goals, such as improved communication, learning about self, finding similar others, and engaging in social play and exchanges. Facebook appeals more in the private and personal domains.

Example 5.5 : Facebook Application Spectrum and Service Functionalities
The social service application spectrum of Facebook is shown by the pie diagram in Figure 5.17. The largest application sector is for communication enhancement, which accounts more than 25% of Facebook applications. The next are five application groups: social comparison and selection, play social games, profile enhancement, and sending gifts. Each of these five areas constitute about 10% of Facebook applications. The

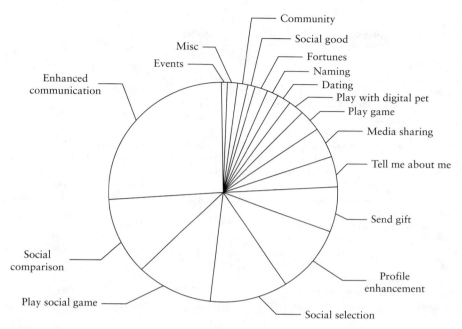

Figure 5.17
The Facebook platform offering over 2.4 million user applications.

Table 5.10
Service functionality of the Facebook platform

Function	Short Description
Profile Pages	Profile picture, bio information, friends list, user's activity log, public messages
Graph Traversal	Access through user's friends list on profile page, with access control
Communication	Send and receive messages among friends, instant messaging, and microblogging
Shared Items	Photo album with built-in access control, embedded outside videos on profile page
Access Control	Access control levels: only me, only friends, friends of friends, and everyone
Special APIs	Games, calendars, mobile clients, etc.

next are two 5% applications: media sharing and tell me about me. It follows with the remaining 15% on many small applications, including dating service, play game, play with digital pet, naming, fortunes, social good, community, music, and events, etc.

The above Facebook applications can be characterized by six service functionalities as summarized in Table 5.10. All Facebook account holders would like to establish personal or organizational profile pages. The profile consists of pictures, bio information, friend circle, bulletin board, and activity logs. Graph traversal is essential to contact friends with fast search engine or personal chains. Communication

Table 5.11
Social media application programming interfaces (APIs)

API Name	Functionality	Protocol Applied	Data Format	Security
Facebook Graph API	Facebook social graph processing, community detection, finding friends, etc.	REST	JSON	OAuth
Google+ API	To provide access to Google+, a social media website with links, status, and photo options	REST	JSON	API key, OAuth
Social Mention API	Programmatic access to interact with Social Mention website, a RESTful API	HTTP	PHP	API key
Delicious API	Allows users to access, edit, and search for bookmarks	REST	JSON, RSS	OAuth, HTTP/ Basic
MySpace API	To access various MySpace functions and integrate application into MySpace	Javascript	Unknown	OAuth
Meetup API	To use the topics, groups, and events created by Meetup in their own applications	REST	JSON, XML KML, RSS	PAith, API key
FindMeOn API v.1,0	Programmatic access to the social media search and management functions of FindMeOn.	HTTP	JSON	API key
Cisco JTAPI	Cisco Java Telephony API allows Java applications to interact with Telephony resources	SOAP, HTTP	XML	SSL Support
YouTube Data API v3.0	Perform actions available on the YouTube website	REST, HTTP	JSON	API key

enables sending and receiving messages among friends, instant messages, and microblogging. Share items includes photo album, videos, etc. Access control allows personalization such as only friends, friends of friends, all, etc. Finally, special APIs are needed to play games, check calendars, mobile clients, etc. Security and privacy control are supported in most Facebook applications. ∎

Programming Interfaces (APIs) for Social Media Applications

*Application programming interfa*ces (APIs) are the first software tools to access a computer, website, or cloud platform. These APIs enable users or programmers to start using the system. Social media APIs are used in social networking, instant messages, dating services, personal, location services, hobbies, travel, crowdsourcing, blogging, chat, messaging, and Avatars, etc. Table 5.11 lists nine representative APIs for social media big data applications. We characterize each API by its functionality, protocol, data format, and security applications.

5.3.3. Social Graph Properties and Representations

The social network is used in social sciences to study relationships between individuals, groups, organizations, or even entire societies. The term is used to describe a social structure determined by such interactions. The ties between constituting members represent the convergence of various social contacts. An axiom to understand social interaction is that it is based on the properties of relations between and within the social group. Due to the existence of many different relations, network analytics are useful in a broad range of social network constructions. In social science, this study is related to anthropology, biology, communication studies, economics, geography, information science, organizational studies, social psychology, sociology, and sociolinguistics.

In general, social networks are self-organizing, emergent, and complex, such that a globally coherent pattern appears from the local interaction of the elements that make up the system. These patterns become more apparent as network size increases. However, a global network analysis of all interpersonal relationships in the world is not feasible. Practical limitations are due to ethics, participant recruitment, and economic considerations.

Levels of Social Media Networking

The nuances of a local system may be lost in a large network analysis, hence the quality of information may be more important than its scale for understanding network properties. Thus, social networks are analyzed at the scale relevant to the researcher's theoretical question. Although levels of analysis are not necessarily mutually exclusive, there are three general levels into which networks may fall: *micro-level, meso-level, and macro-level.* The following example shows their differences in the formation of those social networks.

- *Microsocial network:* At the micro-level, social network research typically begins with an individual, snowballing as social relationships are traced, or may begin with a small group of individuals in a particular social context. Microsocial networks are formed with small social groups or communities. On average, the small group has a hundred or fewer peer nodes. Member nodes in the same group may have close ties with many edge connections. Different communities are loosely connected with many fewer edge connections.

- *Macrosocial networks:* Rather than tracing interpersonal interactions, macro-level social networks generally expand from the outcomes of greater interactions, such as economic or other resources. Large-scale networks are a term somewhat synonymous with "macro-level" social networks. These are often used in social or behavioral sciences in connection with economics classes, professional societies, or political affiliations.

- *Mesosocial networks:* The meso-level theories begin with a population size that falls between the micro- and macro-levels. However, meso-level may also refer to networks that are specifically designed to reveal connections between micro- and macro-levels. Meso-level networks are low density and may exhibit causal processes distinct from interpersonal micro-level networks. The macro-level network graph may far exceed the cutoff boundary being shown at all sides of the network. The circled network groups are at the micro-level, while the thick linkages among micro groups correspond to the meso-level connections. Several micro networks tied to a few central nodes form the so-called meso networks.

Social Graph Characteristics

Social network analysis has emerged as a key technique in modern sociology. Characterizing the existing relationship among a person's social group is the main task in social network analysis. Also, users are facing a so-called "small-world" society, where all people are related in a short chain of social acquaintances, one way or another. All social networks are not so chaotic or random as once assumed, but rather they have underlying structures. Social relationships are often mapped into directed or undirected graphs, sometimes called *acquaintance graphs* or simply *social connection graphs*.

The nodes in a social graph correspond to the users or actors and the graph edges or links refer to the ties or relationships among the nodes. The graphs can be complex and hierarchically structured to reflect relationships at all levels. There can be many kinds of ties between the nodes. Social networks operate from the family level up to national and global levels. There are pros and cons of social networks. Most free societies welcome social networks. For political or religious reasons, some countries block the use of social networks to prevent possible abuses.

Social Network Graph Properties

Social networks play a critical role in problem-solving, running an organization, and the degree to which individuals succeed in achieving their goals. A social network is simply a map of all of relevant ties between all actor nodes. The network can also be used to measure social capital—the value that an individual gets from the social network. These concepts are often displayed in a *social network graph.* An example social network graph is shown in Figure 5.18. The black dots are the nodes (users) and the edges link the nodes under specified tie relationships. Listed below are some interesting properties of a social graph.

- *Node degree, reach, path length, and betweenness:* The *node degree* is the number of immediate node neighbors of a node. The *reach* is defined as the degree to which any member of a network can reach other members of the network. *Path length* measures the distance between pairs of nodes in the network. *Average path length* is the average of these distances between all pairs of nodes. *Betweenness* reveals the extent to which a node lies between other nodes in the network. This measures the number of people who a person is connecting indirectly through their direct links.

- *Closeness and cohesion:* The degree an individual is near all other individuals in a network (directly or indirectly). It reflects the ability to access information through the network members. Thus, closeness is the inverse of the sum of the shortest distances between each individual and every other person in the network. *Cohesion* is the degree to which actors are connected directly to each other by cohesive bonds. Groups are identified as "cliques" if every individual is directly tied to every other individual.

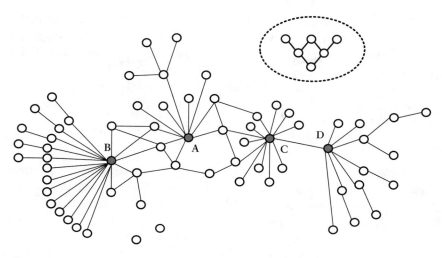

Figure 5.18
The graph representation of account holders in a social network.

- **Centrality and centralization:** Centrality indicates the social power of a node based on how well they "connect" the network. Nodes A, B, and D in Figure 5.18 are all centrality nodes with different node degrees.

- **Social circles or clusters:** This refers to some structured groups. If there is less stringency of direct contact or structurally cohesive blocks, then a social circle can be created either loosely or tightly, depending on the stringency rules applied. Those nodes inside the circle of Figure 5.18 form a cluster. *Clustering coefficient* is the likelihood that two associates of a node are associates themselves.

- **Centralized vs. decentralized networks:** *Centrality* gives a rough indication of the social power of a node based on how well they "connect" the network. *Betweenness*, *closeness*, and *degree* are all measures of centrality. *Centralized networks* have their links dispersed around one or a few nodes, while a *decentralized network* is one in which there is little variation between the number of links each node possesses.

- **Bridge and local bridge:** An edge is a *bridge* if deleting it would cause its endpoints to lie in different clusters or components of a graph. For example, the edge between nodes C and D in Figure 5.18 is a bridge. The endpoints of a *local bridge* share no common neighbors. A local bridge is contained in a cycle.

- **Prestige and radiality:** In a social graph, *prestige* describes a node's centrality. *Degree prestige*, *proximity prestige*, and *status prestige* are all measures of prestige. *Radiality* is the degree a network reaches out and provides novel information and influence.

- **Structural cohesion, equivalence, and hole:** *Structural cohesion* is the minimum number of members who, if removed from a group, would disconnect the group. *Structural equivalence* refers to the extent to which nodes have a common set of linkages to other nodes. These nodes do not have any ties to each other. A *structural hole* can be filled by connecting one or more links to reach other nodes. This is related to social capital: By linking two disconnected people, you can control their communication.

5.3.4 Social Graph Analysis on Smart Clouds

Online social networking services are put together through identity, conversation, sharing, telepresence, relationship, affiliation, etc. These are offered through Internet access and web services. Early online social network services included job hunting, dating, bulletin board services, etc. Traditional online communities are organized in different groups based on different interests and regions, while modern social networking websites are always individual-oriented or follow peer-to-peer interactions. Listed below are some ideas for providing online social networking services:

- Personal page or profiles for each user are linked by social connections.
- There is social graph traversal along specific social links or networks.
- Communication tools are shared between the participants or registered users.
- Special information like music, photos, videos, etc., is shared with friends or professional groups.
- Communities operate in special niche topic areas such as healthcare, sports, hobbies, etc.
- Customized software tools or databases are used to set up social network services.
- Strong customer loyalty creates viral membership growth.
- Social networks have revenues by selling premium memberships and access to premium content.

Consider a 400+ network of e-mail exchanges within a small research laboratory. Only internal e-mail exchanges are considered. The edges correspond to those who have sent e-mail to each other. The number of edges could easily reach 200,000 if fully connected. At the University of Southern California, an e-mail exchange network like this may have to cover 40,000 nodes. This may end up with a connection graph with 1.5 million e-mail exchange edges. If the external e-mails are included, the e-mail network would be significantly enlarged to cover ten millions of nodes on a global scale. Therefore, social networks can grow dynamically to involve billions or hundreds of millions of users.

It is desirable to customize the *online social network* (OSN) to sustain the competition in attracting users. The social network provider should choose a brand name with its own API interfaces and profile variables. The chosen forum categories must be relevant to a sufficiently large user community. The OSN platform must include specific functionalities that make it easy for users to join and enjoy the services. Furthermore, the provider must create an online marketing concept to attract members to join and leave freely. Highly sophisticated software, virtualized data centers, or processing and storage cloud platforms are needed.

The social network community must operate reliably with high availability and performance. Logically, the OSN provides a P2P platform. However, modern popular social networking services are all built with client-server architecture for easy management and maintenance. This means that all blog entries, photos, videos and social network relations are stored and managed by private clouds owned by the service providers. With hundreds of millions of users, the large social network site must maintain large data centers. To serve the clients better, many of the data centers are virtualized to provide standard and personalized cloud services at all levels. The capabilities that an OSN should have are discussed in the following sections.

Filtering Techniques and Recommender Systems

The public demands *recommender systems* in order for movies, tourism, or restaurants to make our daily life activities better organized, convenient, and enjoyable. Social or collaborative filtering of unwanted data can be done by polling the opinions of the users to make decisions based on ratings. Content-based filtering is needed in recommending items based on features of products and ratings by users. Demographic filtering helps decision making based on the demographic information of the users. Finally, knowledge-based filtering makes decisions based on expertise or peer reputation. Hybrid filtering combines the advantages of the above filtering techniques to make even smarter decisions.

Pushing Data Analytics for Cloud/Network Security Enforcement

A hot research area involves applying big data for cyber security enforcement. Big data analytics is needed in network security, enterprise events analytics, and netflow monitoring to identify botnets, persistent threats, data sharing, provenance, and governance techniques that are often wanted for trust management with reputation systems.

Cloud Support of Social Network Applications

In *cyber-physical systems* (CPSs), analytical algorithms can perform more accurately in system configuration, physical knowledge, and working principles. To integrate, manage, and analyze machinery, it is important to handle data more efficiently during the different stages of the machine life cycle. The coupling model between humans and machines is greatly facilitated by the use of cloud storage and analytics systems. This involves sensing, storage, synchronization, synthesis, and service operations.

Smart and Pervasive Use of IoT-enabled Services

Smart and pervasive cloud applications are in high demand by individuals, homes, communities, companies, and governments. These include coordinated calendar, itinerary, job management, events, and *consumer record management* (CRM) services. Other interest areas include cooperative word processing, online presentations, web-based desktops, sharing online documents, data sets, photos, video, databases, and content distribution. Deployment of conventional clusters, grids, P2P, and social networking applications are very much in demand in cloud environments. Earthbound applications may demand elasticity and parallelism to avoid large data movement and reduce storage costs.

5.4 Multicloud Mashup Architecture and Service

A cloud mashup is composed of multiple services with shared data sets and integrated functionalities. For example, the EC2 provided by Amazon Web Service (AWS), the authentication and authorization services provided by Facebook, and the MapReduce service provided by Google can all be mashed up to deliver real-time, personalized driving route recommendation services. To discover qualified services and compose them with guaranteed QoS, we propose an integrated skyline query processing method for building up cloud mashup applications.

A multicloud mashup appears as a web page or web application chain. Multiple clouds use content from more than one source to create a single new service displayed in a single graphical interface. For example, a user could combine the addresses and photographs of their library branches with a Google map to create a map mashup. The term implies easy and fast integration, frequently using open APIs. The main characteristics of a mashup are combination, visualization, and aggregation. It is important to make existing data more useful, for both personal and professional use. To be able to permanently access the data of other services, mashups are generally client applications or hosted online. Mashups can be considered to have an active role in the evolution of social software and Web 2.0. Mashup composition tools are usually simple enough to be used by end users.

The *Open Mashup Alliance* (OMA) is a nonprofit consortium that promotes the adoption of mashup solutions in the enterprise through the evolution of enterprise mashup standards like *Enterprise Mashup Markup Language* (EMML). Enterprise mashup usage is expected to grow tenfold over the next five years. The initial members of the OMA include Adobe Systems, Hewlett-Packard, and Intel, and some technology users like Bank of America and Capgemini. The OMA creates an open and vibrant market for competing runtimes, mashups, and an array of important aftermarket services.

5.4.1 Cloud Mashup Architecture for Agility and Scalability

Hybrid cloud computing leverage occurs on both public and private clouds. Cloud mashup was greatly inspired by using multiple clouds to share the data sets and workload in colocation cloud applications. In a recent study of 1,000 IT executives by the Hybrid Hive, a news site sponsored by Fujitsu and several other partners, hybrid clouds are becoming commonplace. More than 40% of executive respondents reported that they already have a hybrid IT environment in place, while 51% are open to it. Many companies spend one third of their total IT budgets on various types of clouds. Some 80% of IT executives believe in the hybrid infrastructure for the future.

The U.S. National Institute of Standards and Technology (NIST) defines a hybrid cloud as composed of "two or more distinct cloud infrastructures (private, community, or public) that remain unique entities, but are bound together by standardized or proprietary technology that enables data and application portability (e.g., cloud bursting for load balancing between clouds)." Intercloud mashup services are aimed precisely at this direction. The ideal hybrid cloud will make computing resources, on-premises or off-premises, look like one single cloud system. Data privacy and security concerns are the major barriers to applying hybrid clouds or accepting cloud mashup services.

In developing a chain of web applications, web or cloud mashup combines data, presentation, or functionality from two or more sources to create a new service chain. The main characteristics of the mashup are combination, virtualization, and aggregation. In cloud computing, the cloud has captured the computing market with dynamic resource allocations from a pool of VM resources. We have seen the diversity of cloud offerings in Chapter 4. The resource pool can be employed for both parallel and distributed computing, as demonstrated by Amazon EC2 and S3 services. On the other hand, Google's App Engine is primarily driven by web-based service offerings for storage of files, e-mail facility, and messaging, among others.

The AWS and GAE clouds differ not only in their functionalities but also can complement each other for better purposes. This has triggered the idea of mashing up different clouds toward building an *intercloud* or *cloud of clouds* more dynamically. As a matter of fact, cloud mashup offers a more cost-effective solution to new start-ups that do not want to invest in cloud hardware and software to create their own enterprise level data centers or private clouds. The cloud mashup must be designed to support a popular paradigm such as MapReduce on the AWS and yet control it via the GAE through easy-to-operate web interfaces. We will demonstrate how to mashup between GAE and AWS clouds to achieve the desired features of application agility and performance scalability in Example 5.7.

The Idea of Cloud Mashup

Any startup in today's business world needs to keep its operational costs low in the initial years. This allows such businesses to recover initial investments quickly and post profits faster. Thus, it is critical that the company keeps initial costs low. Consider a startup company that works as a social networking portal. It needs lots of data storage space and servers, not to mention the associated cooling requirements and infrastructure, such as a physical building for housing the equipment and power. This could be a moderate to huge initial investment on the part of the company.

One can use the pay-per-use models from public clouds like AWS and GAE to quickly bring the business up to speed. This not only ensures that the loss due to time-to-market is reduced, but also improves the speed with which one can unleash a new idea into the world of business. Mashup use is expanding in the business environment. Today's mashups are typically dataflow systems with the interaction scripted in languages like JavaScript or PHP. The ProgrammableWeb site had, for example, over 2,000 APIs and 5,000 mashups reported in 2010.

Most enterprises need people who can determine what technology resources are needed. They still prefer not to entrust a cloud provider with construction of an enterprise architecture to meet their exact business requirements. A debate between on-premises computing and outsourced cloud services still exists, however, the momentum is toward off-premise. The IT company needs to move away from its current role as a slow-moving centralized provider. Instead, direct corporate governance across the various business lines is becoming a trend. The following example gives some insight into cloud mashup operations."

Example 5.6: A Mashup Service over the AWS and GAE Cloud Platforms

Figure 5.19 shows the concept of mashup between the GAE and AWS platforms. Essentially, one gets user input files from the App Engine and uses the AWS infrastructure for MapReduce. To prove the effectiveness of mashup, the performance of MapReduce on the mashup platform is tested with scalable EC2 resources. We demonstrate the results of AWS-GAE mashup experiments in Figure 5.19. The mashup provider is crucial to link the two cloud platforms together.

The mashup design leverages Google's web agility with the scaling power of AWS EC2. This mashup helps a user to write agile software on the App Engine and use the user inputs to perform parallel computing operations on the AWS. Also, the creator can apply parallel computing operations to a user-owned cluster as well. AWS is not very handy as a scalable web interface because the size of EC2 has to be increased by the subscriber's request. Also, the name server has to be built by the user to isolate the end-server from becoming directly visible on the network. On the other hand, Google is more cost effective in this aspect. ∎

In a typical business, such as eBay, there is a need for computing power to generate relevant results for its consumers to increase their sales. This is beyond what a web-based architecture such as GAE can deliver. So, such a business would need a larger computing "farm" available from Amazon through its AWS offerings. The model allows users to perform a number of computations on a VM. Consider a business running information located

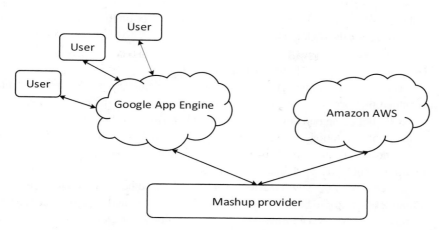

Figure 5.19
The mashup between Google App Engine and Amazon cloud platform.

on an Excel sheet in a Windows host and computation code written on a UNIX-based system. In this case the Google App Engine, which has no capability to "execute" programs, becomes useless. In fact, any executable code needed by a business cannot use the Google model of service. AWS then becomes the preferred way to accomplish this task.

Advantages of Cloud Mashup
A start-up business may offer a web-based application involving large amounts of storage and depending critically on the web page being "up" all the time. The company should consider a cloud provider offering a dynamically scaled (load-based scaling) mechanism, as this would lead to increased availability in the face of a sudden increase in demand common to new start-ups. Also, the ability to quickly and automatically scale down allows the business to keep operational costs low. A business computing platform needs to deliver not only scalable services but also the agility to survive competition. A mashup can combine several platforms or APIs to provide a wider scope of services that allows more flexibility and agility to the users. These two advantages are characterized below.

- *Scalability on the EC2 virtual clusters:* Scaling the implementation of MapReduce can be done in two dimensions: *problem size* and *virtual cluster size*. For the cluster size, the USC experiments run the MapReduce from 1 VM node to 40 VM nodes on the EC2 infrastructure. Thus, scaling is well explored on the EC2 to yield scalable performance.

- *Agility in using the AppEngine interfaces:* A mashup platform is built by combined use of Google App Engine and Amazon Web Services, essentially using the web interfaces by Google and the computing power from Amazon EC2. We use the Google App Engine to create a web page that is capable of uploading documents to the App Engine. Then take the user-uploaded documents and run the MapReduce on the EC2. At the end, the mashup sends the results back to Google users.

Lessons Learned from Cloud Mashup

In creating a scalable and agile mashup, it has been demonstrated that the current most popular cloud platforms hold significant promise for entrepreneurs and established companies alike. By not being tied down to any single platform or the need to be tied to a single flavor of the implementation, the various synergies explored provide insight into what a company would need to do in order to be more scalable with increasing users and data and what is required to be agile in such an environment.

Service-level Agreements (SLAs) must be established between the cloud companies so that a seamless set up can be constructed. The mashup provider has to provide the functionality manually. There is very little security agreement between cloud providers. This could thus become a bottleneck for scaling applications beyond a few hundred users. However, this is exactly where the agility of this approach comes into play by allowing the arrangement to be migrated easily across platform boundaries.

Building a private cloud platform may become even more effective for exploring the scalability and agility of mashup systems, especially when the number of users or data sets grows rapidly. By employing modular data centers, the costs of uploading data across geographically dispersed cloud providers can be alleviated. Wide-range benchmark work is still required to validate the effectiveness of mashup synergies. MapReduce results demonstrate the feasibility of this approach. Other synergies for different models like Dryad and Pig Latin may produce contradictory results due to the differences in computing structure and languages used.

5.4.2 Multicloud Mashup Service Architecture

Listed below are three types of web or cloud mashups, namely *business mashups, consumer mashups*, and *data mashups*, that are briefly introduced below:

- **Business (or enterprise) mashups** define applications that combine their own resources, applications, and data with other external web services. They focus data into a single presentation and allow for collaborative action among businesses and developers. This works well for an agile development project, which requires collaboration between the developers and the customer for implementing the business requirements. Enterprise mashups are secure, visually rich web applications that expose actionable information from diverse internal and external information sources.

- **Consumer mashups** combine data from multiple public sources in the browser and organize it through a simple browser user interface (e.g., WikipediaVision combines Google Maps and a Wikipedia API) [5].

• **Data mashups,** opposite to the consumer mashups, combine similar types of media and information from multiple sources into a single representation. The combination of all these resources creates a new and distinct web service that was not originally provided by either source.

Mashup enablers have also been described as the service and tool providers that make mashups possible. A mashup is enabled by a tool that transforms incompatible IT resources into a form that allows them to be easily combined. Mashup enablers allow powerful techniques and tools for combining data and services to be applied to new kinds of resources. For example, there is a tool for creating an RSS feed from a spreadsheet. Many mashup editors include mashup enablers, for example, Presto Mashup Connectors, Convertigo Web Integrator, or Caspio Bridge.

Cloud mashups have grown rapidly with the introduction of Web 2.0, service-oriented architectures, and big data management. Large cloud data sets are subject to mashup within intercloud services. Mashup applications face an increasing demand for personalized web/ cloud services. Many public or commercial cloud providers compete to satisfy requests for mashup services. The main difficulty comes from the fact that there could be a combinatorial number of possibilities. Consequently, the optimal selection of component services is an NP hard problem and only some suboptimal composite services can be generated.

A cloud mashup is built on top of multiple providers of web, cloud, and big data services. The term refers to a composite cloud application that applies and aggregates data sets or functionalities from more than one source or provider. The motivation is to provide more application agility and scalability by expanding cloud computing with other Internet applications or web services. The design objective is to offer an integrated service by combining several cloud services with related web services offered by social networks and mobile platforms. For example, a cloud mashup can be integrated to form a workflow using AWS, Dropbox, Twitter, and Facebook services. Cloud mashups are built by choosing specific API and data types governed by some desired service functionalities.

Example 5.7: Mashup of Multiple Cloud Services in Healthcare Applications

Suppose each of the tasks handled by an infirmary service is deployed on a separate cloud. The five cloud services form a mashup of integrated healthcare services as identified by a *directed acyclic graph* (DAG), as shown in Figure 5.20. The output of the workflow is the complete process up to the satisfaction of the patient. Each task could be one service provided by one or more web-/cloud-based platforms. Every candidate service is selected from a large service space supported by various cloud functions.

For example, some infirmary services are deployed on a cloud with a fast response time and satisfactory diagnosis results but with a high cost. Patients with similar symptoms need to choose a combination of those five infirmary services considering

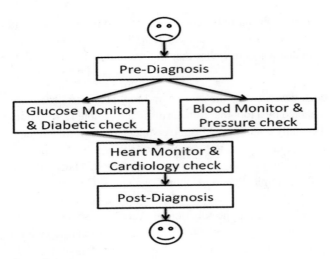

Figure 5.20
Workflow in a mashup of five cloud services for solving outpatient healthcare problems.

the total waiting time and cost involved in the five tasks. In real-life applications, the difficulty lies in the pool of available cloud services being very large. Even worse, a medical check might involve far more tasks compared to the five tasks. If multiple patients choose the same service from the same cloud provider, the waiting list would be long. Correspondingly, the waiting time and cost become unpredictable. Therefore, an efficient method should be developed to help a user choose a composed workflow of cloud services with a guaranteed QoS. ∎

Mashup Architecture Specification

Architecturally, there are two styles of mashups: web-based and server-based. The web-based mashups use the user's web browser to combine and reformat the data. The server-based mashups analyze and reformat the data on a remote server and transmit the data to the user's browser in its final form. In both cases, the architecture of a mashup is divided into three layers:

- *Presentation layer:* This is the user interface of mashups. The technologies used include HTML/XHTML, CSS, JavaScript, Asynchronous JavaScript and XML (Ajax).

- *Web services:* A product's functionality can be accessed using API services. Popular tools used are XMLHttpRequest, XML-RPC, JSON-RPC, SOAP, and REST.

- *Data layer:* This layer handles the data such as sending, storing, and receiving. The tools are XML, JSON, and KML.

Mashups appear to be a variation of a facade pattern. That is, a software engineering design pattern that provides a simplified interface to a larger body of code. Mashups can be used with *software provided as a service* (SaaS). Mainstream businesses are starting to adopt *service-oriented architectures* (SOA) to integrate disparate data by making them available as discrete web services. Web services provide open, standardized protocols to provide a unified means of accessing information from a diverse set of platforms. Web services can be reused to provide completely new services and applications within and across organizations, providing business flexibility.

The quality of composite web services in intercloud applications can be greatly enhanced by fast and optimized skyline query processing. Figure 5.21 illustrates the idea and summarizes the work in three parts: skyline selection, similarity test, and service composition. We select skyline services based on block elimination partitioning of the data space. The skyline may produce a large number of candidate services. To discover the best choice in each skyline subspace, a skyline relaxation method can be used to consider only the representatives in each subspace. The purpose is to accelerate the subsequent QoS-assured services composition.

These three component service classes form a composite cloud service. To reduce the composition time, similarity testing among compatible skyline selections can be used in various skyline sectors. The purpose is to remove redundancy using skyline representatives. Finally, we compose the mashup service as an integrated package for users. The QoS and *quality of experience* (QoE) specify the desired performance requirements in the mashup services.

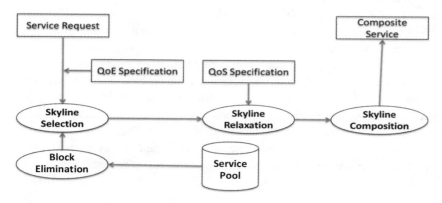

Figure 5.21
Skyline discovery and composition process for intercloud mashup services aided by similarity testing with QoS and QoE assurance.

Quality of Mashup Service (QoMS)

QoMS directly evaluates different performance metric attributes of composite mashup services (Figure 5.21). Take the "online healthcare planner" as an example. One can consider the waiting time, service time, cost, reputation, reliability, and availability for each task. The response time is a major factor of QoMS since it accounts for the communication traffic when a user accesses the services and has a large impact on the service quality. The duration of composite service is neither the optimal nor the actual duration. The first three attributes of a composite service, waiting time, service time, and cost, depend not only on those of its elementary tasks but also on the operations in between, while the last three, i.e., reputation, reliability, and availability, are derived from its elementary attributes.

Quality of Experience (QoE)

How customers are satisfied with the solutions provided by the composite service is a critical part of the evaluation of QoE. For example, the whole medical plan made by the planner is the solution of the composite service, and the quality of the medical plan depends on the solutions of each task t_i, that is, the medical treatment applications, the cloud service providers, etc. People may argue that "reputation" can incorporate how users are satisfied, but it is the quality of service that matters most.

The skyline operators and the MapReduce paradigm have been suggested to support intercloud mashup selection and composition. Previous research integrates the aforementioned two powerful tools to accelerate the service composition process and to achieve high QoS. The goal is to upgrade cloud mashup services and promote the use of big data analytics. The skyline method is especially attractive when choosing qualified web services in a multiattribute decision-making process. The quality of composing web services in a cloud mashup can be greatly enhanced by faster MapReduce skyline query processing.

One problem is that some composition services do not provide a "solution" that is easy to evaluate. We consider QoE for three reasons. First, an increasing number of practical applications fall into solution-related types. Second, more ratings or customers' review scores are available. Third, more interactions can be enabled; a customer can rate different portions of the composition services within the composition procedure. The QoE is defined by the percentile satisfaction level of a service's solution. Each solution is given a score denoting the customer-specified solution quality. The methods of scoring the solution quality fall into two categories: statistics-based or profile-based. The statistics-based methods score a solution from customer voting or reviewing comments. The profile-based methods dynamically estimate a customer's satisfaction level using example pair comparison.

5.4.3 Skyline Discovery of Mashup Services

Given a set Q of data points in d-dimensional QoS space, each dimension represents a performance attribute with values properly ordered. Suppose the lower-valued points are better than the higher-valued ones. A data point P_j is dominated by P_i, if P_i is better than or equal to P_j in all dimensions. Furthermore, P_i must be better than P_j in at least one dimension. All data points that are not dominated by any other point form a subset called the *skyline*. For instance, let us pick two dual dimension points (10, 20) and (20, 10). Because the points do not dominate one another, the two points are parts of the skyline. In the d-dimensional space, a skyline is really a surface that is closest to the origin of the coordinated space. Intuitively, all points on the skyline are more desirable than all off-skyline data points. A skyline query selects the best or most interesting points in all dimensions.

There are several ways to apply MapReduce to upgrade computing efficiency with scalable performance in large-scale skyline query processing. Our approach is based on a novel block-elimination method. Furthermore, we propose a variant of the MapReduce method by adding a process between *Map* and *Reduce*. The idea is illustrated in Figure 5.22 in three steps.

1. ***The map process:*** Service data points are partitioned by the master server (e.g., UDDI) into multiple data blocks based on the QoS demand. The data blocks are dispatched to slave servers for parallel processing.

2. ***Local skyline computation:*** In this process, each slave server generates the local skylines from service data points on its own subdivided data blocks.

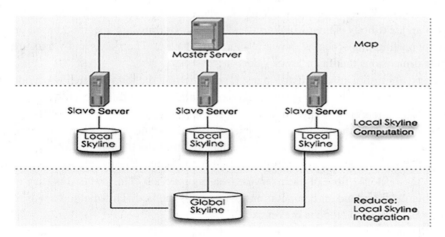

Figure 5.22
MapReduce model for selecting skyline services to optimize QoS.

3. *The reduce process:* In this process, local skylines generated by all the slave servers are merged and integrated into a global skyline, which applies to all services being evaluated.

The quality of the selected skyline service depends on the efficiency of the local skyline computation and the performance of the integration process. Thus, the efficiency and QoS of the MapReduce skyline process depends mainly on how to explore the distributed parallelism to accelerate the Map stage. The efficiency of the mapping depends on data space partitioning. The service data points are partitioned into divided regions. The goal is to achieve load balancing, to fit into the local memory and to avoid repeated computations when old services are dropped and new services are added dynamically. Before the process of *reduce*, we introduce a middle process (local skyline computation) in step 2. The reason is that computing skyline services is expensive if the number of candidate services is extremely large. By introducing the middle process, only local skyline services are delivered to the reduce process in step 3. This will decrease largely the number of services to be processed at the reduce stage.

MapReduce is effective to speed up the skyline query processing process. We need to compare pairwise services in parallel. With MapReduce, the new service is first mapped into a group and added into the local skyline computation. Then all local skylines are integrated into the global skyline at the reduce stage.

Consider two service data points s_1, s_2, in the QoMS space Q. The service s_1 dominates service s_2, if s_1 is better than or equal to s_2 in all attribute dimensions of Q. Furthermore, s_1 must be better than s_2 in at least one attribute dimension. The subset S of services forms the skyline in space Q, if all service points on the skyline are better than or equal to other services along all attribute dimensions. In other words, all skyline services are not dominated by any other service in the space Q. We evaluate three MapReduce skyline methods, denoted as *MR-grid, MR-angular, and MR-block*, where MR stands for MapReduce in all figure labels and text body. Three MapReduce skyline algorithms are specified based on the three data partitioning schemes shown in Figure 5.23(a,b,c). The x-axis and y-axis are two attribute dimensions that favor lower value.

The MR-grid algorithm contains two stages: (1) partitioning the job, in which we divide the data space into some disjoint subspaces and compute the local skyline of each subspace; and (2) merging the job, in which we merge all local skylines to compute the global skyline. Empirically, the number of partitions is set as two times the nodes in the MR-grid algorithm. In the MR-grid, the QoS parameter values in all of the dimensions are used to do the partitioning. For example, we separate the dual-dimensional data space into 16 blocks according to the response time of each service (see Figure 5.23). This method is easy to implement, but many redundant computations exist in this method. This method needs to balance the workload in the reduce process.

In the MR-block method, the data points in the higher orthogonal blocks are dominated. Therefore, we need not compute the local skyline in the blocks that are dominated

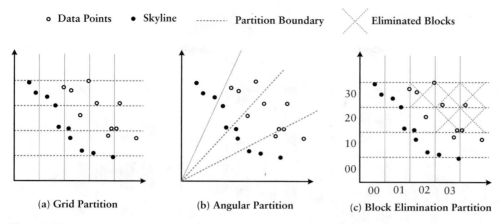

Figure 5.23
Three data partitioning methods for MapReduce skyline query processing. Courtesy of Zhang, Hwang, "Skyline Discovery and Composition of Inter-Cloud Mashup Services," *IEEE Transactions in Service Computing* (April 2016).

by others. There is no dominance relationship between any two angular sectors within the data space.

5.4.4 Dynamic Composition of Mashup Services

The whole service space is first partitioned into *N* disjoint sections. Points within one partition are sent to one Map Task, and each Map Task can process one or more partitions. Map Task outputs the partition number as a key, and a list of local skylines of that particular partition as a value. At the reduce phase, all the local skylines are processed through a Reduce Task, and a global skyline is therefore generated. We emphasize the composition of skyline selected services, which aims at achieving optimized QoMS with respect to a given set of resources and cost constraints. The block-elimination algorithm is improved from the grid partition algorithm.

In what follows, we report the performance results of three MapReduce skyline methods for the composition of skyline-selected web services under QoMS assurance. Our experiments are carried out using both simulated data sets and real *Quality of Web Service* (QWS) data set-simulated data sets, including three categories: random, anti-correlated, and correlated data. The QWS data set comprises measurements of nine QoS attributes over 10,000 real-life web services. The majority of web services are obtained from public sources including UDDI, search engines, and service portals. All experiments are implemented by using a variety of small instances launched in Amazon EC2. The relative performance of the three methods is shown in Figure 5.24.

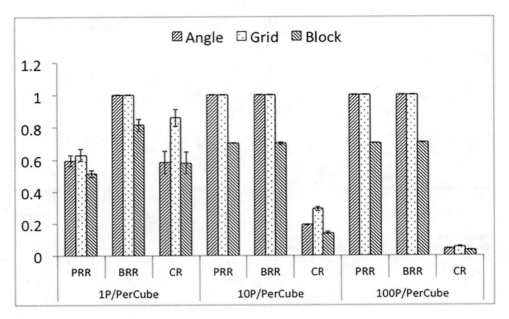

Figure 5.24
Relative performance of three MapReduce methods for cloud mashup performance. Courtesy of Zhang, Hwang, et al. "Skyline Discovery and Composition of Inter-Cloud Mashup Services." *IEEE Transactions in Service Computing* (April 2016).

This mashup method scales well with the growing number of cloud sites involved in the mashup applications. Faster skyline selection, reduced composition time, data set sharing, and resources integration assure the QoS over multiple clouds. We experiment with the QWS benchmark over 10,000 web services along six QoS dimensions. By utilizing block-elimination, data-space partitioning, and service similarity pruning, the skyline process is shortened by three times, when compared with two state-of-the-art methods, as described below.

The process of a skyline search includes two steps: (1) divide the whole search space into small spaces and search within each small space; and (2) send the skyline points of each small space to a node, which computes the overall skyline points. The block-based elimination method reduces a few blocks in step 1, and the other two methods (angle and grid) don't reduce any block. The *point reduction rate* (PPR) is measured by the aggregated local skyline points that are rolled over to step 2, over the total number of points. The *block reduction rate* (BRR) is defined as the blocks containing local skyline points that are rolled over to step 2, over the total number of blocks. We define a *skyline ratio* (SR) as the number of pairs of all of the blocks that need to be pairwise compared over the total number of pairs that have to be calculated in step 2.

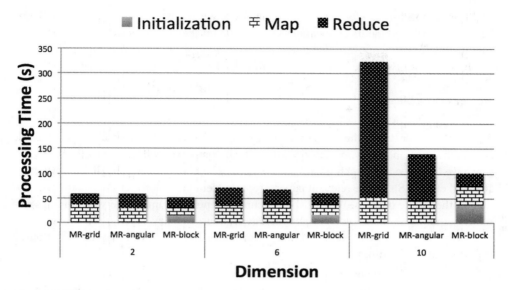

Figure 5.25
Performance of three MapReduce skyline methods over very large data set. Courtesy of Zhang, Hwang, et al., "Skyline Discovery and Composition of Inter-Cloud Mashup Services," *IEEE Transactions in Service Computing* (April 2016).

To evaluate the efficiency of various MapReduce skyline selection methods, we use the basic metric of processing time, which consists of both reduce time and map time. For the MR-block method, the initialization time, which eliminates the blocks that are dominated by others, is also considered. The MR-grid and MR-angular don't have to preprocess the data, thus their initialization times are ignored. We are interested in the processing time used for selecting the optimal or suboptimal skyline services, as the service cardinality (the number of candidate services) becomes very large (100,000 data points for 10,000 composite service requests in the extended QWS dataset). The attribute dimension increases from 2 to 10.

In summary, with a very large service cardinality of 10,000 data points over 10 attributes, our MR-block method outperforms the MR-grid and MR-angular methods by a factor of around 3 and 1.5, respectively. These results clearly demonstrate the advantage of the enhanced block-partitioned MapReduce skyline method, as shown in Figure 5.25.

5.5 Conclusions

In this chapter, we studied cloud-centric IoT architecture and mobile cloud computing. We learned the interaction models among IoT sensing, artificial intelligence, and mobile clouds. Cloudlets for wireless access of remote clouds were introduced. We assessed the progress of AI, smart machines, AR, and VR in recent years. We also reviewed the potential of cloud computing in social media applications. Multicloud mashup services were presented along the lines of service discovery and mashup composition techniques. We emphasized cloud mashups for agility and scalability in real-life cloud and cognitive applications.

Homework Problems

5.1: Study one or two of the websites among Microsoft Research, Apple or iCloud, Google Research, HP Laboratory, or any other high-tech companies whose products or services you have used. Look for technical details of their R&D projects on AI, AR, VR, robotics, IoT, and clouds. Study the relevant papers, reports, demonstrations, or presentations available in the public domain. Write a short technical report to summarize your findings and observations on the technologies applied, algorithm used or developed, products, systems, or services provided. Assess the claimed performance and identify the shortcomings based on your research findings.

5.2: Answer the following updated assessments of GPS technologies and four systems built in the United States, Russia, EU, and China. Wikipedia may be a good source of quick information.

(a) What are the differences in civilian and military applications of various GPS systems?

(b) What are several interesting civilian applications of GPS services?

(c) What are the potential military applications of GPS capabilities?

5.3: In recent years, video analytics have become a hot topic, especially for security check through video tracking, which is useful to protect personal and property safety. Traditional security technology emphasizes real-time response and the effectiveness of verification. Therefore, video presentation with high resolution, no loss, and low delay is the main development direction of the security industry over the past few years. Nowadays, we can see cameras for city surveillance everywhere.

With increasing use of high-definition cameras, how to effectively transmit big amounts of video data has become a key issue. In addition, tracking criminals to obtain their location information is time-consuming and labor-intensive. Please describe how to use artificial intelligence and machine learning technology to analyze massive video samples, automatically track the target, and find the moving path.

5.4: Parkinson's disease (PD) is a chronic disease caused by a movement disorder of the central nervous system. Typically, gait is an important indicator to identify and evaluate PD. In order to evaluate gait changes of the elderly with Parkinson's disease continuously without human intervention, pressure of footstep can be measured when PD patients walk, and the mode of center of pressure (CoP) can be obtained. Try to figure out the differences of

CoP between typical people and PD patients. Discuss the relative merits of the following treatment plans: (a) the pressure sensors are deployed under the PD patient's foot; (b) the pressure sensors are installed on the ground; (c) in order to obtain CoP, the pressure of front, middle, or back parts of foot should be collected; and (d) measure the pressure data when a PD patient is standing or walking.

5.5: Study the intercloud mashup material in Section 5.4. Pick one real-life mashup application in e-business, consumer, and big data applications. Conduct an in-depth study of the chosen mashup application and submit a report consisting of the following technical aspects.

(a) The mashup platform architecture design in three layers for either a web mashup or a service mashup.

(b) The kind of mashup enabler API tools needed and explain their functionality.

(c) The expected gain in performance (QoS or QoE) of the mashup service chain, compared with the use of a single cloud website for the same purpose.

5.6: Study the cloud mesh paper by Shi et al. [21], which was also introduced in Section 5.1.3. Elaborate how to use the cloudlet mesh for distributed intrusion detection and secure transfer of data between mobile device (like a smartphone) and a distance cloud.

5.7: This problem is related to using IoT to promote the green agriculture. Based on a research study from open literature, elaborate on each of the following design requirements. Discuss how to implement each solution with up-to-date wireless, sensor, and GPS technologies.

(a) Real-time collection of a farm's environmental parameters like the temperature, humidity, illumination, soil temperature, soil moisture, and oxygen level in greenhouses, water beds, etc.

(b) Real-time intelligent decision on crop growth, and automatically open or close the environmental control equipment. The deployment of the system provides a scientific basis and effective means for agricultural monitoring, automatic control, and intelligent management.

(c) The system will store and analyze the real-time monitoring data on the server to automatically open or close the specified device, such as remote control watering, switching shutter, adding oxygen or CO_2.

(d) Smart agricultural greenhouses equipped with wireless sensors to monitor the environmental parameters in the greenhouse like air/soil temperature, humidity, moisture, light, and CO_2 concentration.

5.8: We have studied three IoT applications in Examples 5.2–5.3. Investigate another meaningful IoT application in an expert domain of your choice. Submit an investigative report in similar depth as in the examples. Dig out as much technical information as you can from open literature or public sources. Report interesting IoT features, hardware and software advances, interaction models applied, and available performance results both quantitatively and qualitatively. Do not do handweaving reporting. Everything you report must be technically substantiated with experimental evidence and some technical analysis.

5.9: Study the IoT contexts in Table 5.6 for a smart city development. Justify the coded table entries in each row of the table, technically, and discuss how to implement them cost effectively.

5.10: Study two out of nine social media APIs introduced in Table 5.11. Submit a technical report on the details of API functionality, application platform, protocol and data format applied, and security standard used. The best way is to search for very large social-media data applications using the selected APIs. Facebook, Twitter, Google, YouTube, MySpace, or other application program interface (API) example applications are good choices. Report on the application experience and measured performance, if possible.

References

[1] Alrifai, M., D. Skoutas, and T. Risse. "Selecting Skyline Services for QoS-Based Web Service Composition." International Conference on World Wide Web (WWW), 2010.

[2] Bahga, A., and V. Madisetti. *Cloud Computing: A Hands-On Approach*. Bahga and Madisettib, 2014.

[3] Buyya, R., C. S. Yeo, and S. Venugopal. "Market-Oriented Cloud Computing: Vision, Hype, and Reality for Delivering IT Services as Computing Utilities." Proc. of the 10th IEEE International Conference on High Performance Computing and Communication, September 25–27, 2008, Dalian, China.

[4] Chen, K. and D. Ran. "C-RAN: The Road Towards Green RAN," while paper, China Mobile Research Institute, Beijing, China, Oct. 2011.

[5] Chen, M., S. Gonzalez, A. Vasilakos, H. Cao, and V. Leung. "Body Area Networks: A Survey." *ACM/Springer Mobile Networks and Applications* (MONET) 16 no. 2 (2010): 171–193.

[6] Chen, M., Y. Hao, D. Wu, Y. Li, and K. Hwang. "Opportunistic Task Scheduling over Co-Located Clouds in Mobile Environment." *IEEE Service Computing* (December 2016).

[7] Dixit, V. "Cloud Mashup Experiments." EE 657 Final Project Report, University of Southern California, Los Angeles, May 2010.

[8] Dyer, D. "Current Trends/Challenges in Datacenter Thermal Management—A Facilities Perspective." Presentation at ITHERM, San Diego, CA, June 1, 2006.

[9] Foster, I., Y. Zhao, J. Raicu, and S. Lu. "Cloud Computing and Grid Computing 360-Degree Compared." Grid Computing Environments Workshop, November 12–16, 2008.

[10] Greenberg, A., J. Hamilton, D. Maltz, and P. Patel. "The Cost of a Cloud: Research Problems in Datacenter Networks." *ACM SIGCOMM Computer Communication Review* 39 no. 1 (2009).

[11] Gubbi, J., R. Buyya, S. Marusic, and M. Palaniswami. "Internet of Things: A Vision, Architectural Elements and Future Direction." *Future Generation of Computer Systems* 29 (2013): 1645–1660.

[12] Hwang, K., and M. Chen. *Big Data Analytics for Cloud, IoT and Cognitive Learning*. Wiley, 2017.

[13] Hwang, K., G. Fox, and J. Dongarra. *Distributed and Cloud Computing: From Parallel Processing to the Internet of Things*. Morgan Kaufmann, 2011.

[14] Leavitt, N., et al. "Is Cloud Computing Really Ready for Prime Time?," *IEEE Computer* 42 no. 1 (2009): 15–20.

[15] Lee, E. A. "Cyber Physical Systems: Design Challenges." IEEE International Symposium on Object Oriented Real Time Distributed Computing, May 2008.

[16] Linthicum, D. *Cloud Computing and SOA Convergence in Your Enterprise: A Step-by-Step Guide.* Addison Wesley Professional, 2009.

[17] Miller, G. A. "The Cognitive Revolution: A Historical Perspective." *Trends in Cognitive Sciences* 7 (2003): 141–144.

[18] Perera, C., A. Zaslavsky, P. Christen, and D. Georgakopoulos. "Context Aware Computing for the Internet of Things: A Survey." *IEEE Communications in Surveys Tutorials* 16 no. 1 (2013): 414–454.

[19] Rochwerger, B., D. Breitgand, E. Levy, et al. "The RESERVOIR Model and Architecture for Open Federated Cloud Computing." *IBM Systems Journal* (2008).

[20] Satyanarayanan, M., Y. Bahl, R. Caceres, and N. Davis. "The Case of VM-Based Cloudlets in Mobile Computing." *IEEE Pervasive Computing* 4 no. 8 (2009).

[21] Shi, Y., S. Abhilash, and K. Hwang. "Cloudlet Mesh for Securing Mobile Clouds from Intrusions and Network Attacks." The Third IEEE International Conference on Mobile Cloud Computing (MobileCloud), April 2015.

[22] Vlachou, A., C. Doulkeridis, and Y. Kotidis. "Angle-Based Space Partitioning for Efficient Parallel Skyline Computation." Proc. of the 2008 ACM SIGMOD International Conference on Management of Data, 2008.

[23] Wikipedia. "Open Mashup Alliance." https://en.wikipedia.org/wiki/Open_Mashup_Alliance (retrieved August 15, 2016).

[24] Wikipedia. "Mashup (Web application hybrid)." https://en.wikipedia.org/wiki/Mashup (retrieved August 15, 2016).

[25] Wu, Y., M. Su, W. Zheng, K. Hwang, and A. Zomaya. "Associative Big Data Sharing in Community Clouds—The MeePo Approach." *IEEE Cloud Computing Magazine* (January 2016).

[26] Yan, L., Y. Zhang, L. T. Yang, and H. Ning. *The Internet of Things: From RFID to the Next-Generation of Pervasive Networked Systems.* Auerbach Publications, 2008.

[27] Zaslavsky, A., C. Perera, and D. Georgakopoulos. "Sensing as a Service and Big Data." Proc. International Conference on Advanced Cloud Computing (ACC), Bangalore, India, July 2012.

[28] Zhang, F., K. Hwang, S. Khan, and Q. Malluhi. "Skyline Discovery and Composition of Inter-Cloud Mashup Services." *IEEE Transactions in Service Computing* (April 2016).

[29] Zhang, F., M. Sakr, K. Hwang, and S. Khan. "Empirical Discovery of Power-Law Distribution in Map-Reduce Scalability." *IEEE Transactions in Cloud Computing* (in press).

[30] ZigBee Specification. "ZigBee Alliance." http://www.zigbee.org. 2005.

PART III

PRINCIPLES OF MACHINE LEARNING AND ARTIFICIAL INTELLIGENCE MACHINES

Part III features two chapters on the principles of machine learning (ML), deep learning (DL), and artificial intelligence (AI). We study both supervised and unsupervised ML algorithms, and we examine artificial neural networks (ANN) for DL applications. In addition, we study AI machines, smart robots, neuromorphic processors, brain-like computers, augmented reality (AR), and virtual reality (VR). In particular, we present Google's X Lab projects, Brain Project, and DeepMind programs. We assess the recent progress of IBM SyNapse, Deep Blue, Watson, and cognitive initiatives, as well as China's Cambricon neural chips. Chapters 6 and 7 set up the necessary background on ML, DL, and AI machines for the cloud application chapters in Part IV.

Chapter 6: Machine Learning Algorithms and Model Development

Summary: Machine learning refers to the use of computers to recognize data objects and to predict or classify them into similar classes or observed categories. This chapter presents a taxonomy of ML algorithms based on their learning styles and functionality. We study key families of supervised machine learning algorithms—namely regression, classification, decision trees, and Bayesian classifiers. The principles of unsupervised clustering, reinforcement, and semi-supervised algorithms are introduced. Finally, we present the design choices and model optimization for prediction or classification purposes.

Chapter 7: Intelligent Machines and Deep Learning Networks

Summary: AI has become lively in both academia and industry in recent years. We review concrete industrial progress in the area that leads to the design of smart robots, AR and VR, blockchains, intelligent machines, and social graph analysis. We review the AI products or development programs at major companies like Facebook, Samsung, HTC, Huawei, Alibaba, Amazon, and Google. In particular, we study the *Amazon Web Services graphics processing unit* (AWS/GPU) cloud, Google X Lab projects, and blockchain technology to secure business transactions. Then we study many families of ANN for deep learning and cognitive computing.

Chapter **6**

Machine Learning Algorithms and Prediction Model Fitting

6.1 Taxonomy of Machine Learning Methods

The main idea of *machine learning* (ML) is to use computers to learn from massive amounts of data. ML forms the core of *artificial intelligence* (AI), especially in the era of big data. The discipline started from the study of pattern recognition and computational learning theory. This field is highly relevant to statistical decision making and data mining in building AI or expert systems. For tedious or unstructured data, machines can often make better and more unbiased decisions than a human learner. Toward this end, we need to write a computer program based on a model algorithm. Learning from given data objects, one can reveal the categorical class or experience affiliation of future data to be tested. This concept essentially defines ML as an operational term rather than a cognitive term.

To implement an ML task, we need to explore or construct computer algorithms to learn from data and make predictions on data based on their specific features, similarities, or correlations. ML algorithms are operated by building a decision-making model from sample data inputs. The outputs of the ML model are data-driven predictions or decisions. In Section 6.1.1, we classify ML algorithms by their learning style. The style can be a *supervised* approach using some training data, or an *unsupervised* approach exploring hidden structures in data without training data. In Section 6.1.2, we group ML algorithms by their similarities, according to form and function. Both supervised and unsupervised ML methods are plausible in real-life applications.

6.1.1 Categories of Machine Learning Algorithms

We group ML algorithms below by learning paradigm styles and similarity functions applied. First, we group them by learning paradigms, then introduce them based on functionality or modeling methodology.

Classification by Learning Paradigms

ML algorithms can be built with different styles in order to model a problem. The style is dictated by the interaction with the data environment expressed as the input to the model. The data interaction style decides the learning models that a ML algorithm can produce. The user must understand the roles of the input data and the model's construction process. The goal is to select the ML model that can solve the problem with the best prediction result. In this sense, ML sometime overlaps with the goal of data mining. In Figure 6.1, we show three classes of ML algorithms based on different learning styles: *supervised, unsupervised,* and *semi-supervised.* The style is hinged on how training data is used in the learning process.

- *Supervised learning:* The input data is called *training data* with a known label or result, which is depicted by the two types of circles in Figure 6.1(a) within the training data box. A model is constructed through training by using the training data set. The model is improved by receiving feedback predictions. The learning process continues until the model achieves a desired level of accuracy on the training data. Future incoming data (without known labels) is tested on the constructed model. We will introduce various supervised ML algorithms in Section 6.2.

- *Unsupervised learning:* All input data are not labeled with a known result, as shown in Figure 6.1(b). A model is generated by exploring the structures present in the input data. This may be to extract general rules, go through a mathematical process to reduce redundancy, or organize data by similarity testing. Examples of unsupervised ML will be studied in Section 6.3 including clustering, dimension reduction, and *reinforcement learning* (RL).

- *Semi-supervised learning:* In this case, the input data is a mixture of labeled and unlabeled examples, as shown in Figure 6.1(c). The model must learn the structures to organize the data in order to make predictions possible. Such problems and other ML algorithms will be treated under different assumptions on data labeling.

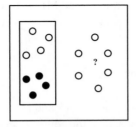 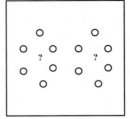 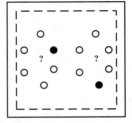

(a) Supervised Learning Algorithm   (b) Unsupervised Learning Algorithm   (c) Semi-supervised Learning Algorithm

Figure 6.1
ML algorithms grouped by different learning styles.

Methodologies for Machine/Deep Learning

ML algorithms are distinguishable by applying different similarity testing functions in the learning process. For example, tree-based methods apply decision trees. A neural network is inspired by artificial neurons in a connectionist brain model. We can handle the ML process subjectively by finding the best fit to solve the decision problem based on the characteristics in the data sets. In what follows, 12 categories of ML algorithms are introduced briefly. The underlying key concepts are illustrated in Figure 6.2.

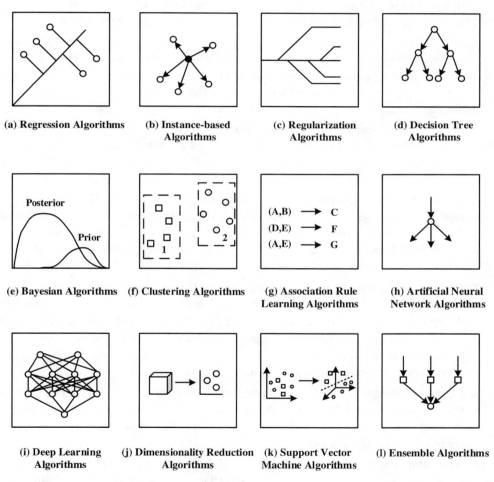

(a) Regression Algorithms   (b) Instance-based Algorithms   (c) Regularization Algorithms   (d) Decision Tree Algorithms

(e) Bayesian Algorithms   (f) Clustering Algorithms   (g) Association Rule Learning Algorithms   (h) Artificial Neural Network Algorithms

(i) Deep Learning Algorithms   (j) Dimensionality Reduction Algorithms   (k) Support Vector Machine Algorithms   (l) Ensemble Algorithms

Figure 6.2
ML algorithms grouped by modeling methodologies.

Some ML algorithms apply training data, including regression, decision trees, Bayesian networks, and support vector machines. Other unsupervised algorithms apply no training data set. Instead, they attempt to reveal hidden structures or properties in the entire input data set. These include clustering methods, association analysis, dimension reduction, and *artificial neural networks* (ANNs).

1. *Regression* offers a supervised approach using statistical learning, as illustrated in Figure 6.2(a). Regression models the relationship between input and output data. The regression process is iteratively refined using an error criterion to make better predictions. This method minimizes the error between predicted value and actual experience in input data.

2. *Instance-based learning* models a decision problem with instances of critical training data, as highlighted by hollow dots in Figure 6.2(b). The data instance is built up with a database of reliable examples. A similarity test is conducted to find the best match to make a prediction. This method is also known as memory-based learning, because representative data instances and similarity measures are stored in the database.

3. *Regularization algorithms* extend from the regression method that regulates the model to reduce complexity. This regularization process acts in favor of simpler models that are also better for generalization. Figure 6.2(c) shows how to find the best prediction model among various design options.

4. *Decision tree method* offers a decision model shown in Figure 6.2(d). The model is based on observation of the data's target values along various feature nodes in a tree-structured decision process. Various decision paths fork in the tree structure until a prediction decision is made hierarchically at the leaf node. Decision trees are trained on given data for better accuracy in solving classification and regression problems.

5. *Bayesian methods* are based on statistical decision theory. They are often applied in pattern recognition, feature extraction, and regression applications. A Bayesian network is shown in Figure 6.2(e), which offers a *directed acyclic graph* (DAG) model represented by a set of statistically independent random variables. Both prior and posterior probabilities are applied in making predictions. Again, the model can be improved with the provisioning of a better training data set.

6. *Clustering analysis* is based on grouping similar data objects as clusters. Two clusters are shown in Figure 6.2(f). Like regression, this method is unsupervised and modeled by using centroid-based clustering and/or hierarchal clustering. All clustering methods are based on similarity testing.

7. *Association rule learning* is unsupervised with training data. Instead, the method generates inference rules that best explain observed relationships between variables in the data. These rules, as shown in Figure 6.2(g), are used to discover useful associations in large multidimensional data sets. These association patterns are often exploited by enterprises or large organizations.

8. *Artificial neural networks* are cognitive models inspired by the structure and function of biological neurons, as shown in Figure 6.2(h). An ANN tries to model the complex relationships between inputs and outputs. This forms a class of pattern matching algorithms that is used for solving DL, regression, and classification problems.

9. *Deep learning methods* extend from ANNs by building much deeper and complex neural networks, as shown in Figure 6.2(i). DL networks are built of multiple layers of interconnected artificial neurons. They are often used to mimic the human brain process in response to light, sound, and visual signals. DL will be explained in Chapter 7. This method is often applied to semi-supervised learning problems, where large data sets contain very little labeled data.

10. *Dimensionality reduction* exploits the inherent structure in the data in an unsupervised manner. The purpose is to summarize or describe data using less information. This is done by visualizing multidimensional data with principal components or dimensions. Figure 6.2(j) shows the reduction from a 3D to a 2D data space. The simplified data can then be applied in a supervised learning method.

11. *Support vector machines (SVMs)* are often used in supervised learning methods for regression and classification applications. Figure 6.2(k) shows how a hyperplane (a surface in a 3D space) is generated to separate the training sample data space into different subspaces. An SVM training algorithm builds a model to predict whether a new sample falls into one category or another.

12. *Ensemble methods* are models composed of multiple weaker models that are independently trained. The prediction results of these models are combined in Figure 6.2(l), which makes the collective prediction more accurate. Much effort is put into what types of weak learners to combine and the ways in which to combine them effectively. The ensemble model consists of mixed learners applying supervised, unsupervised, or semi-supervised algorithms.

6.1.2 Supervised Machine Learning Algorithms

In a supervised ML system, the computer learns from a training data set of {input, output} pairs. The input comes from sample data given in a certain format such as the credit reports of borrowers. The output may be discrete, such as "yes" or "no" to a loan application. The output could be also continuous, such as the probability distribution that the loan can be paid off in a timely manner. The ultimate goal is to work out a reliable ML model that can map or produce the correct outputs from new inputs that were unseen before. The ML system acts like a finely tuned predictor function $g(x)$. The "learning" system is built with a sophisticated algorithm to optimize this function. Given an input data x in a credit report of a borrower, the bank will make a loan decision based on the predicted outcome.

Table 6.1
Four supervised ML algorithms for selected study

ML Algorithm Classes	Algorithm Names (boldfaced ones are covered in this chapter)	Relevant Sections
Regression	**Linear, logistic,** polynomial, stepwise, ordinary least squares regression (OLSR), MARS	6.2.1
Decision Trees	**Decision trees,** random forests, classification and regression tree (CART), ID3	6.2.2
Bayesian Networks	**Bayesian classifier,** Gaussian, multinomial, averaged one-dependence estimators (AODE), Bayesian belief network (BBN)	6.2.3
Support Vector Machines	**SVM** use hyperplane to separate the data space in subspaces to predict new samples falling into which subspace of the hyperplane	6.2.4

In this section, we present four families of important supervised ML algorithms as listed in Table 6.1, where the boldface ones will be studied in subsequent sections. The remaining algorithms are merely listed here for readers to explore further. In solving a classification problem, the inputs are divided into two or more classes, and the learner must produce a model that assigns unseen inputs to one or more of these classes. This is typically tackled in a supervised way. Spam filtering is a good example of classification, where the inputs are e-mails, blogs, or document files and the output classes are "spam" and "non-spam." In regression, also a supervised problem, the outputs are continuous in general but discrete in special cases.

Decision trees are used as a predictive model that maps observations about an item to conclusions about the item's target value. SVMs are built with a set of supervised learning methods, also used in classification and regression. Bayesian networks offer a statistical decision model that represents a set of random variables and their conditional independencies via a DAG. For example, a Bayesian network could represent the probabilistic relationships between diseases and symptoms. Given symptoms, the system computes the probabilities of having various diseases. Many prediction algorithms are used in medical diagnosis to assist doctors, nurses, and patients in the healthcare industry.

6.1.3 Unsupervised Machine Learning Algorithms

Unsupervised learning is typically used in finding special relationships within the data set. There are no training examples used in this process. Instead, the system is given a set of data to find the patterns and correlations therein. Table 6.2 lists some reported ML algorithms that operate without supervision. For example, association rules are generated from input data to identify close-knit groups of friends in a social network database. Details of association analysis or rule-based systems will not be covered in this book.

Table 6.2
Three unsupervised ML algorithms

Algorithm Class	Unsupervised ML Algorithms (boldfaced are covered)	Sections
Clustering Methods	Clustering analysis, **k-means clustering,** hierarchical clustering, expectation maximization (EM), density-based clustering	6.3.1
Dimensionality Reduction	PCA, discriminant analysis, multidimensional scaling (MDS)	6.3.2
Artificial Neural Networks (ANNs)	Deep neural networks (DNN), deep belief network (DBN), recursive neural networks (RNN), convolutional neural networks (CNN)	7.4, 7.5

In clustering, a set of inputs is to be divided into groups. Unlike supervised classification, the groups are not known in advance, making this an unsupervised task. Density estimation finds the distribution of inputs in some space. Dimensionality reduction simplifies the inputs by mapping them into a lower-dimensional space. Various types of ANNs will be treated in Chapter 7 for speech and image understanding and perception applications.

6.2 Supervised Regression and Classification Methods

Regression analysis methods are introduced in this section for ML. First, we present the basic concepts and underlying assumptions. Then, we study linear and logistic regression methods that have been applied frequently in ML. Both mathematical models and numerical examples are provided to clarify the ideas and learning process involved. We will study three families of supervised classification methods: decision trees, Bayesian classifiers, and SVMs. Supervised learning requires a prediction model with an acceptable level of accuracy. The model keeps improving its accuracy by comparing predicted results with the labeled results from the training set. The model constantly adjusts its prediction mechanism until the predicted result reaches a specific level of accuracy.

6.2.1 Linear Regression for Prediction or Forecasting

Regression analysis is widely used in ML for prediction, classification, and forecasting. It essentially performs a sequence of parametric or nonparametric estimations. In other words, the method finds the causal relationship between the input and output variables. Usually, the estimation function can be determined by experience using a priori knowledge or visual observation of the data. We need to calculate the undetermined coefficients of the function by using some error criteria. Furthermore, the regression method can be applied to classify data by predicting the category tag of data.

Regression analysis is aimed at understanding how the typical values of the dependent variables change, while the independent variables are held unchanged. Thus, regression analysis estimates the average value of the dependent variable when the independent variables are fixed. Most regression methods are parametric in nature and have a finite dimension in the analysis space. In this book, we will not deal with nonparametric regression analysis, which may be infinite-dimensional. Like many other ML methods, accuracy or performance depends on the quality of the data set used. In a way, regression offers estimation of continuous response variables, as opposed to the discrete decision values used in classification.

In the formulation of a regression process, the unknown parameters are often denoted as β, which may appear as a scalar or a vector. The independent variables are denoted by a vector X and a dependent variable as Y. When multiple dimensions are involved, these parameters are vectors in form. A regression model establishes the approximated relation between X, β, and Y as follows:

$$Y \approx f(X, \beta). \tag{6.1}$$

The function $f(X, \beta)$ is approximated by the expected value $E(Y|X)$. The regression function f is based on the knowledge of the relationship between a continuous variable Y and vector X. If no such knowledge is available, an approximated form is chosen for f. Consider k components in the vector of unknown parameters β. We have three models to relate the inputs to the outputs, depending on the relative magnitude between the number N of observed data points of the form (X, Y) and the dimension k of the sample space.

1. When $N < k$, most classical regression analysis methods can be applied. Since the defining equation is underdetermined, there is not enough data to recover the unknown parameters β.

2. When $N = k$ and the function f is linear, the equation $Y = f(X, \beta)$ can be solved exactly without approximation, because there are N equations to solve N components in β. The solution is unique as long as the X components are linearly independent. If f is nonlinear, many solutions may exist or no solution at all.

3. In general, we have the situation that $N > k$ data points. This implies that there is enough information in the data that can estimate a unique value for β under an overdetermined situation. The measurement errors ε_i follows a normal distribution. There exists an excess of information contained in $(N - k)$ measurements, known as the *degrees of freedom* of the regression.

Listed below are basic assumptions on regression analysis under various error conditions:

• The sample is representative of the data space involved. The error is a random variable with a mean of zero conditioned over the explanatory input variables.

- The independent target variables are measured with no error. The predictors are linearly independent.
- The errors are uncorrelated and the variance of the error is a constant across observations. If not, a weighted least squares method is needed.

Example 6.1 : Measuring the Height after Tossing a Small Ball in the Air

Consider the example of tossing a small ball in the air. We measure its height of ascent h at the various time instant t. The relationship is modeled as

$$h = \beta_1 t + \beta_2 t^2 + \varepsilon,$$

where β_1 determines the initial velocity of the ball, β_2 is proportional to standard gravity, and ε is due to measurement errors. Here, linear regression is used to estimate the values of β_1 and β_2 from the measured data. This model is nonlinear with respect to the time variable t, but it is linear with respect to parameters β_1 and β_2. ∎

Linear Regression

Linear regression models the relationship between a scalar-dependent variable y and one or more independent variables, denoted by vector X. The case of one input variable is called *simple linear regression* (SLR). For more than one input variable, the process is called *multiple linear regression* (MLR). Here, multiple correlated dependent variables are predicted. A linear predictor function is used to estimate the unknown parameters from data. The model depends linearly on their unknown parameters. We will fit linear regression models with a least squares approach. Linear regression is applied mainly in the following two areas:

1. An approximation process for prediction, forecasting, or error reduction. Predictive linear regression models an observed data set of y and X values. The fitted model makes a prediction of the value of y for future unknown input vector X.

2. To quantify the strength of the relationship between the output y and each input component X_j, we want to assess which X_j is irrelevant to y and which subsets of the X_j contain redundant information about y.

Simple Linear Regression

Consider a set of data points in a 2D sample space. $(x_1, y_1), (x_2, y_2), \ldots, (x_n, y_n)$. If they can be approximated by a straight line, then we obtain the following linear regression expression:

$$y = ax + b + \varepsilon, \tag{6.2}$$

where x is an input variable, y is an output variable in the real number range, a and b are coefficients, and ε is a random error, which follows a normal distribution. The expected result is plotted in Figure 6.3 for the linear regression expression.

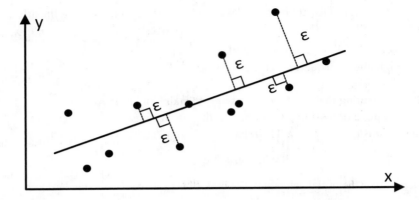

Figure 6.3
Linear regression on a problem with a single input variable over a sample space. 12 data points represented by black circles.

Figure 6.3 shows the residual error of a unitary regression model. The main task for regression analysis is to conduct estimations for coefficient a and b through observation on n groups of input samples. The common method applies a least squares method, and its objective function is given by:

$$\min Q(\hat{a},\hat{b}) = \sum_{i=1}^{n} \varepsilon_i^2 = \sum_{i=1}^{n} [y_i - E(y_i)]^2 = \sum_{i=1}^{n} (y_i - \hat{a}x_i - \hat{b})^2. \tag{6.3}$$

To minimize the sum of squares, we need to calculate the partial derivative of Q with respect to $\hat{a}, \hat{b}$, and make them zero, as shown below:

$$\begin{cases} \dfrac{\partial Q}{\partial \hat{b}} = \sum_{i=1}^{n} (y_i - \hat{a}x_i - \hat{b}) = 0 \\ \dfrac{\partial Q}{\partial \hat{a}} = \sum_{i=1}^{n} (y_i - \hat{a}x_i - \hat{b})x_i = 0 \end{cases} \xrightarrow{\ solve\ } \begin{cases} \hat{a} = \dfrac{\sum_{i=1}^{n} (x_i - \bar{x})(y_i - \bar{y})}{\sum_{i=1}^{n} (x_i - \bar{x})^2}, \\ \hat{b} = \bar{y} - \hat{a}\bar{x} \end{cases} \tag{6.4}$$

where $\bar{x}, \bar{y}$ are mean value for input variable and dependent variable, respectively. After figuring out the model expression, we want to know the fitting degree to assess whether it can express the relationship between the input and output variables. Linear regression can be used not only for prediction but also for classification. However, classification is only used in a binary classification problem. When we figure out the regression equation $y = \hat{a}x + \hat{b}$, we need to figure out the estimated value of the dependent variable for each sample in the training data set; the formula is expressed $\hat{y}=\hat{a}x+\hat{b}$. We decide between the two classes by

$$class = \begin{cases} 1 & y_i > \hat{y}_i \\ 0 & y_i < \hat{y}_i \end{cases} \quad i=1,2,\ldots,n. \tag{6.5}$$

The example in Figure 6.3 corresponds to only one input variable. The approximation is shown by a linear line amid the middle or center of all data points in the data space.

Multiple Linear Regression

Consider the case of m input variables. The output is expressed as a linear combination of the input variables as in Equation 6.6. The ε is an error function with a normal distribution.

$$\begin{cases} y=\beta_0+\beta_1 x_1+\cdots+\beta_m x_m+\varepsilon \\ \varepsilon - N(0,\sigma^2). \end{cases} \tag{6.6}$$

The coefficients $\beta_0, \beta_1, \ldots, \beta_m, \sigma^2$ are unknown as parameters or weights, and ε follows a normal distribution with a zero mean and a standard deviation of σ^2. In a matrix form, we write equation 6.6 by $y=X\beta$, where the input variables and the coefficients are expressed as row vector and column vector, $X=[1,x_1,\ldots,x_m]$, $\beta=[\beta_0,\beta_1,\ldots,\beta_m]^T$, respectively. Our goal is to compute the coefficients by minimizing the following scalar objective function defined over n sample data points:

$$\min Q = \sum_{i=1}^{n} \varepsilon_i^2 = \sum_{i=1}^{n} (y_i-\beta_0-\beta_1 x_{i1}-\cdots-\beta_m x_{im})^2. \tag{6.7}$$

To minimize Q, we need to make the partial derivative of Q with respect to each β_i zero. This process gives:

$$\begin{cases} \dfrac{\partial Q}{\partial \beta_0}=-2\sum_{i=1}^{n}(y_i-\beta_0-\beta_1 x_{i1}-\cdots-\beta_m x_{im})=0 \\ \dfrac{\partial Q}{\partial \beta_j}=-2\sum_{i=1}^{n}(y_i-\beta_0-\beta_1 x_{i1}-\cdots-\beta_m x_{im})x_{ij}=0 \xrightarrow{\text{solve}} \hat{\beta}=(X^T X)^{-1}X^T Y \\ j=1,2,\ldots,m. \end{cases} \tag{6.8}$$

To solve the $m+1$ equations, we will generate the weight vector as follows in a vector formulation:

$$\beta = (X^T X)^{-1} X^T y. \tag{6.9}$$

Therefore, the multiple linear regression equation is obtained as follows:

$$y = X\hat{\beta} = \hat{\beta}_0 + \hat{\beta}_1 x_1 + \cdots + \hat{\beta}_m x_m. \tag{6.10}$$

In fact, the MLR is an extension from SLR; they are identical in nature, but their range of application is different. Unitary regression has limited applications as shown in Example 6.1, while multivariate regression is applicable to many real-life problems as exemplified below.

Example 6.2: Estimate the Density of Pollutant Nitric Oxide in a Spotted Location (contributed by Yue Shi, University of Southern California)

This problem requires estimation of the density of nitric oxide (NO) gas, an air pollutant, in an urban location. Vehicles discharge NO gas during their movement, which creates a pollution problem that is proven harmful to human health. The NO density is attributed to four input variables: *vehicle traffic, temperature, air humidity,* and *wind velocity.* Table 6.3 gives 16 data points collected in various observed spotted locations in the city. We need to apply the multiple linear regression method to estimate the NO

Table 6.3
The Density of Nitric Oxide Measured in Various Observed Areas

Vehicle Traffic (X1)	Temperature (X2)	Air Humidity (X3)	Wind Velocity (X4)	Density of NO (Y)
1300	20	80	0.45	0.066
948	22.5	69	2.00	0.005
1444	23.0	57	0.50	0.076
1440	21.5	79	2.40	0.011
786	26.5	64	1.5	0.001
1084	28.5	59	3.00	0.003
1652	23.0	84	0.40	0.170
1844	26.0	73	1.00	0.140
1756	29.5	72	0.9	0.156
1116	35.0	92	2.80	0.039
1754	30.0	76	0.80	0.120
1656	20.0	83	1.45	0.059
1200	22.5	69	1.80	0.040
1536	23.0	57	1.50	0.087
1500	21.8	77	0.60	0.120
960	24.8	67	1.50	0.039

density in testing a spotted location measured with a data vector of {1436, 28.0, 68, 2.00} for four features {x1, x2, x3, x4}, respectively.

To solve the MLR problem, we can load an open-source program from the following website: https://en.wikipedia.org/wiki/Feature_scaling#Standardization, through a data standardization process. You need to call two API routines: fit(X, y) is used to fit the MLR prediction model with the training data matrix X and y as the target output and predict(X) is used to predict the test data with MLR model applied. We have to go through the following steps:

(1) Using the 16 data points in Table 6.3, we have $X = [1, x_{n1}, x_{n2}, x_{n3}, x_{n4}]^T$ and the weight vector $W = [b, \beta_1, \beta_2, \beta_3, \beta_4]^T$ for $n = 1, 2, \ldots, 16$. For example, for the first row of training data, [1300, 20, 80, 0.45, 0.066], we have $X1 = [1, 1300, 20, 80, 0.45]^T$, which gives the output value $y_1 = 0.066$.

(2) We need to compute $W = [b, \beta_1, \beta_2, \beta_3, \beta_4]^T$ and minimize the *mean square error.*

$$\sum_{n=1}^{N} \left[y_n - \left(b + \beta_1 x_{n1} + \beta_2 x_{n2} + \beta_3 x_{n3} + \beta_4 x_{n4} \right) \right]^2 \beta \sum_{n=1}^{N} \left(y_n - \widetilde{W x_n} \right)^2.$$

The predict (X) code computes the column vector $W = [b, \beta_1, \beta_2, \beta_3, \beta_4]^T$ as in Equation 6.10, where

$$\widetilde{X} = \begin{bmatrix} 1 \ 1300 \ 20 & 80 & 0.45 \\ \vdots & \ddots & \vdots \\ 1 \ 960 \ 24.8 & 67 & 1.5 \end{bmatrix}$$

is a 16×5 matrix directly obtained from the sample data table and $y = [0.066, 0.005, \ldots, 0.039]^T$ is the given column vector of data labels from Table 6.3.

(3) To make the prediction: Let $\hat{y}$ be the prediction results on the testing sample vector $x = [1, 1300, 20, 80, 0.45]^T$. We get $\hat{y} = b + \beta_1 x_1 + \beta_2 x_2 + \beta x_3 + \beta_4 x_4$ by substituting the weight vector obtained from step 2.

(4) The final answer is {$\beta_1 = 0.029$, $\beta_2 = 0.015$, $\beta_3 = 0.002$, $\beta_4 = -0.029$, $b = 0.070$}, and the NO gas density is predicted as $y = 0.065$ or 6.5%. ∎

Logistic Regression Method

A linear regression analysis model can be extended to a broader application for prediction and classification. It is commonly used in fields such as data mining, automatic diagnosis for diseases, and economic predictions. The logistic model may only be used to solve problems of dichotomy. As for logistic classification, the principle is to conduct classification to sample data with a logistic function, known as a sigmoid function, defined by:

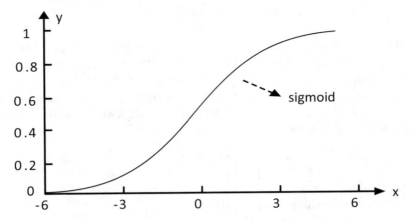

Figure 6.4
The curve of the sigmoid function applied in a regression method.

$$f(x) = \frac{1}{1 + e^{-z}}. \tag{6.11}$$

The input domain of the sigmoid function is $(-\infty, +\infty)$ and the range is $(0, 1)$. In this sense, the sigmoid function is a probability density function for sample data, as shown in Figure 6.4.

The basic idea of logistic regression is to consider vector x with m independent input variables $x = (x_1, x_2, x_3, \ldots, x_m)$. Each dimension of x stands for one attribute (feature) of the sample data (training data). In logistic regression, multiple features of the sample data are combined into one feature by using linear function:

$$z = \beta_0 + \beta_1 x_1 + \beta_2 x_2 + \ldots \beta_m x_m. \tag{6.12}$$

We need to figure out the probability of the feature with designated data and apply the sigmoid function to act on that feature. We obtain the logistic regression as plotted in Figure 6.5:

$$\begin{cases} P(Y=1|x)=\pi(x)=\dfrac{1}{1+e^{-z}} \\ z=\beta_0+\beta_1 x_1+\beta_2 x_2+\cdots\beta_m x_m \end{cases} \rightarrow \begin{cases} x\in 1, \textit{if } P(Y=1|x)>0.5 \\ x\in 0, \textit{if } P(Y=0|x)<0.5 \end{cases} \tag{6.13}$$

Generalized Linear Models (GLMs)

Generalized linear models (GLMs) are a framework for modeling a response variable y that is bounded or discrete. For example, when modeling positive quantities in prices or populations, we may be better off using a log-normal distribution or Poisson distribution. Another situation is to model categorical data, such as candidate nomination in an election process. When modeling ordinal data, such as ratings on a scale from 0 to 10, different

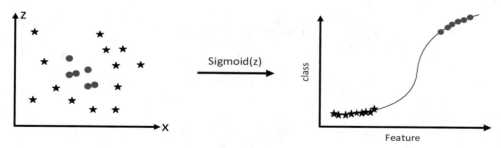

Figure 6.5
Fundamental concept of using logistic regression to classify data elements into two classes.

outcomes are ordered, but the quantity is still a fuzzy term. The GLM allows an arbitrary *link function g* that relates the mean of the response variable to the predictors specified by:

$$E(y) = g(\beta'x). \tag{6.14}$$

Some common examples of GLMs include *Poisson regression* for count data, *probit regression* for binary data, *multinomial logistic regression* and *multinomial probit regression* for categorical data, and *ordered probit regression* for ordinal data. These GLMs are not addressed in this book.

6.2.2   Decision Trees for Machine Learning

Decision tree offers a predictive model in both data mining and ML. We will concentrate on the ML use of decision trees. The goal is to create a model that predicts the value of an output target variable at the leaf nodes of the tree, based on several input variables or attributes at the root and interior nodes of the tree. Decision trees for classification use are known as *classification trees.*

In a classification tree, leaves represent class labels and branches represent conjunctions of attributes that lead to the class labels. The target variable (output) can take two values (such as *yes* or *no*) or multiple discrete values (such as outcomes 1, 2, 3, or 4 of an event). The arcs from a node are labeled with each of the possible values of the attribute. Each leaf of the tree is labeled with a class or a probability distribution over the classes. Decision trees where the target variable assumes continuous values (like real numbers) are called *regression trees.*

Decision trees follow a multilevel tree structure to make decisions at the leaf nodes of a tree; see Figure 6.6 for an illustrated example. In this tree, we need to decide whether or not to go out to play tennis under various weather conditions. The weather conditions are indicated by three attributes: *outlook, humidity,* and *windy.* The outlook is checked at the root, which has three possible outgoing arcs marked as *sunny, overcast,* or *rain.* The humidity is fanning out to two arcs labeled as *> 70* or *not.* The windy values are simply *true* or *false.*

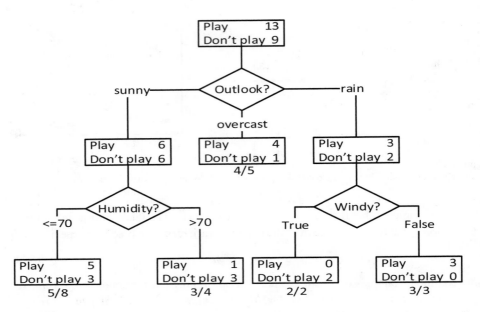

Figure 6.6
Decision tree for deciding whether to play tennis under different whether conditions with probability of final decision at the leaf nodes.

To traverse this tree, one starts from the root to a leaf along a path of one or two levels. Inside each tree node, the target counts are given to determine the probability if a leaf node is reached. For example, if the outlook value is overcast, one reaches a leaf node with a probability of 4/5 to play tennis. On the other hand, if the outlook is sunny and the humidity is above 70, one reaches the leaf node at the extreme left with a probability of 5/8 to play tennis. Similarly, one can also reach other leaf nodes with different probabilities. In the case of a simple prediction decision, the target value could be just class labels (such as *yes* or *no*) without probability indicated.

Decision Tree Learning
The effectiveness of the decision tree is dependent upon the root chosen, or the first attribute for splitting out multiple choices. The successive attribute order applied may lead to entirely different tree topologies. The goal is to cover all correct paths for all labeled sample data provided. The tree must be able to predict accurately for all future testing data that uses the decision tree model. This is a method commonly used in data mining. For simplicity, we assume that all features have finite discrete domains. There is only one target variable called the *classification*. This decision tree is also called a *classification tree*. Each internal (non-leaf) node is labeled with an attribute feature. The arcs coming from an attribute node are labeled with possible attribute values.

Each leaf of the tree is labeled with a class or a probability distribution over the classes. Only discrete values are considered here for classification trees. A tree can be "learned" by splitting the data set into subsets based on an attribute value test. This process is repeated on each derived subset in a recursive manner. The process is completed when the subset at a node belongs to the same class. This greedy algorithm of *top-down induction of decision trees* (TDIDT) is a common strategy for learning decision trees from input data. The regression tree is used if the predicted outcome is continuous, such as a real number. The *classification and regression tree* (CART) is a general term for both of the above trees.

There are three methods, ID3, C4.5, and CART for choosing a top-down approach to constructing the decision tree from the training sample set. We introduce only the ID3 (Iterative Dichotomiser 3) algorithm below. We apply an entropy function to select the most information-rich attribute as the root to grow successive nodes in the decision tree.

ID3 Algorithm Tagging

The core idea of the ID3 algorithm takes the information gain of attribute as the measure and splits the attribute with the largest information gain after splitting to make the output partition on each branch belong to the same class as far as possible. The measure standard of information gain is entropy which depicts the purity of any example set. Given a training set S of positive and negative examples, the *entropy function* of S is defined as follows:

$$Entropy(S) = -p_+ \log_2^{p_+} - p_- \log_2^{p_-}, \qquad (6.15)$$

where p_+ represents positive examples and p_- represents negative examples. The standard measure of effectiveness of training data sets the standard for measuring training example set purity, and the above measure standard is considered an "information gain." This shows the decrease of expected entropy caused by segmented examples. We define the gain $Gain(S, A)$ of an attribute A in set S as follows:

$$Gain(S, A) = Entropy(S) - \sum_{v \in V(A)} \frac{|S_v|}{|S|} Entropy(S_v), \qquad (6.16)$$

where $V(A)$ is the range of A, S is the sample set, and S_v is the sample set with A value equal to v.

Example 6.3: Bank Loan Approval Using Decision Tree with Training Data (contributed by Yue Shi, University of Southern California)

A credit card enables the cardholder to borrow money or pay for a purchase from the card issuing bank. The bank expects a customer to pay it back by a given deadline. The bank keeps statistics of customer payback records. Consider three cardholder attributes: *gender, age,* and *income* as the input variables to a decision process. A sample data set is given in Table 6.4. We can use these sample data points with labeled decisions to construct a decision tree to predict whether a customer will pay in a timely manner or reveal the probability that he or she will do so. Then we can apply the decision tree obtained to a testing customer, characterized by the data vector [Gender: female, Age: 26~40, Income: middle level].

Table 6.4
Credit cardholder data from a card issuing bank

User ID	Gender	Age	Income	Pay Back?
1	Male	>40	High	Yes
2	Female	26~40	High	Yes
3	Male	<15	Low	No
4	Female	15~25	Low	No
5	Male	15~25	Middle	Yes
6	Female	15~25	Middle	Yes
7	Male	26~40	High	Yes
8	Female	26~40	Low	No
9	Male	26~40	Low	Yes
10	Female	<15	Middle	No

The entropy defined in Equation 6.17 leads to the following conditional probability:

$$H[Y|X] = \sum_k P(X = a_k) H[Y|X = a_k], \tag{6.17}$$

where X is the attribute to split (*income*, or *age*, or *gender*), a_k is different values for that random variable, and Y is the final output or decision outcome.

At the root level, if we choose gender as the split attribute, we compute its conditional entropy by:

$$\frac{1}{2} \times \left(-\frac{4}{5} \log \frac{4}{5} - \frac{1}{5} \log \frac{1}{5} \right) + \frac{1}{2} \times \left(-\frac{2}{5} \log \frac{2}{5} - \frac{3}{5} \log \frac{3}{5} \right) = 0.84.$$

If we choose age at the root, we compute the conditional entropy:

$$\frac{1}{10} \times \left(-1 \log 1 - 0 \log 0 \right) + \frac{4}{10} \times \left(-\frac{3}{4} \log \frac{3}{4} - \frac{1}{4} \log \frac{1}{4} \right) +$$
$$\frac{2}{10} \times \left(-1 \log 1 - 0 \log 0 \right) + \frac{3}{10} \times \left(-\frac{2}{3} \log \frac{2}{3} - \frac{1}{3} \log \frac{1}{3} \right) = 0.60.$$

If we choose income at the root, we have the conditional entropy:

$$\frac{3}{10} \times \left(-1 \log 1 - 0 \log 0 \right) + \frac{4}{10} \times \left(-\frac{3}{4} \log \frac{3}{4} - \frac{1}{4} \log \frac{1}{4} \right) +$$
$$\frac{3}{10} \times \left(-\frac{2}{3} \log \frac{2}{3} - \frac{1}{3} \log \frac{1}{3} \right) = 0.60.$$

We select the attribute with the lowest conditional entropy as the root. In this example, the root could be either age or income. This procedure is repeated to the next level of the tree, until all attributes are exhausted, which can cover the entire sample data set. Finally we obtain two decision trees, shown in Figure 6.7. Note that at each level, each training data gets branched to a different leaf node or waits for the next to split. Both trees have at most three levels before reaching the decision leaves; both trees have equal search costs. For an optimal solution, we need to choose the shortest decision tree with the minimum number of levels.

Now, considering the testing customer data: [Gender: female, Age: 26~40, Income: middle level], neither of the two trees can lead to a unique solution. This implies the tree has an over-fitting situation that is heavily biased toward the sample data provided. We will suggest other solutions in Section 6.4 to solve the over-fitting of the prediction model generated. An alternate solution is to shorten the trees by computing the probability at a shortened leaf node based on a majority vote on customers falling in the user category.

For example, we can simply stop the tree construction at the root level by splitting the outgoing edges to three paths corresponding to three possible choices (high, middle, low) from the root in Figure 6.8(a). Or we produce the shortened tree in Figure 6.8(b) with four possible leaf nodes pointed by age values (> 40, 26–40, 15–25, <15), respectively. Then the leaf nodes are marked with probability values. Using either of the shortened decision trees, the testing customer will end up with a *yes* prediction, meaning that the customer will pay back in a timely manner. However, the two trees end up with different probability values predicted for a *yes* vote. In other words, we should use the shortened tree in Figure 6.8(a) as the prediction model. ∎

6.2.3 Bayesian Classifier with Training Samples

Thomas Bayes invented the Bayesian method for classification based on statistical decision theory. We introduce *naive Bayes* and *Bayesian network* in this section. These classifiers improve the accuracy of the classification when used in medical, financial, and many other fields. In this section, we introduce the basics of a Bayesian classifier. Under different conditions, a single ML algorithm cannot reach the specified accuracy requirements. Can we improve the accuracy of the algorithm by combining multiple classifiers in the case of running machine performance? That is known as the *ensemble method*. In order to make reliable decisions, one can combine several simple weak learning methods to improve accuracy beyond 50%.

Consider a pair of random variables: X and Y. Their joint probability $P(X=x, Y=y)$ is related to the conditional probability by $P(X, Y)=P(Y|X) \times P(X)=P(X|Y) \times P(Y)$, thus we can compute the inverse conditional probability as follows:

$$P(Y|X) = \frac{P(X|Y)P(Y)}{P(X)}. \tag{6.18}$$

This is known as *Bayes' theorem*. During classification, the random variable is the class to be decided, and X is the attribute set. We need to compute the class probability $P(Y|X_0)$,

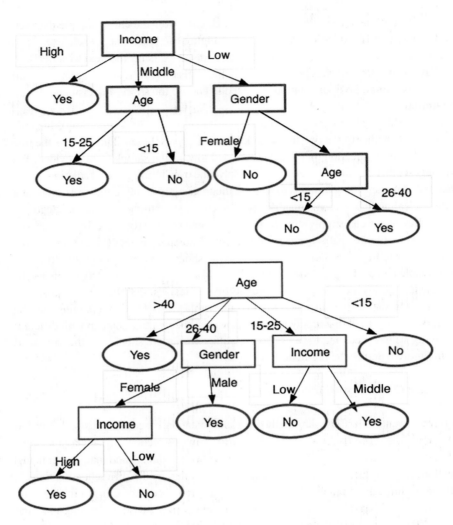

Figure 6.7
Two decision trees constructed using the labeled sample data in Table 6.4. (Artwork courtesy of Yue Shi, USC, 2016).

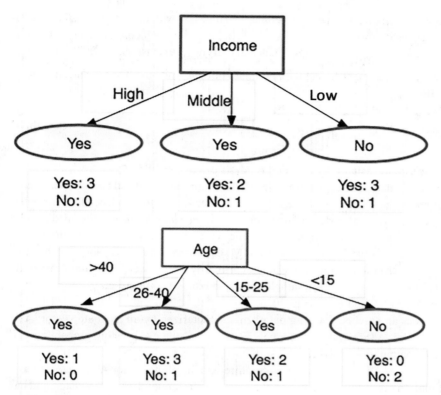

Figure 6.8
Two two-level decision trees stemming out from two different roots with probabilities at leaf nodes decided by vote counts by data entries in Table 6.4. (Artwork courtesy of Yue Shi, USC, 2016).

given the attribute vector X_0 for a testing data item. The maximum value of probability corresponds to that Y is the class for testing data characterized by X_0.

Consider an attribute vector $X = \{X_1, X_2, \ldots, X_k\}$, and l possible values (or classes) for random variable $Y = \{Y_1, Y_2, \ldots, Y_l\}$. We call $P(Y|X)$ as the *posterior probability* and $P(Y)$ the *prior probability* of Y. We assume that all attributes are statistically independent. Thus we can compute the conditional probability as follows:

$$P(X|Y = y) = \prod_{j=1}^{k} P(X_j | Y = y) . \tag{6.19}$$

The naive Bayes classifier calculates the posterior probability for each class Y by:

$$P(Y|X) = \frac{P(Y)P(X|Y)}{P(X)} = \frac{P(Y)\prod_{j=1}^{k} P(X_j | Y)}{P(X)} . \tag{6.20}$$

The Bayesian classification method predicts X to the class with the highest posterior probability. The posterior probability $P(Y_i | X)$, $i = 1, 2, \ldots, l$ for each combination of X and Y, then decides Y_r by finding $\max_{i=1,2,\ldots,l} P(Y_i | X)$, and classifying X to class Y_r. As $P(X)$ is the same for all classes, it is sufficient to find the maximum of the numerator. Thus, we need to compute the following:

$$\max_Y \; P(Y) \prod_{j=1}^{k} P(X_j | Y). \tag{6.21}$$

Example 6.4: Bayesian Classifier and Analysis of Classification Results

The training data is a set of animals. Each data item can be labeled as mammal or non-mammal, but not both. Each data item is characterized by four independent attributes: $\mathbf{A} = <A1, A2, A3, A4> = <$*gives birth, can fly, lives in water, has legs*$>$. We need to build a Bayesian classifier model from the training set. The model will be applied to classify any unlabeled animal as either *mammals* (M) or *non-mammals* (N). Note that the attribute A3: "lives in water" means the animal primarily lives in water, not just occasionally swims in the water. Using the samples in Table 6.5, we compute the *prior probabilities*: P (M) = 6/20 and P (N) = 13/20.

Consider an unlabeled testing data item characterized by an attribute vector: $\mathbf{A}^* = <A1, A2, A3, A4> = <yes, no, yes, no>$. First, we calculate the testing probability values; the computations involved are summarized in Table 6.6.

Since P (M | $\mathbf{A}^*$) > P (N | $\mathbf{A}^*$), this creature with attribute vector $\mathbf{A}^*$ is detected as a mammal. In other words, a creature that gives birth, cannot fly, lives in water, and has no legs is classified as a mammal. Now, let us analyze the accuracy of using the Bayesian classifier by testing four creatures using the above method; see the results in Table 6.6. We obtain the posterior probabilities P(M | A1, A2, A3, A4) and P(N | A1, A2, A3, A4) for each of the four testing animals. Choose the class with highest probability as the predicted class.

Comparing the predicted results with the actual classes, we discover four possible prediction statuses in the rightmost column. The TP (true positive) refers to a true case correctly predicted, TN (true negative) for a true case incorrectly predicted, FP (false positive) means a false case correctly predicted, and FN (false negative) for the false case that is incorrectly predicted. Based on the comparison results, we have the following performance results: TP = 2/4 = 0.5, TN = 1/4 = 0.25, FP = 0, and FN = 1/4 = 0.25. Then, we use two performance metrics to assess the accuracy of the Bayesian classifier.

Prediction accuracy = (TP + TN) / (TP + TN + FP + FN) = 0.75
Prediction error = (FP + FN) / (TP + TN + FP + FN) = 0.25 ∎

The accuracy or error comes from the weak assumption that all attributes are independent. In general, the larger the training set to cover all possible attribute vectors, the higher the prediction accuracy. Furthermore, if any of the individual conditional probability

Table 6.5
Sample data in the training data set for Example 6.4

Name	Give Birth	Can Fly	Live in Water	Have Legs	Class
Human	yes	no	no	yes	mammals
Python	no	no	no	no	non-mammals
Salmon	no	no	yes	no	non-mammals
Whale	yes	no	yes	no	mammals
Frog	no	no	sometimes	yes	non-mammals
Komodo	no	no	no	yes	non-mammals
Bat	yes	yes	no	yes	mammals
Pigeon	no	yes	no	yes	non-mammals
Cat	yes	no	no	yes	mammals
Leopard shark	yes	no	yes	no	non-mammals
Turtle	no	no	sometimes	yes	non-mammals
Penguin	no	no	sometimes	yes	non-mammals
Porcupine	yes	no	no	yes	mammals
Eel	no	no	yes	no	non-mammals
Salamander	no	no	sometimes	yes	non-mammals
Gila monster	no	no	no	yes	non-mammals
Platypus	no	no	no	yes	mammals
Owl	no	yes	no	yes	non-mammals
Dolphin	yes	no	yes	no	mammals
Eagle	no	yes	no	yes	non-mammals

Table 6.6
Pre-test attribute probability for sample data in Table 6.5

Attributes Statistics		Gives Birth		Can Fly		Lives in Water		Has Legs	
		Yes	No	Yes	No	Yes	No	Yes	No
Counts	M	6	1	6	1	2	5	2	5
	N	1	12	10	3	10	3	4	9
Probability	M	6/7	1/7	6/7	1/7	2/7	5/7	2/7	5/7

$P(A_i|C)=N_{ic}/N_c=0$ due to the case that $N_{ic}=0$ from the training data set (Table 6.7), the entire posterior probability becomes zero. This can be avoided by assuming an offset value $P(A_i|C)=(N_{ic}+1)/(N_c+c)=1/(N_c+c)$, where c is number of classes being considered.

6.2.4 Support Vector Machines (SVM)

Support vector offers another approach to classifying multidimensional data sets. Samples on the margin are called the support vectors. We can use a straight line to separate the points

Table 6.7
Predicted results of four animals compared with their actual classes in Example 6.4

Animal Name	Gives Birth	Can Fly	Lives in Water	Has Legs	Predicted Class	Actual Class	Prediction Status
Dog	yes	no	no	yes	M	M	TP
Monostream	no	no	no	yes	N	M	FN
Alligator	no	no	yes	yes	N	N	TN
Horse	yes	no	no	yes	M	M	TP

in 2D space, and use planes to separate points in 3D space. Similarly, we use a hyperplane to separate the points in high-dimensional space. We regard the points in the same area as one class so that we can use SVM to solve the issues of classification. Whereas the original problem may be stated in a finite dimensional space, it often happens that the sets to discriminate are not linearly separable in that space. For this reason, it was proposed that the original finite-dimensional space be mapped into a much higher-dimensional space, presumably making the separation easier in that space. Thus, we can use a hyperplane to cluster these points in high-dimensional space.

Linearly Separable Boundary

Consider a 2D plane with two kinds of data, represented circular and square dots, as shown in Figure 6.9(a). These data are linearly separable; therefore, one straight line is drawn between them. However, infinite straight lines can be drawn, as shown in Figure 6.9(b). How do you find the "best" line, i.e., the one with the minimum classification error? For example, consider the two-class problems in an n-dimensional space.

The two classes are separated by an $(n\text{-}1)$-dimensional hyperplane. Consider a data point D is $(X_1, y_1), \ldots .(X_{|D|}, y_{|D|})$, wherein, X_i is the training sample of n-dimension, with class label y_i. Each y_i can assume a value either $+1$ for one class and/or -1 for the other classes. In this case, the $(n\text{-}1)$-dimensional hyperplane is represented by:

$$w^T x + b = 0, \tag{6.22}$$

where w and b are the parameters and correspond to a straight line in the 2D plane. It is certainly also hoped that the hyperplane can separate the two kinds of data, i.e., all the y_i corresponded by the data points on one side of the hyperplane are -1, and $+1$ on the other side. Make $f(x) = w^T x + b$, use $f(x) > 0$ point pairs for data points with $y = 1$, and $f(x) < 0$ point pairs for data points with $y = -1$.

Maximal Margin Hyperplane

Consider those squares and circles nearest to the decision boundary, as shown in Figure 6.10. Adjust parameters w and b, and two parallel hyperplanes, H_1 and H_2, can be represented by:

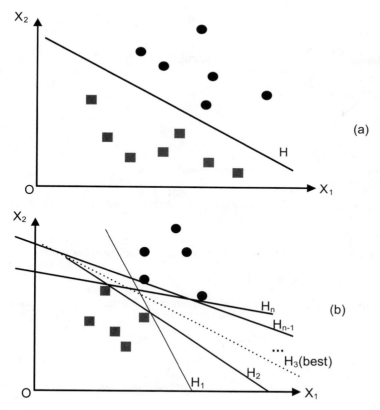

Figure 6.9
The SVM method generates hyperplanes to separate data points in the data space.

$$H_1 : w^T x + b = 1 \quad H_2 : w^T x + b = -1 \tag{6.23}$$

The margin of the decision boundary is given by the distance between those two hyperplanes. To calculate the margin, make x_1 the data point on H_1, and x_2 the data point on H_2, and put x_1 and x_2 into the above formula, then margin d can be obtained by subtracting the two formulas: $w^T(x_1 - x_2) = 2$, therefore: we have $d = 2 / |w|$. Phase of SVM includes estimation of parameters w and b from the training data, and the selected parameters must meet the following two conditions by:

$$\begin{cases} w^T x_i + b \geq 1 & y_i = 1 \\ w^T x_i + b \leq -1 & y_i = -1. \end{cases} \tag{6.24}$$

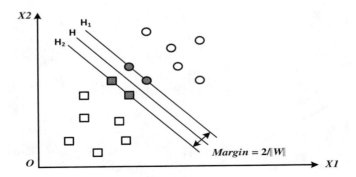

Figure 6.10
A hyperplane (a straight line) that separates the data points into two sides with maximized margin to the dividing line in a 2D data space.

Those two inequalities can be written to the following more compact forms as below:

$$y_i(w^T x_i + b) \geq 1 \quad i = 1, 2, \ldots, N. \tag{6.25}$$

Maximization of the margin is equivalent to minimization of the following objective function:

$$f(w) = \frac{\|w\|^2}{2}. \tag{6.26}$$

Therefore, SVM is obtained by finding the minimum objective function:

$$\min \frac{\|w\|^2}{2}, \quad subject\ to: y_i(w^T x_i + b) \geq 1 \quad i = 1, 2, \ldots, N. \tag{6.27}$$

If we cannot find a hyperplane to separate the data, i.e., the above linear SVM cannot be found a feasible solution, we need to extend the SVM to a nonlinear SVM model through the following two steps: (1) convert the input data to a space of higher dimension through nonlinear mapping; and (2) search the separating hyperplane in the new space. For example, when the low dimensional linear data is inseparable, it can be mapped to a higher dimension to be separable after using the Gaussian function. This is a convex optimization problem because the objective function is quadratic and the constraint condition is linear, and it can be solved through the standard Lagrange multiplier. We may need to adjust the model when the samples are not linearly inseparable. The situation is shown in Figure 6.11.

6.3 Clustering and Dimensionality Reduction Methods

We use a vector quantization method to classify a data set into disjoint clusters without labeled training data. The difficulty lies in how to discover the hidden relationship between unlabeled data elements. Cluster analysis offers the most common unsupervised classification

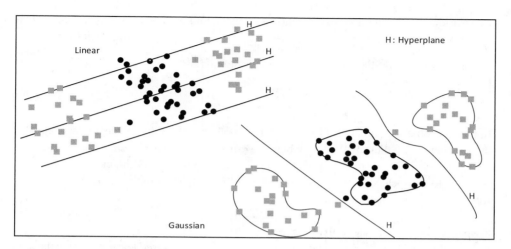

Figure 6.11
The linearly separable hyperplane (upper left) versus nonlinear hyperplanes (curves) that separates the data points in a 2D data space.

method. A clustering method groups data into meaningful subsets called *clusters* without using any training data. This section introduces the *k-means clustering method* of grouping a large set of unrelated data elements (or vectors) into *k* clusters.

6.3.1 Cluster Analysis and K-Means Clustering

Cluster analysis assigns a set of observations to partition a data set into *clusters* based on a Euclidean distance or similarity function. Data elements grouped into the same cluster are similar or have some common properties, according to a predefined similarity metric. The clusters are separated by dissimilar features or properties. Cluster analysis is aimed at separating data for classification purposes. It is an unsupervised classification method.

Assume that the data set D contains n objects in Euclidean space. You need to divide objects in the D into k clusters $C_1, C_2, \ldots, C_k$, making for $1 \leq i, j \leq k$, $C_i \subset D$, $C_i \cap C_j \neq \varnothing$. It is necessary to evaluate the quality of the division by defining an objective function which has the object of high similarity in a cluster and low inter-cluster similarity. In order to embody a cluster more visually, the line heart of a cluster is defined as follows:

$$\bar{x}_{C_i} = \frac{\sum_{i=1}^{n_i} \bar{x}_i}{n_i}, i = 1, 2, \ldots, k, \tag{6.28}$$

where n_i denotes the number of elements in a cluster, and $\vec{x}_i$ denotes the vector coordinate of cluster elements. Then $\bar{x}_{C_i}$ denotes clusters C_i. Use $d(x, y)$ to denote the Euclidean distance between two vectors. The objective function is defined by

$$E = \sum_{i=1}^{k} \sum_{x \in C_i} [d(x, \bar{x}_{C_i})]^2. \tag{6.29}$$

In fact, the objective function E is the error sum of squares of all objects in data sets D to the line heart of a cluster. We study below a *k-nearest neighbor method* for simple clustering, which is easier to implement. A shortcoming of the kNN algorithm is that it is sensitive to the local structure of the data space. This shortcoming is amended by a more sophisticated k-means clustering method.

K-Nearest Neighbor (kNN) Clustering

This is a kind of *lazy learning* method or a type of *instance-based* learning that is the simplest to implement. The objective function is only approximated locally with a deferred classification. The idea is to consider the input data elements as among the k closest training examples in the feature space. The output depends on whether kNN is used for classification or for regression, as defined below:

- For **kNN classification**, an object is classified by a majority vote of its neighbors, meaning the element being classified as a member by the most common among its k nearest neighbors.
- *For* **kNN regression**, the output is the property value for the data object, which is the average of the values of its k nearest neighbors. This means that the data object is weighted by the nearer neighbors.

K-Means Clustering Method

The objective of k-means clustering is described as follows. For a given data set and given k, find a group of clusters $C_1, C_2, \ldots, C_k$ in order to minimize the objective function E:

$$\min E = \min \sum_{i=1}^{k} \sum_{x \in C_i} [d(x, \bar{x}_{C_i})]^2. \tag{6.30}$$

Let S be the set of n data elements and S_i be the *i-th* cluster subset. The clusters, S_i for $I = 1, 2, \ldots k$, are disjoint subsets of S forming a partition of the data set S. K-means clustering is implemented with an iterative refinement technique, also known as Lloyd's Algorithm. Given an initial set of k means $m_1^{(1)}, \ldots, m_k^{(1)}$, the algorithm proceeds by alternating between the following two steps:

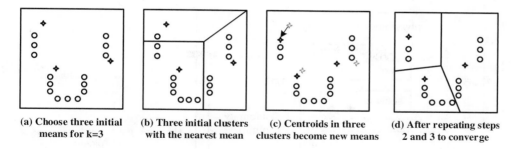

(a) Choose three initial means for k=3 **(b) Three initial clusters with the nearest mean** **(c) Centroids in three clusters become new means** **(d) After repeating steps 2 and 3 to converge**

Figure 6.12
A k-means clustering process that generates three clusters (k = 3) around three means (centroids) in two iterations, where initial and new means are marked by stars.

1. **Assignment step:** Assign each observation to the cluster with mean being the centroid of set S_i to yield the least *within-cluster sum of squares* (WCSS). This is really the squared Euclidean distance at time $t = 1, 2, \ldots \ldots$

$$S_i^{(t)} = \{x_p : \|x_p - m_i^{(t)}\|^2 \le \|x_p - m_j^{(t)}\|^2 \ \forall j, 1 \le j \le k\}. \tag{6.31}$$

2. **Update step:** Calculate the new means at time step $t+1$ as the centroids of the observations in the new clusters:

$$m_i^{(t+1)} = \frac{1}{|S_i^{(t)}|} \sum_{x_j \in S_i^{(t)}} x_j. \tag{6.32}$$

Since the arithmetic mean minimizes the WCSS objective, this algorithm will converge when the assignments no longer reduce the WCSS. Since both steps optimize the WCSS objective, there exists only a finite number of iterations to yield the final partitioning. The algorithm must converge to a (local) optimum. The idea is to assign data objects to the nearest cluster by distance. To construct the clusters iteratively, we use Figure 6.12 to illustrate the initial choice of centroids and four steps to build three clusters out of 15 data points.

1. k initial "means" (in this case $k = 3$) are randomly generated within the data domain.
2. k clusters are created by associating each data point with the nearest mean. The partitions correspond to the Voronoi diagram generated by the means.
3. The centroid of each of the k clusters becomes the new mean.
4. Steps 2 and 3 are repeated until convergence has been reached.

Example 6.5: Cluster Analysis of Hospital Exam Records

Figure 6.13 shows an example of the cluster analysis of a hospital's physical examination records. The physical examination groups are divided into "conformity group" and "nonconformity group" based on clustering of characteristics. Nonconformity may be divided

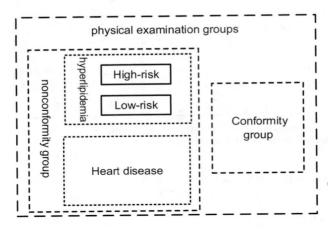

High-risk: patients with high risk of hyperlipidemia
Low-risk: patients with low risk of hyperlipidemia
Conformity group: Normal people in physical examination

Figure 6.13
Clustering of patients into several clusters for receiving different treatment plans.

into a subgroup with hyperlipidemia and another subgroup with heart disease. In the same way, the group with hyperlipidemia is divided into high-risk and low-risk subgroups.

The difference between clustering and classification is, in general, that clustering is an unsupervised learning process and classification is a supervised learning process. Clustering requires determination of the labels by the user rather than using predefined labels. Such an unsupervised clustering is known as *k-means clustering*. ■

Example 6.6: Using K-Means Clustering to Classify Iris Flowers (contributed by Wenhao Zhang, University of Southern California)

Consider solving an iris flower classification problem with k-means clustering for $k = 3$ clusters, given a data set of 150 unlabeled data points on iris flowers. These flowers are classified into three clusters, namely *Iris setosa, Iris versicolour,* and *Iris virginica*. The complete flower data set, denoted as "iris.csv" is from the UC Irvine Machine Learning Repository. There are four features in this data set: (1) sepal length in cm, (2) sepal width in cm, (3) petal length in cm, and (4) petal width in cm.

To simplify the final display of the clustering results, we consider the data points with only two most important features {3, 4}. We identify the clustering centers (centroids) in successive steps, and also draw a 2D Euclidean space diagram (x-axis: petal.length; y-axis: petal.width) to show the final clustering results. The k-means clustering in R code is specified below. A partial data set focusing on features {3, 4} is given in Table 6.8.

```
inputData <- read.csv("./iris.csv") // Read the input data set.

initialCenters <-matrix(c(2, 4, 6, 0.8, 1.6, 2.5), 3, 2) // Select initial means of three clusters.

results <- kmeans(inputData, initialCenters, iter.max = 1, trace = TRUE) // First iteration.
```

Table 6.8
Partial data set for k-means clustering in Example 6.6

petal.length	petal.width
1.4	0.2
1.7	0.3
4.9	1.5
3.5	1.0
6.0	2.5
. . .	. . .

firstCenters <- results$centers //# save the clustering centers after one iteration.

results <- kmeans(inputData, initialCenters, iter.max = 2, trace = TRUE) // Second iteration.

plot(inputData, pch = results$cluster) // Plot the partitioning results after it converges.

points(initialCenters, pch = 16, cex = 2) // Plot the initial centers.

points(firstCenters, pch = 15, cex = 2) // Plot the centers after first iteration.

points(results$centers, pch = 17, cex = 2) // Plot the centers after second iteration, convergence.

The k-means (inputData, 3) program is executed iteratively until convergence is reached. Initially, we choose three distance means that are separated as far apart as possible, shown in Figure 6.14(a). The initial means are (2, 0.8), (4, 1.6), and (6, 2.5). Then we compute its distances with all its neighbors. We form three new clusters, based on the minimum distances criteria applied.

Then we compute the new means (centroids): (1.4, 0.24), (4.2, 1.35), and (5.62, 2.04) among three current cluster members. Since these new means are the same after the second iteration, convergence is reached, as shown in Figure.6.14(b). The three clusters are now distinguished by circles, triangles, and crosses. ∎

6.3.2 Dimensionality Reduction and Reinforcement Learning

This section studies the dimensionality reduction and RL methods. Only the key concepts are introduced here. The RL has been used jointly with DL by the DeepMind AlphaGo program, to be studied in Chapter 9.

Dimensionality Reduction for Machine Learning

With high dimension, the Euclidean distance between any two vectors is used to perform classification, regression, or clustering. This has created a problem of the "curse of

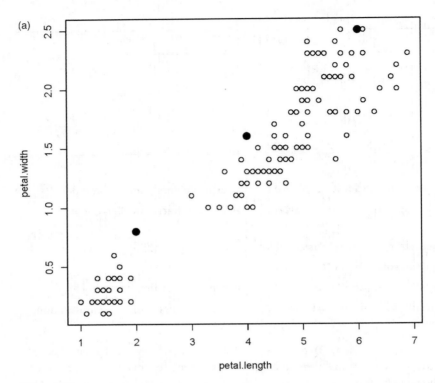

Figure 6.14
K-means clustering of 150 unlabeled patients into three treatment groups for $k = 3$, where (a) shows the choices of initial means in dark circles and (b) shows the final means after two iterations, where the three clusters are identified by circles, triangles, and crosses around their final means shown in dark triangles. (Artwork courtesy of Wenhao Zhang, University of Southern California, 2016).

dimensionality." Many dimensionality reduction algorithms were proposed to solve this problem. Dimensionality reduction transfers the points in high-dimensional space to low-dimensional space through the mapping function to relieve the "curse of dimensionality" within. Dimensionality reduction may not only reduce the correlation of data, but may also accelerate the operation speed of the algorithm (decrease of data volume). Table 6.9 summarizes several dimensionality reduction methods for ML.

The essence of dimensionality reduction is learning a mapping function: $f : x \rightarrow y$ where x is the expression of original data points in vector expression form and y is the expression of low-dimensional vector after data point mapping. Generally, the dimension of y is lower than x. f may be explicit, implicit, linear, or nonlinear.

At present, most dimensionality reduction algorithms process vector expression data while some dimensionality reduction algorithms process high-order tensor expression data.

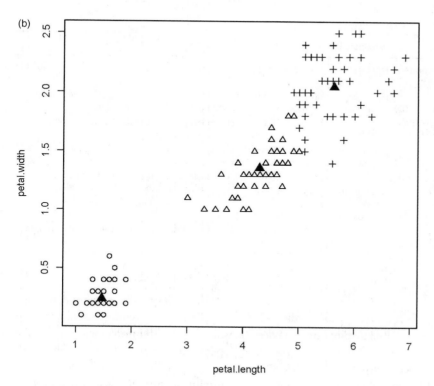

Figure 6.14 *continued*

The reason for using dimensionality reduction data is that there is redundant information and noise information in the original high-dimensional space and it may cause errors and reduce accuracy in practical applications (such as image identification). Through dimensionality reduction, we wish to reduce errors caused by redundant information and improve recognition accuracy (or other applications). Or, we wish to seek the essential structure characteristics of data through dimensionality reduction algorithm. Linear dimensionality reduction includes *principal component analysis* (PCA), and *linear discriminant analysis method* and *nonlinear dimensionality reduction* are represented by locally linear embedding (LLE) and isometric feature mapping methods.

Reinforcement Learning Methods

RL is considered an unsupervised ML algorithm. The correct input/output pairs are never presented, nor are suboptimal actions explicitly corrected. This method expects users to take proactive actions to reinforce the quality of the input data to help the prediction accuracy. This

Table 6.9
Dimensionality reduction methods for ML

Methods	Basic Ideas
Principal Component Analysis (PCA)	Use several aggregate indicators (principal component) to replace all indicators in the original data.
Singular Value Decomposition (SVD)	Take singular value in matrix to resolve. Select the larger singular value and abandon the smaller singular value to reduce matrix dimension.
Factor Analysis (FA)	Find out the intrinsic link of each property through analyzing data structure to find out the generality of property (factor).
Partial Least Squares Method	Integrating the advantages of PCA, canonical correlation analysis method, and multivariate linear regression analysis method.
Discriminate Analysis (DA)	Project the data (points) in high-dimensional space with class labels to low-dimensional space, enabling classification at the low-dimensional space.
Locally Linear Embedding (LLE)	A nonlinear dimensionality reduction algorithm, it may preserve the data in original manifold structure.
Laplacian Eigenmaps	The connected points in the map may be close to each other after dimensionality reduction.

is considered a long-term performance reward. A reinforced learning algorithm demands a policy that links the states of the prediction model to the levels of reinforcement actions to take. The idea of RL is inspired by behavioral psychology. The reinforcement actions also could be related to game theory, control theory, operations research, information theory, crowd intelligence, statistics, and genetic algorithms.

The basic RL model consists of: (1) a set of environment states; (2) a set of actions; (3) rules of transitioning between states; (4) rewarding rules that determine the *scalar immediate reward* of a transition; and (5) observation rules that describe the outputs to the agent. These rules are often stochastic. The observation typically involves the scalar immediate reward associated with the last transition. The agent is assumed to observe the current state fully. In the opposite case, the agent may have only *partial observability* (see Figure 6.15). The full observation is modeled by the *Markov decision process* (MDP), where the conditional probability P(s' | s, a) are known. In the partial observation case, some conditional probabilities are true, while others are unknown due to partial observability.

An agent with RL interacts with its environment in discrete time steps. At each time the agent receives an observation, it then chooses an action from the set of actions available, which is subsequently sent to the environment. The environment moves to a new state and the reward associated with the *transition* RL agent is aimed at collecting as much reward as possible. The agent can choose any action as a function of the history. To act near optimally, the agent must reason about the long-term consequences of its actions.

RL that is well suited to problems include a long-term vs. short-term reward trade-off. It has been applied successfully to various problems, including robot control, elevator

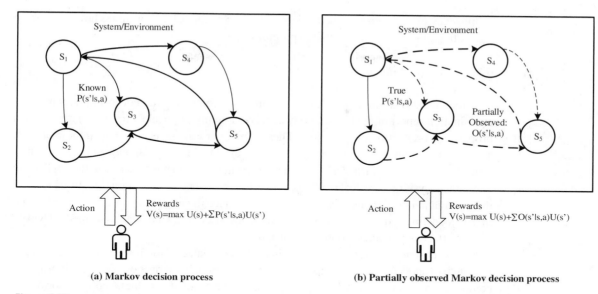

Figure 6.15
The concept of full and partial observations by agents in a reinforcement learning environment.

scheduling, AlphaGo game, checkers, etc. In Chapter 9, we will study how RL is applied with DL in developing the AlphaGo program. In general, RL applies a functional approximation approach to dealing with large environments. This method appeals to the following three-problem environments:

- the environment model is known, but an analytic solution is not available;
- only a simulation-based optimization is given in the environment; and
- information is collected by interacting with the environment with tradeoffs.

The ultimate goal is to reach some form of equilibrium under bounded rationality, similar to that practiced in the MDP with full observation by dynamic programming. Reinforcement actions are not initiated by supervised learning. The emphasis is to achieve online performance. We need to find the proper tradeoff between the exploration of unknown data exploitation and sorted knowledge from available data. To reinforce the learning process, the user must first define what the optimality is. Instead of using brute force, users can use a value-function approach based on Monte Carlo or temporal difference methods. Also, one can consider the direct policy search approach.

We can also consider an *inverse reinforcement learning* (IRL) method based on a trial and error approach. Here, no reward function is given. Instead, the user figures out a policy under some observed behavior. The purpose is to mimic the observed behavior toward optimality. If the IRL process deviates from the observed behavioral course, the trainer needs a contingency plan to return to the track of stability. Section 9.3 demonstrates how to combine DL with RL to produce the AlphaGo program.

6.3.3 Principal Component Analysis

In actual situations, the object has many property compositions. For example, a medical examination report of the human body consists of many physical examination items. Each property is a reflection of the object. There is more or less correlation among these objects, and the correlation causes information overlapping. The high overlapping and correlation of property information (variables or characteristics) may pose many obstacles to the application and data analysis of statistical methods. Property dimensionality reduction is required to solve the information overlapping, which may greatly reduce the number of variables participating in data modeling and will not cause information loss. PCA is a kind of analysis method widely used to effectively reduce variable dimension.

PCA is designed to transfer multiple indicators (variable in the regression) to several aggregate indicators (principal component) with dimensionality reduction ideas. Each principal component may reflect most of the information of the original variables, and the information included is not repeated. Generally, each principal component is the linear combination of the original variable, and each principal component is unrelated. The method may summarize the complex factors into several principal components, while introducing many variables to simplify the problem and obtain scientific and effective data information.

There is information loss in PCA regardless of the decrease in property dimensions. This loss information may be amplified in ML algorithm iteration, causing an inaccuracy of conclusions. Therefore, careful considerations need to be taken into account when using PCA. Principal components are several new variables comprehensively formed by original variables. It is called the *first principal component*, the *second principal component*, etc., according to the information volume in the principal component. There are several relations between principal components and original variables:

1. The principal component retains most of the information from the original variables.
2. The number of principal components is many fewer than that of the original variables.
3. Each principal component is unrelated.
4. Each principal component is the linear combination of the original variables.

The purpose of PCA is to recombine the related variables to a group of new unrelated comprehensive variables to replace the original variables. Generally, the mathematical processing method is the linear combination of original variables as the new comprehensive variables. How does one choose from so many combinations? In PCA, "information" is measured with variance, namely if $Var(F_1)$ is larger, it indicates F_1 contains more information. Therefore, the variance selected in all linear combinations is largest, so F_1 is called the first principal component. If the first principal component is insufficient to represent the information of p variables, we will consider selecting the second linear combination. To effectively reflect the original information, the information in F_1 will not appear in F_2. In the expression $Cov(F_1, F_2) = 0$, F_2 is called the second principal component. We may construct the 3rd, 4th, and p_{th} principal component by doing the same thing.

Supposing there are n evaluation objects (such as the person conducting a physical examination) and m evaluation indicators (such as height, weight, etc.), it is possible to compose a matrix in the size of $n \times m$. It is denoted as: $x = (x_{ij})_{n \times m}$, where $x_i, i = 1, 2, \ldots, m$ is the column vector. The matrix is called the *evaluation matrix*.

After obtaining the evaluation matrix, the general steps of PCA are shown as follows:

1. Calculate the mean value $\bar{x} = \dfrac{1}{n} \sum_{i=1}^{n} x_{ij}$ and variance $S_j = \sqrt{\sum_{i=1}^{n}(x_{ij} - \bar{x}_j)/(n-1)}$ of the original sample data. The mean value and standard deviation will be calculated in columns.

2. Calculate standard data $X_{ij} = \dfrac{(x_{ij} - \bar{x}_j)}{S_j}$ and evaluation matrix changes to the matrix after standardization:

$$
X = \begin{bmatrix}
X_{11} & X_{12} & \cdots & X_{1m} \\
X_{21} & X_{22} & \cdots & X_{2m} \\
\vdots & \vdots & \ddots & \vdots \\
X_{n1} & X_{n2} & \cdots & X_{nm}
\end{bmatrix} = (X_1, X_2, \ldots, X_m).
\tag{6.33}
$$

3. Apply the matrix after standardization to calculate the correlation matrix $C = (c_{ij})_{m \times m}$ of each evaluation indicator (or covariance matrix), thus C is the symmetric and positive matrix. Therefore, $c_{ij} = X_i^T X_j /(n-1)$.

4. Calculate the characteristic value λ and characteristic vector ξ of the correlation matrix (or covariance matrix). Arrange the characteristic values in decreasing order: $\lambda_1 > \lambda_2 > \cdots > \lambda_m$, and arrange characteristic vectors corresponding to the characteristic value. Suppose the j characteristic vector is: $\xi_j = (\xi_{1j}, \xi_{2j}, \ldots, \xi_{mj})^T$, then the j principal component is:

$$
F_j = \xi_j^T X = \xi_{1j} X_1 + \xi_{2j} X_2 + \cdots + \xi_{mj} X_m,
\tag{6.34}
$$

when $j = 1$, F_1 is the first principal component.

5. According to the characteristic value of the correlation matrix, calculate contribution rate η and accumulative contribution rate Q of the principal component:

$$
\eta_i = \frac{\lambda_i}{\lambda_1 + \lambda_1 + \cdots + \lambda_m}, \quad Q_i = \eta_1 + \eta_2 + \cdots + \eta_i, \quad i = 1, 2, \ldots, m.
\tag{6.35}
$$

Finally, according to the contribution rate designated by the user, determine the number of principal components and obtain the principal component of the evaluation matrix. Generally, the contribution rate is 0.85, 0.9, and 0.95. Three different contribution rate levels are determined according to the specific scene. The general steps of PCA are shown below.

Example 6.7: Principal Component Analysis of Patient Data

Table 6.10 gives the set of triglyceride, total cholesterol, high-density lipoprotein cholesterol (HDL-C), low-density lipoprotein cholesterol (LDL-C), age, weight, total protein, and blood sugar data obtained during physical examinations in a certain grade-A hospital of the second class in Wuhan City. Use PCA to determine the principal component of the patients to achieve the dimensionality reduction of data.

Because the data in each column reflect different aspects of the patients undergoing the physical examination and the indicator unit is different, we standardize the original data. For example, the indicator of patient #1 is given as $x'_{11} = \dfrac{x_{11}}{\max(x_1)} = \dfrac{1.05}{6.8} = 0.15$, represented by the following evaluation matrix and correlation matrix:

$$x = \begin{bmatrix} 0.15 & 0.50 & \cdots & 0.77 \\ 0.21 & 0.83 & \cdots & 0.73 \\ \vdots & \vdots & \ddots & \vdots \\ 0.38 & 1 & \cdots & 0.77 \end{bmatrix} \qquad corr(x) = \begin{bmatrix} 1 & 0.40 & \cdots & 0.09 \\ 0.40 & 1 & \cdots & 0.35 \\ \vdots & \vdots & \ddots & \vdots \\ 0.09 & 0.35 & \cdots & 1 \end{bmatrix}$$

Calculate characteristic value and characteristic vector according to the correlation matrix

$$\lambda = [2.96, 2.65, 1.33, 0.62, 0.33, 0.0024, 0.07, 0.036],$$

where the characteristic vector corresponding to the first characteristic value is

$$\xi_1 = [00.42, 0.02, 0.53, 0.06, 0.46, -0.54, 0.07. 0.16]^T.$$

The contribution rate of each principal component is plotted in Figure 6.16. The appointed contribution rate is 85%. ∎

6.3.4 Semi-Supervised Learning Methods

This approach offers a mixture between supervised and unsupervised learning. In this case, the trainer is given an incomplete training data set with some of the target outputs (labels) missing. Transduction is a special case of this principle where the entire set of problem instances is known at learning time, except that part of the targets is missing. In a way, both reinforcement and representation algorithms are subclasses of semi-supervised ML methods. Many ML researchers have found out that the joint use of unlabeled data with a small amount of labeled data can improve learning accuracy.

Table 6.10
Patient data for PCA classification in Example 6.7

Patient ID	Triglycerides	Total Cholesterol	HDL-C	LDL-C	Age	Weight	Total Protein	Blood Sugar
1	1.05	3.28	1.35	1.8	60	56.8	66.8	5.6
2	1.43	5.5	1.66	3.69	68	57.4	79.4	5.3
3	1.16	3.97	1.27	2.55	68	70.7	74.7	5.4
4	6.8	5.95	0.97	2.87	50	80.1	74	5.6
5	3.06	5.25	0.9	3.81	48	82.7	72.4	5.8
6	1.18	5.88	1.77	3.87	53	63.5	78	5.2
7	2.53	6.45	1.43	4.18	57	61.3	75	7.3
8	1.6	5.3	1.27	3.74	47	64.9	73.6	5.4
9	3.02	4.95	0.95	3.53	39	88.2	79	4.6
10	2.57	6.61	1.56	4.27	60	63	80	5.6

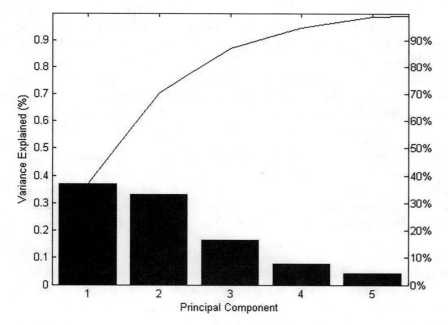

Figure 6.16
Contribution rate of principal components in a dimensionality reduction process.

The discovery of some useful labeled data often demands domain expertise or a set of physical experiments to be conducted. The cost associated with the labeling process prevents the use of a fully labeled training set. In other words, the use of partially labeled data is more plausible. As a matter of fact, semi-supervised learning is closer to human learning due to our ability to handle fuzziness.

Three basic assumptions of semi-supervised learning are provided here. In order to make any use of unlabeled data, we must assume some data distribution. Different semi-supervised learning algorithms may assume different assumptions as outlined below, based on the reports provided in Wikipedia: https://en.wikipedia.org/wiki/Semi-supervised_learning 2016.

1. *Smoothness assumption:* Sample data points which are close to one another are more likely to share a label. This is also generally assumed in supervised learning. This assumption may lead to a preference for geometrically simple decision boundaries. In the case of semi-supervised learning, the smoothness assumption yields a preference for decision boundaries in low-density regions.

2. *Cluster assumption:* The data tends to form discrete clusters, and points in the same cluster are more likely to share a label. One must realize the fact that data sharing a label may be spread across multiple clusters. This assumption is related to feature learning with clustering algorithms.

3. *Manifold assumption:* The data lies on a manifold of much lower dimension than the input space. In this case, we teach the manifold using both the labeled and unlabeled data to avoid the curse of dimensionality. Thus, semi-supervised learning can proceed using distances and densities defined on the manifold.

The manifold assumption is practical when high-dimensional data sets are encountered. For instance, the human voice is controlled by a few vocal cords, and various facial expressions are controlled by a few muscles. We would like in these cases to use distances and smoothness in the natural data space, rather than in the space of all possible acoustic waves or images, respectively. The following example shows the advantage of semi-supervised ML.

Example 6.8: Semi-Supervised Machine Learning

This example was obtained from Wikipedia (https://en.wikipedia.org/wiki/Semi-supervised_learning). The purpose is to show the influence of unlabeled data in semi-supervised learning. The top panel in Figure 6.17 shows a decision boundary we might adopt after seeing only one positive (white circle) and one negative (black circle) example. The bottom panel shows a decision boundary we might adopt if, in addition to the two labeled examples, we were given a collection of unlabeled data (gray circles). This could be viewed as performing clustering and then labeling the clusters with the labeled data, pushing the decision boundary away from high-density regions, or learning an 1D manifold where the data resides. ∎

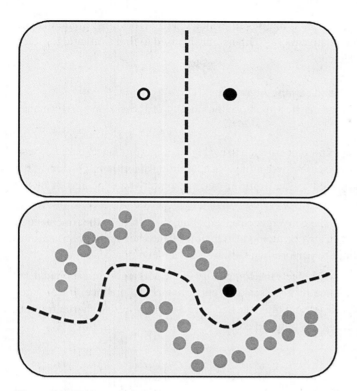

Figure 6.17
Semi-supervised machine learning, where the upper boxes are labeled data for supervised learning and the unlabeled data in the lower box are used in unsupervised clustering or SCM classification.

6.4 Model Development for Machine Learning Applications

Methods to select the right model for ML are studied below. Some strategies and plausible solutions are introduced. We consider data comprehension through visualization, ML algorithm selection, and over-fitting or under-fitting solutions. Finally, we present a procedure for ML algorithm selection. We also discuss the advantages and disadvantages of using different loss functions.

6.4.1 Performance Metrics and Model-Fitting Cases

Each ML algorithm has its own application potential. Given a data set, the performance of a given algorithm may be excellent, but that of another algorithm may be the opposite. Furthermore, changing to a different data set may also change the conclusion drastically. Thus, it is rather difficult to judge which algorithm is more ideal than others in general cases. It is critical to introduce some common metrics to evaluate ML algorithms. Some metrics may be adopted to reveal the relative merits. Others may be used to find similar algorithms that could be easier to implement.

Performance Metrics of Machine Learning Algorithms

We consider three fundamental metrics to assess the quality of the various performance metrics used.

1. *Accuracy:* This is the most important criterion to evaluate ML performance, based on testing the data set. There are two cases: over-fitting or under-fitting algorithms. Obviously, the higher performance exhibited by the training set, the better the expected fit of the algorithm.

2. *Training time:* This refers to the convergence speed of an algorithm, or the time needed to establish the optimality of a working model. Obviously, the shorter the training time, the better the model is built to perform with a lower implementation cost.

3. *Linearity:* This model property reflects the complexity of the ML algorithm applied. Linear performance implies some form of scalable performance. In practice, linear algorithms with lower complexity is more often desired because it may lead to shorter training time or even higher accuracy at a reduced cost.

Machine Learning Performance Scores

In order to quantify the performance of an ML algorithm, we can define some *performance scores*. These scores are normalized as a percentage with 100% for the perfect score and small fractions for lower scores. This score is often a weighted function of all three performance metrics. Different user groups apply different weighting functions to emphasize their preferred choices, such as weighting accuracy as first and training time as second. The performance of an ML algorithm is plotted as a learning performance curve in Figure 6.18.

In this learning curve, the score is shown at the *y*-axis against the training samples or the testing data size on the *x*-axis. There are two competing scores illustrated in such a performance curve. The *training score* is driven by the training data set applied. The *cross validation score* is based on the progressive testing of all incoming data. In general, the training score is higher than the validation score due to the fact that the model is built from the training data set. Figure 6.18 shows an ideal case where the two scores converge quickly after sufficient testing.

Model-Fitting Cases in Machine Learning Process

We consider here two model cases in the process of choosing an acceptable ML algorithm to apply under various performance conditions of the training and testing data sets.

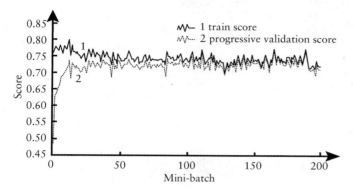

Figure 6.18
Training score and cross validation score match nicely in a well-fitting machine learning model.

- *Over-fitting modeling:* In this case the training score is very high, but the cross validation score is very low for testing data sets applied. As shown in Figure 6.19, the two scores are separated far apart from one another. This status implies that the model fits the training set very closely. However, the model has ignored the noise margins in the validation data set. In other words, the training set is heavily biased on a particular training data set. This sample data set stays far away from common data distribution or characteristics in general applications. In this case, the over-fitting model simply cannot model the testing data accurately.

- *Under-fitting modeling:* In this case the model produced by a given training set ends up with a very low performance score, which is far below the user's expectation. This under-fitting phenomenon implies that a poor training set was chosen and therefore the training model obtained cannot perform well at all on real testing data sets. Consequently, the model obtained is totally unacceptable to users.

6.4.2 Methods to Reduce Model Over-Fitting

The main reason for over-fitting is that the model deliberately memorizes the distribution properties of the training samples. In other words, the model being created is overly biased by the sample data behavior. The over-fitting model scores very high on a particular training set, but scores badly on other data sets. In other words, big score gaps must be closed up across data sets. This section presents several methods for reducing this adverse effect.

Increasing the Training Data Size
Increasing the quantity of samples may make the training set more representative in order to cover more variety and scarcity of data. The increase in samples applied reflects the noise effects better. The mean value of the noise could be reduced to zero. That is, the influence

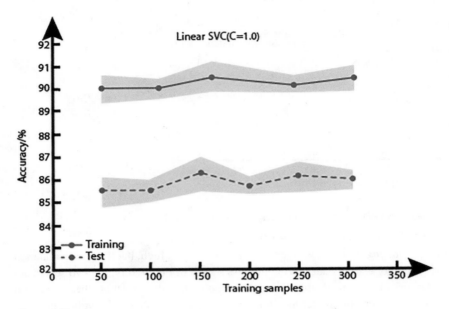

Figure 6.19
The over-fitting case when creating a learning model using the linear SVC algorithm with a small data set up to 150 samples.

of noise on the testing data could be greatly reduced. The common method to increase sample size is to collect more data under the same scenario. Sometimes, manual labeling is added to generate some artificial training samples. For instance, one can apply image recognition, mirror transformation, and rotation to enlarge the sample quantity. Even though these operations may be labor-intensive, the method enhances the dependency of the samples. This will improve the model by avoiding training biases.

Example 6.9: Enlarging the Sample Data Set for the Linear SVC Algorithm

As shown in Figure 6.20, the sample number is now enlarged to 400 from 150. This enlarged data set has resulted in good convergence of the score curves as the data set increases beyond 200. The two scores become very close to one another as the sample data size increases beyond 300. ∎

Under circumstances when small sample data sizes cannot be increased further, we can reduce the noise effect by transforming the existing sample set, such as using a wavelet analysis. The purpose is to reduce the mean noise to zero. In the meantime, the noise variance is also reduced, thus reducing the influence of noise on all data to be tested. As training samples, the difference between training score and cross validation score could be reduced, as demonstrated by the following example.

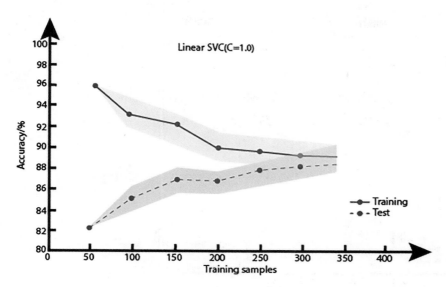

Figure 6.20
Reducing the ML model over-fitting effects by enlarging the training set to 800 samples.

Feature Screening and Dimension Reduction Methods

Sometimes we may have a large training data set that is characterized by many sample features. By revealing the correlation between features, one can cut off some features to reduce the over-fitting effect. Those features with limited representative power are removed. This is called *feature screening* or *dimension reduction*. In fact, we can traverse all combination styles of features and select the more important features. In the case of samples with high dimensionality, association analysis or correlation analysis may be adopted to eliminate some weak features by reducing the dimensions.

Occasionally, it is rather difficult to determine the relationships between orthogonal features. In this case, the PCA algorithm applies dimension reduction. In a case when the dimensionality of feature space is not high, we conduct feature screenings to decrease the complexity of the model. Three methods exist to do so: (1) decrease the degree of polynomial in the ML model; (2) reduce the layers of ANNs and quantity of nodes in each layer; and (3) increase the bandwidth of the RBF-kernel in the SVM algorithm.

> **Example 6.10: Using Fewer Features (Dimensions) to Reduce Over-Fitting Effects**
> One can apply an association analysis to assess various feature impacts in the PCA algorithm. In Figure 6.21, we demonstrate the effects of using fewer features in the linear SVC algorithm. In this case, feature 7 and feature 8 are selected manually after observation of their heavier roles in the learning process ∎

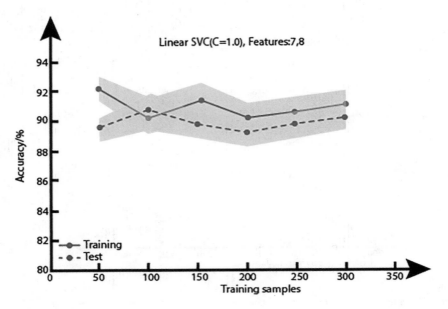

Figure 6.21
Effects of using fewer features in the linear SVC algorithm.

6.4.3 Methods to Avoid Model Under-Fitting

Under-fitting takes place in two situations: (1) the data set is poorly prepared and simply cannot perform well in the training and validation processes; and (2) the ML algorithm is wrongly chosen, considering the nature of the problem environment. Different data sets may appeal to the chosen algorithm differently. An under-fitting problem is difficult to solve completely. The more feasible approach is to find ways to avoid it.

Mixed Parameter Changes

Consider the under-fitting problem when using an SVM model for solving a classification problem. One way is to utilize an ANN to train the system to yield a better model fit. In another example of model under-fitting, we can modify the kernel function to cover the case of nonlinear classification. For example, one can replace a *stochastic gradient descent* (SGD) classifier with a multilayer ANN. In this case, kernel approximation is adopted to complete the task. The following example shows the modification of two parameters in the linear SVC algorithm to yield a better fitting.

> **Example 6.11: Changing the Linear SVC Model with Reduced *C* = 0.1 and L1 Penalty**
> The change in score on data is small after an iteration of 50 mini-batches of sampling data. The scores are low to reflect a status of under-fitting. The performance becomes

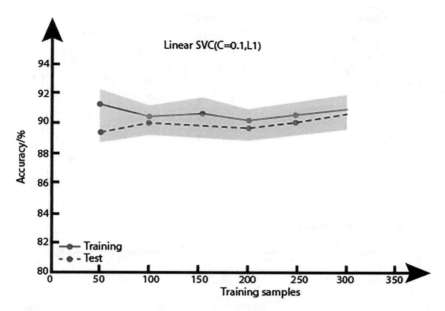

Figure 6.22
The under-fitting results in the linear SVC algorithm where the model score sets a low upper bound on the testing validation scores.

worse in the case of using an under-fitting model. For the linear SVC model, we could reduce the regularization factor C to 0.1 from 1 and apply the L1 regularization penalty. Figure 6.22 plots the improved high scores (around 0.91) in both scores across a wide range of sample data set sizes from 50 to 300. Thus, through a mixed change of model parameters, we end up with a fairly close match between the training and cross validation scores. ∎

6.4.4 Machine Learning Model Selection Options

ML problems also can be viewed as a minimization of some loss function on the training examples. Loss functions express the discrepancy between the trained model prediction and the actual problem instances. For example, the classification problem requires the user to assign a label to instances. The user can then use the trained model to predict the labels of training samples, and loss function then reflects the difference between these two kinds of label sets. Thus, the loss function reveals the effects of losing the expected performance of an ML algorithm. An optimized algorithm should minimize the loss on a training set, while ML is concerned with minimizing the loss on unseen samples. The selection of loss function is critical to obtain a better or optimal prediction model. We consider five design choices of loss functions. Their effects are plotted in Figure 6.23.

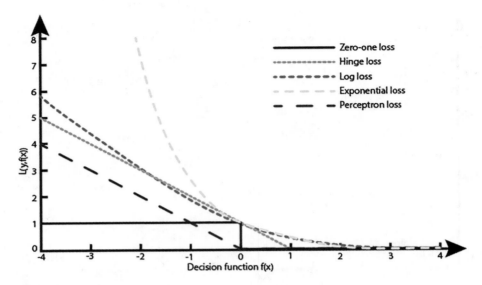

Figure 6.23
Effects of using different loss functions in machine learning model selection.

1. ***Zero-one loss function:*** This policy offers a very sharp division between success and failure. The 0–1 loss function just counts the number of mispredictions in the classification problems. However, it is a non-convex function, and not practical in real-life applications.

2. ***Hinge loss function:*** This is often used in SVM applications for its relative strength to reflect the unusual sensitivity to noise effects. This function is not supported by probabilistic distribution.

3. ***Log loss function:*** This loss function can reflect the probabilistic distribution nicely. In the scenario of multiclass classification, we need to know the confidence of classification. The log loss function is rather suitable. However, its shortcoming lies in lower sensitivity to noise and lack of judgment strength.

4. ***Exponential loss function:*** This has been applied in AdaBoost. It is very sensitive to separation from the crowd and noise. Its prediction style is simple and effective in dealing with boosting algorithms.

5. ***Perceptron loss function:*** This can be regarded as a variation from the hinge loss. Hinge loss poses a heavy penalty to misjudgments of the boundary points, while perceptron loss is satisfied with accurate classification from the sample data. This score ignores the distance from the judgment boundary. The advantage is it is simpler than using the hinge loss function. Its shortcoming lies in the fact that it offers a weaker model to apply to general problems for lack of maximum margin boundary.

Model Modifications or the Ensemble Approach

The PCA algorithm offers a dimension reduction approach for reducing model complexity. One can also consider using several principal components to interconnect the data elements. Besides, the independence of each principal component is strong. Therefore, it greatly reduces the internal connection among the data. The emergence of the ensemble algorithm provides another solution to the under-fitting problem. In a case when each individual model does not perform well on a given data set, one can consider using several algorithms concurrently on the same data set, then choose the one that best fits in performance scores. For example, applying the AdaBoost and decision tree models jointly to improve the accuracy of the prediction results.

Selecting Algorithms for General Data Sets

Given the data sets from a known application domain, we want to select the proper ML algorithm based on the data set characteristics and performance requirement. Three categories of ML algorithms are considered. In general, the following options can be considered in solving under-fitting problems. These methods appeal in particular when one is trying to improve the classification problem since the model performance is so sensitive to the data sets applied. We consider three options to select the data sets. The data set selection is driven by the performance demand.

1. ***Common data sets:*** This option involves dividing the original data set into two parts, with equal characteristics and distributions in the training set and testing set. This subdivision should result in a model performance to avoid either the over-fitting or the under-fitting problems.

2. ***Cross validation:*** Here the original data set is divided into k parts and a part in turn is selected as a test set while the remaining stays as the training set. This demands k validation testing runs. This model performance shows the average accuracy of the model over many subdivided test sets.

3. ***Bootstrap cycle:*** This method involves random sampling with replacement of some data elements repeatedly in different training samples. Let the sampled data be the training set, while the remaining are the test sets. Repeat these sampling cycles k times. This may end up with a weighted mean performance of all test sets.

6.5 Conclusions

ML is in high demand with the rise of data science and the big data industry. In this chapter, we introduced both ML and DL algorithms with illustrative examples. Supervised ML algorithms were applied with training sample data that were labeled. Unsupervised ML algorithms are short of training data. Therefore, it is easier to apply training data to enhance the accuracy of the prediction outcome.

Accuracy is very sensitive to the size of the training data. The training time should remain rather short in order to be effective for real-time applications. For prediction or classification model development, we need to avoid both over-fitting and under-fitting situations. Through data training and feedback loops, one can optimize model parameter selection to reduce errors or cost functions.

Homework Problems

6.1: The user information of a smartphone is given in Table 6.11. For each day, the collected average data includes total call duration (minutes), mobile traffic volume (MB), number of incoming calls, and whether the user is at home or outside (1: home, 0: outside). Given a testing data of A: 90, B: 60, and C: 8, determine whether this person is at home. Likewise, how about another user with calling statistics A: 80, B: 50, and C: 10?

6.2: Physical examination is performed to determine whether patients suffer from hyperlipidemia. The metrics tested include triglycerides, cholesterol, high-density lipoprotein, low-density lipoprotein, etc. Based on the data given in Table 6.12, select a supervised classification model to predict whether or not a patient is suffering from hyperlipidemia.

6.3: Table 6.13 provides the abscissa and ordinate of data points in a ML experiment. Apply the k-means clustering algorithm to subdivide these points into three clusters using the Euclidean distance function. You must identify the centers (centroids) and show the detailed clustering process, step by step. Draw a 2D Euclidean space diagram to show the final partition results on the ten data points and the cluster boundaries.

6.4: We know the advantages of regular exercise, but the weather conditions may prevent us from going outside to do so. Table 6.14 records Cindy's exercise regimen over two weeks. Use the Bayesian network to estimate the probability that Cindy should go play tennis, assuming her partner is available and it is a sunny day.

6.5: In Section 6.4, you studied some selection criteria of ML algorithms to match with the application demands. The purpose was to make predictions, forecasting, or classification

Table 6.11
Part of the application information of a smartphone user

User ID	Total Call Duration (A)	Volume (B)	Frequency (C)	At Home (D)
1	20	45	2	1
2	120	46	4	1
3	90	55	10	0
4	81	56	19	0
5	200	55	8	0

Table 6.12
Physical examination data and the status of hyperlipidemia

Patient ID	Triglycerides	Total Cholesterol	High-Density Lipoprotein	Low-Density Lipoprotein	Hyperlipidemia or Not
1	1.05	3.28	1.35	1.8	No
2	1.43	5.5	1.66	3.69	No
3	1.16	3.97	1.27	2.55	Yes
4	6.8	5.95	0.97	2.87	Yes
5	3.06	5.25	0.9	3.81	Yes
6	1.18	5.88	1.77	3.87	No
7	2.53	6.45	1.43	4.18	Yes
8	1.6	5.3	1.27	3.74	No
9	3.02	4.95	0.95	3.53	Yes
10	2.57	6.61	1.56	4.27	Yes

Table 6.13
Abscissa and ordinate of some data points

Point ID	Abscissa	Ordinate	Point ID	Abscissa	Ordinate
1	0	0	6	4	11
2	2	3	7	6	9
3	4	2	8	8	10
4	0	6	9	12	6
5	3	10	10	7	9

Table 6.14
Cindy's two-week outdoor exercise records

Day	Weather	Play	Day	Weather	Play
1	Sunny	No	8	Rainy	No
2	Overcast	Yes	9	Sunny	Yes
3	Rainy	Yes	10	Rainy	Yes
4	Sunny	Yes	11	Sunny	No
5	Sunny	Yes	12	Overcast	Yes
6	Overcast	Yes	13	Overcast	Yes
7	Rainy	No	14	Rainy	No

of large data sets more accurate or efficient. Briefly answer the following four exercises/ questions on ML algorithm selection. Justify your answers with reasoning or by using example cases.

(a) Compile a table to suggest the key performance metrics that should be applied for each ML algorithm you have learned. Justify your table entries with reasoning by example applications.

(b) How do you define the accuracy (%) as a performance score of a ML method, such as those presented in Figures 6.18–6.22.

(c) Distinguish between over-fitting and under-fitting cases in choosing a ML prediction model.

(d) Define the different loss functions used in plotting those curves in Figure 6.23.

6.6: Justify the true or false choice in the following five statements on three clustering techniques:

(a) K-nearest neighbors (kNN) assumes that nearby points should have the same label.

(b) One major difference between decision tree and kNN is that all features are equally important in kNN.

(c) K-means clustering algorithm always converges to the "right answer."

(d) K-means is guaranteed to converge and guaranteed to converge quickly.

(e) K-means clustering is sensitive to the initialization of the cluster center. (In k-means clustering, we first guess the cluster centers and then update them.)

6.7: When a business makes a loan application from a bank or financial organization, the lender needs to assess the creditability of the borrower. Let $y=0$ denote a borrower with a bad record, while $y=1$ represents a credited borrower. Three features of the borrower are represented by X1, X2, and X3 in Table 6.15. Build a prediction model to test a given customer with a credit record (X1, X2, X3)$=$(−25, 2.5, 0.5). Assess the accuracy of your prediction model.

6.8: When body muscles contract, electromyography (EMG) signals are generated on the skin's surface. EMG signals can be used to control a computer, as a kind of user interface. The purpose is to devise a device that can detect EMG signals characterized by three feature parameters: frequency, strength, and time. Using the data in Table 6.16, you are asked to develop a computer program and use decision tree modeling to extract a set of rules to perform a rule-based classification of the muscle actions or gestures needed to control part of the computer operations, such as power on and off, keyboard, or mouse operations, etc.

6.9: Hyperlipidemia is a common disease, which is caused by high levels of blood lipids. During a physical, triglycerides and total cholesterol in the blood are always used to determine whether the subjects are suffering from hyperlipidemia. Therefore according to the two indexes discussed above, people can be divided into two categories, i.e., healthy people and

Table 6.15
Sampling data of a bank credit report on borrowers

X1	X2	X3	Y	X1	X2	X3	Y
−48.2	6.8	1.6	0	43.0	16.4	1.3	1
−49.2	−17.2	0.3	0	47.0	16.0	1.9	1
−19.2	−36.7	0.8	0	−3.3	4.0	2.7	1
−18.1	−6.5	0.9	0	35.0	20.8	1.9	1
−98.0	−20.8	1.7	0	46.7	12.6	0.9	1
−129.0	−14.2	1.3	0	20.8	12.5	2.4	1
−4.0	−15.8	2.1	0	33.0	23.6	1.5	1
−8.7	−36.3	2.8	0	26.1	10.4	2.1	1
−59.2	−12.8	2.1	0	68.6	13.8	1.6	1
−13.1	−17.6	0.9	0	37.3	33.4	3.5	1
−38.0	1.6	1.2	0	59.0	23.1	5.5	1
−57.9	0.7	0.8	0	49.6	23.8	1.9	1
−8.8	−9.1	0.9	0	12.5	7.0	1.8	1
−64.7	−4.0	0.1	0	37.3	34.1	1.5	1
−11.4	4.8	0.9	0	35.3	4.2	0.9	1

Table 6.16
Experimental data of EMG and corresponding classification of actions

Frequency (F)	Strength (S)	Time (T)	Action (A)
1	810	1	A1
1	864	0.5	A2
1	485	1	A3
1	950	0.5	A2
1	1003	0.5	A2
1	524	1	A3
1	736	0.5	A4
1	661	0.5	A4
2	*	*	A5

patients. Table 6.17 gives the data set of triglyceride and total cholesterol contents of a physical examination in a typical hospital. To divide 18 people into three clusters, we apply a k-means clustering method.

6.10: This problem requires you to develop a decision tree to make a wise decision whether or not to go out to play tennis in a specific weather condition. Table 6.18 gives a set of training samples taken from an exercise log over two weeks. Specify all suitable paths on the decision tree that lead to a decision.

Table 6.17
Hospital's physical checkup data

Serial No.	Triglyceride (mmol/L)	Total Cholesterol (mmol/L)	Serial No.	Triglyceride (mmol/L)	Total Cholesterol (mmol/L)
1	1.33	4.19	10	2.63	5.62
2	1.94	5.47	11	1.95	5.02
3	1.31	4.32	12	1.13	4.34
4	2.48	5.64	13	2.64	5.64
5	1.84	5.17	14	1.86	5.33
6	2.75	6.35	15	1.25	3.18
7	1.45	4.68	16	1.30	4.36
8	1.33	3.96	17	1.94	5.39

Table 6.18
Weather conditions during two weeks of observation

Day	Outlook	Humidity	Windy	Play
1	Sunny	High	Weak	No
2	Sunny	High	Strong	No
3	Overcast	High	Weak	Yes
4	Rain	High	Weak	Yes
5	Rain	Normal	Weak	Yes
6	Rain	Normal	Strong	No
7	Overcast	Normal	Strong	Yes
8	Sunny	High	Weak	No
9	Sunny	Normal	Weak	Yes
10	Rain	Normal	Weak	Yes
11	Sunny	Normal	Strong	Yes
12	Overcast	High	Strong	Yes
13	Overcast	Normal	Weak	Yes
14	Rain	High	Strong	No

References

[1] Alpaydin, E. *Introduction to Machine Learning.* The MIT Press, 2010.

[2] Bishop, C. M. *Pattern Recognition and Machine Learning.* Springer, 2006.

[3] Ding, C. and X. He. "K-means Clustering via Principal Component Analysis." *Proc. of International Conference on Machine Learning* (ICML), 2004: 225–232.

[4] Goldberg, D. E., and J. H. Holland. "Genetic Algorithms and Machine Learning." *Machine Learning* 3 no. 2 (1988): 95–99.

[5] Hutchinson, B., L. Deng, and D. Yu. "Tensor Deep Stacking Networks." *IEEE Transactions on Pattern Analysis and Machine Intelligence* 1–15 (2012): 1944–1957.

[6] Kaelbling, L. P., M. L. Littman, and A. W. Moore. "Reinforcement Learning: A Survey." *Journal of Artificial Intelligence Research* 4 (1996): 237–285.

[7] Langley, P. T. "The Changing Science of Machine Learning." *Machine Learning* 82 no. 3 (2011): 275–279.

[8] MacKay, D. J. *Information Theory, Inference, and Learning Algorithms.* Cambridge University Press, 2003.

[9] Mohri, M., A. Rostamizadeh, and A. Talwalkar. *Foundations of Machine Learning.* MIT Press, 2012.

[10] Vapnik, V. *Statistical Learning Theory.* Wiley-Interscience, 1998.

[11] Witten, I., and E. Frank. *Data Mining: Practical Machine Learning Tools and Techniques.* Morgan Kaufmann, 2011.

[12] Zhang, J., et al. "Evolutionary Computation Meets Machine Learning: A Survey." *IEEE Computational Intelligence Magazine* 6 no. 4 (2011): 68–75.

[13] Zhu, X., and A. Goldberg. *Introduction to Semi-Supervised Learning.* Morgan & Claypool, 2009.

Chapter 7

Intelligent Machines and Deep Learning Networks

7.1 Artificial Intelligence and Smart Machine Development

Artificial intelligence (AI) is estimated to become a $15 billion industry in 2016, and it is growing rapidly. With more than 2,600 companies developing intelligent technology, the value of AI is expected to rise to more than $70 billion by 2020. AI is always a disruptive technology for industrial growth. For example, the U.S. Automobile Association is using AI to protect its users from identity theft and MyFitnessPal at IBM Watson uses it to help users have a more thorough read of their health records. In this section, we assess the smart machines reviewed in the 2016 Gartner Hype Cycle Report. We examine recent advances in AI at Amazon Web Services (AWS) and Google for autonomous driving, flying vehicles for door-to-door merchandise delivery, and cognitive applications. We also review the use of blockchains for securing data transactions in distributed databases.

7.1.1 Analysis of 2016 Gartner Hype Cycle on Smart Machines

Smart machines are truly disruptive technologies. However, they are not ready for the majority of adopters at their current scale. Nevertheless, CIOs and CTOs should still begin to explore them, as the competitive gaps and missed opportunity costs for those that lag behind could be insurmountable. Figure 7.1 shows the Gartner 2016 Hype Cycle for smart machines. In the Hype Cycle, most smart machine technologies are on the rising slope of increasing expectations that may take five to ten years to become mature. These include bots, deep reinforcement learning, digital ethics, virtual personal assistants, cognitive computing, smart robots, and *natural language processing* (NLP).

Neuromorphic hardware, autonomous vehicles, and general-purpose machine intelligence are still a long shot, requiring more than ten years to reach production. Deep neural networks and cognitive expert advisors are the hottest at the peak of inflated expectations, but they are reachable within ten years. Natural language generation, graph analytics, predictive analytics, descriptive analytics, *learning business process outsourcing* (LBPO), and *virtual customer assistants* (VCAs) are at the trough of disillusionment, having improved sharply from the 2015 Hype Cycle. Major suppliers of VCAs include IBM Watson, IPsoft, Microsoft, and Nuance Communications. These smart machines are supposed to adjust their behavior after operational experience. In other words, they should have some machine learning (ML) capability with limited human intervention. Ensemble learning is on the slope of enlightenment. Speech recognition is fairly mature at the plateau of productivity. Other more mature smart machines include *virtual reality* (VR), *augmented reality* (AR), and knowledge management tools. These smart machines are shown by the black circles in Figure 7.1. They may enter the production plateau within two years.

A new field of cloud robotics is on the rise. The approach is to invoke cloud computing, cloud storage, and *Internet of things* (IoT) to become part of a converged infrastructure and shared services for robotics. When connected to the cloud, robots can benefit from the powerful computational, storage, and communication resources of modern data centers in the cloud. Many robots could be connected to a common cloud, which can process and share information concurrently. For example, distributed smart, low-cost, and lightweight robots can be connected to a cloud to form a cloud-centric healthcare system. Humans can also delegate tasks to robots remotely through cloud computing technologies.

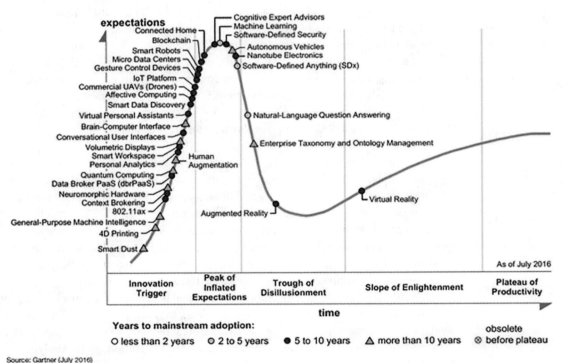

Source: Gartner (July 2016)

Figure 7.1
Gartner 2016 Hype Cycle for smart machines. Courtesy of Gartner Research 2016.

In recent years, the information industry has developed a number of impressive AI machines and systems. Listed below are brief introductions of six of the most impressive AI products and services developed up to 2016. Some of them will be studied further in subsequent sections.

1. AlphaGo program defeated the world Go Champaign in March 2016. The Go is the most complicated chase-board game played on a 19×19 grid by two players placing black and white stones on the board alternatively. At the very first step, there are 361 board points that can be placed. The whole game may end up with 10170 possible choices for the player to consider. The AlphaGo AI program was developed by DeepMind, an AI subsidiary under the Alphabet Company. Technical details are given in Chapter 9. This milestone achievement marked the era that machine intelligence can beat human players in some selected areas.

2. Tesla auto-steering system can send patients for treatment in the nearest hospital emergency room. This autonomic self-driving system can adjust speed, change lanes, and self-brake in response to environment change. It was reported by US National Safety Council in 2015 that human drivers can lead to 13 death accidents out of an average of 100 million miles driven. On the other hand, the autonomous system led to only one death accident in 130 million miles of testing.

3. Accurate prediction of horse race winners. Louis Rosenberg, CEO of Unanimous AI, has developed a collective AI platform to predict the first 5 top winners in Kentucky Derby races in May 2016.

4. Microsoft's language understanding program reached the same error level of 5.9% as a human after 2,000 hours of training over some convolutional and recurrent ANNs. The CNN and RNN will be explained in Section 7.4.

5. The 2016 US presidential election outcome was accurately predicted by MogIA, a new startup AI company in India. MogIA applied 2 million data sets from social media networks to predict that Trump would win the election, which surprised many voters and observers.

6. IBM's Watson Health program has improved the cancer diagnosis accuracy in many testing cases. In Japan, IBM Watson has accurately detected the cancerous blood disease of a female patient. Statistically, the Watson program can detect 1/3 more cases than doctors detect using traditional methods. This advancement will be discussed in Section 7.1.3.

7.1.2 Google's Development of AI Products and Services

So far, Google has maintained the largest user space of AI machines and system support including personalized search engine and expanded cloud services. The development road map that Google has taken is illustrated in Figure 7.2. The timeline shows how Google recruited many top AI scientists and has acquired some existing companies or startups that have demonstrated excellence in AI innovations over big data and cloud resources. In 2013,

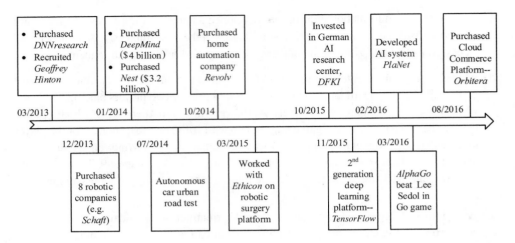

Figure 7.2
Google development timeline in AI-related products and services.

Google acquired DNNresearch and recruited Geoffrey Hinton to join the Google Brain team. Subsequently, Google merged ten robotics and AI companies including the Schaft, DeepMind, and Nest groups.

Since 2015, Google has launched large-scale testing of autonomous vehicles in city traffic environments. The Revolv Company was acquired to expand Google's smart home equipment development. Many top AI experts joined Google to empower AI into Google products and services. This effort ranges from smarter search engines to autonomous cars. Google is also pushing for new advances beyond the post-smartphone era. In 2015, Google teamed up with Ethicon to develop robotic platforms for high-precision surgery and healthcare treatments as evidenced by the investment in DFKI Research in Germany. In 2016, the TensorFlow and PlaNet platforms were developed to promote *deep learning* (DL) applications. The defeat of Korea's top Go player Lee Sedol by AlphaGo and the merging of DeepMind and cloud platform Orbitera are the latest move by Google. This growing trend is expected to continue in the decades to come.

The recent AlphaGo defeat of the top Go champion has reinforced the belief that machine intelligence can beat human intelligence in certain restricted areas. Here, we review the recent progress of AI and robotics including advanced chess and Go programs and self-driving cars. This can be traced back to 60 years of R&D effort in AI including reasoning, knowledge, planning, learning, natural language processing, perception, and the ability to move and manipulate objects in distance. In the twenty-first century, AI techniques became an essential disruptive technology that may change the future of our lives, work, and play.

The ramp-up in cloud computing and the outsourcing of data storage, which has come down significantly in price, has allowed companies to develop and use AI applications.

Mobility and bandwidth ubiquity make it possible for workers to access applications from most remote locations. Finally, our increasingly sophisticated understanding of how the human brain works and our ability to embed brain-like elements into computers have engendered such capabilities as voice and pattern recognition, natural language learning, and ML.

AI applications can be described in three broad categories. The examples to follow will more fully examine these AI initiatives and robotics applications.

1. *Product applications* embed AI in a product or service to provide end-customer benefits. Examples include Netflix's recommendation engine and the use of computer vision to improve car safety.

2. *Process applications* incorporate AI into an organization's workflow to automate processes or augment worker effectiveness. For example, automated voice response systems have been used for some years now to replace human customer service agents.

3. *Insight applications* harness advanced analytical capabilities such as ML to uncover insights that can inform operational and strategic decisions across an organization. For example, Intel employs a predictive algorithm to classify customers into groups with similar needs and buying patterns. Intel estimated that this approach will generate an additional $20 million in revenue once it is rolled out globally.

In recent years, Google has formed or acquired several high technology companies in AI, DL, and robotics areas. Their Brain team, headed by Jeffrey Dean, Geoffrey Hinton, and some other faculty researchers from Stanford University, developed the TensorFlow software platform for DL and cognitive applications. In Section 2.4, we introduce some Google Brain team products. The DeepMind team that joined Google in 2014 will be covered in Chapter 9.

Google X Lab Projects

In 2010, Google founded a semi-secret R&D facility known as Google X (also known simply as "X"), a subsidiary of Alphabet Inc. This X lab is overseen by Google cofounder Sergey Brin and is directed by Astro Teller, also known as the Captain of Moonshots. The lab started with the development of Google's self-driving car. By late 2014, X projects that have been revealed including the self-driving car, Project Wing, Project Glass, and Project Loon, briefly introduced here.

- *Self-driving car:* Google was involved in developing technology for driverless cars. The project was led by Google engineer Sebastian Thrun, director of the Stanford AI Lab and coinventor of Google Street View. Thrun's team at Stanford created the robotic vehicle Stanley, which won the 2005 DARPA Grand Challenge. Google has been lobbying for driverless car laws. As of March 2016, Google has test driven their fleet of vehicles, in autonomous mode, a total of almost 1.5 million miles.

- **Project Wing:** This project aims to rapidly deliver products across a city by using flying vehicles, similar to the Amazon Prime Air concept. At the time of the announcement on August 28, 2014, the project had already been in development secretly at Google for about two years. The flying vehicles take off vertically, then rotate to a horizontal position for flying around. For delivery, it hovers and winches packages down to the ground.

- **Project Glass:** This project develops an AR *head-mounted display* (HMD). The intended purpose of this project is hands-free displaying of current information to smartphone users, allowing for interaction with the Internet via natural language voice commands.

- **Project Loon:** This project aims to bring Internet access to everyone by creating an Internet network of balloons flying through the stratosphere. The balloons fly above the weather and use wireless routers to allow Internet access to those who can't reach it or are in need of help.

In Example 7.1, we will assess the progress of autonomous car and delivery drones at Google X Lab. In general, autonomous cars are also known as self-driving cars or robotic cars. They are motor vehicles that are capable of sensing their environment and navigating without human drivers. An autonomous car detects its surroundings using radar, lidar, GPS, odometry, and computer vision. Such a driverless car is capable of analyzing sensory data to reach its destination without collisions or violating traffic rules. Autonomous cars were tested at Carnegie Mellon University, Mercedes-Benz, Google, and Stanford University in recent years.

A well-designed driverless vehicle may reduce labor costs. It will avoid careless traffic accidents by human drivers due to fatigue or distraction, because it will have a faster reaction time and avoid tailgating and rubbernecking. Autonomous vehicles may eliminate 90% of all auto accidents in the United States and prevent $190 billion in bodily injury or car damage annually. Other advantages could include higher speed limits, smoother rides, and reduced traffic congestion. There are obstacles to the use of autonomous vehicles that may hinder their widespread acceptance. For example, in case of accidents, autonomous cars may lead to disputes concerning liability. New legal framework and government regulations will need to be established before we will see driverless cars on the streets.

Example 7.1 Google Projects on Autonomous Car, Delivery Drone, and Cognitive Computing Services

Figure 7.3(a) shows Google's autonomous car being tested at an intersection. The driver's hands are off the wheel and her foot is away from the brake. It is obvious this testing was carried out at the early experimental stage. The driver stayed in the car in order to prevent an accident, such as hitting a pedestrian on the street. This safety problem was later solved with multiple cameras, better radar signals, and a sophisticated self-driving software system. Tesla offers an autopilot system that cannot detect pedestrians, making it only suitable for restricted highways, not for urban driving.

(a)

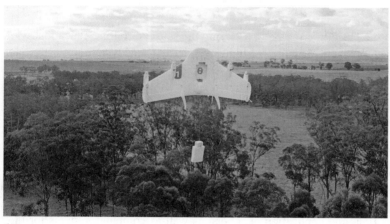

(b)

Figure 7.3

Google's testing projects on autonomous car and delivery drones in 2014. Courtesy of Google, http://www.google
.com. (a) Autonomous car testing at city intersection, (b) Delivery drone under testing.

Google's X Lab has also tested a commercial drone delivery prototype system.
The testing of the delivery drone at Mountainview, California, is shown in Figure 7.3(b).
The merchandise was dropped with a soft landing and then got picked up by a robot
waiting to complete the delivery process. The drone lowers the package to the ground
using a winch. Either the package is smoothly released to the ground directly, or a specially designed ground robot on wheels is notified to move the package to a safe location. The plan is to realize the autonomous delivery system by 2017 as part of Project
Wing at Google. Amazon is also experimenting with similar merchandise delivery
drones.

Other interesting Google X projects include (1) an artificial neural network for speech recognition and computer vision; (2) the web of things, a way of connecting real-world objects to the Internet; and (3) long-lasting smartphone batteries. As of 2015, X Lab has acquired 14 companies, including Redwood Robotics, Meka Robotics, Boston Dynamics, and Jetpac. A number of companies have been acquired and merged into X Lab, covering a diverse range of skills including wind turbines, robotics, artificial intelligence, humanoid robots, robotic arms, and computer vision. ∎

In a 2016 interview, X Lab founder Sebastian Thrun indicated that VR is more concerned with human experience and interaction with our environment, while AI can upgrade the quality of our lives and enhance the efficiency of our work. In other words, AI should be able to promote productivity. In fact, AI may start another industrial revolution by extending the human brain to some sort of "super-brain."

The Udacity Program

Thrun established the Udacity program to look into the future of online education, while Google was devoted to AlphaGo and self-driving cars. Udacity can help improve the quality of education to all who are eager to learn, regardless of gender, age, or ethnicity. This may change the future of the campus-based university system as lifelong education will be made much easier with Udacity. After just five years, Thrun felt that the Udacity education market had already enlarged significantly. This coincides with the *virtual university* concept once advocated by John Hennessy, former president of Stanford University.

Intelligent Robotics

Intelligent robotics is a rapidly growing field. It is a joint discipline covering mechanical engineering, electrical engineering, and computer science. Robotics deals with the design, construction, operation, and application of robots, as well as computer systems for their control, sensory feedback, and information processing. The intention is to replace humans in dangerous environments and manufacturing processes, or to resemble humans in cognition. Many robots are built to do jobs, such as police work or for the military, that are hazardous to people.

Google Neural Machine Translation System (GNMT)

In September 2016, Google announced the GNMT system, which attempts to bridge the gap between human and machine translation. This is another neural approach to achieving real-time language translation such as between Chinese and English.

7.1.3 Cognitive Services at IBM and Other Companies

In this section, we study the AI initiatives undertaken at many IT giants such as IBM and Microsoft. Each company has announced multibillion dollar projects to consolidate their accumulated expertise and promote new products and services that leverage AI, clouds, IoT, and cognitive computing.

IBM Watson Project

In Section 2.4.2, we introduced the IBM SyNAPSE, True, North (TrueNorth), and neuromorphic computer projects. In this section, we review the IBM Watson Project that was launched in 2011. *IBM Watson* is a collective name of an integrated project, which extends from the Deep Blue, SyNAPSE, and brain-like computer projects conducted at several IBM Research Centers at Yorktown Heights (NY), Almaden (CA), and Zurich, Switzerland. The goal is to meet the demands of a cognitive business era. The Watson initiatives are summarized in Table 7.1 in five categories.

IBM Watson aims to build an AI ecosystem for cognitive applications. In fact, IBM has merged the operations of its *global business services* (GBSs) and *global technique service* (GTSs). The purpose is to turn IBM into a company providing business cognitive services with intelligent cloud platform development. On the commercial business side, IBM Watson provides modular services that can cover heathcare, water management, insurance and fraud detection, fashion, and environmental problems.

In cognitive systems, IBM launched programs on natural language processing, information retrieval, knowledge presentation, inference, and machine learning engines that explore distributed parallelism. IBM has claimed that 40 products were developed in these areas. In the medical area, IBM Watson focuses on cancer and tumor diagnosis and detection. Eventually, IBM Health aims to become a large-scale medical and healthcare platform. The goal is to enhance medical diagnosis accuracy and reduce the cost of healthcare expenditures for the general public and rural areas through telemedicine.

Table 7.1
IBM Watson pushing for business cognitive services

Service Categories	Cognitive Service Components
Healthcare Diagnosis	Focus on deep learning on cancers and tumor diagnosis by acquiring big data resources or joint efforts with competing companies.
Quantum Computing	Quantum computing circuit design and platform development to meet future computing and communication demands.
Neuromorphic Chip Developments	Continued efforts on IBM TrueNorth and Zurich artificial phase-change neuromorphic chip design and system testing.
Business Cognitive Services	Disease treatment, water resource management, insurance and fraud detection, fashion environment, corporate merging, etc.
Cloud Computing	Digital advisors, cloud analytics, scientific research, virtual assistants, etc.

AI Programs at Amazon, Facebook, Microsoft, and Twitter

In 2016, AWS announced a new cloud service based on GPU architecture. This cloud is applied mainly in artificial intelligence, earthquake analysis, molecular modeling, genetic engineering, and those applications that demand low-precision arithmetic on massive resources for parallel processing. This GPU cloud differs from EC2, where applications mainly demand massive floating-point operations. The AWS/GPU clouds are designed to support solving complex AI problems through machine learning, extracting new knowledge through big data mining, predictions, or classification, in order to make critical decisions in financing, business, or government.

In the past, GPUs were primarily used to accelerate computer screen display, video games, or entertainment systems. With the growing demands in clouds for machine intelligence, the workloads are changing, dealing with streaming data or social graph analysis. These intelligence-oriented workloads benefit more from horizontal scalability as embedded in large GPU arrays. There exists a sharp difference between GPU clouds and the vertical applications on traditional CPU clouds.

In modern clouds, CPUs and GPUs could even be housed in the same platform, assisted by CUDA parallel processing or OpenCL frameworks. The AWS/GPU cloud initially contained 16 many-core GPUs with 192 GB of video memory. Each GPU has 512 simple cores that can operate in SIMD mode. This GPU cloud is designed to support *affective computing,* which demands the cognitive power to recognize, interpret, process, and simulate human affects or the five senses.

Microsoft, Facebook, and Twitter have also established some AI teams similar to the Google Brain team. They all leverage their accumulated experience by using a massive number of data centers or cloud platforms. Industrial AI programs are emerging as an interdisciplinary field spanning computer sciences, psychology, and cognitive science. For example, emotion management requires social skills assisted by smart robots over IoT platforms of various sizes. Eventually, we hope to predict the actions of other people by understanding their motives and emotional states.

7.1.4 Deep Learning Chips at Intel, Nvidia, and CAS/ICT

Deep learning is the fastest-growing field in artificial intelligence, helping computers make sense of infinite amounts of data in the form of images, sound, and text. Using multiple levels of neural networks, computers now have the capacity to see, learn, and react to complex situations as well or better than humans. This is leading to a profoundly different way of thinking about data, technology, products, and services to be delivered. Forward-looking companies in a variety of industries are adopting deep learning to address massive amounts of data by exploiting improvements in machine learning algorithms and advances in computing hardware.

Intel Ecosystem for AI Information Processing

In 2015, Intel acquired Altera, a *field-programmable gate array* (FPGA) company, in order to expand its chip design for pattern recognition, signal processing, and AI application beyond the traditional CPU and GPU product lines. The intent is to reduce energy consumption and enhance performance cost ratio. Subsequently, Intel acquired human-machine interface company (IDF-Intel Developer Forum) Nervana Systems, a deep learning startup, to cut deeper into the AI field. Table 7.2 summarizes some new Intel product lines that attempt to build an ecosystem for AI chip and system development.

Nvidia GPU Upgrades for Deep Learning

Nvidia has expanded its GPU and software product lines to accelerate deep learning applications. Today's deep learning solutions rely most on using Nvidia GPU chips to process image, handwriting, and voice identification problems. Nvidia recently claimed to have reduced the training time of *deep neural networks* (DNNs) by as much as 12 times, meaning reducing the training time from weeks to a few days. Today, we want computers to not only learn but also to think by themselves. This is opening big opportunities in applications like robots, medicine, and self-driving cars. Table 7.3 lists some Nvidia GPU chips targeting machine learning and neural computing.

Table 7.2
Intel development of an ccosystem for AI chips and systems

Environment	Brief Description
User End	Human-machine interaction (Intel® Edison platform, Intel® Cedar Trail platform, Intel® RealSense™ technology)
Server End	Xeon E5 v4 series CPU; Xeon Phi™ Product Family
Software Service	Intel® Math Kernel Library (Intel® MKL); Intel® Data Analytics Acceleration Library (Intel® DAAL)
Extending Computing Performance	Purchased Altera Corporation; integrated chip featuring Xeon core and FPGA
Business Acquisition	Purchased high-tech companies: Nervana, Movidius, Itseez, etc.

Table 7.3
Nvidia GPU chips targeting machine learning and neural computing

GPU Chip Model	Targeted Applications in Data Centers/Clouds Area
Tesla P100	Deep learning training accelerator for the data center
Tesla P40/P4	Energy-efficient inference accelerator for deep learning
Jstson TKI1TX1	The embedded AI supercomputer for intelligent devices
Drive PX2	Scalable in-vehicle AI supercomputer for autonomous driving

Source: http://www.nvidia.com/object/deep-learning.html#sthash.FQhMYCMb.dpuf

Cambricon Neural Processing Units

We have introduced the early development of the Cambricon accelerator for neural computing in Chapter 2. Now, the design team at China's Institute of Computing Technology has upgraded the accelerator to a *neural processing unit* (NPU) as illustrated in Figure 7.4(a). The instruction pipeline consists of seven stages: namely *fetch, decode, issue, register read, execution, write-back,* and *commit*. The chip applies scratchpad memory and DMA. After the fetch and decode stages, an instruction is injected into an in-order issue queue. After successfully fetching the operands (scalar data, or address/size of vector/matrix data) from the scalar register file, an instruction will be sent to different units depending on the instruction type. Control instructions and scalar computational/logical instructions are sent to the scalar functional unit for direct execution. After write-back to the scalar register file, the instruction is committed from the reorder buffer, as long as it has become the oldest uncommitted instruction.

The NPU chip layout is shown in Figure 7.4(b). The overall area of Cambricon-ACC is 56.24 mm^2. The combinational logic (mainly in vector and matrix functional units) takes

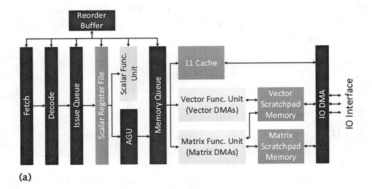

(a)

(b)

Figure 7.4
Cambricom neural processing unit (NPU) built at the Institute of Computing Technology, Beijing, China. Courtesy of Xiaoli Liu, et al., "Cambricon: Instruction Set Architecture for Neural Networks," ACM/IEEE 43rd Annual International Symposium of Computer Architecture (ISCA) 2016. (a) The NPU architecture (b) NPU chip built with TSMC 65nm technology in Taiwan.

32.15% of the chip area. The on-chip memory (mainly vector and matrix scratchpad memories) takes 15.05% of the area, and the matrix function unit and the matrix scratchpad memory accounts for 62.69%. The core instruction pipeline logic, scalar function unit, memory queue, and the vector part account for 9%. The remaining 28.31% is used by the interconnection fabrics. The peak power consumption was measured 1.695 W, which is about 1% of the K40M GPU. Compared with a 128-bit 2 GHz SIMD GPU accelerator, the accelerator chip achieved a speed 117 times faster with a 21-time reduction in power consumption. With an extended 64-chip machine-learning architecture, the team has achieved a speed 450 times faster over an array of GPU chips, with a power reduction of 150 times.

The Cambricon team has proposed a domain-specific *instruction set architecture* (ISA) for NPU. This is a load-store architecture that integrates scalar, vector, matrix, logical, data transfer, and control instructions based on a comprehensive analysis of existing neural network kernel operations. The Cambricon instructions are 64-bit wide. It uses sixty-four 32-bit general-purpose registers for scalars, control, and addressing instructions. To support contiguous, variable-length accesses to vector/matrix data, which are common in neural computations, the designer does not use any vector register files, but keeps data in on-chip scratchpad memory, which is visible to programmers/compilers. Cambricon contains four instruction types: *computational, logical, control*, and *data transfer,* as summarized in Table 7.4. The instruction length is fixed at 64-bit for easier memory alignment and simpler load/store/decoding logic.

Table 7.4
An overview of Cambricon instruction set architecture

Instruction Type		Examples	Operands
Control		jump, conditional branch	register (scalar value), immediate
Data Transfer	Matrix	matrix load/store/move	register (matrix address/size, scalar value), immediate
	Vector	vector load/store/move	register (vector address/size, scalar value), immediate
	Scalar	scalar load/store/move	register (scalar value), immediate
Computational	Matrix	matrix multiply vector, vector multiply matrix, matrix multiply scalar, outer product, matrix add matrix, matrix subtract matrix	register (matrix/vector address/size, scalar value)
	Vector	vector elementary arithmetics (add, subtract, multiply, divide), vector transcendental functions (exponential, logarithmic), dot product, random vector generator, maximum/minimum of a vector	register (vector address/size, scalar value)
	Scalar	scalar elementary arithmetics, scalar transcendental functions	register (scalar value), immediate
Logical	Vector	vector compare (greater than, equal), vector logical operations (and, or, inverter), vector greater than merge	register (vector address/size, scalar)
	Scalar	scalar compare, scalar logical operations	register (scalar), immediate

Because most neural network computations involve neuron and synapse data organized in layers, they are manipulated in a uniform/symmetric manner. Data-level parallelism is enabled by vector/matrix instructions. Customized vector/matrix instructions are specially tailored for neural network operations. Also on-chip scratchpad memory is used to accelerate streaming of dataflow in the ANNs. The Cambricon NPU chip supports a broad range of neural network computations. Comparing the Cambricon with x86 and MIPS across ten kernel neural benchmark operations, the code density of Cambricon is significantly higher. The prototype Cambricon chip has achieved comparable performance/energy efficiency with GPU or other neural computing chips.

7.2 Augmented/Virtual Reality and Blockchain Technology

As shown in Figure 7.5, we humans can experience both a real environment and a virtual environment. In this section, we clarify the concepts of AR, VR, and *mixed reality* (MR). In general, AR is augmented from the real-world environment, where some real sensor-collected signals or data are involved. VR is a computer technology that creates a visual environment, some real and some imagined, within which the users can experience a physical presence and interactions. MR is more a general term that involves both real and virtual environments in the entire spectrum.

7.2.1 Augmented, Mediated, and Virtual Realities (AR, MR, VR)

The world of events can be described as *reality* or *virtuality* (logical) based on their existence in the real-world word or in cyberspace. We characterize them as *real* versus *virtual* events, respectively. These events can be also subdivided as *pure, augmented, mediated,* or *severely mediated* in ascending degree of virtuality from the extreme end of reality. Note that augmented environments are created by computer images, artificial visual effects, or animated events. The mediated events or environments are created out of illusions and special mental conditions. The whole space is simply referred to as a spectrum of reality and virtuality as demonstrated in Figure 7.6.

Here we consider a two-dimensional spectrum of eight cases of reality and virtuality, represented by eight dark dots in the spectrum space. The x-axis displays from *pure reality* (IR) to *pure virtuality* (IV). The y-axis shows variations from pure to augmented and

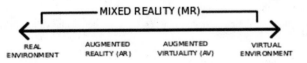

Figure 7.5
The spectrum of real and augmented reality and virtual environments.

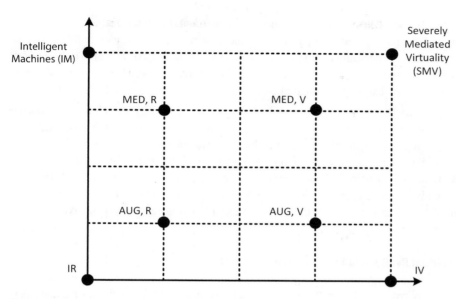

Figure 7.6
Eight combinations of pure, augmented, mediated or virtual models of reality versus virtuality in the application spectrum.

mediated experience environments. The four interior dots have variable degrees of mediation and mediation levels, some are also known as MR as shown in Figure 7.5. At the augmentation level, we have AR and *augmented virtuality* (AV).

At the mediation level, we have *mediated reality* (MED, R) and *mediated virtuality* (MED, V). The augmented environment provides a live view of a physical world environment where elements are *augmented* (or supplemented) by computer-generated sensory input such as sound, video, graphics, or GPS data. Our study will be more focused on the AR and VR cases. The AR is closer to the physical world represented by the four dots at the lower two levels in Figure 7.6. The VR is closer to the mediated world represented by the four dots at the upper two levels in Figure 7.6.

AV and MV are positioned toward the more virtual world, which could be more imaginary. MR and MV demand a higher degree of computer mediation. At the extreme, we have SMV, which is even more difficult to achieve. In general, IV and SMV can be easily confused because different human users may experience them differently due to their mental or emotional conditions. The application areas of AR and VR are reviewed below to clarify some of the ambiguity.

- *Education and training:* Strides are being made in the realm of education, although much more needs to be done. The possibilities of VR and education are endless, and could bring many advantages to students of all ages. Few are currently creating content intended for educational purposes, with most advances being made in the entertainment industry, but many understand and realize the future and the importance of education and VR. For example, U.S. Navy personnel could use a VR parachute training simulator. The use of VR in a training perspective will allow professionals to conduct training in a virtual environment, where they can improve their skills.

- **Video games:** The use of graphics, sound, and input technology in video games can be incorporated into VR. Several VR *head-mounted displays* (HMD) were released for gaming, including the Virtual Boy developed by Nintendo and iGlasses developed by Virtual IO. Several companies are working on a new generation of VR headsets: Oculus Rift is a head-mounted display for gaming purposes, which was acquired by Facebook in 2014. One of its rivals is PlayStation VR by Sony (code named Morpheus). Valve Corporation announced their partnership with HTC Vive to use a VR headset to track the exact position of its users.

7.2.2   Virtual Reality and Product Reviews

VR artificially creates a sensory experience, which can include sight, touch, hearing, and smell. The immersive environment can be made similar to the real world in order to create a lifelike experience, e.g, in simulations for pilot or combat training, or it can differ significantly from reality, such as in VR games. All computer, cloud, and social media providers have their own *application program interface* (API) tools. Readers should visit their websites to learn the specific API tools used in their big data mining, preprocessing, machine learning, and analytics applications.

Among these tools, REST is the most popular protocol, JSON the most used format, and API key is used most for security control. Five product categories are shown: AR, AV, MR, MV, and VR. Table 7.5 lists recent AR/VR/MR products developed by high-tech companies. Those listed are only some representative ones; there are many more for various IT companies and social websites.

In Table 7.5, five product categories are shown: AR, AV, MR, MV, and VR. These include, for example, diminished reality such as computerized welding helmets that filter out and diminish certain parts of a scene. Accelerometer, gyrometer, proximity sensor, and light sensors are built into VR headsets, including, for example, the HTC Vive, Playstation VR, and Samsung Gear VR.

Example 7.2 HTC Vive as VR Game Gear Using 70 Sensors

This is a virtual reality headset released by HTC and Valve in 2016. This headset is designed to turn a room into a 3D space via sensors. The virtual world allows the user to navigate with the ability to walk around, manipulate virtual objects, and experience immersive environments. The device uses two screens, one per eye and uses more than

Table 7.5

Recent AR/VR/MR products developed by high-tech companies

Company	Product	Introduction
Microsoft	HoloLens	A pair of mixed reality head-mounted smart glasses by Microsoft. HoloLens gained popularity for being the first computer running the Windows holographic platform.
Google	Google Cardboard	This is a VR platform by Google for use with a head mount for a smartphone. Named for its foldout cardboard viewer, it is a low-cost system to encourage VR applications.
Facebook	Oculus Rift	Oculus Rift is a VR headset developed and manufactured by Oculus VR, released on March 28, 2016.
Samsung	Gear VR	The Samsung Gear VR is a mobile VR headset developed by Samsung Electronics, in collaboration with Oculus, and manufactured by Samsung.
Sony	PlayStation VR	Known by the code name Project Morpheus during development, it is a VR gaming head-mounted display developed by Sony Interactive Entertainment and manufactured by Sony.
HTC	HTC Vive	This is a VR headset developed by HTC and Valve Corporation in 2016. It is designed to utilize "room scale" technology to turn a room into 3D space via sensors.
Huawei	Huawei VR	Huawei Honor VR was released on May 10, 2016, to support the Honor V8 smartphone.
Alibaba	Buy + Plan	Buy + program uses VR technology to generate an interactive 3D shopping environment with computer graphics systems and auxiliary sensors.

70 sensors including a MEMS gyroscope, accelerometer, and laser position sensors. It can track a space of 225 square ft with a photosensor base station.

The front-facing camera applies the software to identify any moving or static objects in a room. Valve has released its OpenVR *software development kit* (SDK) for users to build software that supports the HTC Vive Developer Edition. For example, Epic Games has used Valve's SteamVR technology to create VR projects. In July 2016, SensoMotoric Instruments (SMI), a computer vision company, integrated its eye tracking technology in the HTC Vive for research and professional applications (see Figure 7.7). ■

7.2.3 Block Chaining for Securing Business Transactions

A *block chain* (also known as *blockchain*) is a distributed database technique, which was recently proposed to secure big data shared in business communities. The idea is to secure a growing list of *blocks* of records from tampering and revision. Each block maintains a timestamp and a link to a previous block. The blockchain serves as the public ledger in all related transactions or chains of actions. The major advantage is to eliminate the use of a trusted third party to secure the transactions. This is extremely useful in automated

Figure 7.7
HTC Vive headset for virtual reality gaming using Valve OpenVR software. Courtesy of HTC, http://www.htc
.com, 2016.

payment services that are practiced in cloud-based business transactions and smart contracts among business partners.

Blockchains have been described as a value-exchange protocol. The blockchain is a decentralized digital ledger that records transactions on thousands of computers globally. The
blockchain-protected transactions cannot be altered retrospectively. A blockchain consists
of blocks that hold batches of valid transactions. Each block includes the hash of the prior
block linked by the blockchain. The linked blocks form a chain. In the past, a similar concept was used in Git, but it does not qualify as a blockchain. The blockchain is parsed by
software to extract relevant information. A blockchain implementation consists of two kinds
of records: *transactions* and *blocks*.

A blockchain is built with transaction blocks that are linked as a chain. Successive transaction blocks are hash-secured to prevent tracing of the transactions for illegal uses. One
can set up a scoring system to prevent other users from access to your private transaction
blocks. Blockchains are built to add new blocks to extend the old blocks rather than over-
writing old blocks. All blocks are distributed and thus eliminate the risk that a central administration could intervene in the transactions. A blockchain is designed to secure online
transactions in five steps:

1. Initiate a digitally signed transaction.

2. Transaction is sent to the miner, which verifies the transaction.

3. Transaction is broadcast to all connected nodes as a block.

4. Network accepts transaction if data is valid.

5. Receiver receives the transaction.

The use of blockchains promises to bring higher efficiencies to global supply chains. Some opponents believe the technology has been hyped with unrealistic claims. In order to mitigate risk, companies are reluctant to place a blockchain at their business core until the technology is truly proven secure. Today's PKI (*public key infrastructure*) system has a security problem in that it relies on the "username/password" system to protect identity. PKI is also decentralized by using public and private keys jointly. The *public key* issued by a *certificate agency* (CA) is used as the user's address on the blockchain. A *private key* is like a password that gives exclusive access to the record by the owner. Transaction data stored on the blockchain is generally considered incorruptible.

Bitcoins sent across the network are recorded as public keys. A private key interacts with blockchains smoothly without conflicts. Every node in a decentralized system has a copy of the blockchain. Data quality is maintained by massive database replication and computational trust. No centralized copy exists and no user is trusted completely. Transactions are broadcast to the network using software. Messages are delivered on a best effort basis. Mining nodes validate transactions and add them to the block being created. Then, the system broadcasts the completed block to other nodes. Blockchains use timestamps such as proof-of-work to serialize the changes.

In a blockchain, the chain with the most cumulative proof is always considered the valid one by the network. In addition to a secure hash-based history, any blockchain database with a higher value can be selected over others. Peers supporting the database don't have exactly the same version of the history at all times, rather they keep the highest scoring version of the database. Whenever a peer receives a higher scoring version, they extend or overwrite their own database and retransmit the improvement to their peers. There is never an absolute guarantee that any particular version will be the best, because blockchains are checking the shared values dynamically and continuously.

On the positive side, a blockchain is applied to any data structure that batches data into timestamped blocks. The system prevents two transactions from spending the same single output in a blockchain. Opponents criticized that such a permissioned system does not support decentralized data verification and thus does not prevent operator tampering and revision. Blockchains may be integrated into a payment system, promoting the use of digital currency and crowdsales. Some blockchain implementations may enable the coding of contracts that will execute when specified conditions are met. Smart contracts can be programmed to perform simple functions.

Example 7.3 Some Reported Applications of Blockchain Technology

Blockchain technology has been applied in cryptocurrencies, including Bitcoin, Black-Coin, Dash, and NXT. Other good applications include payment systems, digital currency, facilitating crowdsales, implementing prediction markets, and offering generic governance tools. Blockchains are expected to disrupt the cloud computing industry. In 2016, the central securities depository of the Russian Federation announced a pilot project based on blockchain technology. Various regulatory bodies in the music industry have started testing models that use blockchain technology for royalty collection and management of copyrights around the world. IBM opened a blockchain innovation research center in Singapore.

By storing data across its network, the blockchain eliminates the risks that come with data being held centrally. Its network lacks centralized points of vulnerability that computer hackers can exploit. Today's Internet security problems are caused by using the "username/password" system. Blockchain security methods use cryptographic technology which may appeal to banks, because it can speed up back office settlement systems. Blockchain may also benefit sharing economic and IoT services, because they involve many collaborating peers.

Other blockchain platforms include Factom, which uses a distributed registry, Gem for decentralized messaging, and MaidSafe for decentralized applications. Storj offers a distributed cloud platform and Tezos offers decentralized voting. In Sweden, use of blockchains in creating a land registry has demonstrated the effectiveness of using blockchains to speed up land sale deals. The Republic of Georgia is piloting a blockchain-based property registry. Some in the insurance industry apply blockchain technology in peer-to-peer insurance practices. Blockchains may also benefit parametric insurance and microinsurance. ∎

7.3 Artificial Neural Networks for Deep Learning

DL simulates operations in deeper layers of ANNs. This is heavily used to extract and learn features from data. Deep neural networks include one input layer, one output layer, and multiple hidden layers. The connection strength between neurons is adjusted in the learning process. Common DL architectures are introduced in subsequent sections, including the basic ANN, *convolutional neural networks* (CNNs), and *recurrent neural networks* (RNNs), amid many possible extensions of these neural networks.

7.3.1 Deep Learning Mimics Human Cognitive Functions

In March 2016, AlphaGo, a computer program developed to play the board game Go, received a great deal of publicity and debate regarding human-machine competition in intelligence. After five rounds of competition, the computer finally beat Lee Sedol, a world-class Go player. Up until then, no professional players had been beaten by Go software. Twenty years ago, the computer Deep Blue used the method of a searching algorithm to beat international chess master Garry Kasparov in an international chess match. However, chess play is much less complex than playing a Go game. Computer-implemented AlphaGo combines reinforcement learning and a value network with a tree search algorithm to make smart decisions in placing the pawns. For the first time, Google AlphaGo has reached almost a human level. This represents a major step in advancing AI to achieve a human level of performance.

Another reported advance was done at the Google Brain project. In June 2012, tens of millions of random images from YouTube were recognized by a computer platform built with over 16,000 CPU cores at Google. They used a training model over a deep neural network built with 1 billion artificial neurons. This model system identified basic features of images, learned how to compose these features, and automatically identified the image of a cat. During the training, the system did not obtain the information, "this is a cat," but it comprehended the concept of "cat" itself.

From the victory of AlphaGo to the success of the Google Brain project, it seems that DL has the capability of self-learning. The meaningful question to ask now is: How can DL compete with humans on self-learning through education? If we want to judge whether a quadrangle is square or not, the rational analytical approach is to seek features of a square, such as the same length for four sides and four 90° corner angles. This requires comprehension of the concept of right angle and the length of the side view, as demonstrated in Figure 7.8. If we show a square image to a child and tell him that this is a square, he would identify a square accurately after several times. The method of rationally identifying a square is similar to the method where feature identification is designed artificially. But the way a child identifies a square follows a perceptual method. In a rational way, it is easy to describe and realize this problem with a computer. However, it's easy for a human to understand many problems in reality, but it's hard for a computer to comprehend and solve these problems in a rational way.

For instance, if we want to identify people through photos using a rational method through the computer, the process requires determining which features in the human face can be used for identification, such as nose, eyes, eyebrows, or mouth. Of course, it is quite difficult to choose appropriate features that can accurately distinguish people. The visual effect in photos can be affected by light, shooting angle, and shading from sunglasses.

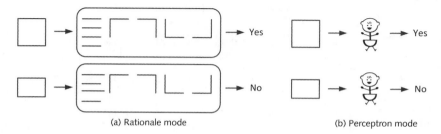

(a) Rationale mode   (b) Perceptron mode

Figure 7.8
Rationale vs. perceptron modes to recognize a square object.

Let's consider a child's recognition of a person as an example. The child does not need to seek the features of the person to be recognized. But, he can accurately identify the person after seeing that person or his/her photos several times. The change of light in photos, difference in shooting angle, and whether sunglasses are worn would not influence the identification. We may therefore interpret that a child recognizes a person by impression. There exists some kind of mapping between the input photos and the output name in a human memory.

With the development of computer applications, people are increasingly aware that a rational or analytical method would be inefficient or impossible when solving many problems in the real world. The mechanism that people do things intuitively seems quite efficient in comparison with modern science and technology. This intuitive method or the method of following one's heart could be simply interpreted as establishing certain mapping between input and output. However, it is still unknown to us how the human brain realizes encoding, processing, and storage of information using 100 billion neurons.

The main contribution of David Hubel and Torsten Wiesel (winners of the 1981 Nobel Prize in Medicine) is that they discovered that information processing of visual systems (i.e., visual cortex) is hierarchical, as shown in Figure 7.9. At Johns Hopkins University in 1958,

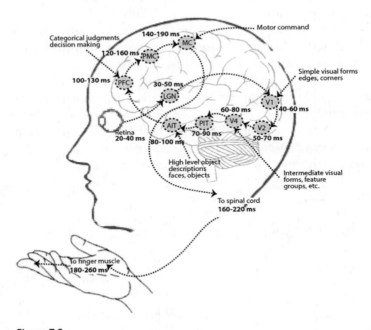

Figure 7.9
Hierarchy signal flows of human visual cortex in the brain, retina, and fingers. (Reprinted with permission from K. Hwang and M. Chen, *Big Data Analytics for Cloud, IoT and Cognitive Computing*, Wiley, 2017.)

they were studying the correspondence between pupil area and neurons in the cerebral cortex. After many experiments, they proved that there is some kind of correspondence between the stimulation received by the pupils and different visual neurons located in the posterior cerebral cortex. They discovered a kind of neuron, named the *orientation selective cell*: when a pupil captures the edge of an object, and if this edge points to a certain direction, the corresponding neurons would be active.

The information processing of the human visual system was interpreted as extracting edge features from area V1, and extracting shape features or some constituent parts of an objective from area V2. Then higher levels of understanding are reached. From low- to high-level features, the abstraction degree increases. A combination of low-level features serves as input to a higher level. Thus, higher-level features reveal more semantics. As abstraction increases, there is less context confusion, which is good for classification or identification purposes.

7.3.2 Evolution of ANNs and Reported Applications

ANNs are also known as *connectionist computing systems*, modeled after human brain structures and functionalities. Even though brain theory is not completely developed, many scientists have experimented on how human learning, memory, and intelligence functions work as a connectionist model. It has been estimated that an average adult may have tens of billions or more biological neurons in the brain. Each neuron is estimated to connect to about 5,000 other neurons. All the neurons interact collectively at different regions in the brain to provide different senses, cognition power, and intelligence functions.

The brain solves problems with large clusters of biological neurons connected by axons. The links between neurons can activate, enforce, or inhibit the connected neurons to produce intelligence. Each individual neuron may have a summation function which combines the values of all its inputs together. There may be a threshold function or limiting function on each connection and on the neuron itself. The connectionist model suggests weighted connection strength that can vary or surpass before the signals can propagate among the neurons. These systems are self-learning and trained rather than explicitly programmed. The ANNs can excel in a number of areas where the traditional computer systems cannot perform well. For example, neural networks have been applied in computer vision and speech recognition. Both are hard to solve using ordinary rule-based programming on today's computers.

Experimental ANN projects typically work with a few thousand to a few million artificial neurons and millions of connections. This is still several orders of magnitude less complex than the human brain and closer to the computing power of a worm. Neural networks typically consist of multiple layers and the signal path traverses from front to back. *Backpropagation* is where the forward stimulation is used to reset weights on the input end of neurons. This is sometimes done in combination with ANN training where the correct result is known. ANNs can be statically or dynamically structured, as studied below. *Dynamic neural networks* are the most advanced. They can form new connections, create new neurons, or disable existing neurons, dynamically.

In symbolic AI, high-level rule-based expert systems are developed with knowledge embodied in *if-then* rules, to low-level (subsymbolic) ML. As mentioned before, if we show a square image to a boy and tell him that this is a square, he would identify a square accurately after several times.

The human brain has a very complicated structure. However, its constitutional unit is a neuron that produces output (excitement) per input. The hierarchical information processing of the human brain is realized through numerous neurons that are interconnected. A *biological neuron* is modeled in Figure 7.10(a), where the left end of the dendrite is connected to the cytomembrane system as input while the right end of the axon is output. What a neuron mainly outputs is an electrical impulse. There are a lot of branches of dendrites and axons, and the end of an axon is often connected to the dendrite of other neurons.

A neuron obtains input from upper-layer neurons, produces output, and transmits it to a neuron in the next layer. If the human brain can be simulated, neurons should be simulated first. Figure 7.10(b) shows the structure of an *artificial neuron*. The inputs to an artificial neuron are all from external stimulating signals, denoted by x_i for $i = 1, 2, \ldots . n$. The artificial neuron calculates a weighted sum of the input signals, where the weights are denoted as w_i for $i = 1, 2, \ldots, n$.

The sigmoid function $y = \text{sig mod}(x) = 1/(1 + e^{-x})$ is applied here, where x represents the sum of weighted inputs. In real-life ANN applications, we list a number of reported applications in several broad categories:

- function or fitness approximation or regression analysis for financial forecasting;
- classification including pattern recognition and novelty detection and sequential decision making;
- big data processing including spam filtering, clustering, medical diagnosis, cancer prediction, etc.;
- smart robotics applications including directing manipulators, gesture detection, and prosthesis; and
- smart control such as game playing, trajectory projection, and autonomous vehicles.

7.3.3 Mathematical Description of an Artificial Neuron

ANN is a kind of abstract mathematical model that aims to reflect the structure and function of the human brain. It is widely used in many fields such as pattern recognition, picture processing, intelligent control, combinatorial optimization, financial prediction and management, communication, robots, and expert systems. There are many similarities

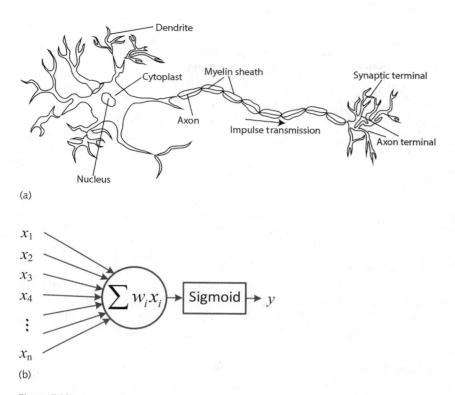

Figure 7.10

Schematic diagrams of biological neuron versus artificial neuron. (a) Biological neuron in human brain (b) Structure of an artificial neuron.

between ANN and biological neural networks in the human brain. ANN consists of a group of connected input/output units. Each connection is expressed as a weighted edge. In the learning stage, we adjust these weights based on the gap between predicted output and labeled test data.

An ANN is typically structured with three types of parameters: (1) the interconnection pattern between the different layers of neurons; (2) the learning process for updating the weights of the interconnections; and (3) the activation function that converts a neuron's weighted input to its output activation.

Single-Layer ANNs

A single-layer ANN is best described by the *perceptron* machine shown in Figure 7.11. The perceptron is a neural network with an input end and an output neuron. By comparison, a multilayer ANN is composed of one input layer, one or more hidden layer(s), and one output layer, as shown later in Figure 7.13.

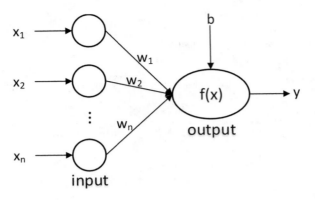

Figure 7.11
Conceptual diagram of a single-layer ANN: the perceptron machine.

Since we stimulate perceptron in the human nervous system, the input node corresponds to the input neuron and the output node corresponds to a decision-making neuron, while weight parameter corresponds to strength of connection between neurons. By constantly stimulating neurons, the human brain can learn unknown knowledge. An activation function, $f(x)$, is used to mimic the stimulation of a neuron in the human brain. This is where the ANN gets its name.

Each input item corresponds to an attribute of things while weight stands for the degree the attribute reflects things. These together with the degree of deviation constitute the input, which is represented by the mathematical equation x listed below. Let function act on x, and the output y is obtained:

$$x = w_1 x_1 + w_2 x_2 + \cdots + w_n x_n + b \rightarrow y = f(x). \tag{7.1}$$

Usually, we may not necessarily obtain ideal results. In the strict sense, $\hat{y}$ should be adopted to stand for input result of perceptron. The equation of the model is $\hat{y} = f(w \cdot x)$, where, w and x are n-dimensional vectors. Typically, a sigmoid function is used for f(x) (Figure 7.12(a)):

$$\text{sig}\,\text{mod}(x) = \frac{1}{1 + e^{-x}} \tag{7.2}$$

or a hyperbolic tangent function is used to represent the function $f(x)$ (Figure 7.12(b)):

$$\tanh(x) = \frac{e^x - e^{-x}}{e^x + e^{-x}}. \tag{7.3}$$

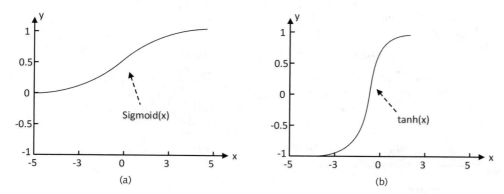

Figure 7.12
Common activation functions for the perceptron. (a) Sigmoid function (b) Hyperbolic tangent function.

7.3.4 Multilayer Artificial Neural Network

A multilayer ANN is composed of one input layer, one or more hidden layer(s), and one output layer, as shown in Figure 7.13. The main unit of an ANN is a neuron. There are a group of connections corresponding to the synapses of biological neurons. The connection strength is expressed by weight value of each connection. The weight value represents activation if it is positive, while it represents suppression when the value is negative. The mathematical equation is:

$$\begin{cases} w = (w_1, w_2, \ldots, w_n) \\ w_i = (w_{i1}, w_{i2}, \ldots, w_{in}) \, i = 1, 2, \ldots n \end{cases} \tag{7.4}$$

The summation function is used to compute the weighted sums for each input signal and, generally, together with an offset or threshold. Its mathematical equation is:

$$\begin{cases} \mu_k = \sum_{j=1}^{n} w_{kj} x_j \\ v_k = \mu_k + b_k \end{cases} \tag{7.5}$$

The nonlinear activation function plays the role of nonlinear mapping and restricts the output amplitude of the neuron within a certain range [often (0, 1) or (−1, 1)]. Its mathematical equation expressed as:

$$y_k = f(v_k). \tag{7.6}$$

where $f(\cdot)$ is an activation function. There is no uniform regulation for the number of hidden layers in an ANN, the number of neurons in input, output, and each hidden layer, or

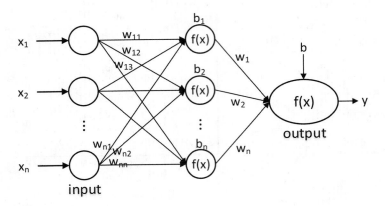

Figure 7.13
Structure of a two-layer artificial neural network.

how to select the activation function of neurons in each layer. And there is no standard for a specific case—that needs to be chosen independently or chosen as per personal experience. Therefore, there is a certain heuristic nature on the choice of network, and this is why ANN is deemed a heuristic algorithm.

Example 7.4 Hyperlipidemia Diagnosis Using an Artificial Neural Network

Table 7.6 gives a data set featuring triglycerides, high-density lipoprotein, low-density lipoprotein, and whether or not a patient has hyperlipidemia (1 for *yes* and 0 for *no*) during a health examination of some people in a grade-A hospital of second class in Wuhan City. Let us attempt to conduct preliminary judgment on whether a person who received a health examination has hyperlipidemia, if his or her health examination data are {3.16, 5.20, 0.97, 3.49} in sequence.

Referring to the data in the table, it is known that this problem is a dichotomy problem (1 for hyperlipidemia or 0 for healthy) with four attributes. Therefore, we can conduct prediction and classification using an ANN.

First, this is a problem of classification, so we set up a class label (1 for hyperlipidemia or 0 for healthy). Second, we need to choose an appropriate model of an ANN. As there is not enough sample data for training in this case, it is not necessary to set up too many hidden layers and neurons. Here, one hidden layer is set up, and the quantity of neurons in each layer is five. The tansig function is chosen as an activation function between the input layer and hidden layer, while the purelin function is chosen as a function between the hidden layer and output layer (choosing other functions has little effect on the results of this case). Its network parameters are listed as the top row headings in Table 7.7.

Table 7.6

Patient examination data for those suspected to have hyperlipidemia

Patient ID	Triglycerides (mmol/L)	Total Cholesterol (mmol/L)	High-Density Lipoprotein (mmol/L)	Low-Density Lipoprotein (mmol/L)	Hyperlipidemia or Not
1	3.62	7	2.75	3.13	1
2	1.65	6.06	1.1	5.15	1
3	1.81	6.62	1.62	4.8	1
4	2.26	5.58	1.67	3.49	1
5	2.65	5.89	1.29	3.83	1
6	1.88	5.4	1.27	3.83	1
7	5.57	6.12	0.98	3.4	1
8	6.13	1	4.14	1.65	0
9	5.97	1.06	4.67	2.82	0
10	6.27	1.17	4.43	1.22	0
11	4.87	1.47	3.04	2.22	0
12	6.2	1.53	4.16	2.84	0
13	5.54	1.36	3.63	1.01	0
14	3.24	1.35	1.82	0.97	0

Table 7.7

Table of parameters for artificial neural network

Neurons at Input Layer	Hidden Layers	Neurons in Hidden Layers	Neurons in Output Layer
4	1	5	1
Permissible Error	Times of Training	Learning Rate	Activation Function
	10000	0.9	Tansig and purelin

We then train the network with the data in Table 7.6, MATLAB is used for programming. The training process is shown in Figure 7.14(a). The error between the actual output of the network in the training process and the ideal output is reduced gradually. A satisfactory state is reached after the second backpropagation. The final training results are shown in Figure 7.14(b). The neural network classifier divides training data into two categories. The training data is divided into both ends and forms two classes.

The results of classification are {1,1,1,1,1,1,1,0,0,0,0,0,0,0}. The accuracy for classification reaches 100%, so this network can be used for prediction. Finally, let's predict whether or not a person whose data is {3.16, 5.20, 0.97, 3.49} has hyperlipidemia with an ANN mentioned above. The result is: *class* = 1. Therefore, we are able establish whether or not a person who received a health examination has hyperlipidemia. ∎

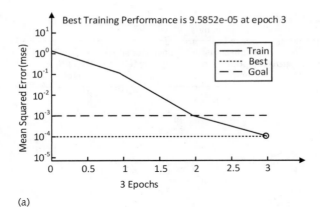

(a)

(b)

Figure 7.14
Training error and results on the ANN in Example 7.4. (a) Training error (b) Training results.

7.3.5 Forward Propagation and Backward Propagation in ANN

As with the perceptron model, how to obtain a set of appropriate weights to let the network have a specific function and a practical application value is important for a multilayer network. Artificial neural network solves this problem with a backpropagation algorithm. Before introducing the backpropagation algorithm, we need to know how the ANN propagates the signals forward from the input end to the output end.

Feedforward Signal Propagation
The input layer transmits toward the hidden layer. As for hidden unit i, its input is h_i^k. Where, h_i^k stands for input of hidden unit i in layer k, b_i^k stands for offset of hidden unit i in layer k. The corresponding output state is shown in Equation (7.7):

$$h_i^k = \sum_{j=1}^{n} w_{ij} x_j + b_i^k \rightarrow H_i^k = f(h_i^k) = f\left(\sum_{j=1}^{n} w_{ij} x_j + b_i \right). \tag{7.7}$$

Equations 7.8 and 7.9 describe how the input data of the neural network are propagated forward. For convenient expression, we often let $x_0 = b$, $\omega_{i0} = 1$. Then the equation of the forward propagation from hidden units of layer k to layer k+1 is:

$$\begin{cases} h_i^{k+1} = \sum_{j=1}^{m_k} w_{ij}^k h_j^k \\ H_i^{k+1} = f(h_i^{k+1}) = f\left(\sum_{j=1}^{n} w_{ij}^k h_j^k \right) \end{cases} \quad i = 1, 2, \ldots, m_{k+1}, \tag{7.8}$$

where m_k stands for quantity of neurons in hidden units of layer k, and w_{ij}^k stands for weight vector matrix from layer k to layer k+1. The final output is obtained as:

$$O_i = f\left(\sum_{j=1}^{m_{M-1}} w_{ij}^{M-1} H_j^{M-1} \right) \quad i = 1, 2, \ldots, m_o, \tag{7.9}$$

where m_o stands for the number of output units (there can be multiple outputs in the artificial neural network, but generally one output would be set up), M stands for the total number of layers of the artificial neural network, and O_i stands for the output of output unit i.

Example 7.5 Forward Propagation-Based Output Prediction in ANN

In an ANN, each set of inputs is modified by unique weights and biases. As shown in Figure 7.15(a), when calculating the activation of the third neuron in the first hidden layer, the first input was modified by a weight of 2, the second by 6, the third by 4, and then a bias of 5 is added on the top. Each activation is unique because each edge has a unique weight and each node has a unique bias.

This simple activation will flood across the entire network. The first set of inputs is passed to the first hidden layer, as shown in Figure 7.15(b). The activations of the first hidden layer pass to the next hidden layer, as shown in Figure 7.15(c). Until it reaches the output layer, the outcome of the classification is determined by the score of each output node, as shown in Figure 7.15(d). Such a procedure of classification in ANN is called forward propagation, which will be repeated for another set of input. ∎

Backward Propagation in Training ANNs

To train an ANN, most algorithms employ some form of gradient descent method using backpropagation to compute the actual gradients. This is done by taking the derivative of the cost function with respect to the network parameters (weights and biases).

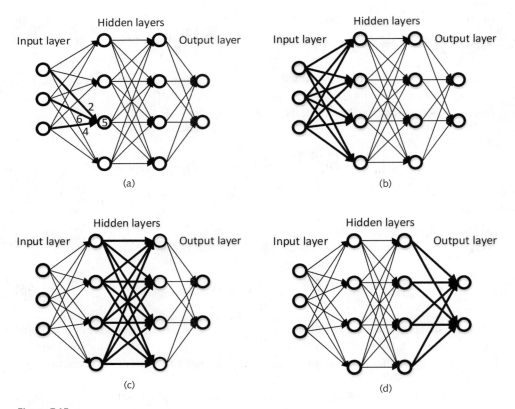

Figure 7.15
Forward propagation-based output prediction in a simple ANN with two hidden layers and four neurons at each layer.

Consider the ANN in Figure 7.16 (Example 7.6) with two hidden layers and four neurons per layer.

Example 7.6 Backward Propagation Based on Weights/Biases Adjustment in ANN

The accuracy of prediction depends on weights and biases. The goal is to make the predicted output as close to actual output as possible. Just like the other machine learning methods, the key to improve accuracy is the training. Let y denote the output of forward propagation, and y^* denote the correct output. The cost is the difference between two, denoted by $(y - y^*)$. After enormous times of training process, the cost should be decreased more and more.

During training, ANN adjusts weights and biases step by step, until the predicted output matches the actual output. To achieve this, three steps are taken.

1. When updating the weights between the first neuron in the output layer and the neurons in the second hidden layer and the bias of the first output neuron, the error between forward propagation of the output and its actual result needs to be calculated first. The error is 3 through computing.

2. Then, the gradient of each weight and bias is calculated. For example, the weights and biases are 5, 3, 7, 2, 6, respectively, as shown in Figure 7.16(a). Then, the corresponding gradients are −3, 5, 2, −4, −7.

3. Finally, the updated weights and biases can be calculated, such as $5 - 0.1 \times (-3) = 5.3$, where 0.1 is the learning rate set by user. In Figure 7.16(b), the bias of the node is revised as follows: $6 - 0.1 \times (-7) = 6.7$.

This simple error will flood across the entire network. As show in Figure 7.16(c), the output error will backward propagate to the second hidden layer and the weight of output layer to the second hidden layer and the bias of the output layer will be updated as well. There is the same operation in Figure 7.16(d), the error of the second hidden layer will backward propagate to the first hidden layer and the weight of the second layer to the first hidden layer and the bias of the second hidden layer will be updated.

Training will repeat these operations until the error is propagated to the input layer and the weight of the first hidden layer to the output layer and the bias of the first hidden layer is updated. At this time, the weights and biases of the whole network are updated, as shown in Figure 7.16(e) Such procedure of updating weights in ANN is called forward propagation, which will be repeated for another set of error. ∎

Next, we will introduce the backpropagation algorithm and how to update the weight w_{ij} through a learning or training process. Ideally, we expect the output of an ANN to be identical with the standard values of the training samples. In reality, it is impossible to accurately achieve this objective. We could only hope the actual output is as close as possible to the ideal output. Then the problem of finding a group of appropriate weights naturally comes down to the problem that $E(W)$ reaches minimum by figuring out appropriate values of W. O_i^s stands for the output result of output unit i if training sample is s, as shown below:

$$E(W) = \frac{1}{2}\sum_{i,s}(T_i^s - O_i^s)^2 = \frac{1}{2}\sum_{i,s}\left(T_i^s - f\left(\sum_{j=1}^{m_{M-1}} w_{ij}^{M-1} H_j^{M-1}\right)\right)^2 \quad (7.10)$$
$$\rightarrow \min E(W)\ i = 1, 2, \ldots, m_o.$$

As for each variable ω_{ij}^k, this is a continuously differentiable nonlinear function. In order to figure out the minimum, we generally adopt the steepest descent method. As per this method, we constantly renew weight in the direction of negative gradient until the conditions set up by the customer are satisfied. The so-called direction of gradient is to figure

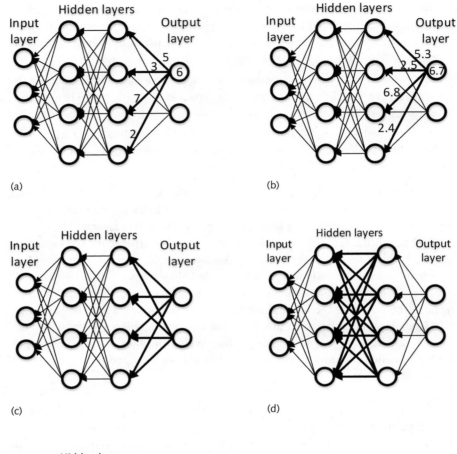

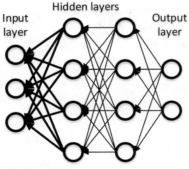

Figure 7.16
Backward propagation based output prediction in a simple ANN with two hidden layers and four neurons per layer.

out partial derivative of function. Assume the weight is $w_{ij}^{(k)}$ after renewal of k times. If $\nabla E(W) \neq 0$, then the renewed weight at time $k+1$ times is expressed by:

$$\nabla E(W) = \frac{\partial E}{\partial w_{ij}^k} \rightarrow w_{ij}^{(k+1)} = w_{ij}^{(k)} - \eta \nabla E(w_{ij}^{(k)}), \tag{7.11}$$

where η is learning rate of that network. It plays the same role as learning rate λ. When $\nabla E(W) = 0$ or $\nabla E(W) < \varepsilon$ (ε is permissible error), it stops renewing. ω_{ij}^k at this time shall be the final weight of the artificial neural network. The process that network constantly adjusts weight is called the learning process of the artificial neural network. The algorithm utilized in this learning process is called the propagation algorithm of the network.

The backward propagation process of the neural network reveals that the error propagation is getting smaller and smaller, which will limit the number of hidden layers in the network. If the number of hidden layers is too large, the error will not be passed to several previous layers in the backward propagation process, which results in the inability to update the corresponding weights and bias.

In 2006, Geoffrey Hinton suggested extending ANN for deep learning. He suggested that each hidden layer include several neurons. The output of the previous layer makes the input of the next layer. Two major observations were made by Hinton: (1) the learning capability to obtain features by deep artificial neural network with multiple hidden layers is strong. What's more, the features obtained by progressive learning in multiple layers can represent data accurately; (2) the layer-wise pretraining method solves difficulties in training ANNs. In the meantime, unsupervised learning is used during layer-wise pretraining.

To solve image and visual recognition problems, deep neural networks are used for dynamic feature recognition. This new technique known as deep learning is simply a rebranding of neural networks. The success of deep learning in recent years depends on the following factors: improvement in algorithm, realizing layer-wise feature extraction, simulating the capability of the human brain in learning, and simulating the hierarchical structure of the human brain during information processing. One can use GPU to support large-scale training of a deep neural network. One may need to process a large amount of training data to prove the prediction accuracy.

In general, we do not know the initial weight value in advance. Therefore, the value of weight must be adjusted dynamically during training. The weight renewal equation is specified by:

$$w_j^{(k+1)} = w_j^{(k)} + \lambda(y_i - \hat{y}_i^{(k)})x_{ij} \quad j = 1, 2, \dots n, \tag{7.12}$$

where $w_j^{(k)}$ is the weight value of input node j after iterations of k times, λ is called *learning rate*, and x_{ij} is the input value of node j in the ith training data sample.

The backpropagation algorithm effectively solves the exclusive-or problem, and more generally the problem of quickly training multilayer neural networks. ANN types vary from those with only one or two layers of single direction logic, to complicated multi-input of many directional feedback loops and layers. Most systems use "weights" to change the parameters of the throughput and the varying connections to the neurons. ANNs are mostly autonomous and learn by input from outside "teachers" or even self-teaching from written-in rules.

ANNs could be operated with supervision or unsupervision, depending on the learning paradigm applied. Three learning paradigms are possible for used in ANNs: namely *supervised deep learning*, *unsupervised deep learning*, and *reinforcement deep learning*, as briefly described below.

- *Supervised deep learning:* Given training data pairs, find a function that matches the samples. A commonly used cost is the mean-squared error. When one tries to minimize this cost using gradient descent for multilayer perceptron, simply apply the backpropagation algorithm to train the neural networks. Supervised deep learning is applied in pattern recognition and regression including speech and gesture recognition.

- *Unsupervised deep learning:* Without labeled training samples, some data x is given and the cost function to be minimized. The cost function depends on the task to model and our a priori assumptions. Tasks that fall within the paradigm of unsupervised deep learning are, in general, estimation problems; the applications include clustering, the estimation of statistical distributions, compression, and filtering.

- *Reinforcement deep learning:* Here, data is usually not given, but generated by an agent's interactions with the environment. At each time, the agent performs an action and the environment generates an observation and an instantaneous cost. The purpose is to discover a *policy* for selecting actions that minimizes some measure of an expected cumulative cost. ANNs are frequently used in reinforcement deep learning as part of an overall algorithm, for example, dynamic programming is coupled with ANNs. Applications using reinforcement learning include control problems, games, and other sequential decision-making tasks.

7.4   Taxonomy of Deep Learning Networks

In this section, we give a taxonomy of all DL networks by dividing them into different connected classes. Then we present static ANNs against dynamic ANNs. In particular, we cover CNNs and RNNs with some examples to illustrate the underlying key concepts involved.

7.4.1   Classes and Types of Deep Learning Networks

We classify ANNs into two major categories: static ANNs and dynamic ANNs. We simply classify them here without getting into the details of each class. ANNs are computational models inspired by biological neural networks. Most ANNs bear some limited resemblance

Table 7.8
Static versus dynamic artificial neural networks

ANN Types	Reported Names of ANNs (check with Wikipedia to find details of each class)
Static ANNs	Neocognitron, McCulloch-Pitts cell, radial basis function (RBF) network; learning vector quantization; perceptron (Adaline model, convolutional neural networks); modular neural networks: committee of machines (COMs); associative neural network (ASNN)
Dynamic ANNs	Feedforward neural network (FFN); recurrent neural networks (RNNs): Hopfield network, Boltzmann machine, simple recurrent networks, echo state network, long short-term memory network, bidirectional RNN, hierarchical RNN, stochastic neural network; Kohonen self-organizing maps; autoencoder; probabilistic neural network (PNN); time delay neural network (TDNN); regulatory feedback neural network (RFNN)

to their much more complex biological counterparts. Some ANNs are static in nature and do not change much with the environment. For example, the perceptron and the neocognitron are statically designed for a fixed purpose.

Some ANNs are dynamically structured, or known as adaptive systems, For example, ANNs used for modeling populations and environments are changing constantly. Dynamic neural networks deal with not only nonlinear multivariate behavior but also time-dependent behavior. Contrary to feedforward networks, RNNs are models with bidirectional data flow. While a feedforward network propagates data linearly from input to output, RNNs also propagate data from later processing stages to earlier stages. RNNs can be used as general sequence processors. In Table 7.8, we list some known ANN types that have been classified as static or dynamic ANNs by Wikipedia in recent years.

7.4.2 Convolutional Neural Networks

A CNN is a feedforward neural network that uses convolution and reduces the quantity of weights in a network and reduces the complexity of calculation compared with a traditional neural network. This kind of network structure is similar to a biological neural network. CNNs require supervised learning and they are widely applied in the voice recognition and image understanding area. The ideas of *convolutions* and *pooling* are introduced next, along with the training process of CNN. The connectivity pattern between its neurons is inspired by the organization of the animal visual cortex.

Individual cortical neurons respond to stimuli in a receptive field. The receptive fields of different neurons partially overlap such that they tile the visual field. This process is approximated by a convolution operation. In general, a CNN is built with many layers of neurons. We need to decide on the number of convolution layers and pooling layers to fit with specific application problems, just like piling up building blocks. Figure 7.17 shows the

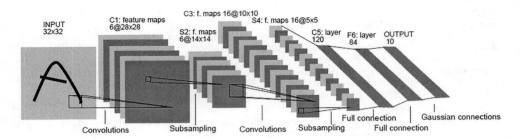

Figure 7.17
Convolutional neural network utilized by LeNet-5. Courtesy of Yann LeCun et al., "Gradient-based Learning Applied to Document Recognition, *Proceedings of the IEEE* 86, no. 11 (1998).

structure of a CNN utilized by LeNet-5. It includes seven layers: three convolution layers, two pooling layers, one fully connected layer, and one output layer.

CNNs may include local or global *pooling layers* to combine the outputs of neuron clusters. The CNN may have various combinations of convolutional and fully connected layers. A convolution operation on a small region of input is aimed at reducing the number of free parameters. This is done by the use of shared weight in convolutional layers. We may use a filter to realize the local connection between input layer and hidden layer. Assume a 10×10 filter is designed to imitate human eyes to feel the local image region. Then a hidden layer neuron is connected to a 10×10 area of the input layer through the filter.

If the hidden layer has 10^6 neurons, the quantity of filter between hidden layer and input layer is 10^6. Each connection corresponds to a 10×10 area of the input layer through a filter. Thus, the connection weight between the input layer and hidden layer becomes $10 \times 10 \times 10^6 = 10^8$. This large quantity of weight parameters poses a computational burden due to the fact that statistic features for one part of an image are the same with those of other parts. This means that the features learned from one part of an image can also be utilized for other parts. Therefore, for all locations of the same image, we can use the same learning features or image filters.

The same filter can be utilized for all locations of an image naturally. 10^6 filters of 10×10 corresponds to different 10^6 areas of 10×10 of an image. If the filters are completely identical, meaning local features are utilized for the whole image, there is one filter with 100 weight parameters between input layer and hidden layer. By sharing weight, the quantity of weight parameter is reduced from 25×10^{10} to 100, which reduces the quantity of weight parameters and computational burden greatly. The concept of local connection and weight sharing enables convolution operations. The filter of 10×10 is viewed as a *convolution kernel* here. When we need to represent more local features, we can use multiple convolution kernels.

A feature map or feature of an image is obtained by convolution. But when using such features to train a classifier directly, we will face the challenge of a huge computational burden.

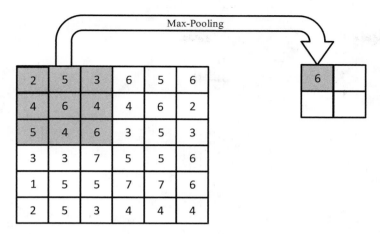

Figure 7.18
The concept of pooling from the 6×6 grid to a 2×2 grid. Source: http://ufldl.stanford.edu/wiki/index.php/UFLDL _Tutorial.

For instance, as for an image of 96×96 pixels, assuming 400 convolution filters are utilized, the convolution dimension is 8×8, and each feature graph includes $(96 - 8 + 1) \times (96 - 8 + 1) = 89^2 = 7,921$ dimensional convolution features. As there are 400 filters, each input image sample would obtain $89^2 \times 400 = 3,168,400$ hidden neurons. This may involve a heavy computation overhead.

Common images have an attribute of static nature. The features that are useful in one image area are very likely to be applicable in another area. Therefore, in order to describe large images, we can conduct aggregation statistics for features at different locations. For instance, people can calculate the mean value (or maximum value) in an area of image. The statistical features obtained by such aggregation cannot only reduce dimensionality but also improve the results (by preventing over-fitting). The operation of such aggregation is called pooling. As per different computational methods, it is divided into mean pooling and maximum pooling. Figure 7.18 shows pooling operation of 3×3 for an image of 6×6; the image is divided into four areas that do not overlap with each other. The result is given on the right after maximum pooling in one area. The feature graph after pooling is 2×2.

Example 7.7 Convolution and Pooling for a Convolutional Neural Network
CNN has been widely used in digital image processing. For example, using DeepID CNN, the recognition rate of the human face can reach a maximum of 99.15% of the correct rate. This technique can play an important role in the search for missing people and the prevention of terrorist crime. Figure 7.19 shows the CNN used. If the given input

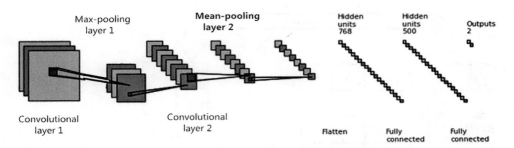

Figure 7.19
Schematic diagrams of a convolutional neural network.

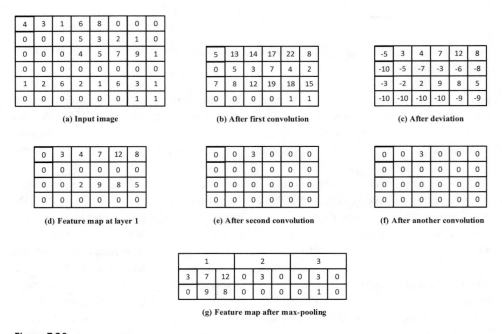

(a) Input image

4	3	1	6	8	0	0	0
0	0	0	5	3	2	1	0
0	0	0	4	5	7	9	1
0	0	0	0	0	0	0	0
1	2	6	2	1	6	3	1
0	0	0	0	0	0	1	1

(b) After first convolution

5	13	14	17	22	8
0	5	3	7	4	2
7	8	12	19	18	15
0	0	0	0	1	1

(c) After deviation

-5	3	4	7	12	8
-10	-5	-7	-3	-6	-8
-3	-2	2	9	8	5
-10	-10	-10	-10	-9	-9

(d) Feature map at layer 1

0	3	4	7	12	8
0	0	0	0	0	0
0	0	2	9	8	5
0	0	0	0	0	0

(e) After second convolution

0	0	3	0	0	0
0	0	0	0	0	0
0	0	0	0	0	0
0	0	0	0	0	0

(f) After another convolution

0	0	3	0	0	0
0	0	0	0	0	0
0	0	0	0	0	0
0	0	0	0	0	0

(g) Feature map after max-pooling

1			2			3		
3	7	12	0	3	0	0	3	0
0	9	8	0	0	0	0	1	0

Figure 7.20
Successive convolutional and pooling steps in building a CNN.

image size, as shown in Figure 7.20(a), is 8×6, we adopt the size of convolution kernels as 3×3 and the size of one feature graph in convolutional layer 1 is $((8-3)+1) \times ((6-3)+1) = 6 \times 4$. Assuming we use three filters, the corresponding weight matrices are:

$$w_1 = \begin{bmatrix} 1 & 0 & 1 \\ 0 & 0 & 0 \\ 1 & 0 & 1 \end{bmatrix}, \; w_2 = \begin{bmatrix} 0 & 0 & 1 \\ 0 & 1 & 0 \\ 0 & 0 & 0 \end{bmatrix}, \; w_3 = \begin{bmatrix} 0 & 0 & 1 \\ 0 & 1 & 0 \\ 1 & 0 & 0 \end{bmatrix}.$$

Assume deviation $b = -10$, the activation function $RELU(x) = \max(0, x)$. In order to obtain the feature graphs of convolutional layer 1, we need the following operations:

1. Use w_1 to perform convolution of input data. The result is showed in Figure 7.20(b).

2. Figure 7.20(c) shows the result with added deviation.

3. After activation, we obtain the feature map 1 of convolutional layer 1, as shown in Figure 7.20(d).

4. Repeating the above steps over weight matrix w_2 and w_3, we get the feature map 2 and 3 of convolutional layer 1, as shown in Figure 7.20(e) and Figure 7.20(f).

In order to obtain the feature graphs of max-pooling layer 1, we choose the maximum value of every nonoverlapping 2×2 area in each output feature map and conduct a 2×2 max-pooling operation. Figure 7.20(g) shows the resulting feature map after the max-pooling at layer 1. ∎

Example 7.8 How a CNN Works with Pooling and Overlapped Processing
We can understand how to realize convolution through the convolution operation for an image of 8×8, as shown in Figure 7.21. The dimension of the convolution kernel is 4×4; and the feature matrix is:

$$w = \begin{pmatrix} 1 & 0 & 1 & 0 \\ 0 & 0 & 1 & 1 \\ 0 & 1 & 0 & 1 \\ 1 & 1 & 0 & 0 \end{pmatrix}.$$

We extract an image x_1 of 4×4 from the image of 8×8 for the convolution operation with the feature matrix. Here, we obtain the value y_1 for the first neuron in the hidden layer by utilizing the equation $y_i = w \times x_i$. The step size of the convolution is set as 1. We continue to extract image x_2 of 4×4, and obtain the value y_2 for the second neuron through the convolution operation. We repeat the aforementioned steps until the traverse of the whole image is completed.

After the calculation for all values of neurons in the hidden layer is completed, a feature map corresponding to a convolution kernel is obtained. Usually, we calculate values of the output feature map in the hidden layer utilizing the activation function. The frequently

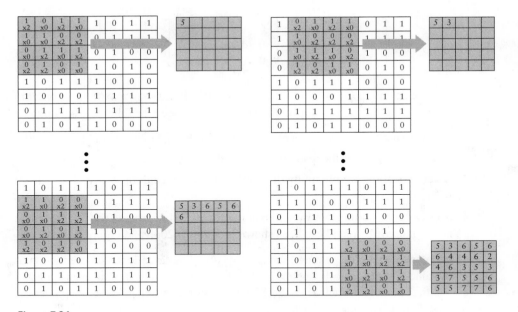

Figure 7.21:
Schematic diagram for a convolutional neural network. Source: http://ufldl.stanford.edu/wiki/index.php/UFLDL _Tutorial.

used activation functions are: sigmoid function $\left[\sigma(x) = \dfrac{1}{1 + e^{-x}} \right]$, hyperbolic tangent function $\left[\tanh(x) = \dfrac{e^x - e^{-x}}{e^x + e^{-x}} \right]$, and RELU function $[\text{RELU}(x) = \max(0, x)]$.

Assume the number of input feature maps x of convolution layer l is n. We adopt the equation $y_j = f\left(\displaystyle\sum_{i=1}^{n} (w_{ij} * x_i + b_i) \right)$ to calculate the output feature map in convolution layer l, where b stands for deviation, w stands for weight matrix, and f stands for activation function. If convolution layer l has m filters, the number of the weight matrix w is $n \times m$, corresponding to the m filters, and the convolution layer l will have m output maps (see Figure 7.21).

The quantity of neurons in the hidden layer is $n_y = \left(\left| \dfrac{n_{l-1} - n_k}{s} \right| + 1 \right) \times \left(\left| \dfrac{m_{l-1} - m_k}{s} \right| + 1 \right) \times m$, where the dimension of input data is $n_{l-1} \times m_{l-1}$, the size of filter is $n_k \times m_k$, the step size of convolution is s (the distance that the convolution moves at each time), and the quantity of filters is m. As shown in Figure 7.21, the items of the schematic diagram of convolution are: 8 * 8 numbers of input data, 4×4 convolution window, 1 step size of convolution, 1 feature map, and the quantity of neurons in hidden layer is:

$$n_l = \left(\left| \frac{8-4}{1} \right| + 1 \right) \times \left(\left| \frac{8-4}{1} \right| + 1 \right) \times 1 = 5 \times 5. \ \blacksquare$$

CNNs are often used in image recognition systems. They have achieved an error rate of 0.23% on the National Institute of Standards and Technology (MNIST) database. The learning process was fast in the MNIST experiments. When applied to facial recognition, they were able to contribute to a large decrease in the error rate. One reported result shows a 97.6% recognition rate on 5,600 still images of more than ten categories. CNNs have been used to assess video quality in an objective way after being manually trained.

ImageNet for large-scale visual recognition is a benchmark in object classification and detection, with millions of images and hundreds of object classes. In the ILSVRC 2014, the winner was GoogLeNet from the DeepDream project. This team achieved a mean average precision of object detection of 0.439329 and a reduced classification error of 0.06656. Their CNNs applied more than 30 layers. Performance of CNN on the ImageNet tests is now close to that of humans. In 2015 a many layered CNN demonstrated the ability to spot faces from a wide range of angles, including upside down, even when partially occluded, with competitive performance.

7.4.3   Connectivity in Deep Neural Networks

Deep learning problems apply deep neural networks, which have forward propagation and reverse learning. There are many types of deep learning architecture. Most of these architectures are used to change the common architecture. In Figure 7.22, we divide deep learning architecture into three types according to the connectionist models of neurons: *fully connected*, *locally connected*, and many other deep learning networks.

- *Fully connected networks:* In the traditional neural network, the connections between layers from input layer, hidden layer, to output layer are fully connected. One neuron in the previous layer connects with every neuron in the next layer. DL architecture like *deep belief networks* (DBNs), *deep Boltzmann machines* (DBMs), *stacked autoencoders* (SAEs), *stacked denoising autoencoders* (SDAEs), *deep stacking networks* (DSNs), and *tensor deep stacking networks* (TDSNs) are fully connected.

- *Locally connected networks:* Locally connected DL architecture means the connection mode between input layer and output layer is locally connected. This kind of DL architecture takes CNN as the representative class. It uses the concept of partial connection and weight sharing of convolutional operation to describe local features. Thus, it reduces the

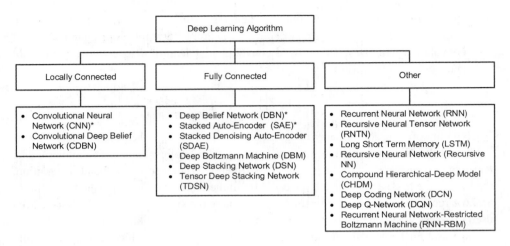

Figure 7.22

A taxonomy of various deep learning neural network models. Reprinted with permission from K. Hwang and M. Chen, *Big Data Analytics for Cloud, IoT and Cognitive Learning*, Wiley, 2017[6].

number of weights greatly. *Convolutional deep belief networks (*CDBNs) are also locally connected.

- ***Other neural networks:*** This class includes RNN, *recursive neural tensor network* (RNTN), *long short-term memory* (LSTM), etc. Other related networks include the *recurrent neural network-restricted Boltzmann machine* (RNN-RBM), *deep Q network* (DQN), *compound hierarchical-deep model* (CHDM), *deep coding network* (DCN), etc. Conventional ANNs, either locally connected or fully connected, may have limited applicability, because they perform badly or become powerless when dealing with data streams.

7.4.4   Recurrent Neural Networks (RNNs)

An RNN is a special class of ANNs, where connections between neurons form a directed cycle, including some self-reflective connections. This creates an internal state of the network which allows it to exhibit some temporal behavior, dynamically. Unlike feedforward neural networks, RNNs use their internal memory to process arbitrary sequences of inputs. This makes them applicable to tasks such as speech or unsegmented connected handwriting recognition. An RNN is created by applying the same set of weights recursively over a graph-like structure. RNNs are trained by the reverse mode of automatic differentiation and have been applied to natural language processing.

An RNN considers current output of a data stream also related to the previous output. That means information processing at the current time needs to consider the output from the last time. Training a single-layer RNN for 100 time steps is equivalent to training a feedforward network with hundreds of layers, as shown in Figure 7.23. When an RNN processes

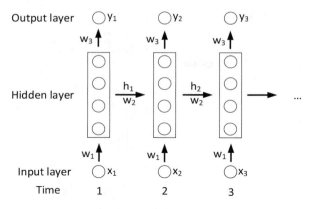

Figure 7.23
The structure of a recurrent neural network (RNN).

a sequence of data, the previous output will feedback as part of the input data. The RNN must remember the previous output for calculating the current output iteratively. There exist connections between the nodes of hidden layers in the network structure. The input of the hidden layer needs to use the output of the input layer and the output of itself iteratively.

Learning Process in Using RNNs

In using an RNN, the gradient descent method can be applied to change each weight in proportion to the derivative of the error with respect to that weight, provided that nonlinear activation functions are differentiable. Various methods for doing so were developed in the past. The standard method is called *backpropagation through time* (BPTT). This is a generalization of backpropagation for feedforward networks. Another approach is to use *real-time recurrent learning* (RTRL). Unlike the BPTT, this algorithm is local in time but not local in space. There is also an online hybrid between BPTT and RTRL with intermediate complexity and there are variants for continuous time. A major problem with gradient descent for standard RNN architectures is that error gradients vanish exponentially quickly with the size of the time lag between important events.

At each time point t, the RNN corresponds to an ANN with three layers. The input and output of RNN at time t are represented as x_t and y_t', respectively, and the hidden layer is represented as h_t. We use the same network parameters (w_1, w_2, w_3) at all times, in which the connection weight between input and hidden layer is w_1, the weight between hidden layer of time $t-1$ and hidden layer of time t is w_2, and the weight between hidden layer and output layer is w_3 (see Figure 7.24). The forward computation is done as follows: the input at time t is x_t, the value h_t of the hidden layer is computed by the current input value x_t, and the value h_{t-1} of the hidden layer at time $t-1$. The output value y_t' is obtained while regarding h_t as the input of the output layer. This figure attempts to reveal the differences between a RNN and an ANN operation.

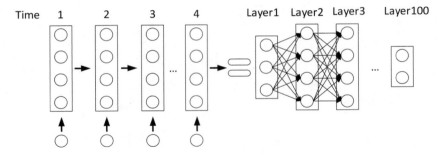

Figure 7.24
Contrast between a recurrent neural network (RNN) and an ANN.

Input and Output Relationship in Different Neural Networks

RNN receives a sequence of inputs and also produces a sequence of outputs. According to different applications, there are different forms of input or output pairs, which are shown in Figure 7.25 in four cases: in Figure 7.25(a), the I/O structure is especially useful for image capturing application. Figure 7.25(b) shows the I/O structure for having multiple inputs with a single output, which matches with document classification.

In Figure 7.25(c), both input and output are sequential. This is practiced in RNN for video streaming applications frame by frame. This architecture is also suitable for statistical prediction of the future situation. In Figure 7.25(d), we input the known data at time 1 and time 2, the prediction starts at time 3. After inputting the data at time 3, we get the output result 1. This implies that we have predicted the data at the next time as 1. In the same way, we get the output result 2 after inputting the data 1 at time 4 and predicting the data at time 5 as 2. In Table 7.9, we list a number of common software libraries developed for using RNNs.

Most deep learning networks are feedforward networks, such as SAE or DBN, which means the signal process flow in one layer is unidirectional from input to output. Unlike feedforward neural networks, RNN receives a sequence of input and also produces sequence values as output. RNN is a neural network including temporal behavior. This implies that the output of a sequence is fed as input to the next input. RNNs appeal to model language or speech recognition processes. The nodes between hidden layers are no longer unconnected but connected, and the inputs of the hidden layer include not only the current input but also the output of the hidden layer from the last time.

7.5 Deep Learning of Other Brain Functions

In this section, we scan through other deep learning neural networks proposed by various researchers in recent years. Brief descriptions of these networks are provided below. In particular, we cover the Boltzmann machines and deep belief networks. When training ANN,

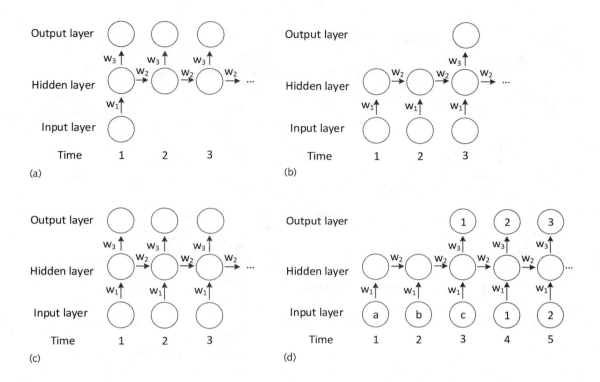

Figure 7.25
Four different forms of input or output applied in different deep learning applications: (a) image capturing (b) document classification (c) classify video frame by frame (d) statistical prediction.

cost value, i.e., the gap between ANN predicted output and actual output, is used to adjust weights and biases over and over throughout the training process. The progress of training follows the tendency of the gradient, which is analogous to a slope. The training process is like rolling a rock down the slope. A rock moves quickly to the surface if the gradient is high. When the gradient is small, the training process of ANN is slow. However, the gradient could potentially vanish back through the nets.

Typically, the gradient is much smaller in the earlier layers. As a result, the early layers are hard to train. However, the early layers correspond to simple patterns and building blocks, especially in facial recognition. The error will propagate in the following layers in ANN. In early years before 2006, there was no way to train ANN, due to the fundamental problem of a vanishing gradient during the training process. Below we introduce the *restricted Boltzmann machine* (RBM), *deep belief network* (DBN) and their training methods and applications.

Table 7.9
Software libraries for deep learning recurrent neural networks

Software Library and Developer	A Brief Description and Developer Information
Caffe (Berkeley Vision and Learning Center)	This package supports both CPU and GPU. Developed in C++, and has Python and MATLAB wrappers.
Deeplearning4j (www.apaxhe.org)	Deep learning in Java and Scala on multi-GPU-enabled Spark. Allows the creation of custom layers. Integrates with Hadoop and Kafka.
TensorFlow (www.tensorflow.org)	Apache 2.0-licensed Theano-like library with support for CPU, GPU, and Google's proprietary TPU and mobile applications.
Theano (deeplearning.net/software/ theano)	The reference deep-learning library for Python with an API largely compatible with the popular NumPy library.
Torch (www.torch.ch)	A scientific computing framework with wide support for machine learning algorithms, written in C and lua, used at Facebook AI Research and Twitter.

Source: en.wikipedia.org/wiki/Recurrent_neural_network

7.5.1 Restricted Boltzmann Machines

RBM is a neural network model that can realize unsupervised learning. It includes two layers, visible layer V and hidden layer H, which are connected by an undirected graph. There is no connection among neurons in the same layer. In this section, we only introduce the V and H as the binary unit. The input of RBM is an m-dimensional vector data V, where $V = (v_1, v_2, \ldots, v_m)$ and $v_i \in \{0.1\}$. v_i stands for binary state of neuron i in the visible layer. The output of RBM is an n-dimensional vector H, where $H = (h_1, h_2, \ldots, h_n)$ and $h_j \in \{0.1\}$. h_j stands for binary state of neuron j in the hidden layer (Figure 7.26).

Now, we give a simple example to understand the learning process of RBM, as shown in Figure 7.27. The goal is to obtain the answer to the following question: Which shapes compose the input graph? There are only two kinds of components in the graph, i.e., square and triangle. Let's use code 1 and code 0 to represent the square shape and the triangle shape, respectively. Let's assume the coding sequences are upper-left corner, upper-right corner, lower-left corner and lower-right corner. Then, the input graph corresponds to a four digit code, i.e., 1011. In Figure 7.26, we show the *mapping* from layer V to layer H. Then we use symmetric mapping and H to reconstruct layer V. The following operations are performed.

1. A code of 1011 is obtained as V. Through mapping, the expression of 01 in layer H is calculated, which means the input graph consists of triangles. Then, symmetrical mapping is adopted to obtain 0011 as the value of V1.

2. To calculate the error between the distribution of V and V1, revise the mapping parameters according to the error.

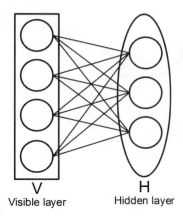

Figure 7.26
The structure of a single stage of a restricted Boltzmann machine (RBM).

3. Repeat step 1 and step 2 with new mapping. Conduct training and establish RBM after completion of training. It includes layer V, layer H and the mapping between the two layers.

From Figure 7.27 we see the need to find good mapping. Now we can use the *contrastive divergence* (CD) algorithm, which can quickly obtain mapping. Mapping means parameters of the RBM network. We define $\theta = (w, bv, bh)$ as mapping, which we learned from the RBM network, w as a link weight between visible layer V and hidden layer H, $w \in R^{m \times n}$. w_{ij} is the link weight between visible neuron i and hidden neuron j, bv is a vector composed of the deviation of each neuron in visible layer, bv_i stands for deviation value of visible neuron i. $bv \in R^m$, bh is a vector composed of deviation of each neuron in hidden layer, $bh \in R^n$. bh_j stands for deviation value of hidden neuron j. The task of learning RBM is to establish RBM network structure or obtain optimal parameter θ^* by CD learning.

7.5.2 Deep Belief Networks

Deep belief network (DBN) is a hybrid deep learning model, which was proposed by Geoffrey Hinton et al. in 2006. Figure 7.28 shows that a DBN includes one visible layer V and n hidden layers. DBN is composed of n stacked RBM, which means the hidden layer of the previous RBM is the visible layer of the next RBM. The original input is visible layer V. This layer V together with hidden layer H_1 consists of one RBM. H_1 is the visible layer V_2 of the second RBM. This hidden layer H_1 together with hidden layer H_2 consists of one RBM and so on. All adjacent layers form a RBM.

In Figure 7.28(a), the visible layer and hidden layer of the top layer are part of an undirected connection, which is called *associative memory*. The RBM visible layer

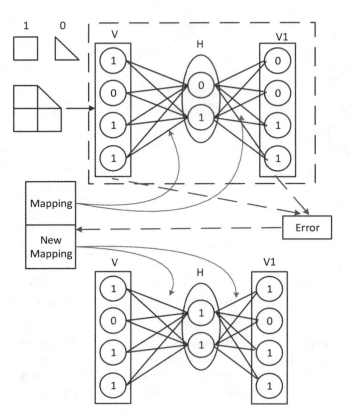

Figure 7.27
Schematic diagram for learning image composition by RBM.

in the top layer consists of hidden layer H_{n-1} in the previous RBM and category labels. The number of neurons in the visible layer above is the sum of the neurons' number in H_{n-1} and the category number. The training of DBN is divided into two parts: unsupervised training and supervised fine-tuning. Unsupervised training uses a large number of data without labels to train RBM one by one. Supervised fine-tuning uses a small amount of data with labels to fine adjust the parameters of each layer in the whole network.

Fine-tuning uses sample data as the input data of the visible layer of DBN and the label of the sample as a part of the visible layer of the top RBM layer. The category labels data y of the sample are expressed with neurons. In other words, if there are m kinds of category labels data of the sample, there will be m neurons to express them. Setting the neuron which

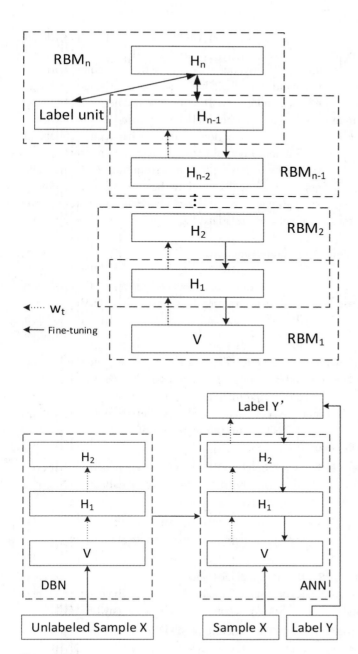

Figure 7.28
The structure of a deep belief network (DBN).

corresponds to the category is equal to 1. BP algorithm can be used to adjust network parameters when utilizing DBN for fine-tuning.

DBN can not only be used to classify directly, but also can use the trained network parameters to conduct artificial neural network initialization. This application mainly includes two parts: unsupervised trained DBN and supervised fine-tuned neural network. As shown in Figure 7.28(b), we can input sample data x without labels and train DBN by the unsupervised training algorithm above to get the connection parameters between each layer. It is the same with DBN to define the number of neural network layers and neurons of each layer. We can use the parameters of DBN which were obtained from training to the initial neural network. Then, we input sample data x with label into the neural network. Finally, we use the correct classification y and y', which we obtained above, to calculate the error and the training method of the neural network, to adjust the parameters of each layer.

7.5.3   Deep Learning to Explore Other Brain Functions

Deep learning is a growing area with hundreds of papers published per year. Many new deep learning networks are proposed or tested for upgrading their capability with various brain functions or cognitive power. We briefly review a few of such new neural network models as follows:

- *Recursive neural tensor networks (RNTNs):* RNTNs are recursive deep neural network structures. RNTNs use a tensor-based composition function for all nodes in a tree structure. This class was suggested for processing input data with variable length or making multistage predictions. RNTNs and RNNs both have recursive behaviors [18]. RNNs are the recursion of time sequence and RNTNs are the recursion of data structure, called *tensors* (to be covered in Chapter 9).

- *Convolutional deep belief networks (CDBNs):* CDBN is a network structure that combines CNN with DBN. It can be utilized to solve the problems of extending DBN to process images with full size and high dimension.

- *Deep Q networks (DQNs):* DQN is a deep neural network structure, which is put forward by Google DeepMind. It combines reinforcement learning methods, Q-learning, and artificial neural networks.

- *Deep Boltzmann machines (DBMs):* DBM includes one visible cell layer and a series of hidden cell layers. There is no connection among the same layer. DBM is a deep structure of stacking several RBMs, and there are undirected connections between any two layers.

- *Stacked denoising autoencoder (SDAE):* The structure of SDAE is similar to a stacked autoencoder. The only difference is changing AE to a denoising autoencoder (DAE). DAE utilizes unsupervised training methods, which includes three steps, i.e., corrupting, encoder, and decoder.

- *Deep stacking networks (DSNs):* DSN uses simple neural network modules to stack deep networks, and the number of modules is uncertain. The output of each module is a category. The input of a module in the first layer is initial data. From the second layer on, the input of modules is the series connection of initial data x and output y of previous layers.

- *Tensor deep stacking networks (TDSNs):* TDSN is the extension of deep stacking networks (DSN). It includes many stacked blocks. Each stacked block includes three layers, i.e., input layer x, two parallel hidden layers h_1 and h_2, and output layer y.

- *Long short-term memory (LSTM):* LSTM is the improvement of RNN, which adds memory modules in hidden layers of basic RNN. LSTM can solve weak influence problems of hidden layers in a previous time point to the hidden layers in a following time point, when using basic RNN for training.

- *Deep predictive coding networks (DPCNs):* DPCN is a hierarchical generative model, which is a deep learning network that can use context data to realize self-updating.

- *Compound hierarchical-deep model:* This model composes deep networks with non-parametric Bayesian models. Features can be learned using deep architectures such as DBN, DBM, stacked autoencoder, etc.

- *Recurrent Neural Network-Restricted Boltzmann Machine (RNN-RBM):* This is a recurrent temporal RBM that has feedback connections that is time varying for extended function beyond RNN and RBM.

7.6 Conclusions

Smart AI machines or robots or systems are very much in demand by the high-tech industry. All major companies are competing for this rapidly growing market. We reviewed the progress made at Amazon, Google, IBM, Intel, Nvidia, etc. in this chapter. Also, we surveyed some AR and VR vendors and their products. Blockchains were introduced for protection of chains of business transactions in a distributed environment like clouds and data centers. Deep learning applies artificial neural networks of various kinds. Convolutional or recursive neural networks are highlighted, especially attractive for implementing cognitive applications. In the remaining chapters we will apply the machine and deep learning algorithms we have learned in Part III. using the available software tools from Hadoop, Spark, and TensorFlow.

Homework Problems

7.1: Visit the Google X Lab website. Find the technical details of all current projects or projects that have been completed. Write a technical report based on your investigative findings.

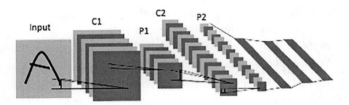

Figure 7.29
Structure diagram of convolutional neural network for image classification.

7.2: Visit the websites of two AR vendors and two VR vendors listed in Table 7.1. Write an investigative report to summarize your technical findings of their product features, functions performed, and technology basis applied.

7.3: Use a CNN (Figure 7.29) to perform image classification. The image has an input layer with 32×32 resolution, and the network includes a convolution layer (C1) and a max-pooling layer (P1). Follow the steps below to carry out the classification task.

(a) Assume the convolution kernel size of C1 in CNN is 5×5, the stride is 3, and the number of feature maps is 6. Calculate the size of each feature map in C1.

(b) The size of the pooling area in P1 is 2×2. Calculate the size of each feature map in a pooling layer.

(c) Let the convolution kernel size of C1 in CNN be 3×3, the stride be 1, and the number of feature maps is 6. Calculate the size of each feature map in C1.

(d) The size of the pooling area in P1 is 3×3. Calculate the size of each feature map in a pooling layer.

7.4: Many gas sensors face a cross-sensitivity problem. For example, a gas sensor is often unable to accurately detect the presence of poison gas. We can solve the problem by using an array of sensors to detect the cross-sensitivity characteristics over an ANN. Table 7.10 gives three gas sensor measurements. Gas condition 1 refers to gas existence and 0 means no gas leakage. Design an ANN model with the given data to distinguish the gas type characterized by X_1: 0.4, X_2: 0.5, and X_3: 0.4.

7.5: Table 7.11 shows the Iris flower data set with only two species: *setosa* (denoted by 1) and *versicolor* (denoted by 0). We can differentiate these data items by their petal length, petal width, sepal length, and sepal width. Design an ANN model to classify the Iris flowers using a clustering approach.

(a) Compute the number of neurons in an input layer of the neural network, and illustrate which flower's features are presented by these neurons, respectively.

Table 7.10
Data of gas sensors and corresponding gas conditions

Sensitivity (X_1)	Sensitivity (X_2)	Sensitivity (X_3)	Gas A (Y_1)	Gas B (Y_2)
0.63	0.56	0.68	1	0
0.55	0.44	0.65	0	1
0.46	0.78	0.64	0	1
0.37	0.55	0.44	1	1
0.58	0.43	0.33	1	0
0.65	0.79	0.35	0	0
0.89	0.35	0.40	0	1
0.58	0.99	0.36	0	1
0.54	0.89	0.32	1	1
0.40	0.55	0.31	1	0
0.69	0.38	0.39	1	0

Table 7.11
Sample data of iris flowers characterized in four attributes

ID. No.	Petal Length	Petal Width	Sepal Length	Sepal Width	Species
1	5.1	3.5	1.4	0.2	1
2	7.0	3.2	4.7	1.4	0
3	5.2	3.4	1.6	0.3	1

(b) Explain the number of neurons in an output layer and how these neurons represent the categories of flowers.

(c) Simply illustrate the process of training and classification and interpret the final clustering results.

7.6: An electronic gas sensor changes its resistance with certain gas. We can determine gas concentration according to the change ratio in resistance, known as sensitivity. However, the resistance of the semiconductor sensor will also vary with temperature and humidity. The sensitivity data set of 16 tests is given in Table 7.12. Use this data set to design an ANN model to assess the gas concentration with $X_1 : 28$, $X_2 : 50$, and $X_3 : 0.4$.

7.7: Assume the handwritten numeral recognition network only has three layers: a convolution layer, a max-pooling layer, and an output layer. If the input is the 8×8 matrix, write a program to calculate the feature graph after the convolution layer and max-pooling layer. The characteristic matrix of the convolution layer must be designed. The pool area is 2×2, and the input matrix of 8×8 is in Table 7.13.

Table 7.12
Temperature, humidity, and gas concentration to measure sensor sensitivity

Temperature (X_1)	Air humidity(X_2)	Sensitivity (X_3)	Concentration of gas (Y)
20	45	0.50	20
22.5	60	0.46	23
23.0	57	0.43	33
21.5	57	0.44	34
26.5	64	0.33	45
28.5	59	0.35	44
23.0	37	0.40	41
26.0	66	0.36	47
29.5	72	0.32	45
35.0	83	0.31	48
30.0	76	0.29	56
20.0	45	0.45	39
22.5	77	0.39	40
23.0	57	0.35	52
21.8	46	0.39	48
24.8	67	0.32	51

Table 7.13
Image data matrix used in Problem 7.7

5	3	17	8	34	137	45	0
0	20	0	0	204	13	0	6
4	0	0	253	0	0	0	2
0	0	198	0	5	0	3	0
6	186	0	146	0	7	0	2
0	139	0	0	176	0	0	0
0	157	0	0	154	0	2	0
4	0	173	182	0	0	0	0

7.8: Given in Figure 7.30, an ANN with linearly activated neurons, i.e., the output y, is a weighted summation of its input signals $y = \sum_{i=1}^{n} w_i x_i$, where w_i is the weight of input signal x_i to that neuron. The numbers at the input arrows at neurons n1 and n2 are the input signals. The numbers at the edges are weights applied on that edge. For example, the edge between n1 and n3 has a weight $w_{13} = -1$. Assume the weights on two input edges are equal to 1.

(a) Calculate the input and output of all neurons (n3, n4, and n5) and the final output of output layer neurons (n6, n7) with respect to input signals (2, 4) to (n1, n2), respectively.

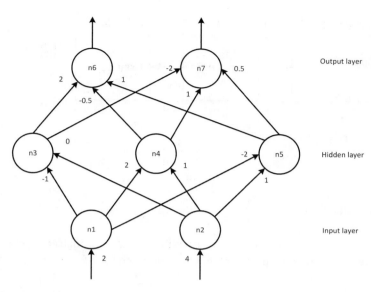

Figure 7.30
An ANN for Problem 7.8.

(b) What is the output of the network if the input signals are changed to (1, 2) for (n1, n2), respectively? Do you have to repeat all the calculations in part(a)? Is there a shortcut to generate the final output in one step based the results obtained in part(a)?

7.9: This problem requires you to use convolutional neural networks (CNNs) to perform image classification tasks. The image has an input layer with 5×5 resolution, and the network includes a convolution layer (C1), a max-pooling layer (P1), and a fully-connected layer. Input binary image as seen here:

$$input\_matrix = \begin{Bmatrix} 1 & 1 & 1 & 0 & 0 \\ 0 & 1 & 1 & 1 & 0 \\ 0 & 0 & 1 & 1 & 1 \\ 1 & 0 & 1 & 0 & 1 \\ 0 & 1 & 0 & 1 & 0 \end{Bmatrix}.$$

Assume the convolution kernel size (also called the receptive field) of C1 is 2×2, the stride is 1, and the number of filters is 1 (see Figure 7.31). You are expected to answer the following problems:

(a) Calculate the number of neurons in the convolutional layer.

(b) Compute the output feature map of this layer, where:

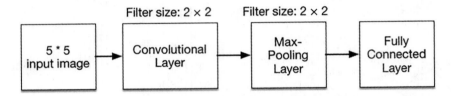

Figure 7.31
The convolutional neural network image for Problem 7.9.

The weight matrix of the filter is $w = \left\{ \begin{array}{cc} 1 & 0 \\ 1 & 1 \end{array} \right\}$.

(c) Define a max-pooling layer with a receptive field with a size of 2×2 matrix. Use a stride of 2 to ensure that there is no overlapping. Compute the output feature map of this layer.

References

[1] Bengio, Y., et al. "Representation Learning: A Review and New Perspectives." *Pattern Analysis and Machine Intelligence* 35 no. 8 (2013): 1798–1828.

[2] Graves, A., A. Mohamed, and G. Hinton. "Speech Recognition with Deep Recurrent Neural Networks: Acoustics, Speech and Signal Processing (ICASSP)." IEEE International Conference on Acoustics, Speech, and Signal Processing (ICASSP) (2013): 6645–6649.

[3] Hinton, G., and R. Salakhutdinov. "Efficient Learning of Deep Boltzmann Machines." Journal of Artificial Intelligence and Statistics 3: (2009): 448–455.

[4] Honglak, L., R. Grosse, R. Ranganath, and A. Y. Ng. "Convolutional Deep Belief Networks for Scalable Unsupervised Learning of Hierarchical Representations." *ICML* (2009): 609–616.

[5] Hutchinson, B., L. Deng, and D. Yu. "Tensor Deep Stacking Networks." *IEEE Transactions on Pattern Analysis and Machine Intelligence* 1–15 (2012): 1944–1957.

[6] Hwang, K., and M. Chen. *Big Data Analytics for Cloud, IoT and Cognitive Computing.* Wiley, 2017.

[7] Kaelbling, L. P., M. L. Littman, and A. W. Moore. "Reinforcement Learning: A Survey." *Journal of Artificial Intelligence Research* vol 4 (1996): 237–285.

[8] LeCun, Y., L. Bottou, Y. Bengio, et al. "Gradient-Based Learning Applied to Document Recognition." *Proceedings of the IEEE* 86 no. 11 (1998): 2278–2324.

[9] Mnih, V., et al. "Human-Level Control through Deep Reinforcement Learning." *Nature* 518 (2015): 529–533.

[10] Rifai, S., Y. Bengio, A. Courville, et al. *Disentangling Factors of Variation for Facial Expression Recognition: Computer Vision—ECCV 2012.* Springer, 2012.

[11] Salakhutdinov, R., A. Mnih, and G. Hinton. "Restricted Boltzmann Machines for Collaborative Filtering." *ACM Proceedings of the 24th International Conference on Machine Learning* (2007): 791–798.

[12] Salakhutdinov, R., J. B. Tenenbaum, and A. Torralba. "Learning with Hierarchical-Deep Models." *IEEE Transactions on Pattern Analysis and Machine Intelligence* 35 no. 8 (2013): 1958–1971.

[13] Schmidhuber, J. "Deep Learning in Neural Networks: An Overview." *Journal of Neural Networks* 61 (2015): 85–117.

[14] Schmidhuber, J. "Learning Complex, Extended Sequences Using the Principle of History Compression." *Journal of Neural Computation* 4 no. 2 (1992): 234–242.

[15] Socher, R., et al. "Recursive Deep Models for Semantic Compositionality over a Sentiment Treebank." Proc. IEEE Conference on Empirical Methods in Natural Language Processing, 2013.

[16] Socher, R., J. Pennington, E. H. Huang, et al. "Semi-supervised Recursive Autoencoders for Predicting Sentiment Distributions." *Proceedings of the Conference on Empirical Methods in Natural Language Processing, Association for Computational Linguistics* (2011): 151–161.

[17] Sun, Y., X. Wang, X. Tang. "Deep Learning Face Representation from Predicting 10,000 Classes." *Proceedings of the IEEE Conference on Computer Vision and Pattern Recognition* (2014): 1891–1898.

[18] Xiaoli, L., et al. "Cambricon: Instruction Set Architecture for Neural Networks." ACM/IEEE 43rd Annual International Symposium of Computer Architecture (ISCA), 2016.

[19] Zhang, J., et al. "Evolutionary Computation Meets Machine Learning: A Survey." *IEEE Computational Intelligence Magazine* 6 no. 4 (2011): 68–75.

PART IV
CLOUD PROGRAMMING AND PERFORMANCE BOOSTERS

This final part presents three chapters on cloud programming paradigms, software tools, and big data application development. Specifically, we will learn the essence of MapReduce, Hadoop, Spark, TensorFlow, and GraphX in Chapters 8 and 9. Other supporting software packages are examined including HDFS, YARN, Mesos, Kubernetes, Storm, AlphaGo, OpenStack, etc. Chapter 10 is devoted to cloud performance, privacy, and security issues. Major public cloud platforms are evaluated by benchmark programs, such as Intel HiBench, CloudSuite, TPC-W, and YCSB. These cloud systems, programming paradigms, machine learning methods, and software tools are illustrated with 90 examples throughout the book.

Chapter 8: Programming with Hadoop and Spark on Clouds

Summary: This chapter is devoted to studying popular software libraries for cloud computing. By extending the MapReduce paradigm to a Java environment, Hadoop becomes more user friendly and widely applied in most cloud platforms. Spark further extends Hadoop from batch mode to streaming execution, machine learning, and graph processing. Hadoop and Spark programming are given by examples running on the AWS cloud. We illustrate how MapReduce, Hadoop, and Spark are used in executing SQL, streaming, MLlib, and GraphX applications.

Chapter 9: TensorFlow, Keras, DeepMind, and Graph Analytics

Summary: This chapter is devoted to studying the principles and tools developed in Google's TensorFlow and DeepMind programs. Google realizes many machine intelligence and cognitive functions in daily-life applications. We will review Google's TensorFlow software platform for developing deep learning systems in speech and image recognition. DeepMind's AlphaGo program applies reinforcement learning to beat the top Go player. The chapter also studies graph-theoretic properties of social networks in social analytics applications. These graph analytics tools are used for big data analysis and solving the community detection problem.

Chapter 10: Cloud Performance, Privacy, and Security

Summary: In this final chapter, we study a wide range of cloud performance issues and benchmark programs. This chapter covers cloud elasticity, throughput, efficiency, scalability, QoS, productivity, and so on. We study various elastic scaling methods including the scale-out, scale-up, and autoscaling schemes. Network threats to cloud platforms are identified and some cloud security enforcement schemes are introduced. In particular, we examine mobile clouds and assess some data privacy preservation schemes. Distributed trust management and reputation systems are introduced to secure data centers where most of the cloud platforms are built today.

Chapter **8**
Cloud Programming with Hadoop and Spark

8.1 Scalable Parallel Computing Over Large Clusters

Cloud programming tools are introduced in this section. We will learn the original Map-Reduce from Google, and the Apache Hadoop and Spark programming models. All of these are open source available to all programmers. They run on a large-scale cluster of servers, either on clouds or on supercomputers. We will review some open-source or commercial software libraries for cloud programming applications.

8.1.1 Characteristics of Scalable Computing

Because handling the whole data flow of parallel and distributed programming is very time-consuming and also needs specialized knowledge of programming, dealing with these issues may affect the productivity of the programmer and may even result in affecting the program's time to market. Furthermore, it may detract the programmer from concentrating on the logic of the program itself. Therefore, parallel and distributed programming paradigms or models are offered to abstract many parts of the data flow from users.

In other words, these models aim to provide users with an abstraction layer to hide implementation details of the data flow, for which users formerly would write codes. Therefore, simplicity of writing parallel programs is an important metric for parallel and distributed programming paradigms. Other motivations behind parallel and distributed programming models are: (1) to improve productivity of programmers; (2) to decrease programs' time to market; (3) to leverage underlying resources more efficiently; (4) to increase system throughput; and (5) to support higher levels of abstraction nodes or workers. The system issues are discussed for running parallel programs in a distributed cluster of servers. Partitioning is applicable to both computation and data as follows:

- **_Computation partitioning:_** Computation partitioning splits a given job or program into smaller tasks. Partitioning greatly depends on correctly identifying portions of the job or program that can be performed concurrently. In other words, upon identifying parallelism in the structure of the program, it can be divided into parts to be run on different workers. Different parts may process different data or a copy of the same data.

- *Data partitioning:* Data partitioning is splitting the input or intermediate data into smaller pieces. Similarly, upon identification of parallelism in the input data, it can also be divided into pieces to be processed on different workers. Data pieces may be processed by different parts of a program or a copy of the same program.

- *Mapping:* Mapping is assigning either the smaller parts of a program or smaller pieces of data to underlying resources. This process that aims to appropriately assign such parts or pieces to be run simultaneously on different workers is usually handled by resource allocators in the system.

- *Synchronization:* Because different workers may perform different tasks, synchronization and coordination between workers is necessary so that race condition is prevented and data dependency between different workers is properly managed. Multiple accesses to a shared resource by different workers may raise race condition, whereas data dependency happens when a worker needs the processed data of other workers.

- *Communication:* Because data dependency is one of the main reasons of communication between workers, communication is always triggered when the intermediate data is ready to be sent among workers.

- *Scheduling:* In a user program, when the computation parts (tasks) or data pieces are more than the available workers, a scheduler selects a sequence of tasks or data pieces to be assigned to the workers. The resource allocator performs the mapping of computation or data pieces to workers, while the scheduler only picks the next part from the queue of unassigned tasks based on a set of rules called scheduling policy.

For multiple jobs or programs, a scheduler selects a sequence of jobs or programs to be run on the distributed computing system. Resources scheduling demands high efficiency in Hadoop and Spark programming. The loose coupling of components in distributed resources makes it possible to schedule elastic *virtual machines* (VMs) to yield higher fault tolerance and scalability than traditional programming models using the *message passing interface* (MPI) library.

8.1.2 From MapReduce to Hadoop and Spark

Cluster computing was meant to encourage general-purpose applications. However, both MapReduce and Hadoop are designed for bipartite graph computing. On the speed side, Spark extends the MapReduce model to support interactive queries and streaming processing using in-memory computing. Spark offers the ability to run computations in memory, which is more efficient than MapReduce running on disks for complex applications. Spark is highly accessible, offering simple *application programming interfaces* (APIs) in Python, Java, Scala,

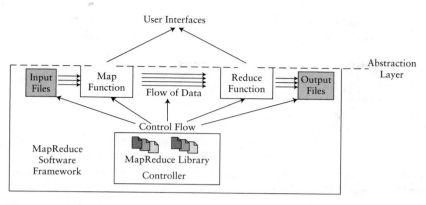

Figure 8.1
MapReduce software framework over the MapReduce pipeline engine.

structured query language (SQL), etc. Spark can run in Hadoop clusters and access any Hadoop data source like Cassandra.

MapReduce is a software framework that supports parallel and distributed computing on large data sets. This software framework abstracts the whole data flow of running a parallel program on a distributed computing system by providing users with two interfaces in the form of two functions: Map and Reduce. Users can override these two functions to interact with and manipulate the data flow of running their programs. Figure 8.1 illustrates the logical data flow from the Map to the Reduce function in MapReduce frameworks. In this framework, the "value" is the actual data and the "key" part is only used to control the data flow.

Workers in a Cluster

Workers are installed in the physical servers in the cloud cluster. They could be VM instances or application containers. The scheduling of these VMs is automatically launched. Note that explicit scheduling is often performed in clouds either for individual worker roles or for gang-scheduling supported in MapReduce. Queues are a critical concept here as they provide a natural way to manage the task assignment in a fault-tolerant distributed environment.

Map and Reduce Functions

MapReduce performs Map and Reduce functions in a pipelined fashion. There has been substantial interest in "data parallel" languages largely aimed at loosely coupled clusters of servers. The language and runtime spawn many task executions simultaneously. MapReduce applies dynamic execution, fault tolerance, and easy-to-use APIs. The following example explains the concept of Map and Reduce functions, separately.

The following map function emits each word *w* plus an associated count of occurrences (just a "1" is recorded in this pseudo-code).

```
map(String key, String value):
  // key: document name
  // value: document contents
  for each word w in value:
    EmitIntermediate(w, "1");
```

The Reduce function merges the word counts by different map workers into a total count as output. Google MapReduce paradigm was written in C. It evolved from use in a search engine to Google App Engine cloud. Hadoop library was developed for MapReduce programming in Java environments. The original Hadoop implements MapReduce in batch mode over distributed disks. The Spark is improved from Hadoop for in-memory processing in both batch and streaming modes over a *directed acyclic graphs*- (DAG) based computing paradigm.

```
reduce(String key, Iterator values):
  // key: a word
  // values: a list of counts
  int result = 0;
  for each v in values:
    result += ParseInt(v);
  Emit(AsString(result));
```

Initially, Google's MapReduce was applied only in fast search engines, and subsequently MapReduce enabled cloud computing. In the past decade, Apache Hadoop has made it possible for big data processing on large server clusters or clouds. Apache Spark frees up many constraints by MapReduce and Hadoop programming in general-purpose batch or streaming applications.

8.1.3   Application Software Libraries for Big Data Processing

We review some open-source software tools and programming projects that are often used to process big data. Most of them have been developed for big data storage, mining, and analysis in academia and industry. Table 8.1 lists the tool names, categories, URLs, languages used, and relevant sections, and major functionality and applications of these tool sets.

We classify the software libraries below into eight categories, namely: *compute engine* (Hadoop, Spark), *data storage* (HDFS, Cassandra), *resource management* (YARN, Mesos), *query engine* (Impala, Spark SQL), *message system* (StormMQ), *data mining* (Weka), *data analytics* (MLlib, Mahout), and *graphic processing* (GraphX). Details of using these software tools can be found in subsequent sections.

Table 8.1
Representative software libraries for big data processing on clouds

Name, Category, Language, Websites, Relevant Sections	Functionality, Applications, and User Community
Hadoop, compute engine, Java http://hadoop.apache.org/, Sec.8.2	Distributed processing of large data sets using Map-Reduce, mainly in batch processing on clouds or large clusters of servers.
Spark, compute with Java, Scala, Python, https://spark.apache.org/, Sec.8.3–8.5	General-purpose compute engine for both streaming and batch processing. Appeals to real-time applications on clouds or large websites.
HDFS, data storage, Java, C, http://hadoop.apache.org, Sec.8.2.4	A distributed file system that provides high-throughput access to application data.
Cassandra, data storage, C/C++, Java, Python, Ruby, http://cassandra.apache.org, Sec. 8.1.3	A distributed NoSQL for mission-critical data with linear scalability and proven fault tolerance on cloud infrastructure.
YARN, resource manager, Java and C, http://hadoop.apache.org, Sec.8.2.5	A new resource manager of Hadoop, which divides the JobTracker into two parts: resource management and job life-cycle management.
Mesos, resource scheduler developed by Google, http://www.google.com, Sec. 8.3	A resource scheduler developed by Google for scalable cluster computing on IaaS clouds.
Impala, query engine, Java, Python, http://www.cloudera.com, Sec. 8.1.3	Analytic database architected specifically to leverage the flexibility and scalability strengths of Hadoop.
Spark SQL, query engine, Python, Scala, Java, R, https://spark.apache.org/, Sec. 8.4	A query processing module in Spark library for structured or relational data sets data.
StormMQ, message system, Java, C++, http://stormmq.com/, sec. 8.1.3	A message queuing platform using Advanced Message Queuing Protocol (AMQP). It provides a hosted, on-premise or cloud solution for M2M apps.
Spark MLlib, Scala, Python, Java, R, https://spark.apache.org/mllib, Sec. 8.5	A machine learning module in Spark library for data analytics applications.
Mahout, data analytics, Scala, Java, http://mahout.apache.org/, Sec. 8.1	A software library for quickly creating scalable performant ML applications. It supports Hadoop and Spark platforms.
Weka, data mining, Java, Python, http://www.cs.waikato.ac.nz, Sec. 8.1	An ML software written in Java. It offers a collection of machine learning algorithms for data processing and mining tasks.
GraphX, graph processing, Scala, Python, Java, R, https://spark.apache.org/graphx, Sec. 8.5	A graph processing module in Spark library for social / media graph processing in streaming and real-time modes.

8.2 Hadoop Programming with YARN and HDFS

In this section, we learn the basic concept of MapReduce for batch processing of large data sets. In batch processing, we deal with a static data set which will not change during execution. For example, streaming data or real-time data cannot be handled well in batch mode. The batch processing considers only static data sets executed in the original MapReduce framework.

8.2.1 The MapReduce Compute Engine

The MapReduce software framework provides an abstraction layer for data and control flow, as illustrated in Figure 8.1. The data flows from the left end to the right end and the control flow is hidden from users. We consider the following data flow steps: data partitioning, mapping and scheduling, synchronization, communication, and output of results. Partitioning is controlled in user programs by specifying the partitioning block size and data fetch patterns.

Here, the data flow in a MapReduce framework is predefined, and the abstraction layer provides two well-defined interfaces in two functions: Map and Reduce, as exemplified below. These mapper and reducer functions can be defined by the user to achieve specific objectives. Therefore, the user overrides the Map and Reduce functions and then invokes the provided MapReduce (Spec & Results) function from the library to start the flow of data. Map and Reduce functions take a specification object, called *Spec*.

This Spec object is first initialized inside the user's program, and then the user writes code to fill it with the names of input and output files, as well as other tuning parameters. This object is also filled with the names of the Map and the Reduce functions. The MapReduce library is essentially the controller of the MapReduce pipeline. This controller coordinates the dataflow from the input end to the output end smoothly in a synchronous manner. The user interfaces (API tools) are used to provide an abstraction to hide the MapReduce software framework from intervention by users, randomly.

Logical Dataflow

The input data to both the Map and the Reduce function have a particular structure. The same argument goes for the output data too. The input data to the Map function is arranged in the form of a (key, value) pair. For example, the key is the line offset within the input file and the value is the content of the line. The output data from the Map function is structured as (key, value) pairs called intermediate (key, value) pairs. In other words, the user-defined Map function processes each input (key, value) pair and produces a number of intermediate (key, value) pairs. Here, the aim is to process all input (key, value) pairs to the Map function in parallel.

In turn, the Reduce function receives the intermediate (key, value) pairs in the form of a group of intermediate values associated with one intermediate key, (key, [set of values]). In fact, the MapReduce framework forms these groups by first sorting the intermediate (key, value) pairs and then grouping values with the same key. It should be noted that sorting the data is done to simplify the grouping process. The Reduce function processes each (key, [set of values]) group and produces a set of (key, value) pairs (zero, one, or more) as output.

Parallel Batch Processing

Each Map server applies a programmer-supplied map function to each input data split (block). Many mapper functions run concurrently on hundreds or thousands of servers or machine instances. Many intermediate key-value pairs are generated. They are stored in local disks for subsequent use. This disk-based handling of intermediate results is the main reason why the original MapReduce was slow on large clusters. The Reduce server collapses the values using another programmer-supplied function, called *reducer*, such as max., min., average, dot product of two vectors, etc.

Formal MapReduce Model

The Map function is applied in parallel to every input (key, value) pair, and produces a new set of intermediate (key, value) pairs as follows:

$$(key_1, val_1) \xrightarrow{Map\ Function} \text{List}(key_2, val_2) \tag{8.1}$$

Then, MapReduce library collects all the produced intermediate (key, value) pairs from all input (key, value) pairs, and sorts them based on the "key" part. It then groups the values of all occurrences of the same key. Finally, the Reduce function is applied in parallel to each group producing the collection of values as output as illustrated below:

$$(key_2, \text{List}(val_2)) \xrightarrow{Reduce\ Function} \text{List}(val_2) \tag{8.2}$$

After grouping all the intermediate data, the values of all occurrences of the same key are sorted and grouped together. As a result, after grouping, each key becomes unique in all intermediate data. Therefore, finding unique keys is the starting point to solving a typical MapReduce problem. Then, the intermediate (key, value) pairs as the output of the map function will be automatically found.

The following examples explain how to define keys and values in MapReduce problems:

1. Count the number of occurrences of each word in a collection of documents in Example 8.1.

2. Count the number of occurrences of words having the same size and the same number of letters in a collection of documents. The unique keys are identified with each word and intermediate value is the word count.

3. Count the number of occurrences of anagrams in a collection of documents.

Anagrams are words that are formed by rearranging the letters of another word. For example, "listen" can be reworked into the word "silent." The unique keys are an alphabetically sorted sequence of letters for each word. The intermediate "value" is the number of occurrences.

The main responsibility of the MapReduce framework is to efficiently run a user's program on a distributed computing system. Therefore, the MapReduce framework meticulously handles all partitioning, mapping, synchronization, communication, and scheduling details of such data flows. We summarize 12 distinct steps in using the MapReduce engine efficiently. MapReduce architecture is built with a master-worker model, shown in Figure 8.2.

Step 1: Data partitioning of input files: MapReduce library splits the input data files into multiple pieces, called *splits* or *blocks*, that match the number of map workers.

Step 2: Fork out the user program to masters and workers: One copy of the user program runs on the master mode. The map and reduce tasks fork out to map and reduce workers, respectively. The master picks idle workers and assigns tasks to them.

Step 3: Assign map tasks and reduce tasks.

Step 4: Read partitioned data blocks into map workers: Each map worker reads its own block of input data. A map worker may handle one or more input data split.

Step 5: Define the mapper function: The Map function receives the input data split as a set of (key, value) pairs to process and produce the intermediate (key, value) pairs.

Steps 6, 7, 8: Perform the operations of the map workers. The MapReduce library generates many copies of a user program and distributes them on available workers. MapReduce applies simple synchronization policy to coordinate map workers with reduce workers, in which the communication between them starts when all map tasks finish.

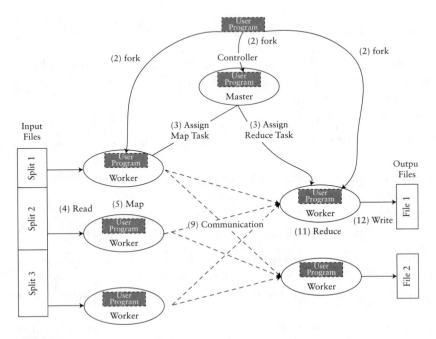

Figure 8.2
Control flow implementation of a MapReduce cluster of workers (servers).

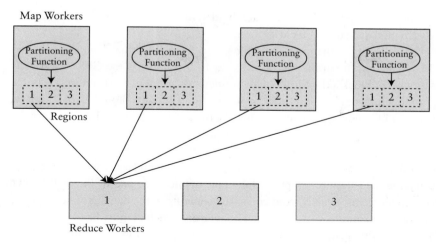

Figure 8.3
The role of MapReduce partitioning functions.

Steps 9, 10: Sort and group (value) pairs: MapReduce framework sorts and groups the intermediate (key, value) pairs before forwarding them to reduce workers. The intermediate (key, value) paired with identical keys are grouped together because all values inside each group should be processed by only one Reduce function to generate the final result.

Step 11: Perform the reduction function: Reduce worker iterates over the grouped (key, value) pairs, and for each unique key, sends the key and corresponding values to the Reduce function. Reduce workers may face a problem of network congestion caused by the reduction or merging operation performed.

Step 12: Write the results to output files: The reduce worker will ouput the final results to output files.

As shown in Figure 8.3, intermediate (key, value) pairs produced by each map worker are partitioned into R regions, which are equal to number of reduce tasks. This guarantees that (key, value) pairs with identical keys are stored in the same region. To implement such a technique, a partitioning function could simply be a hash function (e.g., *Hash(key) mod R*) to forward the data into particular regions.

Compute-Data Locality
MapReduce software framework was first proposed and implemented by Google. The first implementation was coded in C language. The implementation takes advantage of Google File System (GFS) as the underlying layer. MapReduce could perfectly adapt itself to GFS.

GFS is a distributed file system where files are divided into fixed-size blocks (chunks) and blocks are distributed and stored on cluster nodes.

MapReduce library splits the input data (files) into fixed-size blocks, and ideally performs the Map function in parallel on each block. In this case, as the GFS has already stored files as a set of blocks, the MapReduce framework just needs to send a copy of the user's program containing the Map function to the nodes already stored as data blocks. This is the notion of sending computation toward data rather than sending data toward computation.

Example 8.1 Word Count Using MapReduce over Partitioned Data Set

To clarify the data flow, a sample MapReduce application, one of the well-known MapReduce problems, namely word count (the counting of the number of occurrences of each word in a collection of documents), is presented here. Figure 8.4 demonstrates the dataflow of the word count problem for a simple input file containing only two lines as follows:

(1) "most people ignore most poetry."
(2) "most poetry ignores most people."

In this case, the Map function simultaneously produces a number of intermediate (key, value) pairs for each line content so that each word is the intermediate key with "1" as its intermediate value, e.g., (ignore, 1). Then, the MapReduce library collects all the generated intermediate (key, value) pairs and sorts them to group the "1"s for identical words, e.g., (people, [1,1]). Groups are then sent to the Reduce function in parallel so that it can sum up the "1" values for each word and generate the actual number of occurrences for each word in the file, e.g., (people, 2). ∎

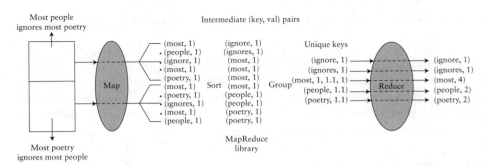

Figure 8.4
The dataflow of a word-count program through the MapReduce engine.

8.2.2   MapReduce for Parallel Matrix Multiplication

In multiplying two $n \times n$ matrices $A = (a_{ij})$ and $B = (b_{ij})$, we need to perform n^2 dot product operations to produce an output matrix $C = (c_{ij})$. Each dot product produces an output element $c_{ij} = a_{i1} \times b_{1j} + a_{i2} \times b_{2j} + \cdots + a_{in} \times b_{nj}$, corresponding to the i-th row vector in matrix A multiplied by the j-th column vector in matrix B. Mathematically, each dot product takes n multiply-and-add (or partial product) time units to complete. Therefore, the total matrix multiply complexity equals $n \times n^2$, since there are n^2 output elements.

In theory, the n^2 dot products are totally independent of each other, and they can be done on n^2 servers in n time units. However, when n is very large, say millions or higher, it is too expensive to build a cluster with n^2 servers. In practice, we consider the use of N servers where $N \ll n^2$. Therefore, the parallel execution time could be done in $n^3 / (n^2/N) = N$ time units. The ideal speedup is expected to be N. In what follows, we illustrate the process of using MapReduce to perform parallel matrix multiplication. For visualization purposes, we consider a small example of $n = 2$ and $N = 3$ in using a MapReduce cluster with two mappers (servers) and one reducer.

Example 8.2 MapReduce Multiplication of Two Matrices

This example shows how to apply the MapReduce method to multiply two 2×2 matrices: $A = (a_{ij})$ and $B = (b_{ij})$ with two mappers and one reducer. We map the first row of matrix A and entire matrix B to one Map server. Then map the second and third rows of matrix A and entire matrix B to the second and third Map servers, respectively. Four keys are used to identify four blocks of data processed:

$$A \times B = \begin{bmatrix} a_{11}, \ a_{12} \\ a_{21}, \ a_{22} \end{bmatrix} \times \begin{bmatrix} b_{11}, \ b_{12} \\ b_{21}, \ b_{22} \end{bmatrix} = \begin{bmatrix} c_{11}, \ c_{12} \\ c_{21}, \ c_{22} \end{bmatrix} = C.$$

A dataflow graph for the MapReduce cascade is given in Figure 8.5. On the left, we partition matrix A and matrix B^T by rows into two blocks, horizontally, where B^T is the transposed matrix of B. The arrows between the row blocks indicate how data blocks are read (mapped) into the two mappers. All intermediate computing results are identified by their <key, value> pairs. Four keys—K_{11}, K_{12}, K_{21}, and K_{22}—are used, simply denoted by the matrix element indices.

We show the generation, sorting, and grouping of four < key, value > pairs by each mapper in two stages. Each short pair <key, value> holds a single partial-product value identified by its key. The long pair holds two partial products identified by each block key. The Reducer is used to sum up the output matrix elements from using four long <key, value(s)> pairs. When the matrix order becomes very large, the time to multiply very large matrices becomes cost prohibitive. Consider each machine instance to have

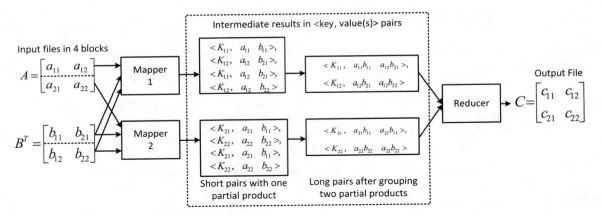

Figure 8.5
MapReduce for parallel matrix multiplication with <key, value> pairs showing as the intermediate results before and after grouping.

six mappers and two reducers. Each mapper handles *n/6* adjacent rows of the input matrix. Each reducer generates *n/2* of the output matrix *C*. ∎

Three parallel computing models are specified in Figure 8.6, namely *map-only, classic MapReduce,* and *iterative MapReduce*. We characterize these models below, along with applications that apply to them.

Map-only Model
A simplified parallel processing mode is the *map-only* execution mode. This model applies to embarrassingly parallel computations by which all subdivided tasks are totally independent from one another. They are carried out in one stage, as shown in Figure 8.6(a). The following are applications suitable for applying a map-parallel model for parallel computing:

- document conversion (e.g., PDF->HTML);
- brute force searches in cryptography;
- parametric sweeps;
- gene assembly; and
- Polar Grid MATLAB data analysis (http://www.polargrid.org).

Classic MapReduce Model

The classic MapReduce is modeled in Figure 8.6(b) for parallel execution of tasks that can be described by two-stage bipartite graphs. Computational tasks suitable to this model are as follows:

- high energy physics (HEP) histograms;
- distributed search;
- distributed sort;
- information retrieval;
- calculation of pairwise distances for sequences (BLAST);
- expectation maximization algorithms;
- linear algebra;
- data mining;
- clustering;
- k-means;
- deterministic annealing clustering; and
- multidimensional scaling (MDS).

Iterative MapReduce Model

The iterative MapReduce is modeled in Figure 8.6(c). This applies the classic MapReduce, iteratively, in many passes through the engine. The best example of iterative MapReduce is the Twister software tool developed at Indiana University. This model has been commercialized by Microsoft. Indiana University has applied Twister in bioinformatics applications. The potentials of Twister are listed as follows:

- expectation maximization algorithms;
- linear algebra;

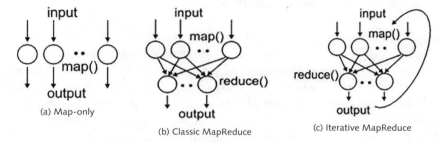

(a) Map-only

(b) Classic MapReduce

(c) Iterative MapReduce

Figure 8.6
Comparison of Map-only, Classic MapReduce, and iterative MapReduce computations.

Table 8.2
MapReduce and its variants in Hadoop and Twister

Features	Google MapReduce	Apache Hadoop	Twister
Execution Mode and Platform	Batch MapReduce on Linux cluster	Batch or real-time MapReduce on Linux cluster	Iterative MapReduce on EC@ or Linux clusters
Data Handling	GFS (Google File System)	HDFS (Hadoop Distributed File System)	Local disks and data management tools
Job Scheduling	Data locality	Data locality; rack aware; dynamic task scheduling	Data locality; static task partitions
HLL Support	Sawzall	Pig Latin	Pregel

- data mining;
- clustering;
- k-means;
- deterministic annealing clustering; and
- multidimensional scaling (MDS).

In Table 8.2, we compare three software packages that are based on using MapReduce. We consider their differences in four technical aspects: execution mode, data handling, job scheduling, and high-level language (HLL) support area. Google MapReduce was written in C language, and is used primarily in batch processing based on the bipartite Map-Reduce graph. It emphasizes data locality and was supported by an HLL Sawzall and GFS and BigTable in Google cloud. Apache Hadoop supports not only batch mode but also real-time applications. Hadoop applies the Hadoop Distributed File System (HDFS) supported by YARN scheduler and Pig Latin. Twister is based on iterative MapReduce that can be applied in parallel tasks described by DAG graphs. Local disks are used in handling distributed data. The language Pregel has been used along with Twister. There is also a commercial version of Twister marketed by Microsoft.

8.2.3 Hadoop Architecture and Recent Extensions

Apache Hadoop is an open-source software library for distributed storage and distributed processing. The package applies very large data sets on computer clusters built from commodity servers. All the modules in Hadoop are designed under the assumption that hardware failures are common and should be automatically handled by the framework. The core of Apache Hadoop consists of a storage part (HDFS) and a processing engine (MapReduce). Hadoop splits files into large blocks and distributes them across nodes in a cluster. To process data, Hadoop transfers packaged code for nodes to process in parallel based on the data that needs to be processed. This approach takes advantage of data locality to allow

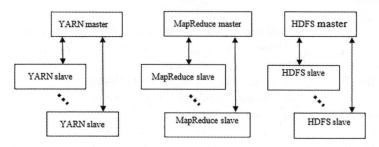

Figure 8.7
Three major functional modules in a Hadoop execution environment.

the data set to be processed faster and more efficiently than it would be in a conventional supercomputer.

The base Apache Hadoop architecture is shown in Figure 8.7. The framework is composed of the following modules: the Hadoop Common package, which provides a file system and OS-level abstractions, a MapReduce engine (either MapReduce/MR1 or YARN/MR2), and the HDFS. The Hadoop Common package contains the necessary Java Archive (JAR) files and scripts needed to start Hadoop.

- *Hadoop Common* contains libraries and utilities needed by other Hadoop modules.
- *Hadoop Distributed File System* is a distributed file system that stores data on commodity machines, providing very high aggregate bandwidth across the cluster.
- *Hadoop YARN* is a resource-management platform responsible for managing computing resources in clusters and using them for the scheduling of users' applications.
- *Hadoop MapReduce engine* is an implementation of the MapReduce programming model for large-scale data processing.

For effective scheduling of work, every Hadoop-compatible file system should provide location awareness: the name of the rack where a worker node is. Hadoop applications can use this information to execute code on the node where the data is, and, failing that, on the same rack/switch to reduce backbone traffic. HDFS uses this method when replicating data for data redundancy across multiple racks. This approach reduces the impact of a rack power outage or switch failure: if one of these hardware failures occurs, the data will remain available.

The Hadoop framework is mostly written in Java programming language with some native code in C and command line utilities written as shell scripts. Although MapReduce Java code is common, any programming language can be used with Hadoop Streaming to implement the "map" and "reduce" parts of the user's program. Other projects in the Hadoop ecosystem expose richer user interfaces.

MapReduce Engine in Hadoop

Hadoop MapReduce engine manages the data flow and control flow of MapReduce jobs over the cloud cluster. This shows the MapReduce engine architecture cooperating with HDFS. The engine has a master/slave architecture consisting of a single JobTracker as master and a number of TaskTrackers as slaves (workers), as shown in Figure 8.8. The JobTracker manages the whole MapReduce job over a cluster and is responsible for monitoring jobs and assigning tasks to TaskTrackers. TaskTracker manages the execution of map and/or reduce tasks on a single computation node in the cluster.

If the work cannot be hosted on the actual node where the data resides, priority is given to nodes in the same rack. This reduces network traffic on the main backbone network. If a TaskTracker fails or times out, that part of the job is rescheduled. The TaskTracker on each node spawns a separate Java Virtual Machine process to prevent the TaskTracker itself from failing if the running job crashes its JVM. A heartbeat is sent from the TaskTracker to the JobTracker every few minutes to check its status. The JobTracker and TaskTracker status and information can be viewed from a web browser.

Each TaskTracker node has a number of simultaneous execution slots, and each executes either a map or a reduce task. Slots are defined as the number of simultaneous threads supported by CPUs of the TaskTracker node. For example, a TaskTracker node with N CPUs, each of which supports M threads, has $M \times N$ simultaneous execution slots. Each data block is processed by one map task running on a single slot. Therefore, there is a one-to-one

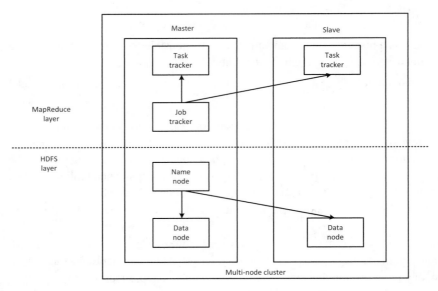

Figure 8.8
Key components in a Hadoop MapReduce engine interacting with the HDFS.

correspondence between map tasks in a TaskTracker and data blocks in the respective DataNode.

A small Hadoop cluster includes a single master and multiple worker nodes. The master node consists of a JobTracker, TaskTracker, NameNode, and DataNode. A slave or *worker node* acts as both a DataNode and TaskTracker, although it is possible to have data-only worker nodes and compute-only worker nodes. Hadoop requires Java Runtime Environment (JRE) 1.6 or higher. The standard startup and shutdown scripts require that Secure Shell (SSH) be set up between nodes in the cluster.

In a larger cluster, HDFS nodes are managed through a dedicated NameNode server to host the file system index and a secondary NameNode that can generate snapshots of the NameNode's memory structures, thereby preventing file-system corruption and loss of data. Similarly, a stand-alone JobTracker server can manage job scheduling across nodes. When Hadoop MapReduce is used with an alternate file system, the NameNode, secondary Name-Node, and DataNode architecture of HDFS are replaced by the file-system-specific equivalents.

The Hadoop library can be deployed in traditional data centers as well as in clouds. The cloud allows organizations to deploy Hadoop without having to acquire hardware or have specific setup expertise. The following cloud providers have currently offered Hadoop services: Microsoft, Amazon, IBM, Google, and Oracle and they are briefly introduced below.

- *Hadoop on Microsoft Azure:* Azure HDInsight is a service that deploys Hadoop on Azure cloud. The HDInsight uses Hortonworks HDP, jointly developed for HDI with Hortonworks. HDI allows programming extensions with .NET. HDInsight also supports the creation of Hadoop clusters using Linux with Ubuntu. It is also possible to run Cloudera or Hortonworks Hadoop clusters on Azure Virtual Machines.

- *Hadoop on Amazon EC2/S3 services:* Hadoop runs well on EC2 and S3. As an example, the *New York Times* used 100 Amazon EC2 instances and a Hadoop application to process 4 TB of raw image TIF data (stored in S3) into 11 million finished PDFs in the space of 24 hr at a computation cost of about $240.

- *Amazon Elastic MapReduce:* The EMR at Amazon runs Hadoop. The system works with provisioning of the Hadoop cluster, running and terminating jobs, and handling data transfer between EC2 (VMs) and S3 (object storage). These are automated by EMR. Apache Hive, built on top of Hadoop, is applied for providing data warehouse services in EMR.

- *Hadoop on CenturyLink Cloud:* The CenturyLink Cloud (CLC) offers Hadoop via a managed and unmanaged model. CLC also offers customers several managed Cloudera Blueprints, the newest managed service being in the CLC with a big data Blueprints portfolio consisting of Cassandra and MongoDB solutions.

Table 8.3
Recent extensions of Hadoop programming tools

Hadoop Core	HLL Extensions	SQL, Analytics	Processing Modes	Database and Resource Managers
HPDS, YARN, MapReduce	Weave, Scalding, Cascalog, Crunch, Cascading, Pig, Sawzall, Dryad	Impala, Hive, R, RHadoop, rhipe, Mahout	Spark, Storm Summingbird, ElephantDB, HBase, Hive	Ambari, HBase, Sqoop, ZooKeeper, Cassandra

Recent Hadoop Extensions

Table 8.3 summarizes recent extensions of Hadoop at various development and user groups. Hadoop library has become the most popular software for cloud users. HDFS is a Hadoop distributed file system, and is also a core component in the Hadoop ecosystem. YARN is the resource manager in a new version of Hadoop. Cloudera Impala provides SQL-based data analytics for Hadoop. Spark is a booming big data analytics platform, which outperforms other counterparts in terms of big data processing by using memory computing. Finally, Mahout and Weka provide open sources for various *machine learning* (ML) algorithms.

Zookeeper, StormMQ, Mesos, and Nagios provide under-layer supporting environments for big data. Hadoop was originally written in Java. Some HLLs are developed for running Hadoop programs. For example, Pig Latin is used to write applications in HLL and get recognized by Hadoop programs. Sawzall is for running MapReduce using the Google App Engine cloud.

Some of the Hadoop extensions, such as Impala and Mahout, are covered in Table 8.1. We will also study the HPDS, YARN, and MapReduce in the Hadoop core (Section 8.3). Most Spark packages are covered in Sections 8.4 and 8.5. The remaining extensions are briefly introduced below:

- *Ambari project* is a collection of web-based tools extending the Hadoop library for provisioning, managing, and monitoring Apache Hadoop clusters. They also support HDFS, MapReduce, Hive, and Sqoop with a dashboard for viewing cluster health and diagnosing their performance.

- *ZooKeeper* is a high-performance coordination service for distributed applications. Pig Latin is a high-level data-flow language used in the AWS Hadoop execution framework.

- *Spark* is an expressive programming model for Hadoop data to be executed in streaming and general graph computation. Hive offers a data warehouse infrastructure that provides data summarization and ad hoc querying in data analytics applications. R, RHadoop, and Rhipe provide support analytics.

- *HLL extensions* for cloud applications include Pig, Sawzall, Dryad, Weave, Scalding, Cascalog, Crunch, and Cascading.

• **Summingbird, Storm, and ElephantDB** offer extensions from the existing processing modes in Hadoop, Cassandra, and HBase to support scalable database applications.

8.2.4 Hadoop Distributed File System

HDFS, inspired by Google GFS, is a distributed file system that organizes files and stores their data on a distributed computing system. HDFS has a master/slave architecture containing a single NameNode as master and a number of DataNodes as workers (slaves). To store a file in this architecture, HDFS splits the file into fixed-size blocks (e.g., 64MB) and stores them on workers (DataNodes). The mapping of blocks to DataNodes is determined by the NameNode. The NameNode (master) also manages the file system's metadata and namespace (Figure 8.9).

In such systems, namespace is the area maintaining the metadata, and metadata refers to all of the information stored by a file system that is needed for the overall management of all files. For example, NameNode in the metadata stores all information regarding the location of input splits/blocks in all DataNodes. Each DataNode, usually one per node in a cluster, manages the storage attached to the node. Each DataNode is responsible for the storing and retrieving of its file blocks.

A Hadoop cluster has nominally a single NameNode plus a cluster of DataNodes, although redundancy options are available for the NameNode due to its criticality. Each DataNode serves up blocks of data over the network using a block protocol specific to HDFS. The file system uses TCP/I = sockets for communication. Clients use *remote procedure call* (RPC) to communicate between each other.

HDFS stores large files in GB or TB across multiple machines. It achieves reliability by replicating the data across multiple hosts, and hence theoretically does not require

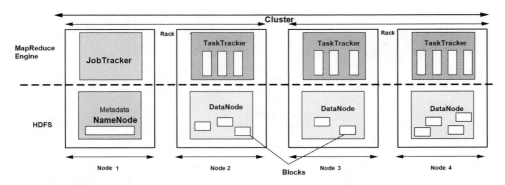

Figure 8.9
HDFS and MapReduce engine installed with, multiple nodes of a Hadoop server cluster.

redundant array of independent disks (RAID) storage on hosts (but to increase I/O performance some RAID configurations are still useful). For example, with a replication value, 3, data is stored on three nodes: two on the same rack, and one on a different rack. Data nodes can talk to each other to rebalance data, move copies around, and keep the replication of data high.

The HDFS file system includes a so-called *secondary NameNode*, a misleading name that some might incorrectly interpret as a backup NameNode for when the primary NameNode goes offline. In fact, the secondary NameNode regularly connects with the primary NameNode and builds snapshots of the primary NameNode's directory information, which the system then saves to local or remote directories. These checkpointed images can be used to restart a failed primary NameNode without having to replay the entire journal of file system actions and then edit the log to create an up-to-date directory structure.

An advantage of using HDFS is data awareness between the JobTracker and TaskTracker. The JobTracker schedules map or reduce jobs to task trackers with an awareness of the data location. For example: if node A contains data (x,y,z) and node B contains data (a,b,c), the JobTracker schedules node B to perform map or reduce tasks on (a,b,c) and node A would be scheduled to perform map or reduce tasks on (x,y,z). This reduces the amount of traffic that goes over the network and prevents unnecessary data transfer.

HDFS is mounted directly with a Filesystem in Userspace (FUSE) virtual file system on Linux and some other Unix systems. File access is achieved through the native Java API, the Thrift API to generate a client in the language of the user's choosing (C++, Java, Python, PHP, Ruby, Erlang, Perl, Haskell, C#, Cocoa, Smalltalk, and OCaml), the command-line interface, browsed through the HDFS-UI web application (web app) over HTTP, or via third-party network client libraries. Several key functions of the HDFS are shown in Figure 8.10.

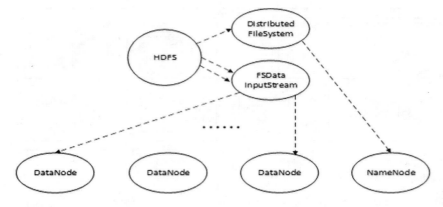

Figure 8.10
HDFS framework and its interaction with data nodes and name nodes.

- **Reading a file:** To read a file in HDFS, a user sends an "open" request to the NameNode to get the location of file blocks. For each file block, the NameNode returns the address of a set of DataNodes containing replica information of the requested file. The number of addresses depends on the number of block replicas. Upon receiving such information, the user calls "read" to connect to the closest DataNode containing the first block of the file. After the first block is streamed from the respective DataNode to the user, the established connection is terminated and the same process is repeated for all blocks of the requested file until the whole file is streamed to the user.

- **Writing to a file:** To write a file in HDFS, a user sends a "create" request to the NameNode to create a new file in the file system namespace. If the file does not exist, the NameNode notifies the user and allows him/her to start writing data to the file by calling the "write" function. The first block of the file is written to an internal queue termed "data queue" while a data streamer monitors its writing into a DataNode.

  Since each file block needs to be replicated by a predefined factor, the data streamer first sends a request to the NameNode to get a list of suitable DataNodes to store replicas of the first block. The steamer then stores the block in the first allocated DataNode. Afterward, the block is forwarded to the second DataNode by the first DataNode. The process will continue until all allocated DataNodes receive a replica of the first block from the previous DataNode. Once this replication process is finalized, the same process will start for the second block and continues until all blocks of the file are stored and replicated on the file system.

- **Block replication:** To reliably store data in HDFS, file blocks are replicated in this system. In other words, HDFS stores a file as a set of blocks and each block is replicated and distributed across the whole cluster. The replication factor is set by the user and is 3 by default.

- **Replica placement:** The placement of replicas is another factor to fulfill the desired fault tolerance in HDFS. Although storing replicas on different DataNodes located in different racks across the whole cluster provides more reliability, it is sometimes ignored as the cost of communication between two nodes in different racks is relatively high in comparison with that of different nodes located in the same rack. Therefore, sometimes HDFS compromises its reliability to achieve lower communication costs. For example, for the default replication factor of three, HDFS stores: (1) one replica in the same node the original data is stored; (2) one replica on a different node but in the same rack; and (3) one replica on a different node in a different rack to provide three copies of the data.

- **Heartbeat and Blockreport message:** Heartbeats and Blockreports are periodic messages sent to the NameNode by each DataNode in a cluster. Receipt of a Heartbeat implies that the DataNode is functioning properly, while each Blockreport contains a list of all blocks on a DataNode. NameNode receives such messages because it is the sole decision maker of all replicas in the system.

8.2.5 Hadoop YARN for Resource Management

YARN is a resource scheduler that allows for distributed processing of large data sets across clusters of computers using simple programming models. It is designed to scale up from single servers to thousands of servers, each offering local computation and storage. The module supports high availability through smart failure detection and management at the application layer.

Figure 8.11 shows three levels of managers built in the YARN. The *resource manager* (RM) looks over the global resources at the highest level by supervising the *node managers* (NM) and *application manager* (AM) at the lower levels. NMs manage VMs and containers. The AM handles a collection of application containers as an orchestration group. YARN was designed to work with Message-Passing Interface (MPI), Hadoop, and Spark libraries.

By default, Hadoop uses first-in-first-out (FIFO) scheduling, and optionally five priority heuristics to schedule jobs from a work queue. The job scheduler was refactored out of the

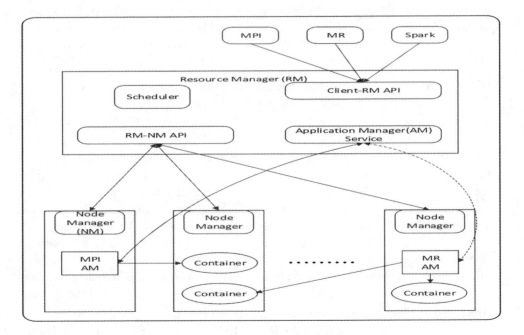

Figure 8.11
The YARN architecture for Hadoop resource management using three levels of managers to manage resources, applications, and nodes hierarchically.

JobTracker, while adding the ability to use an alternate scheduler. Two scheduling policies offer the alternative following choices:

- *Fair Scheduler* was developed by Facebook. The goal of the Fair Scheduler is to provide fast response times for small jobs and *quality of service* (QoS) for production jobs. The Fair Scheduler has three basic concepts: (1) jobs are grouped into pools; (2) each pool is assigned a guaranteed minimum share; and (3) excess capacity is split between jobs. By default, jobs that are uncategorized go into a default pool. Pools have to specify the minimum number of map slots, reduce slots, and a limit on the number of running jobs.

- *Capacity Scheduler* was developed by Yahoo! The Capacity Scheduler supports several features that are similar to the Fair Scheduler. Queues are allocated a fraction of the total resource capacity. Free resources are allocated to queues beyond their total capacity. Within a queue a job with a high level of priority has access to the queue's resources. There is no preemption once a job is running with Hadoop.

> **Example 8.3 Hadoop Implementation of a MapReduce WebVisCounter Program**
> In this example, we present a practical MapReduce program coded in Hadoop termed WebVisCounter. This sample program counts the number of times users connect to or visit a given website using a particular operating system (e.g., Windows XP or Ubuntu Linux). In this case, the input data is shown below. A single line of a typical web server log file has eight fields separated by tabs or spaces with the following meaning:
>
> (1) 176.123.143.12 (IP address of the machine connected)
>
> (2) -- A separator
>
> (3) [10/Sep/2010:01:11:30–1100] (A time stamp of the visit)
>
> (4) "GET /gse/apply/int_research_app_form.pdf HTTP/1.0" (Get request s of the file)
>
> (5) 200 (The status code to reflect success of user's request)
>
> (6) 1363148 (The number of bytes transferred)
>
> (7) "http://www.eng.usyd.edu.au" (User starts here before reaching server)
>
> (8) "Mozilla/4.7[en](WinXp; U)" (The browser used to get the website)
>
> Because the output of interest is the number of times users connect to a given website using a particular operating system, the Map function parses each line to extract the type of the used operating system (e.g., WinXP) as a "key" and assigns a value ("1" in this case) to it. The Reduce function in turn sums up the number of "1"s for each unique "key." ■

8.3   Spark Core and Resilient Distributed Data Sets

Apache Spark is an open-source cluster computing framework. The package was originally developed at the AMPLab at the University of California, Berkeley. Spark extends from batch processing as is the case in Hadoop applications. It extends from a bipartite MapReduce paradigm to pipelined processing of tasks described by DAG. Spark provides an in-memory paradigm to extend Hadoop to streaming, iterative MapReduce, and graph analysis operations. In other word, Spark supports general-purpose parallel computations.

Spark provides an interface for programming the entire clusters with implicit data parallelism and fault tolerance. The idea is centered around a new data structure, called the *resilient distributed dataset* (RDD). This is a read-only multiset of data items distributed over a cluster of machines. The package is maintained in a fault-tolerant way. By removing the limitations imposed in the traditional MapReduce computing paradigm, Spark forces an extended dataflow DAG structure on distributed programs.

A typical Spark application consists of a *driver program* that runs the user's tasks for *parallel executions* on a cluster of servers. The RDDs provide a main abstraction of the Spark execution environment. The RDD offers a collection of data elements partitioned across the nodes of the cluster that can execute the RDD blocks in parallel. RDDs are created by starting with a file in the HDFS or any other Hadoop-supported file system. It is often written as an existing Scala collection in the driver program. Users may also ask Spark to *persist* an RDD in memory, allowing it to be reused efficiently across parallel operations. Also, the RDDs can automatically recover from node failures.

A second abstraction in Spark is *shared variables* that can be used in parallel operations. By default, when Spark runs a function in parallel as a set of tasks on different nodes, it ships a copy of each variable used in the function to each task. Sometimes, a variable needs to be shared across tasks, or between tasks and the driver program. Spark supports two types of shared variables: *broadcast variables*, which can be used to cache a value in memory on all nodes, and *accumulators*, which are variables that are only "added" to, such as counters and sums.

8.3.1   Spark Core for General-Purpose Applications

In this section we introduce the Spark core components and its in-memory execution model for cluster computing.

The Spark Core

As illustrated in Figure 8.12, Spark core provides distributed task dispatching, scheduling, and basic I/O functionalities. These are centered around the RDDs and exposed through APIs for Java, Python, Scala, and R. Spark requires a cluster manager and a distributed storage system. For cluster management, Spark supports its own standalone scheduler,

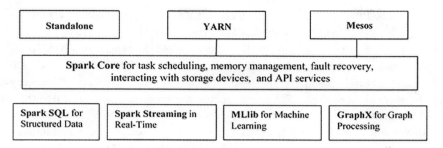

Figure 8.12
The core architecture of the Apache Spark software system.

Hadoop YARN, or Apache Mesos. For distributed storage, Spark can interface with HDFS, MapR File System (MapR-FS), Cassandra, OpenStack Swift, Amazon S3, etc.

Spark also supports a pseudo-distributed local mode, usually used only for development or testing purposes. The distributed storage is not required and the local file system can be used instead. In other words, Spark can run on a single machine with one executor per CPU core. In summary, Spark SQL deals with structured data. Spark Streaming handles live streams of data, MLlib contains common machine learning functionality. GraphX is used for manipulating social network graphs. We will study these features in subsequent subsections.

Spark Distributed Execution Model

To use Spark, developers write a driver program that connects to a cluster of workers, as shown in Figure 8.12. The driver defines one or more RDDs and invokes actions on them. Spark code on the driver also tracks the RDDs' lineage. The workers are cluster servers that can store RDD partitions in RAM across operations. Users provide arguments to RDD operations like map by passing closures (function literals).

Scala represents each closure as a Java object, and these objects can be serialized and loaded on another node to pass the closure across the network. Scala also saves any variables bound in the closure as fields in the Java object. The model reads data blocks from a distributed file system on disks and caches them as persisted RDDs on local RAMs. It is the effective use of the RAMs to hold intermediate computation results that contributes the most to the major speed gain in Spark programming over the traditional Hadoop using distributed local disks.

Iterative data mining demands a user to run multiple ad hoc queries on the same subset of the data. Traditionally, the only way to reuse data between two MapReduce jobs is to write it to an external stable disk storage via a distributed file system. This incurs substantial overhead due to data replication, disk I/O, and serialization. In Spark, this overhead is significantly reduced by caching on the dynamic random access memory (DRAM) in local workers.

In the case of using Pregel for iterative graph computations, one must keep intermediate data in memory, while Hadoop offers an iterative MapReduce interface. However, these frameworks only support specific computation patterns like looping a series of Map-Reduce steps. Data sharing is done implicitly for these patterns. They do not provide abstractions for more general reuse by letting users load several data sets into the memory and run ad hoc queries across them. The Spark execution environment is designed to overcome these difficulties.

Spark was originally written in Scala, which allows concise function syntax and interactive use. Recently, the package has added Java API for standalone application. Readers can refer to development branch on GitHub for more details. Interactive shell is still written in Scala. Spark supports high-level language for the Java VM and object-oriented + functional programming, statically typed. Spark is comparable in speed to Java, but it does not need to write types due to type inference. Spark can interoperate with Java and can use any Java class. It can also call Scala code from Java. See these websites for further information: www.artima.com/scalazine/articles/steps.html, www.artima.com/pins1ed and www.spark project.org/documentation.html.

Example 8.4 Spark Task Scheduling on Scalable Clusters

Figure 8.13 shows the task execution graph of a typical Spark program in three stages. The light-shaded boxes are RDD blocks flowing between task nodes. The dark-shaded boxes are cached partition blocks. *Group by* operation is performed between

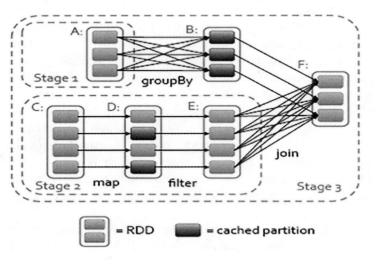

Figure 8.13
A typical task execution DAG graph, showing the scheduling of pipelined operations.

task A and B; *map* between C and D; *filter* between D and E; and *join* at task F as shown by the edges. Parallel execution at task level is implied.

Spark runs general-purpose task graphs such as those characterized by a DAG. Spark operates with cache-aware data reuse and locality. The system offers a partitioning approach to avoid shuffling overheads. Cached RDDs are normally stored as Java objects. Spark supports the fastest access on JVM, but can be larger than ideal. It can also store in serialized format. The scheduling is supported by Hadoop YARN, Google Meso, and the Standalone schedule for Spark applications. ∎

8.3.2 Resilient Distributed Data Sets

Traditionally, MapReduce programs read input data from a disk, map a function across the data, reduce the results of the map, and store reduction results on disk. Spark's RDDs are used as a working set for distributed programs, having the advantage of distributed shared memory, without much relived latency problems. The RDDs facilitate the implementation of iterative algorithms more efficiently. The package also supports interactive and exploratory data analysis. This is particularly beneficial when performing repeated database-style querying of data, a computing paradigm often encountered in ML operations (Figure 8.14).

As a matter fact, Spark was developed to appeal to iterative algorithms often used in training processes in ML applications. MapReduce and Dryad have been adopted for large-scale parallel computing and data analysis. Users write parallel computations using a set of

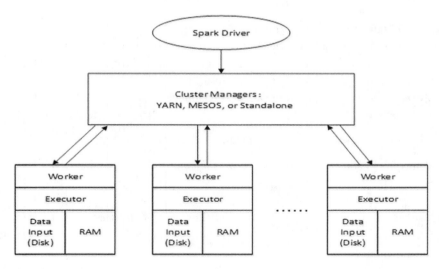

Figure 8.14
Distributed Spark execution model using a cluster of drafted workers (servers).

high-level operators in these programming tools. The driver program invokes parallel operations such as map, filter, or reduce on an RDD by passing a function to Spark. The Spark schedulers distribute the function's execution in parallel on the cluster. For example, the RDDs help implement a *join* operation by producing new RDDs from existing ethernet demarcation devices (EDDs).

The RDDs are immutable and their operations are lazy. In fact, RDDs offer a dynamic data structure for Spark. They enable the cache and distribution of persistent blocks of data around the cluster. New data blocks can be created with join and various Map and Reduce transformation operations. Without RDDs, it is difficult to implement the in-memory Map-Reduce operation in Spark.

Fault tolerance is achieved by tracking the lineage of each RDD or reconstructing the RDDs, in case of some data loss. RDDs can handle any type of Python, Java, or Scala objects. RDDs are used in distributed memory abstraction. This enables programmers to perform in-memory computations on large clusters in a fault-tolerant manner. RDDs are motivated by two types of applications that current computing frameworks handle inefficiently: iterative algorithms and interactive data mining tools. In both cases, keeping data in memory can improve the performance sharply.

As noted earlier, Spark provides two restricted forms of shared variables: *broadcast variables* reference read-only data that needs to be available on all nodes, while *accumulators* are used to program reductions in an imperative style. A typical example of RDD-centric functional programming is given in the following Scala program. Spark's programming abstraction is enabled by effective use of the RDDs.

Example 8.5 Scala Program for Text Processing Using RDDs

This program computes the frequencies of all words occurring in a set of text files and prints the most common ones. Each map, flatMap (a variant of Map) and reduce-ByKey takes an anonymous function that performs a simple operation on a single data item or a pair of items. The program shown here applies its argument to transform an RDD into a new RDD.

val textFiles = spark.wholeTextFiles("somedir")

// Read files from "somedir" into an RDD of (filename, content) pairs.

val contents = textFiles.map(_._2) *// Throw away the filenames.*

val tokens = contents.flatMap(_.split(" ")) *// Split each file into a list of tokens (words).*

val wordFreq = tokens.map((_, 1)).reduceByKey(_ + _)

// Add a count of one to each token, then sum the counts per word type.

wordFreq.map(x => (x._2, x._1)).top(10)

// Get the top 10 words. Swap word and count to sort by count. ∎

To achieve fault tolerance, RDDs provide a restricted form of shared memory, based on coarse-grained transformations rather than fine-grained updates to a shared state. In fact, RDDs are expressive enough to capture a wide class of computations, including recent specialized programming models for iterative jobs, such as Pregel. Data reuse is common in many iterative ML and graph algorithms, including PageRank, k-means clustering, and logistic regression.

Existing abstractions for in-memory storage on clusters, such as distributed shared memory, key-value stores, databases, and Piccolo, offer an interface based on fine-grained updates to a mutable state. With this interface, the only ways to provide fault tolerance are to replicate the data across machines or to log updates across machines. Both approaches are expensive for data-intensive workloads, as they require copying large amounts of data over the cluster network, whose bandwidth is far lower than that of *random access memory* (RAM), and they incur substantial storage overhead.

To understand the benefits of RDDs as a distributed memory abstraction, we compare them against *distributed shared memory* (DSM). In DSM systems, applications read and write to arbitrary locations in a global address space. DSM is a very general abstraction, but this generality makes it harder to implement in an efficient and fault-tolerant manner on commodity clusters. The main difference between RDDs and DSM is that RDDs can only be created through coarse-grained transformations, while DSM reads and writes to each memory location.

This restricts RDDs to applications that perform bulk writes, but allows for more efficient fault tolerance. In particular, RDDs do not need to incur the overhead of checkpointing, as they can be recovered using lineage. Furthermore, only the lost partitions of an RDD need to be recomputed upon failure, and they can be recomputed in parallel on different nodes, without having to roll back the whole program. Another benefit of RDDs is that a system mitigates slow nodes by running backup copies of slow tasks as in MapReduce. Backup tasks would be hard to implement with DSM.

Spark's storage levels are meant to provide different trade-offs between memory usage and CPU efficiency. Spark developers have recommended the following options from which to select:

1. The default storage level (MEMORY_ONLY) is the most CPU-efficient option, allowing operations on the RDDs to run as fast as possible.

2. If not, try using MEMORY_ONLY_SER and selecting a fast serialization library to make the objects much more space-efficient, but still reasonably fast to access with Java and Scala.

3. Do not spill to disk unless the functions that computed your data sets are expensive, or they filter a large amount of the data. Otherwise, recomputing a partition may be as fast as reading it from disk.

4. Use the replicated storage levels if you want fast fault recovery (e.g., if using Spark to serve requests from a web application). *All* the storage levels provide full fault tolerance

by recomputing lost data, but the replicated ones let you continue running tasks on the RDD without waiting to recompute a lost partition.

8.3.3   Spark Programming with RDDs for DAG Tasks

Formally, an RDD is a read-only partitioned collection of data records. RDDs can only be created through deterministic operations on either data in stable storage or from other RDDs. These operations are known as *transformations*. Examples include map, filter, and join. RDDs do not need to be materialized at all times. Instead, an RDD has its lineage about how it was derived from other data sets to compute its partitions from data in stable storage. This is a powerful property, because a program cannot reference an RDD that it cannot reconstruct after a failure.

Spark users can control two other aspects of RDDs: *persistence* and *partitioning*. Users can indicate which RDDs they will reuse and choose an in-memory storage for them. The elements in an RDD can be partitioned across machines based on a key in each record. This is useful for placement optimizations to make two data sets that will be joined together. In Table 8.4, signatures are used to distinguish various operations.

Transformations are lazy operations that define a new RDD. *Actions* launch a computation to return a value to the program or write data to external storage. In join operations, RDDs appear as key-value pairs. The function names are chosen to match with APIs in Scala. For example, map is a one-to-one mapping, while flatMap maps each input value to one or more outputs. The RDD's partition order is identified by a partitioner class. Operations *groupByKey*, *reduceByKey*, and *sort* automatically result in a partitioned RDD.

Spark exposes RDDs through a language-integrated API similar to DryadLINQ used in Azure and FlumeJava. In these cases, each data set is represented as an object. Transformations are invoked on these objects. Programmers start by defining one or more RDDs

Table 8.4
Transformations and actions taken on the RDDs in Spark programming, where Seq(T) denotes a sequence of elements of type T (Source: Zaharia, 2016).

Transformations	$map(f : T \Rightarrow U)$	:	$RDD[T] \Rightarrow RDD[U]$
	$filter(f : T \Rightarrow Bool)$	:	$RDD[T] \Rightarrow RDD[T]$
	$flatMap(f : T \Rightarrow Seq[U])$	:	$RDD[T] \Rightarrow RDD[U]$
	$sample(fraction : Float)$	:	$RDD[T] \Rightarrow RDD[T]$ (Deterministic sampling)
	$groupByKey()$	:	$RDD[(K, V)] \Rightarrow RDD[(K, Seq[V])]$
	$reduceByKey(f : (V, V) \Rightarrow V)$	:	$RDD[(K, V)] \Rightarrow RDD[(K, V)]$
	$union()$	:	$(RDD[T], RDD[T]) \Rightarrow RDD[T]$
	$join()$	:	$(RDD[(K, V)], RDD[(K, W)]) \Rightarrow RDD[(K, (V, W))]$
	$cogroup()$	:	$(RDD[(K, V)], RDD[(K, W)]) \Rightarrow RDD[(K, (Seq[V], Seq[W]))]$
	$crossProduct()$	:	$(RDD[T], RDD[U]) \Rightarrow RDD[(T, U)]$
	$mapValues(f : V \Rightarrow W)$	:	$RDD[(K, V)] \Rightarrow RDD[(K, W)]$ (Preserves partitioning)
	$sort(c : Comparator[K])$	:	$RDD[(K, V)] \Rightarrow RDD[(K, V)]$
	$partitionBy(p : Partitioner[K])$	:	$RDD[(K, V)] \Rightarrow RDD[(K, V)]$
Actions	$count()$	:	$RDD[T] \Rightarrow Long$
	$collect()$	:	$RDD[T] \Rightarrow Seq[T]$
	$reduce(f : (T, T) \Rightarrow T)$	:	$RDD[T] \Rightarrow T$
	$lookup(k : K)$	:	$RDD[(K, V)] \Rightarrow Seq[V]$ (On hash/range partitioned RDDs)
	$save(path : String)$	:	Outputs RDD to a storage system, *e.g.*, HDFS

through transformations on data in stable storage. They can then use these RDDs in action operations that return a value to the application or export data to a storage system. Examples of actions include *count* (which returns the number of elements in the data set), *collect* (which returns the elements themselves), and *save* (which outputs the data set to a storage system).

Spark computes RDDs lazily the first time they are used in an action, so that it can pipeline subsequent transformations. Spark keeps persistent RDDs in memory by default, but it can spill them to disk if there is not enough RAM. Users can also request other persistence strategies, such as storing the RDD only on disk or replicating it across machines, through flags to *persist*. Users can set a persistence priority on each RDD to specify which in-memory data should spill to disk first.

Example 8.6 Lineage Graph for RDDs in PageRank Using Spark

Suppose that a web service is experiencing errors and an operator wants to search terabytes of logs in the HDFS to find the cause. Using Spark, the operator can load just the error messages from the logs into RAM across a set of nodes and query them interactively. This is shown by the first type of the following Scala code: Although individual RDDs are immutable, it is possible to implement a mutable state by having multiple RDDs to represent multiple versions of a data set.

A PageRank algorithm iteratively updates a *rank* (Figure 8.15). The input file *map* links ranks, where the sum is over the scores it received and *N* is the total number of documents. We write the PageRank in Spark as follows:

// Load graph as an RDD of (URL, outlinks) pairs // Build an RDD of (targetURL, float) pairs

// with the contributions sent by each page val contribs = links.join(ranks).

flatMap { (url, (links, rank)) => links.map(dest => (dest, rank/links.size)) }

ranks = contribs.reduceByKey((x,y) => x+y) .mapValues(sum => a/N + (1-a)*sum).

This program was based on the steps shown in Figure 8.15. On each iteration, we create a new rank data set based on the *contribs* and *ranks* from the previous iteration and the static *links data set*. One interesting feature of this graph is that it grows longer with the number. The variables *ranks* and *contribs* in the program point to different RDDs on each iteration as follows:

val links = spark.textFile(. . .).map(. . .).persist() var ranks =

// RDD of (URL, rank) pairs for (i <- 1 to ITERATIONS) { of iterations.

In a job with many iterations, it may be necessary to reliably replicate some of the versions of ranks to reduce fault recovery times. The user can call *persist* with a

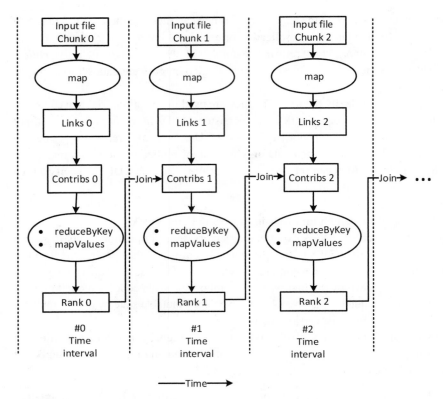

Figure 8.15
The counting process in PageRank algorithm. (Artwork courtesy of Wenhao Zhange, USC, 2016.)

reliable flag to do this. The *links* data set does *not* need to be replicated, because partitions of it can be rebuilt efficiently by rerunning a *map* on blocks of the input file. This data set will typically be much larger than *ranks,* because each document has many links but only one number as its rank, so recovering it using lineage saves time over systems that checkpoint a program entirely in-memory state.

Finally, we can optimize communication in PageRank by controlling the *partitioning* of the RDDs. If we specify a partitioning for links (e.g., hash-partition the link lists by URL across nodes), we can partition ranks in the same way and ensure that the *join* operation between links and ranks requires no communication (as each URL's rank will be on the same machine as its link list). We can also write a custom partitioner class to group pages that link to each other together. Both optimizations can be expressed by calling the *partition,* defined in the following links:

links = spark.textFile(. . .).map(. . .) .partitionBy(myPartFunc).persist()

After this call, the *join* operation between *links* and *ranks* will automatically aggregate the contributions for each URL to the machine with its link lists on, calculate its new rank there, and join it with its links. This type of consistent partitioning across iterations is an optimization in specialized frameworks like Pregel. ∎

Figure 8.16(a) compares the performance of using Spark to assess the PageRank with that of using Hadoop. Three bars are plotted in the comparison experiments: *Basic Spark, Hadoop,* and *Spark with controlled partitioning (optimized).* The iteration time in seconds (s) is shown in the y-axis. The number of machines (workers) is scaled along the x-axis. With 30 machines, the Hadoop takes 171 s, basic Spark takes 72 s, and optimized Spark takes 23 s. Thus, a speed gain in 7.43 is observed. The speedup reduces to 90/14 = 5.7 when 60 machines are used. This is due to the longer overhead experienced when the cluster size is doubled. Figure 8.16(b) shows the relative performance in running a logistic regression application with Hadoop and Spark. One hundred times speedup is observed in Spark over that of Hadoop. In a separate Terasort experiment, the Spark group reported a world record of hundreds of speedup gains of the Spark code over the use of Hadoop.

8.4 Spark SQL and Streaming Programming

In this section, we study the Spark Library for cloud computing. First, we introduce Spark SQL for structured data. We examine the Spark Streaming module for handling life streams of data. Then we study the Spark MLlib for machine learning. Finally, we assess Spark GraphX for graph processing in social media applications.

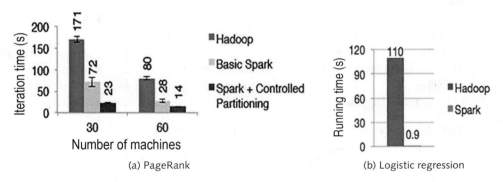

(a) PageRank   (b) Logistic regression

Figure 8.16
Relative performance of running PageRank and logistic regression on Hadoop and Spark separately.

8.4.1 Spark SQL with Structured Data

Spark SQL introduces a data abstraction API called DataFrames (https://spark.apache.org /docs/latest/sqi-programming-guide.html). This package provides support for the processing of structured and relational query processing. Structured data appears mostly in relational databases. Some semi-structured data could be partially structured or use a mixed set of data structures. Spark SQL provides a domain-specific language to manipulate DataFrames in Scala, Java, Python, or R. It mixes SQL queries with Spark programs. Spark SQL can use existing Hive metastore, HiveQL, HiveSerDes, and HiveUDFs, which sit on top of Spark SQL. It also provides SQL language support, with command-line interfaces on the ODBC/ JDBC to use existing *business intelligence* (BI) tools to query the big data. The Impala and Spark SQL are both used for large-scale query processing. The trick for using Spark SQL for query processing is to explore the ability to cache data sets (RDDs) in memory for interactive data analysis. The DataFrames can extract a working set, cache it, and query it, repeatedly. The official website for Spark SQL is: https://spark.apache.org/sql. A typical code to apply functions to results of SQL queries is given below in using Spark SQL:

context = HiveContext(sc)

results = context.sql ("Select * from people")

names = results.map (lambda p: p.name)

Spark SQL includes an optimizer, columnar storage, and code generation to answer queries fast. It can scale to thousands of worker nodes. To get started with Spark SQL, download the Spark package (/downloads.html), which includes the Spark SQL as a module. Then read the Spark SQL and DataFrame guide to learn the API (docs/latest/sqi-programming -guide.html).

Example 8.7 Using DataFrame API for Word Count, Text Search, and Joining Operations
Three example Spark codes are given below to illustrate the Spark applications. The following Spark Python API is applied to count people by age and save countsByAge to S3 in JSON format:

 # Counts people by age

countsByAge = df.groupBy("age").count()

countsByAge.show()

 # Saves countsByAge to S3 in the JSON format.

countsByAge.write.format("json").save("s3a:// . . .")

The following Spark code is used for text search operations:

```
# Creates a DataFrame having a single column named "line"
textFile = sc.textFile("hdfs:// . . .")
df = textFile.map(lambda r: Row(r)).toDF (["line"])
# Counts all the errors
errors = df.filter(col("line").like("%ERROR%"))
# Counts errors mentioning MySQL
errors.count() errors.filter(col("line").like("%MySQL%")).count()
# Fetches the MySQL errors as an array of strings
errors.filter(col("line").like("%MySQL%")).collect()
```

The following code is used for joining of several source files:

```
context.jsonFile("s3n:// . . .")
registerTempTable("json")
results = context.sql(
"""SELECT *
FROM people
JOIN json . . ."""")
```

8.4.2 Spark Streaming with Live Stream of Data

Spark Streaming is a high-level library designed for handling streaming data on most clouds. This library leverages Spark Core's fast scheduling capability to perform streaming analytics. It accepts data in mini-batches. The system performs RDD transformations on those mini-batches of data. This design enables the same set of application code written for batch analytics to be used in streaming analytics. The package can be applied on a large cluster or on a single engine.

Spark Streaming can handle both batch and interactive queries. It enables the reuse of the same code for batch processing, joins streams against historical data, or runs ad hoc queries on the stream state. This makes it possible to build powerful interactive applications in addition to its use in data analytics. The streaming engine is modeled in Figure 8.17. Spark has extended Hadoop to execute not only in batch mode, but also for in-memory computation in streaming and real-time applications.

The streaming module makes it easy to build scalable and fault-tolerant streaming applications. It supports Java, Scala, and Python. The input data streams come from the

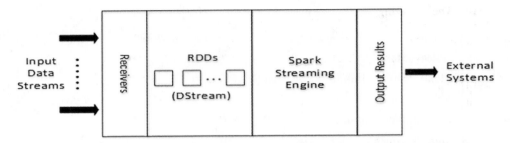

Figure 8.17
Concept of using Spark streaming engine on the DStreams.

left-hand side. The receivers then accept them and convert them into a special type of RDDs, called *Dstreams*. These Dstreams feed into the streaming engine, which could follow the MapReduce or any DAG models. Finally, the answers to queries are output at the right end.

The streaming package can be deployed to read data from HDFS, Flume, Kafka, Twitter, and ZeroMQ sources. The streaming engine can run Spark's Standalone cluster mode or on an EC2 cluster. In a production mode, Spark Streaming uses ZooKeeper and HDFS for high availability. The official website of Spark Streaming is: http://spark.apache .org//streaming. To get started with Spark Streaming, perform the following three steps:

Step 1: Download the entire Spark library from the website: http:/spark.apache.org /downloads.html. Spark Streaming is a working module in this library.

Step 2: Read the Spark Streaming programming guide (/docs/latest/streaming-programming -guide.html). This guide includes a tutorial. It describes the system architecture, configuration, and high availability.

Step 3: Check out example streaming programs in Scala.

To deploy a Spark Streaming application, the first thing is to identify it with a cluster manager to put together the needed machine resources. To package the application, you must compile your streaming application into a JAR. If the application uses advanced sources (e.g., Kafka, Flume, Twitter), then you will have to package the extra artifact they link to, along with their dependencies.

For example, an application using TwitterUtils has to include spark-streaming-twitter_2.10 and all its transitive dependencies in the application JAR. Since the received data must be stored in memory, the executors must be configured with sufficient memory to hold the received data. For example, if you are doing 10-min window operations, the system has to keep at least the last 10 min of data in memory. So the memory requirements for the application depend on the operations performed.

The next step is to deploy *checkpointing*. A directory in the Hadoop API compatible fault-tolerant storage (e.g., HDFS, S3, etc.) must be configured as the checkpoint directory. The streaming application is written in a way that checkpoint information can be used for failure recovery. Finally, we need to configure an automatic restart of the application driver. To automatically recover from a driver failure, the streaming application must monitor the driver process and relaunch the driver if it fails. Different cluster managers apply different tools as specified in what follows.

A Spark application driver can be submitted to run within the Spark Standalone cluster that is, the application driver itself runs on one of the worker nodes. Furthermore, the Standalone cluster manager can be instructed to *supervise* the driver and relaunch it if the driver fails either due to a non-zero exit code or failure of the node running the driver. YARN supports a similar mechanism for automatically restarting an application. Marathon software has been used to achieve this purpose with the use of MESOs as the cluster manager.

In Spark 1.2, a new experimental feature of write ahead logs was introduced for achieving strong fault-tolerance guarantees. If enabled, all the data received from a receiver gets written into a write ahead log in the configuration checkpoint directory. This prevents data loss on driver recovery, thus ensuring zero data loss. This can be enabled by setting the configuration parameter spark.streaming.receiver.writeAheadLogs.enable to true. However, these stronger semantics may come at the cost of the receiving throughput of individual receivers. This can be corrected by running more receivers in parallel to increase aggregate throughput.

The replication of the received data within Spark can be disabled when the write ahead log is enabled as the log is already stored in a replicated storage system. Similar to that of RDDs, transformations allow the data from the input DStream to be modified. DStreams support many of the transformations available on normal Spark RDDs. Some of the common ones are given in Table 8.5 as a working example.

Example 8.8 Two Sample Spark Streaming Applications
The following code is used to *count tweets* on a sliding window:

```
TwitterUtils.createStream( . . . )
.filter(_.getText.contains("Spark"))
.countByWindow(Seconds(5))
```

The following code *finds words* with higher frequency than some historical data:

```
stream.join(historicCounts).filter {
case (word, (curCount, oldCount)) =>
curCount > oldCount ∎
```

Table 8.5
Transformation operators for Spark Streaming applications

Operator	Meaning
Map	Return a new DStream by passing each element of the source DStream through a function *func*.
Filter	Return a new DStream by selecting only the records of the source DStream.
Repartition	Changes the level of parallelism in this DStream by creating more or fewer partitions.
Union	Return a new DStream that contains the union of the elements in the source and other DStream.
Reduce	Return a new DStream of single-element RDDs by aggregating the elements in each RDD of the source DStream using a function *func*. The function must be associative to enable parallelism.
Join	When called on, two DStreams of (K, V) and (K, W) pairs return a new DStream of (K, (V, W)) pairs, with all pairs of elements for each key.
Transform	Return a new DStream by applying an RDD-to-RDD function to every RDD of the source DStream. This can be used to do arbitrary RDD operations on the DStream.

8.4.3 Spark Streaming Application Examples

Spark Streaming is an extension of the core Spark API that enables scalable, high-throughput, fault-tolerant stream processing of live data streams. Data can be ingested from many sources such as Kafka, Flume, Twitter, ZeroMQ, and Kinesis. The TCP sockets can be processed using complex algorithms expressed with *map, reduce, join*, and *window*. Finally, processed data can be pushed out to file systems, databases, and live dashboards. In fact, you can apply Spark's ML and graph processing algorithms on data streams.

Spark supports four programming languages: Scala, Java, Python, and R. You can run Java and Scala examples by passing the class name to Spark's bin/run-example script. For Python, use the command: ./bin/spark-submitexamples/src/main/python/pi.p. For R, use ./bin/spark-submit examples/src/main/r/ dataframe.R. To optimize your programs, the configuration and tuning guides are available to provide information on best practices. They are especially important for making sure that your data is stored in memory in an efficient format. Full API documentation is available in Scala, Java, Python, and R.

Example 8.9 Interactive Search for Error Patterns in Error Message Log

Figure 8.18 shows the use of Spark in loading the error messages from a log into memory, then interactively searching for various error patterns. The first two commands are transforming RDDs. Different RDD blocks are cached in various workers under the coordination of the driver program. The last two commands perform a filtering operation to eliminate the unwanted error patterns. The result is scaled to 1 TB data in 5–7 s. This shows a sharp improvement of 170 s over the use of on disk data.

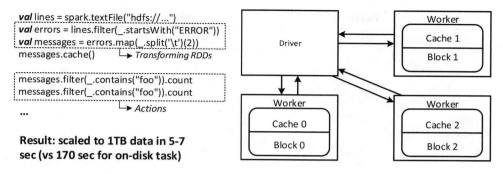

```
val lines = spark.textFile("hdfs://...")
val errors = lines.filter(_.startsWith("ERROR"))
val messages = errors.map(_.split('\t')(2))
messages.cache()            ↳ Transforming RDDs
```

```
messages.filter(_.contains("foo")).count
messages.filter(_.contains("foo")).count
```
...   ↳ Actions

**Result: scaled to 1TB data in 5-7
sec (vs 170 sec for on-disk task)**

Figure 8.18
Interactive search for error patterns in an error message log loaded into worker's memory (Courtesy of Zaharia
et al., 2014).

On November 5, 2014, Databricks announced that a Spark TeraSort benchmark
won the Daytona GraySort contest for 2014. This was a world record on fast sorting
over 1 B data set, as introduced in Example 8.10. ∎

Example 8.10 Spark World Record on TeraSort Benchmark Testing
Spark has been widely slated as the successor to Hadoop MapReduce, and can be
deployed in clusters ranging from just a handful to thousands of nodes. Spark is more
efficient than MapReduce for data that fits in memory. Some organizations were having trouble pushing it to large-scale data sets that could not fit in memory. Therefore,
Databricks has devoted much effort, together with the Spark community, to improve
the stability, scalability, and performance of Spark. Spark works well for gigabytes or
terabytes of data, and it should also work well for petabytes. The results are reported
in Table 8.6.

With help from AWS, the Databricks team participated in the Daytona Gray category, an industry benchmark on how fast a system can sort 100 TB of data (1 trillion
records). The previous world record was 72 min, set by Yahoo! using a Hadoop Map-
Reduce cluster of 2,100 nodes. Using Spark on 206 EC2 nodes, Databricks completed
the benchmark in 23 min. This means that Spark sorted the same data three times
faster using ten times fewer machines.

All the sorting took place on disk (HDFS), without using Spark's in-memory cache.
Additionally, while no official petabyte (PB) sort competition exists, Databricks
pushed Spark further to also sort 1 PB of data (10 trillion records) on 190 machines in
under 4 hr. This PB time beats previously reported results based on Hadoop Map-
Reduce (16 hr on 3,800 machines). This was the first petabyte-scale sort ever done in
a public cloud in 2014. ∎

Table 8.6
Spark TeraSort benchmark results reported in November 5, 2014

Data Features	Hadoop 100 TB	Spark, 100 TB	Spark, 1 PB
Data Size	102.5 TB	100 TB	1,000 TB
Elapsed Time	72 min	23 min	234 min
# Nodes	2,100	206	190
# Cores	50,400	6,592	6,080
# Reducers	10,000	29,000	250,000
Data Rate	1.42 TB/min	4.27 TB/min	4.27 TB/min
Rate/Node	0.67 GB/min	20.7 GB/min	22.5 GB/min

8.5 Spark MLlib for Machine Learning and GraphX for Graph Processing

In this section, we study the ML package, MLlib, and the graph processing package, GraphX, developed with Spark library. Quite a few working examples are illustrated to help readers get started in developing new Spark applications on cloud platforms or even on some local clusters.

8.5.1 Spark MLlib Library for Machine Learning

ML deals with the use of computers to learn the properties of big data. The purpose is to uncover unknown properties, patterns, or hidden knowledge. Specific ML algorithms were treated in Chapter 6. Here, we introduce the basic concept of a ML pipeline. Then we provide some MLlib modules developed with the Spark programming library. Figure 8.19 shows the major components in a typical ML pipeline for supervised ML applications. We consider four major components installed in a smart cloud platform. This ML pipeline is described in five operational steps, including the feedback stage for the purpose of sample data training and prediction model fitting.

Step 1: Input data are divided into two subsets: the training data vs. the test data. Both are stored in the data storage before entering the compute or learning engine.

Step 2: This stage involves data preprocessing operations like filtering, mining, data aggregation, feature extraction, pattern recognition, and some transformation operations.

Step 3: This stage is the learning engine using cloud compute and storage resources. Major operations include data cleaning, model training, and transformation toward the model development under supervision.

Step 4: This stage is aimed at learning model construction and fitting with the problem of environment meeting the learning objectives for prediction or classification, etc.

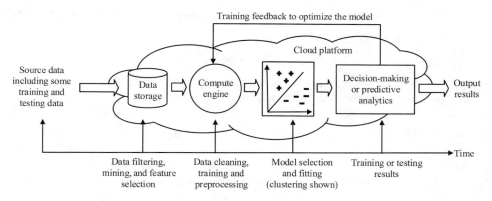

Figure 8.19
The concept of a machine learning pipeline and its training and testing steps.

Step 5: This is the training and testing stage by making decisions or predictions. The training is carried out with feedback to improve the model performance. Then, output the predictive results, if satisfactory.

MLlib is Spark's ML library. Spark MLlib is a distributed ML framework on top of Spark Core. With a distributed memory-based Spark architecture, MLlib was reported nine times faster than the disk-based implementation used by Apache Mahout. This was based on benchmarks completed by the MLlib developers against the *alternating least squares* (ALS) implementations before Mahout itself gained a Spark interface. In general, MLlib scales better than both Mahout and Vowpal Wabbit. Many common machine learning and statistical algorithms have been implemented in MLlib.

Spark ML standardizes APIs for ML algorithms to make it easier to combine multiple algorithms into a single pipeline or workflow. We introduce below key concepts of using the Spark APIs for ML:

• ***ML data set:*** Spark ML uses the SchemaRDD from Spark SQL as a data set which can hold a variety of data types. For example, a data set has different columns storing text, feature vectors, true labels, and predictions.

• ***Transformer:*** A transformer is an algorithm which can transform one SchemaRDD into another. For example, an ML model transforms an RDD with features into another RDD with predictions.

• ***Estimator:*** This algorithm can be fit on a SchemaRDD to produce a transformer. For example, a learning algorithm trains on a data set and produces a prediction model.

• ***Pipeline:*** A pipeline chains multiple transformers and estimators together to specify an ML workflow.

• *Parameter:* All transformers and estimators now share a common API in specifying parameters.

The DAG Pipelines

A pipeline's stage is specified as an ordered array. The examples given below are all for *linear pipelines,* i.e., pipelines in which each stage uses data produced by the previous stage. It is possible to create *nonlinear pipelines* as long as the data flow graph forms a DAG. This graph is currently specified implicitly based on the input and output column names of each stage. If the pipeline forms a DAG, then the stages must be specified in topological order. Since pipelines can operate on data sets with varied types, they cannot use compile-time type checking. Pipelines and pipeline models instead do runtime checking before actually running the pipeline. This type of checking is done using the data set *schema*, a description of the data types of columns in the SchemaRDD.

8.5.2 Some MLlib Application Examples

Table 8.7 lists some important ML algorithm families implemented with Spark MLlib. The summary statistics, correlations, stratified sampling, hypothesis testing, and random data generation are often performed in most ML or data analytics applications. Collaborative filtering techniques including ALS are often needed in the data preprocessing stage. Feature extraction and transformation functions may be applied. At the compute stage, Spark users often apply classification and regression, support vector machines, decision trees, and naive Bayes classifiers.

For unsupervised leaning, we can consider using cluster analysis methods including k-means, and *latent Dirichlet allocation* (LDA). Dimensionality reduction techniques are

Table 8.7
Feature algorithms implemented in Spark ML library

Algorithm	Brief Description
Collaborative Filtering	Alternating least squares (ALS)
Basic Statistics	Summary statistics, correlations, hypothesis testing, random data generation
Classification and Regression	Support vector machines, logistic regression, linear regression, decision trees, random forests, naive Bayes classifiers, gradient-boosted trees, etc.
Dimensionality Reduction	Singular value decomposition (SVD), principal component analysis (PCA)
Clustering Techniques	Streaming k-means, Gaussian mixture, power iteration clustering (PIC), etc.
Feature Extraction and Pattern Mining	Feature extraction and transformation, frequent pattern growth, association rules, PrefixSpan
Evaluation and Optimization	Evaluation metrics, PMML model export, stochastic gradient descent, limited-memory BFGS (L-BFGS)

also used such as *singular value decomposition* (SVD) and *principal component analysis* (PCA). Finally, optimization algorithms may be applied to improve the ML prediction model, such as stochastic gradient descent, limited-memory BFGS. An important task in ML is *model selection*, or using data to find the best model or parameters for a given task. This is also called *tuning*. Pipelines facilitate model selection by making it easy to tune an entire pipeline at once, rather than tuning each element in the pipeline separately.

Currently, Spark MLlib supports model selection using the CrossValidator class, which takes an estimator, a set of ParamMaps, and an evaluator. CrossValidator begins by splitting the data set into a set of *folds*, which are used as separate training and test data sets, e.g., with $k = 3$ folds, CrossValidator will generate 3 (training, test) data set pairs, each of which uses two thirds of the data for training and one third for testing. CrossValidator iterates through the set of ParamMaps. For each ParamMap, it trains the given estimator and evaluates it using the given evaluator. The ParamMap which produces the best evaluation metric is selected as the best model. CrossValidator finally fits the estimator using the best ParamMap and the entire data set.

Example 8.11 Using MLlib for Prediction with Logistic Regression
The following code is used to prediction application outcome using the logistic regression method:

This DataFrame contains the label and # features represented by a vector.

df = sqlContext.createDataFrame (data, ["label", "features"])

 # Set parameters for the algorithm. Here, we limit the number of iterations to 10.

lr = LogisticRegression(maxIter = 10)

 # Fit the model to the data.

model = lr.fit(df)

 # Given a data set, predict each point's label, and show the results.

model.transform(df).show() ■

8.5.3 Spark GraphX for Graph Processing

GraphX is a distributed graph processing framework supported by Spark Core. It provides an API for expressing graph computation that can model the Pregel abstraction. It also provides an optimized runtime support for this abstraction. Like Spark, GraphX initially started as a research project at UC Berkeley's AMPLab and at The Databricks company. The module was later donated to the Apache Software Foundation and the Spark project.

Spark GraphX unifies the *extract, transform, load* (ETL) functions, exploratory analysis, and iterative graph computation as a single system. One can view the same data as both graphs and collections. The package supports *transform* and *join* on graphs with RDDs efficiently. The user can write custom iterative graph algorithms using Pregel API. Visit the Spark website (/docs/latest/grapx-programming-guide.html#pregel-api) for details. Spark users can choose from a growing library of graph algorithms in GraphX. In addition to a highly flexible API, GraphX comes with a variety of graph algorithms such as PageRank, connected components, label propagation, SVD++, strongly connected components, and triangle count.

The growing scale and importance of graph data are driven by the development of numerous *graph processing* systems including Pregel and PowerGraph. By exposing specialized abstractions backed by graph-specific optimizations, these systems can naturally express and efficiently execute iterative graph algorithms like PageRank and community detection on graphs with billions of vertices and edges. The GraphX was built as a library on top of Spark (Figure 8.20). This was done by encoding graphs as collections and then expressing GraphX API on top of standard dataflow operators.

GraphX offers a general method to embed graph computation within distributed dataflow frameworks. The system distills graph computation to a specific *join—map—groupBy* dataflow pattern. By reducing graph computation to a specific pattern, the user can identify the critical path for system optimization. This differs from some general-purpose distributed dataflow frameworks—MapReduce, Spark, Dryad—we have discussed so far. Some rich dataflow operators—*map, reduce, groupBy, join*—are well suited for analyzing unstructured and tabular data.

In general, directly implementing iterative graph algorithms using dataflow operators is a nontrivial task, often requiring multiple stages of complex *joins*. Graph processing systems represent graph-structured data as property graphs, which associate user-defined properties with each vertex and edge. The properties can include metadata (e.g., user profiles and time stamps) and program state (e.g., the PageRank of vertices or inferred affinities). property graphs derived from natural phenomena such as social networks and web graphs

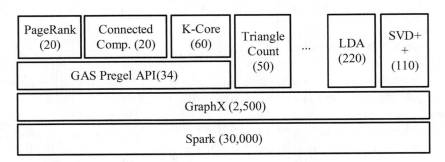

Figure 8.20
GraphX is a thin layer on top of the Spark dataflow framework.

that are often highly skewed and follow power-law degree distributions with several orders of magnitude more edges than vertices.

By 2014, the GraphX had written over 2,500 lines of Scala code, compared with 30,000 in the whole Spark library. Some of GraphX application codes are really short, like 20 lines in PageRank. There are many new GraphX modules being generated by Databricks and other Spark development groups. To get started with GraphX, first download Spark, where GraphX is included as a module. Then read the GraphX programming guide, which includes application examples. Finally, learn how to deploy Spark on a cluster if you would like to run in distributed mode. You can also run locally on a multicore machine without any setup.

Graph processing systems apply a range of graph-partitioning algorithms to minimize communication and balance computation. Gonzalez et al. [6]. demonstrates that *vertex-cut partitioning* performs well on many large natural graphs. Vertex-cut partitioning evenly assigns edges to machines in a way that minimizes the number of times each vertex is cut. Figure 8.21 shows the graph analytics system for pipelined processing of graph views of the same data set. GraphX provides the ability to stay within a single framework throughout the analytics process. Note that the GraphX is shown in use by the GraphLab facility in the compute stage. The system is also fully integrated with the use of Spark and Hadoop resources.

This graph analytics pipeline eliminates the need to learn and support multiple systems or write data interchange formats and plumbing to move between systems. The pipeline supports iteratively *slice, transform,* and *compute* on large graphs as well as to share data-structures across stages of the pipeline. The feedback path is used to improve the analytic model. The gains in performance and scalability for graph computation translate to a tighter analytics feedback loop and therefore a more efficient work flow. To adopt GraphX, the users go to the website of Apache Spark open-source project.

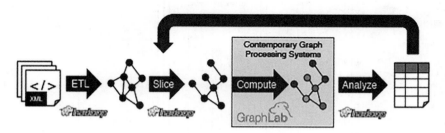

Figure 8.21
Graph analytics for pipelined processing of graph views. Source: Gonzalez et al., "GraphX: Graph Processing in a Distributed Dataflow Framework," 11th USENIX Symposium, OSDI, Bloomfield, CO, October 2014.

8.5.4 Some GraphX Programming Examples

The *property graph* is used in GraphX programming. This is a graph representation model, which is logically represented as a pair of vertex and edge property collections. The *vertex collection* contains the vertex properties uniquely keyed by the vertex identifier. In the GraphX system, vertex identifiers are 64-bit integers which may be derived externally (e.g., user ids) or by applying a hash function to the vertex property (e.g., page URL). The *edge collection* contains the edge properties keyed by the source and destination vertex identifiers. Figure 8.22 shows the concept of distributed graph representation.

The graph (on the left) is represented as a vertex and an edge collection (on the right). The edges are divided into three edge partitions by applying a partition function (e.g., 2D partitioning). The vertices are partitioned by vertex identifiers. Copartitioned with the vertices, GraphX maintains a routing table encoding the edge partitions for each vertex. If vertex 6 and adjacent edges (shown with dotted lines) are restricted from the graph (e.g., by subgraph), they are removed from the corresponding collection by updating the bitmasks thereby enabling index reuse.

The vertex collection is hash-partitioned by the vertex identifiers. To support frequent joins across vertex collections, vertices are stored in a local hash index within each partition. The edge collection is horizontally partitioned by a user-defined partition function. GraphX enables vertex-cut partitioning, which minimizes communication in natural graphs such as social networks and web graphs.

The GraphX programming abstraction extends the Spark dataflow operators by introducing a small set of specialized *graph operators*, summarized in Table 8.8. GraphX inherits the immutability of Spark and therefore all graph operators logically create new collections rather than destructively modifying existing ones.

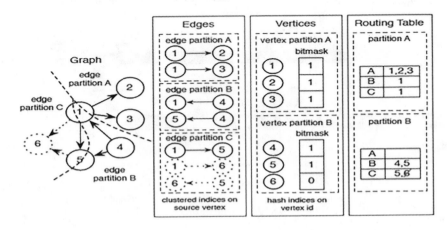

Figure 8.22
Distributed graph representation. Source: Gonzalez et al., "Powergraph: Distributed Graph-Parallel Computation on Natural Graphs," 10th USENIX Symposium, OSDI'12, USENIX Association: 17–30.

Table 8.8

Graph operators that transform vertex and edge collections in Graph

```
class Graph[V, E] {
  // Constructor
  def Graph(v: Collection[(Id, V)],
            e: Collection[(Id, Id, E)])
  // Collection views
  def vertices: Collection[(Id, V)]
  def edges: Collection[(Id, Id, E)]
  def triplets: Collection[Triplet]
  // Graph-parallel computation
  def mrTriplets(f: (Triplet) => M,
      sum: (M, M) => M): Collection[(Id, M)]
  // Convenience functions
  def mapV(f: (Id, V) => V): Graph[V, E]
  def mapE(f: (Id, Id, E) => E): Graph[V, E]
  def leftJoinV(v: Collection[(Id, V)],
      f: (Id, V, V) => V): Graph[V, E]
  def leftJoinE(e: Collection[(Id, Id, E)],
      f: (Id, Id, E, E) => E): Graph[V, E]
  def subgraph(vPred: (Id, V) => Boolean,
      ePred: (Triplet) => Boolean)
    : Graph[V, E]
  def reverse: Graph[V, E]
}
```

Source: Gonzalez et al., "Powergraph: Distributed Graph-Parallel Computation on Natural Graphs," OSDI'12, USENIX Association: 17–30.

Example 8.12 PageRank Graph Processing in Spark GraphX Applications

PageRank measures the importance of each node in a social graph, assuming an edge from u to v represents the endorsement of v's importance by u. For example, if a Twitter user is followed by many others, the user will be ranked highly. GraphX comes with static and dynamic implementations of PageRank as methods on Apache's PageRank object.

Static PageRank runs for a fixed number of iterations, while dynamic PageRank runs until the ranks converge. The GraphOps calls these algorithms directly. Spark GraphX provides an example of a social network data set that we can run PageRank. A set of users is given in graphx/data/users.txt, and a set of relationships between users is given in graphx/data/followers.txt. Spark computes the PageRank of each user as follows:

val graph = **GraphLoader**.edgeListFile(sc, "graphx/data/followers.txt"),

// Load the edges as a graph.

val ranks = graph.pageRank(0.0001).vertices, *// Run PageRank.*

val users = sc.textFile("graphx/data/users.txt").map { line => **val** fields = line.split(",")
(fields(0).toLong, fields(1))}, // *Join the ranks with the usernames.*

val ranksByUsername = users.join(ranks).map {**case** (id, (username, rank))

=> (username, rank)}, // *Join the ranks with the usernames.*

println(ranksByUsername.collect().mkString("\n")), // *Print the result.*

In addition to GraphX, GraphLab and Giraph are also reputable graph analysis packages. GraphX competes in performance with both GraphLab and Giraph systems in Figure 8.23. The 1.5–2.7 times speedup is observed in using GraphX for executing the PageRank algorithm. ∎

Example 8.13 The Use of Map Reduce Triplets (*mrTriplets*) Operator

The mrTriplets (MapReduce Triplets) operator encodes the essential two-stage process of graph parallel computation. Logically, the mrTriplets operator is the composition of the *map* and *groupBy datafow* operators on the triplets view. Figure 8.24 shows the property graph and associated mrTriplets operations as specified in the following Scala code:

val graph: Graph[User, Double]

def mapUDF(t: Triplet[User, Double]) =

    if (t.src.age > t.dst.age) 1 **else** 0

def reduceUDF(a: Int, b: Int): Int = a + b

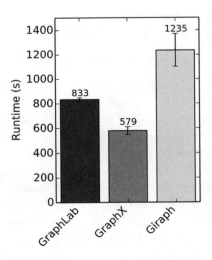

Figure 8.23
Relative PageRank performance on 20 iterations and 3.7 billion of edges. Courtesy of Apache, "MLlib: Apache Spark," www.spark.apache.org.

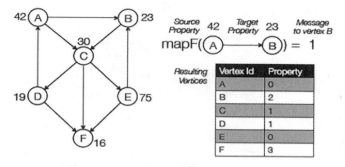

Figure 8.24
Compute the number of older followers of each vertex user.

val seniors: Collection[(Id, Int)] =

graph.mrTriplets(MapUDF, reduceUDF)

The user-defined map function is applied to each triplet, yielding a value which is then aggregated at the destination vertex using the user-defined binary aggregation function as illustrated in the following:

SELECT t.dstId, reduceF(mapF(t)) **AS** msgSum

FROM triplets **AS** t **GROUP BY** t.dstId

In this operation, the mrTriplets operator produces a collection containing the sum of the inbound messages keyed by the destination vertex identifier. For example, in Figure 8.24, we use the mrTriplets operator to compute a collection containing the number of older followers for each user in a social network. Because the resulting collection contains a subset of the vertices in the graph, it can reuse the same indices as the original vertex collection. ∎

Example 8.14 shows how to use social graph analysis to assess user human relationships.

Example 8.14 Graph Analysis of Peer Relations in a Social Network Group
Figure 8.25 shows a social graph among four social entities, identified by numbers 2, 3, 5, and 7 at the vertices. The vertex table describes the positions held by individuals. The edge table describes the working relationship among the source and destination entities. This simply shows how much information that can be conveyed in a simple social graph. ∎

Finally, we assess some performance results reported by Databricks developers of the GraphX analytics system. These results are reported in Gonzales et al. [6]. More details can be found in their paper appeared in the *11th USENIX Symposium on Operating Systems Design and Implementation* [7].

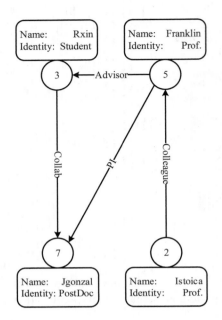

Vertex Table

Id	Property(V)
3	(Rxin, Student)
7	(Jgonzal, PostDoc)
5	(Franklin, Professor)
2	(Istoica, Professor)

Edge Table

SrcId	DstId	Property(e)
3	7	Collaboration
5	3	Advisor
2	5	Colleague
5	7	PI

Figure 8.25
An example property graph used in Spark GraphX programming.

Example 8.15 Comparison of Various Graph Processing Systems

In Figure 8.26, we evaluate the strong scaling performance of GraphX running Page-Rank on the Twitter follower graph. Seven graph systems were evaluated in part(a). With 20 iterations, the best performance comes from GraphLab at Carnegie Mellon University (CMU). This is mainly attributed to the shared memory used in CMU's system. The GraphX scales slightly better than GraphLab given that Spark does not exploit shared memory parallelism and therefore forces the graph to be partitioned across processors rather than machines.

Part(b) plots the effects of using GraphX. As we move from 8–32 machines we see a 3×speedup. However as we move to 64 machines we only see a 3.5×speedup. While this is hardly linear scaling, it is actually slightly better than the 3.2×speedup reported by GraphLab. The poor scaling performance of PageRank has been attributed to high communication overhead relative to the computation time. ∎

8.6 Conclusions

This chapter is devoted to the use of MapReduce, Hadoop, and Spark programming systems for big data applications. We first reviewed the evolution of scalable parallel computing. The principles of MapReduce computing were introduced with working examples. Then, Hadoop library was reviewed and its recent extensions to Hadoop 2

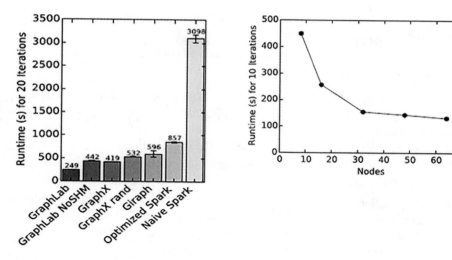

Figure 8.26

Comparison of seven graph processing software systems. Source: Gonzalez et al., "Powergraph: Distributed Graph-Parallel Computation on Natural Graphs," 10th USENIX Symposium, OSDI'12, USENIX Association: 17–30.

were discussed. We studied the Hadoop/MapReduce architecture, including the execution engine, HDFS, and its resource scheduler YARN.

Then we presented Spark Core architecture. The RDDs were introduced for in-memory computing in large clusters. We examined four Spark programming modules for SQL, streaming, ML, and graphic processing applications. The applications of using Hadoop and Spark modules for batch, SQL, streaming, ML, and graph analysis were covered with 15 illustrated examples. Interested readers may refer to the websites of Apache Hadoop and Spark, Databricks, and Cloudera for additional examples.

Homework Problems

8.1: Visit the Google App Engine (GAE) website and download their *software development kit* (SDK). Read the Python or the Java guide to get started. You are asked to develop some new PaaS or SaaS applications in the Google engine. Note that GAE accepts Python, Ruby, and Java programming languages. The platform does not perform IaaS services.

(a) Develop a specific cloud application using available software services like Gmail, Docs, or *customer relationship management* (CRM) on the GAE platform. Test run your applications on the GAE platform.

(b) Report your application development experience and experimental results in terms of some selected performance measures, such as job queuing time, execution time, and resource utilization rate, or some QoS attributes, such as goal achievement, success rate, fault tolerance, and cost-effectiveness.

(c) Change the problem size or data set size and platform configuration to study the scalability and efficiency issues in your GAE experiments.

8.2: Discuss the functional strength and shortcomings in using the following three software packages for building elastic cloud platforms: Eucalyptus, vSphere 5, and Open-Stack. Try to compare them in VM or container creation, container orchestration, virtual clustering, application flexibility, security and availability, and cost-effectiveness concerns. Review public literature to provide evidence of your assessment as an investigative report on the state of the art in cloud software technology.

8.3: Write an application code to run on the Amazon Web Services (AWS) cloud platform for backup storage of a large amount of your personal, family, or company data and records such as photos, video, music, sales receipts, documents, news medium, inventory, market records, financial matters, supply chain information, human resources, and public data sets. Note that strict privacy protection is required here. Minimizing the storage cost is another objective. The access path, software development tools, and AWS services were covered in Chapter 4. You should explain your code development experience and report the results in using the GAE platform.

8.4: In this problem, you will learn how to install Apache Hadoop onto your local computer and set the pseudo-parallel mode. You will test a sample *WordCount* Java code in pseudo-parallel mode in your local computer and full distributed way using AWS EMR. Report what you have learned, and take screen snapshots to show how it successfully ran. Report the output.

The steps to install Apache Hadoop and use *WordCount* example in your local computer in pseudo-parallel mode as follows:

1. Download Hadoop-3.0.0-alpha1.tar.gz in http://apache.claz.org/hadoop/common/hadoop -3.0.0-alpha1/.

2. Follow the instruction here to test the Standalone and psuedo-parallel mode. (Note: TA is only familiar with *NixOS setup. If you have a Windows system, please use VMware player to install Ubuntu virtual machine. A good instruction is written by Bill Cheng: http://merlot.usc.edu/cs402-f16/prepare-kernel/).

3. Some problems you might meet when you set up. For a Mac user, you need to allow access to SSH by going to system preference->sharing, and allowing SSH for all users.

4. You need be able to run the sample hadoop-mapreduce-examples-3.0.0-alpha1.jar in both Standalone and pseudo-parallel mode. Do not stop your NameNode and DataNode daemon.

5. Now that you have finished setting up the pseudo-parallel mode, go to: https://hadoop
   .apache.org/docs/stable/hadoop-mapreduce-client/hadoop-mapreduce-client-core
   /MapReduceTutorial.html. You will use WordCount v2.0 code to test in this pseudo-
   parallel mode.

   Here, you need to set up the environment variables:

   export PATH = ${JAVA_HOME}/bin:${PATH}

   export HADOOP_CLASSPATH = ${JAVA_HOME}/lib/tools.jar

6. Compile the WordCount2.java code and create a JAR:

   bin/hadoop com.sun.tools.javac.Main WordCount2.java
   jar cf wc.jar WordCount*.class

7. Create HDFS input directory and put the input file in the directory:

   bin/hdfs dfs -mkdir wodcount/input

   bin/hdfs dfs -put etc/hadoop/*.xml wordcount/input

8. Run the program:

   bin/hadoop jar wc.jar WordCount2 /user/<your_user name>/wordcount/input /user/<your
   _username>/wordcount/output

   Check the output: bin/hadoop fs -cat /user/<your_username>/wordcount/output/*

   To run in AWS:

1. Go to AWS console, select S3, create a bucket, and upload the JAR, and the input file.
2. Go to AWS console, select EMR service.
3. Create your own cluster; in launch mode, select Setup Execution which will terminate
   the cluster after you finish the job. In added steps, choose the JAR program, and select
   your input folder and the JAR program in S3.
4. Launch the cluster to run it.

8.5: This problem asks you to practice mobile photo uploads to Amazon S3. Explore some
SDK tools on the AWS for using either iOS phone or any Android phone to store photos on
the Amazon S3 cloud and to notify AWS users using the Simple Notification Service (SNS).
Report on the storage/notification service features, your testing results, and app experiences.
Check the website for Android SDK tools. Source Amazon: http://aws.amazon.com/sdkfo
randroid/. You can find iOS and Android SDK tools by checking /sdk-for-ios/ and /sdk-for-
android/, similarly. Use the following three steps to do your experiments:

1. Download the Amazon AWS SDK for Android (or iOS) from the source URL.

2. Check the sample code given in aws-android-sdk-1.6/samples/S3_Uploader, which creates a simple application that lets the user upload images from the phone to an S3 bucket in a user account.

3. These images can be viewed by anyone with access to the URL shared by the user.

You need to perform the following operations and report the results in screen snapshots or using any performance metric you choose to display when using an Android phone. Similarly, for those students using Apple iOS phones, do the following:

1. Try to upload the selected data (image) to the AWS S3 bucket, using the Access key and Security Key credentials provided for the user. This will enable you as an AWS client.

2. Check if the S3 bucket exists with the same name, and create the bucket and put the image in S3 bucket.

3. Show in Browser button and display the image in the browser.

4. Make sure the image is treated as an image file in the web browser.

5. Create a URL for the image in the bucket, so that it can be shared and viewed by other people.

6. Comment on extended applications beyond this experiment.

8.6: Design and request an EC2 configuration on the AWS platform for parallel multiplication of two very large matrices with an order exceeding 50,000.

(a) Report your experimental results including execution time, speed performance, VM instances initiated, compute unit and storage utilization, service charge experienced, etc.

(b). You can also study related issues such as scalability, throughput, efficiency, resource utilization, fault tolerance, and cost-effectiveness in this scientific cloud experiment.

8.7: Choose a data-intensive application such as a large-scale search or business processing application involving crowdsourcing from the general public. Implement the application on one of three cloud platforms: AWS, GAE, or Azure. The major objective is to minimize the execution time of the application. The minor objective is to minimize the user service costs. Assess your compute and storage costs, design experiences, experimental results, and interpret the performance results and QoS results obtained.

8.8: Follow the next six steps to launch and connect to an EC2 instance. Run a sample program retrieved from the AWS site on the EC2 instance installed. Report and discuss the results.

Step 1: Launch an instance: http://docs.aws.amazon.com/AWSEC2/latest/UserGuide/ec2-launch-instance_linux.html.

Step 2: Connect to your EC2 instance. There are three options to take in making this connection:

1. Connect using your browser: http://docs.aws.amazon.com/AWSEC2/latest/UserGuide /ec2-connect-to-instance-linux.html#using-browser.

2. Connect from Windows Putty: http://docs.aws.amazon.com/AWSEC2/latest/UserGuide /putty.html.

3. Connect from Mac or Linux using an SSH client: http://docs.aws.amazon.com /AWSEC2/latest/UserGuide/AccessingInstancesLinux.html.

Step 3: Add a Volume to your EC2 instance: http://docs.aws.amazon.com/AWSEC2/latest /UserGuide/ebs-creating-volume.html;   http://docs.aws.amazon.com/AWSEC2/latest /UserGuide/ebs-attaching-volume.html.

Step 4: Use EC2 instance metadata tool to retrieve a simple bash script consisting of many commands to reveal the instance profile and execution statistics. Simply follow the procedure retrieved from the following link: http://aws.amazon.com/code/Amazon-EC2/1825.

Step 5: Execute three commands selected from the list of 21 commands (shaded area) from the above link. Report the results from executing these three commands. To satisfy your curiosity, you can execute more or all of the commands, but only three corrected ones will be credited.

Step 6: Shut down your EC2 the instance after use. You will be billed continuously if you ignore this step: http://docs.aws.amazon.com/AWSEC2/latest/UserGuide/ec2-clean-up -your-instance.html.

$ ec2-metadata --help
Usage: ec2-metadata
Options:
all--Show all metadata information for this host (also default).
-a/--ami-id The AMI ID used to launch this instance.
-l/--ami-launch-index The index of this instance in the reservation (per AMI).
-m/--ami-manifest-path The manifest path of the AMI with which the instance was launched.
-n/--ancestor-ami-ids The AMI IDs of any instances that were rebundled to create this AMI.
-z/--availability-zone The availability zone in which the instance launched. Same as placement.
-b/--block-device-mapping Defines native device names to use when exposing virtual devices.
-i/--instance-id The ID of this instance.
-t/--instance-type The type of instance to launch. For more information, see Instance Types.

-h/--local-hostname The local hostname of the instance.

-o/--local-ipv4 Public IP address if launched with direct addressing; private IP address if launched with public addressing.

-k/--kernel-id The ID of the kernel launched with this instance, if applicable.

-c/--product-codes Product codes associated with this instance.

-p/--public-hostname The public hostname of the instance.

-v/--public-ipv4 NATted public IP Address.

-u/--public-keys Public keys. Only available if supplied at instance launch time

-r/--ramdisk-id The ID of the RAM disk launched with this instance, if applicable.

-e/--reservation-id The ID of the reservation.

-s/--security-groups Names of the security groups the instance is launched in. Only available if supplied at the instance launch time.

-d/--user-data User-supplied data. Only available if supplied at instance launch time.

8.9: Twister k-means extends the MapReduce programming model iteratively. Many data analysis techniques require iterative computations. For example, k-means clustering is the application where multiple iterations of MapReduce computations are necessary for the overall computation. Twister is an enhanced MapReduce runtime that supports iterative MapReduce computations efficiently. In this assignment you will learn the iterative MapReduce programming model and how to implement the k-means algorithm with Twister.

8.10: Spark can also be used for compute-intensive tasks. This code estimates π by "throwing darts" at a circle. Pick random points in the unit square ((0, 0) to (1,1)) and see how many fall in the unit circle. The fraction should be $\pi / 4$, so use this to get your estimate. A sample code for this purpose is given next. You are asked to run this code in a Hadoop or Spark platform and demonstrate the results and assess their execution times.

```
def sample(p):
    x, y = random(), random()
    return 1 if x*x + y*y < 1, else 0
count = sc.parallelize(xrange(0, NUM_SAMPLES)) .map (sample) \
    .reduce (lambda a, b: a + b)
print "Pi is roughly %f" % (4.0 * count / NUM_SAMPLES
```

8.11: This problem requires you to run a Spark sample program on an Amazon EMR cluster. First, you need to familiarize yourself with AWS Spark library. Visit the following websites to learn how to create, configure, access Spark shell, write a Spark application, and submit a Spark step: http://docs.aws.amazon.com/ElasticMapReduce/latest/DeveloperGuide/emr-spark .html; http://docs.aws.amazon.com/ElasticMapReduce/latest/DeveloperGuide/emr-spark -launch.html; http://docs.aws.amazon.com/ElasticMapReduce/latest/DeveloperGuide/emr -spark-configure.html; http://docs.aws.amazon.com/ElasticMapReduce/latest/DeveloperGuide

/emr-spark-shell.html; http://docs.aws.amazon.com/ElasticMapReduce/latest/DeveloperGuide /emr-spark-application.html; and http://docs.aws.amazon.com/ElasticMapReduce/latest /DeveloperGuide/emr-spark-submit-step.html.

Then, run the following Spark sample code. Report your observed result by showing a screen snapshot. To test the Spark infrastructure installed, you need to sort a Wikistat public data set. The full data set is available online at the website: http://aws.amazon.com/datasets /4182. The data in Wikistat is formatted as follows:

1. Each log file is named with the date and time of collection: *pagecounts-20090430–230000. gz*.

2. Each line in the log file has four fields: projectcode, pagename, pageviews, and bytes. A sample of the type of data stored in Wikistat is given here.

   1.

   en Barack_Obama 997 123091092
   en Barack_Obama%27s_first_100_days 8 850127
   en Barack_Obama,_Jr 1 144103
   en Barack_Obama,_Sr. 37 938821
   en Barack_Obama_%22HOPE%22_poster 4 81005
   en Barack_Obama_%22Hope%22_poster 5 102081

Steps to perform the experiments are given as follows:

1. Create an EMR cluster. Use the settings below:

   (a) Select all software applications: Hadoop 2.6.0, Hive 1.0.0, Mahout 0.10.0, Pig 0.14.0, and Spark 1.4.1.

   (b) Choose instance type m3.xlarge, the number of instances is 3 (1 for master, 2 for cores).

   (c) Select your own EC2 key pair, this will be used for SSH.

2. SSH to your master node. You will know how to SSH to your master node after the cluster is launched successfully.

3. After you have successfully SSH to the master node, type the command spark-shell line scala>.

4. Copy and paste the following commands.

   (a) The first line tells Spark which file to process.

   (b) In the second line, split each data line into multiple fields, taking the first and the second fields (pagetitle and pageview count) and perform a groupBy based on the key (pagetitle).

   (c) The third line caches the data in memory in case we need to re-run this job.

(d) The last line sorts the list and provides the result.

val file = sc.textFile("s3://support.elasticmapreduce/bigdatademo/sample/wiki")

val reducedList = file.map(l => l.split(" ")).map(l => (l(1), l(2).toInt)).reduce
   ByKey(_+_, 3)

reducedList.cache

val sortedList = reducedList.map(x => (x._2, x._1)).sortByKey(false).take(50)

After finishing the task, Spark should return the result similar to the following one:

INFO spark.SparkContext: Job finished: take at:16, took 8.015384737 s

sortedList: Array[(Int, String)] = Array((328476,Special:Search), (217924,Main
   _Page),

(73900,Special:Random), (65047,404_error/),

(55814,%E3%83%A1%E3%82%A4%E3%83%B3%E3%83%9A%E3%83%BC%E3
   %82%B8), (21521,Special:Export/Where_Is_My_Mind), . . .

8.12: Study some reported EC2 or S3 applications on the AWS platform by business or service industry or by large enterprises. For example, Vertica Systems applies EC2 in DBMS (database management system) applications. Eli Lilly uses EC2 in drug development. Animoto offers online service to facilitate personal video production. Contact a few of those service companies for technical implementation and service details. Submit a study report with suggestions on improving the selected compute and storage service applications.

8.13: Using a MapReduce programming model supported in Aneka, develop a program for image filtering of hundreds of photos you have taken using a digital camera. Conduct and report results of scalability experiments by varying the number of computing nodes/ workers and images of different resolutions or file sizes on an Aneka-based enterprise cloud.

8.14: Perform Hadoop Multiply of two 1024×1024 matrices A and B. Use one, two, or three m3.xlarge EC2 machine instances in scale-out experiments. According to Amazon EMR configuration, each m3.xlarge instance is implemented by AWS with six mappers and two reducers by default. See the website: http://docs.aws.com/ElasticMaReduce/latest/Develop mentGuide/TaskConfiguration_h1.03.html for details.

Feel free to scale from one, two, or three m3.xlarge instances to demonstrate the scalable performance. By default, this implies that we scale from a small cluster of six mappers and two reducers to a medium cluster of twelve mappers and four reducers and to a large cluster of eighteen mappers and six reducers in three stages of the EC2 scale-out experiments. Plot the execution time, speedup, and efficiency curves against the cluster size (number of instances) based on your measured results.

8.15: Scala code licensed from the Apache Software Foundation (ASF) is given below. This is a Spark example for streaming applications. Run the code over a chosen input data set on both Hadoop and Spark platforms. Plot the measured results, interpret their physical meanings, and discuss their relative performance in execution time against the cluster size used in your experimental setting.

```
*/
```

```
package org.apache.spark.examples.streaming
import org.apache.log4j.{Level, Logger}
import org.apache.spark.internal.Logging
/** Utility functions for Spark Streaming examples. */
object StreamingExamples extends Logging {
/** Set reasonable logging levels for streaming if the user has not conFigured log4j. */
def setStreamingLogLevels() {
val log4jInitialized = Logger.getRootLogger.getAllAppenders.hasMoreElements
if (!log4jInitialized) {
// First log something to initialize Spark's default logging, then override the logging level.
logInfo("Setting log level to [WARN] for streaming example." +
" To override add a custom log4j.properties to the classpath.")
Logger.getRootLogger.setLevel(Level.WARN)
```

References

[1] Apache. "MLlib: Apache Spark." www.spark.apache.org.

[2] Apache Foundation. "Cluster Mode Overview—Spark 1.2.0 Documentation—Cluster Manager Types." www.apache.org, December 18, 2014.

[3] Chang, F., et al. "BigTable: A Distributed Storage System for Structured Data." Google (2006).

[4] Dean, J., and S. Ghemawat. "MapReduce: Simplified Data Processing on Large Clusters." *OSDI* (2004).

[5] EMC Education Services. *Data Science and Big Data Analytics: Discovering, Analyzing, Visualizing and Presenting Data.* Wiley, 2014.

[6] Gonzalez, J. E., Y. Low, H. Gu, D. Bickson, and C. Guestrin. "Powergraph: Distributed Graph-Parallel Computation on Natural Graphs." OSDI'12, USENIX Association: 17–30.

[7] Gonzalez, J., R. Xin, A. Dave, D. Crankshaw, M. Franklin, and I. Stoica. "GraphX: Graph Processing in a Distributed Dataflow Framework." 11th USENIX Symposium, OSDI, October 2014.

[8] "HDFS: Facebook Has the World's Largest Hadoop Cluster!" Hadoopblog.blogspot.com, May 9, 2010.

[9] Huang, A., and W. Wu. "Mining Ecommerce Graph Data with Spark at Alibaba Taobao." http://databricks .com/blog/2014/08/14/mining-graph-datawith-spark-at-alibaba-taobao.html, 2014.

[10] Hwang, K., and M. Chen. *Big Data Analytics for Cloud, IoT and Cognitive Learning.* Wiley, 2017.

[11] Isard, M., et al. "Dryad: Distributed Data-Parallel Programs from Sequential Building Blocks." *EuroSys* (2007): 59–72.

[12] Lam, C. *Hadoop in Action.* 1st ed. Manning Publications, 2010.

[13] Leskovec, J., et al. "Community Structure in Large Networks: Natural Cluster Sizes and the Absence of Large Well-Defined Clusters." *Internet Mathematics* 6 no. 1 (2008): 29–123.

[14] Low, Y., et al. "Distributed GraphLab: A Framework for Machine Learning and Data Mining in the Cloud." *PVLDB* (2012).

[15] Malewicz, G., et al. "Pregel: A System for Large-Scale Graph Processing." *SIGMOD* (2010): 135–146.

[16] Mondal, J., and A. Deshpande. "Managing Large Dynamic Graphs Efficiently." *Proceedings of the 2012 ACM SIGMOD, International Conference on Management of Data* (2012): 145–156.

[17] Page, L., et al. "The PageRank Citation Ranking: Bringing Order to the Web." *Stanford InfoLab Technical Report* 66 (1999).

[18] Russakovsky, O., J. Deng, H. Su, J. Krause, S. Satheesh, S. Ma, Z. Huang, A. Karpathy, A. Khosla, M. Bernstein, A. C. Berg, and F.-F. Li. "ImageNet Large Scale Visual Recognition Challenge." *International Journal of Computer Vision* (2015).

[19] Ryza, S., et al. *Advanced Analytics with Spark*. O'Reilly, 2015.

[20] "Spark Officially Sets a New Record in Large-Scale Sorting." http://databricks.com/blog/2014/2015spark.

[21] Stanton, I., and G. Kliot. "Streaming Graph Partitioning for Large Distributed Graphs." *Microsoft Research Technical Report MSR-TR-2011–121* (November 2011).

[22] White, T. *Hadoop: The Definitive Guide*. 1st ed. O'Reilly Media, 2009.

[23] Xin, R., J. Rosen, M. Zaharia, M. Franklin, S. Shenker, and I. Stoica. "Shark: SQL and Rich Analytics at Scale" (June 2013).

[24] Yahoo! "Hadoop and Distributed Computing at Yahoo!" April 20, 2011.

[25] Zaharia, M., M. Chowdhury, T. Das, D. Ankur, J. Ma, M. McCauley, J. Michael, S. Shenker, and I. Stoica. "Resilient Distributed Datasets: A Fault-Tolerant Abstraction for In-Memory Cluster Computing." *USENIX Symposium on Networked Systems Design and Implementation*.

[26] Zaharia, M., M. Chowdhury, M. J. Franklin, S. Shenker, and I. Stoica. "Spark: Cluster Computing with Working Sets." *USENIX Workshop on Hot Topics in Cloud Computing (HotCloud)*.

Chapter 9

TensorFlow, Keras, DeepMind, and Graph Analytics

9.1 TensorFlow for Neural Network Computing

This section introduces the key concepts of TensorFlow for machine intelligence. We first study the TensorFlow platforms and their key components in terms of operation steps and sessions. In Section 9.2, we will study the TensorFlow system architecture and review its various installations on all kinds of hosts and explore how to use TensorFlow in deep learning applications. Deep learning is the fastest growing field in artificial intelligence. This field enables computers to make sense of infinite amounts of data in the form of images, sound, and text.

Using multiple levels of neural networks, computers now have the capacity to see, learn, and react to complex situations, often better than humans. For example, how can a safety guard remember 20,000 criminal faces? Computers or clouds can easily identify criminals by performing deep learning operations to extract useful features, make meaningful classifications, and predict accurately.

Much evidence indicates that machine intelligence can beat human intelligence in the big data arena. This leads to a new way of thinking about our data, technology, and the products and services we receive. Forward-looking companies in a variety of industries are adopting deep learning to address exponentially increasing amounts of data by exploiting improvements in machine learning algorithms and advances in computing hardware. This is helping them find new ways to tap into the wealth of data at their fingertips to develop new products, services, and processes—and create a disruptive competitive advantage.

9.1.1 Key Concepts of TensorFlow

TensorFlow is an open-source software library for numerical computation using *data flow graphs* derived from deep neural networks. Graph nodes represent mathematical operations, while the directed edges represent the multidimensional data arrays, known as *tensors*, that flow between the nodes. Using different CPIs, the node computations are distributed to one or more CPUs or GPUs in a computer system, ranging from mobile devices, to desktops, to cloud servers. TensorFlow was originally developed by Google by researchers and engi-neers working on the Brain team. The platform was initially intended to achieve many machine intelligence functions by conducting *machine learning* (ML) on deep neural networks. TensorFlow includes TensorBoard, a data visualization toolkit.

TensorFlow is extending beyond cognitive applications to apply in other fields like health-care, *Internet of things* (IoT), and social media applications. Data flow graphs describe mathematical computation with a *directed acyclic graph* (DAG) of nodes and edges. Nodes typically implement mathematical operations, but can also represent endpoints to feed in data, push out results, or read/write persistent variables. Edges describe the input/output relationships between nodes. These data edges carry the tensors that flow between the nodes as multidimensional data arrays. The flow of tensors through the graph is where TensorFlow gets its name. Nodes are assigned to computational devices and execute asynchronously and in parallel once all the tensors on their incoming edges becomes available.

Google decided to make TensorFlow an open-source DL framework. The main purpose is to promote ML as a key ingredient in the innovative products and technologies of the future. Research in this area is global and growing fast but lacks standard tools. By sharing with the general public, Google developers want to turn the TensorFlow platform into one of the best ML toolboxes in the world. Open TensorFlow standards help exchange research ideas and put ML into new products. Google engineers apply TensorFlow in generating new products and services, as introduced in Section 9.2.

TensorFlow is not a rigid neural networks library. As long as you can express your com-putation as a data flow graph, you easily can use TensorFlow. You construct the graph, and write the inner loop that drives computation. The TensorFlow platform provides useful tools to assemble subgraphs common in neural networks. Users can write their own higher-level libraries on top of TensorFlow. Defining handy new compositions of operators is as easy as writing a Python function.

To implement a machine algorithm, TensorFlow uses a single data flow graph to repre-sent all computational states. Figure 9.1 shows all individual mathematical operations, the parameters and their update rules, and input preprocessing required in such a process. Data flow makes the communication between subcomputations explicit. This will make it easy to execute independent computations in parallel by partitioning the computation across multiple distributed devices. Data flow TensorFlow differs from batch data flow systems in two respects: (1) the model supports multiple concurrent executions on overlapping subgraphs of the total graph; and (2) individual nodes may have a mutable state that can be shared between different executions of the graph.

Mutable state is crucial in a parameter server architecture when training very large ML models. TensorFlow makes it possible to perform instant updates to very large parameters, and propagate those updates to parallel training steps. Data flow with mutable state enables TensorFlow the core operation performed on a parameter server. The mechanism offers ad-ditional flexibility, because it becomes possible to execute many data flow subgraphs on

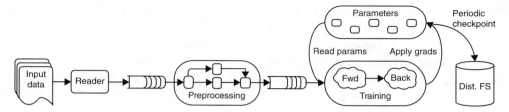

Figure 9.1

TensorFlow data flow graph for a training pipeline in DL applications. Reprinted with permission from M. Abadi et al., "TensorFlow: A System for Large-Scale Machine Learning," Google Brain Team White Paper, November 15, 2015.

the machines hosting the shared model parameters. As shown in Figure 9.1, the training process is done repeatedly over parameters updated with feedback loops. As a result, users can implement different optimization algorithms, consistency schemes, and parallelization strategies in the ML process. A major reference of TensorFlow ideas and implementations can be found in the white paper cited in Figure 9.1 and in other related figures.

Listed below are advantages claimed by Google in making TensorFlow an open-source software platform for machine intelligence. Readers can find good tutorials and application resources on using TensorFlow tools in the open-source website: https://www.tensorflow.org.

- *True portability:* TensorFlow runs on CPUs or GPUs, and on a desktop, server, or even on mobile phones. TensorFlow does not require special hardware to play around with an ML idea. The model can easily take advantage of the elastic scale-up and scale-out capability in clouds or mashup services across many cloud platforms. The model can run as a service in the cloud using docker containers to do TensorFlow computations.

- *Connect research and production:* Google research scientists experiment with new algorithms in TensorFlow, and product teams use TensorFlow to train and serve models live to real customers. Using TensorFlow allows industrial researchers to push ideas to products faster, and allows academic researchers to share code more directly with great reproducibility.

- *Auto-differentiation:* Gradient-based ML algorithms will benefit from TensorFlow's automatic differentiation capabilities. As a TensorFlow user, you define the computations in your predictive model to optimize the objective function. By adding more data, TensorFlow computes the derivatives automatically. The data flow graph is easily extended to visualize the learning steps.

- *Language options:* TensorFlow comes with an easy-to-use Python interface and a C++ interface to execute computational graphs. Users can write stand-alone TensorFlow Python or C++ programs that can keep notes, code, and visualizations logically grouped. It may add new interfaces to use with other favorite languages like Lua, JavaScript, or R.

TensorFlow is designed to perform well on scalable clusters or even on mobile devices that are connected to the data centers and clouds.

Example 9.1 Data Flow Graph and Basic TensorFlow Operations

Figure 9.2 illustrates the key concept of TensorFlow through a sequence of four operations. TensorFlow treats computation as a data flow graph, as shown in Figure 9.2a. The tensors are multidimensional data arrays that are generated by the source nodes and they flow along identified edges to the destination node (Figure 9.2b). In Figure 9.2c, computation states are identified, where *biases* (variables) are feeding into some states to compute the desired gradients, which are often performed in *deep neural network* (DNN) computations. The *learning rates* are the weights applied in DNN learning operations.

Figure 9.2d shows that distributed execution units (CPUs, GPU, etc.) are used to carry out the identified computations in parallel. Both pipelined (temporal) and spatial parallelism are fully explored in the TensorFlow process. In a subsequent section, we will use additional examples and fragment codes to illustrate how TensorFlow works in implementing, language, image, and perception problems. ∎

9.1.2 Tensors, Variables, Feed, and Fetch Operations

A TensorFlow computation is described by a directed graph of nodes and edges. The graph represents a data flow computation, with extensions for allowing some nodes to maintain and update persistent state and for branching and looping control structures. Clients typically construct a computational graph using C++ or Python. In a TensorFlow graph, each node has zero or more inputs and zero or more outputs, representing the instantiation of an operation. Values that flow along normal edges in the graph are called *tensors*.

Basically, we use a directed *graph* to represent computations, *sessions* to frame execution steps, *tensors* to quantify data arrays, *variables* to track states, and *feed* and *fetch* to assign or retrieve values in arbitrary operations. Essentially, TensorFlow is a programming system that uses graphs to specify computation tasks. Nodes in the graph are called "*ops*" (operations). Each *op* gets zero, one, or multiple tensors as its input. It generates similar tensors as the output. Each tensor is a multidimensional data array where the underlying element type is specified or inferred at graph-construction time. Special edges, called *control dependencies*, exist in the graph to control the proper execution timing between source and destination nodes.

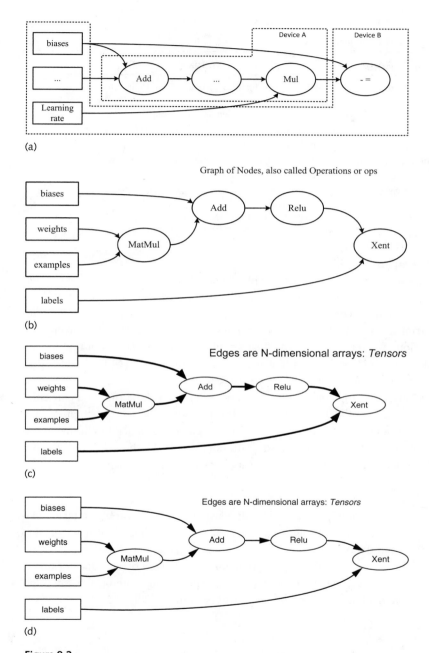

(a)

(b)

(c)

(d)

Figure 9.2
On a data flow graph, tensors flow along the edges to perform pipe lined parallel computations. Distributed execution occurs on multiple devices (CPUs, GPUs, etc.) Reprinted with permission from Jeff Dean, "Large Scale Deep Learning on Intelligent Computer Systems," Google Brain team slide presentation, http:/tensorflow.org /whitepaper2015.pdf.

Table 9.1
Examples of operation types built into TensorFlow core

Category	Examples
Element-wise mathematical operations	Add, Sub, Mul, Div, Exp, Log, Greater, Less, Equal, etc.
Array operations	Concat, SLice, Split, Constant, Rank, Shape, Shuffle, etc.
Matrix operations	MatMul, MatrixInverse, MatrixDeterminant, etc.
Stateful operations	Variable, Assign, AssignAdd, etc.
Neural-net building blocks	SoftMax, Sigmoid, ReLU, Convolution2D, MaxPool, etc.
Checkpointing operations	Save, Restore
Queue and synchronization operations	Enqueue, Dequeue, MutexAcquire, MutexRelease, etc.
Control flow operations	Merge, Switch, Enter, Leave, NextIteration

Operations and Kernels

An *operation* has a name and represents an abstract computation (e.g., "matrix multiply," or "add"). An operation can have *attributes*, and all attributes must be provided or inferred at graph-construction time in order to instantiate a node to perform the operation. One common use of attributes is to make operations polymorphic over different tensor element types (e.g., addition of two tensors of type float vs. addition of two tensors of type int32). Google provides special cloud-based application program interfaces (APIs) for translate, speech, vision, and text applications.

A *kernel* is a particular implementation of an operation that can be run on a particular type of device (e.g., CPU or GPU). A TensorFlow binary defines the sets of operations and kernels available via a registration mechanism. This set can be extended by linking in additional operation and/or kernel definitions/registrations. Table 9.1 shows operation types built into the core of the TensorFlow library.

Tensors

A tensor in an implementation is a typed, multidimensional array. A variety of tensor element types are supported, including signed and unsigned integers ranging in size from 8 to 64 bits, IEEE float and double types, a complex number type, and a string type (an arbitrary byte array). Backing store of the appropriate size is managed by an allocator that is specific to the device on which the tensor resides. Tensor backing store buffers are reference counted and are deallocated when no references remain.

Sessions

Clients programs interact with the TensorFlow system by creating a *session*. To create a computation graph, the session interface supports an *extend* method to augment the current graph managed by the session with additional nodes and edges. Assume the initial graph when a session is created is empty. The other primary operation supported by the session interface is *run*, which takes a set of output names that need to be computed as well as an optional set of tensors to be fed into the graph in place of certain outputs of nodes.

Using the arguments to run, the TensorFlow implementation can compute the transitive closure of all nodes that must be executed in order to compute the outputs that were requested. This allows for the execution of the appropriate nodes in an order that respects their dependencies. Most of our uses of TensorFlow set up a session with a graph once, and then execute the full graph or a few distinct subgraphs thousands or millions of times via the run calls.

Example 9.2 TensorFlow Code Segment

Consider the following example TensorFlow code fragment by the name *tf*. The semantic purpose of this code is described by the computation graph shown in Figure 9.3. We simply trace the code execution to demonstrate the code format from input initialization to data flow and output of computation results.

In general, the computation graph is executed multiple times. The following Python code show the handles of these persistent mutable tensors that can be passed to special operations, like Assign and AssignAdd (equivalent to +=). This makes the mutation of the referenced tensor possible.

```
import tensorflow as tf
b = tf.Variable(tf.zeros([100])) // 100-d vector, initialize to zeroes
W = tf.Variable(tf.random_uniform([784,100],-1,1)) // 784 × 100 matrix w/rnd vals
x = tf.placeholder(name="x") // Placeholder for input
relu = tf.nn.relu(tf.matmul(W, x) + b) // Relu(Wx+b)
C = [ . . . ] // Cost computed as a function of relu
s = tf.Session()
for step in xrange(0, 10):
input = . . . construct 100-D input array . . . // Create 100-d vector for input
result = s.run(C, feed_dict={x: input}) // Fetch cost, feeding x=input
print step, result
```

Most tensors do not survive past a single execution of the graph. However, a *variable* is a special kind of operation that returns a handle to a persistent mutable tensor that survives across executions of a graph. For ML applications of TensorFlow, the parameters are typically stored in tensors and are updated as part of the run of the training graph for the model. ∎

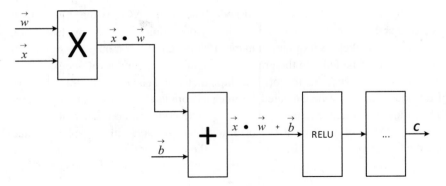

Figure 9.3
Corresponding computation graph for the code in Example 9.2. (Courtesy of Wenhao Zhang, USC, 2016.)

9.1.3   Distributed TensorFlow Execution Environment

In this section, we assess distributed TensorFlow execution environments, ranging from desktop computers to large-scale clusters or cloud platforms. First of all, we have to clarify a number of key terms that are defined hierarchically for the TensorFlow community at www.tensorflow.org.

Clients, Tasks, Jobs, and Cluster

TensorFlow *clients* (users) are identified by the program that builds a TensorFlow graph and constructs a running session. A single client process is called a *task,* corresponding to a specific TensorFlow server. Multiple tasks are often contained in a user *job.* A TensorFlow *cluster* is defined as a collection of related jobs running for a common objective. Therefore, a *TensorFlow cluster* comprises one or more *jobs*, each divided into lists of one or more *tasks*.

A cluster is often dedicated to a particular high-level objective, such as training a neural network, using many machines in parallel. In the TensorFlow framework, a cluster is defined as a "tf.train.ClusterSpec" object. A *parameter server* typically hosts nodes that store and update the variables, while a job named *worker* typically hosts stateless nodes that perform compute-intensive tasks. The tasks in a job typically run on different machines. A *TensorFlow server* is a process running as a tf.train.Server instance, which is a member of a cluster, and exports either "master service" or "worker service."

Master vs. Worker Services and Devices

The *master service* provides remote access to a set of distributed devices and implements the tensorflow::Session interface. Master service can be carried out by any

TensorFlow servers. It is responsible for coordinating the work across one or more *worker services*, which are implemented with a worker_service.proto. All TensorFlow servers (devices) are capable of implementing worker services. Devices are the computational heart of TensorFlow. Each worker is responsible for one or more devices (CPUs or GPUs).

Device names are composed of pieces that identify the device's type, the device's index within the worker, and, in a distributed setting, an identification of the job and task of the worker. For example, device names appear as "/job:localhost/device:cpu:0" or "/job:worker /task:17/device:gpu:3." Device interfaces for CPUs and GPUs are available and new device implementations are handled by a registration mechanism. Each device object is responsible for managing allocation and deallocation of device memory, and for arranging for the execution of any kernels.

Distributed Execution Architecture

The main components in a TensorFlow system are the client, which uses the session interface to communicate with the master, and one or more worker processes. The worker process is responsible for arbitrating access to one or more computational devices (such as CPU cores or GPU cards) and for executing graph nodes on those devices as instructed by the master. Google has both local and distributed implementations of the TensorFlow interface. Two different execution modes are illustrated in Figure 9.4. The use of TPU accelerators can improve the TensorFlow system performance significantly.

A local implementation is used when the client, the master, and the worker all run on a single machine in the context of a single operating system process (possibly with multiple

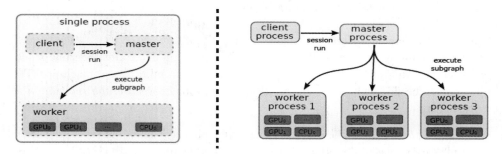

Figure 9.4

TensorFlow execution environment: single machine vs. distributed multiple machines. (Reprinted with permission from M. Abadi et al., "TensorFlow: A System for Large-Scale Machine Learning," Google Brain Team White Paper, November 15, 2015.)

devices, if, for example, the machine has many GPU cards installed). Distributed implementation shares most of the code with the local implementation, but extends it with support for an environment where the client, the master, and the workers can all be in different processes on different machines. In the distributed environment, these different tasks are *containers* in jobs managed by a cluster scheduling system. One can start a TensorFlow server as a single-process "cluster" using the tf.train.Server.create_local_server() method.

Creating a TensorFlow Cluster

A TensorFlow cluster is a set of "tasks" that participate in the distributed execution of a TensorFlow graph. Each task is associated with a TensorFlow "server," which contains a "master" that can be used to create sessions, and a "worker" that executes operations in the graph. A cluster can also be divided into one or more "jobs," where each job contains one or more tasks. To create a cluster, you start one TensorFlow server per task in the cluster. Each task typically runs on a different machine, but you can run multiple tasks on the same machine (e.g., to control different GPU devices). The following actions take place in a cluster.

- Create a tf.train.ClusterSpec that describes all of the tasks in the cluster. This should be the same for each task.

- Create a tf.train.Server, passing the tf.train.ClusterSpec to the constructor, and identifying the local task with a job name and task index.

- Create a tf.train.Server instance in each task. This instance contains local devices, connections to other tasks in its tf.train.ClusterSpec, and a session target to perform the distributed computation. Each server is a member of a specific job and has a task index within that job. All servers can communicate with each other in the cluster.

Replicated Training in TensorFlow

The model training involves multiple tasks in a worker job that trains the same model on different mini-batches of data. All tasks typically run on different machines. The training can be done with either *in-graph replication* or *between-graph replication* as outlined here.

- ***In-graph replication:*** The client builds a single tf.Graph that contains one set of parameters and multiple copies of the compute-intensive part of the model, each pinned to a different task in /job:worker.

- ***Between-graph replication:*** A separate client handles each /job:worker task, typically in the same process as the worker task. Each client builds a similar graph containing the parameters and a single copy of the compute-intensive part of the model, pinned to the local task in /job:worker.

In the previous two approaches, the training can be completed in two different ways. *Asynchronous training* applies to both replication methods in that each replica of the graph has an independent training loop that executes without coordination. *Synchronous training* requires that all replicas read the same values for the current parameters, compute gradients in parallel, and then apply them together. It is compatible only with in-graph replication. For example, one can use gradient averaging as in the CIFAR-10 multi-GPU trainer. For between-graph replication, one can apply the tf.train.SyncReplicasOptimizer in the TensorFlow system.

Stochastic gradient descent (SGD) is an important method in ML. SGD is robust in asynchrony, and previous systems trained deep neural networks using asynchronous parameter updates. The previous assumption was that an asynchronous update is more scalable, resulting in higher throughput at the cost of training steps using stale data. Some have recently revisited the assumption that synchronous training does not scale. Since GPUs enable training with hundreds, rather than thousands, of machines, it may be possible to train a model synchronously in less time than asynchronous training on the same machines.

As illustrated in the lower part of Figure 9.5, asynchronous data parallelism, each worker reads the current value when the step begins, and applies its gradient to the different current value at the end. The dashed lines indicate the separate synchronization signals applied. This approach ensures high utilization, but the individual steps use stale information, making each step less effective. The synchronous cases use queues to coordinate execution. A blocking queue acts as a barrier to ensure that all workers read the same parameter version, and a second queue accumulates multiple gradient updates accordingly.

The synchronous control accumulates updates from all workers before applying them, but this may slow down workers and limit overall throughput. To mitigate the stragglers, the TensorFlow group at Google implemented backup workers which are similar to MapReduce backup tasks in that MapReduce starts backup tasks reactively. By detecting a straggler, backup workers run proactively, and the aggregation takes the first m of n updates produced. The SGD samples train data randomly, so each worker processes a different random batch.

9.1.4 Execution Sessions in TensorFlow Programs

In this section, we use some TensorFlow code segments to illustrate how TensorFlow works. TensorFlow supports C, C++, and Python programming languages. Presently, Python appeals primarily to specific TensorFlow operations in terms of providing auxiliary functions to simplify the graph construction. These functions are not yet supported by C or C++. The session libraries for the three languages are consistent. The first step is to specify the source operation (op), which requires no extra input such as constant. The outputs of the source op

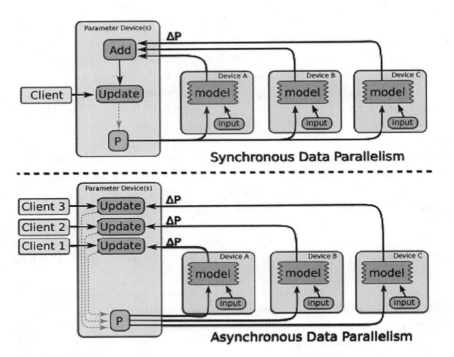

Figure 9.5
Synchronous and asynchronous data-parallel training methods. (Reprinted with permission from M. Abadi et al., "TensorFlow: A System for Large-Scale Machine Learning," Google Brain Team White Paper, November 15, 2015.)

feed into other ops. In Python, the value returned from an op generator is output to another op as input.

Our purpose is to guide users to develop DL applications. The TensorFlow graph describes the computation processes involved. Each session must be initiated to distribute the ops to CPU or GPU devices. The op method must be specified to return with new tensors generated. In Python code, the returned tensor is specified by:

<a rel = "nofollow" href="http://www.numpy.org/""="""style ="box-sizing: border-box; background-color: transparent; color: rgb(45, 133, 202)";> numpy.ndarray.

In C and C++, the returned tensor is simply a tensorflow::Tensor case. In the development stage, the op execution is described by a subgraph. In the execution stage, the session execution is applied to carry out the op specified. For example, during the construction stage a computation graph is created to train the neural network. Then the training op is used, repeatedly, during the execution stage. TensorFlow Python has a default graph, by which the op generator can add more nodes. The following code segment is used to manage such graphs. We first create a constant() node op to generate a 1×2 matrix and add it into a default graph. Then, we create a matmul() op using matrix1 and matrix2 as input, and return the value "product" as the matrix multiply result.

```
import tensorflow as tf
matrix1 = tf.conatant ([3., 3.] ])
matrix2 = tf.conatant ([2.], [2., ] ])
product = tf.matmul (matrix1, matrix2)
```

The above code generates a default graph with three nodes: two constant() ops and a matmul() op. You need to initiate a session graph, which requires creation of a session object. If there are no other parameters, the session API will just initiate the default graph automatically. This is done with the following code segment. The session is responsible for handling all input to the op node. The function applied is run(product), which triggers three ops to participate in the execution. The return value result is a NumPy "ndarray" object.

```
sess = tf.Session()
result = sess.run(product)
print result
sess.close()
```

To close up a session, all resources must be released during the following code segment:

```
with tf.Session(*) as sess:
result = sess.run([product])
print result
```

The TensorFlow system allocates the available CPU or GPU to execute the flow graph automatically. If there is more than one available GPU, the user may need to narrow down to a particular GPU, if needed.

```
with tf.Session() assess:
with tf.device("/gpu:1):
matrix1 = tf.constant([[3.,3.11)
matrix2 = tf.constant([[2.], [2.]])
product = tf.matmul(matrix1, matrix2)
```

Devices are identified by "/cpu:0," "/gpu:0," "gpu:1," etc. In an interactive environment Python applies a session to initiate the graph using Session.run() or using InteractiveSession to replace Session. One can also use Tensor.eval() or Operation.run() to replace Session.run(). The following code segment shows how to enter interactive TensorFlow Session using the run() op to initate "x" and how to add a subtraction sub op to output the result:

```
import tensorflow as if
sess = tf.InteractiveSession()
x = tf.Variable([1.0, 2.0])
a = tf.Variable([3.0, 3.0])
x.initialize.run()
sub = tf.sub(x, a)
print sub.eval ()
# ==> [-2. -1.]
```

Static Tensors vs. Variables

Tensors are a data structure flowing among computation nodes in a data flow graph. They appear as multidimensional data arrays or tables. Each tensor is characterized by static rank, shape, and type. *Variables* are used to handle the dynamic information needed in graph execution. In general, statistical parameters are treated as a set of variables. For example, you can treat the weights applied in an *artificial neural network* (ANN) as variables stored in a tensor. During the training period, repeated use of the graph model is needed to update the weight tensors.

Fetch vs. Feed Operations

To retrieve output results, you can use a session run() to adjust the graph, inputting some tensors to help *fetch* the result. The previous example fetches only a single node state. You can also fetch multiple tensors to get multiple results. In a single op execution, one can get all the results at the same time. Tensors can be stored as constants or variables. A *feed* mechanism is introduced in TensorFlow; this enables the replacement of some tensors by patchup tensors. The feed tensor can be used by run() as a new input parameter. Feed is effective to adjust the model under certain conditions. When a method is done, the feed disappears immediately. This allows one to treat some special operations as feed operations by using the label tf.placeholder() for a larger-scale example of feeds.

9.2 TensorFlow System for Deep Learning

It is fair to say that deep neural networks play a crucial role in understanding speech, images, language, and vision applications. Both pretrained models and APIs must have low overhead and be easy to use in ML system development. In what follows, we check some of the DL systems developed by the Google Brain team for various big data applications. Among these, we see DL applications in Android apps, drug discovery, Gmail, image understanding, maps, natural language understanding, photos, robotics research, speech, and YouTube, among many others.

Among 50 internal product development teams at Google, the interest in using DL was measured by the number of unique project directories containing model description files. That number increased from 150 in 2013 to 1,200 in 2015. In general, three approaches are adopted in cognitive computing apps.

1. Apply a software library on clouds or supercomputers for ML and neuroinformatics studies.
2. Use representation and algorithms to relate the inputs and outputs of artificial neural computers.
3. Design hardware neural chips to implement brain-like computers for ML and intelligence.

9.2.1 Layered TensorFlow System Architecture

At Google, the TensorFlow project historically has gone through three stages of development. These advances reflect the leadership roles by some top scientists or pioneering engineers at Google research teams.

DistBelief

Google Brain built DistBelief as a first-generation, proprietary, ML system in 2011. More than 50 teams at Google and other Alphabet companies have deployed DistBelief's DL neural networks in Google's commercial products, including Google Search, Google Voice Search, advertising, Google Photos, Google Maps, Google Street View, Google Translate, and YouTube.

Google assigned computer scientists Geoffrey Hinton and Jeffrey Dean to lead the effort to simplify and refactor the codebase of DistBelief into a faster, more robust application-grade library, known as TensorFlow. In 2009, the team led by Hinton was able to reduce the amount of errors in neural networks which used DistBelief, by at least 25 percent. This is attributed to scientific breakthroughs in generalized backpropagation.

TensorFlow

The name TensorFlow is derived from the tensor flowing operations which neural networks perform on multidimensional data arrays. These arrays are referred to as "tensors," which is not identical to the mathematical concept of tensors. The purpose is to train neural networks to detect and decipher patterns and correlations, in a timely manner. The earlier TensorFlow implementation runs on single devices. Now, TensorFlow can run on multiple CPUs and GPUs, which can be easily built in big data centers or cloud clusters.

TensorFlow is a software platform that supports CUDA programming in general-purpose computing on GPU. It runs on 64-bit Linux or Mac OS X desktop or server systems. It also runs on mobile computing platforms, including Android and Apple's iOS. TensorFlow computations are expressed as *stateful data flow graphs* (SDG). Many teams at Google have migrated from DistBelief to TensorFlow for research and production uses. This library of algorithms originated from Google's need to instruct computer systems, known as neural networks, to learn and reason similar to the way humans do, so that new applications can be derived to mimic many human sensing and comprehension functions.

Tensor Processing Unit (TPU)

In May 2016, Google announced a custom *application specific integrated circuit* (ASIC) chip they built specifically for ML-tailored TensorFlow programming. They installed *tensor processing units* (TPUs) inside their data centers for more than a year, and have found that they deliver an order of magnitude performance gain per watt in ML operations. The TPU is a programmable device concentrating on a high volume of low-precision (e.g., 8-bit) arithmetic, therefore it is more applicable for inference rather than training. Support of this open-sourced TensorFlow package can be found at: https://github.com/google/gemmlowp. Android support of TensorFlow is available for mobile execution, and iOS support will come soon.

The TensorFlow source code is an extensible and cross-platform library. Figure 9.6 shows the layered system architecture. A thin C API separates user-level languages from the core library. The core TensorFlow library is implemented in C++ for portability and performance. The system works with many operating systems including Linux, Mac OS X, Android, and iOS, running on the x86 and ARM-based CPU architectures as well as NVIDIA's Kepler, Maxwell, and Pascal GPU microarchitectures. The master translates user requests into execution across a set of tasks. Multiple masters could work on different sets of CPU and GPU devices.

Given a graph and a step definition, the master partitions the graph into multiple subgraphs for each participating device, and caches these subgraphs so that they can be used in subsequent steps. Since the master sees the overall computation as a step, it applies standard optimizations such as common subexpression elimination and constant folding. It then coordinates execution of the optimized subgraphs across a set of tasks. The data flow executor in each task handles requests from the master, and schedules the execution of the kernels that comprise a local subgraph. The layered architecture of the TensorFlow system is given in Figure 9.6.

To optimize the data flow execution of large-scale and fine-grained graphs with low overhead, the team dispatched approximately 2 million null operations per second. The data flow executor dispatches kernels to local devices and runs kernels in parallel when possible to the Google Brain. They use multiple cores in a CPU device, or multiple streams on

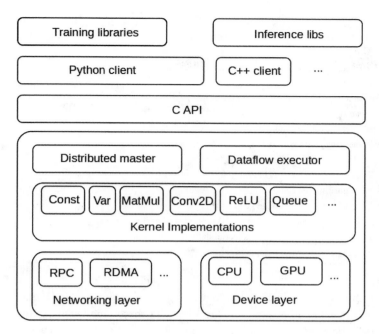

Figure 9.6
The layered architecture of TensorFlow architecture. (Reprinted with permission from M. Abadi et al., "Tensor-Flow: A System for Large-Scale Machine Learning," Google Brain Team White Paper, November 15, 2015.)

a GPU. The runtime contains over 200 standard operations, including mathematical, array manipulation, control flow, and state management operations.

Many of the operation kernels are implemented using *Eigen::Tensor*, which applies C++ templates to generate efficient parallel code for multicore CPUs and many-core GPUs. Google engineers liberally use libraries like cuDNN to implement kernels where a more efficient specialization is possible. They have also implemented support for quantization. This enables faster inference in environments such as mobile devices and high-throughput data center applications. They also use the *gemmlowp,* a low-precision matrix multiplication library to accelerate the quantized computation.

The TensorFlow system specializes in *send* and *receive* operations for each pair of source and destination device types. Transfers between local CPU and GPU devices use the cudaMemcpyAsync() API to overlap computation and data transfer; transfers between two local GPUs use DMA to relieve pressure on the host. For transfers between tasks, Tensor-Flow supports multiple protocols, including RPC over TCP, and RDMA over Converged Ethernet. GPU-to-GPU communication that uses collective operations is also being investigated. Typically, users compose standard operations to build higher-level abstractions, such as neural network layers, optimization algorithms, and shared embedding computations.

Table 9.2
Some available TensorFlow models for machine learning applications

Model Name	Brief Description
Autoencoder	Various autoencoders
Inception	Deep convolutional networks for computer vision
Nameignizer	Recognize and generate names
Neural_GPU	Highly parallel neural computer
Privacy	Privacy-preserving student models from multiple teachers
Resnet	Deep and wide residual networks
Slim	Image classification models in TF-Slim
Swivel	The Swivel algorithm for generating word embeddings
Syntaxnet	Neural models of natural language syntax
Textsum	Sequence-to-sequence with attention model for text summarization
Transformer	Spatial transformer network allowing spatial data manipulation
Im2txt	Image-to-text neural network for image captioning

TensorFlow supports multiple client languages. They have prioritized support for Python and C++ because Google internal users are most familiar with these languages. As features become more established, they are typically ported to C++ so that users can access an optimized implementation from all client languages. If it is difficult or inefficient to represent a subcomputation as a composition of operations, users can register additional kernels that provide an efficient implementation written in C++. Google engineers have built several tools that aid users. These include serving infrastructure for running inference in production and a *visualization dashboard* that enables users to follow the progress of a training run.

In Table 9.2, we list some well-developed TensorFlow models for various ML applications. Only a brief description is given here to each ML application. Details of each ML model can be found at the TensorFlow website (https://www.tensorflow.org), where tutorials are given to show implementation details.

9.2.2 TensorFlow Installation on Various Host Machines

In this section, we explain the procedures to install or release binaries or how to build TensorFlow programs. Note that TensorFlow can only be installed in an Ubuntu Linux 64-bit host or a Mac OS X system host. If you have a Windows system, you should install first the VM: Workstation Player 12, from the VMware website: https://my.vmware.com/web/vmware/free#desktop_end_user_computing/ vmware_workstation_player/12_0 . Then you can install the Ubuntu 14.04 TensorFlow edition in the VM being installed (http://releases.ubuntu.com/14.04/).

You may want to visit the TensorFlow website to seek help if needed. The open-source website is: https://www.tensorflow.org/versions/r0.10/get_started/basic_usage.html. On this site, you can learn how TensorFlow works, how to represent computations as graphs, how to execute graphs in the context of sessions, how to represent data as tensors, how to maintain state with variables, and how to use feeds and fetches to get data into or out of arbitrary operations. Python options to install TensorFlow on various hosts or clouds are given as follows:

- **Linux CPU-only:** Python 2 (build history) / Python 3.4 (build history) / Python 3.5 (build history).
- **Linux GPU:** Python 2 (build history) / Python 3.4 (build history) / Python 3.5 (build history).
- **Mac CPU-only:** Python 2 (build history) / Python 3 (build history).
- **Mac GPU:** Python 2 (build history) / Python 3 (build history).
- **Android:** (build history).

The following procedure is suggested to install Ubuntu 14.04 in VMware Workstation Player 12: http://merlot.usc.edu/cs402-f16/prepare-kernel/#player.

1. Download Python 3.5 from https://www.python.org/downloads/. Choose the OS you have on your host. Set the default Python 3.5 with the command: $ alias python=python3.

2. Install pip using the following commands:

   # Ubuntu/Linux 64-bit

   $ sudo apt-get install python-pip python-dev

   # Mac OS X

   $ sudo easy_install pip

   $ sudo easy_install --upgrade six

3. Select the correct binary for CPU only, if you want to use the CUDA. You could install the GPU version and follow the installation instructions with following commands:

   # Ubuntu/Linux 64-bit, CPU only, Python 3.5

   $ export

   TF_BINARY_URL=https://storage.googleapis.com/tensorflow/linux/cpu/tensorflow
   -0.10. 0rc0-cp35-cp35m-linux_x86_64.whl

   # Mac OS X, CPU only, Python 3.4 or 3.5:

   $ export

   TF_BINARY_URL=https://storage.googleapis.com/tensorflow/mac/cpu/
   tensorflow-0.10.0rc0-py3-none-any.whl

4. Install TensorFlow using the command:

```
# Python 3
$ sudo pip3 install --upgrade $TF_BINARY_URL
```

5. Test TensorFlow from the command line:

```
$ python
. . . // import tensorflow as tf //
hello = tf.constant('Hello, TensorFlow!')
sess = tf.Session()
print(sess.run(hello))
Hello, TensorFlow!
a = tf.constant(10)
b = tf.constant(32)
print(sess.run(a + b))
```

Visit https://www.tensorflow.org/versions/r0.10/get_started/os_setup.html for other installations. Go to https://www.tensorflow.org/versions/r0.10/get_started/basic_usage.html to learn more about TensorFlow. Table 9.2 shows a repository of various application models contributed by TensorFlower developers or users. Some additional details can be found at: www.tensorflow.org.

9.2.3   TensorFlow Ecosystem for Distributed Resources Sharing

The TensorFlow platform needs an ecosystem that can support the integration of open-source frameworks in the following four software solutions for distributed execution of TensorFlow programs:

- Cluster manager provides docker containers for distributed TensorFlow execution.
- Use of Kubernetes in distributed execution of TensorFlow modules.
- Mesos deployment of Marathon for distributed execution of TensorFlow modules.
- Provides TFRecord documents with InputFormat/OutFormat in Hadoop MapReduce and Spark programs.

Specifically, we use several working TensorFlow code segments to explain how to integrate TensorFlow programs with some available open-source software frameworks.

Example 9.3 Flag Signaling Opportunity for Distributed TensorFlow Execution
Defining signals is often needed to inform a worker of the roles played by other workers in the distributed TensorFlow execution environment. The following code sets up often used flags for this purpose. The meaning of those flags is given in the attached comments.

```
# Flags for configuring the task
flags.DEFINE_integer("task_index". None.
                "Worker task index. should be >=0. task_index=0 is"
                "the master worker task the performs the variable"
                "initialization.")
flags.DEFINE_string("ps_hosts". None.
                "Comma-separated list of hostname:port pairs")
flags.DEFINE_string("worker_hosts". None.
                "Comma-separated list of hostname:port pairs")
flags.DEFINE_string("job_name". None. "job name: worker or ps"). ∎
```

Example 9.4 Linking Servers with Their Workers or Parameter Servers

Very often, when a TensorFlow program opens up its own server, the server needs to be closely united with its parameter servers. This is due to the fact that many worker and parameter servers (PS jobs) are often sharing frequently used code segments. The following sequence of code segments achieves this goal:

```
# Construct the cluster and start the server
ps_spec=FLAGS.ps_hosts.split(".")
worker_spec=FLAGS.worker_hosts.split(".")

cluster=tf.train.ClusterSpec((
    "ps": ps_spec.
    "worker": worker_spec))

server=tf.train.Server(
    cluster.job_name=FLAGS.job_name, task_index=FLAGS.task_index)
if FLAGS.job_name= = "ps":
    server.joint) ∎
```

Example 9.5 Between-Graph Replication for Installing Jinja Modules

Data flow graph replication is often performed in TensorFlow programming. In this case, each worker constructs its own graph and operates on the graph independently. At most they share the gradients with some parameter servers. It would be beneficial if they could be better coupled together to reduce the graph costs. The situation is described in Figure 9.7, where two clients work with their servers and associated workers by sharing the parameter servers (PS).

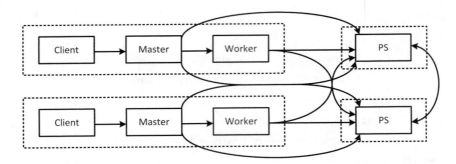

Figure 9.7
Between-graph replication for distributed Tensor execution.

The following code is needed to set up the environment to train model graph construction:

with tf.device(tf.train.replica_device_setter(

  worker_device="/job:worker/task:%d" % FLAGS.task_index,

  cluster=cluster)):

Construct the TensorFlow graph.# Run the TensorFlow graph.

To enable such a TensorFlow graph construction, the Jinja model must be installed as exemplified in the following code segment:

On Ubuntu

sudo apt-get install python-jinja2

On most other platforms

sudo pip install Jinja2 ∎

9.2.4 TensorFlow for Handwritten Digit Recognition

A well-known application of TensorFlow is the automated recognition of handwritten (scripted) digits by a computer using a ML approach. At the TensorFlow website, https://www .tensorflow.org/versions/r0.10/tutorials/mnist/tf/index.html, one can find an open benchmark of such a program over the MNIST data set of handwritten numerals. This program is traced below as an example of a TensorFlow application using a simple feed-forward neural network with the MNIST data set. TensorFlow is basically a neural network library. The system applies to any problem that can be expressed by a data flow graph. Other suitable applications include image processing, speech and language understanding, photo recognition, and captioning.

The objective is to run a TensorFlow program for classifying handwritten digits from the MNIST data set. You need to first find the TensorFlow packages by running the following command:

```
$ python -c 'import os; import inspect; import tensorflow;
print(os.path.dirname(inspect.getfile(tensorflow)))'
```

You obtain the TensorFlow package path specified by /usr/local/lib/python2.7/dist-packages/tensorflow. After that, you can run the convolutional.py demo using the following command:

```
# Using 'python -m' to find the program in the Python search path:
$ python -m tensorflow.models.image.mnist.convolutional.
Extracting data/train-images-idx3-ubyte.gz,
Extracting the data/train-labels-idx1-ubyte.gz,
Extracting the data/t10k-images-idx3-ubyte.gz.,
Extracting data/t10k-labels-idx1-ubyte.gz, etc . . .
```

You can alternatively pass the path to the model program file to the Python interpreter (make sure to use the Python distribution you installed with # TensorFlow to, for example, . . . /python3.X/ . . . for Python 3).

```
$ python /usr/local/lib/python2.7/dist-packages/tensorflow/models/image
/mnist/convolutional.py
```

Note that you need to substitute /usr/local/lib/python2.7/dist-packages/tensorflow with the actual path for the tensorflow package obtained above. Visit https://www.tensorflow.org/versions/r0.10/get_started/os_setup.html if using other installation methods. The following example shows how to use TensorFlow in programming an ANN, called the *MNIST classifier*:

Example 9.6 Programming an ANN for Handwritten Digit Recognition by TensorFlow
We consider the construction of a four-layer ANN, called the *MNIST classifier*. There are four steps to construct their ANN. We specify the procedure of each step, separately, using pseudo codes with comments, which are rather close to Python codes.

Step 1: Collect the data. We use the MNIST data which is taken from Yann LeCun's website (http://yann.lecun.com/index.html). TensorFlow has included some Python code (named input_data.py). The data will be installed when running the downloaded files. We import it just by a Python code import input_data. The Python codes and explanation are specified in the following steps:

```
# import tensorflow, numpy and input_data to this program
import tensorflow as tf
import numpy as np
```

```
import input_data
# load the data
mnist = input_data.read_data_sets("MNIST_data/," one_hot=True)
trX, trY, teX, teY = mnist.train.images, mnist.train.labels, mnist.test.images,
mnist.test.labels
```

Step 2: Construct the ANN model. We select a four-layer neural network to construct the classifier, which contains one input layer, two hidden layers, and one output layer. The Python code for this step is given below. The following code defines the model explicitly. There are two hidden layers and three dropouts. The dropout means that some node weight does not work in the network; the work of those nodes is temporarily considered as part of the network structure, but its weight was preserved (only temporarily, not updated). The tf.matmul is a multiply function. The tf.nn.relu is a kind of activation function.

```
// The following is for weight initialization in the ANN construction
def init_weights(shape):
return tf.Variable(tf.random_normal(shape, stddev=0.01))
def model(X, w_h, w_h2, w_o, p_drop_input, p_drop_hidden):
X = tf.nn.dropout(X, p_drop_input) #dropout
h = tf.nn.relu(tf.matmul(X, w_h))
h = tf.nn.dropout(h, p_drop_hidden) # dropout
h2 = tf.nn.relu(tf.matmul(h, w_h2))
h2 = tf.nn.dropout(h2, p_drop_hidden) # dropout
return tf.matmul(h2, w_o)
```

The following code defines the placeholder. X is not a specific value, it is a placeholder, a value that we will input when we ask TensorFlow to run a computation. We want to input any number of MNIST images, each flattened into a 784-dimensional vector. We represent this as a 2D tensor of floating-point numbers, with a shape [None, 784]. (Here, None means that a dimension can be of any length.) Similarly, Y is a 10-dimensional vector that stands for 10 numbers. Through weight initialization, the entity w_h is a 784×625, w_h2 a 625×625, and w_o a 625×10 matrix.

```
X = tf.placeholder("float," [None, 784])
Y = tf.placeholder("float," [None, 10])
w_h = init_weights([784, 625])
w_h2 = init_weights([625, 625])
```

w_o = init_weights([625, 10]) // Define p_keep as the probability of dropout:

p_keep_input = tf.placeholder("float")

p_keep_hidden = tf.placeholder("float") // The model is set as follows:

py_x = model(X, w_h, w_h2, w_o, p_keep_input, p_keep_hidden)

Step 3: Train the model. By comparing the output of training data and its labels, the algorithm will adjust the parameters of the network. The Python code is given below. This part defines the cross_entropy as a loss function. Then we ask Tensor-Flow to minimize cross_entropy using the RMSPropOptimizer algorithm. Argmax is an extremely useful function that gives you the index of the highest entry in a tensor along some axis. For example, tf.argmax(y,1) is the label our model has for each input, while tf.argmax(y_,1) is the correct label. We can use tf.equal to check if the prediction is correct.

cost = tf.reduce_mean(tf.nn.softmax_cross_entropy_with_logits(py_x, Y))

train_op = tf.train.RMSPropOptimizer(0.001, 0.9).minimize(cost)

predict_op = tf.argmax(py_x, 1) //Create a session object to launch the graph

sess = tf.Session()

init = tf.initialize_all_variables()

sess.run(init)

for i in range(100):

for start, end in zip(range(0, len(trX), 128), range(128, len(trX), 128)):

sess.run(train_op, feed_dict = {X: trX[start:end], Y: trY[start:end], p_keep_input: 0.8, p_keep_hidden: 0.5})

print i, np.mean(np.argmax(teY, axis=1) == sess.run(predict_op, feed_dict={X: teX, Y: teY, p_keep_input: 1.0, p_keep_hidden: 1.0}

endfor

endfor

Step 4: Test the network. The algorithm will compare the output of the test data and its corresponding label and calculate its accuracy. The training data is used to train the parameters of the model, but the test data is not used to train the parameters. Therefore, we can use test data to get the accuracy of the train model. As shown in Figure 9.8, the accuracy becomes higher after each training. After training the system multiple times, the accuracy of 0.9851 was achieved as shown in Figure 9.8. ∎

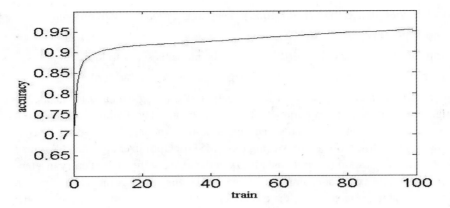

Figure 9.8
Results of TensorFlow based on programming an artificial neural network.

9.2.5   TensorFlow Applications for Cognitive Services

Given a computation graph, one of the main responsibilities of the TensorFlow implementation is to map the computation onto the set of available devices. A simplified version of this algorithm is presented here. One input to the placement algorithm is a cost model, which contains estimates of the sizes (in bytes). Single machine and distributed system structures input and output tensors for each graph node, along with estimates of the computation time required for each node when presented with its input tensors. Distributed execution of a graph is very similar to multidevice execution. After device placement, a subgraph is created per device.

TensorFlow Steps in Developing Machine Learning at Google

TensorFlow provides a Python API, as well as a less documented C/C++ API. Among the broad spectrum of applications, TensorFlow is proven successful in automated image captioning software, such as DeepDream. Google officially implemented RankBrain on October 26, 2015. This package is fully backed by TensorFlow. It handles a substantial number of search queries, replacing the static algorithm to obtain faster and more accurate search results. Specific requirements in a ML system follow:

1. Ease of expressing ML ideas or algorithms as data flow graphs

2. Enables scalable ML system development to handle ever increasing data sets

3. Can run experiments on multiple cloud platforms with high portability

4. Is easy to share and reproduces search, classification, and prediction results

TensorFlow was applied by 50 Google internal teams in developing new service products.

A Data Flow Graph for Machine Learning Systems

The computation in ML or DL systems is often described as a data flow graph. The following example is borrowed from Jeff Dean's slide presentation (http://tensorflow.org/white paper2015.pdf). We use this sequence of graphs in Figure 9.2 to illustrate four major steps in TensorFlow operations: TensorFlow treats computation as a data flow graph where the tensors (multidimensional data arrays) flow along identified edges to enable successive computation steps at various execution states. Distributed execution is made possible on multiple devices (processes, machines, GPUs, etc.).

Google has suggested four ways to get started with ML development.

1. Use a cloud-based API (for vision, speech, etc.).

2. Run a trained model.

3. Use an existing model structure for fine-tuning your data set.

4. Develop your own ML models for new problems.

The Google Brain team developed TensorFlow with the emphasis on dealing with large data sets that demand huge amounts of computation.

TensorFlow is an open-source software library for ML in various kinds of perceptual and language understanding tasks. It is a second-generation API, which is currently used by 50 Google teams responsible for many Google products for speech recognition, Gmail, Google Photos, and Search. These teams had previously used DistBelief, a first-generation API. TensorFlow was originally developed by the Google Brain team for Google's research and production purposes. The package was released in 2015 under the Apache 2.0 open-source license.

Here, acoustic speech signals are fed into the system as input. Through repeated learning from the deep recurrent neural network (DRNN) system, text output as a question: "How cold is it outside?" is generated automatically. Apple's Siri system also has built such conversational capabilities. *Deep convolutional neural networks* (DCNNs) are also proven very useful for this purpose. In addition, object recognition and detection are of equal importance. This is part of the traditional field of pattern recognition and image processing domain. Deeper convolution and scalable object detection offer viable approaches to solve the problem on modern clouds.

Machine translation can be done by sequence to sequence the learning process with neural networks. Neural machine translation has been worked out at Google. Language modeling was also conducted with a one-billion-word benchmark. The approach is to measure progress in statistical language modeling. Another exciting area is automatic parsing grammar as a foreign language. The whole purpose of ANNs is to learn a complicated function from data. ANNs have formed a hot research field in the past thirty years.

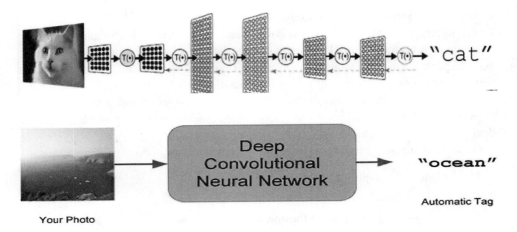

Figure 9.9
Using a deep convolution neural network to recognize a particular image out of millions of photos belonging to different or similar classes. (a) Reconizing a cat (not a dog), (b) Distinguishing an ocean view from many other views. (Courtesy of Jeff Dean, Google Brain Team, 2016.)

Example 9.7 The Use of Google's ImageNet for Image Understanding

ANN models, especially DCNNs, are undergoing a reincarnation. They offer a collection of simple, trainable mathematical functions that are compatible with many variants of ML. Figure 9.9 shows the idea of using a DCNN to recognize a "cat" or an "ocean" from a thousand classes over millions of photo images. Image captioning has been in high demand in Google search requests.

Searching for a personal photo without tags is equivalent to the task of identifying one image out of 1,000 different classes. The work was carried out at Google using ImageNet. Another project using GoogLeNet also emphasizes a deeper convolution approach in the inception area. Neural networks have made rapid progress in image recognition. The ImageNet project challenges many classification tasks. The Inception team using GoogLeNet reduced the error rate to 6.66% in 2014. ∎

In what follows, we present the concept of *big query* from Google. Then we use TensorFlow to construct the computation graph for an image recognition system. First, we go through an example development to trace the process in working steps.

Building a Computation Graph with TensorFlow Tools

TensorFlow is an open-source software library for easier programing, which allows you to express your computation as a data flow graph. Nodes in the graph are called ops and data flowing through the graph are represented as a tensor, which is a typed multidimensional array. We need to create a session to execute ops in the graph. During the executions of the

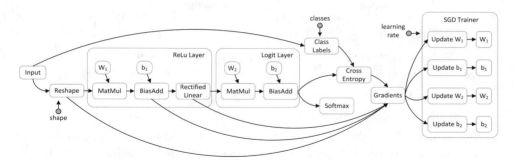

Figure 9.10
The image recognition model expressed as a TensorFlow graph. (Courtesy of Jeff Dean, Google Brain Team.)

graph, we use variables to maintain the state, and we can fetch or feed a tensor directly from or into any operation in the graph by using the fetch or feed mechanism in TensorFlow.

The first step of TensorFlow programs is to build a graph with ops. An op takes zero or more tensors, performs some computations, and produces zero or more tensors. To execute ops in the graph, we need a session to launch the graph, which is the second step of TensorFlow programs. A session places the graph ops onto devices, such as CPUs or GPUs, provides methods to execute them, and returns tensors produced by ops.

Figure 9.10 describes the computation graph of TensorFlow. First, we use the Reshape op to translate the input to make it available for training in TensorFlow, then we conduct the MatMul and BiasAdd ops on W1 and b1, respectively. We use Cross Entropy to compute the loss between the computed output and the original label, and update W and b by finding the minimum loss through gradient descending. All these ops are a kind of computing unit. We set these units and confirm the way they compose, like stringing gates together one by one. The way one uses a session to execute the graph is the same as electrifying the gate circuits, however, instead we give data to the op units and then they form the data flow.

We then keep adding more nodes to decode the file data as an image, to cast the integers into floating point values, to resize, and then finally to run the subtraction and division operations on the pixel values.

Image Recognition using TensorFlow

We use GoogleNet Inception-v3 (http://arxiv.org/pdf/1512.00567v3.pdf) to train the ImageNet (http://www.image-net.org/). There are 1,000 categories in the whole image set. In this example, we will use the pretrained Inception-v3 as a model, and one image in a data set as a test case, to describe the process of image classification using TensorFlow. Figure 9.10 shows a 800×608 RGB image used as an input for recognition purposes. The process of building a TensorFlow graph using C++ follows.

1. We create an object b of GraphDefBuilder, which is used to specify a model to run or load data as specified by the following code segment:

```
Status ReadTensorFromImageFile(string file_name, const int input_height,
const int input_width, const float input_mean, const float input_std),
td::vector<Tensor>* out_tensors)
tensorflow::GraphDefBuilder b;
```

2. We need to create nodes for the model we want to run. These nodes load, resize, and scale the pixel values to make the original image fit the input condition of the model. The first node we create is just a Const op that is used to hold a tensor with the file name of the image we want to load.

```
string input_name = "file_reader";
string output_name = "normalized";
tensorflow::Node* file_reader =tensorflow::ops::ReadFile(tensorflow::ops
Const(file_name, b.opts()),b.opts().WithName(input_name));
const int wanted_channels = 3;
tensorflow::Node* image_reader;
if (tensorflow::StringPiece(file_name).ends_with(".png")) {
image_reader = tensorflow::ops::DecodePng( file_reader,
     b.opts().WithAttr("channels",wanted_channels).WithName("png_reader"));}
     else { image_reader = tensorflow::ops::DecodeJpeg( file_reader,
b.opts().WithAttr("channels", wanted_channels).WithName("jpeg_reader"));}
tensorflow::Node* float_caster = tensorflow::ops::Cast(
image_reader, tensorflow::DT_FLOAT, b.opts().WithName("float_caster"));
tensorflow::Node* dims_expander = tensorflow::ops::ExpandDims(
float_caster, tensorflow::ops::Const(0, b.opts()), b.opts());
tensorflow::Node* resized = tensorflow::ops::ResizeBilinear(
dims_expander, tensorflow::ops::Const({input_height, input_width},
b.opts().WithName("size")), b.opts());
tensorflow::ops::Div(
tensorflow::ops::Sub(
resized, tensorflow::ops::Const({input_mean}, b.opts()), b.opts()),
tensorflow::ops::Const({input_std}, b.opts()),
b.opts().WithName(output_name));
```

3. In the end, all the information about model definition is stored in b variable; we use ToGraphDef function to turn it into a full graph definition: tensorflow::GraphDef graph.

4. We create a session object which is the interface of running the graph and run it. At the same time, we need to specify which node we want to get the output from, and where to put the output data.

In this example, we get a vector of tensor objects that is just an input image. This is a tensor of multidimensional array holds a 609-pixel high, 800-pixel wide, three-channel image. We download the GraphDef file for model definition, then compile, load, and run the C++ codes we can get the final predicted classification:

```
wget
https://storage.googleapis.com/download.tensorflow.org/models/ inception_
dec_2015.zip –O
tensorflow/examples/label_image/data/inception_dec_2015.zip
unzip tensorflow/examples/label_image/data/inception_dec_2015.zip -d
tensorflow/examples/label_image/data/
bazel build tensorflow/examples/label_image/ . . .
bazel-bin/tensorflow/examples/label_image/label_image
```

The result is: a cabbage butterfly (644):0.908836, which represents the index of best score and corresponding score respectively from all the categories (Figure 9.11). From the result we can see that the model correctly recognized the cabbage butterfly in the picture with the score as high as 0.90. The above example shows how image recognition works with

Figure 9.11
Sample image tested through the TensorFlow image recognition system at Google.

TensorFlow using the pretrained model. Another interesting area is to combine vision with translation or to combine vision with robotics intelligence. This will be critical to the autonomous vehicle driving projects, which are actively pursued at Google, Baidu, and other research centers. For example, we want the robots to learn hand-eye coordination through a DL system onboard a car. Some progress has already been demonstrated in several ongoing projects in the United States and China.

9.3 Google's DeepMind and Other AI Programs

In this section, we study the DeepMind technology that is currently in use in Google *artificial intelligence* (AI) programs. The *reinforcement DL* (RDL) scheme is presented along with its applications in AlphaGo and other programs at Google cloud. In 2010, a British AI company started the DeepMind Technologies, which received the "Company of The Year" award by Cambridge Computer Laboratory in the United Kingdom. Subsequently, DeepMind was acquired by Google in 2014.

9.3.1 Reinforcement Deep Learning Algorithm

As introduced in Section 9.1.2, the reinforcement deep learning process is mainly displayed by interactions between the learning agent and its working environment. The reinforcement learning offers an algorithm to solve sequential decision-making problems. The cumulative reward is maximized by software agents after taking a series of actions in a working environment. Without knowing any rules in advance, an agent observes the current environmental state and tries some actions to improve the DL process. A reward is the feedback to the agent by adjusting its action strategy. After numerous adjustments, the reinforcement algorithm obtains the knowledge of optimal actions to achieve the best results for a specific situation in the decision environment.

Figure 9.12 shows the interaction of an agent and its environment during the learning process. At each time t, the agent receives a state s_t. and executes an action a_t. Then, it receives an observation o_t. and a reward r_t associated with the action. The environment is typically formulated as a *Markov decision process* (MDP) to allow the agent to interact with it. After receiving an action, the environment emits a state and a scalar reward. The goal of reinforcement learning is to accumulate the rewards as much as possible at successive steps. A sequence of observation, action, and reward, $\{o_1, r_1, a_1, \ldots, a_{t-1}, o_t, r_t\}$, forms an experience, while the state is a function of the experience, i.e.,

$$s_t = f(o_1, r_1, a_1, \ldots, a_{t-1}, o_t, r_t)$$

AlphaGo's algorithm uses a *Monte Carlo tree search* (MCTS) to find its moves based on knowledge previously "learned" by ML. A DL ANN is used by extensive training, both

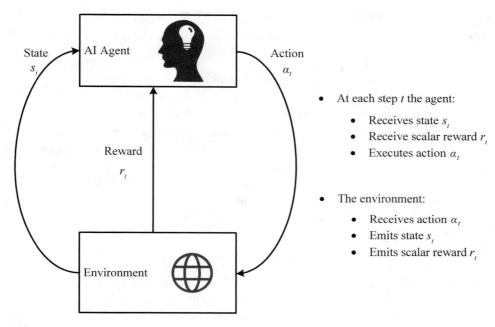

Figure 9.12
Interaction of an agent and environment in DL. (Reprinted with permission from David Silver, "Deep Reinforcement Learning," http://www0.cs.ucl.ac.uk/staff/d.silver/web/Resources_files/deep_rl.pdf, May 8, 2015.)

from human and computer play. The MCTS is guided by a *value network* and a *policy network,* both implemented using deep neural network technology. A limited amount of game-specific feature detection is applied to the input at the preprocessing stage, before it is sent to the neural networks.

The system's neural networks were initially bootstrapped from human gameplay expertise. AlphaGo was initially trained to mimic human play by attempting to match the moves of expert players from recorded historical games, using a database of around 30 million moves. Once it had reached a certain degree of proficiency, it was trained further by being set to play large numbers of games against other instances of itself. This was done with reinforcement learning to improve its play with the purpose of trying to avoid wasting the opponent's time. The program is programmed to resign if its assessment of win probability falls beneath a given threshold. For the AlphaGo–Lee Sedol 2016 match, the resignation threshold was set at 20%.

At the 33rd International Conference on Machine Learning (ICML 2016), Silver et al. presented the application details of DeepMind by using the reinforcement deep learning (RDL) approach. Specifically, a value function, policy, and model are represented by a deep neural network. In a RDL approach, AI is achieved by reinforcement learning and DL jointly. The human-level task can be solved by a single agent with reinforcement learning to achieve the objective set by the DL mechanism. After the action is selected by the agent, policy, value function, and model play important roles in its performance.

1. **Policy** is a behavior function selecting actions given states. There are two typical policies. One is the deterministic policy, which definitely executes some action a under a specific state s, i.e., $a = \pi(s)$. The other is stochastic policy, which means there is a probability to perform some action a under state s, i.e., $\pi(a \mid s) = P[a \mid s]$.

2. **Value function** predicts the future reward and evaluates the efficacy of an action or state, i.e., $Q\pi(s, a)$ is the expected total reward from state s and action a under policy π. It calculates the expected value of the accumulated reward obtained in future states, i.e., $t+1, t+2, t+3 \ldots$, etc. However, the future reward is discounted as time passes. The discount-factor $\gamma \in [0,1]$ is applied to decrease the award in a future state. The goal is to obtain the maximum value of $Q\pi(s, a)$. The optimal policy is obtained by maximizing the value function as follows:

$$Q^*(s, a) = E\left[r_{t+1} + \gamma \max_{a_{t+1}} Q^*(s_{t+1}, a_{t+1}) \mid s, a\right].$$

Equation (9.2) was attributed to Bellman, who uses dynamic programming to achieve the optimal value through multiple iterations. Give an action a under state s, a reward r_{t+1} is obtained at state s_{t+1}. In order to achieve the maximum Q-value, the state s_{t+1} needs to be optimal. Similarly, the Q value of state s_{t+2} should be optimized to guarantee the optimal Q-value of state s_{t+2}, etc. The iterative process goes on until the final state. When the number of states and actions is small, a state action table can be built to record the optimal Q-value. For infinite states, the approximation function is needed to represent the relationship among state, action, and value. A neural network is the best choice for this purpose.

The *deep Q-network* (DQN) provides three stable solutions to overcome the above problem.

1. Use experience replay to break correlations in data and go back to an *independent and identically distributed* (IID) setting. We store all past policies in replay memory and learn from them.

2. Freeze the target Q-network to avoid oscillations and break correlations between the Q-network and target.

3. Clip rewards or normalize network adaptively to a sensible range. This demands the use of a robust gradient method.

9.3.2 Interaction Between Policy Network and Value Network

This project applies convolutional deep networks that learn to play video games in a fashion that mimics the short-term memory of the human brain. Go is a very complex game for both human players and computers due to its huge search space. In 1997, IBM's computer

Deep Blue beat world chess champion Garry Kasparov in an open match. Ever since then, the strongest AI program to play Go only reached about amateur 5-dan level, which still could not beat a professional Go player without handicaps. For example, the software program Zen, running on a four PC cluster, beat Masaki Takemiya (9p) two times at five- and four-stones handicaps. The program Crazy Stone beat Yoshio Ishida (9p) at a four-stones handicap.

The Go game is played with black and white stones on a 19×19 mesh board. The game has a search tree complexity equal to b^d, where b is the game's breadth (number of the illegal moves at each state) and d is the depth (number of moves before the game is over). This means that brute force search is impossible for computers to evaluate who is winning. No computers had ever beaten human Go players until March 2016. In fact, Go is much more complex than any other games such as chess. This is attributed to the much larger number of possibilities on the Go game board. The complexity involves deep steps that even professional players cannot keep track of beyond certain steps with possible rewards accurately evaluated.

The AlphaGo research project was formed around 2014 to test how well a neural network using DL could compete against professional Go players. It represented a significant improvement over previous Go programs. AlphaGo running on multiple computers won 500 games played against other Go programs. The distributed system used in the October 2015 match was using 1,202 CPUs and 176 GPUs. In January 2016, the team published a paper in the journal *Nature* that describes the algorithms used in AlphaGo. In March 2016, this computer program beat Lee Sedol, a 9-dan world Go player by 4 to 1 in a five-game match. AlphaGo was not specifically trained to face Lee, and it won the game entirely by machine intelligence without handicap. Although it lost to Lee in the fourth game, Lee resigned the final game.

The AlphaGo and Lee Sedol match proves that computers can be trained to formalize the human intelligence process. In addition to the Go match, seven Atari video games—Pong, Breakout, Space Invaders, Seaquest, Beam Rider, Enduro, and Q*bert—were also tested using similar computer programs. All of these games involve strategic thinking out of imperfect or uncertainty information contents. DeepMind claims that their AI program is not preprogrammed. Each move is limited to 2 s. The program learns from experience using only raw pixels as data input. Technically, the program uses DL on a convolutional neural network.

The Google DeepMind program is aimed at solving very difficult intelligence problems that leverage ML and neuroscience systems. Google's DeepMind has combined DL and reinforcement algorithms to achieve human level performance in several innovative AI applications. The new algorithm is called RDL, which adopts a group of agents to select the best actions. The first RDL approach was known as the *deep Q-network* (DQN), proposed by David Silver of DeepMind. He is also one of the AlphaGo authors. The DQN combines *convolutional neural networks* (CNN) and Q-network algorithms. The Q-network is used to assess the reward after an agent executes a specific action.

The intelligence program learns to play the game right after a sufficient number of learning plays. For most games, DeepMind plays well below the current world record. For example, the application of DeepMind program to 3D video games, such as Doom, is still under development in 2016. According to DeepMind cofounder Mustafa Suleyman, DeepMind Technologies is also extending their applications to a DeepMind Health program. This program is mainly designed to provide clinical services to the healthcare community. This will open up intelligent healthcare services, which will benefit patients. In what follows, we introduce the DeepMind approach by combining DL with reinforcement learning ideas. Then we examine the algorithms used in AlphGo and in the Flappy Bird game, including their implementation and learning processes.

CNN Construction in AlphaGo and Its Training Process

The Go game is played on a 19×19 grid board as shown in Figure 9.13. Black and white stones are placed on the board, one at a time by two players alternately. Once the stones of the same color are fully surrounded by the opponent's stones, they will be removed from the board. The winner ends up with control of the larger areas. It is essentially a seize-and-control game. The game involves a large search space in every move of the stone. A CNN can be built based on the successive insertions of the stones in the strategic grid locations from the left-hand side to the right.

The DeepMind team has proposed a novel scheme *Q-learning* based on reinforcement learning. Figure 9.14 shows the schematic system diagram of Google's reinforcement learning architecture, known as Gorila. This system was implemented on large clusters of servers at Google. With 64 search threads, a distributed cluster of 1,930 CPUs and 280 GPUs was used in the AlphaGo and Lee Sedol competition. Parallel acting generates new interactions

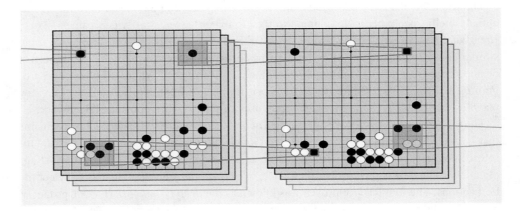

Figure 9.13
Convolutional neural network construction over the Go playing board.

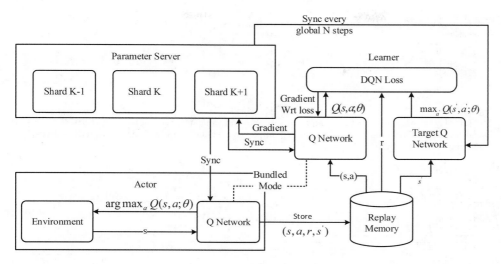

Figure 9.14
The Gorila architecture for implementing the Google reinforcement learning system. (Courtesy of David Silver, "Deep Reinforcement Learning," http://www0.cs.ucl.ac.uk/staff/d.silver/web/Resources_files/deep_rl .pdf, May 8, 2015.)

with distributed replay memory to save iterations. Parallel learning computes gradients from replayed iterations. The distributed CNN updates the network with gradients.

AlphaGo program is built with four parts: *policy network, fast rollout, value network,* and *MCTS*. The fast rollout network is trained by linear modeling utilizing local features, and has high speed but low accuracy, while policy network has low speed but high accuracy, which is implemented using DCNN based on global features. Value network estimates who will win given the current state, black chessman, or white chessman. MCTS combines the three parts above.

Figure 9.15 illustrates the neural network training process using human experts. The learn pipeline flows from the left to the right. Expert successive positions serve as the inputs. The policy network starts with a supervised learning algorithm to maximize likelihood by stochastic gradient descent. After self-play, the policy network is reinforced using the RL algorithm. The system then moves to generate self-play data to feed the value network to assess its rewarding values. This process is repeated until the winning condition is met.

9.3.3 Reinforcement Learning in the AlphaGo Program

In Figure 9.16, we provide a schematic block diagram to illustrate the data flow in the AlphaGo program in three learning stages.

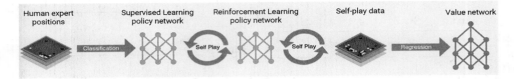

Figure 9.15
The self-play training pipeline between policy networks and value networks by human experts. (Courtesy of David Silver, "Deep Reinforcement Learning," http://www0.cs.ucl.ac.uk/staff/d.silver/web/Resources_files /deep_rl.pdf, May 8, 2015.)

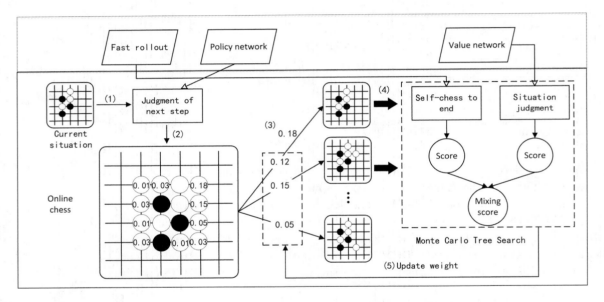

Figure 9.16
The online playing process of the AlphaGo game. (Artwork courtesy of Junbo Zhang, Huazhong University of Science and Technology, China 2016.)

> **Stage 1:** This stage performs offline DL, as shown on the left side of Figure 9.16. A supervised DL method is implemented against a professional player's chess manual. The purpose is to perform two tasks in parallel.
>
> 1. Local feature extraction with linear model training to generate fast rollout for use in the Monte Carlo tree search.
>
> 2. Run feature graph in 48 passes with the DEAL learning model to update the policy network for use in the next two stages and in the online execution process.

Stage 2: This stage updates the previous policy network through reinforcement learning to an enhanced edition of the policy network, ready for use in Stage 3. A self-chess manual is used to sample the random walk from step u-1 to step u to be carried out Stage 3.

Stage 3: This stage applies the self-chess manual at step u in three parallel tasks to mark victory or defeat, extract useful features, and current chessman color.

The outputs of the three tasks are merged to feed into the DL logistic regression model in order to work with value network. The updated rollout, policy network, and value network will be used in the online execution process in five steps.

How AlphaGo Beat the Champion Go Player Lee Sedol

In Figure 9.16, we show five execution steps in the online AlphaGo program. Essentially, these steps use the updated policy network to make a decision in the next stone placement using the MCTS.

Step 1: Extract feature based on current state of placed stones.

Step 2: Estimate the probability of each empty location that would be located with policy network.

Step 3: Compute the weight for the next move on each empty location based on the initial value probability.

Step 4: Check the value network and fast rollout network to update scores. Here fast rollout demands high speed rather than high accuracy. Repeat this score process iteratively after each move in the match. The rate of winning is estimated at each insertion location. The value network gets the estimated result on each state.

Step 5: Choose the decision with a maximum weight to make the next move. The update of these weights can be done in parallel. If the times of visiting a location exceed a certain value, the next step is searched on the next layer in the Monte Carlo tree.

The MCTS performs the following tasks using the value network and policy network, collaboratively:

1. Choose several possible strategies that the opponent would choose for the next move based on the current situation.

2. Judging the strategies of the opponent, choose a move that benefits most to traverse the right subtree. The search tree of AlphaGo will not expand all the nodes, except along the optimal path of the subtree traversed.

3. Estimate the probability of winning using the value network to estimate the best action in the next move. A MCTS needs to predict deeper results along the tree layers. The mutually supportive results of these two networks are key for AlphaGo to win the game.

4. After deciding the best action, estimate the possible next moves of the opponent and corresponding strategies through policy network based on the location of the best action.

In summary, AlphaGo's algorithm combines DL and reinforcement learning, trained with human players and machine Go manuals. The reinforcement learning method is based on the MCTS on the value network and the policy network, which are both implemented with deep neural networks:

> **Example 9.8 Reported Performance Results on Monte Carlo Tree Search**
> The MCTS process essentially exhausts all possible moves and rewards. Building a large lookahead search tree to cover millions of possibilities, the 19×19 AlphaGo programs use MCTS to end up with the accuracy listed in Figure 9.17(a). The value network is trained to predict expert human moves, using the large database of professional Go games. Figure 9.17(b) compares the winning rates of four competing Go programs in this context.
>
> The predictive accuracy of the 12-layer CNN reaches 55%, which is a significant improvement over the 31% and 39% predictive accuracy reported for earlier Go programs. The neural network is considerably stronger than the traditional search-based program GNU Go, and its performance is on a par with MoGo for 100,000 rollouts per move. The Pachi runs a reduced search of 10,000 rollouts per move. It wins about 11% of games against Pachi with 100,000 rollouts per move. ∎

9.3.4 DeepMind Health Project in the United Kingdom

In 2016, the Google DeepMind team announced the launch of a DeepMind Health research partnership with Moorfields Eye Hospital and the National Health Service (NHS) Foundation in London. This opened up the opportunity for DeepMind to serve the healthcare industry. The NHS Foundation Trust is one of the world's leading eye hospitals with a 200-year track record in clinical care, research, and education. This collaboration was inspired by

Program	Accuracy		Program	Winning rate
Human 6-dan	~ 52%		GNU Go	97%
12-layer ConvNet	55%		MoGo (100k)	46%
8-layer ConvNet*	44%		Pachi (10k)	47%
Prior state-of-the-art	31-39%		Pachi (100k)	11%

Figure 9.17
(a) Accuracy comparison, (b) Winning rates of four different AlphaGo programs. (Reprinted with permission from David Silver, "Deep Reinforcement Learning," http://www0.cs.ucl.ac.uk/staff/d.silver/web/Resources _files/deep_rl.pdf, May 8, 2015.)

the desire to explore how high-tech and the medical industry could work together to solve two specific conditions that cause sight loss: *diabetic retinopathy* and *age-related macular degeneration* (AMD). Together, this move may affect more than 625,000 people in the UK and over 100 million people worldwide.

It is estimated that 9% of the world's adult population is affected by diabetes. Diabetes is also the leading cause of blindness in the working age population. Diabetic patients are 25 times more likely to suffer some kind of sight loss. Early detection and treatment can prevent 98% of severe visual loss resulting from diabetes. AMD is the most common cause of blindness in the UK. By 2020, blinding from AMD is estimated to reach 200 million cases. Eyecare professionals use digital scans of the fundus (the back of the eye) and scans called *optical coherence tomography* (OCT) to diagnose and determine the correct treatment. These scans are highly complex and take a long time for eye doctors to analyze.

The joint DeepMind and NHS effort attempts to explore how ML could help analyze these scans efficiently and effectively, leading to earlier detection and intervention for patients and reducing the number of cases of sight deterioration. The two will work on 1 million anonymized eye scans and some related anonymous information about eye condition and disease management. This means that a patient's identity can be kept separate from the scans. Furthermore, historic scans may be used to improve future cases. Even though the joint work is still at an early stage, the long-term impacts are obvious.

The DeepMind Health program was founded to move AI technology into healthcare so that it can positively affect people's lives across the world. It will help talented clinicians get the tools and support they need to continue to provide world-class care. Front-line nurses, doctors, and other healthcare professionals can also get technical assistance. DeepMind Health will support clinicians by providing the technical expertise needed to build and scale technologies that will help them provide the best possible care to their patients. These tools can also help projects like Hark and *acute kidney injury* (AKI) detection. Ultimately, the joint team aims to give nurses and doctors more time to focus on more important issues. The following list provides several principles that developers have identified:

- *Valuing clinician and patient expertise:* The program will be used to assist nurses, doctors, and patients. However, it will be more useful to clinical experts and staffs. The tools will be driven by the needs and insights of those involved in frontline care.

- *Stand behind the National Health Service:* The goal is to build world-class technologies that support direct patient care with clinical applications. The British NHS believes that healthcare should be universally available and free at the point of use. DeepMind Health's work will support and strengthen that principle.

- *Build technologies that work together:* Effective healthcare technologies must work well with existing systems while supporting further innovation by clinicians and technologists. This is the basic guideline for the joint team from NHS and DeepMind Heath. They will protect the confidentiality of patient data, even though the innovation system will be widely shared across national boundaries.

Two core patient safety issues are identified by the developing team: (1) *detection* and (2) *intervention*. Detection aims at helping hospitals recognize the early signs of patient deterioration so that the right medical interventions can be made at the right time. Currently, the work has already started on the detection of AKI. Tackling AKI has been identified by the NHS as a clinical priority. DeepMind Health has also acquired another Hark which helps clinicians with more effective intervention.

9.4   Predictive Software, Keras, DIGITS, and Graph Libraries

This section is devoted to predictive software libraries. We will study Keras for supporting TensorFlow computing, DIGITS for neural network learning, and some graph analytics for social media applications. A sound TensorFlow ecosystem must be designed to integrate with various open-source frameworks. We assess distributed execution environments using GPUs and CPUs for deep learning applications. We evaluate the ecosystem that promotes resource sharing among many neural learning tasks handled by servers, workers, or parameter servers. Graph analytics is used to uncover insights embedded in social media networks.

9.4.1   Predictive Software Libraries for Cognitive Applications

Some commercial predictive analytics tools are introduced below. These tools are indispensable in social media and business applications of big data resources. They can be applied in many important real applications that use data mining, machine learning, and statistics techniques to extract information from business or government data sets. The purpose is to reveal hidden patterns and trends and predict future outcomes. Both open-source and commercial analytics tools are available from large or small software companies or research organizations, such as IBM, SAP, Oracle, MATLAB, SAS, and Predixion.

Predictive Analytics Applications
Important applications of predictive analytics software are listed below. Most of them are related to financial matters, marketing analysis, heathcare, social management, etc. Both regression and machine learning techniques are often applied in implementing these applications.

- Analytical *customer relationship management* (CRM).
- Clinical decision support and disease prediction.
- Fraud detection, loan approval, and collection analytics.

- Child protection, healthcare, and eldercare.
- Customer retention and direct marketing.
- Portfolio, product, or economic prediction.
- Underwriting and risk management.

Commercial Software for Predictive Analytics

In Table 9.3, we summarize the functionality and application domains of five representative predictive analytics software packages. These are selected from 31 analytics from: https://www.predictiveanalyticstoday.com.

IBM offers a predictive analytics portfolio that meets the specific needs of different users. This package includes the IBM SPSS Analytic Server, Data Collection, Statistics and Modeler, Analytical Decision Management, Social Media Analytics, and IBM Analytic Answers. The IBM SPSS Modeler offers an extensive predictive analytics platform that is designed to bring predictive intelligence to decisions made by individuals, groups, systems, and the enterprise. The solution provides a range of advanced algorithms and techniques that include text analytics, entity analytics, decision management, and optimization. IBM SPSS Statistics is an integrated family of products that addresses the entire analytical process, from planning to data collection to analysis, reporting, and deployment.

SAP Predictive Analytics helps to analyze customers, provide targeted products and services, and reduce risk. This software works with the existing data environment as well as with the SAP BusinessObjects BI platform to mine and analyze the business data,

Table 9.3
Top five commercial predictive analytics software systems

Software Name	Functionality and Application Domains
IBM Predictive Analytics	Predictive analytics portfolio from IBM includes SPSS Modeler, Analytical Decision Management, Social Media Analytics, SPSS Data Collection, Statistics, Analytic Server, and Analytic Answers.
SAS Predictive Analytics	SAS supports predictive, descriptive modeling, data mining, text analytics, forecasting, optimization, simulation, and experimental design.
SAP Predictive Analytics	SAP Predictive Analytics software works with the existing data environment as well as with the SAP BusinessObjects BI platform to mine and analyze the business data, anticipate business changes, and drive smarter and more strategic decision making.
GraphLab Create	A machine learning platform from Dato that enables data scientists and app developers to easily create intelligent apps at scale.
Predixion	The first cloud-based predictive modeling platform released in 2010. It supports end-to-end predictive analytics capabilities, from data shaping to deployment. Models evolved from machine learning libraries by Microsoft SQL Server Analysis Services, R, and Apache Mahout.

Source: https://www.predictiveanalyticstoday.com/what-is-predictive-analytics/

anticipate business changes, and drive smarter and more strategic decision making. They perform intuitive, iterative, or real-time predictive modeling, advanced data visualization and integration. GraphLab Create is a machine learning platform that enables data scientists and application developers to easily create intelligent applications at scale. The package offers to clean the data, develop features, train a model, and create a predictive service.

Oracle data mining (ODM) contains several data mining and data analysis algorithms for classification, prediction, regression, associations, feature selection, anomaly detection, feature extraction, and specialized analytics. It also provides a means for the creation, management, and operational deployment of data mining models inside the database environment. The Oracle Spreadsheet add-in provides predictive analytics operations within a Microsoft Excel spreadsheet.

Predixion released the first cloud-based predictive modeling platform in 2010. Predixion Insight is available in public, private, or hybrid cloud environments as well as on premises, and it supports complete end-to-end predictive analytics capabilities from data shaping to deployment. Models in Predixion are created leveraging various integrated machine learning libraries such as Microsoft SQL Server Analysis Services, R, or Apache Mahout. The SAS software for predictive analytics applications is described in Example 9.9.

Example 9.9 SAS Analytics for Predictive and Descriptive Modeling
SAS Predictive Analytics provides a commercial software package for integrated predictive, descriptive modeling, data mining, text analytics, forecasting, optimization, simulation, and experimental design. The application domains of SAS Analytics include predictive analytics, data mining, visual analytics, forecasting, econometrics, and time series analysis. The package can also be applied in model management and monitoring, operations research, quality improvement, statistics, text analytics, and analytics for Microsoft Office.

The predictive analytics and data mining components are used to build descriptive and predictive models and deploy results throughout an enterprise. Their functionalities include exploratory data analysis, model development and deployment, high-performance data mining, credit analysis, analytics acceleration, scoring acceleration and model management and monitoring. The SAS Enterprise Miner streamlines the data mining process to create accurate models. The SAS output dashboard displays tables, histograms, ROC charts, and range diagrams in reporting prediction results. ∎

9.4.2   Keras Library and DIGITS 5 for Deep Learning

In this section, we study the Keras software library for deep learning with TensorFlow and Theano platforms. Then we study the DIGITS 5 software tools developed by NVIDIA for accelerating the training of deep neural networks on distributed GPU devices.

Keras: A High-Level Deep Learning Library

Keras is a high-level neural networks library, written in Python. The system is capable of running on either TensorFlow or Theano. The Keras developer focuses on enabling fast experimentation in deep learning with various types of deep neural networks. The library allows for easy and fast prototyping through total modularity, minimalism, and extensibility. Specifically, it supports both convolutional networks and recurrent networks, as well as combinations of the two most important neural networks. Arbitrary connectivity schemes are supported, including multi-input and multi-output training. The system runs seamlessly on CPU and GPU. Listed below are guiding principles in using the Keras library:

- **Modularity:** A model is understood as a sequence or a graph of stand-alone, fully configurable modules that can be plugged together with as little restriction as possible. In particular, neural layers, cost functions, optimizers, initialization schemes, activation functions, and regularization schemes are all stand-alone modules that you can combine to create new models.

- **Minimalism:** Each module should be kept short and simple. Every piece of code should be transparent upon first reading. No black magic: it hurts iteration speed and ability to innovate.

- **Easy extensibility:** New modules are dead simple to add (as new classes and functions), and existing modules provide ample examples. The ability to easily create new modules allows for total expressiveness, making Keras suitable for advanced research.

- **Work with Python:** Python uses no separate configuration files in a declarative format. Models are described in Python code, which is compact, easy to debug, and allows for easy extensibility.

The Keras home page is located at https://keras.io. There are two types of models available in Keras: the *sequential model* and the *model class* used with functional APIs. These models have a number of methods in common: *model.summary()* prints a summary representation of the model and *model.get_config()* returns a dictionary containing the configuration of the model. Other commands like *model.get_weights()* returns a list of all weight tensors in the model as NumPy arrays. The *model.set_weights(weights)* sets the values of the weights of the model, from a list of NumPy arrays. The arrays in the list should have the same shape as those returned by *get_weights()*. Finally, the *model.to_json()* returns a representation of the model as a JSON string.

DIGITS 5 for Segmentation Workflow in GPU-Based Deep Learning

In 2016, NVIDIA announced a new software platform, known as NVIDIA DIGITS 5. This platform supports the training of neural networks in GPU-based deep learning applications. In many ways, this software package completes the TensorFlow approach in promoting distributed parallel execution on multiple GPU devices. This software platform has been designed with the following two important functions for neural network computing:

1. A completely integrated system for segmentation workflow in neural network applications. The system creates a database for photo image segmentation that enables the visualization of the output image from a segmented neural network.

2. DIGITS model store is an open-source online knowledge base. It can download network description and pretraining models.

We explore below the object of image segmentation. We introduce the steps to use DIGITS 5 to train a neural network to understand and set up the Synthia data set to synthesize cars, pedestrians, road signs, and any other objects on city streets. This feature is critically important to accelerate deep learning in guiding self-driving cars that read and understand images taken from the on-board cameras. NVIDIA has been a pioneer in accelerating deep learning with GPU hardware supported by deep learning software tools for a number of years. The following example explains the key concept involved.

Example 9.10 Instance-Aware Image Segmentation in Neural Learning

Instance-aware image segmentation (IAIS) refers to the segmentation of a given image into multiple segments or component parts. The neural network can learn the skeleton boundary of each subdivided image segment. This is very useful in practical imaging understanding applications. As shown in Figure 9.18, the IAIS system must be able to understand each class of image segments, even under the condition that some segment boundaries are fuzzy and not clearly distinguishable from surrounding image segments.

The left image has five persons lined up in a photo shot. The middle image is the segmented images of the five persons that are attached to each other without clear boundaries among them. The rightmost image is the same image after IAIS treatment. Now their skeleton boundaries are plotted with edge extraction and labeling by different

Figure 9.18
This five-person photo is taken from the PASCAL VOC database. The image segmentation is shown in the middle image. The instance-segmented image shown on the right is for identification purposes. (Courtesy of www.nvidia.com, 2016.)

colors for different persons. The color labeling is one way to distinguish the individuals. This is the main concept of instance segmentation. Facebook SharkMask has applied this technique to do image understanding and captioning. ∎

Today's deep learning solutions rely almost exclusively on NVIDIA GPU-accelerated computing to train and speed up challenging applications such as image, handwriting, and voice identification. A deep learning system with NVIDIA GPUs encourages parallel execution of image workloads. This can speed up networks by 10 to 75 times over using traditional CPUs. This has reduced the time of many image data training iterations from several weeks to just days. NVIDIA has claimed that GPUs can achieve a 12 times improvement in training deep neural networks (DNNs) over the use of CPU devices.

In general, the GPU approach offers faster AI application development. As a matter fact, today's computers can perform not only learning operations, but also some kind of thinking in the image recognition process. This opens up opportunities in applications for robots, medicine, and self-driving cars. You can quickly design and deploy deep learning applications with real-time responses. GPUs are largely used in desktops, notebooks, servers, and supercomputers around the world. Now even GPU clouds have appeared in Amazon, IBM, and Microsoft cloud platforms. The following example shows a complete training solution in playing multiparty games.

Example 9.11 Cloud Gaming on Small PCs by Many Players

Most of today's games are designed with a pipeline of GPU devices. NVIDIA GeForce GPU has been applied in many games in streaming mode. For example, many PC games are played with GPU support. There are more than 80 games for PC users to choose from. Cloud gaming is becoming popular; it is especially attractive for online games involving large number of players scattered in different places. The most common methods of cloud gaming use video streaming and file streaming.

Cloud gaming is also known as *gaming on demand* supported by video streaming of games onto computers, consoles, and mobile devices. This is similar to *video on demand,* through the use of a thin client computer. The actual game is stored, executed, and rendered on a remote cloud owned by the gaming company. The rendering video results are streamed directly to the consumers' computers. This greatly reduces the cost of gaming on expensive computers. The gaming signals are connected to big home TV screens for playback or display purposes. Companies that use this type of cloud gaming include NVIDIA (GeForce NOW), Playkey, PlayGiga, CiiNOW, Ubitus, Playcast Media Systems, Gaikai and OnLive. ∎

Graph-Parallel Computation Models

We introduce below the basic concept of social graph query processing. Then we assess several graph-parallel computation models proposed in recent years.

Relationship Detection on Social Graphs

To understand the *strength of relationship* one often asks the following questions: How often do nodes or individuals communicate with each other? What other nodes or individuals tend to join that conversation? How much "weight" should be given a type of node, based on the analysis you're conducting? To assess the *direction of relationship*, one asks another set of questions: Who typically initiates the conversation? Is it a two-way conversation, or does one always lead? How often and in what situations does the conversation get forwarded to others? Example 9.12 clarifies these concepts.

Example 9.12 Graph Analytics for Revealing Human Relationships in Social Networks

In Figure 9.19, Alice is a member of the chess group and knows Bob, who is also a member of the chess group. There can be a set of ancillary data (metadata) that is also captured about the relationship, such as how long they have known each other and how long they have been members of the same group. Nodes represent entities such as people, businesses, accounts, devices, ATMs, or any other item you might want to track as part of a network. Properties are pertinent information that relate to nodes.

Edges are the lines that connect nodes to nodes or nodes to properties and they represent the strength and "direction" of the relationship between the two nodes.

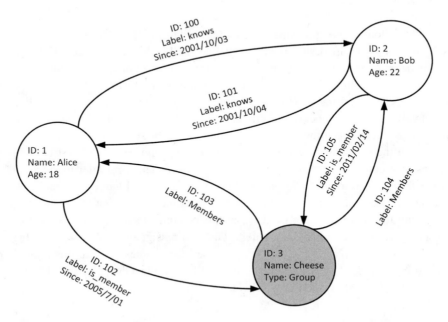

Figure 9.19
Graph analytics for revealing peer relationships in a social group. (Courtesy of Bill Schmarzo, "Graph Analytics 101," EMC2, January 2014.)

Most of the important information is really stored in the edges. Meaningful patterns emerge when one examines the connections and interconnections of nodes, properties, and edges. ∎

Graphs provide a way of organizing data to highlight relationships between people on a social network or devices on an IoT. Analytical techniques can reveal groups of related entities, identify the central influencer in a social network, or identify complex patterns of behavior indicative of advocacy or fraud. As an example, instead of focusing on the prevalence of keywords in a web page, the Google PageRank system leverages the relationships between web pages and prioritizing results from highly authoritative sites, which has contributed to the fast and accurate response to search queries hosted on the Google search engine.

Social media networks such as Facebook and LinkedIn are driven by a fundamental focus on relationships and connections. For example, Facebook users can now use the service's Graph Search to find friends of friends who live in the same city or like the same baseball team, and the site frequently suggests "people you may know" based on the mutual connections that two unconnected individuals have established. LinkedIn focuses on helping business professionals grow their social networks by helping them find key contacts or prospects that are connected to existing friends or colleagues, and allowing users to leverage those existing relationships to form new connections.

Likewise, the ability to comprehend and assess such relationships is a key component driving the world of business analytics. For example, business managers frequently want to know the answers to questions such as:

- Who are the social influencers who have the most social power to influence the perspectives of others?

- Who are the social drivers and who are their typical followers based upon the topic of discussion?

- What is a person's interest in a crime database that may be related to another person of interest?

- Based on known suspicious behavior in a corporate network, how can we identify malicious hacking attacks?

- Which of an organization's partners have a financial exposure to the failure of another company?

9.4.3 Graph-Parallel Computations on Clouds

From social networks to web-scale computing, we can leverage graph data in many ways. The traditional *data-parallel model* used in Hadoop and Spark emphasizes merging data (reduction operation) from large tables of numerical data. The growing scale in using graph

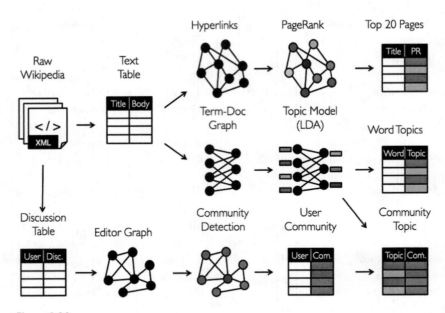

Figure 9.20

Converting raw data to tables and graphs before they are analyzed by graph algorithms. (Courtesy of Apache Foundation, "Cluster Mode Overview—Spark 1.2.0 Documentation—Cluster Manager Types," www.apache .org, December 18, 2014.)

data in the social media industry and scientific community has driven the development of numerous new *graph-parallel systems*, notably the Giraph, GraphLab and GraphX applications. By introducing new techniques to partition and distribute graphs, these systems can efficiently execute sophisticated graph algorithm orders of magnitude faster than using traditional data-parallel systems. Figure 9.20 shows the transformation of XML raw data from text tables or decision tables to graph representations before certain graph algorithms can be applied to produce the desired answers to those data or graph queries.

The graph representations may appear as hyperlinks, term-doc graphs, or community detection graphs. The graph algorithm applied could be PageRank, topic modeling (LDA), or user community statistics. PageRank may respond to a user query with the top 20 web pages. LDA reveals the most relevant word topics or the community topics. Community detection also generates the answers as community topics. Note that some graph algorithms like LDA can produce results in different formats.

Graph-parallel computation on clouds may result in substantial performance gains in terms of speed and accuracy. However, they experience some difficulty in exploring the resources in important stages of a typical graph-analytics pipeline. This situation is illustrated in Figure 9.21. The data flows from the left to the right in the graph analytics

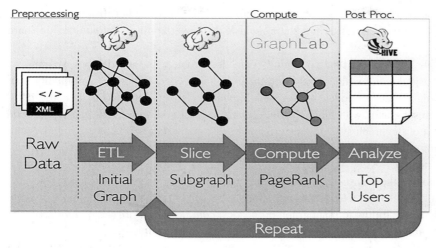

Figure 9.21
A typical graph analytics pipeline consisting of five functional stages. (Courtesy of Apache Foundation, "Cluster Mode Overview—Spark 1.2.0 Documentation—Cluster Manager Types," www.apache.org, December 18, 2014.)

pipeline consisting of five stages. The first three stages apply Hadoop to perform some preprocessing tasks, namely using the ETL to construct the initial graph from the XML raw data and then partition it (using Slice) into subgraphs over the raw data. The fourth stage is for compute using GraphLab tools (like PageRank). The final stage applies Hive to analyze the graph-parallel computation results.

Note that the results could provide feedback to the Slice stage for repeated fine-tuning operations to optimize the query answers. As a consequence, it is often necessary to move between table and graph views of the same physical data and to leverage the properties of each view to express results. However, existing graph analytics pipelines must be composed of graph-parallel and data-parallel subsystems. This may lead to extensive data movement and duplication. Thus, the graph programming model can be rather complex and hierarchically structured on the clouds. Sometimes cloud mashup services are needed to do a better job.

9.4.4   Community Detection in Social networks

In social science, a *community* (or a *cluster*) is formed by a group of people under some bounding relations. Detecting communities is of great importance in sociology, biology, and computer science. The community structure is often represented by *social graphs*. Each social graph for a well-formed community is organized as a set of *nodes* (*vertices*) with many *edges* joining internal nodes of the community and few edges linking to external nodes in the original global graph. The communities could be either disjoint or overlapping. Disjoint communities do not share nodes, while overlapping communities do share some nodes.

For simplicity, to present the community detection problem and its solutions we consider here only disjoint communities, by which there are more edges inside the community than edges linking to external nodes in the social graph under study. In terms of autonomy, communities are subgraphs with higher cohesion with internal nodes and very light connection with the rest of the graph system. We focus on the subgraph representing a community with some common properties. The formation of a community subgraph follows some similarity function among its nodes. As illustrated in Figure 9.22, six graph operations can change the graph topology. Like a human community, the social graph can also vary during its life cycle.

Communities are defined as self-maintained subgraphs in a global graph. For social network analysis, we follow four subgraph properties: *complete mutuality, reachability, node degree,* and *internal* vs. *external cohesion* in defining a community graph. The global criteria to identify communities varies with different community formation rules. The global graph may have some global property that is shared by neighboring communities. However, each community subgraph may have its unique rules to form the community structure. A random subgraph is expected to have no such structure.

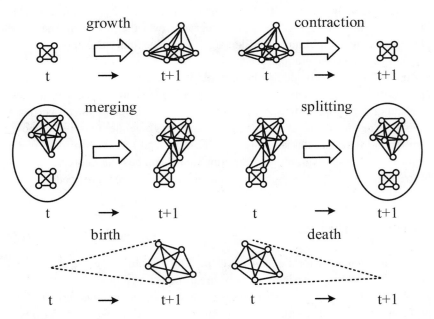

Figure 9.22
Community graph operations: birth, death, growth, merging, splitting, and contraction.

Community detection refers to the process of detecting the existence of a community structure in a large social graph. A *null model* is used to verify whether the graph being studied displays a particular community structure or not. The most popular null model corresponds to random subgraphs of the global graph. Random subgraphs have edges that are rewired randomly. However, its node degree matches that of the global graph. This null model is the basic concept behind the concept of *modularity* of the original graph. A social graph with good modularity implies that it can be easily partitioned into many subgraphs for parallel processing by the cluster servers.

Modularity enables the detection of a community structure. *Graph clustering* is often performed based on modularity properties. Various clustering techniques—basic clustering, k-means, and hierarchical clustering—can be applied here for detecting communities. A social subgraph is a community if the number of edges inside the subgraph exceeds that of a random subgraph in a null model. This expected number is an average over all possible realizations of the null model. Node similarity is a way to group nodes to form a community. For example, one can compute the similarity between each node pair of vertices by some predefined criterion. Another important measure of node similarity is based on properties of random walks on graphs.

Example 9.13 High-School Community Detection Based on Grade Classes

This example shows a simple social graph by grouping high-school students based on their grade classes. Each grade class is called a *community* here. The problem of community detection here is to distinguish the grade classes based on the courses students are taking during the same year. This is an overlapping community detection problem because some students could be labeled as being in two or more grades. The graph shown in Figure 9.23 partitions 69 students into six grades, labeled grade 7 to grade 12. The edges demonstrate their classroom relations by who is taking the same common courses. Obviously, students in the same grade are often taking a similar set of courses. Therefore, there exist more internal edge connections among them.

Due to age differences or scheduling conflicts, some courses are shared by students across adjacent grade levels or even two or more levels apart due to their study progress. These are shown by the cross-grade or distance edge connections. Of course, there are fewer cross-grade edges than internal edges in the same grade community. It turns out that grade 7 and grade 12 students are easier to separate from the rest. In grades 9 and 10, students have more cross edges than those of other grades. This social graph clearly demonstrates the differences between internal and external edges affiliated with different grade communities. The boundary between communities can be detected by distributed connections among the students. ∎

To detect community affiliation in a social graph, we understand that nonoverlapping communities are easier to detect than the overlapping cases. Three methods are listed for

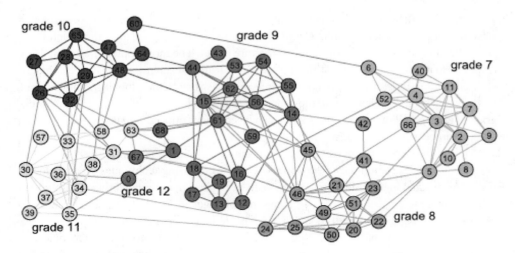

Figure 9.23
High school community formation based on grade membership. (Courtesy of J. Xie et al., "Overlapping Community Detection in Networks." *ACM Computing Survey,* August 2013.)

detecting community in a social graph. These methods are distinguished by the membership affiliation rules applied, and the results of the three methods are based on *spin-spin interactions, random walks*, and *synchronization*.

Spin-spin model: A spinning system is used to spin among q possible states. The interaction is ferromagnetic, i.e., it favors spin alignment, so at zero temperature all spins are in the same state. If antiferromagnetic interactions are also present, the ground state of the system may not be the one where all spins are aligned, but a state where different spin values coexist, in homogeneous clusters. With community structure, and the interactions between neighboring spins, it is likely that the structural clusters could be recovered from like-valued spin clusters of the system, as there are many more interactions inside communities than outside.

Random walks: Random walks are useful to find communities. If a graph has a strong community structure, a random walker spends a long time inside a community due to the high density of internal edges and consequent number of paths that could be followed. Here we describe the most popular clustering algorithms based on random walks. All of them can be trivially extended to the case of weighted graphs.

Synchronization: In a synchronized state, the units of the system are in the same or similar state(s) at every time. Synchronization has also been applied to find communities in graphs. If oscillators are placed at the vertices, with initial random phases and nearest-neighbor interactions, oscillators in the same community synchronize first, whereas a full synchronization requires a longer time. So, if one follows the time evolution of the process, states with synchronized clusters of vertices can be quite stable and long-lived, so they can be easily recognized.

The ultimate goal of clustering algorithms is to try and infer properties of, and relationships between, vertices that are not available from direct observation/measurement. There are also applications aimed at understanding real systems. Some results have been mentioned in the previous sections. This section is designed to give a flavor of what can be done by using clustering algorithms. Therefore, the list of works presented here is by no means exhaustive. Most studies focus on biological and social networks. We mention a few applications to other types of networks as well.

Other social media networks also exist in today's IT world. These networks briefly introduced here also generate bi-data sets that can feed into clouds in making analytics decisions.

- **Collaboration networks:** In such a social network, individuals are linked together for common interest or business collaborations. Collaboration is done through an implicit objective concept of acquaintance. For instance, one may consider a person to be a friend, while the latter may disagree. A formal collaboration team is put together through special agreement or attachment. The best example is the virtual organization involving IBM, Apple, and Motorola in developing the PowerPC computer series in the past.

  The analysis of the structure of scientific collaboration networks has exerted a big influence on the development of modern network science. Scientific collaboration is associated with coauthorship. Two scientists are linked if they have coauthored at least one paper together. Information about coauthorship can be extracted from large databases of published works in various fields. Some of the collaboration networks are attached to private clouds for intellectual copyright protection.

- **Citation networks:** These have been used to understand the citation patterns of authors and to disclose relationships between disciplines. The system was tested on a citation network of over 6,000 scientific journals to derive a map of science. They used a clustering technique based on compressing the information on random walks taking place on the citation graph. A random walk follows the flow of citations from one field to another, and the fields emerge naturally from the clustering analysis.

- **Legislative networks:** These networks enable one to deduce association between politicians through their parliamentary activity, which may or may not be related to party affiliation. Numerous studies on this subject were done by using library data from the U.S. Congress. They examined the community structure of networks of committees in the U.S. House of Representatives. Committees sharing common members are connected by weighted edges. Hierarchical clustering reveals close connections between some of the committees.

The detection of such a dynamically changing social community is much more involved than that of static or disjoint communities. There is no consensus about a quantitative definition of the concept of overlapping community because it depends on the method adopted. Intuitively, one would expect that community clusters share nodes at their borders. This idea has inspired many interesting detection algorithms. Dynamic social graphs that vary in time are also more difficult to evaluate. This could be studied using time-stamped data sets. Tracking the evolution of community structure in time is crucial to uncover how communities are generated and how they interact with each other dynamically.

9.5 Conclusions

In this chapter, we have learned the operating principles and software tools developed by the Google TensorFlow and DeepMind programs. The Google Brain team has created quite a few machine intelligence and cognitive functions with these tools. The group continues the work on many other AI and robotics applications. The DeepMind AlphaGo program applied reinforcement deep learning to beat the top Go player. They are also extending the work to DeepMind for healthcare applications. We also studied the role played by Keras software library in streamlining TensorFlow computations in an integrated deep learning environment.

These advances in machine learning programming prove that well-trained machines can augment human intelligence in many ways. We have also studied the graph-theoretic properties of social networks. Many social media analytics tools are reviewed and demonstrated by large-scale big data analysis applications. In particular we addressed community detection issues and presented some solutions using the Spark libraries in streaming mode.

Throughout the book, we have emphasized the use of smart cloud resources for machine learning and AI applications. The programming tools Hadoop, Spark and TensorFlow, Keras, DIGITS, and graph analytics presented in this chapter will help readers achieve these goals.

Homework Problems

9.1: Choose a data-intensive application such as large-scale searching or business processing involving crowdsourcing from the general public. Implement the application on one of three cloud platforms: AWS, GAE, or Azure. The major objective is to minimize the execution time of the application. The minor objective is to minimize the user service costs. Assess your compute and storage costs, design experiences, and experimental results, and interpret the performance results and QoS results obtained.

9.2: AlexNet, a network architecture proposed by Alex, won the championship in the ImageNet Large Visual Recognition Challenge in 2012. AlexNet is an improvement of a CNN network model for image recognition. Use the TensorFlow platform and repeat the AlexNet experiments with TensorFlow. See https://www.tensorflow.org/ for recent progress in this area at Google. This homework requires you to load or create program codes and show the steps of building an AlexNet for handwritten digital recognition with the TensorFlow platform.

9.3: Using the open-source BigQuery in TensorFlow, predict the amount of taxis needed in New York. You may finish this homework with the following steps:

Step 1: Get the data set: the history data of total number of taxi rides and the weather data from the National Oceanic and Atmospheric Administration (NOAA), such as position, the lowest and highest temperature, rainfall, etc. Then, merge the weather data and the taxi-riding numbers.

Step 2: Construct a DL neural network and do the test. You can use 80% of the data set as training and the rest for testing (of course, you can decide the partition of the data set based on your case). Build and save the model with TensorFlow, and use the test set to estimate it. If the result is far from the expected result, you can redesign your network model.

Step 3: Apply the trained model. When we get the weather data for the next 24 hours, we can directly pass the predicting factors (such as position, the lowest and highest temperature, rainfall, etc.) into the network model, then we can predict the taxi demands for that day.

9.4: Visit the website of the Google Brain teams (g.com/brain) or TensorFlow platform https://www.tensorflow.org/. Uncover technical details on Android applications that have explored DL and/or TensorFlow platforms at Google. Study the relevant papers, reports, or presentations available at Google or via public domain. Write a short technical report to summarize your findings and observations on the DNN applied, DL algorithm used or developed, and any products or prototype systems built at Google. It would be interesting if you can assess the claimed performance and identify shortcomings based on the fact finding and mining information you have studied.

9.5: Repeat Problem 9.4 on Gmail, Map, or YouTube applications by the Google Brain teams. This is really a research-oriented study. You can work on one, two, or all three applications based on the time you have.

9.6: Repeat Problems 9.4 and 9.5 on drug discovery or on photo services you find by the Google Brain teams.

9.7: Repeat Problems 9.4 and 9.5 on images or natural language understanding by the Google Brain teams.

9.8: Repeat Problems 9.4 and 9.5 on speech translation or robotics research by the Google Brain teams.

References

[1] Abadi, M., et al. "TensorFlow: A System for Large-Scale Machine Learning." Google Brain Team White Paper. https://www.tensorflow.org, November 15, 2015.

[2] Apache Foundation. "Cluster Mode Overview—Spark 1.2.0 Documentation—Cluster Manager Types." www.apache.org, December 18, 2014.

[3] Bengio, Y., Y. LeCun, and G. Hinton. "Deep Learning." *Nature* 521 (2015): 436–444.

[4] Dean, J. "Large Scale Deep Learning on Intelligent Computer Systems." Google Brain Team Slide Presentation, http:/tensorflow.org/whitepaper2015.pdf.

[5] Deng, L., and D. Yu. "Deep Learning: Methods and Applications." *Foundations and Trends in Signal Processing* 7 no. 3–4 (2014).

[6] Derek, I., C. Rose, and T. Karnowski. "Deep Machine Learning—A New Frontier in Artificial Intelligence Research." *IEEE Computational Intelligence Magazine* (2013).

[7] Gonzalas, J. E., Y. Low, H. Gu, D. Bickson, and C. Guestrin. "Powergraph: Distributed Graph-Parallel Computation on Natural Graphs." USENIX Symposium, OSDI'12, USENIX Association: 17–30.

[8] Google TensorFlow Group. "TensorFlow Tutorials." http://www.tensorflow.org, 2016.

[9] Hansen, D., et al. *Analyzing Social Media Networks with NodeXL*. Morgan Kaufmann, 2010.

[10] Hwang, K., and M. Chen. *Big Data Analytics for Cloud, IoT and Cognitive Learning*. Wiley, 2017.

[11] Jouppi, N. "Google Supercharges Machine Learning Tasks with TPU Custom Chip." Google Cloud Platform Blog, May 18, 2016.

[12] Pinheiro, C. A. R. *Social Network Analysis in Telecommunications*. Wiley, 2011.

[13] Russakovsky, O., J. Deng, H. Su, J. Krause, S. Satheesh, S. Ma, Z. Huang, A. Karpathy, A. Khosla, M. Bernstein, A. C. Berg, and F. Li. "ImageNet Large Scale Visual Recognition Challenge." *International Journal of Computer Vision* (2015).

[14] Schmarzo, B. "Graph Analytics 101." *EMC Infocus*, January 28, 2014.

[15] Silver, D. "Deep Reinforcement Learning." http://www0.cs.ucl.ac.uk/staff/d.silver/web/Resources_files/deep_rl.pdf, May 8, 2015.

[16] Silver, D., A. Huang, C. Maddison, A. Guez, L. Sifre, G. Driessche, J. Schrittwieser, I. Antonoglou, and V. Panneershelvam. "Mastering the Game of Go with Deep Neural Networks and Tree Search." *Nature* 529 no. 7587 (2016): 484–489.

[17] Wikipedia. "DeepMind." https://en.wikipedia.org/wiki/Google_DeepMind, July 2016.

[18] Xie, J., et al. "Overlapping Community Detection in Networks." *ACM Computing Survey* (August 2013).

[19] Xu, G., et al. *Web Mining and Social Networking: Techniques and Applications*. Springer, 2010.

Chapter 10

Cloud Performance, Security, and Data Privacy

10.1 Introduction

When cloud computing was first introduced in 2007, many computer scientists and professionals raised doubts on its performance and exposure to network security threats. We study a number of plausible solutions to sustaining the promised high-throughput performance of using clouds. We will learn techniques to defend clouds against network attacks and how to prevent a user's sensitive data from being leaked to the general public.

10.1.1 What Are Cloud Performance and QoS?

Until recently, the original cloud design goals were only partially fulfilled. We were still climbing a steep hill to deliver sustained cloud productivity. Elastic and dynamic resource provisioning are the foundation of cloud performance to reduce the cost of leased resources and maximize utilization. The National Institute of Standards and Technology (NIST) has identified that cloud computing demands scalable performance, economies of scale, measurable productivity, high availability, and energy efficiency. With guaranteed *service-level agreement* (SLA), the cloud automatically allocates more resources using *scale-up* or *scale-out* when the workload increases beyond a certain threshold. The system releases unused resources using *scale-down* or *scale-in* when the workload reduces.

The data center comprises a large number of servers that provide resources to meet service demands. In the case of using clouds to support social, business, education, and government operations, there are many *quality of service* (QoS) parameters to consider in cloud services, such as response time, cost of leasing resources, service level agreement, reliability guarantees, system availability, and trust/security assurance. In particular, QoS requirements cannot be static and may change over time due to continuing changes in business operations and operating requirements. In summary, both cloud users and providers must be satisfied with high QoS.

Cloud computing enables a new business model that supports on-demand, pay-for-use, and economies of scale IT services over the Internet. Internet cloud works as a service factory built around virtualized data centers. Lack of trust between users and providers has hindered the universal acceptance of the clouds as outsourced computing services. Cloud platforms are built dynamically, with provisioned hardware, software, network, and data sets through virtualization. The idea is to migrate desktop computing to a service-oriented platform using virtual server clusters at data centers. To satisfy multitenancy, the cloud ecosystem must be designed to be secure, trustworthy, and dependable.

To model cloud performance, we need to use real-life benchmark programs and test them on existing public clouds. We evaluate various cloud platforms over scale-out and scale-up workloads. Analytical expressions are derived to define the elasticity, scalability, productivity, efficiency, availability, and QoS of cloud systems. We test five cloud benchmarks: Yahoo! YCSB, CloudSuite, HiBench, BenchClouds, and TPC-W on Amazon Elastic Computer Cloud (EC2) supported with Elastic MapReduce (EMR) services.

BenchClouds is a new benchmark developed at the University of Southern California (USC) targeted at processing social media workloads running on hybrid clouds or mashups. We aim to reveal the effects of elasticity on scalable performance, QoS, and productivity in major cloud classes.

1. Sustained performance of clouds comes mainly from fast elastic resources provided to match with workload variations. Scaling-out should be practiced when the elasticity is high and scaling-up acts to use more powerful nodes with higher efficiency.

2. To achieve productive services, the choice of scale-up or scale-out solutions should be based on workload patterns. We observed high performance in scaling-out benchmarking with HiBench and BenchClouds experiments.

3. Scale-out reconfiguration overhead is much lower than those experienced in scale-up experiments. However, scaling-up is found to be more cost-effective in YCSB and TPC-W experiments.

4. Cloud productivity is greatly attributed to system elasticity, efficiency, QoS, and scalability. Cloud providers must guarantee the performance for quota-abiding users who comply with the SLA.

Cloud performance can guide the design and upgrade of existing and future cloud systems. The trust management issues on intercloud mashup services are very complex to handle, especially when the clouds are built over globally distributed data centers, such as nine Amazon Web Services (AWS) EC2 sites located in various regions worldwide.

10.1.2 How Do You Secure Clouds and Protect Shared Data?

In reality, trust is a social problem, not a purely technical issue. However, it is believed that technology can enhance the trust, justice, reputation, credibility, and assurance in Internet applications. For web and cloud services, trust and security must be established first to alleviate the worries of large numbers of users. We propose a reputation-based trust management scheme augmented by data coloring and software watermarking. We require a healthy cloud ecosystem to be free from abuse, violence, cheating, hacking, viruses, rumors, pornography, spam, privacy, and copyright violations. Both public and private clouds demand *"trusted zones"* for data, *virtual machines* (VM), and *user identity*.

Trust and security have hindered the acceptance of cloud platforms for business computing. Protected clouds must first secure virtualized data center resources, uphold user privacy, and preserve data integrity. The authors suggest using a *trust overlay network* (TON) over multiple data centers. The purpose is to implement a reputation system for establishing trust between service providers and data owners. Data coloring and software watermarking techniques are suggested to protect shared data objects and massively distributed software modules. These techniques safeguard multi-way authentications, enable single sign-on in the cloud, and tighten the access control of sensitive data in both public and private clouds.

Clouds demand security and copyright protection. These are crucial to their acceptance by a digital society. This section introduces system vulnerability, network threats, defense countermeasures, and copyright protection in distributed or cloud computing systems.

Threats to Systems and Networks

Network viruses have threatened many users in widespread attacks. These incidents create a worm epidemic by pulling down many routers and servers. In addition, attacks cause billions of dollars in losses for business, government, and services. Various attack types and the potential damages to users are summarized in Figure 10.1. Information leakage leads to the loss of confidentiality. Loss of data integrity may be caused by user alteration, a Trojan horse, and service spoofing attacks. The *denial of service* (DoS) results in loss of system operation and Internet connections.

Lack of authentication or authorization leads to illegitimate use of computing resources by attackers. Open resources like data centers, *peer-to-peer* (P2P) networks, grid, and cloud infrastructures could well become the next targets. Users need to protect clusters, grids, clouds, and P2P systems. Otherwise, no users dare to use or trust them for outsourced work. Malicious intrusions to these systems may destroy valuable host, network, and storage resources. Internet anomalies found in routers, gateways, and distributed hosts may hinder the acceptance of these public-resource computing services.

Security Responsibilities

Three security requirements are considered below: *confidentiality, integrity,* and *availability* for most Internet service providers and cloud users. In *software as a service* (SaaS), *platform as a service* (PaaS), and *infrastructure as a service* (IaaS), the providers gradually release the responsibilities of security control to the cloud users. In summary, the SaaS model relies on the cloud provider to perform all security functions. On the other extreme,

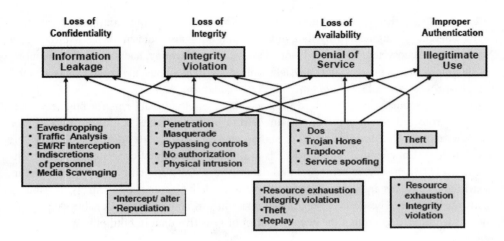

Figure 10.1
Various system attacks and network threats to cyberspace including clouds.

the IaaS model wants the users to assume almost all security functions except leaving the availability to the hands of the providers. The PaaS model relies on the provider to maintain data integrity and availability, but burdens the user with confidentiality and privacy control.

System Defense Technologies

Three generations of network defense technologies have appeared in the past. In the first generation, tools were designed to prevent or avoid intrusions. These tools usually manifested as access control policies or tokens, cryptographic systems, etc. However, the intruder could always penetrate a secure system because there was always a weakest link in the security provisioning process. The second generation detects intrusions as they happen to exercise remedial actions. These techniques include firewalls, *intrusion detection systems* (IDS), *public key infrastructure* (PKI) service, and reputation systems. The third generation provides more intelligent responses to intrusions.

Copyright Protection

Collusive piracy is the main source of intellectual property violations within the boundary of a P2P network. Paid clients (colluders) may illegally share copyrighted content files with unpaid clients (pirates). Online piracy has hindered the use of open P2P networks for commercial content delivery. One can develop a proactive content poisoning scheme to stop colluders and pirates from alleged copyright infringements in P2P file sharing. Pirates are detected with identity-based signatures and time-stamped tokens. The scheme stops collusive piracy without hurting legitimate P2P clients. Grid and cloud security, P2P reputation systems, and copyright protection are all related.

Data Protection Infrastructure

Security infrastructure is needed to support safeguard web and cloud services. At the user level, one needs to perform trust negotiation and reputation aggregation over all users. At the application end, we need to establish security precautions in worm containment and intrusion detection against virus, worm, and *distributed denial of service* (DDoS) attacks. We need also deploy mechanisms to prevent online piracy and copyright violations of digital contents.

There is a division of security responsibilities between cloud providers and users for the three cloud service models. The providers are totally responsible for maintaining the platform availability. IaaS users are more responsible for confidentiality issues. The IaaS providers pay more support for data integrity. In PaaS and SaaS services, providers and users are equally responsible for preserving data integrity and confidentiality.

10.2 Cloud Performance Metrics and Benchmarks

We present generic cloud performance models for evaluating Iaas, PaaS, SaaS, and mashup or hybrid clouds. We test clouds with real-life benchmark programs and propose some new performance metrics. Our benchmark experiments are conducted mainly on IaaS cloud platforms over scale-out and scale-up workloads. Cloud benchmarking results are analyzed with efficiency, elasticity, QoS, productivity, and scalability.

Cloud scaling is enabled by using virtualized resources. Hence, the scale of computing power needs to be calculated at the abstraction level of virtual resources. To handle a workload composed of a large number of small jobs, performance concerns are the average response time and throughput, rather than completion time of individual tasks. Hence, scalability needs to upgrade system capability to handle a large number of small users. Cloud productivity is tied to the performance cost ratio. Cloud relies on a virtualization technique to enable elastic resource provisioning or deprovisioning. Hence, the effectiveness of virtualization becomes crucial to cloud performance.

10.2.1 Auto-Scaling, Scale-Out, and Scale-Up Strategies

Due to multitenant demands, clouds are facing all sorts of workloads including multitasking, batch processing, streaming, data mining, and analytics. The cloud workload must be matched with adequately configured resources to achieve high performance and sustained productivity. Clouds are used primarily for data-intensive and latency-sensitive jobs, search engines, OLTP/business processing, social media networking, data warehousing, and big data analytics. Cloud workloads are characterized by their data set size, algorithms, memory-access pattern, and service model applied. We demonstrate three cloud resource scaling techniques in Figure 10.2.

The *auto-scaling* shown in Figure 10.2(c) is a brute-force strategy to increase or decrease resources in a cloud. The idea is to add more machine instances when a specific resource (like CPU) utilization rate exceeds a preset threshold during a fixed observation period. Practicing auto-scaling can enhance cloud performance at the expense of always provisioning more resources above the workload demand. As seen from Figure 10.2(c), auto-scaling is easy to implement with a utilization-thresholding approach. However, it tends to waste more in over-provisioned resources. We illustrate the ideas of scaling-up resources in Figure 10.2(a) and scaling-out resources in Figure 10.2(b). These scaling strategies and their possible mixtures are characterized as follows:

- **Auto-scaling** strategy applies a threshold to increase the machine instance automatically, once the instance utilization rate exceeds a preset threshold (say 85%) for a preset period (say 100 s). Auto-scaling tends to over-provision resources to satisfy the user at runtime.

- **Scale-out** strategy allows for the adding of more machine instances or processing nodes of the same type based on the quota agreed to in the SLA. Obviously, scaling-out applies more to the use of homogeneous clusters with identical nodes.

- **Scale-up** strategy is implemented with scaling the cloud from using small nodes to more powerful nodes with better processors, memory, or storage.

Mixed scaling strategy allows one to scale-up (or scale-down) the instance type and adjust the instance quantity by scale-out (or scale-in) resources at the same time. Mixed scaling works better using a heterogenous cluster. We will evaluate the relative performance of the three scaling strategies in subsequent sections. In general, the scale-up approach takes longer overhead to reconfigure and has the lowest elasticity among all scaling approaches. Scaling-up or down takes a longer time and thus results in both over-provisioning and under-provisioning of resources, as seen by the shaded areas above or below the workload curve.

The scale-out strategy matches the workload variation closely. Thus, it has the lowest over- or under-provisioning of resources. The auto-scaling wastes a lot in over-provisioning, however it will not cause any interruption in committed client services. The benchmark results support these claims. This is the main reason why scale-out is more practiced in cloud platforms than the scale-up approach.

Differences in Scaling Strategies
Elastic scaling applies only to virtualized resources (VMs and containers), due their low overhead in reconfiguration. For physical clusters, the scaling-out or scaling-up takes too

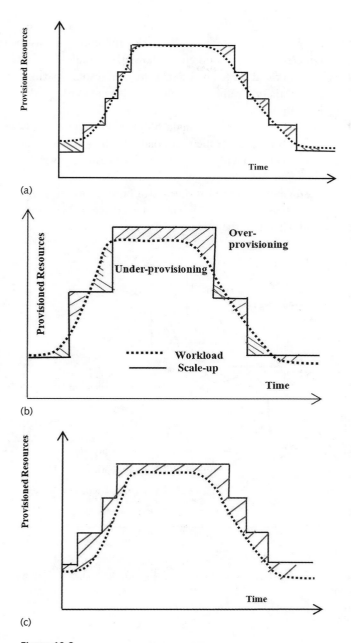

Figure 10.2

Auto-scaling, scale-out, and scale-up machine instance resources in elastic clouds, where over/under-provisioning is shown by shaded areas above/below the workload. (Reprinted from Hwang et al.,"Cloud Performance Modeling with Benchmark Evaluation of Elastic Scaling Strategies," *IEEE Transactions on Parallel and Distributed Systems,* January 2016.)

long to reconfigure. Therefore, scaling is not cost-effective to perform over physical nodes. In Figure 10.3, we use an example workload variation to show the differences in elastic scale-out and scale-up scaling strategies. The thin solid curve shows the actual workload variation. The thick curve above the workload curve corresponds to ideal resource scaling with automated elasticity. This ideal elasticity is rather difficult to implement in reality due to unknown workload variation until runtime.

In reality, we implement the scale-out scheme (shown in dash-dot step lines) for its low overhead and small incremental growth by tracing the workload variation closely. The scale-up scheme (shown in dashed lines) takes a longer period before updating. This is due to its higher overhead that is encountered when switching from small machine instances to larger ones. However, it offers a quantum jump in resources in order to avoid under-provisioning. In general, we see that scale-out results in much lower over-provisioning than scale-up of resources in a cloud. Note that the infrastructure cost is directly proportional to the resource amount provisioned.

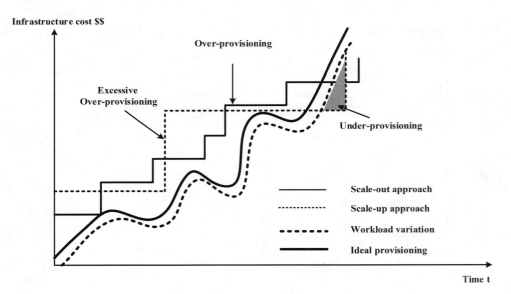

Figure 10.3
Performance cost analysis of three elastic scaling strategies: scale-out, scale-up, and auto-scaling against the workload variations.

Table 10.1
Cloud benchmarks, workloads, metrics applied, and systems tested

Benchmark and Developer	Reported Applications and Workloads	Performance Metrics	Clouds Applied and Workload Generation
BenchCloud at USC	Social media applications with big data processing	Speedup, efficiency, QoS, scalability	AWS EC2, Twitter API-workload
CloudSuite at EPFL, Lausanne	Data/graphics analytics, media streaming, and web services	Latency, WIPS, speedup, efficiency, scalability	AWS, GAE, Faban workload generator
HiBench at Intel	Terasort, word count, DFSIO, Nutch indexing, page rank, etc.	Speed, HDFS bandwidth, utilizations (CPU, memory, IO)	Hadoop Random Text Writer, k-Means Data Set
TPC-W by Trans. Proc. Council	Web search and analytical query processing	WIPS, $/WIPS, TPS (transactions per second), QoS, efficiency	AWS EC2, Rackspace, TPC client workload
YCSB by Yahoo!	Synthetic workload, data services	Latency, throughput, speedup, scalability, replication impact	Microsoft Azure, AWS, HBase, Shared MySQL

Cloud Benchmark Suites Tested

Table 10.1 summarizes the five open-source cloud benchmark suites we tested. The Yahoo YCSB and TPC-W were developed by industry. BenchCloud and CloudSuite were developed in academia. CloudSuite was developed at EPFL in Lausanne, Switzerland. All source codes and data sets are available in these open-source benchmarks. BenchCloud is still under development at USC. This suite collects users' programs and data sets mainly from social media applications. HiBench is specifically tailored for running Hadoop programs on most clouds. The suite was developed for measuring the speed, throughput, HDFS bandwidth, and resource utilization in a large suite of programs. The YCSB is a Yahoo! cloud-serving benchmark.

Example 10.1 Intel HiBench Micro Benchmark for Big Data Processing

HiBench is a set of micro benchmarks specifically tailored for testing Hadoop/Spark programs based on the MapReduce paradigm. The suite was developed at Intel for measuring the speed, throughput, HDFS bandwidth, and resources utilization in sort, word count, page ranking, Bayesian classifier, and distributed I/O workloads. Details of HiBench programs can be found at: https://github.com/intel-hadoop/HiBench. HiBench consists of ten cloud benchmark programs as listed here.

- *Sort:* This workload sorts text input data randomly generated using TexWriter.

- *WordCount:* This counts the occurrence of each word in the input text data using TexWriter.

- **TeraSort:** This is standard benchmark generated by Hadoop TeraGen program.
- **Sleep:** This workload sleeps an amount of seconds in each task to test framework scheduler.
- **Scan, join, and aggregate:** SQL query processing with five Hive OLAP queries.
- **PageRank:** Benchmarks PageRank algorithm implemented in Spark-MLlib/Hadoop examples.
- **Nutch indexing:** Large-scale search indexing using MapReduce on Nutch search engine.
- **Bayesian classifier:** This workload benchmarks naive Bayesian classification algorithm implemented in Spark-MLlib/Mahout examples.
- **K-means clustering:** This tests the K-means clustering algorithm for knowledge discovery and data mining in Mahout 0.7 or Spark MLlib.
- **Enhanced DFSIO:** This tests the HDFS throughput on Hadoop write and read operations simultaneously. It measures the average I/O rate of each map task and the aggregated throughput.

The first four programs are micro benchmarks. Scan, join, and aggregation are for SQL processing. PageRank and Nutch indexing are web search benchmarks. The Bayesian classifier and k-means clustering are for machine learning (ML), and the DFSIO program is a HDFS benchmark. ∎

Example 10.2 CloudSuite Benchmark at EPFL in Lausanne, Switzerland

CloudSuite is a collection of benchmark programs from local and other sources. The suite was compiled by the faculty and researchers at the École Polytechnique Fédérale de Lausanne (EPFL) for testing scale-out workloads on the clouds. Benchmark programs collected in CloudSuite include: data analytics, data caching, data serving, graph analytics, media streaming, software testing, web search, and web serving. Details of these programs can be found at: http://parsa.epfl.ch/cloudsuite.html.∎

Other cloud benchmarks include CloudCmp, Phoronix, CloudStone, and C-Meter. Two commercial cloud evaluations were conducted recently. Nine large cloud providers were evaluated by BitCurrent and 144 cloud sites were examined by CloudHarmonics. However, the performance metrics they have applied are far from being adequate to cover the QoS and productivity in clouds.

Example 10.3 The TPC-W Benchmark for Testing Cloud/Web Services

The Transaction Processing Performance Council (TPC) has developed a large number of benchmarks (labeled as C, D, E, H, Energy, W, etc.) for measuring computer, database, and web-service performance. TPC-C and SPECweb are the most notable ones in measuring the performance of e-commerce servers. In February 2000, the TPC-W benchmark was introduced for testing cloud workload. The TPC-W consists of 14 web interactions to browse, search, display, update, and order commercial products. The primary performance metric is the number of *web interactions per second* (WIPS) or ($/WIPS) for cost measures. Details can be found here: http://www.tpc.org /tpcw/default.asp.■

10.2.2 Cloud Performance Metrics

We apply an extended concept of performance to include capabilities and productivity. Capabilities and performance are necessary to upgrade the productivity of a cloud. In Table 10.2, we divide cloud performance metrics into three levels: *performance, capabilities*, and *productivity*. The basic performance level consists of traditional metrics such as speed, speedup, efficiency, utilization, etc. Cloud capabilities are marked by network latency, data throughput, storage capacity, data analytics, and system recoverability. The third level deals with cloud productivity, which is revealed by QoS, SLA, security, power, cost, availability, etc. Table 10.2 summarizes the metrics grouped at three performance abstraction levels.

   Most basic performance metrics and capability measures have been defined in the past. Some elasticity, productivity, and scalability measures are newly proposed here. We will demonstrate the power of using those new metrics in evaluating cloud performance in subsequent sections.

Basic Performance Metrics

These include traditional performance measures of speed, speedup, efficiency, etc., for parallel and distributed computing.

- *Speed (S_r):* Number of *millions of operations per second* (Mops). The operation could be integer or floating-point such as *mega floating-point operations per second* (MFlops). The speed is also known as *throughput* by some benchmarks such as *millions of web interactions per second* (WIPS), etc.
- *Speedup (S_u):* Speed gain of using multiple nodes.
- *Efficiency (E):* Percentage of peak performance achieved.
- *Utilization (U):* Busy resources (CPU, memory, storage).
- *Scalability (S):* Scaling ability to upgrade performance.

Cloud Capabilities

These are macroscopic metrics that describe the hardware, software, reconfiguration, and networking capabilities of a cloud. These metrics are good indicators of cloud performance.

Table 10.2
Performance, capability, and productivity metrics for evaluating clouds

Abstraction Level	Performance Metric	Notation (Eq. #)	Brief Definitions with Representative Units or Probabilities
Basic Performance Metrics	*Execution time*	T_e	Time elapsed during program or job execution (seconds, hours)
	Speed	S_r	Number of operations executed per second (PFlops, TPS, WIPS, etc.)
	Speedup	S_u	Speed gain of using more processing nodes over a single node
	Efficiency	E	Percentage of max. performance (speedup or utilization) (%)
	Scalability	S (Eq.10.5)	The ability to scale-up resources for gain in system performance
	Elasticity	E_1 (Eq.10.14)	Dynamic interval of auto-scaling resources with workload variation
Cloud Capabilities	*Latency*	T	Wait time from job submission to receiving the first response (seconds)
	Throughput	H	Average number of jobs/tasks/operations per unit time (PFops, WIPS)
	Bandwidth	B	Data transfer rate or I/O processing speed (MB/s, Gbps)
	Storage capacity	S_g	Storage capacity with virtual disks to serve many user groups
	Software tooling	S_w	Software portability and API and SDK tools for cloud apps
	Big data analytics	A_n	The ability to uncover hidden information and predict the future
	Recoverability	R_c	Recovery rate or the capability to recover from failure or disaster (%)
Cloud Productivity	*QoS of cloud*	QoS	The satisfaction rate of a cloud service or benchmark testing (%)
	Power demand	W	Power consumption of a cloud computing system (MWatt)
	Service cost	$Cost$	The price per cloud service (compute, storage, etc.) provided ($/hour)
	SLA/Security	L	Compliance of SLA, security, privacy, or copyright regulations
	Availability	A	Percentage of time the system is up to deliver useful work (%)
	Productivity	P (Eq.4)	Cloud service performance per unit cost (TFlops/$, WIPS/$, etc.)

- **Latency (T):** System response time or access latency.
- **Bandwidth (B):** This is data transfer rate or I/O rate.
- **Elasticity (E_l):** The ability to scale-up/down or scale-in/out to match with workload variation.
- **Software (S_w):** Software portability, API, and SDK tooling.
- **Big data analytics (A_n):** The ability to uncover hidden information or predict trends in big data.
- **Cloud productivity:** Related to many technical and economic factors such as QoS, availability, power efficiency, and cost-performance ratios.
- **Quality of Service (QoS):** Satisfaction with user services.
- **System availability (A):** The system up time per year.
- **Service costs (C_o):** User renting costs and provider cost.
- **Power demand (W).** Cloud power consumption (MWatt).
- **SLA/Security (L).** Compliance of SLA, security, etc.
- **Productivity (P).** QoS-satisfied performance per unit cost.

Cloud Efficiency and Productivity

We specify a cloud configuration on the resources provisioned at a given time instance. The configuration is described by a resources matrix as follows:

$$\Lambda = \begin{matrix} & \begin{matrix} v_1 & v_2 & \cdots & v_k \end{matrix} \\ \begin{matrix} r_1 \\ r_2 \\ \cdots \\ r_m \end{matrix} & \begin{pmatrix} a_{11} & a_{12} & \cdots & a_{1k} \\ a_{21} & a_{22} & \cdots & a_{2k} \\ \cdots & \cdots & \cdots & \cdots \\ a_{m1} & a_{m2} & \cdots & a_{mk} \end{pmatrix} \end{matrix}, \tag{10.1}$$

where $V = \{v_j \mid j = 1, 2, \ldots, k\}$ are machine instances; $R = \{r_i \mid i = 1, 2, \ldots, m\}$ are resources types in instances; and a_{ij} ($1 \leq i \leq m, 1 \leq j \leq k$) are the resource quantity.

Elastic Compute Unit (ECU) by AWS

With comparable QoS and cost estimation, scalability is directly proportional to productivity. Therefore, we will demonstrate the measured productivity results and skip the scalability plots in subsequent sections. Table 10.3 shows some machine instances applied in our experiments on Amazon EC2. The provider rents resources by instance types and quantity. AWS has defined a term ECU (*EC2 compute unit)* in Table 10.3 to quantify the

Table 10.3
The ECU rating of machine instance types in Amazon EC2 in 2014

Instance Type	ECU	Virtual Cores	Memory (GB)	Storage (GB)	Price ($/hour)
m1.small	1	1	1.7	1×160	0.044
m1.medium	2	1	3.7	1×410	0.087
m3.medium	3	1	3.75	1×4 SSD	0.07
m1.xlarge	8	4	15	4×420	0.350
m3.xlarge	13	4	15	2×40 (SSD)	0.280
c1.xlarge	20	8	7	4×420 (SSD)	0.520
c3.xlarge	14	4	7.5	2×40 (SSD)	0.210

computing power of each instance type. By a 2009 standard, 1 ECU instance is equivalent to a CPU with 1.2 GHz Xeon processor.

Memory and storage capacity also affect the ECU count. For example, a system may rent three instances on EC2 for general purpose applications with two instance types. We use an instance vector $V = \{m1.large, m3.large\}$ built with $a_{m1.large} = 1$ and $a_{m3.large} = 2$ instances. To assess the cost effectiveness, we also list the instance renting prices in 2014.

Consider a cluster configuration Λ. Let $T(1)$ be the execution time of an application code on a 1-ECU instance. Let $T(\Lambda)$ be the execution time of the same code on a virtual cluster Λ. The speedup is defined by $Speedup (\Lambda) = T(1) / T(\Lambda)$. Assume that the cluster is built with n instance types. The type-I has n_i instances, each with an ECU count c_i. We calculate the total cluster ECU count by:

$$N(\Lambda) = \sum_{i=1}^{i=n} n_i \times c_i .$$

(10.2)

This $N(\Lambda)$ count sets a ceiling of the cluster speedup. Now, we are ready to define the *cloud efficiency* for the cluster Λ in question as follows:

$$Efficiency (\Lambda) = Speedup (\Lambda) / N(\Lambda) = T(1) / \left\{ T(\Lambda) \times \sum_{i=1}^{i=n} n_i \times c_i \right\}.$$

(10.3)

In general, cloud *productivity* is driven by three technical factors: (1) system performance such as throughput in terms of transactions per second or response time; (2) system availability as an indicator of QoS measured by percentage of uptime; and (3) cost for rented resources measured by price. Let Λ be a cloud configuration in use. We define cloud *productivity* by three factors, all of which are functions of Λ:

$$P(\Lambda) = \frac{p(\Lambda) \times \omega(\Lambda)}{C(\Lambda)}, \tag{10.4}$$

where $p(\Lambda)$ is a *performance* metric used, which could be the speed or throughput selected from Table 10.3. The $\omega(\Lambda)$ is the QoS of the cloud. For simplicity, one can approximate the QoS by the *service availability* measure. According to a CloudHarmonics Report on 144 cloud websites, more than half have 99% or higher availability. The $C(\Lambda)$ is the user cost to rent resources to form the virtual cluster Λ.

Production-Driven Scalability

For different workloads, scalable performance is often tied to different resource types, even though instances are often provisioned in configuration packages. The performance of CPU-bound jobs is primarily decided by machine instance numbers. Memory-bound problems are limited by the memory (including cache) allocated within the machine instances. The storage-bound problems are limited by network latency and disk storage and I/O bandwidth encountered.

Cloud scalability is driven by the productivity and QoS of a cloud system. This measure is inversely proportional to the service costs. As we scale from configuration $\Lambda1$ to another $\Lambda2$, this metric evaluates the economy of scale by a pair of productivity ratios. The higher the value of a scalability measure, the more opportunity exists to target the desired scaling scheme.

$$S(\Lambda1, \Lambda2) = \frac{P(\Lambda2)}{P(\Lambda1)} = \frac{p(\Lambda2) \times \omega(\Lambda2) \times C(\Lambda1)}{p(\Lambda1) \times \omega(\Lambda1) \times C(\Lambda2)}. \tag{10.5}$$

10.2.3 Cloud Performance Models Expressed in Radar Charts

Depending on the cloud service models applied, the resources can be controlled by users, vendors, or by both jointly. As a comparison, control of desktop computing systems falls into the hands of users, except the control of a networking facility which is shared. This adds a great burden on the part of users. The control of cloud resources shifts the burden from users to vendors as we change to IaaS, PaaS, and SaaS clouds. First, we introduce a generic cloud performance model. Then we will show how to extend or refine the generic framework to model all types of cloud computing services. The performance of a cloud, denoted as **F**(*Cloud*), is modeled by a *performance function* **F**, consisting of a 5-tuple expression.

$$F\ (Cloud) = \{Service\ Model,\ Service\ Offerings,\ Performance,$$
$$Capabilities,\ Availability\}, \tag{10.6}$$

where the *Cloud* is identified by the cloud site name. The *service model* could be one or more of the available service modes such as IaaS, PaaS, SaaS, *data as a service* (DaaS), *testing as a service* (TaaS), *healthcare as a service* (HaaS), *network as a service* (NaaS), *location as a service* (LaaS), and *communication as a service* (CaaS), etc.

The *performance* here refers to a subset of performance metrics selected from the first column in Table 10.2. To illustrate the modeling ideas, we first specify three basic cloud service models, namely IaaS, PaaS, and SaaS. Then we show how to extend the model to cover hybrid clouds or cloud mashups. Figure 10.4 shows three radar charts for three cloud service models. Each spoke of the polygon represents an attribute dimension. The attribute scale is proportional to the directional length along the spoke. The further away from the center, the higher performance is expressed in a scale from 0 to 5, where value "0" means the least performance and "5" the highest.

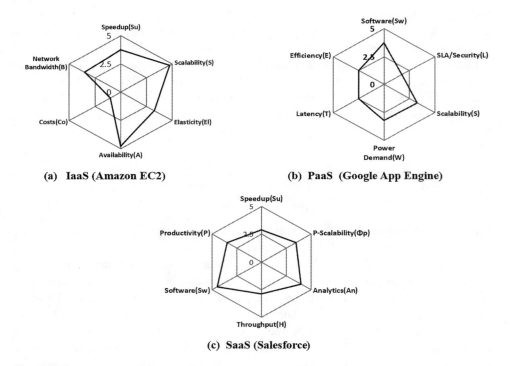

Figure 10.4
Performance maps of various clouds, where data points are extracted from reported Amazon EC2, Google App Engine, and Salesforce clouds. (Courtesy of Hwang et al.,"Cloud Performance Modeling with Benchmark Evaluation of Elastic Scaling Strategies," *IEEE Transactions on Parallel and Distributed Systems,* January 2016.)

The polygon area offers an average or approximated indicator of the overall performance of the cloud along those dimensions. Let $\{p_i \mid i = 1, 2, \ldots, n\}$ be a set of n performance attributes. In general, the larger the area of the polygon (Equation 10.7), the higher the average performance. Here we assume that all six dimensions are equally weighted:

$$Area = 0.5 \times \sin(2\pi / \mathrm{n}) \times \sum p_i \times p_{i+1}. \tag{10.7}$$

Three cloud configurations are evaluated in Figure 10.4 along different sets of performance metrics. They differ in resources provisioned, performance level achieved, performance results recorded, etc. The runtime conditions cannot be fully predicted or captured by users.

IaaS Performance Model

We test the following set of performance attributes in evaluating an IaaS cloud. This model specification could be specially tailored to special user groups or providers. In general, we suggest a 5-tuple to model the performance of an infrastructure IaaS cloud:

$$F\ (Infrastructure\ cloud) = \{< IaaS >, < Compute,\ Storage >,$$
$$< S_w,\ E_l,\ S >, < B >, < A,\ C_o >\}, \tag{10.8}$$

where the six metrics are selected from Table 10.2. Figure 10.4(a) shows the Amazon EC2 performance map, where the polygon data points are extracted and normalized from previous reports. With some modifications, the model can be applied to evaluate other IaaS clouds, such as Rackspace, GoGrid, FlexiScale, or Joyent.

PaaS and SaaS Performance Models

The PaaS cloud platforms are used mainly in developing user applications. Therefore, in Equation (10.9), a special set of performance metrics are selected, different from those used to evaluate IaaS models. For application developers, the major concern is programmability or the effective use of *software development kits* (SDK). Again, the dimensional performance is based on previous reports:

$$F\ (Platform\ Cloud) = \{< PaaS >, < Apps\ Development,\ TaaS>,$$
$$< E,\ S >, < B,\ S_w >, < W,\ L >\}, \tag{10.9}$$

where the six performance metrics are selected from Table 10.2. This model can modified to evaluate many PaaS platforms like Microsoft Azure, Google App Engine, Salesforce .com, and Amazon EMR.

Multitenant architecture is reflected in a SaaS model. It allows for a single software instance to be shared by many tenants. Each user may work in a dedicated environment. Common issues of concern that relate to SaaS performance are presented here. For simplicity, Equation (10.10) shows the SaaS map model in six performance dimensions:

$$F\ (Application\ Cloud) = \{< SaaS >, < Marketing,\ Social\ Media >,$$
$$< Su,\ \Phi_p >, < H,\ S_w,\ A_n >, < P >\}. \tag{10.10}$$

Modeling Hybrid Clouds or Mashup

Private clouds are used by organization or enterprise employees. They are used for re-
search/development, providing messaging, communication as a service (CaaS), etc. Private
clouds have better security, cost factors, and availability and private cloud users are more
concerned about raw speed, utilization, and productivity. Hybrid clouds are built with a
private cloud interacting closely with some public clouds. They are also known as cloud
mashups. Equation (10.11) is an example performance model for hybrid clouds or mashups:

$$F\ (Hybrid\ Cloud) = \{< IaaS,\ PaaS,\ SaaS >, < Social\ Media,$$
$$Compute,\ Backup\ Storage,\ etc. >, < S_u,\ U,\ E,\ \Phi,\ S_r,\ T_e >,$$
$$< T,\ H,\ B,\ S_g,\ S_w >, < A,\ C_o >\}, \tag{10.11}$$

where the six metrics are selected from Table 10.2. In Figure 10.4(c), we plot two performance
polygons for Salesforce in CRM (*customer relation management*) applications. The data are
points extrapolated from [4, 10, 21, 36]. This model can be modified to evaluate many SaaS
clouds like Gmail, IBM Lotus Live, Microsoft Dynamic CRM, Salesforce CRM, etc.

The first relative performance model is specified in Equation (10.12). The objective is to
compare the relative performance of several benchmark suites running on the same cloud
platform. This model specified in Equation (10.12) was applied to compare the performance of HiBench and BenchClouds.

$$F\ (YCSB,\ CloudStone,\ BenchCloud)$$
$$= \{< AWS\ EC2\ and\ S3>, <YCSB,\ CS,\ BC >,$$
$$< Raw\ Speed\ (S_r),\ Utilization\ (U),$$
$$Service\ Costs\ (C_0),\ Productivity\ (P) >\} \tag{10.12}$$

Consider k cloud platforms $< C_1,\ C_2,\ \ldots\ C_k >$ which are under testing by p benchmark
programs $< B_1,\ B_2,\ \ldots,\ B_p >$. Assume that the clouds are tested by m performance metrics
$< M_1,\ M_2,\ \ldots,\ M_m >$. The following model (Equation 10.13) reveals the relative performance of multiple cloud platforms. For example, EC2 and Rackspace are evaluated in
Figure 10.4(b) for the case of choosing $k = 2$, $p = 1$, and $m = 6$.

$$F\ (C_1,\ C_2,\ \ldots,C_k) = \{< C_1,\ C_2,\ \ldots,\ C_k >, < B_1,\ B_2,\ \ldots,\ B_p >,$$
$$< M_1,\ M_2,\ \ldots,\ M_m >\}. \tag{10.13}$$

In Figure 10.5, the performance of nine cloud sites is plotted by Bitcurrent in terms of
response time to HTTP requests across five countries. There are four EC2 sites in APAC,
EU, US east, and US west tested. Other cloud providers are GoGrid, Google AppEngine,
Joyent (in UK), Rackspace, and Azure. In general, latency is confined between 200 and 580

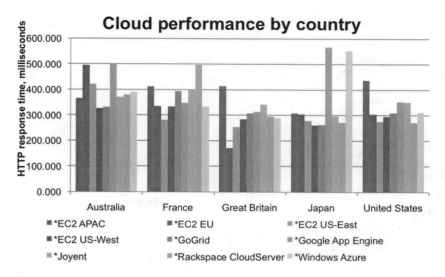

Figure 10.5
HTTP response time (in ms) of nine public clouds in five countries. (Source: Bitcurrent, Inc., "Cloud Computing Performance Report," http://www.bitcurrent.com, 2010.)

ms. It takes less time to access these clouds from the UK; in Australia and France the access times are higher. In all regions, the Google AppEngine takes a longer time to access from Australia and Japan. The EC2 EU has the longest access time from Australia.

Expressed Concerns of Cloud User Group

We can use the radar chart to compare the concerns by major user groups. In Figure 10.6(a,b,c), six cloud user groups are distinguished by various polygons on the radar chart. G2000 refers to users in large organizations. Large web business includes Facebook, Twitter, AWS cloud, etc. Public companies and government or nonprofit users form two other user groups. Private or regional users and startup users are the remaining groups. User concerns are expressed along 11 dimensions, such as: data privacy, infrastructure control, high cost, poor performance, etc. On each dimension, the scale is plotted from 0 for "no concern" at the center to 3.5 for the highest concern. The higher the value, the more concern expressed.

The dimension of "just do not like it" refers to biased users who resent using clouds regardless of other factors. Obviously, data privacy is a major concern among all groups. The private regional or non-tech users are most concerned about data privacy, lock-in problems, and poor performance. The public companies have escalation, data privacy, and networking cost concerns. Surprisingly, job security and high costs are of less concern for all groups. These data were surveyed by Bitcurrent Inc. in 2010, when clouds were newly introduced. Now that clouds have become more mature and more commonly used, the concerns may have shifted to some extent.

(a) G2000 vs. government or nonprofit organization

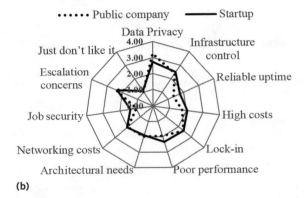

(b)

(c)

Figure 10.6
A Keviate graph (radar chart) for expressing 11 concerns by 6 cloud user groups. Source: Bitcurrent, Inc., "Cloud Computing Performance Report," 2010.

10.3   Performance Analysis of Cloud Benchmark Results

Some cloud benchmark performances are assessed below. We first analyze the elasticity issues. Then we compare the relative performance of scale-out vs. scale-up workloads.

10.3.1   Elastic Analysis of Scalable Cloud Performance

Elasticity cannot be achieved without virtualization. Multitenancy architecture demands elastic resources with auto-scaling to yield scalable performance. Differences in virtualization abstraction levels (IaaS, PaaS, SaaS) affect system reconfiguration capability or the elasticity of the cloud system. In the past, physical computer resources may have taken a long time to reconfigure. Thus, the elasticity was very low due to large reconfiguration overhead. Elasticity was introduced to evaluate cloud scalability, using two questions:

(1) How fast or timely is it to change the resources state in a cloud?

(2) How precisely are the resources provisioned to address the workload variations?

Elasticity is illustrated in Figure 10.7(a) where the elasticity is measured with two parameters: *speed* and *precision*. *Speed* is calculated by the time delay (θ) of the provisioning or de-provisioning process, while precision is the offset (μ) with under- or over-provisioning. *Elasticity* was defined by Herbst et al. [12] as the degree to which a system is able to adapt to workload changes by provisioning or de-provisioning resources automatically. This implies that at each time the available resources match the current demand as closely as possible. Let θ be the average time to switch from an under-provisioned state to an elevated state and μ be the average percentage of under-provisioned resources during the scaling process. The elasticity is defined by the following expression:

$$E_l = 1 / (\theta \times \mu). \tag{10.14}$$

Figure 10.7(b) plots the elasticity as a function of the reconfiguration overhead (θ) under different provisioning offsets (μ) from the actual scaling curve. When the offset is small ($\mu = 10\%$), the elasticity drops sharply as the overhead (θ) increases. When the offset gets to 70%, the elasticity drops to 0.04 from 0.25, when the average provisioning time θ is at 40 s. The elasticity stays rather flat and low as θ increases. In order to increase the elasticity of a cloud system, we should minimize the provisioning time and keep the offset as low as possible. The elasticity is a necessary condition for scalability, but not sufficient. The built-in auto-scaling mechanism is greatly affected by the elasticity measure. The resource usage and instance replication affect the cloud performance greatly.

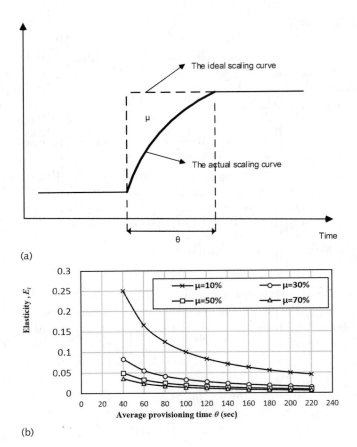

Figure 10.7
Elastic cloud resource provisioning, where θ is the overhead time and μ is the offset between actual scaling and an auto-scaling process. (a) Elastic resource scaling, (b) Elasticity vs. scaling speed. (Courtesy of Herbst et al., International Conference on Autonomic Computing [ICAC], January 2013.)

10.3.2 Scale-Out, Scale-Up, and Mixed Scaling Performance

Extensive cloud benchmark experiments have tested the Amazon AWS EC2 with EMR library support. These experiments tested five benchmarks: BenchCloud, YCSB, Cloud-Suite, HiBench, and TPC-W, as listed in Table 10.1. The purpose was to check the performance of EC2 under different benchmark programs over varying data sizes. The experimental setting applied a fixed instance type to scale-out. For scale-up experiments, we had to change the instance types by program direction. Manual scaling was applied under program control in all experiments. Auto-scaling was not applied in scaling experiments on EC2 due to its brute force provisioning policy. Some load-balancing was automatically practiced on the EC2 under the control of the EMR library.

Example 10.4. AWS EC2 Scale-Out Performance Tested by TPC-W Benchmark

In scale-out experiments, the same machine instance is replicated in many copies. Figure 10.8 reports the TPC-W scale-out experimental results. The TPC-W consists of programs for testing web and cloud services in business transactions. Scale-out workload is assumed from 200 to 4,000 user transactions. Four throughput curves are given in Figure 10.8(a); the system scales well to 550 WIPS with 4,000 users, but gets saturated at 20 instances.

The fewer the transactions, the lower the achievable throughput and the earlier it gets saturated. For example, with 200 user transactions, the throughput does not scale well and is almost flat at the bottom with increasing cluster size. With 800 transactions, the throughput scales to 100 WIPS and becomes flat at 4 machine instances. With 2,400 transactions, the throughput increases to 300 WIPS before it becomes saturated at 12 nodes.

The saturated performance with large cluster size is also reflected by the productivity curves plotted in Figure 10.8(b). In other words, the productivity scales to the peak before it drops rapidly. In the case of 4,000 users, the productivity drops from a peak of 0.8 at 20 nodes to 0.55 with 32 nodes. The conclusion from these plots is that the TPC-W benchmark results demonstrate that both throughput and production are scalable only if the user transactions are sufficiently large to keep the cloud instances busy. ■

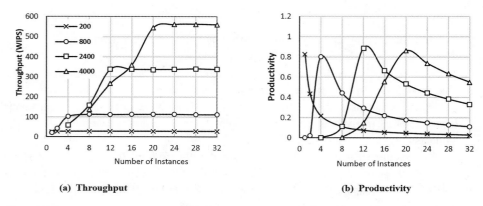

(a) Throughput   (b) Productivity

Figure 10.8

Scale-out performance of TPC-W benchmark on Amazon EC2 cloud. (Courtesy of Hwang et al., "Cloud Performance Modeling with Benchmark Evaluation of Elastic Scaling Strategies," *IEEE Transactions on Parallel and Distributed Systems,* January 2016.)

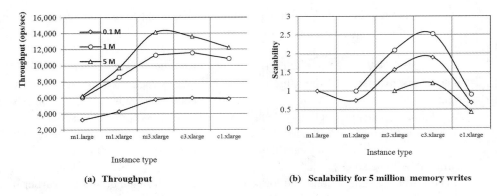

(a) Throughput

(b) Scalability for 5 million memory writes

Figure 10.9
Scale-up performance of Yahoo! YCSB on EC2. (Courtesy of Hwang et al., "Cloud Performance Modeling with Benchmark Evaluation of Elastic Scaling Strategies," *IEEE Transactions on Parallel and Distributed Systems,* January 2016.)

In scale-up experiments, we upgrade the machine instances from small to medium and extra-large types, as given in Table 10.3, in order of increasing computing power (ECU and vCPU), memory, and storage capacities. Of course, the resource cost increases from small to large instances, accordingly. Three scale-up experiments can be performed on the EC2 by running YCSB, HiBench, and TPC-W, respectively. The results of TPC-W scale-up experiments are reported in Figure 10.9, the system scales up in a sequence from *m*1.*small instance to m*1.*medium, m*3.*medium, m*1.*large, and m*1.*xlarge* instances. Auto-scaling cannot be implemented to automate the scaling-up process due to heavy overhead or low elasticity encountered.

Example 10.5. Scale-Up Performance Tested by Yahoo! YCSB Benchmark
The Yahoo! YCSB is part of the CloudSuite data serving benchmark on AWS HBase 0.92.0 cluster. Figures 10.9(a,b) report throughput and scalability respectively. The cluster scales up to *m*3.*large* nodes. Figure 10.9(a) shows that for all three workloads, performance increases apparently when scaling up from *m*1.*large* to *m*3.*xlarge* instance, however for *c*3.*xlarge* and *c*1.*xlarge*, throughput and execution time almost remain the same as *m*3.*xlarge* instance.

From Figure 10.9(b), the efficiency drops rapidly from *m*1.*large* to *m*1.*xlarge* and from *c*3.*xlarge* to *c*1.*xlarge*. This is due to the fact that scaling-up does not catch the hardware resources increase. We plot the scalability in Figure 10.9(b) for 5M memory operations. Here, we the set the QoS (cloud availability) to be 100%. As we scale-up, the productivity reaches the peak values for all workloads at *c*3.*xlarge*. The message being conveyed is that YCSB shows heavy memory-intensive database operations, and we can reach the highest productivity at *c*3.*xlarge* instance. ∎

Example 10.6. Mixed Scale-Up and Scale-Out Performance

For mixed scaling, four cluster configurations are specified along the *x*-axis in Figure 10.10. The leftmost cluster has eight *small* instances with a total ECU count of eight. The next has four *medium* and four *small* instances with 12 ECUs. The next one has three *large* and two *medium* instances with 16 ECUs. The right cluster has three *xlarge* and two *large* instances with 32 ECUs.

Obviously, the mixed scaling strategy offers much more flexibility in mapping applications with large workload variation. The speed of mixed scaling is the highest among the three methods. The efficiency varies similarly as the scale-up case. However, due to significant increases in computing capacity, the renting cost also increases proportionally. The productivity thus may drop to some extent with a sharp increase in costs. Applying the relative performance models in Equations (10.11) and (10.12), we compare three benchmark programs: HiBench, YCSB, and BenchCloud and two cloud platforms, EC2 and Rackspace. These comparative studies reveal the strength and weakness in different benchmarks or cloud platforms. ■

10.3.3 Relative Merits of Scaling Strategies

The enterprise cloud is used by many users within an organization. Each user may build some strategic applications on the cloud. The user demands customized partition of the data, logic, and database in the metadata representation. Many such private clouds are built with leased resources from public clouds. Cloud mashup results from the need to use multiple clouds simultaneously or in a sequence. For example, an industrial supply chain may involve the use of different cloud resources or services at different stages of the chain. There exists a public repository of thousands of service APIs and mashups for web commerce

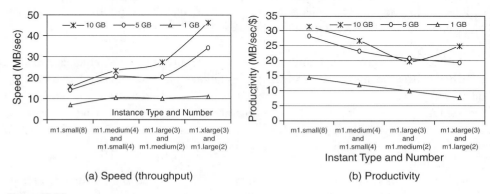

(a) Speed (throughput)   (b) Productivity

Figure 10.10

HiBench WordCount performance results on four EC2 clusters with mixed scale-up and scale-out nodes shown on the *x*-axis. (Reprinted with permission from Hwang et al., "Cloud Performance Modeling with Benchmark Evaluation of Elastic Scaling Strategies," *IEEE Transactions on Parallel and Distributed Systems*, January 2016.)

services. Popular APIs include Google Maps, Twitter, YouTube, Amazon eCommerce, and Salesforce.com.

Example 10.7. Comparing Three Scaling Strategies on Cloud Performance

Scaling-out, scaling-up, and mixed strategies are evaluated in Figure 10.11. We compare their relative merits through executing two benchmark programs, Sort and WordCount in HiBench suite, on the AWS EC2 platform. The workload for these two programs has 10 GB of data elements. We measure the HiBench performance of these two programs along six performance dimensions: throughput, scalability, QoS, productivity, costs, and efficiency.

The QoS is mainly indicated by system availability which was recorded at 99.95–100% for all cluster configurations. In terms of cost, WordCount, the scale-out small cluster (solid polygons in Figure 10.11(a, d) has the smallest service costs. The scale-up clusters in Figure 10.11(b, e) cost more and the mixed cluster is the most expensive one to implement. Mixed scaling demands a lot more consideration on tradeoffs between performance and cost incurred.

Speedwise, all mixed strategy for Sort (Figures 10.11c and 10.11e) have the fastest throughput (or speed). The WordCount program shows slow throughput in all cases. The scale-up cluster shows very high efficiency for WordCount. The Sort clusters (dash-line polygons) show poor efficiency and throughput except high throughput for the mixed mode for sorting very large clusters in Figure 10.11(f). In Figure 10.11(a), we see higher productivity for the large cluster (16 nodes) configuration.

The peak values are application-dependent. Different benchmarks may lead to different conclusions. In general, scaling-out should be practiced when the elasticity speed is high. These performance maps are compared in terms of their polygon area values. Under each scaling case, we compare two cluster configurations. The polygon areas reported simply provide a means to compare the relative performance of cluster configurations with a common benchmark. ∎

In Table 10.4, we give a qualitative assessment of the three scaling techniques evaluated in HiBench experiments on various EC2 configurations. The assessment is based on those quantitative measures reported in previous sections. We take a macroscopic view of the reported numerical results to reach some generalized observations on cloud performance under various operating constraints. Overall, we find that scaling-out is the easiest one to implement on homogeneous clusters. The elasticity overhead is also lower in these cluster configurations.

Scaling-up is more complex to implement than scaling-out due to the switching of node types. This will reduce the elasticity speed and prolong the reconfiguration overhead. The mixed scaling is the most difficult one to implement but offers the best flexibility due to the switching of node types.

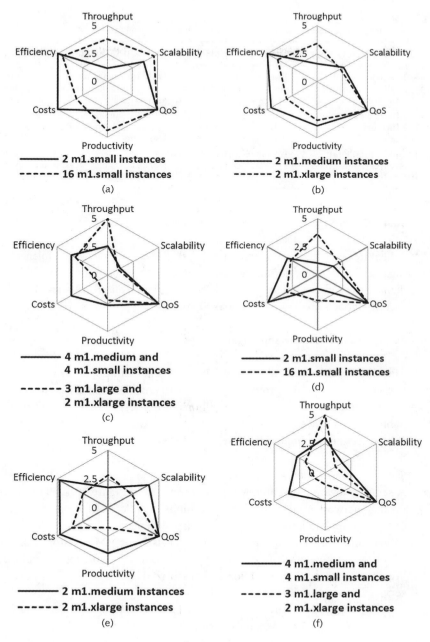

Figure 10.11
Performance of two HiBench programs on two EC2 clusters. (Reprinted with permission from Hwang et al., "Cloud Performance Modeling with Benchmark Evaluation of Elastic Scaling Strategies," *IEEE Transactions on Parallel and Distributed Systems*, January 2016.)

Table 10.4
Scaling techniques based on HiBench benchmarking findings on the EC2

Impact Factors	Scale-Out Technique	Scale-Up Technique	Mixed Scaling
Elasticity Speed, Scaling Complexity, and Overhead	Fast elasticity, possibly supported by auto-scaling and heuristics	High overhead to reconfigure and cannot support auto-scaling	Most difficult to scale with wide range of machine instances
Effects on Performance, Efficiency, and Scalability	Expect scalable performance if the application can exploit parallelism	Switching among heterogeneous nodes may reduce scalability	Flexible app, low efficiency and resource utilization
QoS, Costs, Fault Recovery, and Cloud Productivity	Cost the least, easy to recover, incremental productivity	More cost-effective, but reduced QoS may weaken productivity	High costs, difficult to recover, expect the highest productivity

10.4 Cloud Security and Data Privacy Protection

A healthy cloud ecosystem is required to free users from abuses, violence, cheating, hacking, viruses, rumors, pornography, spasm, privacy, and copyright violations. The security demands of three cloud service models—IaaS, PaaS, and SaaS—are described here. These security models are based on various SLAs between providers and users.

10.4.1 Cloud Security and Privacy Issues

Malware-based attacks like worms, viruses, and *denial of service* (DoS) exploit the system vulnerabilities and provide intruders with unauthorized access to critical information. Risky cloud platforms may cause billions of dollars in losses for businesses and disrupt public services. We propose below a security-aware cloud architecture and identify the five protection mechanisms needed.

Security-Aware Cloud Architecture
A security-aware cloud architecture is proposed in Figure 10.12. This architecture helps insulate network attacks through the establishment of trusted operational zones for various cloud applications. Security compliance demands the protection of all data center servers and storage areas. We protect hypervisors or VM monitors from software-based attacks and safeguard data and information from theft, corruption, and natural disasters. We provide strong authentication and authorized access to sensitive data and on-demand services.

Those suggested security and privacy features are summarized here as design objectives of a trusted and dependable cloud:

- *Virtual network security and trust negotiation:* Virtual network security protects VMs in virtualized data centers. The scheme also prevents data loss to other tenants. Cross

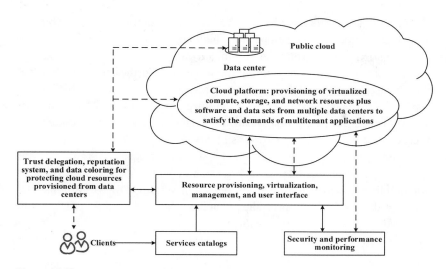

Figure 10.12

A security-aware cloud platform built with virtual machines, storage, and networking resources over data center servers. (Reprinted from Hwang and Li, "Trusted Cloud Computing with Secure Resources and Data Coloring," *IEEE Internet Computing* 14 no. 5, September 2010.)

certificates must be used to delegate trust across PKI domains for data centers. Trust negotiation among different certification authorities (CAs) resolves policy conflicts.

- **Worm containment and DDoS Defense:** Internet worm containment and distributed defense against DDoS attacks are necessary to insulate infrastructure from malware, Trojans, and cybercriminals. This demands the joining of identities with the public clouds.

- **Reputation systems for data centers:** Reputation system could be built with P2P technology. One can build a hierarchy of reputation systems among virtualized data centers and distributed file systems as introduced in Figure 10.12. Intellectual copyright is protected by piracy prevention with proactive content poisoning.

- **Data coloring and software watermarking:** This refers to the use of data coloring at the software file or data object level. This requires the segregation of user access and the insulation of sensitive information from provider accesses.

Security Defense of Virtual Resources

Virtualization enhances cloud security. But VMs add an additional layer of software that could become a single point of failure. With virtualization, a single physical machine can be divided or partitioned into multiple VMs (e.g., server consolidation). This provides each VM with better security isolation and each partition is protected from DDoS attacks by other partitions. Security attacks in one VM are isolated and contained from affecting the other VMs. VM failures do not propagate to other VMs. Hypervisor provides the visibility of the guest OS, with complete guest isolation. Thus, fault containment and failure isolation of VMs provide a more secure and robust environment.

Sandbox provides a trusted zone for running the programs. Furthermore, sandbox can provide a tightly controlled set of resources for the guest operating systems, which allows a security testbed to test the application codes from third-party vendors. With virtualization, the VM is decoupled from the physical hardware. The entire VM can be represented as a software component and can be regarded as binary or digital data. This implies that the VM can be saved, cloned, encrypted, moved, or restored with ease. VMs enable higher availability and faster disaster recovery. Live migration of VMs was suggested by many researchers for building a distributed intrusion detection system (DIDS). Multiple IDS VMs can be deployed at various resource sites including the data centers. DIDS design demands trust negation among PKI domains. Security policy conflicts must be resolved at design time and updated periodically.

Live Migration and Open Virtual Format

We suggest live migration of VMs specifically designed for building DIDs. Multiple IDS VMs can be deployed at various resource sites including the data centers. DIDS design demands trust negation among PKI domains. Security policy conflicts must be resolved at design time and updated periodically. A defense scheme is needed to protect user data from server attacks. The user private data must not be leaked to other users without permission.

Security threats may be aimed at VMs, guest OS, and software running on the cloud. IDS attempts to stop the attacks before they take effect. Both signature matching and anomaly detection can be implemented on VMs dedicated for building IDS. Signature-matching IDS is more mature, but requires frequent updating of the signature databases. Network anomaly detection reveals abnormal traffic patterns, such as unauthorized episodes of TCP connection sequences, against normal traffic patterns. Distributed IDSs are needed to combat both types of intrusions.

Example 10.8. Man-in-the-Middle Attacks on Virtual Machines

Consider VM migration from a host machine A to another host machine B via a vulnerable network. In a man-in-the-middle attack, the attacker can view the VM contents being migrated, steal sensitive data, or even modify the VM-specific contents including the OS and application states. The VM migration is shown in Figure 10.13 from one host machine to another. An attacker can launch an active attack to insert a *VM-based rootkit* (VMBR) into the migrating VM, which can subvert the entire operation of the migration process without the knowledge of the guest OS and embedded application. ∎

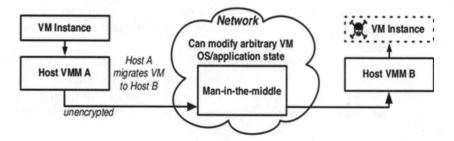

Figure 10.13

A virtual machine (VM) migrating from a host A to a host B through a vulnerable network threatened by a man-in-the-middle attack to modify the VM template and OS state.

10.4.2 Cloud Security Infrastructure

Servers in the cloud can be *physical machines* (PMs) or VMs. User interfaces are applied to request services. The provisioning tool carves out the systems from the cloud to satisfy the requested service. A security-aware cloud architecture demands security enforcement. Malware-based attacks such as network worms, viruses, and DDoS attacks exploit system vulnerabilities. These attacks compromise system functionalities or provide the intruders unauthorized access to critical information. Thus, security defense is needed to protect all cluster servers and data centers. Some cloud components that demand special security protection are as follows:

- Protection of servers from malicious software attacks like worms, viruses, and malwares.
- Protection of hypervisors or VM monitors from software-based attacks and vulnerabilities.
- Protection of VMs and monitors from service disruption and denial of service attacks.
- Protection of data and information from theft, corruption, and natural disasters.
- Provision of authenticated and authorized access to critical data and services.

Public and private clouds demand different levels of security enforcement. Different SLAs are distinguished by variable degrees of shared responsibility between cloud providers and users. Critical security issues include data integrity, user confidentiality, and trust among providers, individual users, and user groups. We assess below the security demands of three popular cloud service models—Iaas, Paas, and Saas. Figure 10.14 characterizes various security, privacy, and copyright protection measures demanded by three cloud service models.

Many protection features listed in Figure 10.14 are well established in grid and network-based computing systems. They can be applied to protect clouds as well. Useful features include the securing of cloud computing with copyrighted contents, data coloring, watermarking, VM management, trust overlay construction, and reputation systems specifically designed for protecting data centers. These new protection features are presented in subsequent sections.

IaaS is sitting at the innermost implementation layer, which is extended to form the PaaS layer by adding OS and middleware. PaaS is further extended to the SaaS model by creating applications on data, content, and metadata using special APIs. This implies that SaaS demands all protection functions at all levels. IaaS demands protection mainly at the networking, trusted computing, and compute/storage levels. PaaS embodies IaaS support plus additional protection at the resource management level.

Securing Infrastructure as a Service

This model allows users to lease compute, storage, networks, and other resources in a virtualized environment. The user does not manage or control the underlying cloud infrastructure but has control over OS, storage, deployed applications, and possibly select networking

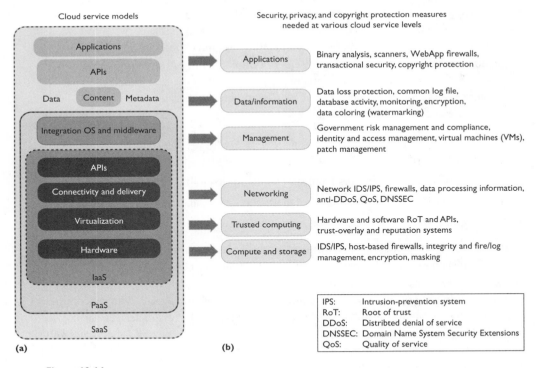

Figure 10.14
Cloud service models on the left and corresponding security measures on the right: The IaaS is at the innermost level, PaaS at the mid-level, and SaaS at the widest level including all resources. (Reprinted from Hwang and Li, "Trusted Cloud Computing with Secure Resources and Data Coloring," *IEEE Internet Computing* 14 no. 5, September 2010.)

components. Amazon EC2 is a good example. At the cloud infrastructure level, network security can be enforced with IDS, firewalls, antivirus, and DDoS defense.

Securing Platform as a Service

The cloud platform is built on top of IaaS with system integration and virtualization middleware support. The platform allows the user to deploy user-built software applications onto the cloud infrastructure using programming languages and software tools supported by the provider (e.g., Java, Python, .NET). The user does not manage the underlying cloud infrastructure. PaaS is pushed by Google App Engine and Microsoft Azure. This level requires securing the VMs provisioned, enforce security compliance, manage potential risk, and establish trust among all cloud users and providers.

Securing Software as a Service

This is browser-initiated application software used by over thousands or more cloud customers. On the customer side, there is no upfront investment in servers or software licensing. On the provider side, costs are rather low, compared with conventional hosting of user applications. SaaS, as heavily pushed by Google, Microsoft, Salesforce, etc., demands the protection of data from being lost, distorted, or stolen. Transactional security and copyright compliance are designed to protect all intellectual property rights. Data encryption and coloring offer options to uphold data integrity and user privacy.

Security Challenges in Virtual Machines

Traditional network attacks include buffer overflows, DoS attacks, DoS, spyware, malware, rootkits, Trojans, and worms. In a cloud environment, newer attacks may result from hypervisor malware, guest hopping and hijacking, or VM rootkits. Another one is the man-in-the-middle attack for VM migrations. In general, passive attacks attempt to steal sensitive data or passwords. Active attacks manipulate the kernel data structures. IDS can be *network-based IDS* (NIDS) or *host-based IDS* (HIDS). Program shepherding can be applied to control and verify the code execution. Other defense technology includes using DynamoRIO dynamic optimization infrastructure, or VMware vSafe and vShield tools, security compliance for hypervisors, and using Intel vPro technology. Others apply a hardened OS environment or use isolated execution and sandboxing.

Cloud Defense Methods

Virtualization enhances cloud security. However, VMs add an additional layer of software that could become a single point of failure. With virtualization, a single physical machine can be divided or partitioned into multiple VMs (e.g., server consolidation). This provides each VM with better security isolation and each partition is protected from DoS attacks by other partitions. Security attacks in one VM are isolated and contained from affecting the other VMs. In Table 10.5, eight protection schemes are listed to secure public clouds and data centers.

Trust negotiation is often done at the SLA level. PKI service could be augmented with data center reputation systems. Worm and DDoS attacks must be contained. It is harder to establish security in the cloud due to the fact all data and software are shared by default.

Example 10.9. EMC Establishment of Trust Zones for Protection of Virtual Clusters Provisioned to Multiple Tenants

EMC and VMware have joined to build the security middleware for trust management in distributed system and private clouds. The concept of "trusted zones" was established as part of the virtual infrastructure. Figure 10.15 illustrates the concept of creating *trust zones* for the virtual clusters (multiple App and OS for each tenant) provisioned in separate virtual environments. The physical infrastructure is shown at the bottom marked as cloud provider. The virtual clusters or infrastructures are shown

Table 10.5
Physical and cybersecurity protection at cloud/data centers

Protection Schemes	Brief Description and Deployment Suggestions
Secure Data Centers and Cloud Sites	Choose hazard-free location, enforce building safety. Avoid windows, keep buffer zone around the site, bomb detection, camera surveillance, earthquake-proof, etc.
Redundant Utilities at Multiple Sites	Multiple power and supplies, alternate network connections, multiple databases at separate sites, data consistency, data watermarking, user authentication, etc.
Trust Delegation and Negotiation	Cross certificates must be used to delegate trust across PKI domains for various data centers. Trust negotiation among the CAs needed to resolve policy conflicts.
Worm Containment and DDoS Defense	Internet worm containment and distributed defense against DDoS attacks are necessary to secure all data centers and cloud platforms.
Reputation System for Data Centers	Reputation system could be built with P2P technology. One can build a hierarchy of reputation systems from data centers to distributed file systems.
Fine-Grain File Access Control	This refers to fine-grain access control at the file or object level. This bulks up the security protection beyond firewalls and intrusion detection systems.
Copyright and Piracy Protection	Piracy prevention achieved with peer collusion prevention, filtering of poisoned content, non-destructive read, alteration detection, etc.
Privacy Protection	User authentication, biometric identification, intrusion detection, and disaster recovery; privacy enforcement by data watermarking, data classification, etc.

in the upper boxes for two tenants. The public cloud is associated with the globe user communities at the top.

The security functions and actions are taken at the four levels from the users to the providers. The small circles between the four boxes refer to interactions between users and providers and among the users themselves. The arrowed boxes on the right are those functions and actions applied between the tenant environments, the provider, and the global communities. The security measures insulate the tenant zones and isolate the VM in the virtual zones. The main innovation here is to establish the trust zones among virtual clusters. The end result is to enable end-to-end security and compliance across the virtual clusters dedicated to different tenants. ∎

Data Integrity and Privacy Protection

Users desire a software environment that provides many useful tools to build cloud applications over large data sets. In addition to application software for clouds, users need some security and privacy protection software for using the cloud.

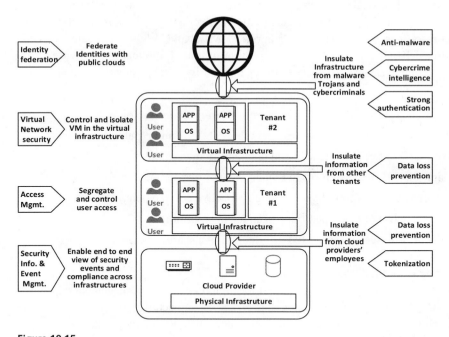

Figure 10.15

Techniques for establishing trusted zones for virtual cluster insulation and VM isolation. (Courtesy of L. Nick, EMC presentation, Tsinghua University, May 25, 2010.)

- Special APIs for authenticating users and sending e-mail using commercial accounts.
- Fine-grain access control to protect data integrity and deter intruders or hackers.
- Protect shared data sets from malicious alteration, deletion, or copyright violation.
- Securing the ISP or *cloud service providers* (CSP) from invading user privacy.
- Personal firewalls at user ends. Keep shared data sets from Java, JavaScript, and ActiveX applets.
- Privacy policy consistent with CSP's policy. Protect against identity theft, spyware, and web bugs.
- VPN channels between resource sites to secure transmission of critical data objects.

Privacy and Copyright Protection

The user gets predictable configuration before actual system integration. Yahoo's Pipes was an example of lightweight cloud platforms. With shared files and data sets, privacy, security, and copyright could be compromised in a cloud-computing environment. Users need to work in a software environment that provides many useful tools to build cloud applications over large data sets. Google platform essentially applies in-house software to protect resources. The Amazon EC2 applies HMEC and X.509 certificates in securing resources. It is necessary to protect browser-initiated application software in the cloud environment. Several security features desired in a secure cloud are identified as follows:

- Dynamic web services with full support from secure web technologies.
- Establish trust between users and providers through SLA and reputation systems.
- Effective user identity management and data-access management.
- Single sign-on and single sign-off to reduce security enforcement overhead.
- Auditing and copyright compliance through proactive enforcement.
- Shifting the control of data operations from client environment to cloud providers.
- Protection of sensitive and regulated information in a shared environment.

Data Coloring and Cloud Watermarking

In the past, watermarking was mainly used for digital copyright management. As shown in Figure 10.16(b), the system generates a special color for each data object. Data coloring means labeling each data object by a unique color. Differently colored data objects are thus distinguishable. The user identification is also colored to be matched with the data colors. This color-matching process can be applied to implement different trust management events. Cloud storage provides a process for the generation, embedding, and extraction of the watermarks in colored objects.

Proactive Solutions to Data Lock-In Problem

Cloud computing moves both the computation and data to the server clusters maintained by cloud service providers. Once the data is moved into the cloud, users cannot easily extract their data and programs from cloud servers to run on another platform. This leads to a data lock-in problem. This has hindered the use of cloud computing. The data lock-in is attributed to two causes:

1. **Lack of interoperability:** Each cloud vendor has their proprietary API that limits users to extract data once submitted.

2. **Lack of application compatibility:** Most computing clouds expect users to write new applications from scratch when they switch cloud platforms.

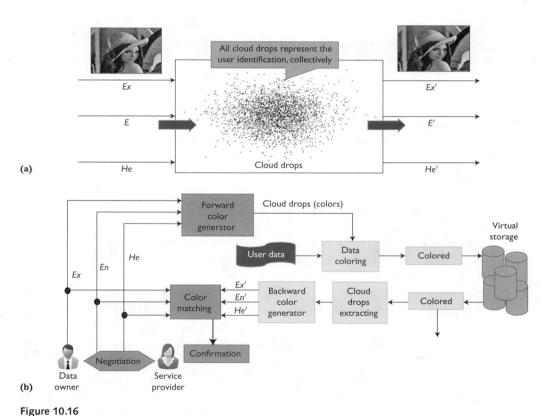

Figure 10.16

Data coloring for trusted access of shared data in an open cloud environment. (Reprinted from Hwang and Li, "Trusted Cloud Computing with Secure Resources and Data Coloring," *IEEE Internet Computing* 14 no. 5, September 2010.)

One possible solution to data lock-in is the use of standardized cloud APIs. This requires building standardized virtual platforms that adhere to open virtual format (OVF)—a platform-independent, efficient, extensible, and open format for VMs. This will enable efficient, secure software distribution, facilitating the mobility of VMs. Using OVF, one can move the data from one application to another. This will enhance QoS and thus enable cross-cloud applications, allowing workload migration among data centers to user-specific storage. By deploying applications, user can access and intermix the applications across different cloud services.

Example 10.10 Data Coloring for Access Control of Shared Big Data in Public Clouds
In general, data protection is done by encryption or decryption, which is computationally expensive. Data coloring takes a minimum amount of calculations to color or decolor the data objects. Cryptography and data coloring can be used jointly. We extend this model to add unique data colors to protect large data sets in the cloud. To guard cloud security, we combine the advantages of secured cloud storage and software watermarking through data coloring and trust negotiation.

The concept of data coloring is illustrated in Figure 10.16. The lady's image is the data object being protected. The forward and backward color generation processes are shown in Figure 10.16(a,b). Data coloring is found much more cost effective for protecting big data in clouds. Computationally, it is much less complicated than using encryption to secure data. The two approaches can be used jointly to provide double protection. ∎

10.4.3 Mobile Clouds and Security Threats

As shown in Figure 10.17, the user carrying a mobile device moves across heterogeneous mobile computing environments, such as cellular networks, mobile ad hoc networks, body area networks, vehicular networks, etc. However, the resource-constrained nature of the mobile device, especially limited battery life, has been a stumbling block for the user to enjoy further improvements of mobile applications and services. Special cloudlets [27] were introduced to serve as wireless gateways between mobile users and the Internet. These cloudlets can be used to offload computations or web services to remote clouds safely.

The combination of mobile communication and mobile clouds is paving the way to many more useful applications in our daily lives. In other words, heavy-duty computations initiated by "small" mobile devices could be carried out by "large" clouds. In the example illustrated, the users move in the physical world. Meanwhile, the abundant data is collected through *Internet of things* (IoT) sensing in various mobile environments. These sensing signals must be directed to the cloud for data storage. Virtualized data objects are created

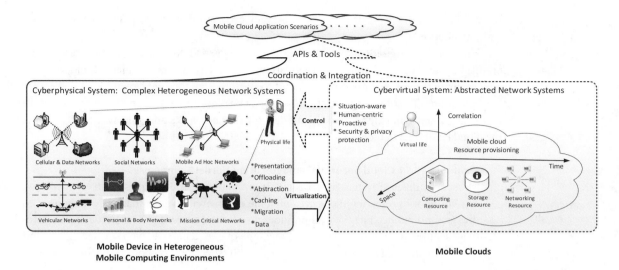

Figure 10.17

The capabilities of a mobile device are enhanced by mobile clouds in a heterogeneous mobile computing environment. (Courtesy of Hwang and Chen, Big Data Analytics for Cloud, IoT, and Cognitive Computing, Wiley, 2017.)

in the cloud for the user. By taking advantage of the abundant resources in the cloud platforms, data mining and ML algorithms are often developed to analyze the mobile user's situation and take timely actions proactively. At the bottom of Figure 10.17, a *cyberphysical system* (CPS) is deployed to have integrated execution of many mobile applications.

The support of mobility, data protection, security infrastructure, and trust management is needed in mobile computing and cloud-centric IoT applications. The purpose is to safeguard these cloud computing services in a fixed or mobile distributed computing environment. Mobility support includes special air interface and mobile API designs and the use of *wireless PKI* for mobile access of cloud platforms. *Virtual private networks* (VPNs) can be also used to secure cloud platforms.

10.5 Trust Management in Clouds and Datacenters

A lack of trust between service providers and cloud users has hindered the universal acceptance of cloud computing as a service on demand. In the past, trust models have been developed to protect mainly e-commerce and online shopping provided by, for example, eBay and Amazon. For web and cloud services, trust and security become even more demanding, because leaving user applications completely to the cloud providers has faced strong resistance by most PC and server users. Cloud platforms become worrisome to some users due to lack of privacy protection, security assurance, and copyright protection.

Using common sense, one can see that technology can enhance trust, justice, reputation, credit, and assurance in Internet applications. As a virtual environment, a cloud poses new security threats that are more difficult to contain than the traditional client and server configurations. To solve these trust problems, a new data-protection model is presented. In many cases, one can extend the trust models for P2P networks and grid systems to protect the clouds and data centers.

Example 10.11 Cloud Security Deployment by Vordel Company

A security defense system by Vordel is shown in Figure 10.18. This system was deployed by Vordel for protecting the access of some commercial clouds that are widely open to the general public. The firewall provides an external shielding. The Vordel XML gateway secures the application server, message queue, database, web service client, and browser with HTTP, JMS, SQL, XML, and SSL security protocols, respectively. ∎

10.5.1 Distributed Intrusion and Anomaly Detection

Data security is the weakest link in all cloud models. We need new cloud security standards to apply common API tools to cope with the data lock-in problem and network attacks or abuses. The IaaS model represented by Amazon EC2 is most sensitive to external attacks. The role-based interface tools alleviate the complexity of the provisioning system. For example, the IBM Blue Cloud provisions through a role-based web portal. A SaaS bureau may order secretarial services from a common cloud platform. Many IT companies are now offering cloud services with no guaranteed security.

Defense against DDoS Flooding Attacks

A DDoS defense system must be designed to cover multiple network domains spanned by a given cloud platform. These network domains cover the edge networks where cloud resources are connected. DDoS attacks come with widespread worms. The flooding traffic is large enough to crash the victim server by buffer overflow, disk exhaustion, connection saturation, etc. A flooding attack pattern is shown in Figure 10.19(a). Here, the hidden attacker launched the attack from many zombies toward a victim server at the bottom router R_0.

The flooding traffic flows essentially with a tree pattern shown in Figure 10.19(b). Successive attack-transit routers along the tree reveal the abnormal surge of traffic. This DDoS defense system is based on change-point detection by all routers. Based on the anomaly pattern detected in covered network domains, the scheme detects a DDoS attack before the victim is overwhelmed. The detection scheme is suitable for protecting cloud core networks. The provider-level cooperation eliminates the need of intervention by edge networks.

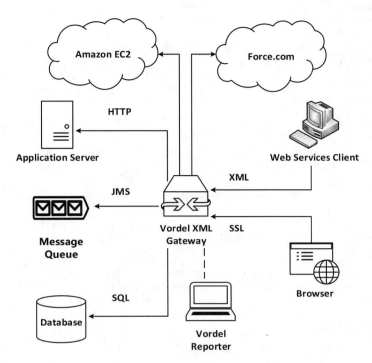

Figure 10.18
A Vordel security structure with XML gateway plus external firewall to safeguard the access of Amazon EC2 and Force.com cloud platforms. Source: Vordel Company.

10.5.2 Reputation-Based Trust Management in Clouds

Trust is a personal opinion, which is very subjective and often biased. Trust can be transitive but not necessarily symmetric between two parties. Reputation is a public opinion, which is more objective and often relies on a large opinion aggregation process to evaluate. Reputation may change or decay over time. Recent reputation should be given more preference than an older image. In this section, we review the reputation systems for protecting data centers or cloud user communities.

Reputation System Design Options
An overview of design options of reputation systems is given in Figure 10.20. The public opinion of the character or standing (such as honest behavior or reliability) of an entity could be the reputation of a person, agent, product, or service. It represents a collective evaluation

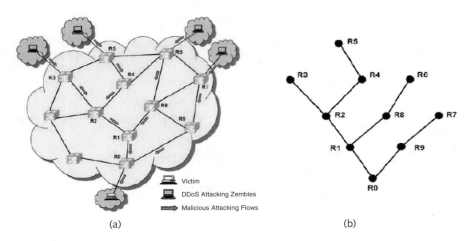

(a)   (b)

Figure 10.19

DDoS attacks and defense by change-point detection at all routers on the flooding tree. Reprinted with permission from Chen et al., "Collaborative Detection of DDoS Attacks over Multiple Network Domains," *IEEE Transactions on Parallel and Distributed Systems* (June 2007). (a) Traffic flow pattern of DDoS attach, (b) The attack traffic flow tree over ten routers.

by a group of people/agents and resource owners. Many reputation systems have been proposed in the past mainly for P2P, multi-agent, or e-commerce systems.

To address the reputation systems for cloud services, a systematic approach is based on the design criteria and administration of the reputation systems. Figure 10.20 shows a two-tier classification of existing reputation systems that have been proposed in recent years. Most of them were designed for P2P or social networks. These reputation systems can be converted for protecting cloud computing applications. In general, the reputation systems are classified as *centralized* or *distributed* depending on how they are implemented. In a centralized system, a single central authority is responsible for managing the reputation system, while the distributed model involves multiple control centers working collectively. Reputation-based trust management and techniques for securing P2P and social networks could be merged to defend data centers and cloud platforms against attacks from the open network.

A centralized reputation system is easier to implement, but demands more powerful and reliable server resources, while a distributed reputation system is much more complex to build. Distributed systems are more scalable and reliable for handling failures. At the second tier, reputation systems are further classified by the scope of reputation evaluation. The *user-oriented* reputation systems focus on individual users or agents. Most P2P reputation systems belong to this category. In data centers, the reputation system is modeled for the resource site as a whole. This reputation system applies to products or services offered by the cloud. Commercial reputation systems have been built by eBay, Google, and Amazon in connection with the services they provide. These are centralized reputation systems.

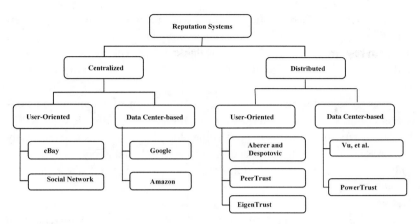

Figure 10.20
Design options of reputation systems for social networks and cloud platforms.

Distributed reputation systems are mostly developed by the academic research communities. The EigenTrust reputation system was developed at Stanford University using the trust matrix approach. The PeerTrust system was developed at Georgia Institute of Technology for supporting e-commerce applications. The PowerTrust system was developed at the University of Southern California based on the power law characteristic of Internet traffic for P2P applications. Other systems in Figure 10.20 are also for P2P reputation evaluation.

Reputation Systems for Clouds

Redesigning the above reputation systems for protecting data centers offers new opportunities for their expanded applications beyond the P2P networks. Data consistency is checked across multiple databases. Copyright protection secures wide-area content distributions. To separate user data from specific SaaS programs, the providers take the most responsibility in maintaining data integrity and consistency. Users can switch among different services using their own data. Only the users have the keys to access the requested data.

The data objects must be uniquely named to ensure global consistency. To ensure data consistency, unauthorized updates of data objects by other cloud users are prohibited. The reputation system can be implemented with a TON. A hierarchy of P2P reputation systems is suggested to protect cloud resources at the site level and data objects at the file level. This demands both coarse-grained and fine-grained access control of shared resources. These reputation systems keep track of security breaches at all levels.

The reputation system must be designed to benefit both cloud users and the data centers. Data objects used in cloud computing reside in multiple data centers over a *storage-area network* (SAN). In the past, most reputation systems were designed for P2P social networking or for online shopping services. These reputation systems can be converted to protect cloud platform resources or user applications on the cloud. The five security mechanisms presented earlier can be greatly assisted by using the reputation system specifically designed for data centers.

However, it is possible to add social tools like reputation systems to support safe cloning of VMs. The snapshot control is based on the defined *recovery point objective* (RPO). Users demand new security mechanisms to protect the cloud. For example, one can apply secured information logging, migrate over secured virtual LAN, and apply error-correcting code (ECC) based encryption for secured migration.

Trust Overlay Networks

Reputation represents a collective evaluation by users and resource owners. Many reputation systems have been proposed in the past for P2P, multi-agent, or e-commerce systems. To support trusted cloud services, Hwang and Li [17] suggested building a TON to model the trust relationships among data center modules. This trust overlay could be structured with DHT (*distributed hash table*) to achieve fast aggregation of the global reputations out of a large number of local reputation scores. Here, the designer needs to have two layers for fast reputation aggregation, updating, and dissemination to all users.

At the bottom layer is the trust overlay for distributed trust negotiation and reputation aggregation over multiple resource sites. This layer handles user/server authentication, access authorization, trust delegation, and data integrity control. At the top layer is an overlay for fast virus/worm signature generation and dissemination and for piracy detection. This overlay facilitates worm containment and intrusion detection systems against virus, worm, and DDoS attacks. The content poisoning technique is reputation-based. That protection scheme can be easily extended to stop copyright violations in a cloud environment surrounding the data centers.

The reputation system enables trusted interactions between cloud users and data center owners. Privacy is enforced by matching colored user identification with the colored data objects. The use of content poisoning was suggested to protect copyright of digital contents. The security-aware cloud architecture (Figure 10.12) is specially tailored to protect virtualized cloud infrastructure. The trust of provided cloud platforms comes from not only SLA, but also effective enforcement of security policies and deployment of countermeasures to defend against network attacks. Figure 10.21 shows the TON architecture for securing multiple data centers in a large-scale cloud or across multiple clouds.

By varying the security control standards, one can cope with the dynamic variation of the cloud operating conditions. The designer is aimed at a trusted cloud environment to assure high-quality services including security. The cloud security trend is to apply virtualization support for security enforcement in data centers. Both reputation systems and

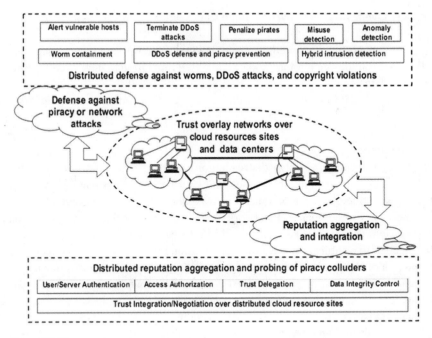

Figure 10.21

DHT-based trust overlay network built over cloud resources from multiple data centers for trust management and distributed security enforcement. (Reprinted from Hwang and Li, "Trusted Cloud Computing with Secure Resources and Data Coloring," *IEEE Internet Computing* 14 no. 5, September 2010.)

data watermarking mechanisms can protect data center access at the coarse-grain file level and to limit the data access at the fine-grain file level.

In the long run, a new SaaS is desired. This "SaaS" is crucial to the universal acceptance of web-scale cloud computing in personal, business, community, and government applications. Internet clouds are certainly in line with IT globalization and efficient computing outsourcing. However, the interoperability among different clouds relies on a common operational standard by building a healthy cloud ecosystem.

The lower box in Figure 10.21 shows the use of the TON for distributed reputation aggregation and probing of privacy colluders over distributed resource sites. These include user/server authentication, access authorization of sensitive data in multiple data centers, trust deletion among user groups, and data integrity control to prevent stealing or deletion of shared data. The upper box consists of a security countermeasure module for distributed defense against worm spreading, DDoS attacks, and copyright violations.

10.5.3 P2P Trust Overlay Network over Multiple Data Centers

This section defines a trust matrix among peers and describes how to aggregate the global reputation. The goal is to design a robust and scalable P2P reputation system over multiple data centers. Each data center is considered a peer entity with a collective reputation score among its users. Here, P2P interactions refer data center-to-data center exchange of trust score.

Peer Trust Characteristics

There are two ways to model the trust or distrust among peers: *trust* and *reputation*. Trust refers to the belief of one peer in another, based on his or her direct experiences with the peer. Reputation is a collective opinion on a peer by other peers based on recommendations. To face the reality of an open P2P network, one has to assume that the participating peers in a P2P system do not trust each other unless proven otherwise. A fair *reputation system* is thus needed to establish the trust or distrust among the peers, based on recorded historical behaviors of the peers. The purpose is to distinguish good peers from the bad ones through a scientific screening process. The quality of the reputation system is primarily indicated by its accuracy and effectiveness to update periodically.

Trust Matrix for Computing Reputations

Consider an overlay network for global reputation aggregation in a P2P system over five data center peers, denoted by nodes N1, N2, . . . , N5 of a directed graph shown in Figure 10.22. The trust relationships among the peers are represented by a square *trust matrix* shown in equation 10.15. Here, $m_{ij}(t)$ is the *local score* issued by node i in evaluating node j at time t. All trust scores are fractions in the range (0, 1) with 0 meaning no trust (or no contact) and 1 for 100% trust. For the five-node network, the following trust matrix at certain time t is achieved. Note that all row sums are 1. A zero entry, $m_{ij}(t) = 0$, means that node i does not evaluate node j for lack of direct contact. The diagonal scores are all zero, meaning no peer evaluates himself.

$$M(t) = \begin{bmatrix} 0 & 0 & 0 & 0.2 & 0.8 \\ 0.6 & 0 & 0 & 0 & 0.4 \\ 0 & 0.7 & 0 & 0 & 0.3 \\ 0 & 0 & 0 & 0 & 0 \\ 0.9 & 0 & 0 & 0.1 & 0 \end{bmatrix} \tag{10.15}$$

The edge labels are the *local scores* issued between all (source, destination) pairs. The fraction value inside each node in Figure 10.22 is the *global reputation score* of that peer at time t. This global score is resulted from aggregating all local scores issued by all peers toward the peer being evaluated. However, all local scores must be weighted by their own

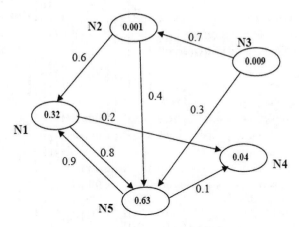

Figure 10.22
A directed graph showing the trust relationship among five data centers in a P2P trust overlay network.

global reputations. In other words, the global reputation is the weighted sum of all local scores. For clarity, all the global reputation scores are normalized so that their sum is always a "1." For example, the global scores of the five peers are represented by a *reputation vector* of five components which add up to 1.

$$V(t) = \{v_1(t), v_2(t), v_3(t), v_4(t), v_5(t)\} = \{0.32, 0.001, 0.009, 0.04, 0.63\} \quad (10.16)$$

Reputation Systems

A reputation system calculates the global reputation score of a peer by considering the opinions (i.e., feedback) from all other peers who have interacted with this peer. After a peer completes a transaction, for example, downloading a music file, the peer will provide his or her feedback for other peers to use in future transactions. By making the reputation scores publicly available, peers are able to make informed decisions about which peers to trust.

The eBay reputation system is a simple and successful one since it has a centralized authority to manage all user feedback scores. However, in an open and decentralized P2P system, peers will not have any centralized authority to maintain and distribute reputation information. Instead, most existing P2P reputation systems calculate global reputation scores by aggregating peer feedback in a fully distributed manner. Building an efficient P2P reputation system is a challenging task due to several intrinsic requirements of large-scale P2P systems.

To measure peers' reputations, one can set up an evaluation system. After each transaction, the two participant parties evaluate each other by giving an honest score. Each peer's reputation can be retrieved from the vote system. However, not every peer is trustworthy. The scores from malicious peers are useless, while the scores from more trustworthy peers are more useful. This advises us to assign different weights to votes based on the voting peers' reputations. It should be noted that a peer's reputation may be different from other different peers. The reputations can be expressed with a reputation matrix.

Global Reputation Aggregation

As global reputation scores are aggregated from local feedback, the distribution property of feedback plays a significant role in the design of an efficient reputation system. Surprisingly, most previous work either ignored the distribution of peer feedback or assumed an arbitrary random distribution, which could be misleading. To achieve global reputation scores, each peer calculates its own parts and all peers cooperatively compute a global matrix. For example, at time $t+1$, the global reputation score of node N5 is computed as follows:

$$v_5(t+1) = m_{15}(t) \times v_1(t) + m_{25}(t) \times v_2(t) + m_{35}(t) \times v_3(t)$$
$$= 0.8 \times 0.32 + 0.4 \times 0.001 + 0.3 \times 0.009 = 0.2573. \qquad (10.17)$$

Similarly, the remaining global scores for the other four peers are computed to yield the following updated global reputation vector:

$$V(t+1) = \{v_1(t+1),\ v_2(t+1),\ v_3(t+1),\ v_4(t+1),\ v_5(t+1)\}$$
$$= \{0.5673,\ 0.0063,\ 0,\ 0.1370,\ 0.2573\}. \qquad (10.18)$$

The above vector is unnormalized. Dividing each peer score by the total sum of all component scores, one can obtain the following *normalized global reputation vector*. Note that the sum of the five peer reputation scores should be 1 in the normalized vector.

$$V(t+1) = \{v_1(t+1),\ v_2(t+1),\ v_3(t+1),\ v_4(t+1),\ v_5(t+1)\}$$
$$= \{0.5862,\ 0.0065,\ 0,\ 0.1416,\ 0.2657\}. \qquad (10.19)$$

Three Reputation Systems for Data Centers

The PeerTrust system was developed at the Georgia Institute of Technology. The system computes the reputation score of a given peer as the average feedback weighted by the scores of the originators. Five trust attributes were suggested in this system. The EigenTrust system was developed at Stanford University, which aggregates reputation information using the eigenvector of the trust matrix over the peers. EigenTrust relies on a good choice of some pretrusted peers. This assumption may be overly optimistic in a distributed computing environment because the pretrusted peers (or data centers) may change with time (see Table 10.6).

Table 10.6
Comparison of three P2P reputation systems

Reputation System	Local Trust Evaluation	Global Reputation Aggregation	Implementation Overhead	Scalability & Reliability
EigenTrust at Stanford University	Uses sum of positive and negative ratings	Uses pretrusted peers to compute global scores from trust matrix	Moderate overhead experienced in assigning score managers and in messaging for global score aggregation	Limited scalability and reliability if pretrusted peers leave
PeerTrust at Georgia Institute of Technology	Normalized rating on each transaction	Peer calculates trust score over five factors in a distributed manner	Moderate overhead experienced in global score calculation over five factors and on the establishment of the trust manager	Partially scalable and resistant to malicious peers
PowerTrust at USC	Uses Bayesian method to generate local trust scores	Distributed ranking of power nodes and LRW strategy to aggregate global reputation scores	Low overhead in using locality-preserving hashing to locate power nodes. Global aggregation time drops sharply with look-ahead random walk strategy applied	Highly scalable and robust with dynamic peer joint and departure

Example 10.12. PowerTrust—A Scalable Reputation System over Multiple Data Centers

The PowerTrust reputation system [31] was developed at the University of Southern California. TON is a virtual network on top of a P2P system. A TON is represented by a directed overlay graph. The graph nodes correspond to the peers. The directed edges or links are labeled with the feedback scores between two interacting peers. The feedback score is issued by a peer (source of the link) for the service provided by the interacting peer (destination of the link).

The major building blocks in a PowerTrust system are shown in Figure 10.23. First, a TON is built on top of all peers (nodes) in a P2P system. All peers evaluate each other, whenever a transaction takes place between a peer pair. Therefore, all peers frequently send *local trust scores* among themselves. These scores are considered as the raw data input to the PowerTrust system. The system supposes to aggregate the local scores to calculate the global reputation score of each participating peer.

All global scores form a *reputation vector*, $V = (v_1, v_2, v_3, \ldots, v_n)$, which is the output of the PowerTrust system. All global scores are normalized with $\sum_i v_i = 1$,

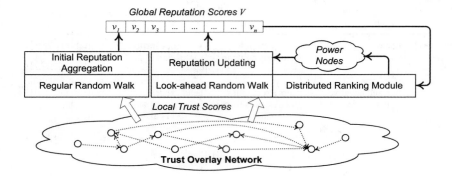

Figure 10.23
Function modules in the PowerTrust reputation system for local score collection and global reputation score aggregation. (Reprinted from Zhou and Hwang, "PowerTrust: A Robust and Scalable Reputation System for Trusted Peer-to-Peer Computing," *IEEE Transactions on Parallel and Distributed Systems (TPDS)* 18 no. 4, April 2007.)

where $i = 1, 2, \ldots, n$ and n is the TON network size. The system is built with five functional modules as shown in Figure 10.23. The *regular random walk* module supports the *initial reputation aggregation*. The *look-ahead random walk* (LRW) module is used to update the reputation score, periodically.

To this end, the LRW also works with a *distributed ranking module* to identify the power nodes. The system leverages the power nodes to update the global scores reputation. PowerTrust achieves high aggregation speed and accuracy, robustness to resist malicious peers, and high scalability to support large-scale P2P applications. ∎

Reputation Convergence

The *convergence overhead* is measured as the number of iterations before the global reputation convergence. Convergence means that the distance between two consecutive reputation vectors is smaller than the threshold. The EigenTrust approach relies on a few pretrusted nodes to compute the global reputations. They assume that some peers are known to be trustworthy, essentially among the very first few peers joining the system.

For fairness, the same number of power nodes equal to that of pretrusted nodes used in EigenTrust are chosen. The power nodes in PowerTrust and the pretrusted node in EigenTrust are allowed to leave freely. A sharp drop of iteration count in using PowerTrust to a flat small number less than 50 is observed, when α increases from 0.15 to 1, while the EigenTrust still requires more than 100 iterations to converge. The EigenTrust system converges very slowly. The system cannot guarantee its convergence when the pretrusted nodes are allowed to leave the system freely.

In the PowerTrust system, the power nodes are re-elected after each aggregation round. Based on the distributed ranking mechanism, the score managers of the departing power nodes notify the system to replace them in a timely fashion with other more qualified power nodes. The decrease of computation overhead means significant traffic reduction on the network, and less work for all peers involved. The low overhead in using the PowerTrust system makes it attractive in performing highly scalable P2P applications.

10.6 Conclusions

Even though cloud computing use has become widespread these days, most cloud users are still worried about the security threats and privacy violations. This worry comes mainly from the fact that resources and data are shared among many users in the public domain. Cloud security and privacy protection still have many open issues yet to be solved. IoT technology and big data techniques can be applied to alleviate some of these problems. In particular, the mobile clouds are most vulnerable. Cloud mesh may augment Wi-Fi mesh in this regard. The cloud-based radio access network may have more security measures in 5G mobile systems. Cloud mashup services are projected to grow rapidly in the coming decade due to the growing population of public clouds. The skyline discovery and composition of cloud mashup services can be greatly upgraded, if ML and data analytics are applied for online business.

In general, high performance promotes cloud productivity, but the converse may not necessarily hold. The QoS in clouds is based on user preferences. Different users may set their own satisfaction threshold for the QoS they can accept. The efficiency is controlled by the providers considering the interest of all users at the same time. Overall, one can say that the scaling-out strategy is the easiest one to implement on modern clouds. The elasticity overhead is lower in these cloud configurations. Scaling-up is more complex to implement than scaling-out due to the switching between node types. This will reduce the elasticity speed and prolong the reconfiguration overhead. Mixed scaling is the most difficult one to implement but offers the best application flexibility.

Homework Problems

10.1: Visit the Microsoft Azure Developer Center. You can download the Azure development kit to run a local version of Azure. Design an application experiment and test run on a local computer, such as your desktop or notebook computer, or on a university workstation or server. Report your experiment experiences in using the Azure platform.

10.2: This problem asks readers to gain concrete hands-on cloud application experiences by running the following two HiBench micro benchmarks: Sort and WordCount, on the EC2 of the AWS cloud. Your benchmark experiments should apply the MapReduce paradigm using the Hadoop software library. You will perform scale-out experiments on the EC2. You need to plot the measured benchmark performance in terms of execution time, speedup, efficiency, and scalability, etc., as the EC2 cluster increases from 1 to 4, 8, 12, and 16.

10.3: Repeat Problem 10.2 for scaling-up experiments on Sort and WordCount by changing the EC2 machine instances from small to medium, large, and extra-large types. Now, you will perform scale-up experiments on the EC2. You need to plot the measured benchmark performance in terms of execution time, speedup, efficiency, and scalability, etc., as the number of machine instances changes from small to extra-large configurations.

10.4: Repeat Problem 10.2 for scaling-up experiments on TeraSort and Sleep programs by changing the EC2 machine instances from small to medium, large, and extra-large types. Perform scale-up experiments on the EC2. You need to plot the measured benchmark performance in terms of execution time, speedup, efficiency, scalability, etc. as the number of machine instances changes from small to extra-large configurations.

10.5: Run the following three SQL programs: Scan, Join, and Aggregate in HiBench suite. Execute the SQL codes on the EC2 of the AWS cloud. Your benchmark experiments should apply the MapReduce paradigm using the Hadoop software library. You will perform scale-out experiments on the EC2. You need to plot the measured benchmark performance in terms of execution time, speedup, efficiency, scalability, etc., as the number of machine instances in EC2 increases from 1 to 4, 8, 12, and 16.

10.6: Run the following two HiBench Web Search benchmarks: PageRank and Nutch indexing on the EC2 of the AWS cloud. Your benchmark experiments should apply the MapReduce paradigm using the Hadoop software library. You will perform scale-out experiments on the EC2. You need to plot the measured benchmark performance in terms of execution time, speedup, efficiency, scalability, etc., as the number of machine instances in EC2 increases from 1 to 4, 8, 12, and 16.

10.7: Run the HDFS program enhanced DFSIO in the HiBench suite on the EC2 of the AWS cloud. Your benchmark experiments should apply the MapReduce paradigm using the Hadoop software library. You will perform scale-out experiments on the EC2. Plot the measured benchmark performance in terms of execution time, speedup, efficiency, scalability, etc., as the EC2 increases from 1 to 4, 8, 12, and 16 instances.

10.8: This problem requires you to develop a new meaningful benchmark application program hosted and executed on the AWS platform. The application area can be selected from the following four application domains. You can use any languages to develop new web 2.0 services or cloud mashup, or big data analytics applications.

- Cloud-based mobile computing/communications.
- Social-media applications on the AWS Cloud.
- Big data mining and analytics apps for critical decision making.
- Campus-wide educational services hosted on the AWS.

10.9: This problem requires you to develop a new meaningful benchmark application program hosted and executed on the AWS platform. The application area can be selected from the following four application domains. You can use any programming languages supported by AWS to develop the new application.

• Healthcare applications on the cloud

• Cloud-assisted IoT applications

• Location-sensitive or geographical information services

• Any new MapReduce, Hadoop, and Spark apps on AWS

10.10: Test the relative performance of using two public clouds: the AWS and Salesforce clouds. You can choose any benchmark programs you have learned in this chapter. For example, you can use the TPC-W benchmark to evaluate large-scale web search or business processing of social media data sets. Assume that the major benchmarking objective is to minimize the execution time or service costs of the chosen applications.

1. Run the service on the AWS platform.

2. Run the service on the Salesforce cloud.

3. Compare your compute and storage costs and experimental results on the two chosen clouds. Report their relative performance and QoS results measured.

10.11: The Magnum is a good software project to realize container orchestration and host clustering on OpenStack Nova machine instances. Check with the OpenStack website to follow up on the latest release of the Magnum source codes. Write a short technical report to summarize your research findings.

10.12: Consider two cluster configurations $V(1)$ and $V(2)$ of an EC2 cloud. The performance of these cluster configurations is measured by their *system throughputs $T(1)$ and $T(2)$*. The QoS is measured by their *availabilities $A(1)$ and $A(2)$*, respectively. Assume that the configuration costs are given as $C(1)$ and $C(2)$, respectively.

1. Derive two formula to express the *productivity $P(1)$ and $P(2)$* of these two clusters with configurations $V(1)$ and $V(2)$, respectively.

2. Suppose the cloud system is scaled up from configuration $V(1)$ to configuration $V(2)$. Can you express the *scalability* of this cloud?

References

[1] Bahar, A., A. Habib, and M. Islam. "Security Architecture for Mobile Cloud Computing." *International Journal of Scientific Knowledge* 3 (2013): 11–17.

[2] Bai, X., Y. Wang, G. Dai, W. T. Tsai, and Y. Chen. "A Framework for Contract-Based Collaborative Verification and Validation of Web Services." In *Component-Based Software Engineering*. Springer, 2007.

[3] Binnig, C., D. Kossmann, T. Kraska, and S. Loesing. "How Is the Weather Tomorrow?: Towards a Benchmark for the Cloud." ACM Second International Workshop on Testing Database Systems, Providence, RI, June 29, 2009.

[4] Bitcurrent, Inc. "Cloud Computing Performance Report." http://www.bitcurrent.com, 2010.

[5] Cai, M., K. Hwang, Y. K. Kwok, S. Song, and Y. Chen. "Collaborative Internet Worm Containment." *IEEE Security and Privacy* (2005): 25–33.

[6] Chen, Y., K. Hwang, and W. S. Ku. "Collaborative Detection of DDoS Attacks over Multiple Network Domains." *IEEE Transactions on Parallel and Distributed Systems* (June 2007).

[7] Cloud Security Alliance. "Trusted Cloud Initiative (TCI)." https://research.cloudsecurityalliance.org/tci, 2013.

[8] CloudHarmony. "Benchmark Evaluation of 114 Public Clouds." http://cloudharmony.com/clouds, 2014.

[9] Cooper, B., A. Silberstein, E. Tam, R. Ramakrishnan, and R. Sears. "Benchmarking Cloud Serving Systems with YCSB." *Proc. of the 1st ACM Symposium on Cloud Computing* (2010): 143–154.

[10] Farber, M., and S. Kounev. "Existing Cloud Benchmark Efforts and Proposed Next Steps." Presentation at Karlsruhe Institute for Technology (KIT), Karlsruhe, Germany, August 31, 2011.

[11] Ferdman, M., et al. "Clearing the Clouds: A Study of Emerging Scale-Out Workloads on Modern Hardware." ACM 17th Int'l Conf. on Architectural Support for Programming Languages and Operating System (ASPLOS), London, England, March 2012.

[12] Herbst, N., S. Kounev, and R. Reussner. "Elasticity in Cloud Computing: What It Is, and What It Is Not." International Conference on Autonomic Computing (ICAC 2013), San Jose, CA, June 2013.

[13] Hill, M. "What Is Scalability?" *ACM SIGARCH Computer Architecture News* 18 no. 4 (December 1990).

[14] Huang, S., J. Huang, J. Dai, T. Xie, and B. Hong. "The HiBench Benchmark Suite: Characterization of the MapReduce-Based Data Analysis." International Conference on Data Engineering Workshops, Long Beach, CA, March 1–6, 2010.

[15] Hwang, K., X. Bai, Y. Shi, M. Y. Li, W. G. Chen, and Y. W. Wu. "Cloud Performance Modeling with Benchmark Evaluation of Elastic Scaling Strategies." *IEEE Transactions on Parallel and Distributed Systems* (January 2016).

[16] Hwang, K., G. Fox, and J. Dongarra. *Distributed and Cloud Computing.* Morgan Kaufmann, 2012.

[17] Hwang, K., and D. Li. "Trusted Cloud Computing with Secure Resources and Data Coloring." *IEEE Internet Computing* 14 no. 5 (September 2010).

[18] Hwang, K., Y. Shi, and X. Bai. "Scale-Out and Scale-Up Techniques for Cloud Performance and Productivity." IEEE Cloud Computing Science, Technology and Applications (CloudCom 2014), Workshop on Emerging Issues in Clouds, Singapore, December 18, 2014.

[19] Hwang, K., and Z. Xu. "Scalable Parallel Computing." In *Performance Benchmarking.* McGraw-Hill, 1998.

[20] Iosup, A., S. Ostermann, M. Yigitbasi, R. Prodan, T. Fahringer, and D. Epema. "Performance Analysis of Cloud Computing Services for Many-Tasks Scientific Computing." *IEEE Transactions on Parallel and Distributed Systems* 22 no. 6 (June 2011).

[21] Kamvar, D., T. Schlosser, and H. Garcia-Molina. "The EigenTrust Algorithm for Reputation Management in P2P Networks." Proc. of the 12th International Conference on World Wide Web, Budapest, Hungary, May 20–24, 2003.

[22] Krebs, R., C. Momm, and S. Knounev. "Metrics and Techniques for Quantifying Performance Isolation in Cloud Environments." ACM QoSA'12, Bertinoro, Italy, June 25–28, 2012.

[23] Ostermann, S., A. Iosup, N. Yigitbasi, R. Prodan, T. Fahringer, and D. Epema. "A Performance Analysis of EC2 Cloud Computing Services for Scientific Computing." *Proc. of the International Conference on Cloud Computing.* Springer, 2010.

[24] Satyanarayanan, M., P. Bahl, R. Caceres, and N. Davies. "The Case for VM-Based Cloudlets in Mobile Computing." *IEEE Pervasive Computing* 8 no. 4 (2009): 14–23.

[25] Shi, Y., S. Abhilash, and K. Hwang. "Cloudlet Mesh for Securing Mobile Clouds from Intrusions and Network Attacks." Third IEEE International Conference on Mobile Cloud Computing (MobileCloud), San Francisco, CA, April 2, 2015.

[26] Smith, W. *TCP-W: Benchmarking: An E-commerce Solution.* Intel, 2005.

[27] Sobel, W., S. Subramanyam, A. Sucharitakul, J. Nguyen, H. Wong, S. Patil, and D. Patterson. "Cloudstone: Multi-platform, Multi-language Benchmark and Measurement Tools for Web 2.0." Proc. of First Workshop on Cloud Computing and Applications, October 2008.

[28] Song, S., K. Hwang, R. Zhou, and Y. K. Kwok. "Trusted P2P Transactions with Fuzzy Reputation Aggregation." *IEEE Internet Computing,* Special Issue on Security for P2P and AD Hoc Networks 9 (November/December 2005).

[29] Xiong, L., and L. Liu. "PeerTrust: Supporting Reputation-Based Trust for Peer-to-Peer Electronic Communities." *IEEE Transactions on Knowledge and Data Engineering* (2004): 843–857.

[30] Yigitbasi, N., A. Iosup, D. Epema, and S. Ostermann. "C-Meter: A Framework for Performance Analysis of Computing Clouds." *IEEE/ACM Proc. of 9th International Symposium on Cluster Computing and the Grid (CCGrid)* (June 2009).

[31] Zhou, R., and K. Hwang. "PowerTrust: A Robust and Scalable Reputation System for Trusted Peer-to-Peer Computing." *IEEE Transactions on Parallel and Distributed Systems (TPDS)* 18 no. 4 (2007): 460–473.

Index

Note: Figures and tables are indicated by " f " and " t " respectively, following page numbers.